THE FIRST AMERICAN REPUBLIC
1774-1789
The First Fourteen American Presidents Before Washington

Thomas Patrick Chorlton

authorHOUSE®

AuthorHouse™
1663 Liberty Drive
Bloomington, IN 47403
www.authorhouse.com
Phone: 1-800-839-8640

First published by AuthorHouse 4/25/2011

ISBN: 978-1-4567-5387-0 (e)
ISBN: 978-1-4567-5388-7 (dj)
ISBN: 978-1-4567-5389-4 (sc)

Library of Congress Control Number: 2011904304

Printed in the United States of America

Front jacket photo of Independence Hall by Daniel Ucko.
All other photographs, unless otherwise indicated,
are from the "Tom Chorlton Collection."
Map from AN ENCYCLOPEDIA OF WORLD HISTORY, 6/e edited by Peter N. Stearns. Copyright (c) 2001 by Houghton Mifflin Harcourt Publishing Company. Reprinted by permission of Houghton Mifflin Harcourt Publishing Company. All rights reserved.
Cover design by Janelle Gonyea.

This book is set in Caslon, as in the Declaration of Independence.

This book is printed on acid-free paper.

"Why follow where the road may lead ?
Go, instead, where there is no path
and leave a trail..."

- Ralph Waldo Emerson

This Book is dedicated to my
Mother & Father
with profound gratitude and love.

TABLE OF CONTENTS

"It's about sex and revenge, except for a short chapter on the Continental Congress."

Preface

THE FIRST AMERICAN REPUBLIC

1774 - 1789

Every Frenchman knows that these are the days of the Fifth French Republic. It was founded by Charles de Gaulle in September 1958 when a new French Constitution was overwhelmingly approved by the voters. Its origins stretch back to the days of the French Revolution which gave birth to the First Republic (1792-95) and the three subsequent attempts at republican government which were intermixed with Bourbons and Bonapartes over the past two centuries.

During that same period the United States of America has been blessed to live under only one Constitution that went into effect in 1789. In March of that year our first national bicameral legislature was established--late, as always, due to the lack of a quorum--and the following month our first modern President was sworn into office at Federal Hall in New York City. But this was our second attempt at a republican form of government.

What few Americans realize is that we had a fully functioning national government prior to 1789. It was called the Continental Congress and it was, in every respect, the First American Republic (1774-1789).

It began on September 5, 1774, when elected delegates from eleven of the American colonies first assembled in Philadelphia in direct defiance of both the King and Parliament. Surprisingly, this First American Republic is most often dismissed in text books and popular history as a failed attempt at self-government. And yet, it was during that fifteen year period that we won the war against the strongest empire on Earth, established organized government as far west as the Mississippi River, built alliances with some of the great powers of Europe and transformed thirteen separate entities into a national confederation. The very lessons we learned during that period, and the men who served as congressional delegates, provided us with the wisdom to craft the Constitution we live under today.

When the Continental Congress initially met in 1774, its very first order of business was to elect one of its own members to serve as President.

He functioned as Head of State, much as the Presidents of Germany and Italy do today. He signed all official documents, received all official visitors and represented the emerging nation at official events and through extensive correspondence. While Congress retained all other executive, legislative and judicial functions, the President even presided over its deliberations. Eventually, a house, carriage and servants were provided for the President as a sign of national pride and respect.

In all, fourteen distinguished individuals were chosen by their peers for this unique and awesome responsibility. They were the giants of their age, men of power, wealth and experience who often led their new nation through extremely difficult days largely on the strength of their character. For far too long they have been lost to history.

This is their story.

Thomas Patrick Chorlton
February 26, 2011

PO Box 1892
Folly Beach, SC 29439
www.firstamericanrepublic.com

"We lost the American colonies because we lacked the statesmanship to know the time and the manner of yielding what it is impossible to keep."

- Queen Elizabeth II
July 6, 1976

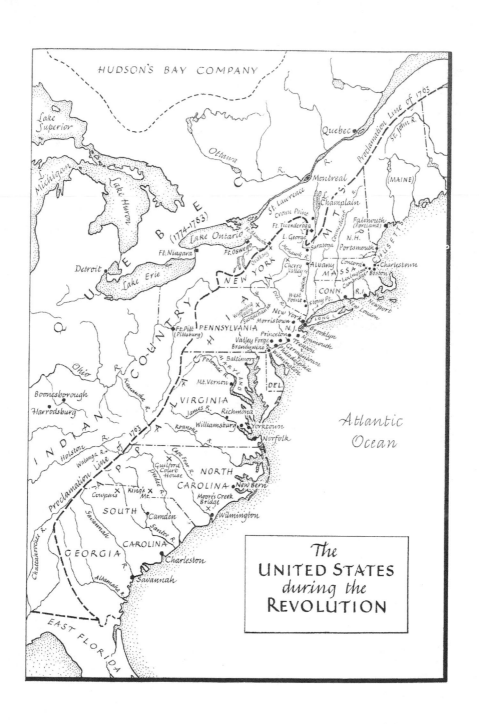

The
UNITED STATES
during the
REVOLUTION

IN THE BEGINNING

"What is Past is Prologue"

Liberty and greed were the twin goals that drove the European colonization of North America.[1] For the great empires, it was the quest for ever more power and dominance on the World stage. For individuals, it was the dream of wealth beyond status or birth or, for many others, the struggle for personal or religious freedom in the face of hostility or even persecution at home.

In America, during the late 16th Century, the British made several unsuccessful attempts to establish colonies along the Atlantic coast while, back home in England, Shakespeare was composing his immortal verse. When the latest explorers finally did reach Virginia on April 26, 1607, they named their first permanent settlement Jamestown (founded on May 14)[2] in honor of their new king, James I, who had ascended the throne of England four years earlier.[3] They came for commercial reasons on behalf of the Virginia Company.[4] Their adventure, however, transformed the history of the World. For the next 167 years, British subjects rapidly expanded across the Atlantic seaboard of North America while remaining loyal subjects of their King.

One year after the founding of Jamestown, Samuel de Champlain raised the French flag at Quebec in July 1608.[5] The titanic struggle over North America between Europe's two greatest powers had begun.

During that same period, a joint stock company known as the Merchant Adventurers put up most of the capital to finance a voyage to establish a colony at the mouth of the Hudson River. Unlike Jamestown, however, success came through the determination of a group of English separatists who were motivated by the quest for religious liberty. When these Pilgrims arrived at Cape Cod in November 1620 (far north of their original destination) they drew up the Mayflower Compact, "by which they formed themselves into a body politic and agreed to enact laws for the welfare of the colony. They selected John Carver as their first governor. (When Gov. Carver died six months later, William Bradford was elected to replace him. Gov. Bradford served until his death in May 1657.)"[6]

On November 11, 1620, in what is today Provincetown Harbor, forty-one men (excluding the seamen who would eventually return to England, those too ill to participate and women and children) signed the Mayflower Compact on board ship before they set foot on land.[7] As author Nathaniel Philbrick observes in his history of the Pilgrims, "It is deeply ironic that the document many consider to mark the beginning of what would one day be called the United States came from a people who had more in common with a cult than a democratic society."[8] Nevertheless, these brave souls, against all possible odds, did indeed plant the seeds of democracy in the New World.

The number of British colonies continued to grow despite dramatic political and social upheaval in England where Civil War broke out in 1642 and ultimately led to the beheading of King Charles I in 1649. Two years later, at the Battle of Worcester, Oliver Cromwell defeated those loyal to Charles II and the young king fled to France. At the same time, Parliament issued the first in a long series of Navigation Acts to make certain that Britain kept a tight grip on all issues pertaining to American trade. It was the Age of Mercantilism during which private enterprise had to meet the demands of government, not the consumer. By May 1660, the King had been restored to his throne.[9] Three years later, the newest trade legislation, the Staple Act, included a list of enumerated articles along with the mandate that most goods imported by British colonies had to be shipped on British ships and pass through the British Isles.

Primary responsibility for North American affairs evolved during the century and a half of British domination. Initially, the Privy Council directly handled matters such as the granting of royal charters. In 1672, as commerce became increasingly important, the government appointed customs commissioners in each of the colonies to try to prevent colonial merchants from evading British duties by shipping tobacco and other targeted items to Europe through other colonial ports. The Navigation Act of 1696 once again attempted to tighten the system by transferring authority to the newly created Board of Commissioners for Trade and Plantations, commonly referred to as the Board of Trade. Eventually, the position of Secretary of State for the Southern Department was established to include the Atlantic seaboard. Finally, in 1768, with the appointment of the Earl of Hillsborough, control was consolidated into an even more powerful position under a new Secretary of State for the American Department.[10]

In the eyes of the British Government, the American colonies existed solely for the benefit of the Mother Country. Trade was the lifeblood of that relationship. An amusing example was demonstrated in The Hat Act of 1732 which prohibited the "export of hats from one colony to another and imposed other restrictions on the growing colonial hat industry for the benefit of English manufacturers."[11] The following year, The Molasses Act was established to protect the British West Indies' sugar and molasses trade from foreign competition, but, in the process, it also threatened the destruction of New England's highly profitable rum industry. Widespread smuggling resulted. Britain responded in 1755 by authorizing the use of Writs of Assistance which were, in effect, search warrants.

The Writs gave customs officials the authority to request assistance from colonial officers in order to search private homes and warehouses. This process led directly to the first unambiguous assertion of American Rights on February 24, 1761. On that date, James Otis, Jr. (one of the most prominent lawyers in Boston and the godfather of American Independence) argued in court that such writs were "against the fundamental principles of law..." and that "a man who is quiet, is as secure in his house, as a prince in his castle..."[12] Otis asserted that even Parliament could not enact legislation contrary to Natural Law. In doing so, he laid the foundation for Jefferson's basic argument in the Declaration of Independence fifteen years later. Fortunately, attorney John Adams was there to witness Otis' oration and to preserve parts of it for posterity. Adams described the experience sixty years later when he wrote that "Otis was a flame of fire!...He burned everything before him. American independence was then and there born..."[13]

On the world stage, developments in America were often secondary to the clash of empires on the European continent. Those distant battles, however, eventually spilled over to America and, on one occasion, actually began with developments in the New World. For Great Britain, the year 1689 was pivotal. Internally, Parliament forced the last Catholic monarch, James II, from the throne and asserted, on its own authority, the Declaration of Rights which usurped many of the king's prerogatives. It then selected James' daughter Mary to reign with William (her husband and first cousin) as joint monarchs.[14] Externally, this radical transformation led Britain to join the alliance against Louis XIV of France in the War of the League of Augsburg, known in America as King William's War. Fighting continued between French Canada and the British colonies until 1697. Three years later, when Charles II of Spain died, his death led to renewed hostilities throughout Europe, known as the War of the Spanish Succession. The American phase of that war, which began a year later, was called Queen Anne's War (Benjamin Franklin, the oldest of America's future patriot leaders, was born in the midst of that conflict in January 1706). When the Treaty of Utrecht was finally signed in 1713, France ceded to Britain Newfoundland, Nova Scotia and the Hudson Bay territory, but France retained control over Quebec.[15]

In 1732, the initial phase of British colonization in The New World came to a close when Georgia, the last of the original American colonies, was chartered by King George II.[16] Two future American Presidents, Richard Henry Lee and George Washington, were born that same year. At the end of the decade, however, Europe was thrown into even greater turmoil with the death of the last of the Hapsburg Emperors, Charles VI. As a result, the War of the Austrian Succession raged on in Europe from 1740-48, and included more plot twists than a Dickens novel. Three years after Charles' death the fighting once again spread to America and brought British and French forces and their respective Indian allies into combat on various frontiers. It was known in America as King George's War (1743-48). Combat ended with the Treaty of Aix-la-Chapelle in October 1748, helping to elevate Prussia to major power status.[17] (That same year, Peyton Randolph, who would become the first President of the Continental Congress, was appointed as the King's Attorney for the Colony of Virginia.)

In America, however, diplomatic agreements did little to defuse the simmering situation along the borders between New France and the British colonies. Nova Scotia, the Cherokee country, the Ohio River Valley and other locations continued to be pressure points as the incursion of French trappers and hunters from Quebec increasingly collided with the westward expansion of British American colonization. In the spring of 1754, the first skirmish--in what proved to be the final showdown between British and French interests in America--broke out along the Ohio River Valley.

"The Ohio Company was a group of land speculators, many of them of the best Virginia families, organized to exploit and colonize the Ohio Valley."[18] Greed was the driving force. Since Virginia's Lt. Governor Robert Dinwiddie was himself a shareholder in the company, he freely used his political authority to further the company's commercial interests.[19] In early 1754, Dinwiddie gave orders that a fort should be built at the Forks of the Ohio River (near present day Pittsburgh) in order to protect his company's investment from hostile Indians, French traders and even conflicting claims from Pennsylvania. In April, he sent additional troops to reinforce his new fort. Dinwiddie appointed 22 year old George Washington, a lieutenant colonel in the Virginia Militia, to serve as second in command to Col. Joshua Fry.[20]

What the Governor did not know was that approximately 500 Frenchmen were already in the process of ejecting the Virginians from the half-completed fort and renaming it Fort Duquesne. As Washington led a contingent of 60 men from the new regiment toward their destination, they met their comrades fleeing from the fort. Despite this sudden reversal,

Washington decided to push forward. On May 27, 1754, he conducted a surprise attack on a small French contingent, killing the French commander, Jumonville, and nine other men.[21]

The French claimed that their fallen leader had been murdered under a flag of truce. The Virginians rejected this charge and built a new base, Fort Necessity, near the Cumberland Road just east of what is today Uniontown, Pennsylvania. As the rest of the Virginia forces gathered at this new location, Washington assumed command on the death of Col. Fry. The new fort, however, did not last long. On July 3, 1754, Fort Necessity was attacked by a combined force of nearly 900 French and Indians. Washington and his troops were forced to surrender the next day, July 4, 1754 (exactly twenty-two years prior to the adoption of the Declaration of Independence).[22]

At precisely that same time (June 19-July 10, 1754), representatives from seven of the American colonies (Connecticut, Massachusetts, Maryland, New Hampshire, New York, Pennsylvania and Rhode Island) were meeting in Albany, NY at the request of the British authorities. The Albany Convention represented the first formal attempt to develop coordinated action among the American colonies. Its initial goal was to retain the allegiance of the Iroquois Indians during conflicts involving the French. The Convention's most memorable development, however, was the adoption of the Albany Plan of Union which was crafted by a committee and revised by Benjamin Franklin.[23] The Plan called for the creation of a President-General appointed by the King and the election of a Grand Council by the colonies which would be subject to veto by either the King or the President-General. Even though the plan was rejected at the time by both the British Government as well as the individual colonies, twenty years later a version of this proposal would resurface as the Galloway Plan during a pivotal moment in the First Continental Congress.[24]

One year after Washington's surrender, while attempting to recapture Fort Duquesne (July 9, 1755), Gen. Edward Braddock, the commander-in-chief of all British troops in America, lost his life in the Battle of the Wilderness.[25] It was a tremendous defeat for the British and Americans (914 out of 1,373 soldiers were killed or wounded). It also provided a glimpse into the future since it included two American soldiers who would join forces during the American Revolution, Washington and Horatio Gates, as well as the man they would initially confront, Thomas Gage.

Unlike previous wars which had begun in Europe and then spread to America, the French & Indian War raged for two years along the American frontier before it ignited a full scale European conflict. Finally, in the spring of 1756, Great Britain officially declared war on France and the Seven Years War (1756-63), which eventually reached as far as India, began. During its bloody course, Britain and its ally Prussia, under Frederick the Great, battled against the alliance of France, Russia, Austria, Sweden and Saxony.

Initially, the British War Cabinet was headed by the Duke of Newcastle, a seasoned politician who served for years as the First Lord of the Treasury. He was known as "a consummate master of parliamentary tactics."[26] His poor grasp of foreign affairs, however, led to a leadership coalition with William Pitt the Elder, one of the giants of modern British history. What Pitt clearly understood was that this war would be the defining moment for the British Empire in North America. As the government's dominant figure, Pitt therefore pledged to commit all of Britain's resources to its ultimate triumph. True to his word, Pitt spared no cost in his single-minded pursuit of victory.[27]

While Prussia focused on the European battle front, one of Pitt's primary goals was to finally drive the French out of Canada. In 1759, British Gen. James Wolfe led a lengthy attack against the fortress-city of Quebec, which was being guarded by the Marquis de Montcalm and the French Army. After weeks of failure and frustration, Wolfe repositioned his troops on the cliffs above and to the west of the city's walls in an area known as the Plains of Abraham. On September 13, 1759, it was there that the British defeated the French, and both commanders, Wolfe and Montcalm, lost their lives.[28] Five days later, Quebec surrendered. That same year, Britain recaptured Fort Duquesne, rebuilt it and renamed it Fort Pitt, the cornerstone of today's city of Pittsburgh. Twelve months after the fall of Quebec, Montreal became the last major French settlement to surrender on September 8, 1760.[29] New France had vanished from the map of North America.

In the wake of these events, the war itself was interrupted by even more pressing political developments at home. On October 25, 1760, King George II died. He was succeeded by his 22 year old grandson, George III, the first of Britain's Hanoverian monarchs who actually spoke fluent English. Unlike his royal German predecessors, the new king also had a much better grasp of the nuances of parliamentary politics after years of careful tutoring by Lord Bute.[30] Even though the progressive Whig Party clearly dominated the Tories in the House of Commons,[31] the young king wasted no time in nurturing an informal network of legislators who became known as "The King's Friends."[32] Through the judicious distribution of royal favors, lands and titles, George III learned how to maximize his influence on critical issues of state.

The eager young King frequently clashed with his imperious first minister over both policies and personalities. Lord Bute, the King's closest advisor, termed the war "bloody & expensive" and urged an honorable peace.[33] In response, Pitt simply ignored the country's mounting debt (the war was costing Britain approximately £20,000,000 per year).[34] Pitt even advocated the expansion of the war to include Spain. This battle of wills was finally resolved when Pitt resigned in disgust on October 5, 1761.[35] His resignation marked the beginning of what became known as the "revolving door ministry" during which the leadership of the government frequently changed hands during the remainder of the decade.

The accession of Czar Peter III to the Russian throne the following year was a stroke of good luck for Britain and its ally. In March 1762, the new Czar switched sides to support Prussia, thereby placing even more pressure on France. Within weeks, an armistice was signed among the great powers and work began on a final peace agreement. That December, the House of Commons gave its support to the preliminary peace treaty by a vote of 319-65.[36]

Finally, on February 10, 1763, the Treaty of Paris was signed and the Seven Years War came to an end. Pitt's dream had been fulfilled. The British Lion now reigned supreme. But, as Dartmouth Professor Colin Calloway states, "the challenges of governing a continent from an island strained British politics" and imposed new challenges throughout the Empire.[37] The British national debt had exploded to £130,000,000.[38] (According to the conversion process developed by journalist and historian David A. Price, based on a research paper developed by the Economic Policy and Statistics Section of the House of Commons Library, the 1763 British debt in 21st Century Dollars would have equaled approximately $25,000,000,000.)[39]

The rest of the decade would have to be devoted to servicing the debt just to keep the country solvent. To accomplish this thankless task, the King turned to George Grenville, Pitt's brother-in-law, a man who was far more attentive to details than his famous relative but totally lacked Pitt's vision and popularity.

As the new First Lord of the Treasury, Grenville was determined to raise revenue from every conceivable source, including America. In his opinion the American colonists had gained the most from the elimination of the French along their frontier and therefore the colonies should be willing to pay their fair share of the cost of the war. To the Americans, however, the defeat of the French seemed part of Britain's global strategy. The colonists also believed that direct taxation of America by Parliament was prohibited by the British Constitution since the American colonies were not represented in that body. This debate continued to intensify until it broke out into full scale revolution a decade later. Britain had indeed won the war, but at what cost?

Dissent was heard in London, as well. John Wilkes, a Member of the House of Commons and publisher of a periodical known as *The North Briton*, spoke out against the impact of the war. In issue No. 45 (April 23, 1763), Wilkes went so far as to denounce the King's assertion that the peace treaty was honorable.[40] For his courage, Wilkes was thrown into the Tower of London. His supporters would march to the prison each day, always in groups of 45, to commemorate Issue No. 45 of the North Briton which had initiated his notoriety. Sometimes the daily theme would be quite imaginative, such as "45 virgins for Wilkes." This peculiar tradition was even repeated on the streets of Charleston, South Carolina in October 1768.[41]

Over the next quarter century, the slogan "Wilkes and Liberty!" rang out as the anthem of the rights of all Englishmen to his loyal supporters both in Britain and America. Each time he was ejected from Parliament Wilkes became more popular.[42] Ultimately, after years of struggle and occasional imprisonment, Wilkes became the Lord Mayor of London (with a population of approximately 800,000) and the King himself was forced to share the stage with Wilkes during some official ceremonies. To Americans, Wilkes was both a friend and a hero. In 1769, the South Carolina legislature even contributed £1,500 to his defense over the vehement opposition of the Royal Governor.[43]

In addition to the debate over paying for the war, the other major impact of peace in America was the opportunity for the colonies and colonists to head west without the fear of facing French resistance. For over one and a half centuries, the acquisition of land had been a major driving force for British Americans. Now, to ambitious Americans of all classes, that dream appeared nearly inexhaustible. The King and his ministers, however, viewed the situation very differently. On October 7, 1763, George III issued the British North American Proclamation which pledged to respect Indian claims west of the Appalachian Mountains and established those mountains as the western boundary for the existing British colonies.[44] Land west of that line would be under London's direct control. Despite this royal decree, Americans continued to covet what they would one day refer to as their "manifest destiny."[45]

And so, before the ink had dried on the Treaty of Paris, battle lines had been drawn between Great Britain and her American colonies. Did Parliament have the authority and the ability to force the Americans to help pay for the last war? Would the Americans respect the limits on westward expansion established by the Crown? Or, would Grenville and his successors manage to snatch defeat from the jaws of victory?

The great 20th Century historian Barbara Tuchman answered those questions in a book she insightfully titled *The March of Folly*. Tuchman defines "folly" as the pursuit of policy contrary to self-interest. She attributes the American Revolution to failed British Government policy because, in her judgment: "In the end Britain made rebels where there had been none."[46] The decade after official peace was declared became an unbroken series of disastrous blunders on the part of the British Government. At every step, the King and Parliament seriously miscalculated the impact of their policies on their American subjects.

This downward spiral began with the passage of Grenville's American Revenue Act in the spring of 1764.[47] Even though it was known in the colonies as the Sugar Act and viewed by Parliament as an extension of the earlier Molasses Act (1733), it actually taxed a wide variety of items including non-British textiles, coffee, indigo, iron, hides, whale fins, raw silk and potash. It also doubled the duties on foreign goods that were reshipped from England to her colonies and prohibited the importation of French wines in America. But, since Americans had become notorious for undermining earlier trade acts through smuggling and other illegal activities, Grenville took additional steps to make certain that this time the legislation would produce the much needed revenue. He therefore revitalized the customs system, established a new Vice-Admiralty Court to guarantee convictions beyond the reach of American juries, and gained parliamentary approval for the Currency Act which was designed to prohibit the colonies from paying their debts to British merchants with depreciated colonial currency.[48]

In practice, the Currency Act led to a critical shortage of British Pounds throughout America. As a result, the colonists were repeatedly reminded of how heavy handed British authority could be. Tight money also made it far more difficult for Americans to gain real financial independence at home. In the short run, this was a good fit with British colonial policy which wanted to keep America dependent upon the Mother Country. In the long term, however, it had exactly the opposite effect.

When the Massachusetts House of Representatives next met on October 18, 1764, James Otis was prepared to respond to Grenville's legislation. Speaking on behalf of Americans throughout the colonies, Otis introduced a petition denouncing taxation without representation, a phrase that would become the battle cry of Americans as the struggle progressed. Otis argued that one of the fundamental principles of Britain's unwritten Constitution was that no Englishman could be taxed without his consent. Therefore, since the American colonies had neither voice nor vote in Parliament, Otis reasoned that only the colonial legislatures could levy taxes on the colonists. Thomas Hutchinson, the American-born Lt. Governor of Massachusetts, tried to head off a direct confrontation by suggesting that milder language be used requesting a favor from the King rather than asserting a right. Otis held firm.

In Virginia, Richard Henry Lee, a future president, echoed those same sentiments when he wrote to a friend that " '...the right to be governed by laws made by our representatives, and the illegality of taxation without consent,' are such essential principles of the British constitution, that it is a matter of wonder how men, who have almost imbibed them in their mother's milk...should be of opinion that the people of America were to be taxed without consulting their representatives!"[49] In mid-December 1764, Lee's denunciation of taxation without representation was approved by the Virginia House of Burgesses.[50] That same month, in *The Grievances of the American Colonies Candidly Examined*, Gov. Stephen Hopkins of Rhode Island asserted that Parliament's power had its limits. True to his word, Gov. Hopkins refused to execute the act when it officially went into effect the following year.[51]

Even though the word "revenue" was part of the official title of Grenville's 1764 legislation, many loyalists argued that both the Sugar Act and the Currency Act were simply the latest in Parliament's long established prerogative in matters pertaining to trade and navigation. These "external" taxes, they maintained, did not violate any constitutional provisions because they were nothing more than the orderly management of the empire's trade. Others insisted that Parliament's supremacy had been clearly established in 1689 when King James II was deposed and that the American colonies, therefore, had no legal basis for challenging its actions under any circumstances.

Despite the intensity of this debate, Grenville continued to devote his energy to devising additional ways to force the Americans to pay what he considered to be their fair share of Britain's war debt. Overall, taxes at the end of the French & Indian War averaged 26 shillings per person in Britain compared with only one shilling per head in America.[52] Given those statistics, Parliament was hardly impressed by American claims that the colonies were overtaxed. Therefore, in early 1765, Grenville took the fateful step of introducing the American Stamp Act which sailed through the House of Commons with little debate. Britain itself had had a stamp tax since the end of the previous century.[53] Grenville viewed the legislation as simply the extension of a proven revenue measure to America. George III was too ill at the time to sign the legislation, but it received the Royal

Assent by commission on March 22, 1765. It was scheduled to go into effect in America on November 1 of that year.

Under its provisions, most legal documents as well as a wide variety of other items would have to bear the stamp for the transaction to be legal. (A stamp tax remains to this day on each pack of cigarettes sold in the United States as well as playing cards and hard liquor.) By distributing a little financial pain over a wide range of activities, Grenville anticipated less resistance from the Americans. Even Benjamin Franklin in London, who unsuccessfully argued against the proposal while serving as a colonial lobbyist, initially misjudged his countrymen's response.[54] Once again, however, British miscalculation produced exactly the opposite of Grenville's objective. By spreading the burden to everyone, the Stamp Act gave Americans across the continent common cause. To make matters even worse, Grenville unwittingly guaranteed well-publicized opposition to the Act by foolishly mandating that even newspapers must pay the tax.

Grenville's plan to employ colonists as Stamp Collectors rather than British officials also backfired. Instead of making the new tax easier to enforce because it was being managed by prominent Americans, it guaranteed that Stamp agents would risk everything if they failed to heed the intense opposition of their fellow citizens.

To the Americans, for the first time in their history, Britain was attempting to impose an "internal" tax on the colonies; a tax specifically designed to raise revenue without the pretense of regulating overseas trade. The cry of "taxation without representation" took on even greater significance as American opposition to the new tax began to build almost immediately. In several colonies, prominent citizens seized the moment by transforming mob anger into political groups known as the Sons of Liberty.

Sam Adams in Massachusetts and Christopher Gadsden in South Carolina were among the most creative in harnessing this power.[55] One by one, most of the designated Stamp Collectors were threatened and intimidated into resigning their positions even before the Act went into effect. Violence was common. Some supporters of the legislation were literally tarred and feathered.

On May 29, 1765, Patrick Henry, a new member of the Virginia House of Burgesses (who turned 29 that same day) introduced seven provocative resolutions denouncing the Stamp Act. During the debate, Henry stunned his colleagues by stating that "Tarquin and Caesar had each his Brutus, Charles the First his Cromwell, and George the Third may profit by their example!" When some members of the legislature shouted "Treason! Treason!" Henry responded with the immortal phrase: "If this be treason, make the most of it!"[56] Two days later, after Henry left Williamsburg, the House rescinded its support for his most assertive resolutions. All seven, however, appeared in newspapers across America thereby creating the false impression that Virginia, the oldest and largest of the colonies, had clearly taken the lead in opposition to the Stamp Act.

One week later, in Massachusetts, James Otis introduced the proposal which led to the creation of the Stamp Act Congress which was held in New York City that October. Even before that Congress convened, however, Grenville's ministry collapsed in July 1765. He was replaced by the Marquis of Rockingham, a former protégé of Pitt, who had the unenviable task of trying to repair relations with America while continuing to assert Parliament's supremacy. Since word of Grenville's fate did not reach the American coast for several weeks, protests across the colonies continued to grow throughout the month of August. In Massachusetts, Gov. Bernard wrote that "The power and authority of government is really at an end."[57] On the evening of August 26, 1765, Lt. Gov. Thomas Hutchinson of Massachusetts watched helplessly as his new mansion in Boston was destroyed by a mob.[58]

In the midst of these developments, the Stamp Act Congress opened in New York City on October 7, 1765. For the first time in American history, the colonies came together of their own volition, over the objections of the Crown, to debate issues of profound continental concern. Connecticut, Delaware, Maryland, New Jersey, New York, Pennsylvania, Rhode Island and South Carolina sent a total of 28 delegates. The gathering, which served as an obvious benchmark for the convening of the Continental Congress nine years later, concluded its work in just two weeks. It issued an Address to the King, a Memorial to the House of Lords, a Petition to the House of Commons and a Declaration of Rights and Grievances. The latter document (written in part by Thomas McKean, a future President of the Continental Congress)[59] denied Parliament's authority to levy a tax on the colonies and condemned the provision in the Stamp Act permitting Admiralty Courts to try American citizens for violating the Act.

With great political astuteness, the Declaration also pointed out that "the restrictions imposed by several late Acts of Parliament on the trade of these colonies will render them unable to purchase the manufactures of Great Britain."[60] In the end, this proved to be the most persuasive argument of all since English businessmen carried far more influence in Parliament than thirteen colonies three thousand miles away. On January 17, 1766, London Merchants submitted their own Petition against the Stamp Act and pleaded with their friends and colleagues in the House of Commons to revoke the legislation.[61]

What made believers out of hardened British businessmen was the remarkable effectiveness of an American boycott of British goods and the unprecedented rejection of British authority. By the date the Stamp Act was scheduled to go into effect (November 1, 1765) only Georgia attempted to implement parts of the legislation. In the other twelve colonies, the Stamp Collectors had long since resigned or had pledged not to enforce the Act. The stamps themselves were kept under lock and key, often at undisclosed locations. The King well understood the importance of the issue. In December 1765, he wrote in his personal correspondence that the crisis was "...undoubtedly the most serious matter that ever came before Parliament."[62]

In London, January 1766 proved to be a critical month. The Rockingham ministry was determined to repeal the Stamp Act, but reports of the riots throughout America gave the government tremendous concern over the future of British authority itself. When Parliament reconvened on January 14, the drama began immediately when the ailing William Pitt returned to the House of Commons. He denounced the Stamp Act as unconstitutional: "...my opinion...is, that the Stamp Act be repealed absolutely, totally, and immediately...because it was founded on an erroneous principle. At the same time," Pitt argued, "let the sovereign authority of this country over the colonies, be asserted in as strong terms as can be devised, and be made to extend to every point of legislation whatsoever..." Speaking for the opposition, Grenville angrily challenged Pitt to "tell me when the Americans were emancipated?" Pitt responded: "I have been charged with giving birth to sedition in America..I rejoice that America has resisted... the gentleman asks, when were the colonies emancipated? But I desire to know, when were they made slaves?"[63]

On January 28, Benjamin Franklin, the best known American lobbyist (who, for nearly two decades, resided in London where he represented several of the American colonies), also urged repeal in his testimony before a committee of the House of Commons. His remarks proved prophetic. "Many arguments have been lately used here [in Parliament] to shew [sic]... that if you have no right to tax them [Americans] internally, you have none to tax them externally, or make any other law to bind them. At present they do not reason so, but in time they may possibly be convinced by these arguments."[64]

By mid-March, both houses of Parliament had reluctantly voted to put an end to the ordeal. Finally, on March 18, 1766, George III gave his royal assent. The Stamp Act was dead.[65] As part of the process, however, Parliament did follow Pitt's advice by passing the Declaratory Act that same day. In the new legislation, Parliament did indeed assert its authority to legislate concerning all matters pertaining to America. At the time it was, at best, a fig leaf; an attempt to camouflage Parliament's humiliation. In America, the Declaratory Act was almost completely ignored. Its potential impact was lost in the public jubilation over a rare colonial victory. On May 19, 1766, the Boston Gazette reported that repeal of the Stamp Act touched off "the greatest and most universal joy that was ever felt on the continent of America."[66] In Williamsburg, Lt. Gov. Fauquier presented fireworks and a formal ball at the Governor's Mansion to celebrate the repeal.

The mood was dramatically different in London. The Rockingham Ministry collapsed in June and was replaced a month later by Pitt's second administration. In the hope of persuading his former foe to return to government, George III tempted Pitt with a peerage. Foolishly, William Pitt, popularly known as "The Great Commoner," succumbed to the temptation and was henceforth known as the Earl of Chatham. As he took his seat in the House of Lords, his influence with both the people and the Commons noticeably diminished.[67] Shocked by his lack of public support for the first time in his long and distinguished career, and still racked by poor health, Chatham gradually withdrew from much of the work of his own Ministry despite the bread riots which rocked England that November. In the midst of this political void, Charles Townshend (popularly known in some circles as "Champagne Charlie"[68]) became the new Chancellor of the Exchequer in early 1767.

In his determination to improve the government's bottom line, Townshend boasted that he knew how to raise revenue from America. According to his proposal, since Americans successfully resisted paying one "internal" tax, then he would impose a wide range of "external" taxes on them. The long history of trade and navigation acts provided the perfect example for his plan and the new Declaratory Act clearly gave Parliament the authority to enforce such legislation. The Townshend Acts passed Parliament in late June 1767. They placed new duties on a wide range of items exported to America including glass, lead, tea and paper. The legislation then went one fateful step further by directing that the funds raised through this system should be used to pay the salaries of Royal officials in each American colony. If permitted to stand, this new provision would deny the colonial assemblies one of their few effective tools in dealing with royal officials; i.e., the threat of withholding an official's salary when a disagreement broke out between the executive and legislature. The Acts finally went into effect on November 20, 1767, but by then Charles Townshend was already dead. A rising young member of the Commons,

Frederick North, replaced Townshend and thereby also inherited the burden of implementing the new taxes.[69]

Opposition arose at once. In the *Pennsylvania Chronicle*, John Dickinson began a series of "Letters from a Farmer in Pennsylvania to the Inhabitants of the British Colonies" in which he carefully and persuasively laid out the arguments against the Townshend Acts.[70] The Letters were reproduced widely throughout the colonies in 1768 and established Dickinson as a major public figure. Simultaneously, a boycott of British goods began to spread along the Atlantic coast. Still tasting victory from the repeal of the Stamp Act, Americans believed that they could force Parliament to back down again. American merchants, who dreaded the price they would be forced to pay again in diminished profits, led the opposition.

At the end of 1767, Chatham's health forced him to resign from the government and he again retired to his country estate. The Duke of Grafton, considered a friend of the colonies, formed a new ministry.[71] Early the next year, the new office of Secretary of State for the Colonies was created in an attempt to better manage American affairs. Lord Hillsborough was the first to hold the position.

On March 4, 1768, Massachusetts Gov. Bernard wrote to Hillsborough that "I have perceived that the wickedness of some and the folly of others will in the end bring troops here..."[72] Within three months, Bernard's fears were realized when the HMS Romney (a British man-of-war) arrived in Boston Harbor to help stop wide-spread smuggling. At the same time, Hillsborough ordered Gen. Gage in New York to send at least one regiment to Boston.[73] That same June, debate in the Massachusetts House of Representatives reached a fever pitch when James Otis referred to the British House of Commons as "a parcel of button-makers...pensioners, pimps and whore-masters."[74] In July, Pennsylvania Speaker Joseph Galloway openly opposed the boycott but he was publicly denounced by Charles Thomson, one of the major leaders of the colony's opposition who later became Secretary of the Conti-nental Congress. Philadelphia ultimately joined Boston and New York in pledging non-importation of British goods.

By late summer 1768, Secretary Hillsborough ordered that two more British regiments should be sent to Boston. On September 5, the *Boston Gazette* ran an article threatening that if troops came "we will put our lives in our hands."[75] Despite this saber rattling, reinforcements did arrive from Nova Scotia on October 1, 1768. A month later, Gen. Gage reported to Hillsborough that quiet was returning to Boston. But James Otis again offered a glimpse of the future when he wrote: "...you [Great Britain] cannot in the end ruin the colonies...we have been a free people, and if you will not let us remain so any longer, we shall be a great people."[76]

Despite the outrage expressed in many of the colonial legislatures, the Townshend Acts remained a less visible target than their predecessor two years earlier. As an "external tax on trade," fewer Americans were aware of them because most of the impact was indirect. The presence of well armed British troops also helped to sober the opposition. Since Hillsborough was eager to defuse the situation, in May 1769 he informed the colonial governors that most of the Townshend duties would be ended and that no new taxes would be proposed. By July 1769, Gen. Gage reported that the Boston crisis had passed and he started removing troops.

In early 1770, the British Government turned over once again. The Duke of Grafton resigned; Lord Chatham (William Pitt) returned to the House of Lords; and, the able and ambitious Frederick North, still Chancellor of the Exchequer, became the head of His Majesty's Government at the age of 38. Despite the courtesy title of "Lord," by which he was popularly known, North was actually the first member of the House of Commons to head the government since Grenville. But, as one of the "King's Friends," he not only enjoyed the support of his Sovereign, he was also weighed down by a profound sense of loyalty to George III. One analyst has speculated that "...the confidential tone of the king's letters seems to show that there was an unusual intimacy between them, which may account for North's compliance."[77] The fact that North was only six years older than the young King could well have contributed to this remarkable sense of camaraderie. In any case, Lord North's elevation began a twelve year odyssey that, despite his best intentions, ended badly for him, the empire and the sovereign he loved.

Initially, North's goal was to orchestrate a period of benign neglect for those he viewed as self-indulgent Americans. Due to his previous position, he knew better than most that all of the recent attempts to extract revenue from North America had resulted in far more pain than gain for the Mother Country. North was determined to change course and thereby reestablish the authority of the British Government. His first step was to repeal all but one of the hated Townshend Acts which he did on March 5, 1770.[78]

In one of history's many ironies, that date is still honored in America, not for events in London, but for the "massacre" that took place that same day, 3,000 miles away, in Boston. The basic facts of the event are clear. The British soldiers involved were part of the force sent by Hillsborough to enforce the Townshend Acts and maintain order in the Massachusetts capital. The citizens of Boston deeply resented the troops and often taunted them. On the night of March 5, that sparring spun out of control. "A stick flew out of the darkness, striking the gun barrel of Private Hugh

Montgomery. He stepped back, or slipped on the icy street, and fired his weapon. Knocked to the ground, he screamed to the other soldiers, 'Fire! Fire!'" Fearing for their lives, the soldiers did open fire on the mob and five Americans were killed, including Crispus Attucks, the first African-American to die in the revolution.[79] Sam Adams immediately saw the enormous propaganda potential that the incident provided. He prepared his own account of what he termed "The Boston Massacre" and distributed it as widely as possible, including the next ship to England. As a result of his quick action, Sam Adams' version of events was circulated throughout both England and America weeks before the Massachusetts Government's official report was released.

The most bizarre twist to the story is that it was Sam Adams' younger cousin, John, who was persuaded to assist in the defense of the British troops when they came to trial. The final verdict acquitted the commander and four of his men, convicted two others of manslaughter, and ordered the dismissal of the remaining two soldiers.[80] John Adams' reputation as an American patriot combined with the news of the repeal of the Townshend Acts (which reached Boston prior to the trial) helped to defuse what could have become open warfare.

The seeds of a future confrontation, however, had been planted on that date, as well. Even though the Townshend Acts were gone, Lord North decided to retain the tax on tea in order to reaffirm the spirit of the Declaratory Act. At first, Boston, New York and Philadelphia pledged to continue the boycott until it, too, was repealed. But by July, American merchants felt confident enough to start importing British goods once again. In October, even Boston finally capitulated. At the end of that month, John Dickinson wrote from Pennsylvania to Arthur Lee in London that "My countrymen have been provoked, but not quite enough..."[81]

As the new year began, the resistance had faded and a period of near tranquility settled over the American colonies for most of the next two years. Lord North's goal of reducing tension between Britain and America seemed remarkably successful. Even events surrounding the destruction of the British revenue ship Gaspée off the coast of Rhode Island in June 1772 failed to significantly reignite popular passion. It did, however, help to underscore the need for more effective communication both within and between the colonies. In November 1772, Massachusetts formed a Committee of Correspondence to facilitate regular communication among its towns and villages. The following March, the Virginia House urged the creation of a Committee of Correspondence among all 13 colonies.[82] By mid-summer 1773, Connecticut, Massachusetts, New Hampshire, Rhode Island and South Carolina had responded positively to Virginia's call. By the end of the year, most of the remaining colonies had also joined. At the same time, Sam Adams and Thomas Cushing of Massachusetts began to suggest that what was really needed was a formal meeting of a colonial congress. By July 1773, even Benjamin Franklin and Arthur Lee, America's two major lobbyists overseas, expressed support for the idea.[83]

One of the most reliable accounts of the American Revolution, which provided "a detailed record of the progress of the conflict between Britain and America, year by year as it developed,"[84] was the English publication known as the *Annual Register*. During 1771-73, it was "virtually silent on American affairs."[85] During that period, the British Empire's focus had turned to India and the growing financial crisis of the East India Company, which served as the surrogate for British authority in that region of the world. Under the mercantile system, the financial health of the government and the company were tightly entwined. In the spring of 1773, to help the company unload its huge surplus of tea at a profit, Lord North permitted the company to sell its tea in American without paying the English tax while, at the same time, he intended to tightly enforce the tea duty on the American colonies.[86] Through such a process, the East India tea would still be cheaper than the Dutch tea which colonists like John Hancock regularly smuggled along the East Coast. Special agents were appointed to enforce the new program in America's major ports.

Between October and early December 1773, popular sentiment and a revival of the Sons of Liberty forced most of the Tea Agents to resign and the tea to be impounded in Philadelphia, New York and Charleston. In Boston, however, the Tea Agents surprisingly refused to step down. As a result, Sam Adams and his fellow patriots were more determined than ever to prevent the unloading of their cargo. On the night of December 16, 1773, the Sons of Liberty, dressed as Mohawk Indians to provide a partial disguise, boarded three ships in Boston Harbor and dumped 342 chests of tea into the bay.[87] News of the Boston Tea Party quickly spread through America and across the Atlantic. Some, like George Washington, a member of the Virginia House of Burgesses, were "shocked to read of the Boston Tea Party because he believed it would encourage the British to further excesses."[88] Sam Adams and his followers, however, were convinced that the tea duty had to be stopped at all cost and that their symbolic action had roused America from its slumber. Unlike Washington, they delighted in what they considered to be Britain's extreme overreaction two months later because it finally forced Americans to take sides.

When word of the incident reached London, both the King and Parliament erupted in outrage. They agreed that it was time to firmly reassert British authority over America by making an example out of

Massachusetts. In March, Parliament passed the Boston Port Act, the first of four legislative measures which were vilified as the "Intolerable Acts" in the colonies. The Boston Port Act, in effect, closed Boston's Harbor, the colony's economic lifeline. Gen. Thomas Gage was then appointed the new Governor of Massachusetts. He arrived on May 13, 1774. That night, the Boston Town Meeting demanded that all trade with Great Britain be suspended immediately throughout the colonies.[89] They next urged that a congress be called to discuss other appropriate actions. Massachusetts' best known messenger, Paul Revere, then carried the proposal to New York City and on to Philadelphia. Conservatives and merchants in both places shuddered at the thought of yet another boycott. They therefore urged that a meeting of the colonies should precede any further action. In doing so, they hoped to diminish the impact of the New England radicals by electing delegates closer to their own views. On May 27, 1774, members of the Virginia House of Burgesses also endorsed the revised proposal and then issued an invitation to the other 12 colonies to elect delegates to a Continental Congress which would meet that fall in Philadelphia.[90]

Throughout that summer, as one colony after another elected delegates to the upcoming congress, Parliament continued to stoke the fire of rebellion by approving three more Intolerable Acts. On May 20, 1774, it cut to the very heart of American Rights by adopting the Massachusetts Government Act which abrogated the colony's Royal Charter of 1691. That same day, it approved the Administration of Justice Act which was designed to transfer some colonial trials to other locations or even to England itself in order to increase convictions. And, on June 2, it added insult to injury by expanding the Quartering Act under which Americans were responsible for providing barracks and supplies for the same British troops who were there to enforce the other harsh measures.[91]

A fifth piece of legislation, the Quebec Act, was also approved during this period. Even though it had been under discussion long before the Boston Tea Party, the Quebec Act was viewed in America as yet another slap in the face. It extended Canada's boundary to the Ohio River, land long coveted by British Americans, and granted French Canadians the right to continue to practice their Catholic faith which the vast majority of British Americans considered a treasonous allegiance to a foreign power, the Pope. In the opinion of many historians, the Quebec Act was perhaps the primary reason that Canadians remained loyal to Britain throughout the American Revolution despite repeated efforts by the Continental Congress to either conquer or seduce its northern neighbors.[92]

By the end of the summer, only Georgia had resisted attempts to elect delegates and participate in the congress. On August 20, 1774, the four

Massachusetts delegates (Sam Adams, John Adams, Thomas Cushing and Robert Treat Paine) arrived in New York City to a hero's welcome.[93] For six days they were celebrated everywhere they went. As the news from London grew worse, Massachusetts increasingly became a symbol of American resistance. Finally, on August 29, the four delegates entered Philadelphia to another warm welcome. Since they had wisely agreed among themselves to tone down their usual fiery rhetoric, they made a positive impression on their fellow delegates from across the continent. Without a moment's delay, the Massachusetts men began an endless round of private dinner parties and late nights in public taverns in order to size up their distinguished colleagues.[94] Back home in Boston, Gov. Gage-- still the military commander of British forces in North America--wrote to Lord Dartmouth on September 2, 1774, that "...Civil Government is near its end..."[95]

George III and his ministers had hoped to intimidate the other American colonies by making a brutal example of Massachusetts. Instead, they forced even cautious legislators and conservative merchants to join together for their mutual defense. Once again, British miscalculation had led to folly. After 167 years, the period of American colonial submission had come to an end.

On September 5, 1774, a new era began.

Introduction

IN THE BEGINNING

Notes

Abbreviation Key

JCC
Ford, Worthington C., et. al. eds., *Journals of the Continental Congress, 1774-1789*; 34 volumes, Washington, D.C.: National Archives, 1904-37.

PHL
Hamer, Philip M., et al., eds., *The Papers of Henry Laurens*, 16 volumes, Columbia, SC: University of South Carolina Press, 1968-2003.

LDC
Smith, Paul H., et al., eds., *Letters of Delegates to Congress, 1774-1789*; 25 volumes, Washington, D.C.: Library of Congress, 1976-2000.

[1] Daniel M. Friedenberg, Life, Liberty and the Pursuit of Land, (Prometheus Books, Buffalo, NY, 1992), p. 13. In his preface, Friedenberg states that "in a fundamental sense, the history of the United States is land munching in every direction..."

[2] David A. Price, Love and Hate in Jamestown, (Alfred A. Knopf, New York, 2003), pp. 27 & 36,

[3] W. E. Lunt, History of England, 3rd ed. (Harper & Brothers, New York, 1947) pp. 387-388. When Elizabeth I died without an heir, Parliament selected James, the son of Henry VIII's great-niece, Mary Queen of Scots. At that time, James was already King of Scotland--James VI--but he became James I when he accepted the English crown and thereby began the House of Stuart (1603-1714). It was James' great-grandson--a German Prince--who eventually succeeded to the British Throne as George I over a century later (1714). James is best known today for the edition of the Bible which bears his name.

[4] Price, op. cit., p. 3.

[5] Edward P. Hamilton, The French and Indian Wars, (Doubleday & Company, Garden City, NY, 1962) p. 22.

[6] Nathaniel Philbrick, Mayflower, (Viking, New York, 2006), pp. 20-21. Of the 102 passengers, only approximately 50 were religious separatists (p. 29). According to Philbrick, half of the Mayflower's passengers were dead four months after they landed in the New World (p. 46). See also: William L. Langer, Editor, "The English in North America," An Encyclopedia of World History (Houghton Mifflin Company, Boston, 1972) 5th Edition, p. 549.

[7] Philbrick, op., cit., pp. 42-43.

[8] Philbrick, op., cit., p. 40.

[9] Simon Schama, A History of Britain: The Wars of the British 1603-1776, vol. 2 (Hyperion, New York, 2001) pp. 242-253. On September 3, 1758, exactly seven years after the Battle of Worcester--when Charles II was driven into exile--Oliver Cromwell died. Twenty-one months later, that same Charles II entered London in triumph and reclaimed the British Throne.

[10] J. Steven Watson, The Reign of George III, 1760-1815, (The Clarendon Press, Oxford, 1960) p. 576.

[11] Mark Mayo Boatner III, Encyclopedia of the American Revolution (David McKay Company, New York, 1974) p. 774.

[12] Henry Steele Commager, Editor, James Otis, "Speech Against the Writs of Assistance," Documents of American History (Appleton-Century-Crofts, New York, 1963), 7th edition, pp. 45-47.

[13] Lynn Montross, The Reluctant Rebels (Harper & Brothers Publishers, New York, 1950), p, 20.

[14] Schama, op. cit., pp. 320-321.

[15] Langer, op. cit., pp. 554-555.

[16] Delaware, which was technically the last of the original colonies, functioned as a separate entity for decades before being conveyed to William Penn by the Duke of York (the future James II) in 1682. In 1704, it began the process of reclaiming its independence from Pennsylvania when it was granted its own legislature. In 1710, it also initiated its own Executive Council. It did not complete the process, however, until full statehood was declared in 1776.

[17] Langer, op. cit., pp. 554-555.

[18] Hamilton, op. cit., p. 148.

[19] William Benton, Publisher, Encyclopaedia Britannica (Encyclopaedia Britannica, Inc., Chicago, 1966), Vol. 7, pp. 458-459.

[20] James Thomas Flexner, George Washington: The Forge of Experience (1732-1775), p. 81.

[21] Hamilton, op.cit., p. 148.

[22] Flexner, op. cit., pp, 104-106.

[23] Herbert L. Osgood, The American Colonies in the Eighteenth Century, vol. 4 (Peter Smith, Gloucester, MA, 1958) p. 317.

[24] For additional information on the Galloway Plan of Union, see Chapter 2.

[25] Osgood, op. cit., pp. 349-350.

[26] Boatner, op. cit., p. 782.

[27] Watson, op. cit., pp. 72-74.

[28] Hamilton, op. cit., pp. 288-289.

[29] Walter R. Borneman, The French & Indian War (HarperCollins, New York, 2006), p. 251.

[30] Watson, op. cit., pp. 4-5.

[31] Watson, op. cit., p. 51.

[32] Stanley Ayling, George the Third (Alfred A. Knopf, New York, 1972) pp. 72-74. For nearly two and a half centuries, historians, biographers and students of British history have debated the real role George III played in parliamentary affairs. Some have concluded that he was either passive or simply inept and, in either case, exerted little significant influence on his ministers. Others believe that he was a remarkably subtle --yet effective--politician thanks, in no small part, to the tutoring of Lord Bute. The transformation of The Great Commoner, William Pitt, into the partially declawed Lord Chatham would seem to support the latter conclusion. The King, like his royal predecessors, did indeed have many favors to dispense. Unlike them, however, George III had a better grasp of the parliamentary system and the nation. Some might argue that except for his streak of stubbornness and his serious health problems he might have been one of the best politicians of his age.

[33] As cited in Reed Browning, The Duke of Newcastle, (Yale University Press, New Haven, 1975), p. 276.

[34] Browning, op. cit., p. 276.

[35] Watson, op. cit., p. 74.

[36] Watson, op. cit., p. 88.

[37] Colin G. Calloway, The Scratch of a Pen, (Oxford University Press, Oxford, 2006), p. 11.

[38] Calloway, op. cit., p. 20.

[39] Price, op. cit., pp. 239-241.

[40] Louis Kronenberger, The Extraordinary Mr. Wilkes (New English Library, London, 1974) p. 35.

[41] See Chapter 2.

[42] Montross, op. cit., pp. 61-63. Wilkes was an irreverent popular hero who drove the entire British establishment mad. "Wilkes' enemies, who were legion, accused him of being an ambitious demagogue rather than a sincere reformer--a charge supported by many of his own cynicisms. At any rate, he proved his courage as well as ability, and in 1763 the cry 'Wilkes and liberty!' became the rally call of the London mob."

[43] Kinloch Bull, Jr., The Oligarchs in Colonial and Revolutionary Charleston (University of South Carolina Press, Columbia, SC, 1991) p. 152.

[44] Allan Nevins, The American States During and After the Revolution (The Macmillan Company, New York, 1927) p. 24.

[45] Richard B. Morris, Editor, Encyclopedia of American History, (Harper & Row, Publishers, New York, 1961), p. 193. The term "Manifest Destiny" was made popular in 1845 in reference to the debate over the Northwest boundary of the United States.

[46] Barbara W. Tuchman, The March of Folly (Alfred A. Knopf, New York, 1984) pp. 127-231. In Chapter Four, Tuchman speculates on what might have happened if Britain and the United States had retained some formal ties. Is it possible, she asks, that such "a preponderance of transatlantic power" might have "...spared the world the Great War of 1914-18 and its unending sequels." Other chapters deal with the fall of Troy; the provocation of the Renaissance Popes which led to the Protestant Reformation; and, United States policy in Vietnam.

[47] Lawrence Henry Gipson, The Coming of the Revolution, 1763-75, (Harper & Row, New York, 1954) pp. 65-66.

[48] Boatner, op. cit., p. 313.

[49] James Curtis Ballagh, Editor, The Letters of Richard Henry Lee, 1762-78, vol. 1 (The Macmillan Company, New York, 1911) p. 6; Richard Henry Lee to a gentleman in London, May 31, 1764.

[50] Oliver Perry Chitwood, Richard Henry Lee, Statesman of the Revolution (West Virginia University Library, Morgantown, WV, 1967) p. 32.

[51] Morris, op. cit., p. 75.

[52] Calloway, op. cit., p. 12.

[53] Gipson, op. cit., p. 70.

[54] Walter Isaacson, Benjamin Franklin: An American Life, (Simon & Schuster, New York, 2003), pp. 222-223. When Franklin failed to dissuade Grenville from adopting the Stamp Act, he took a more pragmatic approach, even nominating a close colleague in Pennsylvania to be that colony's Stamp Agent. His friend, John Hughes, quickly regretted the appointment and Franklin's reputation was momentarily tarnished.

[55] Richard Walsh, Charleston's Sons of Liberty, (University of South Carolina Press, Columbia, 1959), pp. 32-33.

[56] A. J. Langguth, Patriots: The Men Who Started the American Revolution, (Simon and Schuster, New York, 1988) p. 69. While there remains some confusion over the exact number of Resolutions introduced by Patrick Henry, perhaps the most credible source remains John C. Miller, Origins of the American Revolution, (Little, Brown and Company, Boston, 1943), pp. 122-126.

[57] John R. Galvin, <u>Three Men of Boston</u> (Thomas Y. Crowell Company, New York, 1976) p. 108.

[58] Galvin, op. cit., p. 103.

[59] See Chapter 7.

[60] "Resolutions of the Stamp Act Congress," <u>Documents of American History</u>, ed. Henry Steele Commager, 7th ed., (Appleton-Century-Crofts, New York, 1963) p. 58.

[61] Commager, op. cit., "Petition of London Merchants Against the Stamp Act," p. 59-60.

[62] Bonamy Dobree, Editor, <u>The Letters of King George III</u> (London, 1935) p. 33; George III to Henry Conway, 5 December 1765. See also: David H. Murdoch, Editor, <u>Rebellion in America: A contemporary British Viewpoint, 1765-1783</u>, (Clio Books, Santa Barbara, CA, 1979), p. 39.

[63] Gipson, op. cit., pp. 109-110.

[64] Gipson, op. cit., p. 110.

[65] Jack P. Greene and J. R. Pole, Editors, <u>The Blackwell Encyclopedia of the American Revolution</u> (Basil Blackwell, Inc., Cambridge, MA, 1991), pp. 121-122.

[66] Galvin, op. cit., p. 127.

[67] Lillian B. Miller, <u>"The Dye is Now Cast"</u> (Smithsonian Institution Press, Washington, DC, 1975) p. 150.

[68] Thomas Fleming, <u>Liberty, The American Revolution</u> (Viking, New York, 1997) pp. 64-65.

[69] Watson, op. cit., p. 129.

[70] Claude H. Van Tyne, <u>The Causes of the War of Independence</u> (Houghton Mifflin Company, Boston, 1922) pp. 252-3.

[71] Lillian B. Miller, op. cit., p. 175.

[72] Galvin, op. cit., p. 149.

[73] Gipson, op. cit., p. 189.

[74] Galvin, op. cit., p. 163.

[75] *Boston Gazette*, September 5, 1768.

[76] Thomas Tudor, <u>The Life of James Otis</u> (Boston, 1823) p. 35; James Otis to Arthur Jones, November 1768.

[77] Boatner, op. cit., p. 811.

[78] Langer, op. cit., p. 558.

[79] Greene, op. cit., pp. 140-141; Robert J. Chaffin, "The Townshend Acts Crisis, 1767-1770."

[80] Page Smith, John Adams (Doubleday & Company, New York, 1962), Vol.1, p. 125.

[81] Jack N. Rakove, The Beginnings of National Politics (Alfred A. Knopf, New York, 1979) p. 7.

[82] Nevins, op. cit., p. 27.

[83] Rakove, op. cit., p. 12.

[84] David H. Murdoch, ed., Rebellion in America: A contemporary British Viewpoint, 1765-1783, (Clio Books, Santa Barbara, CA, 1979) p. 1.

[85] Murdoch, op. cit., p. 113.

[86] Brian Gardner, The East India Company (Dorset Press, New York, 1971) pp. 110-111.

[87] Schama, op. cit., p. 469.

[88] James Thomas Flexner, Washington: The Indispensable Man, (Little, Brown & Company, Boston, 1974) p. 58.

[89] Edmund Cody Burnett, The Continental Congress (The Macmillan Company, New York, 1941) p. 19.

[90] Harry M. Ward, The American Revolution, Nationhood Achieved, 1763-1788 (St. Martin's Press, New York, 1995) p. 51.

[91] Greene, op. cit., pp. 201-202.

[92] Frank Arthur Mumby, George III and the American Revolution: The Beginnings (Kraus Reprint Company, New York, 1970) p. 329.

[93] Montross, op. cit., p. 30.

[94] L. H. Butterfield, Editor, Diary and Autobiography of John Adams (The Belknap Press, Cambridge, 1961), p. 114.

[95] Lawrence Henry Gipson, The Triumphant Empire: Britain Sails Into the Storm, (New York, 1965), p. 163; Thomas Gage to Lord Dartmouth, September 2, 1774.

THE FIRST AMERICAN REPUBLIC: 1774-1789

Thomas Patrick Chorlton

PRESIDENT	1	2	3	4	5	6	7	8	9	10	11	12	13	14	15	16	17
RANDOLPH	1721	1775	54	N	Y	Y	1774	53	1	$$	Y	N	1	0	N	N	N
MIDDLETON	1717	1784	67	N	N	N	1774	57	1	$$$	Y	N	3	12	N	N	N
HANCOCK	1737	1793	56	N	Y	N	1775	38	30	$$$	Y	Y	1	2	Y	Y	N
LAURENS	1724	1792	68	N	Y	Y	1777	53	13	$$$	N	N	1	12	N	Y	N
JAY	1745	1829	83	N	Y	N	1778	32	10	$$	N	Y	1	7	N	N	N
HUNTINGTON	1731	1796	64	N	N	N	1779	48	23	$$	N	Y	1	0	Y	Y	N
McKEAN	1734	1817	83	N	N	N	1781	47	5	$$	Y	Y	2	6	Y	Y	N
HANSON	1721	1783	62	N	N	N	1781	60	12	$$	N	N	1	8	N	Y	N
BOUDINOT	1740	1821	81	N	N	N	1782	42	12	$$$	N	N	1	2	N	N	N
MIFFLIN	1744	1800	56	N	Y	N	1783	39	9	$$	Y	Y	1	0	N	N	Y
RH LEE	1732	1794	62	N	Y	N	1784	52	12	$$	Y	N	2	9	Y	Y	N
GORHAM	1738	1796	58	N	N	N	1786	48	6	$$	Y	N	1	9	N	N	Y
ST. CLAIR	1736	1818	82	Y	Y	Y	1787	50	9	$	N	Y	1	7	N	N	N
GRIFFIN	1748	1810	62	N	Y	Y	1788	39	15	$	N	N	1	4	N	N	N
SECRETARY																	
THOMSON	1729	1824	94	Y	Y	N	1774	45	175	$$	N	N	2	2	*	*	N

1. Birth Year
2. Death Year
3. Age at death
4. Born in Europe
5. Traveled in Europe
6. Attended Inns of Court in London
7. Year elected President
8. Age when elected
9. Months as President
10. Personal Fortune during life
11. Speaker of his Colony/State
12. Served as Governor
13. Number of Wives
14. Number of Children
15. Signed Decl. of Independence
16. Signed Articles of Confederation
17. Signed US Constitution
*   Thomson certified document

xliii

Peyton Randolph

Chapter 1

President
PEYTON RANDOLPH
of
VIRGINIA

First Among Equals

By the morning of Monday, September 5, 1774, most of the delegates to the Continental Congress had arrived in Philadelphia. North Carolina would present its credentials nine days later. Georgia wouldn't join for a year. [1] Some members had been in the city for several days, eager to meet and evaluate their colleagues from the other colonies. A few, such as Sam and John Adams of Massachusetts, were already well known by reputation. In contrast, Joseph Galloway, the Speaker of the Pennsylvania House of Representatives, and Peyton Randolph, the Speaker of Virginia's House of Burgesses, were best known because of their elective positions. The most famous American, however, was not there that morning. Benjamin Franklin was still living in London where he had already served for 15 years as an agent for several of the colonies. [2]

The 43 men who did gather that cool, damp morning at Smith's City Tavern (Philadelphia's newest and finest)[3] were well aware that they were about to take a fateful step into history. [4] The King himself had denounced their gathering. Parliament could easily decide to use the full weight of the British Empire against them as it had recently done to the colony of Massachusetts. The path ahead was perilous. No one dared to utter the word "independence," and few would have identified with such a cause. Some of the more conservative delegates were there expressly to sidetrack any discussion of the issue if it should arise. What they all agreed on was the critical need for immediate reform in the British Government's relationship with its American colonies. These men took their rights and their status as British citizens very seriously. They prayed that their King and his government would do so, as well.

As John Adams recorded in his diary: "At Ten, The Delegates all met at the City Tavern, and walked to the Carpenters Hall" three blocks away.

1

It was the closer of the two meeting places that had been offered to the delegates for their deliberations. The other, the Pennsylvania State House, was two blocks further west. Even before Congress officially opened, the political tug of war had begun. Adams and others feared that if they accepted the State House they might also be pressured into accepting their host, Speaker Galloway, as their first elected leader. Since Galloway was known to have loyalist tendencies, many of the delegates wanted to avoid such a trap.[5] If a tavern closer to the State House had been selected as the gathering place that morning, the course of American history might well have been altered. Instead, when the delegates inspected Carpenters Hall "The General Cry was, that this was a good Room, and the question was put, whether We were satisfied with this Room, and it passed in the Affirmative." But, "A very few were for the Negative and they were chiefly from Pennsylvania and New York."[6]

Once the meeting hall had been selected, the first order of business was to elect one individual to preside over their deliberations and to represent the body as a whole. As the oldest and largest of the 13 colonies, Virginia held the unique distinction of being first among equals. Even though Town Meetings in New York, Massachusetts and Pennsylvania had earlier endorsed the idea of holding a continent wide meeting, it was Virginia that had issued the call for the colonies to convene a Congress.[7] Therefore, it is hardly surprising that the delegates turned to Virginia when selecting their first leader. John Adams and other savvy New England delegates also realized that a truly united response to the crisis at home demanded visible leadership from other regions, especially the South.

It was equally obvious which member of Virginia's delegation would receive this honor. In each of the colonies, the Speaker of the House was the highest elected official. Even though the Virginia delegation included six other distinguished members (Richard Bland, Benjamin Harrison, Patrick Henry, Richard Henry Lee, Edmund Pendleton and George Washington) there was no question that Peyton Randolph, Speaker of the Virginia House of Burgesses, headed their delegation. Fortunately, he was a man of great distinction and extensive government experience.

Thomas Lynch, Sr. of South Carolina made the nomination. Adams recorded that historic moment: "Then Mr. Lynch arose, and said there was a Gentleman present who had presided with great Dignity over a very respectable Society, greatly to the Advantage of America, and he therefore proposed that the Hon. Peyton Randolph Esqr., one of the Delegates from Virginia, and the late Speaker of their House of Burgesses, should be appointed Chairman and he doubted not it would be unanimous.--The

Question was put and he was unanimously chosen. Mr. Randolph then took the Chair..."[8]

Charles Thomson of Pennsylvania was then elected Secretary. Silas Deane of Connecticut described the implications of Thomson's election to his wife that same day: "This proceeding, is highly agreeable to...Citizens in general, but mortifying to the last Degree To Mr. Galloway and his Party, Thompson [sic] being his Sworn opposite as You may say, & by his means, prevented being one of the Congress, for this province."[9] Galloway, who clearly leaned toward the loyalist position, and Thomson, popularly known as "the Sam Adams of Philadelphia,"[10] had long been bitter political rivals. By blocking Thomson's election as a delegate to Congress, Galloway had hoped to eliminate Thomson's influence over events. Exactly the opposite happened. Thomson's election as Secretary gave him a unique role during the entire fifteen-year history of Congress.[11]

In his "Notes of Debates," New York Delegate James Duane described what happened next: "A question was then put what Title the Convention should assume & it was agred that it should be called the Congress. Another Question was put what shoud [sic] be the Stile of Mr Randolph & it was agreed that he should be called the President."[12] Caesar Rodney of Delaware also shared his thoughts on Congress during its first week. On September 9 he wrote to his brother Thomas: "...in short it is the greatest Assembly...that ever was Collected in America." Rodney also observed that "the Bostonians who (we know) have been Condemned by Many for their Violence, are Moderate men..."[13]

When Congress resumed at ten o'clock the following morning, Patrick Henry of Virginia rose to declare that "Government is dissolved...We are in a State of Nature..."[14] A new era had indeed begun for America and for the World.

As Congress then began its deliberations, few men, if any, could have been better prepared for the presidency. Peyton Randolph's long and distinguished career as Attorney General and Speaker of the Virginia House of Burgesses, America's oldest legislature, helped him to develop and refine the skills and subtlety that were essential for effective leadership. His reputation for firmness yet fairness was also well known. And, his first-hand experience in dealing with Parliament and the British Government during earlier years in London was invaluable. As a large and well educated man, Peyton's demeanor itself commanded authority and respect. In his biography of the Randolph Family, H. L. Eckenrode described Peyton as "...tall and powerful and red-faced, a veritable ox of a man..."[15] Of special importance to his 18th Century contemporaries, the Randolph name was second to none throughout the colonies.

The Randolph Family first arrived in Virginia in 1642 when 19 year old Henry Randolph left Northamptonshire to seek his fame and fortune in the New World. He eventually became Clerk of the Virginia House of Burgesses and married the Speaker's daughter. In 1669, Henry and his wife relocated to England, but the childless couple returned to Virginia before he died in 1672. Even though their time back in England was fairly brief, it apparently inspired Henry's 18 year old nephew, William, to follow in his uncle's footsteps by emigrating to America. Today, we refer to that eager young teenager as William of Turkey Island, the founder of the Randolph Dynasty in Virginia. "He began life without an acre and before he died he owned 10,000 acres."[16] William and his wife Mary Isham also raised nine children. Remarkably, all lived well into adulthood. Each of their seven sons received his own estate upon William's death in 1711, and their two daughters married with large dowries.

William's fifth oldest son, John Randolph of Tazewell Hall, studied law at London's prestigious Inns of Court and became Virginia's Attorney General. Twice he was sent back to England to represent the colony on urgent legislative business. The British Government was so impressed with his ability that he was the only native Virginian ever to be knighted by the King. In 1736, Sir John Randolph was unanimously elected Speaker of the House of Burgesses. But, one year later, at the height of his career, Sir John died suddenly at the age of 44.[17]

Sir John's son, Peyton, was born in Virginia in 1721 and was educated in Williamsburg at the College of William and Mary. Then, following in his father's foot-steps, he traveled to England in 1739 to study law at the Inns of Court. Upon Peyton's return to America, he was called to the bar on February 10, 1742. In recognition of his ability and in deference to his family ties, Peyton was appointed to his father's former position as Virginia's Attorney General on May 7, 1744.[18]

The following March, the young attorney married Elizabeth Harrison, known throughout her life as Betty, but called Bess by her devoted husband. She was the oldest of nine children of the late Col. Benjamin Harrison of Berkeley Plantation. Her brother Benjamin, who became one of Peyton's close political colleagues, was known for uttering "plain truths"[19] in an era that delighted in elocution. That same brother's youngest son, William Henry Harrison, went on to become the 9th President of the United States (1841) under the Second Republic; and, President Harrison's grandson, another Benjamin, served as the 23rd President (1889-93). Bess and Peyton, however, remained childless (but later they informally adopted Peyton's 22 year old nephew, Edmund Randolph, when Peyton's younger brother and his family fled to England in the early days of the American Revolution).[20]

In 1745, at the age of 24, Peyton inherited various properties and plantations outside of Williamsburg from his late father's estate. The income they generated (along with his private law practice) permitted him to devote most of his attention to public affairs. In August 1747, Peyton also became a Vestryman at Bruton Parish Church in Williamsburg and, two years later, he "was commissioned one of the justices to serve on the bench in the regular monthly courts" of York County..." For the next few years his name headed the list of justices, and he was present at almost every session..."[21] Many years later, Peyton's cousin Thomas Jefferson sketched this profile of his famous relative:

"He was indeed a most excellent man; and none was ever more beloved and respected by his friends. Somewhat cold and coy towards strangers, but of the sweetest affability when ripened into acquaintance. Of Attic pleasantry in conversation, always good humored and conciliatory. With a sound and logical head, he was well read in the law; and his opinions when consulted, were highly regarded, presenting always a learned and sound view of the subject, but generally, too, a listlessness to go into its thorough development; for being heavy and inert in body, he was rather too indolent and careless for business, which occasioned him to get a smaller proportion of it at the bar than his abilities would otherwise have commanded. Indeed, after his appointment as Attorney General, he did not seem to court, nor scarcely to welcome business. In that office he considered himself equally charged with the rights of the colony as with those of the crown; and in criminal prosecutions exaggerating nothing he aimed at a candid and just state of the transaction, believing it more a duty to save an innocent than to convict a guilty man. Although not eloquent, his mater was so substantial that no man commanded more attention..."[22]

Peyton's legislative career began in the summer of 1748 when the citizens of Williamsburg elected him to represent them in the House of Burgesses, the lower house of Virginia's General Assembly. When the legislature met that October, he was appointed to the powerful and prestigious Committee on Privileges and Elections.

The Assembly adjourned the following May as the ailing Lt. Gov. Gooch ended his long and distinguished tenure in the colony (1727-1749) and prepared to return to England. His replacement, Lt. Gov. Robert Dinwiddie, finally convened a new Assembly in April 1752. This time, Peyton was elected to represent the College of William and Mary, his alma mater.

That same month, Lt. Gov. Dinwiddie initiated a plan to enhance his own income by collecting a fee of one pistole [approximately 20 shillings] for affixing the seal of the colony on all land patents issued in Virginia.[23] After consulting the Council, Dinwiddie believed that the new fee clearly fell within his prerogative. Under pressure from their constituents, however, members of the House of Burgesses viewed the pistole fee as an illegal tax which had been imposed without their approval. The issue came to a head when the second session of the General Assembly met on November 1, 1753. In early December, the Burgesses expressed their outrage in an Address to the King; and then, on Monday, December 17, they officially appointed Peyton Randolph as their agent "to negotiate the Affairs of this Colony, in Great-Britain."[24] It was an extremely delicate situation. Since Peyton left Virginia without the Lt. Governor's permission, Dinwiddie declared that he had forfeited his position as Attorney General.

In early January 1754, Peyton set out on "a long and difficult winter voyage across the North Atlantic."[25] He arrived in London in February and started to lobby on behalf of his cause. On April 2, the Board of Trade held a hearing on the issue as part of a larger review of frontier defense. Peyton's efforts were negated from the start, however, because the Board refused to accept his credentials as an agent of the General Assembly and therefore denied him permission to present the case against the pistole fee on behalf of the House of Burgesses. The next day he again appeared before the Board, this time to explain his absence from his duties as Attorney General without the Lt. Governor's permission. In June, just as the French & Indian War broke out along the American frontier, Peyton was once again summoned by the Board and informed that the King considered his office as Attorney General to be vacant.[26] On July 3, 1754, the Board of Trade informed Dinwiddie that they had ruled in the Governor's favor, but they placed several restrictions on his conduct pertaining to the fee. They also made clear that they favored Peyton's reappointment as Attorney General in order "to quiet the Minds of the People..." On February 10, 1755, Lt. Gov. Dinwiddie reported back to the Board that he had indeed reinstated Peyton as Virginia's Attorney General even though it was "very disagreeable" to him. On May 13, the Board of Trade gave its final approval.[27]

Unrepentant, Peyton reported on his mission in person to the House of Burgesses. In response, his colleagues offered their thanks "for his faithful Discharge of the Trust reposed in him by this House."[28] What he apparently never did receive was the £2,500 which was originally promised by his fellow Burgesses to cover his expenses. But, as a result of his lobbying efforts in London, Peyton had become one of the few American leaders who was well known throughout the British Government and, in turn, knew Parliament and the Privy Council first-hand.

During the General Assembly's spring session in 1756, Peyton, once again the colony's Attorney General, also became Chairman of the Committee on Privileges and Elections, one of the most powerful positions in the House of Burgesses. That May, he took on a completely different responsibility when he announced that he was organizing a large group of prominent Virginia gentlemen to serve under his military command. They became known as the Associators. Because the French and Indian War had been raging on Virginia's frontier for nearly two years by then, the colonial Militia was eager to mobilize new recruits. While no one expected these pampered aristocrats to become an effective fighting force, even Lt. Gov. Dinwiddie encouraged them as "a brave Example for the other People" and hoped that they would "be of Service in annimating [sic] the lower Class..."[29] None were engaged in direct combat. All returned safely to their regular careers.

Peyton then assumed a role better suited to his education and upbringing when he became a member of the Board of Visitors at the College of William and Mary. In 1757, he was also elected by his peers to serve a term as College Rector.[30]

Two years later, Peyton was seriously ill as reported by Maria Byrd, a close family friend: "Poor Mr. Attorney he has had a very long fit of sickness, he looks dreadfully...He complained of a trembling in his Body & that neither Bark nor Doctors could move his Feavers."[31] With time, Peyton's health did improve.

In November 1761, Peyton was again elected by the City of Williamsburg to the General Assembly. Three years later in mid-1764, as word of Parliament's proposed Stamp Act began to circulate, Peyton and the recently established Committee of Correspondence directed their new agent in London to vigorously oppose any such measure. That October, Peyton served as Chairman of the Committee of the Whole as the House of Burgesses debated its formal response to the latest reports from London. He then chaired the ad hoc committee that prepared an Address to the King and Memorials to both Houses of Parliament in strong opposition to the bill. On December 18, 1764, the Virginia legislature gave final approval to the documents.[32]

Colonial protests, however, fell on deaf ears. Parliament approved the Stamp Act in early 1765. It was scheduled to go into effect that November. As leaders of the House of Burgesses began to focus on strategies for winning repeal, some of the younger members of the House felt that stronger measures were required. On May 29, while Peyton was again presiding over the Committee of the Whole, Patrick Henry delivered a diatribe denouncing the Act. It was reputedly one of the most riveting speeches in that legislature's long history. Some of his colleagues considered it to be treasonous.[33] The following day, after many of the Burgesses had already left for home, five of Henry's seven resolutions were approved, the last by a single vote. Nearly a half century later, Thomas Jefferson recorded the scene: "...Peyton Randolph (then Attorney General) came out at the door where I was standing, and exclaimed, 'By God, I would have given one hundred guineas for a single vote!'"[34]

Patrick Henry's final resolution was actually rescinded on May 31 after he also left town. Nevertheless, newspapers across America printed all seven resolutions as though they truly expressed the sentiment of that distinguished body.[35] The inaccurate report had a profound impact throughout the colonies. It appeared that Virginia was leading the opposition to the Act.

In May 1766, while the resistance to the Stamp Act continued to rage, the House of Burgesses itself was severely shaken by the sudden death of its powerful Speaker, John Robinson. By custom, he had also served as Colonial Treasurer. Almost immediately, rumors of Robinson's involvement in a financial scandal began to spread throughout Virginia. As a result, the offices were separated later that year.[36]

The two men who competed to replace Robinson as Speaker would both eventually serve with distinction as Presidents of the Continental Congress. Peyton, however, held a wide lead over the younger Richard Henry Lee who was recognized as one of the leaders of the insurgents.[37] Lt. Gov. Fauquier, who had replaced Dinwiddie in 1758, had a far more cordial relationship with Peyton than did his predecessor. He reported to the Board of Trade that "my wishes for success attend him."[38] Fauquier's hopes were fulfilled. Peyton Randolph was elected Speaker of the Virginia House of Burgesses on November 6, 1766.[39] What would have shocked all concerned, however, was that after a century and a half, the Burgesses had just chosen the last man who would hold that prestigious office, the highest elective position in the colony. For his part, Peyton must have considered it the pinnacle of his public career. How could he have anticipated that a new and even greater continental responsibility awaited him in the future?

Even though Peyton had to relinquish the office of Attorney General, it did remain in the Randolph family when his younger brother, John, was appointed by the King to take his place.[40]

As the new Speaker, Peyton wisely consolidated his authority by increasing the size of the legislature's permanent committees, thereby offering the younger members a seat at the table.[41] He also deftly handled the Robinson scandal by appointing a distinguished ad hoc committee of the House, including Richard Henry Lee and Patrick Henry (two of

Robinson's harshest critics) to uncover and publicize the details. "Personally, he [Peyton] took comfort in the fact that the amount he had borrowed from Robinson was but a fraction of the sum which Robinson had borrowed from him."[42]

When the Stamp Act was finally withdrawn by Parliament in 1766, the new Speaker sent the official thanks of the House of Burgesses to the King. But, within a year, the battle over taxes resumed when the Townshend Acts came up for debate.[43] The colony of Massachusetts responded by enacting yet another non-importation agreement and then sent a "circular letter" urging other colonial legislatures to follow its lead. As Speaker, Peyton placed the correspondence before the House and carefully monitored the legislative responses as they developed in Virginia and throughout the other colonies. By mid-April 1768, a Petition to the King and Memorials to both Houses of Parliament had been approved by the Virginia House and even the Governor's Council. Since Lt. Gov. Fauquier had died in March, Virginia's opposition to the new taxes was even officially placed before the Throne because the President of the Governor's Council, John Blair, was serving as Acting Governor.[44]

In October 1768, the Baron de Botetourt arrived in Williamsburg as the first Royal Governor to personally lead the colony since 1689. Unlike most of his predecessors--who had chosen to remain in Britain where they collected the spoils of office while their Lt. Governors ruled in their place--Gov. Botetourt took his duties very seriously. As a result, the new governor was exceptionally well received despite policy differences. Peyton and his wife were among the select few who hosted a private dinner in the Baron's honor.[45]

As required by law upon the installation of a new governor, elections were held and the new General Assembly opened in May 1769, with Peyton once again serving as Speaker. Despite the genuine affection that had already begun to develop between Gov. Botetourt and the people,[46] colonial Virginians were even more determined than ever to protect and advance their liberties after years of interference from London. At the opening of the legislature, instead of "petitioning" the governor for all the rights and privileges normally accorded to the House of Burgesses, Peyton replaced the notion of supplication with assertion when he "...[laid] claim to all of their ancient rights and privileges..."[47] For the next few days, he and the House then went out of their way to camouflage their preparation of a response to the Massachusetts circular letter concerning another boycott. Finally, on Tuesday, May 16, 1769, the House of Burgesses adopted four resolutions that came to be known as the Virginia Resolves. They contained "little of the filial devotion of the year before, but a blunt statement of rights."[48] As Speaker, Peyton ordered that they be printed in the Virginia Gazette.

On Wednesday morning, the Royal Governor summoned the full House to meet with him at once in the upstairs Council Chamber. His message was clear and direct: "Mr. Speaker, and gentlemen of the House of Burgesses: I have heard your resolves and augur ill of their effect; you have made it my duty to dissolve you; and you are dissolved accordingly."[49] As the elected representatives of the people filed out of the Capitol, they regrouped at Raleigh Tavern, only one long block down Duke of Gloucester Street. There they reconvened as a quasi-legislative group and unanimously elected Peyton to serve as their moderator. They completed their work the following day, May 18, when they adopted a formal Association which pledged loyalty to the Crown but denounced the Townshend Acts and urged merchants and citizens to boycott the importation of British goods. Peyton was the first to sign the document followed by 87 of his fellow Burgesses.[50] In the months that followed, he also continued to carry on correspondence with leaders throughout Virginia as well as the other colonies.

Despite the growing tension between Britain and her American colonies, Peyton set out that same summer on a special mission for the Crown. Almost two years earlier he had been appointed by the King to a commission "to resolve a long-standing boundary dispute between New York and New Jersey. After numerous postponements, the members finally agreed to meet on July 19, 1769, in New York City."[51] The journey afforded Peyton the opportunity to visit Philadelphia and New York for the first time and to make the acquaintance of other colonial leaders. On of his new contacts was the commission's young clerk, New York attorney John Jay, who would join Peyton again at the opening of the Continental Congress in 1774 and would ultimately follow him as President several years later.[52] Overall, the trip was a golden opportunity for Peyton to learn first hand the concerns of his northern colleagues and for them to develop an appreciation for the highest elected official in the South.

On September 7, while still in New York, Peyton was reelected to the House of Burgesses from the City of Williamsburg. Before his work on the commission was completed, however, he had to return home on September 27 to prepare for the opening of the new General Assembly. When it finally convened on November 7, 1769, Gov. Botetourt was pleased to confirm the rumor that most of the Townsend taxes would soon be repealed by Parliament. Even though the fundamental constitutional issue of Britain's right to tax the colonies remained unresolved, the Burgesses were encouraged by what they perceived as the success of their latest boycott. As the tumultuous decade came to an end, they celebrated with an elegant Christmas Ball in the Capitol at which, in a spirit of solidarity with their husbands, "Mrs. Randolph and the wives of the other burgesses were all 'cheerfully dressed in Virginia cloth.'"[53]

On March 5, 1770, all of the Townsend taxes were repealed except for the tax on tea. That same day, in Massachusetts, five Americans were killed by British troops in what became known as the Boston Massacre.[54] A group of Virginia's Burgesses and some of the colony's leading merchants reacted to these developments by designing yet another new non-importation agreement. Peyton again served as moderator of the debate and signed the final document.[55] Despite the ongoing conflict, hostility did gradually subside as Lord North, the newest leader of the British Government, strove to defuse British-American tensions. At first, North was surprisingly successful. Under his leadership, the early 1770s actually became a period of benign neglect in Britain's relationship with her American colonies.[56]

In that atmosphere, Peyton was able to devote more attention to local concerns. In the summer of 1770, he headed the building committee for a new Lunatic Asylum. The following summer, he served on a committee to erect a statue in honor of Lord Botetourt, the late governor who had died on October 15, 1770, and had been buried in the crypt beneath the chapel at the College of William and Mary. That statue still stands today in the school's library.[57] In July 1771, as the late governor was being immortalized in stone, the last man who would hold that title arrived in the colony. In keeping with the spirit of the moment, Gov. Dunmore's tenure began amicably. The honeymoon, however, did not last.[58]

Peyton also continued his service as a member of the college's Board of Visitors where he helped to oversee the construction of a new building on campus. In early January 1773, he even took time to answer some of his correspondence, a chore he usually dreaded: "I must own, I don't like the business of writing, not from idleness neither, but because I had rather read the productions of any man's brain than those of my own...The best news I can tell you is, that Williamsburg begins to brighten up and look very clever, and I think it will be worth your while to come and enjoy the wholesome air that breathes through it for a week or a fortnight... Bess desires to be remembered to you. She is in but an indifferent state of health..."[59]

On March 12, 1773, this brief period of tranquility began to fade as Americans refocussed on the larger world and its unresolved issues. On that date, in response to a request from the Massachusetts House of Representatives, the Burgesses reestablished their Committee of Correspondence and joined in urging all of the other colonies to do likewise. Peyton was appointed chairman of that eleven-member body. At the committee's first meeting the following day, the three members who lived closest to Williamsburg were selected to deal with emergency situations. Peyton was chosen to head that group, as well.[60]

Under Peyton's leadership, Virginia's Committee of Correspondence began at once to develop communication between the colonies on a wide range of issues, both legislative and political. Gov. Hutchinson of Massachusetts understood, perhaps better than the correspondents themselves, the implications of such regular contact: "It was an act," he wrote, "which ought to have been considered as an avowal of independency, because it could be justified only upon principles of independence."[61]

The importance of the new committees became clear to all as news began to spread concerning the Tea Act. This law granted the East India Company exclusive rights to the American market and called for the enforcement of the three-pence duty on all tea sold. The British Government appointed special Tea Agents to implement the new law; but, in Philadelphia, New York and Charleston they were intimidated into resigning and the tea was never distributed. The Boston agents, however, refused to resign. As a result, Sam Adams and his Sons of Liberty took matters into their own hands on the evening of December 16, 1773, the night before the tea was scheduled to be unloaded. Their Boston Tea Party lit the fuse which led directly to revolution.[62]

Throughout that winter and spring, political leaders across the colonies braced themselves for Parliament's reaction to Boston's bold defiance. The Virginia General Assembly (which met on May 5, 1774) was certainly no exception. In mid-May, news of the Boston Port Act finally reached Williamsburg. The British Government's response was even harsher than had been anticipated. By closing Boston Harbor, Parliament was intentionally destroying that colony's economic lifeline. As Gen. Thomas Gage, the newly appointed military governor of Massachusetts, reported to his superiors in London: "The act staggered the most presumptuous."[63]

As the crisis unfolded, Peyton tried to avoid provoking Gov. Dunmore long enough for the House to quietly craft a substantive response to Parliament. But, on the evening of Monday, May 23, a group of younger Burgesses (including Thomas Jefferson, Richard Henry Lee and Patrick Henry) took matters into their own hands once again by drafting a resolution which called for Virginia to observe a "Day of Fasting" on June 1, the day the Boston Port Act was scheduled to go into effect. Thomas Jefferson described the event in the autobiography he penned decades later:

"The lead in the house on these subjects being no longer

left to the old members... and myself, agreeing that we must boldly take an unequivocal stand in the line with Massachusetts...We were under conviction of the necessity of arousing our people from the lethargy into which they had fallen as to passing events; and thought that the appointment of a day of general fasting & prayer would be most likely to call up & alarm their attention."[64]

The resolution was introduced and unanimously adopted by the House the following day. That Thursday, May 26, when the Virginia Gazette printed the resolution, Gov. Dunmore angrily dissolved the Assembly. On Friday, the members of the House demonstrated their outrage by reconvening at Raleigh Tavern (as they had in 1769) where they once again selected Peyton to serve as moderator. They voted to establish a new "Association" which would implement yet another boycott of British goods. And then they took an additional step. Virginia called for a continent-wide congress.

The Burgesses recommended to the Committee of Correspondence that they "communicate, with their several corresponding committees, on the expedience of appointing deputies from the several colonies of British America, to meet in general congress, at such place annually as shall be thought most convenient; there to deliberate on those general measures which the united interests of America may from time to time require."[65]

As chair, Peyton headed a list of 89 Burgesses who signed the resolution. He and the other members of the Committee of Correspondence then prepared copies of the resolution for each of the other colonies in time for that Saturday's afternoon post.[66] Less than a day later an express rider came to Peyton's home to deliver letters from Boston, Philadelphia and Annapolis which urgently requested an even more comprehensive boycott than the one Virginia had just approved.[67] Peyton responded by holding two meetings on Monday, May 30. In the morning, the 25 Burgesses who were still in Williamsburg met to review the news from the north and issued a call on their own authority for a general meeting of all members of the House of Burgesses to be held on August 1. That afternoon, the citizens of Williamsburg, Peyton's constituents, met at the Court House and unanimously approved the measures taken earlier that day.[68]

Two days later, on the designated "Day of Fasting," Burgesses and citizens met together at that same Court House and marched in procession behind their Speaker to Bruton Parish Church, only a block away, "where an excellent Sermon, well adapted to the present unhappy Disputes between Great Britain and her Colonies, was preached..."[69] Even as the Boston Port

Act went into effect, colonists across America were demonstrating their solidarity with their New England brothers. Parliament's goal of divide and conquer was a failure from the start.

When Gov. Dunmore called for new elections that same summer, the people of Williamsburg informed Peyton that it would not be necessary for him to campaign since "it is to your singular Merit alone you are indebted for the unbought Suffrages of a free People..."[70] On the following Wednesday, July 13, after the voters had unanimously reelected him, they hosted a special dinner in Peyton's honor at Raleigh Tavern. Afterwards they escorted him back to his own home "where they gave three cheers, and then departed, wishing him long to live to enjoy those honours which have been so justly conferred upon him by his countrymen."[71]

Virginia's first revolutionary Convention officially opened on Monday, August 1, 1774. As always, Peyton was elected to chair the meeting. After six days of intense deliberations, the Convention approved an expanded boycott which would include exports as well as imports over the next year. It also elected seven delegates who would represent Virginia at the upcoming Continental Congress the following month. Peyton's selection to that body was unanimous and, as chair of Virginia's First Convention, he was also "...empowered, on any future occasion that may, in his opinion, require it, [to] convene the several delegates of this colony at such time and place..."[72]

Peyton and three of his fellow delegates (Harrison, Lee and Bland) arrived in Philadelphia on Friday, September 2, 1774.[73] The spirit of the moment was perhaps best captured that evening in John Adams' diary: "After Coffee, We went to the Tavern, where we were introduced to Peyton Randolph, Esqr., Speaker of Virginia, Coll. Harrison, Richard Henry Lee, Esq., and Coll. Bland. Randolph is a large, well looking Man. Lee is a tall, spare Man. Bland is a learned, bookish Man. These Gentlemen from Virginia appear to be the most spirited and consistent, of any. Harrison said he would have come on foot rather than not come. Bland said he would have gone, upon this Occasion, if it had been to Jericho."[74]

Another eyewitness account was provided by Silas Deane, a delegate from Connecticut, in detailed letters he wrote to his wife as the new Congress began: "Mr. Randolph, our worthy President, may be rising of sixty, of noble appearance, and presides with dignity."[75] To Deane, Peyton seemed "designed by Nature for the Business; of an affable, open, & majestic deportment, large in size, though not out of Proportion, he commands respect, & Esteem, by his very aspect, independent of the high Character he sustains."[76] Deane made only one factual error, Peyton was only 53, not 60. As so often happens, Peyton's girth added both age as well as authority to his appearance.

As President, Peyton presided over Congress as it debated voting representation and adopted rules of procedure. The first critical issue that came before the delegates pertained to developments in Massachusetts where the situation continued to deteriorate because of the British military occupation. An unfounded rumor reached Philadelphia early in September that Boston had been bombarded and that "a half dozen colonists had been killed."[77] That report proved to be false, but the reality of British occupation led Suffolk County, Massachusetts, which included Boston, to approve a series of 19 Resolves that authorized the use of force against the British, if necessary.[78] Paul Revere delivered the Suffolk County Resolves to Congress on Saturday morning, September 17. Despite the fact that the more conservative delegates were, in the view of historian Merrill Jensen, "aghast at resolves which, in effect, declared independence and pointed in the direction of open warfare...they were caught in a dilemma."[79] To oppose the resolutions might create the impression that Congress actually supported the British occupation, the exact opposite of its stated purpose.

Therefore, despite individual misgivings, the Continental Congress unanimously voted to approve the Suffolk Resolves that same afternoon. Peyton immediately wrote to Joseph Warren, the leader of the resistance, enclosing a copy of the congressional resolution, urging that it "be communicated to the Committee of Correspondence for the Town of Boston."[80] In his Diary, John Adams described this as "one of the happiest Days of my Life...This Day convinced me that America will support the Massachusetts or perish with her."[81]

During Peyton's tenure as President, Congress also defined American Rights and established the comprehensive boycott known as the Continental Association, the very action that conservative merchants most dreaded. Under its provisions, imports would cease on December 1, exports would be terminated on September 10 of the following year, and even consumption of existing goods would be actively discouraged. Local committees were authorized to monitor compliance.

As President, Peyton was also the first to sign the Address to the People of Great Britain on October 21, 1774.[82] The following day, while the First Continental Congress debated the petition to the King, Peyton reluctantly relinquished the presidency in order to return to Virginia. As Speaker, he had to preside over the next scheduled session of the House of Burgesses in Williamsburg to prevent Gov. Dunmore from further mischief at home.[83] As Peyton and his two fellow delegates, Harrison and Bland, departed Philadelphia on Monday morning, October 24, they assigned their proxies to one of the remaining members of their delegation: "We Depute Colo George Washington to sign our Names to any of the Proceedings of the Congress."[84]

Peyton and his traveling companions arrived in Williamsburg six days later.[85] For a variety of reasons, the opening of the General Assembly was repeatedly postponed by the Governor and did not actually begin until June 1775. For Peyton, however, no rest was in sight. On November 10, 1774, he and his fellow delegates reported on their congressional work to a gathering of several hundred merchants who had assembled at the Capitol. Despite the negative impact it would have on their profits, the businessmen expressed their approval of the continentwide boycott and promised to do their part by abiding by its provisions.[86] In December, Peyton was chosen as chairman of the Williamsburg committee to oversee the boycott in the capital city.[87]

Throughout these hectic months, Peyton and his congressional colleagues grew increasingly anxious to learn how their petitions had been received in London, especially in the wake of the recent British election which had enhanced Lord North's majority.[88] "We are all gaping for intelligence from the new parliament," Peyton wrote in early January.[89] In the hope of avoiding unnecessary conflict, he also urged that any "miscreants" who were caught violating the Association's boycott should be persuaded rather than punished. "I have advised the gentlest methods in bringing them to a sense of their misconduct, " Peyton wrote in February 1775. "Rigorous methods sou'd be avoided till obstinate opposition calls on us to take care that the public shall not suffer."[90]

At Peyton's call, the Second Virginia Convention met at St. John's Church in Richmond on March 20, 1775. Peyton was once again elected Convention President and reelected as a delegate to the Second Continental Congress. Thomas Jefferson was then selected as his alternate in case Peyton was unable to complete his term in Philadelphia because of his Virginia responsibilities. The members approved the resolutions that had been adopted by Congress and then took the fateful step of appointing a committee to prepare a plan for arming and training Virginians for self-defense.[91] What set this Convention apart from all the other assemblies being held throughout the colonies were the immortal words spoken so passionately by Patrick Henry that still stir the American soul more than two centuries later: "I know not what course others may take; but as for me, give me liberty or give me death!"[92]

After returning to Williamsburg, Peyton was immediately confronted with two new crises. In mid-April 1775, Virginia Delegate Edmund Pendleton even speculated that Peyton might not return to Congress because of a recent "disturbance in the City [Williamsburg], by the Slaves."[93] And then, during the night of April 21, 1775, an even greater threat shattered the peace when Gov. Dunmore secretly moved twenty barrels of gunpowder from the city's public magazine to the safety of a British ship. Patrick Henry and units of the Virginia Militia threatened to march on the Capital if the people's property was not immediately returned. Peyton met privately with the Governor in an attempt to defuse the situation. Ultimately, Peyton crafted a compromise whereby Gov. Dunmore issued a bill of exchange for £330, the estimated value of the powder. Throughout the crisis, Peyton was deeply concerned "that violent measures may produce effects which God only knows the consequences of."[94]

As the tension mounted across America, Peyton, as the first President of Congress, also came under increased pressure from British authorities as well as local loyalists. On April 29, 1775, the Virginia Gazette "published news of a royal proclamation instructing General Gage in Boston to arrest the leading 'rebels' in Massachusetts and Philadelphia and supplying blank commissions for the execution of those captured. Among the names explicitly recommended for the commissions were the two Adamses, Hancock, Dickinson, Randolph, and Middleton - a 'black list' Gage was supposed to keep secret."[95] Earlier that same year, a small pamphlet had been published by James Rivington entitled "PILLS FOR THE DELEGATES: OR THE CHAIRMAN CHASTISED." A collection of four letters which had previously appeared in the Massachusetts Gazette in late 1774, it was addressed to "Peyton Randolph, Esq; on his Conduct, as President of the General Congress..." Its author, "Grotius," not only denounced the work of the Congress but also stated that "it is indeed whispered, that Mr. Randolph is very far from approving of many things adopted by Peyton Randolph, Esq; President of the Congress..."[96]

It was actually Peyton's younger brother John, the Attorney General, who grew increasingly uneasy as Peyton became publicly identified as a leader of the rebellion. Before the end of 1775, John Randolph lost hope in a peaceful settlement and reluctantly left for England with his immediate family. Only the Attorney General's oldest son, Edmund, chose to remain in Virginia with his famous uncle and aunt to fight for the patriot cause. The separation was extremely painful for the entire family.

In a farewell note to Attorney General Randolph, Thomas Jefferson tried to find some hopeful sign in his friend's departure: "Looking with fondness towards a reconciliation with Great Britain, I cannot help hoping you may be able to contribute towards expediting this good work...I wish they were thoroughly and minutely acquainted with every circumstance relative to America as it exists in truth. I am persuaded this would go far towards disposing them to reconciliation." Jefferson, reflecting the view of most of his congressional colleagues, then stated that he still wished for reunion with the Mother Country. "I am sincerely one of those," he wrote less than a year before he authored the Declaration of Independence, "and would rather be in dependance on Great Britain, properly limited, than on any nation upon earth, or than on no nation. But, I am one of those too who rather than submit to the right of legislating for us assumed by the British parliament, and which late experience has shewn they will so cruelly exercise, would lend my hand to sink the whole island in the ocean."[97]

In the midst of this personal and political turmoil, Peyton set aside his own safety when duty called. The citizens of Williamsburg, however, insisted that a special honor guard of "250 of the first Gentlemen" must escort "the good old Speaker" as he set out for Philadelphia in late April 1775.[98]

When he did arrive in Philadelphia, Peyton was unanimously reelected President as the Second Continental Congress opened on May 10, 1775.[99] Unlike the previous Fall, Congress now met at the Pennsylvania State House.[100] In addition to a new location, the Delegates also welcomed several new members, including Benjamin Franklin, who had just returned from his long and distinguished career as America's chief lobbyist in London; and, John Hancock, the wealthiest merchant in New England who would soon leave his indelible mark on Congress and the presidency.[101]

During these first weeks back in Philadelphia, Peyton dined most evenings at City Tavern along with several of his Virginia colleagues and delegates from Delaware, Maryland and New York. George Read of Delaware described the arrangements to his wife: "...a few of us have established A table for each day in the Week save Saturday when there is A general dinner."[102]

One of the original delegates who did not return was former Pennsylvania Speaker Joseph Galloway. He denounced the work of the First Congress and refused to participate any further.[103] As his loyalist sentiments became increasingly well known, Galloway became the target of public outrage. The situation was perhaps best described in a private letter written by North Carolina Delegate Joseph Hewes: "Galloway has turned apostate...he has lost the Confidence of all ranks of People. A few days ago a Box was left at his Lodgings in this City directed for Jos. Galloway Esqr. He opened it before several Gentleman then present and was much surprised to find it contained a Halter with a note in these words 'all the Satisfaction you can now give your injured Country is to make a proper use of this and rid the World of a Damned Scoundrell.'""[104]

The mood of Congress had also significantly shifted since the previous autumn. Not only had the King and Parliament dismissed Congress' earlier petitions but American forces on Lake Champlain had just captured Fort Ticonderoga. The greatest impact, however, resulted from the fact that British troops had fired on the Massachusetts Militia at Lexington and Concord on April 19, and the Americans had repaid the British in kind. Blood had been spilled. Forty-nine Americans were killed and another 41 were wounded on that first day of the Revolutionary War. British losses were estimated at 19 Officers and 250 soldiers killed or wounded. As a result, Boston became an active battlefield just as the delegates assembled in Philadelphia.[105]

After two intense weeks, Peyton again felt obligated to resign the presidency when he received word that Gov. Dunmore had set June 1 as the date for the General Assembly's next session. Former President Henry Middleton was offered the chair but declined because of poor health.[106] The delegates then turned to New England and elected John Hancock of Massachusetts to serve as their third President. One month later, Thomas Jefferson would enter Congress for the first time to replace Peyton as a member of the Virginia Delegation.[107]

Once again, Peyton was accorded protection as he departed on May 24 for his journey home. When he arrived in Williamsburg, "...bells began to ring as our worthy Delegate entered the city..." The following morning, the Volunteer Company of Williamsburg gathered to welcome Peyton and to pledge that they would "...most cheerfully hazard our lives in the protection of one who has so often encountered every danger and difficulty in the service of his countrymen. May Heaven grant you long to live THE FATHER OF YOUR COUNTRY, and the friend to freedom and humanity!"[108]

Events now moved at lightning speed. The final session of the Virginia House of Burgesses did open on June 1, 1775, and Peyton was immediately reelected as Speaker. Only a week later, Gov. Dunmore, "fearing for his own personal safety," abandoned Williamsburg and took refuge on a British ship anchored off Yorktown.[109] On Friday, June 23, Peyton called a meeting of the citizens of Williamsburg and urged them to station militia throughout the city to protect it from a surprise attack by loyalists. That Saturday, June 24, 1775, the Virginia House of Burgesses, America's oldest legislature, completed 156 years of service to the commonwealth when it met to transact business for the last time.[110]

The following Monday, Peyton again switched hats when, as President of the Virginia Convention, he issued the call for that body to reconvene. When it opened in Richmond on July 17, Peyton again presided as President but his exhaustion was obvious to all. Nevertheless, on August 11, 1775, Peyton once again received the most votes (89) when the Convention elected seven delegates to Congress for the coming year.[111] By mid-August, after missing several days due to poor health, he was persuaded by his colleagues to return early to Williamsburg in order to regain his strength. Pinkney's Virginia Gazette reported the story in its next edition: "Last Saturday [August 19], about 2 o'clock, the Hon. Peyton Randolph Esq. with his lady arrived at his house in this city from Richmond, the gentlemen of the Convention having recommended it to him to retire for the present from the fatigue of business, on account of his being much indisposed, and as the time of his departure for the General Continental Congress was nearly approaching."[112]

After a week at home, Peyton felt strong enough to again set out for Philadelphia. Accompanied by his loving wife and two other couples, he said farewell to Williamsburg for the last time on Sunday, August 27, 1775. Despite the good company, the journey was even more taxing than usual because two carriages broke down along the way. When Peyton did arrive in Philadelphia he learned that a quorum had not yet been attained for the conduct of business.[113] Finally, on Wednesday, September 13, the new session of the Continental Congress began when the first delegates from Georgia presented their credentials.[114] All thirteen colonies were represented at last.

Peyton was warmly received upon his return, but, to the displeasure of many, President Hancock did not offer to relinquish the chair. John Adams reported that "Mr Randolph, our former President is here, and Sits very humbly in his Seat, while our new one continues in the Chair, without Seeming to feel the Impropriety."[115] Shortly after Congress met, however, Peyton was confined with a fever" for several days.[116]

By September 22 he was apparently well enough to be appointed along with John Adams, Benjamin Franklin and John Jay as a member of a congressional committee responsible for examining "the state of the trade of America."[117] During debate from floor on October 7, Peyton introduced a motion that "all the orders of the day should be read every morning."[118] And on October 15, he joined John Rutledge and three others on a committee "to consider farther ways and means of promoting the manufacture of saltpetre."[119] Peyton's last recorded participation in congressional debate was on Friday, October 20.[120] The next day, in a letter to a friend, John Adams described Peyton as "The old Gentn...who is not credulous nor inthusiastical but very steady, Solid and grave..."[121]

And then it was over. On Sunday evening, October 22, while dining with Mrs. Randolph, Thomas Jefferson[122] and other friends at the home of Harry Hill, three miles outside of Philadelphia, Peyton "was taken with a choaking & one Side of his Face was distorted & about eight He expired."[123] America's first President was dead.

When Congress met the next morning, the delegates were deeply shocked and saddened to learn that their colleague and mentor was gone. Francis Lightfoot Lee expressed his thoughts to a fellow Virginian: "You know his Virtues & will lament the loss of the friend and Patriot. I am so concern'd that I cant think of politicks."[124] Thomas Cushing of Massachusetts wrote: "Our Late President Mr. Randolph dyed yesterday... he was a worthy Character, he was sinsible, a Gentleman of an even Temper and of sound Judgement; he dyed engaged in a good Cause."[125] On hearing the news, Richard Henry Lee immediately notified George Washington: "Tis with infinite concern I inform you that our good old Speaker Peyton Randolph Esqr...was taken during the course of dinner with the dead palsey, and at 9 oClock at night died without a groan." Putting aside their earlier political rivalry, Lee added that "Thus has American liberty lost a powerful Advocate, and human nature a sincere friend."[126]

Before voting to adjourn out of respect for their fallen leader, the delegates resolved "That this Congress will attend his funeral as mourners, with a crape round their left arm...That this Congress continue in Mourning for the space of one month. That a Comm[ittee]...be appointed to superintend the funeral." Henry Middleton, Stephen Hopkins and Samuel Chase were selected for that assignment.[127]

That same day, John Adams paid tribute to Peyton's memory in a letter to James Warren: "As this Gentleman Sustained very deservedly One of the first American Characters, as he was the first President of the united Colonies, and as he was universally esteemed for his great Virtues and shining Abilities, the Congress have determined to shew his Memory and Remains all possible Demonstrations of Respect" Adams then added his impression of Peyton after he relinquished the presidency: "This venerable Sage, I assure you, since he has stood upon the same Floor with the rest of Us has rose in the Esteem of all. He was attentive, judicious and his Knowledge, Eloquence, and classical Correctness shewed Us the able and experienced Statesman and Senator, wheras his former station had in a great Measure concealed these and shewed Us chiefly the upright and impartial Moderator of Debate." In conclusion, Adams wrote that "Mr. Randolph was as firm, stable and consistent a Patriot as any here--the Loss must be very great to Virginia in Particular and the Continent in general."[128]

That Tuesday afternoon, October 24, 1775, America witnessed its first State Funeral as President Hancock and the entire Continental Congress led a long line of dignitaries in solemn procession behind the casket of its first President. As one eyewitness reported: "On the day his Remains were interred there was a greater collection of People than I had ever seen. The three Battalions were under Arms. Their Standards and Colours were furled with black Gauze: their Drums muffled, and covered with Gauze. The Bells at Christ Church were muffled. There, Mr. Duché preached a most excellent Sermon:-thence the Corpse was carried to the Burying-yard, the way being lined on each side by the Battalions..."[129] Delegate Josiah Bartlett of New Hampshire informed his wife that "...it is Supposed to be much the greatest funeral that Ever was in America."[130]

In his Will, Peyton left most of his estate to his dear wife Bess with the provision that on her death it would pass to his brother John and then on to his favorite nephew, Edmund. "When his personal property was inventoried and appraised, his holdings in York, Charlotte, and James City Counties amounted to £12,980, including over one hundred slaves valued at £685."[131]

Thirteen months after Peyton's death, Edmund Randolph personally escorted his uncle's body back home to Virginia which, by then, had officially declared statehood. On Tuesday, November 26, 1776, "...the remains of our late amiable and beloved fellow citizen, the Hon. Peyton Randolph, esq: were conveyed in a hearse to the College chapel, attended by the worshipful brotherhood of Freemasons, both Houses of Assembly, a number of other gentlemen, and the inhabitants of this city. The body was received from the hearse by six gentlemen of the House of Delegates, who conveyed it to the family vault in the chapel..."[132]

Mrs. Randolph continued to live in their Williamsburg home for the rest of her life. In the Autumn of 1781, she graciously hosted Count Rochambeau when he and Gen. Washington set up headquarters in the city during the siege of Yorktown. Finally, in 1783--having lived just long enough to celebrate her new nation's victory in its struggle for independence--the widow of America's first President quietly passed away.[133] Both she and Peyton's brother John (whose remains were brought home to Virginia after his death in England) along with Peyton and his father, Sir John, now rest in the crypt beneath Wren Chapel at the College of William and Mary.[134]

In her Will, Mrs. Randolph appropriated £130 for a suitable monument to the memory of her husband to be erected as soon as possible in the chapel of the College of William and Mary opposite to that of Peyton's father, Sir John Randolph. To this day, her request remains unfulfilled. No monument to America's First President is located inside the chapel above Peyton's crypt. In the catacomb below, a simple large red brick tomb marks Peyton's final resting place.[135]

After his wife's death, Peyton's estate was auctioned on February 13, 1783. Thomas Jefferson took that opportunity to purchase Peyton's personal library. Those books became part of the extensive collection which Jefferson eventually sold to the national government as the foundation for the Library of Congress.[136]

Four decades later, the Peyton Randolph House hosted its last revolutionary hero. On October 20-21, 1824, the elderly Marquis de Lafayette stayed there while visiting Williamsburg during his triumphant year-long tour of America.[137]

After Peyton's death, the Randolph Clan continued to play a dominant role in America's political life. His favorite nephew, Edmund, went on to become Governor of Virginia (the first of three Randolphs who served in that office) and the first Attorney General of the United States. Edmund subsequently succeeded his cousin, Thomas Jefferson, as Secretary of State, a position which brought both of them nothing but heartache. Another of Edmund's cousin, John Randolph of Roanoke (1773-1833), became a dominant and often controversial figure in the US House of Representatives. America's most prominent Chief Justice, John Marshall (1755-1835), was also a Randolph, much to the consternation of his cousin President Jefferson. In an ironic twist of fate, during the Civil War both the Confederate Secretary of War, George Wythe Randolph (1818-1867), and its Commanding General, Robert E. Lee (1807-1870), were also related by blood to America's first President. One of the last known Randolph descendants to hold high office was Francis Biddle (1886-1968), the Attorney General during Franklin D. Roosevelt's final two terms.

Today, through the dedication of the Colonial Williamsburg Foundation, Peyton Randolph's home still stands overlooking Market Square as it has for more than two and a half centuries. The original high-back Speaker's Chair, from which he guided the fate of Virginia through its most perilous decade, continues to dominate the House of Burgesses in the reconstructed Capitol. Peyton's greatest legacy, however, in the words of John Adams, is that he was "...that eminent American, and most worthy Man The Honourable Peyton Randolph Esqr our first venerable President..."[138]

President Peyton Randolph's Home in the heart of
Colonial Williamsburg, Virginia

President Peyton Randolph is buried in the crypt of the
Chapel at the College of William & Mary in
Colonial Williamsburg, Virginia.

WHILE PEYTON RANDOLPH
WAS PRESIDENT

September–October 1774
May 1775

On Tuesday, September 6, 1774, Congress unanimously determined that before it could argue effectively that its rights had been violated, it must first delineate what those specific rights were and from whence they came. It therefore established a grand committee, consisting of two members from each colony, "to State the rights of the Colonies in general, the several instances in which these rights are violated or infringed, and the means most proper to be pursued for obtaining a restoration of them."[139] The Committee on American Rights and Grievances was chaired by Stephen Hopkins of Rhode Island and included both John and Sam Adams as well as three future Presidents of Congress: John Jay, Thomas McKean and Richard Henry Lee.[140] Its final report, which was adopted by Congress on October 14, is viewed by some as America's first constitution.[141]

The committee boldly declared that "the inhabitants of the English Colonies in North America, by the immutable laws of nature, the principles of the English constitution, and the several charters or compacts...are entitled to life, liberty, & property, and they have never ceded to any sovereign power whatever, a right to dispose of either without their consent."[142] The document then outlined each and every instance, since the close of the French & Indian War in 1763, in which American rights have been violated.

During Peyton Randolph's presidency, Congress also established the Continental Association, which called for a boycott of British goods and ultimately the prohibition on exports to Britain. In addition; Congress appointed committees to draw up an Address to the People of Great Britain; a Letter to the Inhabitants of the Province of Quebec; a Memorial to the Inhabitants of the British Colonies; and, it began work on a Petition to the King. It was a very productive first step on what proved to be "a journey of a thousand miles."[143]

In London, King George III told his faithful First Minister, Lord North, that "the dye is now cast, the colonies must either submit or triumph..."[144] For once, the King was exactly right. Even Lord Dartmouth, the Secretary of State for the Colonies, who was surprisingly sympathetic to the Americans, denounced Congress since it was not legally constituted. He condemned its work in advance as "propositions that lead to inevitable destruction."[145] Meanwhile, Gen. Thomas Gage, the Military Governor of Massachusetts, pleaded with his superiors in London for additional British troops.[146]

Along the American Frontier, relations between colonial settlers and the indigenous Indians again reached the boiling point. In the Fall of 1774, Virginia Gov. Dunmore took time away from the political crisis in Williamsburg to order a thousand militia to march to the confluence of the Ohio and Kanawha Rivers. On October 10, Chief Cornstalk and his Shawnee warriors were defeated at Point Pleasant in what is popularly known as Dunmore's War. Even though both sides suffered heavy losses, the colonial victory helped to stabilize a large part of the Frontier, and thereby enabled more Americans "to concentrate against the British instead of the Indians" when the Revolutionary War began a few months later.[147] It was hardly the outcome that Gov. Dunmore had in mind.

Back in Massachusetts, the Suffolk County Resolves of September were followed by the opening of what became the colony's First Provincial Congress on October 5, 1774. Two hundred and sixty representatives from across Massachusetts had initially come to Salem at the call of Gov. Gage for the opening of the new legislative session. When fear of opposition forced the Governor to cancel the meeting at the last moment, the delegates resisted by forming themselves into a convention and declaring themselves the protectors of the province's "peace welfare and prosperity." They elected John Hancock as their chairman.[148]

That process led directly to the Minutemen who shed their blood at Lexington Green and Concord Bridge the following spring.

Chapter 1

President
PEYTON RANDOLPH
of
VIRGINIA

Notes

Abbreviation Key

JCC   Journals of the Continental Congress
LDC   Letters of Delegates to Congress
PHL   The Papers of Henry Laurens

[1] JCC, Vol. I, (Library of Congress, US Government Printing Office, 1904), p.30. North Carolina did not arrive until September 14, 1774. Ibid., Vol. II, p. 240. Georgia did not participate until September 13, 1775.

[2] James Grant Wilson & John Fiske, Appleton's Cyclopaedia of American Biography (D. Appleton and Company, New York, 1887), Vol. II, pp. 529-531. Benjamin Franklin first came to England in 1757 "to plead the cause of the [Pennsylvania] assembly before the privy council." He returned to Philadelphia in 1762, but traveled to London again in 1764 and did not return to America until May 5, 1775, only five days before the opening of the Second Continental Congress.

[3] LDC, Vol. 1, Paul H. Smith, Editor (Library of Congress, Washington, DC, 1976), p. 13; Robert Treat Paine's Diary, August 29-September 5, 1774. See also: L. H. Butterfield, Editor, Diary and Autobiography of John Adams, (The Belknap Press, Cambridge, 1961), Vol. 2, pp. 114-115. John Adams described Daniel Smith's City Tavern as "the most genteel one in America." According to Butterfield's footnote, City Tavern was "furnished 'in the style of the best London taverns.'" It stood on the west side of Second Street between Walnut and Chestnut Streets. See also: Walter Staib, The City Tavern Cookbook (Running Press, Philadelphia, 2009), pp. 6-7. City Tavern opened in December 1773, the same month that the Boston Tea Party took place. It consisted of five levels, including three dining rooms and five lodging rooms. It played a critical role throughout the sessions of the Continental Congress that were held in Philadelphia. The original Tavern was razed in 1854, but an historically accurate replica was constructed on the same site in 1975. Walter Staib later received congressional approval to operate the Tavern which he reopened on July 4, 1994, "featuring eighteenth-century style gourmet cuisine."

[4] JCC, Vol. I, pp. 21-25. Two future Presidents of Congress--Richard Henry Lee of Virginia and Thomas McKean of Delaware--did not attend until the following day, September 6, 1774, even though their credentials were accepted along with their delegations on the opening day, September 5, 1774. Several other delegates arrived during the session.

LDC, Vol. 1, pp. xxvi-xxxii. A total of 56 delegates participated in the First Continental Congress (September 5-October 26, 1774).

[5] Merrill Jensen, The Founding of a Nation: A History of the American Revolution, 1763-1776, (Oxford University Press, New York, 1968), pp. "The decision to meet at Carpenters Hall... [was] highly agreeable to the mechanics and citizens in general, but mortifying to the last degree to Mr. Galloway and his party...Both decisions had been made before Congress met, for the methods of the Caucus Club [informal meetings 'out of doors' among John Adams and kindred spirits] worked quite as well in Philadelphia as in Boston..."

[6] Butterfield, op. cit., Vol. 2, p. 122.

[7] Journals of House of Burgesses, 1773-1776, pp. xiv-xv.

[8] Butterfield, op. cit., Vol. 2, p. 123.

[9] LDC, op. cit., Vol. 1, p. 20; Silas Deane to Elizabeth Deane, August 31-September 5, 1774.

[10] Butterfield, op. cit., Vol. 2, p. 115; John Adams Diary entry, August 30, 1774.

[11] J. Edwin Hendricks, Charles Thomson and the Making of a New Nation: 1729-1824, (Associated University Presses, Inc., Cranbury, NJ, 1979), p. 111. Thomson's election as Secretary helped to seal Galloway's fate. Thomson of Pennsylvania was not a delegate. Galloway had blocked his membership due to Thomson's progressive credentials and his political opposition to Galloway's leadership. Two conservative members of the New York Delegation tried to come to Galloway's rescue. Both James Duane and John Jay (a future president) argued that the Secretary should be an elected member of Congress. Others, however, insisted that the Secretary's responsibilities would preclude his full participation and thereby deny his colony adequate representation. Galloway and his supporters finally backed off and Charles Thomson, known to some as the "Sam Adams of Philadelphia," was unanimously elected Secretary of Congress. See also: Chapter 15.

[12] LDC, op. cit., Vol. 1, p. 25, James Duane's Notes of Debates, Monday, 5 September 1774, Philadelphia.

[13] LDC, op. cit., Vol. 1, p. 58; Caesar Rodney to Thomas Rodney, September 9, 1774.

[14] Edmund Cody Burnett, The Continental Congress, (The Macmillan Company, New York, 1941), p. 37.

[15] H. J. Eckenrode, The Randolphs: The Story of a Virginia Family, (Bobbs-Merrill Company, Indianapolis, 1946), p. 89.

[16] Eckenrode, op. cit., pp. 31-33. The exact date of William Randolph's (1651-1711) arrival in Virginia is uncertain, but it seems logical that his Uncle Henry's visit to England was instrumental in the teenager's decision to move to the New World.

[17] Jonathan Daniels, The Randolphs of Virginia: America's Foremost Family, (Doubleday & Company, Inc., Garden City, 1972), p.48.

[18] Peyton Randolph House History: Block 28, Colonial Lots 207 & 237 (Colonial Williamsburg Foundation, Williamsburg), p. 86. Report prepared by Mary Stephenson (May 1952), revised by Jane Carson (December 1967), The exact date of Peyton Randolph's appointment as Attorney General is not clear. Some historians list 1748 rather than 1744. The generally reliable Peyton Randolph House History, however, concludes that it was most likely 1744.

[19] Woodrow Wilson, George Washington, (Harper & Brothers Publishing, New York, 1924), p. 172.

[20] Daniels, op. cit., pp. xviii, 67. Peyton's older brother, Beverly Randolph--named after Peyton's mother, Susanna Beverly--apparently lived in England his entire adult life. He is seldom mentioned in articles pertaining to the Randolph Family or the Revolution-ary Era. Peyton also had a younger sister named Mary who was married three times.

[21] Peyton Randolph House History, op. cit., p. 88-89.

[22] Andrew A. Lipscomb and Albert E. Bergh, Editors, The Writings of Thomas Jefferson (Washington, 1903) Vol. XVIII, p. 139-40.

[23] Virginius Dabney, Virginia: The New Dominion, (Doubleday & Company, inc., Garden City, 1971), pp. 100-101.

[24] Edmund Randolph, History of Virginia, (The University Press of Virginia, Charlottesville, 1970), p. 161.

[25] John J. Reardon, Peyton Randolph: 1721-1775, One Who Presided, (Carolina Academic Press, Durham, NC, 1982) p. 11.

[26] Peyton Randolph House History, op. cit., p. 95.

[27] Peyton Randolph House History, op. cit., pp. 96-97.

[28] Journals of House of Burgesses, 1752-1758, pp. 250-251.

[29] Official Records, II, pp. 411, 427; Dinwiddie to James Abercromby, May 10, 1756; and, to Horatio Sharpe, May 24, 1756.

[30] Peyton Randolph House History, op. cit., p.104.

[31] Virginia Magazine, XXXVIII (1930), pp. 348-349; Maria Byrd to her son, William Byrd III, September 23, 1759.

[32] Peyton Randolph House History, op. cit., p. 109.

[33] See Introduction.

[34] Lipscomb, op. cit., Vol. XIV, pp. 162-172; Thomas Jefferson to William Wirt, August 14, 1814.

[35] John C. Miller, Origins of the American Revolution, (Little, Brown and Company, Boston, 1943), pp. 122-126.

[36] John J. Reardon, Edmund Randolph, (Macmillan Publishing Co., Inc., New York, 1974), p. 9.

[37] For a biographical sketch of Richard Henry Lee, see Chapter 11.

[38] Journals of House of Burgesses, 1766-1769, pp. xiv-xv; Lt. Gov. Fauquier to Board of Trade, May 11, 1766.

[39] Journals of House of Burgesses, op. cit., p. 11.

[40] Daniels, op. cit., p. 78.

[41] Reardon, Peyton Randolph, op. cit., p. 28.

[42] Reardon, Peyton Randolph, op. cit., p. 29.

[43] See Introduction.

[44] Jensen, op. cit., pp. 251-252.

[45] Reardon, Peyton Randolph, op. cit., p. 32.

[46] Dumas Malone, Jefferson the Virginian, (Little, Brown & Co., Boston, 1948), pp. 129 & 139.

[47] Reardon, Peyton Randolph, op. cit., p. 32.

[48] Lucille Griffith, The Virginia House of Burgesses: 1750-1774, (University of Alabama Press, University, AL, 1970), pp. 41-42.

[49] Journals of House of Burgesses, 1766-1769, pp. 215, 218.

[50] Reardon, Peyton Randolph, op. cit., p. 35.

[51] Reardon, Peyton Randolph, op. cit., p. 37.

[52] Walter Stahr, John Jay: Founding Father (Hambledon & London, New York, 2005), pp. 25-26.

[53] Reardon, op. cit.., p. 37.

[54] See Introduction.

[55] Reardon, Peyton Randolph, op. cit., pp. 37-38.

[56] See Introduction.

[57] The original statue of Lord Botetourt still stands today in the College Library after surviving the outdoors for nearly two centuries. An exact replica can now be found at the center of the quadrangle in front of the Wren Building on the College campus. Gov. Botetourt is also the only Royal Governor to be buried at the College. His grave is within a few feet of the final resting place of Peyton Randolph.

[58] Edmund Randolph, op. cit., pp. 196-197.

[59] Charles F. Jenkins Collection, Old Congress, Historical Society of Pennsylvania; Peyton Randolph to Landon Carter, January 13, 1773.

[60] Allan Nevins, The American States During and After the Revolution: 1775-1789, (The Macmillan Company, New York, 1927), p. 27.

[61] Thomas Hutchinson, The History of...Massachusetts Bay... (Boston, 1764-1828), Vol. III, p. 397.

[62] See Introduction.

[63] C. F. Carter, ed., *The Correspondence of General Thomas Gage* in Yale Historical Publications (New Haven, 1931-1933) I, p. 355; Gen. Gage to Lord Dartmouth, Boston, May 19, 1774.

[64] Merrill D. Peterson, Editor, Thomas Jefferson, Writings, (The Library of America, New York, 1984), pp. 7-8.

[65] Journals of House of Burgesses, 1773-1776, pp. xiv-xv.

[66] Journals of House of Burgesses, 1773-1776, p. 138; Minutes of Committee of Correspondence.

[67] *Virginia Gazette* (Purdie and Dixon), June 2, 1774, p. 2.

[68] Peyton Randolph House History, op. cit., p. 121.

[69] *Virginia Gazette* (Purdie and Dixon), June 2, 1774, p. 2.

[70] *Virginia Gazette* (Purdie and Dixon), July 7, 1774, p. 2

[71] *Virginia Gazette* (Rind), July 14, 1774, p. 3

[72] Reardon, Peyton Randolph, op. cit., p. 48.

[73] Peyton Randolph House History, op. cit., pp. 124-125. The other Virginia delegates "rode in two days later, on Sunday [September 4, 1774]."

[74] Butterfield, op. cit., pp.119-120.

[75] LDC, op. cit., Vol. 1, p. 61; Silas Deane to Elizabeth Deane, September 10-11, 1774.

[76] LDC, op. cit., Vol. 1, p. 23; Silas Deane to Elizabeth Deane, August 31-September 5, 1774.

[77] Jack N. Rakove, The Beginnings of National Politics, (Alfred A. Knopf, New York, 1979), p. 44.

[78] JCC, op. cit., Vol. 1,op. cit., pp. 31-39.

[79] Jensen, op. cit., p. 495.

[80] LDC, op. cit., Vol. 1, p. 76; Peyton Randolph to Joseph Warren, September 17, 1774.

[81] Butterfield, op. cit., pp. 134-135.

[82] JCC, op. cit., Vol. 1,pp. 15-102. For additional discussion of the Galloway Plan, see Chapter 3. See also: Edmond Randolph, op. cit., p. 211.

[83] LDC, op. cit., Vol. 1, p. 227; Silas Deane to Jonathan Trumbull, Sr., October 22, 1774. For a biographical sketch of Henry Middleton, see Chapter 2.

[84] LDC, op. cit., Vol. 1, op. cit., p. 245; Virginia Delegates to George Washington, October 24, 1774.

[85] *Virginia Gazette* (Purdie and Dixon), November 3, 1774, p. 1. Randolph, Harrison and Bland didn't leave Philadelphia until Monday, October 24, 1774.

[86] *Virginia Gazette* (Purdie and Dixon), op. cit., November 10, 1774, p. 1.

[87] Peyton Randolph House History, op. cit., p. 128.

[88] Lillian B. Miller, "The Dye is Now Cast" (Smithsonian Institution Press, Washington, DC, 1975), pp. 148-150.

[89] As cited in Rakove, op. cit., pp. 71-72; Peyton Randolph to Landon Carter, January 6, 1775.

[90] Rakove, op. cit., p. 51.

[91] Reardon, Peyton Randolph, op. cit., p. 57. See also: Edmund Randolph, op. cit., p. 209.

[92] David J. Brewer, ed., The World's Best Orations (Fred P. Kaiser, St. Louis, 1899), Vol. VII, p. 2477: Patrick Henry's immortal "Liberty or Death" Speech to the Virginia Convention in Richmond, Virginia, March 23, 1775.

[93] LDC, op. cit., Vol. 1, p. 330; Edmund Pendleton to George Washington, April 21, 1775.

[94] As cited in Reardon, Peyton Randolph, op. cit., p. 59.

[95] Peyton Randolph House History, op. cit., pp. 129-130.

[96] The real identity of "Grotius," the author, remains unknown but is likely drawn from Hugo Grotius (1583-1645), a Dutch jurist and politician in the early days of the ill-fated Dutch Republic (1602-1810), who is considered by many as the father of International Law. James Rivington (17224-1802), the pamphlet's printer, first spied for Britain but eventually became a double agent for Washington. In 1781, at Washington's urging, Rivington helped to convince British Commanding General Clinton that Washington's troops were preparing for a major attack on New York, thereby denying Cornwallis the reinforcements at Yorktown which might have prevented the American victory there.

[97] LDC, op. cit., Vol. 1, pp. 707-708; Thomas Jefferson to John Randolph, August 25, 1775.

[98] *Virginia Gazette* (Purdie), May 12, 1775, suppl., p. 1.

[99] JCC, op. cit., Vol. II, p. 12.

[100] LDC, op. cit.,Vol. 1, p. 338; Robert Treat Paine's Diary, May 10, 1775.

[101] JCC, op. cit., Vol. II, pp. 11-12.

[102] LDC, op. cit., Vol. 1, p. 358; George Read to Gertrude Read, May 18, 1775.

[103] John E. Ferling, The Loyalist Mind: Joseph Galloway and the American Revolution, (The Pennsylvania State University Press, University Park, 1977) p. 34. By opening day, former Pennsylvania Speaker Joseph Galloway had resigned from both the legislature as well as Congress and had retired to the countryside. Before long he would begin to actively support the British. See also, LDC, Vol. 1, pp. 295-296; Joseph Galloway to Samuel Verplanck, January 14, 1775.

[104] LDC, op. cit., Vol. 1, p. 342; Joseph Hewes to Samuel Johnston, May 11, 1775.

[105] Encyclopedia of the American Revolution, Mark M. Boatner III, ed., (David McKay Company, Inc., New York, 1974), p. 631. In addition to the 49 Americans killed on April 19, 1775, 39 to 41 were wounded and five were listed as missing. British losses are estimated at 19 officers and 250 soldiers killed or wounded out of 1,800.

[106] LDC, op. cit., Vol. 1, p. 406; Samuel Ward's Diary, May 24, 1775.

[107] LDC, op. cit., Vol. 1, p. 535; Samuel Ward to Henry Ward, June 22, 1775.

[108] *Virginia Gazette* (Dixon), June 3, 1775, p. 3; and, (Pinkney), June 1, 1775, p. 3; and, (Purdie), June 2, 1775, suppl., p. 3.

[109] *Virginia Gazette* (Purdie), June 9, 1775, Supplement.

[110] Journals of House of Burgesses, 1773-1776, pp. 280-283.

[111] JCC, Vol. II, p. 243. Richard Henry Lee came in second with 88 votes; Thomas Jefferson was third with 85. In seventh place was the noted Virginia lawyer George Wythe with 58 votes.

[112] *Virginia Gazette* (Pinkney), August 25, 1775, p. 6.

[113] LDC, op. cit., Vol. 2, p. 6; Richard Smith's Diary, September 12, 1775.

[114] JCC, op. cit.,Vol. II, p. 240.

[115] LDC, op. cit., Vol. 2, p. 30; John Adams letter to James Warren, September 19, 1775, p. 30.

[116] LDC, op. cit., Vol. 2, p. 27; Samuel Ward to George Washington, September 17, 1775.

[117] JCC, op. cit.,Vol. II, p. 259.

[118] JCC, op. cit., Vol. II, p. 486.

[119] JCC, op. cit., Vol. II, p. 296.

[120] JCC, op. cit., Vol. II, p. 496.

[121] LDC, op. cit., Vol. 2, p. 226; John Adams to James Warren, October 21, 1775.

[122] Malone, op. cit., p. 211.

[123] LDC, op. cit., Vol. 2, p. 247; Samuel Ward to Henry Ward, October 24, 1775.

[124] LDC, op. cit., Vol. 2, p. 228; Francis Lightfoot Lee to Landon Carter, October 22, 1775.

[125] LDC, op. cit., Vol. 2, p.240; Thomas Cushing to William Cooper, October 23, 1775.

[126] LDC, op. cit., Vol. 2, pp. 229-230; Richard Henry Lee to George Washington, October 22/23, 1775.

[127] JCC, op. cit., Vol. III, pp. 302-303, October 23, 1775.

[128] LDC, op. cit., Vol. 2, p. 232; John Adams to James Warren, October 23, 1775.

[129] LDC, op. cit., Vol. 2, p. 303, Footnote: Solomon Drowne to Miss Sally Drowne, November 12, 1775.

[130] LDC, op. cit., Vol. 2, p. 252; Josiah Bartlett to Mary Bartlett, October 25, 1775.

[131] Reardon, Peyton Randolph, op. cit., p. 69.

[132] *Virginia Gazette* (Purdie), November 29, 1776, p. 2.

[133] Peyton Randolph House History, op. cit., p. 145. See also: Peyton Randolph House at Colonial Williamsburg, Colonial Williamsburg Web Page, (http://www.colonial Williamsburg.com/Almanack/places/hb/hbran.cfm).

[134] Personal inspection by the author of the crypt under the Wren Chapel at the College of William & Mary. See also "Tomb Notes," provided by the College.

[135] Peyton Randolph House History, op. cit., p. 145.

[136] Colonial Williamsburg Web Page, (http://www.colonial Williamsburg.com/Almanack/people/bios/biorapey.cfm), p. 6.

[137] Colonial Williamsburg Web Page, (http://www.colonial Williamsburg.com/Almanack/places/hb/hbran.cfm), p. 4.

[138] LDC, op. cit., Vol. 2, p. 232; John Adams to James Warren, October 23, 1775.

WHILE PEYTON RANDOLPH WAS PRESIDENT

Notes

Abbreviation Key

JCC   Journals of the Continental Congress
LDC   Letters of Delegates to Congress
PHL   The Papers of Henry Laurens

[139] Worthington Chauncey Ford, ed., JCC, (Government Printing Office, Washington, DC, 1904), Vol. 1, p. 26.

[140] JCC, op. cit., Vol. 1, p. 28.

[141] Stephen A. Cambone, Noble Sentiments and Manly Eloquence: The First Continental Congress and the Decision for American Independence, (Ph. D. Dissertation, Claremont Graduate School, 1981), pp. 186-188.

[142] JCC, op. cit., Vol. 1, p. 67.

[143] Confucius: "A journey of a thousand miles begins with a single step."

[144] Frank Arthur Mumby, George III and the American Revolution: The Beginnings, (Constable & Company Ltd., London, 1924), p. 346. George III to Lord North, September 11, 1774.

[145] B. D. Bargar, Lord Dartmouth and the American Revolution, (The University of South Carolina Press, Columbia, 1965), p. 147. Lord Dartmouth to Gov. Dunmore, 3 August 1774.

[146] Merrill Jensen, The Founding of a Nation (Oxford University Press, New York, 1968), p. 570.

[147] Virginius Dabney, Virginia: The New Dominion, (Doubleday & Company, Inc., Garden City, NY, 1971), pp. 123-125.

[148] William M. Fowler, Jr., The Baron of Beacon Hill (Houghton Mifflin Company, Boston, 1980), pp. 176-177.

Henry Middleton

Chapter 2

President
HENRY MIDDLETON
of
SOUTH CAROLINA

The Pivotal Moment

Things happen for a reason.

On October 22, 1774, as the First Continental Congress was nearing its conclusion, delegates from all twelve colonies in attendance unanimously elected Henry Middleton of South Carolina to serve as their new president. And yet, for over two centuries, historians have never asked the most obvious question concerning this remarkable development. Why?

Why did the delegates turn once again to the South to select their new president rather than to the New England region, the major focus of their deliberations; or, to Pennsylvania or Massachusetts, which had much larger populations? Why did Congress pass over those who had clearly established themselves as the leaders of the debate (e.g., John Adams, John Dickinson, Ned Rutledge, Joseph Galloway) in favor of one of its older and more reserved members? At this precise moment in history, when the Petition to the King was under debate, why was Henry Middleton of South Carolina selected by his peers to preside over their final, critical days?[1]

Even Middleton Family scholars have tended to disregard this amazing development since Henry's active term of office was a total of only five days. (The First Continental Congress completed its work and adjourned on October 26, 1774.) What they and other historians have failed to recognize is the importance of the selection itself. Henry Middleton was elected as the second President of the Continental Congress because he was precisely the right man at that specific moment in the history of his newly emerging country.

The immediate steps which led to Henry's election were actually taken four weeks earlier. It was then that Joseph Galloway, Speaker of the Pennsylvania General Assembly, and the head of his state's congressional delegation, introduced his "Plan of Union."

Galloway was a protégée of Benjamin Franklin. He presided over their powerful political faction in Philadelphia during Franklin's long absences overseas. Galloway, however, "proved an ineffective leader,"[2] and exhibited little of Franklin's charm. In stark contrast to his mentor, Galloway seemed to grow more politically conservative with age. Even prior to their arrival in Congress, John Adams and the other New England delegates had been alerted to Galloway's loyalist tendencies by his numerous political enemies.[3]

During the Summer of 1774, Galloway had joined forces with his perennial enemy, Pennsylvania Governor John Penn, to stack the colony's delegation to the Continental Congress with conservative members like himself.[4] But, once Congress was underway, Galloway forced himself to vote for the Suffolk County Resolutions (which supported Massachusetts resistance to British troops). He even supported the call for a boycott of British goods entering America in order to stay within the congressional mainstream long enough to introduce his Plan of Union on September 28, 1774.[5]

Galloway's goal was to offer his colleagues an alternative to the endless tug-of-war with the Mother Country, a battle he believed the Americans could never win. His Plan bore a close resemblance to one developed by Franklin years earlier which had been adopted at the Albany Conference in 1754.[6] According to its provisions, Great Britain would concede some power to the colonists by creating an American legislature which would be inferior to Parliament. It would consist of a "President General" appointed by the King and a "Grand Council" elected by the colonial assemblies. The Grand Council would only deal with domestic issues. Both the President General and the British Parliament would have veto power over proposed legislation and the King would remain as Head of State.[7] [Canada and Australia would find parts of his plan surprisingly familiar two centuries later.]

The Galloway Plan attracted support in Congress from some of the more conservative faction. John Jay of New York, a future President, and his colleague James Duane proudly seconded its introduction. Ned Rutledge of South Carolina considered it "almost a perfect Plan."[8] After lengthy debate, however, Congress was still divided and "a motion was made and adopted to have the plan 'lye upon the table,' presumably to be taken up for reconsideration at any later appropriate time."[9]

John Adams and the more radical faction were horrified. They clearly understood that if Galloway's Plan were adopted it would sidetrack the momentum for true self-government in the American colonies and would likely strengthen London's control through the illusion of representation. While it was still too early for anyone in Congress to even mention the word "independence," adoption of the Galloway Plan would terminate that critical debate before it had even begun. Adams and his allies were also alarmed by the fact that the influential South Carolina delegation seemed to be evenly divided between the Rutledge brothers who clearly identified with the conservatives while Gadsden and Lynch championed the more radical cause. South Carolina's fifth and deciding vote was Henry Middleton.[10] With little time to spare, Adams had to undermine support for the Galloway Plan, especially in the South Carolina delegation, before the Plan came back to Congress for a final vote.

As other congressional issues continued to unfold, a golden opportunity presented itself to Adams in late October when Peyton Randolph, the First President of the Continental Congress, was called home to Williamsburg to resume his role as Speaker of the Virginia House of Burgesses. The office of President was open once again. Adams wasted no time in making good use of that prestigious position. To a generation of powerful and prosperous men who gloried in their reputations and saw their respective colonies as their true homeland, the selection of the second President of the Continental Congress had significant cachet value for the individual selected, as well as his colony.[11]

Even though he left few fingerprints, John Adams knew how to orchestrate events as he repeatedly demonstrated throughout his congressional career. It was Adams who would hand pick Washington as the best available choice for Commander-in-Chief of the Continental Army in 1775; and, Adams who would personally select Jefferson to write the Declaration of Independence in 1776.[12] In a preview of those developments, Adams realized that the surest way to prevent the adoption of the Galloway Plan in late 1774 was to win over South Carolina. The key to that goal was Henry Middleton, the colony's most distinguished planter-politician who had been elected to Congress with the support of all South Carolina factions.[13] Henry Middleton, the Paterfamilias of South Carolina, who had not yet identified with either political faction, was clearly the deciding vote. His "silent and reserved" personality,[14] extensive family connections, immense fortune and lifetime of political experience made him the perfect choice to succeed Randolph.

The agreement was most likely finalized on Friday evening, October 21, 1774, at "a meeting at the City Tavern the night before the measure was to be discussed again."[15] The following morning, Henry Middleton of South Carolina was elected as the Second President of the Continental Congress.[16] When the body then resumed its debate on Galloway's proposal, support for the Plan had not only evaporated but the motion to reconsider was rejected and the delegates subsequently decided not to include Galloway's Plan in the minutes.[17] A dangerous detour on the road to independence had been averted.

In a sense, the Middleton Family had been preparing for that pivotal moment for nearly a century. Henry's ancestors had played a central role throughout the evolution of their colony. His grandfather, Edward Middleton, arrived in the Carolinas in 1678, only eight years after its founding.[18] Edward's younger brother, Arthur, immigrated the following year. Born in England, the brothers had been successful merchants on the Island of Barbados, but their dream of building vast fortunes there was limited by the small size of the island and the fact that most of the desirable land had already been purchased. Like many other English businessmen on Barbados, they concluded that their best hope for fame and fortune was to relocate to the newly established Carolina colony on the mainland.[19]

In September 1678, shortly after he arrived, Edward Middleton obtained a landgrant for 1,780 acres at the head of Yeamans Creek (soon to be known as Goose Creek) which flows into the Cooper River approximately fourteen miles north of Charleston. The new Middleton plantation was "larger than any existing plantation on Barbados."[20] The area, which had already become popular with other transplants from the island, became the base of both political and financial clout for former Barbadians who gradually became known as "Goose Creek Men."[21]

Within three months of his arrival in South Carolina, Edward Middleton obtained a seat on the Grand Council, the only governing body in the colony. Thus began almost two centuries of Middleton Family influence at the highest levels of colonial and state government.

In July 1679, Edward Middleton took an even more fateful step when he married Sarah Fowell, the wealthy widow of a close friend. Through his new wife, he inherited control over much of her late husband's estate. Middleton also continued to acquire as much property as possible. By 1680, "Edward had amassed 4,130 acres in landgrants plus a prime commercial lot on Charleston's waterfront."[22] He and his new wife built their home, eventually known as The Oaks, close to the north bank of Goose Creek. In 1683, Middleton acquired yet another important position when he was named as an Assistant Judge for Berkeley County. Thus, in only five years, Edward Middleton had firmly established himself as both a political and financial power and the head of one of the colony's most promising founding families.

Arthur Middleton established his home along the south bank of Goose Creek where he earned a reputation as the more reckless member of the family. Having participated in the slave trade while living in Barbados, the younger Middleton illegally engaged in the Indian slave trade in the

Carolinas. When word reached the South Carolina Proprietors in London, they wrote to Governor West on March 31, 1684, that Arthur Middleton should be removed from his seat on the Council "for disobeying our orders in sending away [enslaving] the Indians..."[23]

On December 7, 1682, 35 year old Arthur Middleton married Mary Smyth, the widow of John Smyth of Boochae Plantation who had also served on the Grand Council. Their union, however, produced no children. Mary, widowed for the second time in 1685 after Arthur Middleton's death, went on to marry into yet another of the most powerful Goose Creek families when she became the bride of Ralph Izard and bore him a son who carried on the Izard Family name. Since Arthur Middleton had left his entire estate to his widow she, in turn, left it to her third and final husband. As a result, the wealth that Edward Middleton's younger brother had worked so hard to accumulate was largely transferred to the Izard Family.

Tragically, both Middleton brothers died unexpectedly in 1685. Edward Middleton, however, did leave an heir. His son, Arthur, was born in 1682. After his father's death, young Arthur was lovingly cared for by his mother, even after she remarried another wealthy plantation owner, Job Howe. As the young boy grew to maturity, so, too, did the South Carolina economy. After years of trial and error, the wealthy Carolina planters finally identified rice as the perfect cash crop for their region. "By 1699, the province achieved a favorable balance of trade for the first time."[24] It was into this prosperous environment that young Arthur Middleton, now in his late teens, began to lay claim to his inheritance at the dawn of a new century.

In February 1704, young Middleton followed in his father's footsteps when he began his lifelong quest to expand his landholdings throughout the colony. On July 23, 1706, at the age of 24, he purchased from his mother his late father's plantation home, The Oaks. He "sealed the indenture between himself and his mother with the Middleton coat of arms by virtue of his signet ring."[25] That same year, he donated four acres of land for a rectory to the newly established St. James Parish in Goose Creek. In appreciation, "the vestry presented an enclosed pew...to Arthur and his heirs."[26] (Three centuries later, that pew is still used today by Middleton descendants when St. James Goose Creek holds it's annual service on the Sunday after Easter.)[27]

And then, on October 29, 1706, Arthur Middleton began what would become the most famous branch of his family when he married Sarah Amory, the orphaned daughter of Jonathan Amory, the former leader of the Goose Creek men in the Commons House, South Carolina's new elected assembly. Sarah had been raised by the Rhett Family at their townhouse on East Bay in the heart of Charleston after most of her own family had died of disease. Over sixteen years of marriage, Sarah Middleton gave birth to eight children, but only three lived to maturity: William (b. 1710), Henry, the future President (b. 1717), and Thomas (b. 1719).

Arthur Middleton's public career also began in 1706 when he was elected to represent his home county of Berkeley in the Commons House. The following year, he became a vestryman of the new St. James Parish in Goose Creek, a position with political as well as religious implications.

In July 1710, Arthur Middleton left for London to attend to both public and private affairs. While some speculate that he might have been sent to England as a child, this was his first documented journey. His agenda included a meeting with the Lords Proprietors of South Carolina (who controlled the colony) concerning the recently disputed election of a temporary governor. Of even greater importance, he went to claim his place as head of the older English branch of the Middleton Family because of the recent deaths of both his uncle and his half-brother. A few years later, he entrusted his young son William to the care of his British relatives. (By custom, it was common for wealthy South Carolina families to place their eldest sons with family members back in England both to attain a better education and to avoid the fevers which so often plagued the colony.)

When Arthur Middleton returned home to Charleston, he carried with him a document signed by Lord Carteret, one of the Lords Proprietors, confirming Middleton's appointment as Carteret's deputy on the Proprietary Council. He had also been commissioned as a naval officer. For the next few years, Arthur Middleton's public service included work on committees concerning the establishment of free schools, the development of a provincial library and the construction of the statehouse in Charleston.[28] Basking in his enhanced personal and political status, he resumed his aggressive acquisition of land as soon as he returned from London.

On April 15, 1715, when the Yamassee Indians began to revolt against the treatment they suffered from traders and some colonial authorities, Arthur Middleton's role as the recently appointed Commissioner of Indian Affairs became critical. He traveled north to successfully negotiate with Virginia Gov. Spotswood over the urgency for military assistance. At the same time, his wife and family fled to Charleston for safety. Once the threat was contained, however, popular anger arose over the lack of adequate assistance from the Lords Proprietors during times of crises. In 1716, a petition was addressed to the King signed by members of the South Carolina Commons House. Despite his high position and close association with the Proprietors, Arthur Middleton also signed. It urged that the Proprietors be removed and that the colony "may be added to those under your [Majesty's] happy protection..."[29]

On December 10, 1719, Arthur Middleton was chosen as Speaker of the newly elected Commons House. Later that same day, due to a parliamentary battle, Gov. Johnson dissolved the Commons House. In response, its members declared themselves to be the legal representatives of the people and met as a convention. They promptly elected Speaker Middleton as their president and presiding officer. Finally, in August 1720, the Privy Council in London took over responsibility for the colony of South Carolina in the name of the King. The Speaker and his colleagues had won.[30]

Just as political victory over the Proprietors was secured, personal tragedy befell the Middleton Family. Sarah Amory Middleton, Arthur's wife and the mother of his children, died in late 1721. Their deep love is clearly reflected in this excerpt from a letter he wrote the following March: "It is the greatest lost [sic] that could have befallen me in this world..."[31]

When the first Royal Governor arrived in Charleston in May 1721, he brought with him a list of newly appointed councilmembers, including Arthur Middleton. In an unusually democratic procedure, Middleton was subsequently elected by his council colleagues to serve as their President.[32] Four years later, as the battle for power between the Commons House and the Governor's Council grew more intense over the issue of paper currency, the Royal Governor returned to England for a year's sabbatical. Being next in line of succession, Arthur Middleton became Acting Governor of South Carolina in May 1725.[33]

Middleton's term as Governor was anything but peaceful. Historian M. Eugene Sirmans states in his study of Colonial South Carolina that "The council shared Middleton's timidity, and together they permitted South Carolina's government to drift." In sharp contrast "...the Commons House of Assembly was not the least bit timid."[34] Under these circumstances, the Commons House even censured the Acting Governor in an attempt to diminish his authority. Despite their differences, the House briefly put aside political warfare when it joined with Gov. Middleton and the Council in resisting a renewed effort by the former Lords Proprietors in their attempt to regain control over the colony. By November 1725, however, the protracted battle over issuing paper currency to relieve the constant shortage of legal tender became even more intense between the Commons House on one side and the Acting Governor and his Council on the other.[35]

In 1727, a severe economic crisis hit the colony. As a result, an anti-tax association was formed, headed by Landgrave Thomas Smith, a member of the Council.[36] He claimed that as the eldest member of the Council he should be the Acting Governor. When it became clear that Smith might use physical force to remove Gov. Middleton, Smith was arrested. In outrage, many of Smith's supporters marched on Charleston that June. To maintain order, the militia was called out, but it refused to confront the mob.[37]

The tug of war between the various legislative and political factions continued to intensify. The colonial Chief Justice, who sided with Gov. Middleton, also became a frequent target of the Commons House. In May 1728, the House sent an official messenger to forcefully apprehend the Chief Justice while he was meeting with the Governor and his Council. Gov. Middleton, at the end of his patience, disbanded the Commons House. From then until a new Royal Governor finally arrived in 1730, South Carolina Government was locked in a stalemate.

Fortunately, Arthur Middleton did have a new wife and companion to help him through these extremely difficult years. On August 23, 1723, he had married Sarah Morton, the widow of a fellow counselor. She not only helped to oversee developments at The Oaks and his various plantations during his long absences in the city, but the new Mrs. Middleton also proved to be a loving and devoted mother to his two young sons, Henry and Thomas, who were still at home. Finally, in 1729, Middleton's oldest son, William, returned from his nineteen year upbringing in England to claim his place as the future heir of the Middleton Family. The following April, William Middleton began his own family when he wed Mary Izard whose grandmother had been the widow of his great-uncle. On April 14, 1731, the young couple presented Arthur Middleton with his first grandchild whom they named Sarah in honor of his father's first wife.[38]

While Arthur Middleton continued to expand his landholdings and grew increasingly wealthy from his extensive rice plantations throughout the area, his son William built a magnificent new country home which he named Crowfield after one of his family's great English estates.[39] The young couple, however, suffered one tragedy after another. Three of their children died in infancy between 1732-34. And then, on June 14, 1734, William Middleton's young wife also died. He and his only surviving child, Sarah, struggled on alone for the next three years. But, on August 5, 1737, seven year old Sarah also passed away.[40] William Middleton's young family was gone in less than a decade. Yet still, there was more grief.

Only one month after the loss of his last child, William's father died at the age of fifty-six.[41] Arthur Middleton was buried behind the chancel of St. James Goose Creek. In his will, he generously provided for his widow and all three of his sons. But, since his eldest son William already had his own estate, the second son, Henry, ultimately inherited The Oaks, the Middleton Family homestead.

Despite his bereavement, William Middleton began again. On November 10, 1737, he married Mary Morton, the daughter of his stepmother by her third husband. Sadly, disaster struck one final time when his second wife died less than a year later.[42]

William Middleton's political fortunes were also tested. In 1737, he challenged his recent defeat for a seat in the Commons House (probably due to that body's lingering hostility toward his father's term as Acting Governor). But, in 1740, he was named to the Governor's Council, the third generation of Middletons to hold that high office.

Later in the decade, William Middleton somehow found the strength to try again to build a new family. In 1747, he married Sarah Wilkinson. Two years later she bore him a son whom they named William.[43] A second son, Thomas, was born in 1753. At the same time, the young father learned that he had inherited even more property in England because of the death of elderly relatives. After all that he had suffered in America, William Middleton decided to return to England to claim his latest inheritance.[44] On February 25, 1754, he sold his Plantation in Goose Creek as he prepared to relocate.[45] He and his family sailed for England on April 5, 1754, taking with them his nephew Arthur, his brother Henry's oldest son. Fifteen months later, William Middleton wrote from England to officially resign his position as a member of the Governor's Council. He had decided to make his English estate his permanent home. He never returned to South Carolina.

As the second son of Arthur Middleton (1681-1737), Henry would have been destined to play only a supporting role in the history of South Carolina. But, because his older brother had emigrated to England, Henry assumed center stage during the Revolutionary Era. Because of his vast fortune, his acquisition of valuable properties through three marriages, his ownership of the family homestead, The Oaks, and the intermarriage of his seven grown children to many of the other great South Carolina Families, Henry ultimately attained a unique status which was unrivaled by any of his contemporaries.

"When Henry became twenty-one in 1738 he received his inheritance from his father. His estate totaled 4848 1/3 acres."[46] As one of the most eligible young men in the Charleston area, he began to court Mary Williams (popularly known as Molly) the daughter of John Williams, another wealthy plantation aristocrat. It was through Henry's marriage to Molly in the summer of 1741 that he took charge of the Ashley River estate that today proudly bears his name: Middleton Place. Molly's wealthy father, who had no male heir, actually willed the property to his daughter, with the proviso that ultimate ownership would pass to Mary's oldest son. But, over the next twenty years, while Henry served as master of Middleton Place, he added two more large structures (one flanker on each side of the existing mansion)[47] to house his extensive library and to provide extra bedrooms for male visitors. Henry's dream, however, was the transformation of that great estate into a showplace of brilliant natural beauty. Toward that goal, Henry directed the most extensive landscaping project ever seen in the colonies. It is estimated that 100 slaves labored for a decade under a professional English landscape artist to create the gardens and the terraced lawn which still leads to the elegant butterfly lakes and the Ashley River.[48]

In 1742, both Henry and his younger brother, Thomas, entered public service as elected members of the 13th Royal Assembly of the Commons House. At the same time, their older brother William (before his departure for England) was a member of the Governor's Council. Henry and Thomas declined reelection two years later in order to devote more attention to their plantations during tough economic times. By 1747, however, both Henry and his younger brother resumed their public careers when they did accept election to the 15th Royal Assembly. That same year, Henry was elected Speaker of the Commons House, the highest elected office in the colony.[49] During this period, he also served as a Justice of the Peace. In 1754, Henry was again chosen as Speaker. When elected for a third time in 1755, he declined to serve for health reasons. But, on December 22, 1755, six months after his elder brother had resigned the position, Henry Middleton was appointed by the King as a member of the Governor's Council. Word of Henry's appointment arrived just as the French & Indian War in America evolved into a full scale confrontation between England and France in what became known in Europe as the Seven Years War (1756-63).[50] At the same time, the new Royal Governor, William Henry Lyttleton, increasingly alienated even his own Council through his autocratic style and lack of deference to local political customs and traditions.[51]

The year 1742 also proved to be the turning point in Henry Middleton's family life when his wife Mary gave birth to the first of their twelve children on June 26. They named him Arthur after Henry's father. Thirty-four years later this infant would proudly add his signature to the Declaration of Independence.

Unfortunately, their next three children died before their first birthdays. Their second daughter, Mary, lived less than two and a half years. Next came another son, Williams, who died before he turned seven. Miraculously, the rest of their children all lived to maturity: Henrietta, known as Hetty (1750-1792); Thomas (1753-1797); Hester, known as Hess (1754-1789); Sarah, known as Sally (1756-1784); another Mary (1757-1825); and, Susannah, known as Sukey (1760-1834). Through marriage to many of the other great families of South Carolina (i.e., Izard, Rutledge, Manigault, Drayton, Pinckney, Smith and Parker), Henry's seven surviving descendants helped to elevate their wealthy and politically influential father--now head of the Middleton Family of South Carolina--to the status of patriarch.

Henry's loving wife, however, did not live long enough to see her grandchildren. After twenty years of marriage and a dozen pregnancies, Mary Williams Middleton died at the age of 40 on January 9, 1761. She was buried at Middleton Place. Despite his grief, Henry still needed a mother for his large family and a companion to help with his extensive estates. In 1762, at the age of 45, he took as his second wife Maria Henrietta Bull, the daughter of the former Lt. Governor, William Bull, Sr., and sister of the current Acting Governor, William Bull II.[52] The two most powerful South Carolina families were thereby directly linked through marriage. For the next decade, Henry and his second wife lived at the pinnacle of colonial society just as the ties between Britain and its American empire began to unravel.

On Christmas Eve 1763, two years after his mother's death, Arthur Middleton, Henry's oldest son, returned from his formal education in England. As the primary heir of both his late mother as well as his father, Arthur was presented with Middleton Place as his personal estate. The following year, at the age of 22, Arthur married into another of the most prominent Goose Creek families when he took Mary Izard (known as Polly) as his young bride. The fourth generation of Middletons in South Carolina was now solidly established.

During these years, Henry and his second wife, Maria, apparently spent more time than usual at their Charleston home at 69 Broad Street. They worshiped on Sundays at the newly completed St. Michael's Church just down the street.[53] By 1765, however, Henry had relocated his family to yet another plantation only seven miles from Charleston which became known as The Retreat. As he devoted more of his time to public service and his brood of lovely daughters, he still continued to oversee his various rice and indigo plantations, his numerous slaves and the men he carefully selected to manage his landholdings. That same year, with the death of his stepmother, Sarah Wilkinson Middleton, Henry, his two brothers and their children each inherited part of her sizable fortune.[54]

This financial windfall, however, was not enough to cover the massive debts left by Henry's brother Thomas when he died suddenly on December

17, 1766. Thomas Middleton had increasingly pursued his fortune as a merchant and slave trader. He left broken lives and financial ruin in his wake. Henry was forced to devote months of anguish attempting to settle his brother's estate as equitably as possible. Henry Laurens, the most successful South Carolina merchant of the era and himself a future President of the Continental Congress, had been a harsh business critic of Thomas Middleton, but, in a letter dated October 30, 1767, Laurens gave Thomas' brother Henry high praise: "That gentleman is in all respects, as a man of honor, understanding, and precision in business very well qualified for such a Trust..."[55]

In 1768, after selling The Retreat, Henry returned to his ancestral home at The Oaks in Goose Creek where his stepmother had resided until her death. At the age of 51, Henry would live out the final 16 years of his life where it began, in St. James Parish, Goose Creek.

The following year was largely devoted to travel for both Henry and his oldest son. Arthur Middleton and his wife Mary sailed for England on May 25, 1769, for what turned into a three-year European holiday. Henry, his wife and two of his young daughters left less than a month later to escape to the cooler climate of Rhode Island during one of the driest summers in South Carolina memory. They did not return to Charleston until the following November, after a brief visit to Philadelphia.[56] Even if this lengthy journey had no intentional political overtones, Henry's exposure to the issues and leaders of the North must have left an impact.

The last half of the decade had been a period of political upheaval throughout all thirteen colonies. In March 1765, the British Parliament passed the notorious Stamp Act, London's first attempt to directly tax the American colonies in order to raise revenue without camouflaging their actions under the heading of trade legislation.[57] Like all the other colonial legislatures, the Commons House in South Carolina was outraged at what it perceived to be Britain's violation of colonial rights. Christopher Gadsden, the Sam Adams of the South, organized popular resistance by mobilizing his own band of the Sons of Liberty.[58] That October, Gadsden, Thomas Lynch, Sr. and John Rutledge attended the Stamp Act Congress in New York as the official representatives of South Carolina, one of nine colonies to participate.[59] By November 1, 1765, when the stamps were scheduled to go into effect, mob violence had already forced the South Carolina stamp agents to resign. Even the Port of Charleston, the colony's commercial lifeline, ceased operation. In January 1766, the Commons House officially petitioned Lt. Gov. Bull (Henry's brother-in-law who was again serving as Acting Governor) to set aside the stamps and reopen the port. In clear defiance of the Lt. Governor, Henry was one of only two members of the Governor's Council who voted with the Commons House to reopen the Port. The crisis was temporarily resolved when Parliament finally acceded to the plea of British merchants by revoking the hated law. By mid-1767, however, the battle lines reemerged with Parliament's approval of the Townshend Acts which imposed a tax on various imports and devoted part of that tax to directly paying Royal Officials in America.[60] Yet another American boycott of British goods was initiated. In October 1769, South Carolina established the Non-Importation Association to enforce the boycott. Despite being a member of the Governor's Council, Henry did sign the document and publicly joined the boycott.[61]

In fact, as the 1760s drew to an end, Henry grew closer to the more populist position of the Commons House and further from the loyalist leadership of his brother-in-law, the Acting Governor. Their policy differences grew into a seismic split at the highest levels of the South Carolina oligarchy.[62] It initially surfaced in October 1768, when a group of Charleston workmen marched down Broad Street in support of John Wilkes, then a relatively obscure British politician who had been imprisoned in London for criticizing the Royal Government over its infringement of liberties.[63] Wilkes' fame grew as the debate over taxation without representation intensified throughout the American colonies. In December 1769, as a sign of support, the South Carolina Commons House voted £1,500 to assist Wilkes with his legal expenses. What few knew at the time was that Henry Middleton, still a member of the Governor's Council, provided for the transfer of those funds through his elder brother William who lived in England. In his letter of transmittal, Henry wrote to his brother that "I hope our purses will always be opened when wanted in so good a cause..."[64]

The breaking point for Henry finally came over the reappointment of one of his old nemesis to the Council. Years earlier, when William Wragg had been dismissed from the Governor's Council in 1756, it had seriously injured the Council's reputation. Now, to make amends for that earlier insult, the Secretary of State for the American Colonies ordered Acting Gov. Bull to readmit Wragg to his former seat. At a Council meeting on January 24, 1770, Bull interpreted his instructions from London to imply that Wragg should regain his seniority, as well. Not only was Henry outraged by the fact that the readmission would give Wragg seniority over Henry, but Wragg's denunciation of the Non-Importation Association would further alienate the Council from the Commons House. Finally, on September 14, 1770, The Hon. Henry Middleton publicly broke with the loyalist establishment of his colony when he submitted his formal resignation from the Council. It was, indeed, the end of an era. The

Middleton Family had served on the Council for three generations, only a few years shy of the founding of the colony. As events would soon prove, Henry's resignation was also a prophetic transition for South Carolina itself.[65]

Free of his public responsibilities for the first time in many years, Henry's relatively quiet life during the early 1770s closely paralleled British-American relations during that same tranquil period. Henry attended to his vast landholdings which included twenty plantations consisting of approximately 50,000 acres which were worked by 800 slaves.[66] He also devoted more time to his extended family. Back in London, Lord North, the new leader of His Majesty's Government, orchestrated the demise of all but one of the Townshend duties (i.e., the tax on tea) and carefully steered a course to avoid further confrontation with America.

One year after Henry's letter of resignation from the Council, Arthur and Mary Middleton returned to Charleston from their extensive European tour. They brought with them Henry's first grandchild, a boy named in his honor, who had been born in London one year earlier. The Christmas Season of 1771 might well have been one of Henry's happiest moments as three generations of his family gathered to celebrate the holidays. But, just two months later, tragedy struck yet again when Henry's second wife, Maria Henrietta Middleton, died. She was only 49 years old and the only mother Henry's youngest daughters had ever known. Later that year, Arthur and Mary Middleton named their first daughter after Arthur's stepmother.

One of Henry's major preoccupations during 1773 was the courtship of his daughters who, by now, had grown into young women of great charm and reputation. On September 28, 1773, Sally became the first to wed when she married Charles Cotesworth Pinckney, a young lawyer from one of Charleston's most distinguished families. The new bride moved into Pinckney Mansion which, because of its grandeur, had previously been leased by several Royal Governors. The following year began with the return of Henry's second son, Thomas, who had completed his schooling in London. And then, Henry's two oldest daughters married into equally distinguished families. In February 1774, Hess became the wife of plantation heir and physician Charles Drayton. One week later, Henrietta wed prominent attorney Ned Rutledge who would soon serve with her father in the First Continental Congress. Thus began the Middleton-Pinckney-Rutledge block in the Commons House.

By July 1774, political events overwhelmed private affairs. That month a special meeting was convened in Charleston to debate Virginia's call for a continent-wide conference (in response to the Intolerable Acts which had been imposed on Massachusetts).[67] Boston's leaders were also urging another massive protest against British goods. While there was widespread support for the conference, major division developed over the financial impact of yet another boycott. Ultimately, the more radical faction elected three of their own to serve as delegates: Christopher Gadsden, Thomas Lynch, Sr. and Ned Rutledge (Henry's new son-in-law who would soon be identified with the more conservative block). All factions joined in unanimous support for John Rutledge (Ned's older brother) and Henry.[68] On Saturday, July 24, 1774, Henry, now titular head of the South Carolina delegation by right of age and status, and his son Thomas, left Charleston by ship for Philadelphia. His daughter Henrietta and her husband Ned Rutledge joined them. On August 2, the Commons House met in an exceptionally early session at 8 am to ratify South Carolina's delegation and to appropriate funds for their journey. By the time the Governor realized what was happening and dismissed the assembly, it had already completed its work.[69]

On September 2, after he had settled into his lodgings in Philadelphia, Henry dined at the home of Thomas Mifflin of Pennsylvania. Later that same evening they met Peyton Randolph and Richard Henry Lee of Virginia at the City Tavern. All four men were destined to serve as Presidents during the First American Republic.[70]

Finally, on Monday, September 5, 1774, the delegates from eleven colonies (North Carolina and Georgia were not represented that morning) met at 10 am at City Tavern and marched as a group to Carpenters Hall where, in its first official act as the Continental Congress, Thomas Lynch, Sr. of South Carolina nominated Peyton Randolph of Virginia to serve as its first President.[71]

During the weeks that followed, the other members of the South Carolina delegation became vocal participants in the debates over non-importation of British goods, a declaration of American rights and other critical issues. But Henry, unlike so many of his congressional colleagues, was noted for his restraint. He obviously felt no need to offer his opinion on every topic. In the debate over limiting American exports to Britain, however, Henry did join with Lynch and the Rutledge brothers in demanding that rice--his colony's economic lifeline and the foundation of his own fortune--be exempted from the list of prohibited commodities. Congress reluctantly agreed in order to guarantee South Carolina 's continued participation.[72]

And then, as described earlier, Henry was elected by his peers to serve as the second President of the Continental Congress when Peyton Randolph was called home to Williamsburg. Henry presided over the final debate on the Petition to the King. It was Henry Middleton's signature as President of Congress that George III first saw as that document was presented to His Majesty later that year.[73]

The South Carolina delegation arrived back in Charleston by ship on November 6, 1774. The following January the Speaker of the South Carolina Commons House praised the five delegates: "Posterity will pay a just tribute to your Memories, and will revere the Names of the Members of the Continental Congress."[74] A newly created South Carolina Provincial Congress (which soon replaced the colonial Commons House) met to review and implement the resolutions from Philadelphia. Henry and his two sons were elected as members of this new legislature. For the past two centuries, numerous sources, including the memorial tablet at St. James Goose Creek, have incorrectly listed Henry as the president of this new Provincial Congress during 1775-76. Not only did he not serve as head of that legislative body, Henry and his Continental Congress colleagues from South Carolina were reelected by that same Provincial Congress and returned to Pennsylvania in the spring of 1775.[75]

When the second Continental Congress met on May 10, 1775, Peyton Randolph was reelected as President but he resigned the office two weeks later when duty again demanded his return to Williamsburg. As before, on May 24, 1775, Henry was asked to replace Randolph, but this time he declined the office because of his delicate health.[76] The delegates then turned to New England and elected John Hancock of Massachusetts as their third President.

In July 1775, while serving in Philadelphia, Henry shared his thoughts and concerns with his son Arthur. In one of his few surviving letters, Henry informed his son that he had purchased "woollens...for cloathing your Uncles Negroes." He told Arthur that even though the price of the cloth was higher than usual, "I thought it was better to purchase them, than let the Negroes suffer of want of cloathing." In the same letter he mentioned that he was intending to travel to New York to see a sick friend, Mr. Fenwicke, and that "I am really under much concern for poor Mrs. Fenwicke and greatly pity her Situation."[77]

Henry continued as a member of Congress while the first Continental Army was established and he and his fellow delegates selected George Washington as Commander-in-Chief. When former President Peyton Randolph died unexpectedly in Philadelphia that October, former President Henry Middleton was one of three members appointed by Congress to superintend America's first state funeral.[78]

On Sunday, November 5, 1775, Henry and John Rutledge left Congress early to return home by land to avoid capture by the British Navy. They had succeeded in winning Congress' approval for the establishment of four regiments to defend South Carolina and Georgia. Meanwhile, back in South Carolina, Royal Government had completely collapsed. On September 15, Lord William Campbell, the last Royal Governor, had dissolved the Commons House from the safety of a British man-of-war in Charleston Harbor.[79]

Even before his return, Henry and his son Arthur were elected to South Carolina's Council of Safety.[80] Henry also returned home as the sole surviving son of his generation. His older brother William had died in England on September 7, 1775. At the start of the new year, however, Henry reaffirmed his lust for life when he married for the third and final time. His new wife, Lady Mary McKenzie Drayton Ainslie, was the daughter of the late Earl of Cromartie and, like Henry, she had been twice widowed.

In February 1776, when the Provincial Congress of South Carolina met again, Henry Middleton and John Rutledge reported to the members that the Continental Congress had instructed them to form a new state government. On February 11, Henry and his son Arthur were elected to the committee to design that new government. Five days later, when delegates were again being elected to the national Congress, Henry thanked those assembled for the honor of having twice served in that capacity, but declined renomination to a third term due to the toll the travel took on his health. Not surprisingly, Henry's son Arthur was elected to fill his father's seat in Philadelphia.[81] Henry did, however, accept election to the Legislative Council (the new upper house of state government), but he resisted the suggestion that he also serve as President of that body.[82] By now, Henry Middleton was 59 years old. More than half of his life had already been devoted to public service.

On June 28, 1776, Charleston had repelled Britain's first attempt at invasion. on May 24, 1775,For the next four years, life in the Low Country resumed some limited semblance of normalcy as South Carolina supported the American cause while the war continued to rage in the northern and mid-Atlantic states. Christmas 1777 provided a rare opportunity for the rapidly expanding Middleton Family to gather together at home. By now, all except Henry's youngest son and daughter had married and the proud patriarch had gathered around him two grandsons who bore his name.[83]

One year later the reality of the war again began to overtake local affairs. The British invaded Georgia in December 1778. Savannah fell at the end of that month. Charleston was next. As the British marched through South Carolina, various plantations were captured or destroyed, including some of Henry's vast landholdings. Eventually, Middleton Place along the Ashley River and The Oaks, near the Cooper River, were both looted and vandalized by the King's troops. At one point, most of the Middleton women and grandchildren fled to Hampton Plantation, forty miles north of Charleston, in search of safety while the Middleton men remained behind to prepare for the defense of the city. Even though the British briefly withdrew to await reinforcements, their ultimate goal was clearly Charleston.

Because of his age and poor health, Henry resisted the burden of any further public service but he continued to strongly support the American cause by extending sizable personal loans to the new state during its time of trial. On November 1, 1779, for example, Henry loaned the young government 100,000 pounds currency.[84]

At the end of 1779, the British commanding general, Sir Henry Clinton, left New York with 8,700 soldiers and 5,000 sailors and marines to augment the forces already assembled in Savannah. By February 1780, the final invasion of the Low Country had begun. This time, Henry personally took his wife and daughters to safety at one of his distant plantations 120 miles from the capital. On April 13, the British bombardment of Charleston began. One month later, after heated debates between American Gen. Benjamin Lincoln and the revolutionary leaders, Charleston surrendered.[85]

Approximately 5,500 Continentals and militia became prisoners.[86] It was the greatest American military defeat of the war. Gen. Clinton declared the inhabitants of Charleston to be prisoners of war but initially allowed them to remain neutral. On June 3, however, after many who had fled returned to the city (including Henry and his daughters), Gen. Clinton reversed his position and demanded that all residents must reaffirm loyalty to the King.[87] As family patriarch and a former President, Henry must have faced an intense internal struggle over how best to meet this challenge. Finally, on October 8, 1780, Henry Middleton submitted the following carefully-crafted letter to Gen. Clinton:

> "Sir, before the unnatural contest between Great Britain and America took place, I was happy and gloried in the appellation of a British subject, nor should I have held myself absolved from the oath of allegiance which I had taken had not the colonists been so severely treated as to be deprived of the support and protection of the Crown by Acts of Parliament and thereby left at liberty to shift for themselves and provide for their own security...I must candidly confess, Sir, that although I have long most

sincerely lamented it as a misfortune to both countries
and ardently wished it never had a beginning, I have found
it difficult to divest myself entirely of all partiality for a
cause in which I have been so long engaged. But, since this
country [South Carolina] has submitted to His Majesty's
arms, I have not endeavored by any means to keep up the
spirit of independence and have considered myself under
Sir Henry's [sic] Clinton's proclamation of the 3rd of June
as restored to all the rights and duties belonging to a citizen
and inhabitant and while this country shall remain a part
of the British Empire I will demean myself as becomes a
true and faithful subject and give such proofs as I am able
of my allegiance and attachment to His Majesty's person
and government."[88]

Henry's carefully crafted correspondence was not accepted by the
British. He and many other South Carolina leaders were finally forced to
make an unambiguous statement of loyalty. Informed of this development
while still being held a prisoner by the British, Henry Laurens, the fourth
President, was less than sympathetic to his colleague's dilemma. Laurens'
reaction was that "Mr. Middleton, although he has been a President of
Congress, loves his rice fields."[89] Meanwhile, Henry's son Arthur and his
son-in-law Ned Rutledge, both of whom refused to sign any statement,
were among the revolutionary leaders who were briefly held in the dungeon
of The Exchange Building in Charleston and then transported to the
fortress prison in St. Augustine, Florida where they were kept for nearly a
year. Another son-in-law, Charles Cotesworth Pinckney, was under house
arrest at Snee Farm outside of Charleston. Compounding this personal
and political tragedy, three of Henry's grandchildren died before the end
of the year.

With a large family to protect and provide for, Henry, once again,
had little time to grieve. During 1781, he sold several of his landholdings
(including his Charleston home) in order to raise enough cash to help the
family through the occupation. Necessity kept him focused. Even after the
British surrendered at Yorktown in October 1781, Charleston remained
occupied while peace terms were negotiated in Paris.

When the South Carolina General Assembly finally reconvened outside
of Charleston on January 8, 1782 (the first time since the occupation began)
a critical new issue arose. Many patriots who had refused to take the British
oath urged harsh action against those who had signed. Punishment ranged
from confiscation of property to enforcement of heavy fines. Henry's name

was conspicuously absent from all such lists despite his reluctant but public capitulation. Even his son's political enemies did not dare to challenge the head of the state's most powerful family. In retirement, Henry continued to cast a large shadow from the relative seclusion of The Oaks.[90]

Charleston's liberation finally came on December 14, 1782, as American Gen. Nathanael Greene led his troops into the capital on the heels of the British evacuation. The war was over. Years of reconstruction were ahead, but Henry and his family had survived. Both father and eldest son reestablished homes in the city while beginning the process of repairing their plantations. According to surviving tax records from 1783, Henry still held at least 27,871 acres of land throughout the state and claimed 259 slaves.[91] Henry's youngest son, Thomas, gave the family additional cause to celebrate when, on April 8, 1783, he took Ann Manigault for his wife. Ann's father, one of the few Charlestonians to rival Henry's fortune, was also a former Speaker of the Commons House.

During the final year of his life Henry made certain that his affairs were in order by rewriting his will on April 16, 1784. Three weeks later he suffered one last family sorrow when his daughter Sally, wife of Charles Cotesworth Pinckney, passed away. And then, at 2:30 on the afternoon of June 13, 1784, Henry Middleton died quietly at his home in Charleston. He was 67 years old, the dominant figure of one of his new nation's greatest families during its revolutionary era. Like his father, President Henry Middleton was laid to rest behind the chancel in the churchyard of St. James Goose Creek, less than a mile from The Oaks.

Arthur Middleton, Henry's oldest son, survived his father by only two and a half years. He had taken Henry's seat in the Continental Congress in 1776 when his father declined to accept reelection. As a result, Arthur Middleton's place in history was carved in stone the day he signed the Declaration of Independence. He died on January 1, 1787, at the age of 44. His remains were eventually interred in a massive tomb in the gardens of Middleton Place alongside his mother. Arthur Middleton was survived by his wife Mary, two sons and six daughters.

Not surprisingly, Arthur Middleton's girls married into other leading South Carolina families. Two eventually extended the Middleton clan to neighboring states and a third lived at prestigious Grosvenor Square in London. His youngest surviving child, John Izard Middleton, was born less than two years before his father's death. He was known as "the first American classical archaeologist"[92] and lived most of his life as a gentleman historian and painter in France and Italy. His book on Latin antiquities, *Grecian Remains in Italy*, was published in 1812. Amazingly, another volume of his sketches, *The Roman Remains*, finally reached the printer in 1997, nearly two centuries later. John Izard Middleton died in Paris in 1849. Today, several of his paintings are prominently displayed in the front hall of the surviving flanker at Middleton Place.

Arthur Middleton's oldest son, Henry Middleton, carried on his grandfather's name and the family's commitment to public service. From 1802 to 1812, he was elected a State Representative and State Senator and then Governor of South Carolina. Gov. Middleton later was elected to two terms as a Member of Congress and then served as Minister to Russia for the next decade under Presidents James Monroe, John Quincy Adams and Andrew Jackson. He returned to South Carolina in 1830 and became a leader of the Union Party in strong opposition to those, like John C. Calhoun, who advocated the principle of state nullification.[93] Upon his death in June 1846, Governor Middleton was laid to rest with full public honors. While Gov. Middleton's youngest son remained in the United States Navy throughout the Civil War and ultimately retired as a Rear Admiral, two of the Governor's other sons, John and Williams, sided with the Confederacy by signing the Ordinance of Succession. It was Williams (1809-83) who began the daunting challenge of rebuilding Middleton Place after a detachment of Sherman's Army ransacked the estate and burnt the main buildings during the final months of the war.[94]

Thomas Middleton, President Henry Middleton's younger surviving son, inherited the ancestral homestead, The Oaks, when his father died. But, despite a prominent public career, he eventually sold the estate in order to make new investments which produced mixed results. Like his older brother Arthur, Thomas Middleton only lived to the age of 44. He died on August 19, 1797, and was laid to rest next to his father and grandfather at St. James Goose Creek. He was survived by his wife Anne, three sons and two daughters. His oldest grandson, Nathaniel Russell Middleton, became the President of the College of Charleston in 1858. A half century later, Thomas Middleton's great-great grandson, J. J. Pringle Smith,[95] inherited what remained of Middleton Place, and he and his wife devoted the rest of their lives to recreating the gardens and recapturing the grandeur of an earlier era. Through their devotion, in 1941 Middleton Place was awarded the prestigious Bulkley Medal by the Garden Club of America "in commemoration of 200 years of enduring beauty."[96]

President Middleton's sons-in-law also continued to distinguish themselves and their family through public service. Charles Cotesworth Pinckney, Sally's husband, was a delegate to the Constitutional Convention in 1787 and the South Carolina Ratification Convention in 1788. He declined requests that he serve as Secretary of War or Secretary of State during the 1790s, but he did agree to become US Minister to France in

1796. In 1800, he was the unsuccessful candidate of the Federalist Party for Vice President when Jefferson beat Adams; and, in 1804 and 1808, he was defeated by Jefferson and then Madison for the Presidency. He died in 1825 and is buried at St. Michael's graveyard in the heart of historic Charleston.

Edward "Ned" Rutledge, Henrietta's husband, served with Henry in the First Continental Congress in 1774 along with his older brother John Rutledge. Like Arthur Middleton, Ned Rutledge also signed the Declaration of Independence. In September 1776, he, John Adams and Benjamin Franklin represented Congress at the eleventh-hour Peace Conference which was called by the British Commander, Gen. Howe. That November, Ned Rutledge returned to South Carolina to become a military officer in defense of his state. Like his close friend and brother-in-law, Arthur Middleton, Ned Rutledge was also arrested when Charleston fell in 1780. They were confined in the prison at St. Augustine, Florida. Rutledge was a member of the South Carolina Ratification Convention in 1788 and, ten years later, he was elected Governor of South Carolina (a position held previously by his brother, John). Both Rutledge brothers died in 1800. Today, Ned Rutledge is buried in the churchyard of St. Philip's and his older brother John is interred three blocks away at St. Michael's. Their magnificent mansions have been converted into elegant bed and breakfast establishments and still face each other on Broad Street in the center of historic Charleston.

Charles Drayton, Hester's husband, was eleven years her senior. He was the second son of John Drayton, the founder of Drayton Hall Plantation which still stands today near Middleton Place. He received a degree in medicine from the University of Edinburgh and served as a doctor upon his return to Charleston. Unlike most of the extended family, Charles showed little interest in political service. He did serve in the state militia prior to the occupation of Charleston in 1780, but, unlike Pinckney and Rutledge, he reluctantly signed the petition to the King for restoration as a British subject in order to stay close to his family.

Peter Smith and Mary Middleton were wed in November 1776. They lived on a 800 acre plantation in Goose Creek, prior to the fall of Charleston. In 1790, Peter was elected to the South Carolina State Senate representing the same ancestral base at St. James Goose Creek from which so many Middletons had served.[97]

Sukey, Henry's youngest daughter, married John Parker on Christmas Eve 1786, two years after her father's death. Her husband, a lawyer, served in the Continental Congress from 1786-88. Today, his family's Memorial Tablet hangs next to the Middleton Tablet at St. James Goose Creek and his descendants still serve with distinction on the Vestry of that great old historic church just as they and the Middletons did nearly three centuries ago.[98]

President Henry Middleton's home at 69 Broad Street in the heart of Charleston is long gone, but, only a short distance from that location, Henry's pew (No. 60) at St. Michael's Church, still welcomes the faithful as it has for the past 250 years.

The Middleton Family's great mansion, The Oaks, was destroyed by fire around 1840. The building which now stands at that site is still known as "The Oaks Plantation Athletic & Country Club" and the magnificent boulevard of Live Oak trees which were planted during the 18th Century still grace the long drive to its front door.

Nearby, St. James Goose Creek, one of the oldest surviving churches in South Carolina (established by an Act of Assembly in 1706 and completed in 1719) has just been lovingly restored to its simple yet elegant beauty. It also has the distinction of being the longest functioning church in the state since services are still held once every year on the Sunday after Easter. Direct descendants of the great Goose Creek families, including the Middletons and the Parkers, still fill the pews where their revolutionary ancestors once sat. It is truly history come to life. Behind the pulpit hang the two large tablets of worship which were donated by William Middleton in 1758. On the south wall, a memorial tablet perpetuates the memory of Edward Middleton, who first came to the new colony in 1678; his son Arthur, who served as President of the Governor's Council and Acting Governor in the 1720s; Arthur's son, Henry, who was chosen as his new nation's second president; and, Henry's youngest son, Thomas. "The last three of whom... rest as to their earthly part without the eastern wall of this church adjacent to the chancel."[99]

By far, however, Henry's best known memorial is his magnificent old estate along the Ashley River which he lovingly transformed into a showplace of breathtaking natural beauty and which is now designated as a National Historic Landmark. In 1975, it was turned over to a non-profit foundation which has opened the plantation to the public. It is there that his son Arthur and Henry's first wife are buried.[100] Even the mindless desecration during the Civil War which destroyed most of Henry's personal papers and two of the plantation's great buildings could not undo Henry's enduring legacy.[101] Today, when the people of Charleston celebrate great occasions with picnic lunches, outdoor concerts and majestic fireworks, they still gather in the thousands under the stars at historic Middleton Place.[102]

President HENRY MIDDLETON is buried at St. James Goose Creek in South Carolina. After more than three centuries, services are still held once every year on the Sunday after Easter.

Middleton Place, President Middleton's home from 1741-1761, is America's oldest landscaped gardens. Today, it is a National Historic Landmark. (Photo reprinted with permission from the Middleton Place Foundation.)

WHILE HENRY MIDDLETON
WAS PRESIDENT

October 1774

President Henry Middleton presided over the final debate on the Petition to the King, the last and most critical document approved by the First Continental Congress prior to adjournment on October 26, 1774. Even though the Delegates continued to pledge loyalty to His Majesty, they denied Parliament's authority to either tax the colonies or to interfere with colonial self-government. Parts of the Petition were surprisingly bold: "The apprehension of being degraded into a state of servitude from the preeminent rank of English freemen...excites emotions in our breasts, which though we cannot describe, we should not wish to conceal."[103]

As President, Henry was the first to sign. The Petition, however, did not reach London until mid-December. By then, word of the Suffolk Resolves had already spread through the top echelons of the British Government. Lord Dartmouth's reaction was typical: "If these resolves... are to be depended on, they [the Americans] have declared war against us..."[104]

When the Petition to the King finally did arrive, it was accompanied by copies of the Continental Association (i.e., the boycott) and the various letters and memorials to the People of Great Britain and others. After a conversation with Lord North, who's Government had just won a renewed mandate through parliamentary elections, former Massachusetts Gov. Thomas Hutchinson concluded that the British Government might have used the milder portions of the Petition to try to defuse the crisis, but that the other documents were simply too incendiary to permit compromise.[105]

As Pennsylvania Speaker Joseph Galloway distanced himself from the Patriot cause, he repeatedly pointed out that the American pledge to remain loyal to the King while rejecting Parliament's right to govern the colonies was simply impossible under the British Constitution. He argued that the delicate balance which existed between King, Lords and Commons could not be separated without toppling the entire constitutional structure.[106] George III underscored this point in his speech from the Throne when he opened the new Parliament in November 1774: "...[Parliament] may depend on my firm and steadfast resolution to withstand every attempt to weaken or impair the supreme authority of this Legislature over all the dominions of my crown..."[107] John Wilkes, the champion of British liberty, condemned the King's speech as "America's death warrent..."[108]

Despite the rush to reprisals, two parliamentary giants tried one last time to defuse the crisis. The Earl of Chatham (William Pitt) spoke in the House of Lords on January 20, 1775, urging that British troops be withdrawn from America as the first step toward reconciliation. He then introduced legislation to meet most of America's demands, including recognition of the Continental Congress, while reasserting the supremacy of Parliament. His bill was rejected by a vote of 61-32.[109] In the House of Commons, Edmund Burke's efforts met the same fate. So, too, did secret negotiations that were being conducted between Benjamin Franklin and leaders of the British Government throughout that Winter.[110] The dye had indeed been cast.

Finally, on February 2, 1775, Lord North urged that Massachusetts be declared in a state of rebellion.[111] Gov. Gage was instructed to arrest the ringleaders and to seize the colony's military supplies. The appearance of British Troops on Lexington Green early on the morning of April 19, 1775 was the direct result of that policy. The shots that day which spilled American blood were truly heard around the World.

Chapter 2

President
HENRY MIDDLETON
of
SOUTH CAROLINA

Notes

Abbreviation Key

JCC   Journals of the Continental Congress
LDC   Letters of Delegates to Congress
PHL   The Papers of Henry Laurens

[1] Paul H. Smith, Editor, LDC (Library of Congress, Washington, DC, 1976), Vol. 1, p. 234. Secretary Thomson's notes for October 22, 1774, which are contained in the New York Historical Society's manuscript collection, are fragmentary and incomplete.

[2] Jack N. Rakove, The Beginnings of National Politics (Alfred A. Knopf, New York, 1979), pp. 52-62.

[3] L. H. Butterfield et al., Editors, The Adams Papers, Diary and Autobiography of John Adams (The Belknap Press, Cambridge, 1961), Vol. 2, pp. 138, 148-9. See also: LDC, Vol. 1, op. cit., p. xxxi. Joseph Galloway's letter of resignation as a Delegate to the Continental Congress was accepted on May 12, 1775, two days after the Second Congress began. By the end of that year Galloway had actively joined the Loyalist side and he subsequently played a major role in helping the British to govern the city of Philadelphia during their occupation of the American capital in 1777-78.

[4] John E. Ferling, The Loyalist Mind: Joseph Galloway and the American Revolution (The Pennsylvania State University Press, University Park, 1977), p. 25.

[5] LDC, op. cit., Vol. 1, p. 222. Joseph Galloway... "subsequently protested that he had only reluctantly signed the association [the boycott agreement]."

[6] Walter Isaacson, Benjamin Franklin: An American Life (Simon & Schuster, New York, 2003), pp. 158-162. See also: Introduction, p. 8.

[7] LDC, op. cit., Vol. 1, pp. 117-119; Joseph Galloway's Plan of Union, September 28, 1774.

[8] Joseph Galloway, A Candid Examination of the Mutual Claims of Great Britain and the Colonies... (New York, 1775), pp. 53-54.

[9] LDC, op. cit., Vol. 1, p. 113.

[10] H. James Henderson, <u>Party Politics in the Continental Congress</u> (McGraw-Hill Book Company, New York, 1974), Table 1: Radical and Conservative Factions in the First Continental Congress, p. 46.

[11] <u>JCC</u>, op. cit., Vol. 12, p. 1222. In recognition of the status associated with the office of President, four years later--December 16, 1778--the former Presidents were requested to "lay before the Board of Treasury accounts of their expenditures in support of their households while they respectively exercised the office of President, in order to their being adjusted and paid out of the public treasury." The delegates also decided that a house should be hired and servants provided for the President at public expense.

[12] David McCullough, <u>John Adams</u> (Simon & Schuster, New York, 2001), p. 120. John Adams was rightly known as the "Atlas of Independence" since he often orchestrated the major developments inside the Continental Congress. He realized, however, that he was not personally popular with some of the delegates, so he tried to camouflage his role in some of the most important developments. Nevertheless, it was John Adams who hand selected George Washington to be the Commander-in-Chief of the new Continental Army (because Washington did not "look" ambitious), just as he convinced Thomas Jefferson to author the Declaration of Independence and he persuaded Richard Henry Lee to ride to Richmond to obtain a resolution for independence from the Virginia Convention. Thanks to David McCullough's excellent biography, at long last John Adams is starting to receive the recognition he so richly deserves.

[13] George Winston Lane, Jr., <u>The Middletons of Eighteenth Century South Carolina: A Colonial Dynasty, 1678-1787</u> (Doctoral dissertation, Emory University, 1990), p. 447. Since no formal biography of Henry Middleton has been published, Dr. Lane's 826 page doctoral dissertation on the Middleton Family during the 18th Century has been very helpful in filling that gap.

[14] <u>LDC</u>, op. cit., Vol. 1, p. 4.

[15] Cornelia Meigs, <u>The Violent Men</u> (The Macmillan Company, New York, 1949), p. 63.

[16] <u>JCC</u>, op. cit., Vol. I, p. 102.

[17] <u>LDC</u>, op. cit., Vol. 1, p. 116.

[18] <u>Merriam Webster's Geographical Dictionary</u>, (Merriam-Webster, Inc., Springfield, MA, 1998), p. 840. In 1663, King Charles II gave eight noblemen proprietorship over the Carolinas. The Carolinas were not officially separated into North and South until 1712.

[19] Lane, op. cit., pp. 30-32.

[20] Lane, op. cit., p. 34.

[21] Walter Edgar, <u>South Carolina: A History</u> (University of South Carolina Press, Columbia, 1998), pp. 84-85.

[22] Lane, op. cit.., p. 38.

[23] Lane, op. cit.., p. 53.

[24] Lane, op. cit.., p. 70.

[25] Lane, op. cit., p. 73.

[26] Lane, op. cit.., p. 76.

[27] St. James Goose Creek did celebrate its 300th Anniversary on Sunday, April 23, 2006. Charleston attorney Philip Middleton and his wife were there for the service, seated in the Middleton pew once occupied by President Henry Middleton in the 18th Century. The Rev. Doctor William Paterson Rhett, Jr., the descendant of another prominent South Carolina family (the family that raised President Henry Middleton's mother after she had been orphaned), officiated at the tricentennial service.

[28] Lane, op. cit.., p. 58.

[29] M. Eugene Sirmans, Colonial South Carolina: A Political History 1663-1763 (The University of North Carolina Press, Chapel Hill, 1966), p. 117.

[30] Edgar, op. cit., p. 111.

[31] Amory Papers, Library of Congress; Arthur Middleton to Thomas Amory, Charleston, March 9, 1722.

[32] Sirmans, op. cit., p. 138.

[33] Edgar, op. cit., p. 112.

[34] Sirmans, op. cit., p. 151.

[35] Sirmans, op. cit., pp. 153-155.

[36] Webster's Third New International Dictionary (Encyclopaedia Britannica, Inc., Chicago, 1961), p. 1268. The title Landgrave in South Carolina referred to someone who ranked just below the Lords Proprietors.

[37] Webster's Third New International Dictionary, p. 156.

[38] As cited in Lane, op. cit., p. 164.

[39] Samuel Gaillard Stoney, Plantations of the Carolina Low Country (Dover Publication, Inc., New York, 1964), pp. 56-7.

[40] Lane, op. cit., pp. 185-186.

[41] Lane, op. cit., p. 187.

[42] Lane, op. cit., p. 204.

[43] William and Sarah Middleton's son is now known to history as William Fowle Middleton.

[44] William's return to England did, in a sense, fulfill the original dream of both his grandfather and his great uncle. Their goal, like many who left Britain for Barbados

and the Carolinas during the 17th Century, was to make their fortune in the New World and then some day return home as wealthy men to live out their lives in familiar surroundings.

[45] Lane, op. cit., p. 256. In 1784, John Middleton, William Middleton's son (Henry's nephew), bought his father's former plantation. It remained in the family for over a century. In 2003, the City of Goose Creek purchased a portion of the property from a private development corporation in order to convert it into a municipal golf course.

[46] Lane, op. cit., p. 206.

[47] According to Middleton Place sources, current research at Middleton Place might indicate an even earlier date of construction for the original house. It might have been built by John Williams' father-in-law, John Cattell, from whom he obtained the property.

[48] *Middleton Place*, Middleton Place National Historic Landmark, Inc. and The Middleton Place Foundation, Charleston, SC, p. 26.

[49] Kinloch Bull, Jr., The Oligarchs in Colonial and Revolutionary Charleston (University of South Carolina Press, Columbia, 1991), p. 25.

[50] For additional information on the Seven Years War, see Introduction.

[51] See Introduction. See also: Bull, op. cit., p. 46.

[52] Langdon Cheves, Middletons of South Carolina (Revised 1979, Harriott Cheves Leland, Director of Research, Middleton Place Foundation), p. 242.

[53] George W. Williams, St. Michael's Charleston, 1751-1951 With Supplements 1951-2001 (College of Charleston Library, Charleston, 2001). St. Michael's Episcopal Church still stands today at the corner of Meeting and Broad Streets in the heart of historic Charleston. It is the oldest church building in Charleston and still one of the most active congregations.

[54] Lane, op. cit., pp. 334-5.

[55] George C. Rogers, Jr., Editor, PHL (University of South Carolina Press, Columbia, 1976), Vol. 5, p.696; Henry Laurens to Thomas and Richard Millerson & Co., May 25, 1768.

[56] As cited in Lane, op. cit., pp. 398-399.

[57] See Introduction.

[58] Richard Walsh, Charleston's Sons of Liberty: A Study of the Artisans,1763-1789 (University of South Carolina Press, Columbia, 1959), p. 26.

[59] C. A. Weslager, The Stamp Act Congress, (University of Delaware Press, London, 1976), p. 92. John Rutledge, at the age of 26, was the youngest member of The Stamp Act Congress in 1765. For additional information on The Stamp Act Congress, see the Introduction, pp. 17-18; and, Chapter 7, pp. 209-211.

[60] For more information on the Townsend Acts, see Introduction.

[61] Bull, op. cit., p. 164.

[62] Bull, op. cit., p. 17: "...the Bulls embarked on what was to become a dense network of family and political alliances. The two other families principally involved were the Draytons and the Middletons...These wealthy-families were the oligarchs..."

[63] See Introduction.

[64] As cited in Lane, op. cit., p. 402; Henry Middleton to William Middleton, December 11, 1769.

[65] Bull, op. cit., pp. 153-4.

[66] James Grant Wilson, Editor, Appletons' Cyclopaedia of American Biography (D. Appleton and Company, New York, 1888), p. 317.

[67] For more information on the Intolerable Acts, see Introduction, pp. 26-28.

[68] Lane, op. cit., p. 447.

[69] Bull, op. cit., p. 200.

[70] LDC, op. cit., Vol. 1, p. 7.

[71] JCC, op. cit., Vol. I, p. 14.

[72] Frank W. Ryan, Jr., "The Role of South Carolina in the First Continental Congress," The South Carolina Historical Magazine, Vol. LX, No. 3, July 1959, The South Carolina Historical Society, Charleston, SC, p. 148.

[73] JCC, op. cit., Vol. I, Illustration of "Signatures to the Petition to the King" following p. 120.

[74] Journal of the Commons House of Assembly, South Carolina Archives, Vol. XXXIX, pp. 190-191. These sentiments were delivered by Speaker Rawlins Lowndes.

[75] In addition to the Middleton Memorial Tablet at St. James Goose Creek, other credible sources that list Henry Middleton as the President of the South Carolina Provincial Congress (1775-76) include Appletons' Cyclopaedia of American Biography (1888), and the South Carolina Historical and Genealogical Magazine (1900), which was reprinted by the Middleton Place Foundation "Occasional Essays," Vol. 1, No. 2 (1979). In fact, according to its Official Journal, the only three men to serve as President of the South Carolina Provincial Congress during its brief transitional existence (1775-76) were Col. Charles Pinckney [uncle of Charles Cotesworth Pinckney], Henry Laurens [a future President of the Continental Congress] and William Henry Drayton.

[76] A. J. Langguth, Patriots: The Men Who Started the American Revolution (Simon and Schuster, New York, 1988), p. 267.

[77] LDC, op.; cit., Vol. 1, p. 595; Henry Middleton to Arthur Middleton, July 6, 1775.

[78] JCC, op. cit., Vol. III, p. 303.

[79] Edgar, op. cit., pp. 224-225.

[80] William Edwin Hemphill, Editor, Extracts from the Journals of the Provincial Congress of South Carolina, 1775-76 (The State Records of South Carolina, Columbia, 1960), p. 132.

[81] John H. Hazelton, The Declaration of Independence: Its History, (Dodd, Mead and Company, New York, 1906), p. 510.

[82] Lane, op. cit., pp. 503-5.

[83] Lane, op. cit., p. 533.

[84] As cited in Lane, op. cit., p. 557. Pinckney Family Papers, 3rd Ser., Charleston Historical Society; Maurice Simons, John Rutledge and Pierce Butler to Henry Middleton and his heirs, Bond for 100,000 pounds currency, November 1, 1779.

[85] Edgar, op. cit., pp. 232-233.

[86] Gregory D. Massey, John Laurens and the American Revolution, (University of South Carolina Press, Columbia, SC, 2000), p. 162.

[87] Sir Henry Clinton, The American Campaign (Yale University Press, New Haven, 1954), pp. 181-2. See also: Henry Lee, The American Revolution in the South, (Arno Press, New York, 1969), p. 193.

[88] As cited in Lane, op. cit., p. 575-576; Henry Middleton to Lieut.- Colonel Nisbet Balfour [Commandant of Charleston], (enclosed in James Simpson to William Knox, December 31, 1780), in Davies, Documents, 18 (1780): 183.

[89] Laurens Papers, op. cit., Vol. 15, p.383; Henry Laurens, "Journal and Narrative of Capture and Confinement in the Tower of London," November 5, 1781,

[90] American Papers, South Carolina Historical Society; Edward Rutledge to Arthur Middleton, February 26, 1782. See also: Barnwell, "Middleton Papers," South Carolina Historical Society, 27, (January, 1926), p. 8. See also: Biographical Directory of the South Carolina House of Representatives, Vol. II, The Commons House of Assembly, 1692-1775. See also: Walter B. Edgar, Editor (University of South Carolina Press, Columbia, 1976), p. 459.

[91] Lane, op. cit., p. 652.

[92] Charles R. Mack and Lynn Robertson, Editors, The Roman Remains, by John Izard Middleton, (University of South Carolina Press, Columbia, 1997), Introduction. This description is attributed to Charles Eliot Norton who, in 1885, was "one of the foremost cultural historians in the United States and Harvard University's first professor of fine arts."

[93] Edward McGrady, Jr., Editor, Eminent and Representative Men of the Carolinas of the Nineteenth Century, Vol. 1, (Brant & Fuller, Madison, 1892), [This volume was reproduced from an 1892 Edition in the South Caroliniana Library at the University of South Carolina, Columbia], pp. 553-4.

[94] *Middleton Place*, op. cit., p. 20.

[95] Through the complicated family connections common to that era, in which first cousins frequently married, J. J. Pringle Smith was actually descended from three of President Henry Middleton's children.

[96] Barbara Doyle, Editor, "The Glory of the Garden...Shall Never Pass Away," Middleton Place Compendium, Vol. 1, 1979-83, (An Anthology of Articles Originally Appearing in The Middleton Place Notebook), p. 7.

[97] John F. Haley, Staff Director, Biographical Directory of the American Congress 1774-1961 (US Government Printing Office, Washington, DC, 1961), p. 1425.

[98] The Parker Family Tablet at St. James Goose Creek memorializes the first John Parker who died before 1695 and his son, grandson, great-grandson (Sukey's husband) and great-great-grandson (President Henry Middleton's grandson), all of whom were also named John.

[99] This inscription is contained on a large stone tablet which is embedded in the south wall of St. James Goose Creek, the Middleton Family Church which is located approximately one mile from the Middleton homestead, The Oaks.

[100] In addition to Henry's first wife, Mary Williams Middleton, and their son, Arthur, Henry's grandson, Governor Henry Middleton, and Henry's great-grandson, Williams Middleton, are also buried in this tomb. Middleton Place, (published by the Middleton Place National Historic Landmark, Inc. and The Middleton Place Foundation, Charleston, South Carolina, 1976), p. 20.

[101] An Historic Marker on the grounds of Middleton Place states: "The main house and both dependencies were looted and burned by a party of the 56th New York Volunteers on February 22, 1865. The central dwelling and north flanker were completely destroyed, their fragile walls leveled two decades later in the Great Earthquake of 1886. The south flanker was less severely damaged in the Civil War fire, allowing Williams Middleton to restore it in the 1870s for use as the family's residence and thereby stabilizing it sufficiently to survive the Great Earthquake."

[102] Charleston's international cultural celebration known as The Spoleto Festival is held for seventeen days from late May through mid-June every year. The closing ceremony, known as The Festival Finale, is always held at Middleton Place the final night starting with picnic lunches at 3 pm followed by the Spoleto Festival Orchestra at 8 pm and concluding with exceptional fireworks after the concert. Thousands gather every year under the stars to participate in this revered Charleston tradition.

WHILE HENRY MIDDLETON WAS PRESIDENT

Notes

Abbreviation Key

JCC   Journals of the Continental Congress
LDC   Letters of Delegates to Congress
PHL   The Papers of Henry Laurens

[103] Worthington Chauncey Ford, ed., JCC (Government Printing Office, Washington, DC, 1904), Vol. I, p. 118.

[104] Peter O. Hutchinson, ed., The Diary and Letters of His Excellency Thomas Hutchinson (Houghton, Mifflin & Co., Boston, 1884), Reprint edition, (New York: AMS Press, 1973), Vol. 1, p. 284.

[105] Stephen A. Cambone, Doctoral Dissertation, Noble Sentiments and Manly Eloquence: The First Continental Congress and the Decision for American Independence (Claremont Graduate School, 1981), pp. 217-218.

[106] John E. Ferling, The Loyalist Mind: Joseph Galloway and the American Revolution (The Pennsylvania State University Press, University Park, 1977), pp. 83-84.

[107] Lawrence Harvey Gipson, The British Empire Before the American Revolution (Alfred A. Knopf, New York, 1965), Vol. XII, The Triumphant Empire, p. 273.

[108] As cited in Pauline Maier, From Resistance to Revolution, Colonial Radicals and the Development of American Opposition to Britain, 1765-1776 (London, 1972), p. 236. See also: as cited in Lillian B. Miller, ed., The Dye is Now Cast (Smithsonian Institution Press, Washington, DC, 1975), p. 150.

[109] Stanley Ayling, The Elder Pitt (David McKay Company, Inc., New York, 1976), p. 416. See also: J. C. Long, Mr. Pitt and America's Birthright (Frederick A. Stokes Company, New York, 1940), p. 514.

[110] Walter Isaacson, Benjamin Franklin: An American Life (Simon & Schuster, New York, 2003), pp. 283-289.

[111] Bernard Donoughue, British Politics and the American Revolution (Macmillan & Co., Ltd., London, 1964), pp. 238-239. Horace Walpole, influential Member of the House of Commons, called North's proposal "a vote for civil war." See also: Allan Nevins, The American States During and After the Revolution (The Macmillan Company, NY, 1927), p. 66.

Chapter 3

President
JOHN HANCOCK
of
MASSACHUSETTS

Disguised Immortality

It is a national shame that only one of the original fourteen presidents is universally known today, and that even he has been immortalized not because of his unique contribution to the founding of the nation but because of his autograph. In fact, the name John Hancock has become synonymous with requesting a signature on any document. But few ever ask why he was accorded the honor of being the first to sign the Declaration of Independence. In a strange twist of fate, despite the fact that he has become a household name, few realize that he once served as Head of State. Like his thirteen distinguished colleagues, President John Hancock has also been lost to history.

Unlike Randolph and Middleton, however, John was not born into wealth and power. He was the son and grandson of Congregational ministers. His humble birth in rural Massachusetts held no clue to the enormous fame and fortune he would ultimately attain. Like Benjamin Franklin, John became one of the most remarkable examples of early American success and perhaps the best politician of the Revolutionary Era. John's family, however, began life at the bottom rung of society. His great-great-grandfather, Nathaniel Hancock, Sr., arrived in America in 1634, little more than a decade after the Pilgrims landed at Cape Cod Harbor.[1] He settled in what became the village of Cambridge where the first college in America was founded two years later. This close proximity to Harvard afforded his descendants a unique opportunity to advance in colonial society.

His only surviving son, Nathaniel Jr., one of eight children, was born in 1639. He became a shoemaker by trade and was later elected the town constable, the first Hancock to hold public office. At the age of 29, the young Hancock joined the Cambridge Congregational Church and eventually became a deacon. It was a fateful step since his family's association with the church over the next two generations also helped to elevate his descendants from obscurity.

Deacon Hancock's second son, John, became the first Hancock to attend Harvard College which was then viewed as a seminary as much as a secular institution.[2] After graduation young Hancock did enter the ministry and, in 1698, he was called to serve as pastor of the Congregational Church in what became the village of Lexington. For the next 54 years he lovingly yet firmly dominated both his congregation and his community, earning the honorary title of "Bishop" despite its disturbing Anglican overtones.[3]

In 1700, the young "Bishop" married Elizabeth Clark, a minister's daughter. The first of their five children, John Jr., was born in 1702. John the son also attended Harvard and studied for the ministry. Eventually, the Bishop's third and youngest son, Ebenezer, did likewise. His middle son, however, was not afforded that same opportunity because of family finances. Instead, in July 1717, fourteen year old Thomas Hancock was sent to Boston as an apprentice to learn the craft of book binding. Inspired by his father's strong personality, young Thomas eagerly applied that same self-confidence to the world of business.

The "Bishop's" eldest son, however, was more intimidated than inspired by his father's authoritarian style. In 1726, after several years of searching, Pastor John Hancock was eventually called to the pulpit at the North Congregational Parish of Braintree which is today known as Quincy. In December 1733, he married Mary Hawke Thaxter, the widow of a deceased minister. Over the next decade, she gave birth to a daughter and two sons. John III, the middle child and future president, was born on January 23, 1737 (new style),[4] at the Braintree parsonage.

One of young John's earliest neighbors and playmates was John Adams, 15 months his senior. Since the Adams family was also a member of the same congregation, Pastor Hancock had the unique distinction of baptizing two of the giants of the American Revolution.[5] Throughout their long and intensely eventful lives, these two boys--who once romped together in the woods of rural Massachusetts--would share a love-hate relationship which left its indelible imprint on the course of history.

At the age of seven, John Hancock's idyllic lifestyle came to an abrupt end when his father suddenly died in May 1744. By the following year it was decided that his mother and two siblings would move to Lexington to live with his grandfather, but that John would be sent to Boston to stay with his Uncle Thomas. It was the turning point in John's life.

Thomas Hancock was, at the age of 42, one of the richest and most successful merchants in New England. Years earlier, when he had completed his apprenticeship, he had eagerly set out on his own as an independent book seller. He quickly expanded his inventory to include a much wider variety of imported items and became heavily involved in transatlantic shipping ventures. The House of Hancock ultimately included vast real estate holdings, such as Hancock Wharf in Boston harbor, as well as complex financial services for British and American merchants.[6]

In 1730, his business partner's daughter, Lydia, became Thomas Hancock's wife.[7] Despite his wealth and success, however, Hancock's lowly birth initially precluded the young couple's acceptance by the top strata of Boston society. Thomas Hancock responded by establishing an even higher standard of extravagance. The three story stone mansion he built in 1737 across from Boston Common[8] and the magnificent carriages he ordered from England, all bearing the Hancock Crest, raised the bar for those who dared to compete. He left standing orders with his English agents that items intended for his personal use were to be of "the very best kind, cost what it will."[9] To another business partner he wrote: "Neither do I intend to Spare any Cost or pains in making my Gardens Beautiful or Profitable."[10]

In March 1740, Thomas Hancock extended his influence into the political realm when he was elected to the position of Boston selectman, the forerunner of today's city councilman. His reelection over the next 13 years attests to both his popularity and his dedication to public service.[11]

Despite his prestigious reputation throughout New England and along the Atlantic Coast, The Hancocks of Beacon Hill had no children to share in their blessings. The House of Hancock had no heir.

Into this void stepped the young fatherless nephew. Seven-year-old John was the answer to his uncle's prayer. He brought laughter and excitement to the Boston mansion and guaranteed that Thomas Hancock's legacy would live on. In return, Uncle Thomas spared no expense in lavishing the very best on the lad. John apparently adapted with ease. He eventually exceeded even his extravagant uncle in conspicuous consumption.

The first step in John's transformation from country bumpkin to Boston Brahmin was a proper education. In July 1745, John was enrolled in the elite Boston Latin School. Following the regular school day, John and his classmates would then walk to Abiah Holbrook's classroom off campus where they were taught the fine art of penmanship. It was there, under Holbrook's strict supervision, that John perfected the signature that has become a national emblem.[12] He graduated in the spring of 1750 and entered Harvard College that August. There, after a lifetime of religious indoctrination, one of John's professors, Edward Wigglesworth, actually urged his students to reexamine various theological doctrines. This fresh approach to religion might well have appealed to the serious young student. Even though all of John's "closest adult male relatives" (except for his Uncle Thomas) "were active Congregational ministers,"[13] there is no indication that religion played any significant role in John's adult life beyond its social implications.[14]

John graduated from Harvard College in July 1754. At the age of 17, armed with the best formal education America could provide, John returned to his new family on Beacon Hill, eager to make a name for himself. He immediately began a six year apprenticeship under his uncle's personal tutelage. Even John Adams, his childhood friend and frequent critic, had to admit that John was "Wholly devoted to business, he was as regular and punctual at his store as the sun in his course."[15] Uncle Thomas viewed young John as "a sober, modest, young gentleman," whose "industry, abilities for business and good behavior,"[16] demonstrated his determination to succeed. John, however, best described his attitude toward business when he offered advice to his younger brother Ebenezer: "...give great attention to business and let your Conduct be such as to merit the Esteem of all about you, and remember that the Diligent Hand maketh Rich."[17]

John's apprenticeship coincided exactly with the French & Indian War which was a financial boon for the House of Hancock. In many respects, in the 18th Century, it functioned during times of war as an early incarnation of 21st Century corporate giants such as Halliburton. "By this time" according to one Hancock biographer, "[Thomas] Hancock and his distasteful but indispensable partner, Apthorp, were so generally recognized as the military provisioners of the British government in America that they no longer had to dicker for contracts."[18] John carefully observed how his uncle deftly transformed military developments and political connections into increased profits. In 1757, when Thomas Pownall was appointed by the King as the new Governor of Massachusetts, Thomas Hancock wasted no time in forming a strong alliance with the new chief executive. As a result, Thomas Hancock was selected as a member of the prestigious Governor's Council the following year. By 1760, however, the end of the war was in sight and Gov. Pownall's brief tenure also came to an end. As always, Uncle Thomas adjusted to the situation and continued to thrive despite occasional setbacks. He was the consummate pragmatist. It was a lesson that his bright young nephew also applied throughout his life.

On June 3, 1760, Gov. Pownall left Boston for England. Included in his party was 23 year old John Hancock. As a favor to John's uncle, Pownall had agreed to keep an eye on the lad during his maiden voyage. The purpose of John's journey was threefold. First, he was directed to settle several business accounts which could best be handled in person.

Second, he was urged to observe political and financial developments in London in order to anticipate future commercial opportunities. And, most importantly, John, as the heir apparent to the House of Hancock, was directed to introduce himself to his uncle's business associates.[19]

At first John was delighted with London. He pursued both business and pleasure and apparently spared few expenses, as his uncle frequently pointed out.[20] But, in October 1760, the raucous life of the capital came to an abrupt halt with the death of King George II. Theatres closed and the nation went into mourning. For John, the initial excitement of observing these historic events quickly turned to boredom. Nevertheless, he began to petition his uncle to permit him to extend his visit until the coronation of the new king. Thomas Hancock reluctantly agreed. But, when the ceremony was postponed for several more months, even John decided that it was time for him to return to America. He wrote in March 1761 that "I am almost satiated with London...I shall with satisfaction bid adieu to this grand place with all its pleasurable enjoyments and tempting scenes." In terms that his enemies would frequently hurl at him, John concluded that Londoners were too "showy" and "superficial."[21] In August 1761, John headed home to Boston.

Having seen the world, John was more eager than ever to make a name for himself in the commercial realm. Finally, on January 1, 1763, Thomas Hancock notified his business associates that "I have this Day Taken my nephew, Mr. John Hancock, into Partnership with me, having had long experience of his up-rightness & great Abilities for business."[22]

John's first target as a full partner was an attempt to corner the lucrative market for North American whale oil. With his uncle's blessing, he significantly expanded the company's involvement in all aspects of the trade from New England whalers to London wharfs. But, despite his determination, John's inexperience and the intensity of his competition led to less than satisfactory results over several years.[23] It was a hard-learned lesson in the value of caution which he would never forget.

On August 1, 1764, only 19 months after announcing his nephew's promotion, Thomas Hancock collapsed while entering the Council Chamber and died later that afternoon. According to the provisions of his will, John inherited his uncle's vast business holdings and thereby became one of the wealthiest men in New England. Less than two weeks later his fortune was further enhanced when his widowed aunt transferred to him most of her own inheritance--including the Hancock Mansion--"in consideration of that Love and Affection that I have for my said Nephew..."[24]

For the rest of her life, Aunt Lydia devoted herself to John's happiness and success just as she had done for her late beloved husband. She continued to manage the mansion with a firm hand and to oversee their servants and slaves. (The Hancocks had at least five slaves: Molly, Agniss, Cato, Prince Holmes and Hannibal. John even brought gifts for all of them when he returned from London. Cato, for example, received a cap and a French Horn. When Thomas Hancock died, he left small bequests to his slaves and authorized Cato's freedom when he reached the age of 33.) As John took over his uncle's business, he also "...ordered a Negro named Frank from London to be his personal servant." According to biographer Herbert S. Allan, John conducted this purchase "just as he would have requisitioned a batch of Irish butter." (A moss-covered slab in Boston's Old Granary Burying Ground near John's own tomb marks the spot where Frank was buried in 1771.)[25]

Aunt Lydia also served as John's hostess at their frequent formal dinners and eagerly took charge of John's matrimonial prospects. Even though the 27 year old merchant king was without question the most eligible bachelor in Boston, John continued to exhibit no interest in courting, and even less in marriage. Until recent years, an individual's sexual orientation was seldom alluded to in the study of American biography. If John Hancock had been a 21st Century politician, however, the issue would almost certainly have been raised. What is remarkable is that even in the 18th Century, John's harshest contemporary critic, John Mein, the former publisher of the *Boston Chronicle*, actually did speculate on John's sex life in one of the many diatribes he spewed forth attacking revolutionary leaders: "When... [Hancock] was in London...He...drank tea every day with the housemaid, and on Sunday escorted her to White Conduit House [a social club]...but his old schoolfellows and intimates know that though nature had bestowed upon him a human figure, she had denied him the powers of manhood. The girl was therefore in perfect safety."[26]

A century later, it was reported in the *Boston Evening Transcript* of February 11, 1884, that Professor Warren of Dover, New Jersey stated that "A gentleman was engaged...by descendants of Hancock to gather material to write a history of Hancock's life." According to Warren, "Material was collected and read, when the members of the family immediately offered the writer $1,000 to hand over the work and not make further investigation. The writer took the money, and the book was never published."[27]

What John did enjoy was the companionship he found in various male social clubs and taverns through which he also expanded his network of commercial and political associates. Two of his earliest contacts were Thomas Cushing, a prominent member of the House of Representatives who remained loyal to John for the rest of his life, and James Otis, the godfather of the American Revolution, who first spoke out against British tyranny in 1761.[28]

In March 1765, John continued to follow in his late uncle's footsteps when he was elected as one of Boston's seven selectmen.[29] From that moment, politics began to slowly consume his life. Parliament's enactment of the American Stamp Act in 1765 proved to be the catalyst for John's transformation.

In July 1765, John wrote to former Gov. Pownall that "I seldom meddle with Politicks, & indeed have not Time now to Say anything on that head [the Stamp Act]."[30] His initial interest in Britain's attempt to raise revenue from the colonies focused almost exclusively on its impact on his business empire. But, by that fall, John became increasingly cognizant of the Act's frontal assault on American liberties. John's political awakening was reflected in a letter he wrote to Massachusetts Gov. Barnard that October: "...I will not be a slave. I have a Right to the Libertys & Privileges of the English Constitution, & I as an Englishman will enjoy them."[31]

John first tested the political waters in that fall's special election to the Massachusetts House of Representatives. He came in a disappointing fourth. What no one knew at the time, however, was that John Hancock would never again lose at the ballot box. His populist instincts combined with his generous public philanthropy quickly won over support from the majority of Bostonians. The following March he was easily reelected as a Boston selectman and on May 6, 1766, as news of the Stamp Act's repeal began to reach Boston, John did indeed win election to the Massachusetts House along with his new associates: Otis, Cushing and Sam Adams. (In the election just one year later, John came in first among his Boston colleagues.[32])

John's primary tutor during this critical period was none other than Sam Adams, "The Grand Incendiary" of the Revolutionary Era.[33] Adams was eager to convert the young tycoon to his cause in order to tap John's deep pockets and his extensive commercial connections. Sam Adams was instrumental in John's election to the Massachusetts House in 1766. Later that election day, as reported years later by John Adams, the Adams cousins were walking past the Hancock Mansion on Beacon Hill when Sam Adams wryly commented that "This town has done a wise thing to-day...they have made that young man's fortune their own!"[34] John Hancock, on the other hand, delighted in the attention Adams and his cronies showered on him. Some of John's personal and professional rivals began to deride him as little more than Sam Adams' puppet. Before long, however, this incongruous couple became the yin and yang of Massachusetts politics.

Over time Sam Adams began to worry about his wealthy disciple.

John repeatedly demonstrated a remarkable grasp of popular sentiment and easily courted public support through lavish banquets and contributions to worthy causes. And, unlike Adams, John had little interest in political philosophy. His practical mind always focused instead on tangible results. In 1767, just as the two men began to drift apart, Parliament once again presented a common enemy when it passed the Townshend Acts, another foolish attempt to raise revenue in America.[35] Almost immediately John joined Adams in calling for a new boycott of British goods. His fellow merchants, however, were less than enthusiastic and public support was initially weak.

John refused to let the issue die. When five commissioners arrived in Boston to oversee implementation of the new acts, John publicly harassed them at every opportunity. His landslide reelection to the Massachusetts House in May 1768 convinced him that public sentiment was beginning to turn in his favor. That same month, however, the Romney, a British man-of-war, entered Boston Harbor to put down any attempt at local defiance. In June the commissioners took advantage of the Romney's presence and seized one of John's ships, the Liberty, as it entered the harbor. "A large angry mob spontaneously appeared on Hancock's wharf and tried to prevent the seizure."[36] The battle over the "Liberty Affair" had just begun.

During the next twelve months John Hancock demonstrated dignity and defiance as the British authorities tried every tactic to prove that he had "landed goods illegally before making a proper entry at the Customs House."[37] As usual, British shortsightedness produced the opposite result. The boycott which few Bostonians supported a year earlier was now signed by sixty local merchants on August 1, 1768.[38] Some also demanded that Gov. Bernard be recalled. Instead, more fuel was thrown on the fire when two British regiments arrived in Boston that Fall. Through it all, John urged peaceful resistance as his reputation soared throughout the colonies. Finally, on November 3, 1768, he was arrested and formally charged with smuggling. Unwittingly, the British had conferred on John the one thing which even his vast fortune could not buy, the status of martyr for American liberty.

John's trial dragged on from that November through the following March. As his legal counsel, he hired one of the best young attorneys in the colony, none other than his old boyhood companion, John Adams, Sam's younger cousin. Finally, on March 5, 1769 the prosecution moved to dismiss all of the charges.[39] Thanks to the failed attempt to intimidate and destroy him, John Hancock was catapulted to the front ranks of American patriots where he would remain for the rest of his life. Even John Wilkes, the symbol of the struggle for liberty back in Britain, wrote to express his support for John's "known zeal to the cause of his country, which our common enemies desire to punish, when they cannot suppress it."[40]

John no longer had to rely on Sam Adams and the more radical wing of the popular movement. As a result of the "Liberty Affair," his political base was solid in its own right. John's growing independence, however, angered the radicals who began to raise questions concerning his true patriotism. He was also attacked from the right when his old antagonist John Mein of the *Boston Chronicle* ran a series of articles lambasting John as "Johnny Dupe, Esq.: alias the Milch-Cow of the Well Disposed."[41]

Throughout 1769, John feared that the presence of the additional British troops could easily lead to bloodshed if the mob taunted them beyond their endurance. That is exactly what happened on the evening of March 5, 1770 (exactly one year after his trial ended) when a British guard, who was surrounded by an angry mob, called for reinforcements. The incident led to the death of five Americans and the Sam Adams-inspired version of The Boston Massacre which intentionally omitted any mention of the mob's harassment of the British soldier. Ironically, back in London, the hated Townshend taxes (except for the tax on tea) were repealed that same day.[42]

What could have easily lit the fuse of revolution was temporarily extinguished by the end of the year when none other than John Adams successfully defended the British soldiers against the massacre charges. As Adams stated so eloquently at the trial, "facts are stubborn things... and whatever our wishes, our inclinations, or the dictums of our passions, they cannot alter the state of facts and evidence."[43] The commemoration of the Massacre, however, would continue to stoke the revolutionary fire in the years ahead.

Overall, the early 1770s marked a period of benign neglect concerning British policy toward North America. Lord North, now head of His Majesty's government, honestly desired a respite from the constant feuding over one failed tax policy after another.[44] During this political lull, John's Aunt Lydia managed to matchmake an engagement between her wealthy nephew and Dorothy Quincy, whom everyone called Dolly. But, as biographer Herbert Allen states, "it might not have ripened into marriage four years later but for the constant nurture of John's foster mother, who seems to have adopted Dolly, too."[45] As the long courtship wore on, the brilliant young military officer Aaron Burr also began to show interest in Dolly. Over a century ago, Dolly's biographer described the scene: "Aunt Lydia...immediately took alarm. She apprehended delay, if not peril, to her cherished plans...[she] never allowed them a moment in each other's society without a chaperon."[46]

By 1771, John's health had also become an issue. He perfected the art of utilizing his periodic bouts of gout to his political advantage. From late spring through the fall John often thwarted the plans of the radicals by claiming to be indisposed due to his condition. Thomas Hutchinson, now Governor of Massachusetts, took delight in what he perceived as estrangement between the leaders of the opposition. After John's overwhelming reelection to the Massachusetts House in 1772, Hutchinson felt confident enough to reverse his earlier hostility toward the "Merchant King."[47] He finally approved the selection of John Hancock to the prestigious Governor's Council, the position once held by John's uncle. But, to Hutchinson's horror--and great popular applause--John publicly turned down the governor's appointment and announced that he would remain a representative of the people.[48] Once again, John demonstrated his remarkable political instincts.

While John's popularity continued to soar, Gov. Hutchinson's long political career started to unravel in early 1773 when inflammatory letters he had written to British officials a few years earlier began to surface in Boston after being leaked by Benjamin Franklin in London.[49] That May, Sam Adams enthusiastically predicted that the governor "never will be able to recover..."[50] Within a year, Hutchinson was gone.

As events unfolded, in 1773 the Virginia House of Burgesses urged all thirteen colonial legislatures to establish regular ongoing lines of communication through the creation of intercolonial Committees of Correspondence. In Massachusetts, John was elected as one of the fifteen members of that new committee. As the hero of the "Liberty Affair," he was already one of the best known Americans. Now, as an active correspondent with his colleagues across the continent, John was able to further expand his political network.

In June 1773, news reached Boston that the British Parliament had once again unwittingly played into the hands of Sam Adams. Lord North's new policy, which gave the East India Company the exclusive right to sell tea to America, also called for enforcement of the existing tea duty which had been largely ignored through smuggling.[51] The Boston radicals were elated as they began to mobilize renewed popular opposition to government policy. Thanks in large measure to his loyal captain, James Scott, John's ships in London refused to carry the controversial cargo even before word of the latest legislation arrived in America.[52] Once the radicals did begin their resistance, John was thus able to keep at arm's length from their more extreme endeavors without jeopardizing his patriot credentials.

On December 7, the last of the three ships carrying the damnable tea entered Boston Harbor. If the tea duties were not paid by midnight December 16, "the cargoes would be legally confiscated by the Customs

House and brought ashore."[53] While John publicly called for calm,[54] Sam Adams and his Sons of Liberty took matters into their own hands. On the evening of December 16, only hours before the deadline, the Sons of Liberty, disguised as Mohawk Indians, boarded the three ships and tossed all 342 chests of tea into Boston Harbor.[55]

News of the Boston Tea Party angered and outraged a wide cross section of British and American citizens from George III to George Washington (who feared that it would trigger even greater problems with the Mother Country).[56] For the next few months, Bostonians anxiously awaited Parliament's response to so bold an act of defiance. At first, John withdrew to his mansion as he carefully evaluated public sentiment and waited for the right moment to speak out. Then, on March 5, 1774, he accepted the town's invitation to deliver the annual oration to commemorate the fourth anniversary of the Boston Massacre. As he "rose from his sickbed," John swept away any lingering doubt concerning his true allegiance. He urged an overflow audience of 2,000 fellow Bostonians to "Remember, my friends, from whom you sprang...I conjure you by all that is dear, by all that is honorable, by all that is sacred, not only that ye pray, but that ye act; that, if necessary, ye fight, and even die, for the prosperity of our Jerusalem."[57]

The citizens of Boston responded by unanimously reelecting John to the House of Representatives a few weeks later. Two months after the Massacre Oration, Boston's worst nightmare did come true as news of the Boston Port Act reached America. In this first of four Intolerable Acts passed by Parliament,[58] the British Government closed Boston Harbor to all commercial activity. The Tea Party had achieved its goal. There was no longer any neutral ground.

As Massachusetts reached out to her sister colonies for support, John characteristically resumed his low profile throughout May and June 1774. His great genius was in articulating the will of the people, not converting them to a specific direction. He understood the value of patience as the radicals and the more conservative merchants hotly debated the proper course. By July, John reemerged as a member of the group that drafted the response to the Intolerable Acts. He was then selected by the people to serve on Boston's Committee of Safety which helped to enforce the resolutions approved by the Town Meetings. The radicals, however, still feared John's popular base of support. They excluded him from the delegation to the First Continental Congress that was elected not by popular vote but by the Massachusetts House of Representatives.

Biographer Harlow Giles Unger offers a dramatically different interpretation of events surrounding John's failure to attend the First Continental Congress. According to Unger, when another delegate (James

Bowdoin) fell ill, many urged John to take his place but he refused, "insisting that Boston needed at least one leader at home to command patriot forces and represent the city at a forthcoming provincial congress." Unger contends that John even hosted a farewell banquet for the four remaining delegates. [59] Given John's lifelong passion for appearing at the center of great events, Unger's interpretation rings hollow. The fact that the Hancock name was already known throughout the continent because of John's defiance during the "Liberty Affair" might well have given his distinguished colleagues pause lest they be overshadowed by him in Philadelphia. (In fact, that is exactly what happened nine months later when John was finally added to the Massachusetts Delegation.)

Nevertheless, during September and October 1774, while John and Sam Adams, Robert Treat Paine and Thomas Cushing represented Massachusetts at the Philadelphia Congress, John Hancock further consolidated his own leadership throughout the colony. On October 5, the members of the General Assembly gathered in Salem in defiance of Gov. Gage's order that they be disbanded. The next day these elected representatives voted to transform themselves into a new legislative body and elected John Hancock as their first chairman. When a larger group reconvened a week later in Concord, John was formally elected as the first President of the Massachusetts Provincial Congress. [60] For the next two months he presided over this revolutionary body as it debated the future of the colony and ultimately approved the boycott of British goods (known as the Continental Association) which had been adopted by the Continental Congress only weeks earlier.

During these critical days, John was also elected chairman of the newly created Massachusetts Committee of Safety which operated in many respects as a shadow government. Its most pressing business was to create and supply a proposed 15,000 man state militia for the defense of the colony. By the time the Massachusetts Delegation returned from Philadelphia in early November, Sam Adams must have been shocked by the degree to which his former protégée had consolidated his own political base. Not surprisingly, John was quickly added to the slate of delegates who were elected to represent the colony when the Philadelphia Congress was scheduled to resume the following May.

In the months leading up to the resumption of the Continental Congress, the Second Provincial Congress of Massachusetts met in Cambridge in February 1775. John was again elected to serve as president. As British pressure increased, the Congress moved to Concord later that spring while John Hancock and Sam Adams sought protection from repeated personal threats by retreating to the parsonage in nearby Lexington where John's late grandfather, the "Bishop," once ruled supreme.[61] Aunt Lydia and John's fiancee joined them there as a growing number of citizens began to flee Boston. (The Hancock-Clarke House where they stayed still stands today within sight of Lexington Green. Even the bed that John Hancock and Sam Adams shared the evening of April 18, 1775 [a common practice in the 18th Century] can be seen in the "parlor-bedroom" on the first floor.)[62]

It was there at the parsonage, very early on the morning of April 19, 1775, that Paul Revere arrived at full gallop to warn them that British troops were on their way to Lexington to arrest the two patriot leaders and to confiscate the military provisions being stored at Concord. In the confusion, John and his radical colleague just barely escaped, only minutes before the first shot of the revolution was fired less than two blocks away on Lexington Green.

Over the next few days John desperately tried to piece together news of the bloody developments at Lexington and Concord as he and Adams continued to elude the British troops. He was delighted to hear that the King's Army had been pushed back to Boston and that the patriot militia was in hot pursuit. Finally, on April 24, John was reunited with Aunt Lydia and Dolly at Worcester. After attending to last minute details pertaining to the Committee of Safety as well as his commercial affairs, John and his party headed south toward Philadelphia and the opening of the Second Continental Congress. Along the way he left Aunt Lydia and Dolly in the safe care of relatives in Fairfield, Connecticut.

When the Massachusetts Delegation reached New York City in early May, thousands of people lined the streets to greet them. As John proudly wrote to Dolly, "...the carriage of your humble servant, of course, being first in the Procession."[63] That scene was repeated a few days later when John, his colleagues and the delegates from New York and Connecticut arrived in Philadelphia on May 10, 1775. That same evening the work of the Congress resumed and Peyton Randolph of Virginia was again elected President. Because of recent developments, however, Congress' focus shifted to the battlefield as the delegates eagerly listened to first hand accounts from Massachusetts. Theoretical debate had given way to harsh reality.

On the morning of May 24, President Randolph was again called back to Virginia when he received word that Gov. Dunmore intended to reopen the House of Burgesses over which Randolph still presided as Speaker. Once again, former President Middleton of South Carolina was asked to assume the chair in Randolph's absence but this time Middleton declined due to poor health.[64] Congress then turned to New England and to the former President of the Massachusetts Provincial Congress, John Hancock, who was by now one of the best known patriots in America. With little debate, he was elected unanimously as the third President of the Continental Congress.[65]

Unlike Randolph and Middleton, who had assumed the mantle of national leadership near the end of their long and distinguished lives, John was extremely eager to carve out his own unique place in history early in his career. As a young man of 38, he brought energy and ability to the presidency while he tirelessly transformed the office from that of elder statesman to chief executive. Over the next two and a half years, John, more than any other single individual, established the foundation of the modern presidency.

John took an active interest in every aspect of Congress and carried on an exhaustive correspondence with absent delegates, state officials, military officers and foreign contacts. He considered it his duty "to see every resolve of Congress executed..."[66] To his friends on the Massachusetts Committee of Safety, John apologized for his lack of personal correspondence: "When I can get a Leisure hour I will write you & all my Friends. Docr Church knows how I was hurried, & it still Continues."[67]

Through it all, John's pragmatic approach freed him from the often bitter factions which developed over policy. Even though Sam and John Adams soon regretted that they had promoted their less fiery colleague for the position, most delegates appreciated John's impartiality during debates and his natural gregariousness in social settings. He was already the consummate politician who knew how to ingratiate himself without diminishing the dignity of his office. Both his wealth and personality made his task much easier; but, beneath it all, he never abandoned the intense work ethic which he had also inherited from his uncle. After the long hours of meetings each day and the frequent social gatherings most evenings, John would still burn the midnight oil as he carried out his official duties late into the night.[68]

Less than three weeks after his election as president, John's reputation was further enhanced by none other than Gen. Gage who offered a pardon "to all persons who shall forthwith lay down their arms..." with the exception of John Hancock and Sam Adams "whose offenses are of too flagitous a nature to admit of any other consideration than that of condign punishment."[69]

At the same time, however, John's dream of adding military glory to his meteoric rise was dashed when John Adams orchestrated the selection of George Washington of Virginia to be the Commander-in-Chief of the newly created Continental Army. Adams later wrote that "Whether he [John Hancock] thought, An Election, a Compliment due to him and intended to have the honor of declining it or whether he would have accepted I know not." Adams did admit that John's "exertions, sacrifices, and general merits in the cause of his country had been incomparably greater than those of Colonel Washington."[70] But, unlike John, Washington had prior military experience as a member of the Virginia Militia at the start of the French & Indian War.[71] The very fact that Washington was from Virginia, the oldest and largest of the colonies, was also key. In addition, Adams understood that a continental army must have true geographic balance in order to win support from all regions.

Despite his disappointment, John's skills were unquestionably better suited to parliamentary procedures than battlefield campaigns. Even though he never completely forgave Adams for what he considered personal disloyalty by an old friend, John, as president, extended every courtesy to Gen. Washington and conducted their relationships throughout the war on a thoroughly professional basis.[72]

On Sunday morning, June 18, 1775, only days after Washington's appointment, John wrote to his old friend Joseph Warren, the new President of the Massachusetts Provincial Congress, the office John himself had recently held. (What John did not know at the time was that his friend had been killed the previous day at the Battle of Bunker [Breeds] Hill.) John began his correspondence by mentioning his new responsibilities: "I intended writing you a long Letter, but am prevented, by my Attention to the orders of Congress...I have great Duty to Do, but I will persevere even to the Destruction of my Constitution." Then, without any hint of animosity, John informed Warren that: "The Congress have Appointed George Washington Esqr. General & Commander in Chief of the Continental Army, his Commission is made out, & I shall Sign it tomorrow, he is a Gentn. you will all like. I submit to you the propriety of providing a suitable place for his Residence, & the mode of his Reception. Pray tell Genl. Ward of this with my Respects, & that we all Expect to hear that the Military Movements of the Day of his Arrival will be such as to do him & the Commandr in Chief great honour...Would it not be proper to have a Troop at the Entrance of our Province to Escort him down, & then the Foot ready to Receive him. Pray do him every honour..."[73]

Washington attested to their excellent rapport two-and-a-half years later when John completed his presidential service. Washington wrote to the departing President: "In the progress of that intercourse which has necessarily subsisted between us, the manner in which you have conducted on your part, accompanied with every expression of politeness and regard to me, gives you a claim to my warmest acknowledgements."[74] And, when

John requested an armed guard for his journey home, Washington wrote: "I have ordered Cornet Buckmer, with 12 Dragons, to attend you as an escort and to receive your commands. For this purpose you will be pleased to retain them, as long as you may consider their attendance necessary."[75]

Even though John clearly enjoyed his public duties, his living arrangements were completely unacceptable. Never before had he been forced to manage his own household. He missed Aunt Lydia's steady hand at home and grew increasingly irritated over the lack of correspondence from his fiancee. On June 10, 1775, he wrote: "My dear Dolly...I have ask'd [a] million questions & not an answer to one...I Really Take it extreme unkind...I want long Letters...I will forgive the past if you will mend in future."[76] She seldom did.

Despite the lengthy delay and their obvious hesitation, Aunt Lydia prevailed. On the evening of August 28, 1775, while Congress was in recess and John was traveling home through New England, Aunt Lydia arranged for John and Dolly to be married in what biographer Harlow Giles Unger described as "a quite dispassionate ceremony" while visiting relatives in Fairfield, Connecticut.[77] The man known for his lavish banquets on almost every occasion took this fateful step without the slightest formal celebration. Upon hearing the news, John Adams expressed his shock to a close Massachusetts friend: "Be it known to you then that two of the most unlikely Things, within the whole Congress of Possibility, have really, and actually happened. The first is the Suden Marriage of our President..."[78]

Only a few days after their wedding John and his bride returned to Philadelphia. Dolly's presence assuaged John's loneliness, and her demeanor clearly met the demands of her new role as hostess to the nation. John Adams found her behavior to be "easy and genteel."[79] By necessity, she even assisted the President on some official duties late at night. "For months after their wedding, Dolly and her husband spent their evenings engaged with scissors as they trimmed the rough edges off the bills of credit printed by Congress. After each one was properly cut and signed by the President, they packed them up in bundles..."[80] Congress eventually relieved her of those tedious chores by appropriating funds for additional staff.

Their union easily evolved into a comfortable partnership. Overall, those two strong-willed individuals enjoyed their life in the public eye, not unlike prominent "power couples" in the nation's capital today. During their 18 years of marriage, Dolly gave birth to both a daughter and a son; but, tragically, both died very young. As a result, most of their married life was consumed by government service. (It is interesting to note that over the past two centuries, only two First Ladies from the First Republic have had biographies devoted to them: Dolly Quincy Hancock and Sarah Livingston Jay, the wife of the fifth President.)[81]

At the start of 1776, Thomas Paine published his small salient pamphlet, Common Sense. At first, many of the Founding Fathers, including John, failed to grasp its revolutionary impact. On January 17, John sent a copy to his friend and colleague Thomas Cushing in Boston: "I inclose you a pamphlet which makes much Talk here, said to be wrote by an English Gentleman Resident here by the name of Paine, & I believe him the Author, I Send it for your and Friend's Amusement."[82] The arguments Paine made, however, proved powerful and persuasive to the average man. Unlike the delegates to Congress, Thomas Paine did not hesitate to call the King a tyrant; and, in one of many brilliant passages, he argued that "the fate of Charles the First [beheading] hath only made kings more subtle--not more just."[83]

By late January, John informed Gen. Washington that "By the latest advices from England it appears that administration are determined to exert themselves and to send a considerable force against us next Spring, though at the same time they pretend to say that they will offer terms of accommodations..."[84] That spring the President extended an invitation to General and Mrs. Washington to be his guests on their next visit to Philadelphia.[85]

In April 1776, John confided to a friend that "I thought I had known heretofore what it was to be hurried in Business, but my Department...is a Department of great Business & constant Attention." John added that "Night and Day have I a Levee, I determine to persevere, tho' it is really hurtful to my health." On a happier note, John mentioned that "I am going to move into the most Airy Elegant house in the City, havg. had the Offer of it, ready furnished by the Owners...a polite offer to use the House, Furnishing, Gardens, Stables &c at will, & the Compliment of the Use."[86] John and Dolly's new home, near the intersection of Arch and Fourth Streets, suited them well.[87] As in Boston, the Hancock mansion quickly became the social center of the capital. Unfortunately, his dear Aunt Lydia did not live long enough to visit her nephew and his new bride in Philadelphia. She died "very suddenly" that spring while visiting relatives in Connecticut.[88]

In June 1776, Congress echoed many of Paine's arguments as it finally debated American independence. John proudly presided as the new nation inched closer each day toward total separation from the British Empire. When the vote finally came on July 2, 1776 (the true Independence Day), John enthusias-tically embraced full emancipation and, as President, he and Secretary Charles Thomson were the only officers to attach their names to the document immediately after its approval, thereby sealing their fate should the cause of independence fail. Then, on August 2, the official engrossed copy of the Declaration was ready for the delegates to sign.[89] With the stroke of a quill pen, John's signature on that parchment became perhaps the most famous in all of recorded history.[90]

On July 6, John began the process of distributing copies of the Declaration of Independence to each of the States. "Altho it is not possible to foresee the Consequences of Human Action," he told them, "yet it is nevertheless a Duty we owe ourselves and Posterity in all our public Counsels, to decide in the best Manner we are able, and to trust the Event to that Being who controuls both Causes and Events so as to bring about his own Determinations." In closing, John stated: "The important Consequences to the American States from this Declaration of Independence, considered as the Ground & Foundation of a future Government, will naturally suggest the Propriety of proclaiming it in such a Manner, that the People may be universally informed of it."[91] That same day, John sent a copy of the Declaration to Gen. Washington with the request that "you will have it proclaimed at the Head of the Army in the Way you shall think most proper."[92]

In the midst of all his official correspondence, John somehow made time to share his thoughts with his good friend William Cooper, Boston's Town Clerk: "Could you exactly know my particular Scituation, and how much of the Day and Night I devote to the Execution of publick Business I am Confident you and my Friends would readily excuse my not writing. I am really so greatly Engag'd, and Business fast increasing in my Department that I have not a moment to myself."[93] Under the circumstances, this was perhaps one of the few times in his remarkable life that John could be accused of understatement. For once, even John Adams completely concurred with John's evaluation of events. In mid-July, John Adams wrote to his wife Abigail that "Never--Never in my whole Life, had I so many Cares upon my Mind at once."[94]

Less than two weeks later the congressional committee which was assigned "to prepare and digest the form of a confederation" laid before Congress its proposal for "Articles of Confederation and Perpetual Union."[95] The debate dragged on for months as Congress and its president dealt with an ever increasing workload. On July 19, for example, John received a peace proposal from Lord Richard Howe, the commanding admiral of the British Navy along the North American coast. Congress' negative response can best be understood through the letter Benjamin Franklin sent to his old friend Howe the next day: "The Official Dispatches to which you refer me, contain nothing more than what we had seen in the Act of

Parliament, viz. Offers of Pardon upon Submission; which I was sorry to find, as it must give your Lordship Pain to be sent so far on so hopeless a Business. Directing Pardons to be offered the Colonies, who are the very Parties injured, expresses indeed that Opinion of our Ignorance, Baseness, & Insensibility which your uninform'd and proud Nation has long been pleased to entertain of us; but it can have no other Effect than that of increasing our Resentment."[96]

Britain responded to the rejection of its Peace Commission by increasing its military pressure. On December 12, Congress was forced to flee to Baltimore to avoid the threat of capture by British troops. John described the turmoil to a close friend one month later: "My Scituation, upon Leaving Philada. was really distressing, you well know the State of my Family at that time, a Wife but Nine Days in Bed, a little Infant just Breath'd in the World...On arrival I had no house prepar'd, Mr. Purviance was so obliging as to Take us in, & we Remain'd there Ten Dys..."[97] There, despite woefully inadequate accommodations, a committee of five was appointed "to prepare and report a plan for obtaining foreign assistance."[98] And it was in Baltimore, on Christmas Day 1776, that John pleaded with the States for reinforcements: "I beseech you therefore by all that is sacred--by that Love of Liberty and your Country, which you have always manifested --by those Ties of Honour which bind you to the Common Cause...and finally--by your Regard for suceeding Generations, that you will, without a Moment's Delay, exert yourselves to forward the Troops for Ticonderoga from your States..."[99]

On March 7, 1777, John was finally able to return to Philadelphia where Congress resumed its deliberations a week later.[100] Dolly and their infant daughter arrived by the end of the month but, due to the renewed threat of invasion and their little girl's poor health, she and their daughter headed back to New England where baby Lydia died that August.[101]

On June 14, 1777, the new flag, mistakenly attributed to Betsy Ross, was adopted as the official American standard.[102] Two months later, British Gen. William Howe entered Chesapeake Bay to begin his assault on America's Capital. By then, John was thoroughly exhausted and aching to return home to Boston after nearly two-and-a-half years of continuous service at the epicenter of the revolution. First, however, Congress had to flee Philadelphia yet again. On September 17, John described the scene to his wife as the British Army approached: "Nothing could have happened more fortunate, than your leaving this City at the time you did, for in a very few days we were much Alarm'd, & proceeded to Pack up all our publick Papers, to be ready in case we were under the necessity of Removing...I Expect Congress will this Day Adjourn to Lancaster...The Enemy are within 26 or 30 miles of us, & an Action Expected as soon as the weather clears up...I am greatly hurried."[103]

Six days later Gen. Howe and his troops did capture the American capital. Congress briefly reconvened late that month in Lancaster, Pennsylvania for one session, but then quickly moved across the Susquehanna for the added security the river provided and resumed its work at York, 90 miles from Philadelphia. Once again, John shared the details with Dolly when he wrote to her from York on October 1: "...very soon after you left me our Alarms began & continued Day & night until the morng. of the 19th Sepr. when about one oClock (& I was not in bed, nor had my Cloaths off for three Nights before) I Rec'd an Express from the General's aid De Camp recommending the immediate Removal of Congress, as the Enemy had it in their power to throw a party that Night into the City. I instantly gave the alarm, Rous'd the Members...and after having fix'd my Packages, Papers &c in the Waggons and Sent them off, about 3 oClock in the morning I Set off myself..."[104]

Despite the tremendous humiliation of having to abandon the national capital, the gloom began to lift on October 20 when Congress received news of the glorious American victory at Saratoga, New York and the capture of Gen. Burgoyne's British Army.[105] Gen. Horatio Gates, the American commander at Saratoga, became the hero of the hour (even though Gen. Benedict Arnold deserved much of the credit). Gates' good fortune stood in stark contrast to the failure of Gen. Washington's troops to protect Philadelphia.[106]

During his final days as President, John deftly presided over the deliberations concerning the proposed Articles of Confederation. And then, on October 29, as John took his leave of Congress, he became the first President to deliver a farewell address (even though he made clear his intention to return): "Gentlemen...I think I shall be forgiven if I say I have spared no pains, expence, or labour, to gratify your wishes, and to accomplish the views of Congress. My health being much impaired, I find some relaxation absolutely necessary, after such constant application; I must therefore request your indulgence for leave of absence for two months. But I cannot take my departure, gentlemen, without expressing my thanks for the civility and politeness I have experienced from you...I pray heaven, that unanimity and perseverance may go hand in hand in this house..."[107] In response, his colleagues introduced a formal resolution of thanks for his dedicated service which passed over the objection of his old nemesis, Sam Adams.[108] Henry Laurens of Charleston, the most prominent merchant of the South, was elected to succeed John.

On his journey north, John met Dolly at Hartford, Connecticut. A few days later, on Wednesday, November 19, 1777, a military honor guard escorted their carriage through the streets of Boston as cheering crowds and bells and cannons welcomed them home.[109] As Hancock biographer Harlow Giles Unger wrote: "In contrast, no one even noticed the Adamses when they got to Massachusetts a few days later."[110] Retirement, however, was the furthest thing from John's mind. After a period of rest and recuperation from his latest bout of gout, John had every intention of plunging back into Massachusetts politics by becoming his state's first popularly elected governor. It was his opponents' worst nightmare.

Almost immediately, the citizens of Massachusetts demonstrated both their support and respect for their national hero by reelecting John to the State legislature, unanimously selecting him as Moderator for their Town Meetings and reelecting him as a delegate to the Continental Congress. In return, John renewed his philanthropy to the city's poor and he actively helped to rebuild Boston in the wake of the British occupation. He also publicly announced that he would accept "Continentals" issued by Congress as repayment for debts owed to him even though the value of that paper currency continued to drop.[111] Despite these efforts, John's gubernatorial dream was temporarily deferred in the spring of 1778 when the voters of Massachusetts rejected the newly proposed State Constitution. In characteristic fashion, John had kept at arm's length from the debate and came through the referendum more popular than ever. His enemies were once again dumbfounded. James Warren compared John to the hated former Gov. Hutchinson when he wrote to Sam Adams that John "... certainly equals him in Ambition and Exceeds him in Vanity."[112]

On June 7, 1778, Warren again denounced the former President when he described John's late departure for Philadelphia by comparing it to "the Pomp and retinue of an Eastern Prince..."[113] The preparations for the journey, however, took almost as long as the time John spent back in Philadelphia, which had recently been abandoned by the British. Since it became clear that President Laurens had no intention of resigning his office in deference to John (just as John had refused to step down in 1775 when former President Peyton Randolph returned to Congress), John, unlike Randolph, felt that his continued presence as just a delegate was beneath his dignity.[114] Therefore, after celebrating the second anniversary of the Declaration of Independence with his congressional friends, John and Dolly left for Boston to pursue other ambitions.

Two years earlier, while still serving in Congress, John had been elected by the Massachusetts legislature as his state's major general.[115] As soon as John and Dolly returned home from Philadelphia, he finally had the opportunity to don his bright new uniform and lead his state militia in the liberation of British occupied Newport, Rhode Island. But, by August 1778, the entire campaign under American Gen. John Sullivan collapsed because of a series of mishaps and poor coordination with the French Fleet. As always, John enjoyed the ceremony, but he actually played only a minor role in the campaign itself. He did, however, help to save the critical alliance with France. While Gen. Sullivan and other American military leaders publicly demeaned the French for their halfhearted support, John hosted several banquets at his mansion on Beacon Hill in honor of the Vice Admiral, the Comte d'Estaing, and his French officers. The French returned the compliment. D'Estaing referred to John as "the true friend of France in America, a great statesman and an able General."[116]

In June 1779, John added yet another star to his political galaxy when he was elected Speaker of the Massachusetts House. Later that summer he also attended the State Constitutional Convention in Cambridge, but intentionally kept a low profile while John Adams almost single handedly authored what became perhaps the best state constitution in the country. To John Hancock's delight, it provided for a strong executive with veto power over legislation and command over the state militia. The document was subsequently approved by the voters of Massachusetts and in September 1780, John Hancock won an overwhelming victory as the state's first freely elected Governor with an astonishing 91% of the vote.[117]

John truly loved serving as governor and applied his experience and skill toward setting broad policies rather than engaging in the rough and tumble of day to day legislative combat. Year after year he continued to win reelection as his health gradually failed and he grew prematurely old. On November 14, 1783, as the Peace Treaty with Great Britain was finally ratified, John wrote to one of his oldest and dearest friends, Captain James Scott, the loyal employee who had commanded so many ships on behalf of the House of Hancock over the years: "...one thing I can truly Boast, I sat out upon honest Principles & strictly adhered to them to the close of the contest, and this I defy malice itself to controvert. I have lost many thousand sterling, but, thank God, my country is saved and by the smile of Heaven I am a free & Independent man..."[118]

On January 29, 1785, John shocked friends and foes alike when he suddenly resigned as Governor, supposedly because of poor health. His close ally, Lt. Gov. Thomas Cushing, succeeded to the office, but was narrowly defeated in the next election later that spring. Some speculated that John's real motivation was his gradual decline in popular support. Others considered it a brilliant political ploy to revitalize his image. John's numerous supporters in Boston immediately elected him to represent them in the new State Legislature which, in turn, elected him yet again as a delegate to the Continental Congress. During his two year sabbatical from the governor's office John even managed to get reelected as President of the Continental Congress on November 23, 1785, without ever having traveled to New York where Congress was then meeting.[119] For the next six months he repeatedly promised to take up his national duties as soon as his health would permit; but, in June 1786, John finally submitted his resignation for the term he had never begun.[120]

Throughout that summer and fall, John completely withdrew from public affairs as the uprising by financially hard pressed Western Massachusetts farmers grew into the open warfare known as Shays Rebellion. Sam Adams and his close colleague Gov. Bowdoin dealt harshly with the rebels and politically alienated western voters in the process. It was also during those dark days that John's young son died of a head injury while ice skating in early 1787. John confided to Gen. Knox that his "Situation is totally deranged by the untimely Death of my Dear and Promising Boy."[121]

In their grief, John and Dolly decided to travel to New York and Philadelphia to escape from their sorrow as best they could. Political foes, however, immediately speculated on the real meaning of John's renewed visibility. It soon became clear that he had decided to return to the governor's office. At the Spring 1787 election, in the wake of Shays Rebellion and its political fallout, John easily defeated the incumbent, reclaimed the governorship and immediately pardoned all rebels who were still in jail. His leniency was welcomed by many of his constituents but some revolutionary colleagues such as James Madison condemned him as "an idolater of popularity."[122]

In May 1787, shortly after John returned to the Governor's office, the Constitutional Convention opened in Philadelphia. By now, having served as Governor for over four years, John strongly supported states rights but, as a former President of Congress, he also understood far better than most the pragmatic demands of national government. In characteristic fashion, he initially kept his views on the proposed Constitution to himself. That December he was elected as a delegate to the Massachusetts Ratification Convention and on January 9, 1788, at its opening session, John was selected to serve as Convention President. Since only five of the required nine states had already ratified the new Constitution, and since the outcome in Virginia and New York was far from certain, the Massachusetts vote was of critical importance. History had come full circle. The future of the young nation once again rested with Massachusetts where the revolution first began.

After the Ratification Convention opened, John retired to his home to continue his recuperation and reflection while weeks of heated debate ensued. Supporters of the Constitution such as Rufus King feared that "our prospects are gloomy, but hope is not entirely extinguished."[123] Finally, on January 31, 1788, John was literally carried into the Convention.[124] After consultations with all factions, he publicly endorsed the Constitution and proposed that nine specific amendments should be recommended for adoption by the new government once it was established. Six days later Massachusetts formally approved the new charter by a vote of 187-168. In his long career, this was perhaps the greatest moment of John Hancock's public life. As his biographer Robert Finkelstein states: "...in the final analysis it was Hancock's prestige and influence which successfully decided the issue..."[125] If Massachusetts had not ratified, the new Constitution would probably have been doomed.

That same popularity, however, helped to unravel any dreams John might have had for one final election to national office. Federalists across the country such as Hamilton and Madison feared that Hancock alone could rival Washington's popularity and they therefore selected John Adams, another Massachusetts patriot who was equally deserving yet far less charismatic, to be the new government's first Vice President.[126]

Ever the pragmatist, John rededicated the remaining years of his life to his state and extended an olive branch to some of his harshest critics by endorsing none other than Sam Adams for Lt. Governor in the 1789 election. They won overwhelmingly.[127] Later that year, however, there was one last major controversy when Washington paid an official visit to Massachusetts. Because of his increasingly poor health, Gov. Hancock invited President Washington, his former subordinate, to call on him at his Beacon Hill Mansion. Washington took great offense at what he perceived to be a breach of protocol and demanded that the Governor must first visit him. John quickly sensed a lack of popular support for his position and did indeed "take the first step," but with the flare worthy of a death scene from Hamlet.[128] He then returned home and eagerly awaited his rival's departure.

John continued to serve as Governor for the remainder of his life. It is ironic that it was only John's death on October 8, 1793, that permitted his former mentor and once bitter rival, Lt. Gov. Sam Adams, to finally succeed to the state's highest office. Predictably, John's funeral was the largest ever seen in Boston. Over 20,000 mourners from all walks of life followed Vice President John Adams and Gov. Sam Adams in the formal procession from Beacon Hill to Granary Burying Ground one block from Boston Common. What is astonishing is that it took 103 years before a monument was finally erected over John's grave. Like all of his presidential colleagues from the First Republic, even John Hancock was largely forgotten by an ungrateful nation.

Unlike Middleton, John left no direct descendants. The Hancock name streaked across the sky like a meteor as a great new nation was born and then it faded into history. Three years after his death, his widow scandalized the upper crust of Boston society when she married one of John's oldest friends and former employees, Captain James Scott. Years later, once again a widow, Dolly (who lived until 1830) sold the great mansion and moved to Federal Street. It was there, in 1824, that the elderly Marquis de Lafayette, on his Grand Tour of the Nation, stopped his carriage during his welcoming parade to personally pay his respects to the widow of the deceased President.

In old age, even John Adams mellowed as he reflected on his oldest friend and often bitterest adversary. "I could melt into Tears," Adams wrote, "when I hear his Name...If Benevolence, Charity, Generosity were ever personified in North America, they were in John Hancock."[129] Five years later Adams wrote to another friend: "I can say, with truth, that I profoundly admired him, and more profoundly loved him."[130] John Hancock's greatest legacy, however, remains the American Presidency itself. He, more than any other individual, built the initial foundation upon which the Chief Executive of the most powerful nation on Earth still stands.

President John Hancock's
Monument & Grave at the
Old Granary Burial Ground
Boston, Massachusetts

WHILE JOHN HANCOCK
WAS PRESIDENT

May 1775 - October 1777

As John Hancock assumed the presidency in late May 1775, word reached the Continental Congress that Fort Ticonderoga on Lake Champlain had fallen to the Americans.[131] Early the next month, Virginia Gov. Dunmore and his family fled to the safety of a British warship at Yorktown.[132] By the end of the year, most of the Royal Governors across America had mimicked Dunmore's humiliating example. Political authority across the continent had clearly shifted to the Americans.

In Philadelphia, John Adams orchestrated the selection of George Washington of Virginia to be Commander-in-Chief of the newly created Continental Army.[133] The fact that Washington did not look ambitious was especially significant to Adams. The General received his official commission on June 17, 1775, the same day that the Battle of Breed's Hill in Boston (incorrectly known as The Battle of Bunker Hill) was being won by the British at a terrible cost to the King's officers and enlisted men.[134] One week later, as Gen. Washington and his senior staff rode off to war, Thomas Jefferson was arriving in Philadelphia to begin his duties as Virginia's newest Delegate.[135]

On July 6, having reluctantly unsheathed its sword, Congress adopted the "Declaration on Taking Arms" in order to present America's case before the world. In the document's most memorable line, the Delegates boldly pledged that they were "resolved to dye Free-men rather than live Slaves."[136] The following week, Congress also approved a "Speech to the Six Confederate Indian Nations," urging them to remain neutral in the White Man's War.[137]

Despite the fact that blood had already been shed on both sides, John Dickinson of Pennsylvania pleaded with his fellow delegates to lay their cause before the King one last time. On July 8, 1775, the Olive Branch Petition, as revised by Dickinson and approved by Congress, began its ill-fated journey across the Atlantic.[138] The Petition reached the office of Lord Dartmouth, Secretary of State for the Colonies, in London on August 21. Dartmouth, however, was away on holiday. On August 23, without having seen the Petition, "the Privy Council approved the proclamation for suppressing rebellion and sedition in America."[139] Dartmouth returned on September 1, but by then it was too late. Any serious hope of reconciliation had vanished.

On October 10, 1775, Gen. William Howe very reluctantly replaced the ineffective Gen. Thomas Gage as Commander-in-Chief of British forces in America.[140] Three days later, after months of bickering, Congress also took additional military action when it voted to launch the first American Navy.[141]

That November, American Gen. Montgomery captured Montreal as part of Congress' goal of incorporating Canada into the new union.[142] But, at the end of December, Montgomery lost his life and America lost its last hope for victory over Canada when Quebec repelled his attempted invasion on New Year's Eve.[143]

Back in London, salt was poured into open wounds on December 22 when George III signed Parliament's Prohibitory Act which removed the colonies from the King's protection, prohibited all trade with America and authorized the seizure of American ships.[144]

The pivotal year of 1776 began with the publication of Thomas Paine's explosive pamphlet *Common Sense*.[145] That same January, American troops delivered 59 cannons from Fort Ticonderoga to Gen. Washington in Boston after Gen. Henry Knox led a superhuman slog through the wilderness.[146] After the cannons were secretly positioned against the British warships, Gen. Howe had little choice but to evacuate Boston Harbor on Sunday, March 17.[147] The siege of New England was over as the war moved South.

In mid-May, Congress urged all of the remaining colonies to establish new constitutions.[148] In early June, Richard Henry Lee (once again at the urging of Adams) introduced the Virginia Resolution which called for Independence, Foreign Alliances and Confederation. Congress established separate committees to deal with each of the three proposals. While the Delegates debated their future course, the British attempted to initiate a southern strategy by landing 3,000 troops outside of Charleston. It failed. On June 28, 1776, the South Carolina Militia and its trusty palmetto fort withstood the British assault and saved Charleston from invasion for the next four years.[149]

Finally, on Monday, July 1, 1776, Congress began its decisive debate on independence. The preliminary vote at the end of the first day showed nine States in favor, Delaware split, Pennsylvania and South Carolina opposed and New York forced to abstain because of the lack of instructions from the New York Assembly.[150] John Adams and his allies exerted herculean efforts late into the night to win over the remaining Delegates.[151] They were victorious. When the final count was taken the next day, July 2, the vote was 12 in favor and one abstention. Independence had been officially approved, at last.

Congress then turned to the proposed declaration which would announce to all the world the necessity for that fateful step. Jefferson watched in agony from the back of the room as various phrases and whole passages of his proposed proclamation were ripped apart or revised.[152] By Thursday morning, July 4, Congress finally voted to approve the Declaration of Independence.[153] On July 8, the document was first read to the citizens of Philadelphia from the steps of the Pennsylvania State House where Congress was meeting. The very next day, the New York Provincial Congress voted for independence and thereby made the declaration unanimous.[154]

As the fate of the new nation was being crafted in Philadelphia, 7,800 Hessian mercenary troops landed on Long Island, NY on August 12 to join Gen. Howe's British forces.[155] Later that month, the Revolutionary War nearly turned into a decisive defeat for the Americans there in New York when Gen. Washington came within hours of losing much of his army. Overconfidence on the part of the British plus American good fortune enabled Washington to evacuate 9,500 Continental troops in the dead of night.[156] That December Washington retook the initiative when he crossed the Delaware River and captured or killed 940 Hessians at Trenton on Christmas Day.[157]

Just as John was preparing to relinquish the presidency, news reached Congress that Gen. Horatio Gates and his American Army had won a tremendous victory in mid-October over British Gen. Johnny Burgoyne at Saratoga, New York.[158] It was a desperately-needed morale boost for Congress as well as the Army and a tremendous shock to British leaders on both sides of the Atlantic. In Paris, Franklin would effectively use the news to finally persuade the French King to join America in a formal alliance.[159]

Chapter 3

President
JOHN HANCOCK
of
MASSACHUSETTS

Notes

Abbreviation Key

JCC   Journals of the Continental Congress
LDC   Letters of Delegates to Congress
PHL   The Papers of Henry Laurens

[1] Nathaniel Philbrick, Mayflower, (Viking, New York, 2006), p. 43.

[2] Robert Zeus Finkelstein, Merchant, Revolutionary, and Statesman (Ph.D. Dissertation, University of Massachusetts, 1981), p. 8: "In the seventeenth century over half its [Harvard's] graduates became ministers..."

[3] Herbert S. Allan, John Hancock: Patriot in Purple, (The Macmillan Company, New York, 1948), p. 5.

[4] William Benton, Publisher, Encyclopedia Britannica (Chicago, 1966), Vol. 4, p. 619. Great Britain adopted the Gregorian Calendar (New Style) by Act of Parliament in 1751. By law, eleven days were added starting on September 3, 1752 which thereby became September 14, 1752. Portugal, Spain and France had already done so in 1582, over a century earlier.

[5] Harlow Giles Unger, John Hancock: Merchant King and American Patriot, (John Wiley & Sons, Inc., New York, 2000), p. 14. See also: Page Smith, John Adams (Doubleday & Co., Garden City, NY, 1962), Vol. 1, p. 9.

[6] William T. Baxter, The House of Hancock, (Harvard University Press, Cambridge, 1945), pp. xx-xxi.

[7] Lydia Henchman was 11 years younger than her new husband, Thomas Hancock.

[8] During the British occupation of Boston (1775-76) Gen. William Howe seized the Hancock Mansion for his personal residence but took remarkable care in accounting for its contents when he and his troops were forced out of the city.

[9] Abram English Brown, John Hancock: His Book (Lee and Shepard Publishers, Boston, 1898), p. 38; Thomas Hancock to Messrs. Jonathan Barnard & Company, November 25, 1763.

[10] As cited in William M. Fowler, Jr., The Baron of Beacon Hill (Houghton Mifflin Company, Boston, 1979), p. 14; Thomas Hancock to James Glin, December 20, 1736.

[11] Fowler, op. cit., p. 14.

[12] Fowler, op, cit., p. 21.

[13] Finkelstein, op. cit., p 21.

[14] Fowler, op. cit., pp. 9 & 35. Thomas and Lydia Hancock and their adopted son, John, were regular members of the Brattle Square Church and major contributors but both Thomas and John seemed to view their participation as simply another aspect of their civic lives.

[15] Charles Francis Adams, ed., The Works of John Adams (Little, Brown & Co., Boston, 1851-1865), Vol. X, pp. 258-259; John Adams to William Tudor, June 1, 1817.

[16] As cited in Unger, op. cit., p. 54; Thomas Hancock to Christopher Kilby, May 23, 1760.

[17] As cited in Allann, op. cit., p. 67; John Hancock to Ebenezer Hancock, December 27, 1760. (Massachusetts Historical Society, Proceedings. Vol. 43, December 1909-1910, p. 194.)

[18] Allan, op. cit., p. 61.

[19] Unger, op. cit., p. 54.

[20] As cited in Allan, op. cit., pp. 68-69; John Hancock to Thomas Hancock, January 14, 1761.

[21] As cited in Allan, op. cit., pp. 69-70; John Hancock to Rev. Daniel Perkins, March 2, 1761.

[22] As cited in Finkelstein, op. cit., p. 98; Thomas Hancock to Messrs Jonathan Barnard and Co., January 1, 1763. See also: Francis Hurtubis, Jr., "First Inauguration of John Hancock, "Bostonian Society Publications, 2nd ser., I (1916), p. 43.

[23] Fowler, op. cit., pp. 46-47.

[24] Boston Public Library; Lydia Henchman Hancock's Transfer of Ownership, August 10, 1764.

[25] Fowler, op. cit., pp. 8, 45 & 48. See also: Allan, op. cit., pp. 72 & 86. Even John's birth father, Pastor John Hancock, bought a slave named Jeffrey.

[26] As cited in Allan, op. cit., p. 68. (John R. Alden, "John Mein: Scourge of Patriots," *Colonial Society of Massachusetts, Publications*, Vol. XXXIV (1943), p. 596.) See also: Fowler, op. cit., pp. 43-44.

[27] *Boston Evening Transcript*, Monday, February 11, 1884, p. 2. (Provided by Middlebury College Interlibrary Loan; Call # film 198.)

28 See Introduction.

29 Fowler, op. cit., p. 55.

30 Massachusetts Historical Society, Hancock Family Miscellaneous Papers; John Hancock to Thomas Pownall, July 6, 1765.

31 As cite in Fowler, op. cit., pp. 60-61; John Hancock to Barnard and Harrison, October 14, 22, 1765.

32 Unger, op. cit., p. 111.

33 Paul Lewis, The Grand Incendiary, A Biography of Samuel Adams, (The Dial Press, New York, 1973).

34 Adams, op. cit., Vol. X, p. 260; John Adams to William Tudor.

35 See Introduction for additional details on the Townshend Acts.

36 Finkelstein, op. cit., p.187.

37 Finkelstein, op. cit., p.192.

38 Unger, op. cit., p. 123.

39 Baxter, op. citl,, pp. 266-268.

40 Publications of the Colonial Society of Massachusetts, (The Merrymount Press, Boston, 1943), Vol. XXXIV, p. 414; John Wilkes to William Palfrey [John Hancock's chief assistant], July 24, 1769, "John Wilkes and William Palfrey," See also: Introduction, pp. 10-11 and Chapter 2, p. 65, for more on "Wilkes and Liberty."

41 *Boston Chronicle*, October 26, 1769, Vol. II, No. 43.

42 To save face, Parliament passed the Declaratory Act in 1766 at the same time that it revoked the hated Stamp Act. In similar fashion, it retained the tax on tea on March 5, 1770, to underscore its authority to tax American trade even though it revoked all of the other Townshend taxes. Unintentionally, it led to the Boston Tea Party on December 16, 1773, and the loss of the American colonies.

43 David McCullough, John Adams, (Simon & Schuster, New York, 2001), p. 68.

44 See Introduction.

45 Allan, op. cit., p. 159.

46 Ellen C. D. Q. Woodbury, Doroth Quincy, Wife of John Hancock, (The Neale Publishing Company, Washington, DC, 1905), pp. 90-91.

47 Unger, op. cit., John Hancock, Merchant King and American Patriot is the title of Unger's biography.

48 John Hancock chose wisely by rejecting Gov. Hutchinson's offer. In Britain, the King

had made a similar offer to William Pitt, the Great Commoner, by elevating him to the House of Lords as the Earl of Chatham. Pitt's popularity and influence never recovered from the honor.

[49] Walter Isaacson, <u>Benjamin Franklin, An American Life</u>, (Simon & Schuster, New York, 2003), pp. 271-272.

[50] Harry Alonzo Cushing, Editor., <u>Writings of Samuel Adams</u> (G. P. Putnam's Sons, New York, 1907), Vol. III, pp. 39-40; Sam Adams to Arthur Lee, May 17, 1773.

[51] See Introduction, p. 21-22. See also: Brian Gardner, <u>The East india Company</u> (Dorset Press,New York,1871), pp. 110-111.

[52] Abram English Brown, <u>John Hancock: His Book</u> (Lee and Shepard Publishers, Boston, 1898), p. 178. As always, the faithful Captain Scott served his friend and employer exceptionally well. John Hancock to Haley & Hopkins, December 21, 1773.

[53] Finkelstein, op. cit., p. 262.

[54] John Hancock's real role in the Boston Tea Party remains a topic of debate. While some authors believe that he was deeply involved but retained public deniability, there is little hard evidence to support this theory.

[55] See Introduction.

[56] James Thomas Flexner, <u>George Washington: The Forge of Experience (1732-1775)</u>, (Little, Brown & Company, Boston, 1965), p. 320.

[57] <u>The World's Best Orations</u>, David J. Brewer, Editor, (Fred P. Kaiser, St. Louis, 1899), Vol. VI, pp. 2399-2400. See also: <u>John Hancock's Life and Speeches</u>, Paul D. Brandes, ed., (The Scarecrow Press, Inc., Lanham, MD, 1996), pp. 205-219.

[58] For more information on the Coercive [aka Intolerable] Acts, see Introduction, pp. 22-23.

[59] Unger, op. cit., p. 182.

[60] Brandes, op. cit., pp. 131-132.

[61] S. Lawrence Whpple, *The Hancock-Clarke House, Parsonage and Home*, (Lexington Historical Society, 1984), p. 6.

[62] Paul H. Smith, Editor, <u>LDC</u> (Library of Congress, Washington, DC, 1976), Vol. 1, p. 344; Caesar Rodney to Thomas Rodney, May 11, 1775.

[63] *Magazine of American History*, Vol. 19 (June 1888), pp. 509-510; John Hancock to Dorothy Quincy, May 7, 1775.

[64] <u>LDC</u>, op. cit., Vol. 1, p. 406; Samuel Ward's Diary, May 24, 1775.

[65] Worthington Chauncey Ford, Editor, <u>JCC</u> (Library of Congress, Washington, DC, 1905), Vol. 2, pp. 58-59.

[66] LDC, op. cit., Vol. 4, p. 541; John Hancock to John Bradford, July 25, 1776.

[67] LDC, op. cit., Vol. 1, p. 580; John Hancock to the Massachusetts Committee of Safety, July 4, 1775.

[68] Jennings B. Sanders, The Presidency of the Continental Congress, (Peter Smith, Gloucester, Massachusetts, 1971), pp. 34-35.

[69] Peter Force, Editor, American Archives (M. St. Clair Clarke & Peter Force, Washington, DC, 1839), 4th series, Vol. II, pp. 968-970; "Proclamation by General Gage," June 12, 1775.

[70] L. H. Butterfield, Editor, Diary and Autobiography of John Adams (The Belknap Press, Cambridge, 1961), Vol. 3, pp. 321-322.

[71] See Introduction.

[72] Burnett, op. cit., p. 83.

[73] LDC, op. cit., Vol. 1, pp. 507-508; John Hancock to Joseph Warren, June 18, 1775.

[74] John C. Fitzpatrick, Editor, The Writings of George Washington, 1745-1799, (Government Printing Office, Washington, DC, 1933), Vol. 9, p. 414; George Washington to John Hancock, October 22, 1777.

[75] Fitzpatrick, op. cit.,. pp. 495-496; George Washington to John Hancock, November 2, 1777.

[76] Brown, op. cit., pp. 202-204; John Hancock to Dorothy Quincy, June 10, 1775.

[77] Woodbury, op. cit., p. 92. See also: Unger, op. cit., p. 218.

[78] LDC, op. cit., Vol. 2, p. 24; John Adams to James Warren, September 17, 1775. (The second amazing event John Adams described to James Warren was that his cousin, Sam Adams, had finally learned to ride a horse.)

[79] LDC, op. cit., Vol. 2, p. 296; John Adams to Abigail Adams, November 4, 1775.

[80] Finkelstein, op. cit., p. 306.

[81] Woodbury, op. cit. See also: Lois Hobart, Patriot's Lady: The Life of Sarah Livingston Jay, (Funk & Wagnalls Company, Inc., New York, 1960).

[82] LDC, op. cit., Vol. 3, pp. 105-106; John Hancock to Thomas Cushing, January 17, 1776.

[83] Thomas Paine, Basic Writings of Thomas Paine: Common Sense, (Willey Book Company, New York, 1942), p. 8.

[84] LDC, op. cit., Vol. 3, p.165; John Hancock to George Washington, January 29, 1776.

[85] LDC, op. cit., Vol. 4, p. 9; John Hancock to George Washington, May 16, 1776.

[86] LDC, op. cit., Vol. 3, p. 561; John Hanson to William Palfrey, April 20, 1776.

[87] LDC, op. cit., Vol. 4, p. 9.; John Hancock to George Washington, May 16, 1776.

[88] LDC, op. cit., Vol. 4, p. 26; John Hancock to Thomas Cushing, May 17, 1776.

[89] American independence was actually approved by the Continental Congress on July 2, 1776. The date that is universally celebrated as the anniversary of independence--July 4-- was the day that the declaration announcing independence was adopted. The actual birthday of the country, however, was September 5, 1774, the opening day of the First Continental Congress. From that date to the present, the United Colonies/States has been self-governing.

[90] Perhaps the only rival for the title of "most famous signature" in all of Western History could be that of King John's on the Magna Carta in 1215.

[91] LDC, op. cit., Vol. 4, p. 396; John Hancock to Certain States, July 6, 1776.

[92] LDC, op. cit., Vol. 4, p. 397; John Hancock to George Washington, July 6, 1776.

[93] LDC, op. cit., Vol. 4, p. 394; John Hancock to William Cooper, July 6, 1776.

[94] LDC, op. cit., Vol. 4, p. 465; John Adams to Abigail Adams, July 16, 1776.

[95] Edmund Cody Burnett, The Continental Congress (The Macmillan Company, New York, 1941), pp. 213-219. The Articles of Confederation were submitted to the full body on July 12, 1776.

[96] LDC, op. cit., Vol. 4, pp. 498-499; Benjamin Franklin to Lord Howe, July 20, 1776.

[97] LDC, op. cit., Vol. 6, p. 91; John Hancock to Robert Treat Paine, January 13, 1777.

[98] JCC, op. cit., Vol. VI, p. 1039. One of the five committee members was Richard Henry Lee of Virginia, a future President.

[99] LDC, op. cit., Vol. 5, p. 663; John Hancock to Certain States, December 25, 1776.

[100] LDC, op. cit., Vol. 6, p. 409; John Adams to Abigail Adams, March 7, 1777.

[101] Unger, op. cit., p. 255.

[102] JCC, op. cit., Vol. VIII, p. 464. See also: Mark M. Boatner, Editor, Encyclopedia of the American Revolution, (David McKay Company, Inc., New York, 1974), pp. 369-370. "Although Betsy is known to have made flags, the one...popularly called the Betsy Ross flag, is not among the many that historians consider seriously as a contender for the honor of being 'the first Stars and Stripes.'"

[103] LDC, op. cit., Vol. 7, pp. 685-686; John Hancock to Dorothy Hancock, September 17 1777.

[104] LDC, op. cit., Vol. 8, p. 38; John Hancock to Dorothy Hancock, October 1, 1777.

[105] LDC, op. cit., Vol. 8, p. xiii, Chronology of Congress.

[106] Clare Brandt, The Man in the Mirror: A Life of Benedict Arnold, (Random House, New York, 1994), pp. 126-141.

[107] JCC, op. cit., Vol. IX, pp. 846 & 852-853; October 28, 1777 and October 31, 1777.

[108] Sanders, op. cit., pp, 13-14.

[109] *Independent Chronicle*, November 21, 1777.

[110] Unger, op. cit., p. 261.

[111] *Independent Chronicle*, January 29, 1778.

[112] Warren-Adams Letters, Massachusetts Historical Society, No. 73, Vol. II, p. 42; James Warren to Sam Adams, August 18, 1778.

[113] Warren-Adams Letters, op. cit., p. 20; James Warren to John Adams, June 7, 1778.

[114] See Chapter 1. The irony is that it was John Hancock who had done exactly the same thing to his predecessor, Peyton Randolph, when Hancock refused to step down from the presidency upon Randolph's return to Philadelphia in September 1775.

[115] LDC, op. cit., Vol. 3, p. 245, footnote 1. John Hancock had been appointed major general of the Massachusetts Militia on February 8, 1776.

[116] As cited in Douglas Southall Freeman, George Washington, (Charles Scribners Sons, New York, 1952), Vol. 5, p. 70; "Probate Report to Sartins," November 5, 1778.

[117] In the same year--1780--Thomas Jefferson was also elected Governor of Virginia. While Hancock never lost popular support or an election for the remainder of his life, Jefferson narrowly escaped censure by his state legislature after two disappointing terms as his state's wartime chief executive.

[118] John Hancock: His Book, op. cit., p. 233; John Hancock to James Scott, November 14, 1783.

[119] JCC, op. cit., Vol. XXIX, p. 883. See also: Burnett, op. cit., p. 640. David Ramsay of South Carolina was selected to serve as chairman pending the arrival of President Hancock.

[120] JCC, op. cit. (1934) Vol. XXX, p. 328; June 5, 1786.

[121] Knox Papers, Massachusetts Historical Society, Boston, Massachusetts, Vol. 20, p. 21; John Hancock to Henry Knox, March 14, 1787.

[122] LDC, op. cit., Vol. 24, p. 249; James Madison to Thomas Jefferson, April 23, 1787.

[123] King Papers, New York Historical Society; Rufus King to James Madison, January 20 & 23, 1788.

[124] Jeffrey St. John, A Child of Fortune, (Jameson Books, Inc., Ottawa, IL, 1990) p. 125.

[125] Finkelstein, op. cit., p. 380.

[126] Hamilton Papers, Vol. V, p. 231; Alexander Hamilton to T. Sedgwick, November 9, 1788.

[127] Lewis, op. cit., pp. 367-368.

[128] James Thomas Flexner, George Washington and the New Nation (1783-1793), (Little, Brown and Company, Boston, 1970), p. 230.

[129] *Pennsylvania Magazine of History and Biography*, (The Historical Society of Pennsylvania, Philadelphia, 1936), Vol. 60, No. 4, p. 435; John Adams to Richard Rush, July 31, 1812.

[130] Adams, op. cit., pp. 258-259.

WHILE JOHN HANCOCK WAS PRESIDENT

Notes

Abbreviation Key

JCC   Journals of the Continental Congress
LDC   Letters of Delegates to Congress
PHL   The Papers of Henry Laurens

[131] Worthington Chauncey Ford, ed., JCC, (Government Printing Office, Washington, DC, 1905), Vol. II, p. 55. Fort Ticonderoga was captured by American forces on May 10, 1775. News of the capture reached the Continental Congress on May 18.

[132] Ivor Noël Hume, 1775: Another Part of the Field, (Eyre & Spottiswoode, London, 1966), pp. 222-223.

[133] Page Smith, John Adams, (Doubleday & Company, Inc., Garden City, NY, 1962), Vol. I, pp. 200-201. Initially, even Peyton Randolph of Virginia, the former President, argued that since most of the troops currently fighting were from New England that it would be most appropriate to appoint a Commander-in-Chief from that same region. See also: David McCllough, John Adams, (Simon & Schuster, New York, 2001), p. 20. See also: Cornelia Meigs, The Violent Men, (The Macmillan Company, New York, 1949), pp. 113-116. "The Members of Congress, though they finally achieved a unanimous vote on the adoption of the army and the appointment of a commander-in-chief, did not do so without much struggle and dissension."

[134] Thomas J. Fleming, Now We Are Enemies, (St. Martin's Press, New York, 1960), pp. 328-329. The British lost 226 killed, 828 wounded, "almost fifty per cent of their attacking force...even more crushing were the casualties in their officer corps.. 92 out of the approximately 250 officers in the fight." The Americans lost 140 dead and 301 wounded.

[135] Merrill D.Peterson, Thomas Jefferson (Oxford University Press, New York, 1970), p. 79.

[136] JCC, op. cit., p. 155.

[137] JCC, op. cit., pp. 177-183.

[138] H. James Henderson, Party Politics in the Continental Congress, (McGraw-Hill Book Company, New York, 1974), p. 49. Even John Adams was persuaded to sign the Petition in order to present a united front. Adams knew, however, that if and when the Petition failed, the more conservative Delegates would lose much of their influence in Congress.

[139] B. D. Bargar, <u>Lord Dartmouth and the American Revolution</u>, (The University of South Carolina Press, Columbia, 1965), p. 155.

[140] Frank Arthur Mumby, <u>George III and the American Revolution: The Beginnings</u>, (Constable & Company Ltd., London, 1924), pp. 385-386. "General Howe himself had no heart for the business...On being told that it was a command, Howe reluctantly obeyed..."

[141] William M. Fowler, Jr., <u>Rebels Under Sail</u>, (Charles Scribner's Sons, New York, 1976), pp. 46-55. As usual, John Adams was a prime motivating force.

[142] Edmund Cody Burnett, <u>The Continental Congress</u>, (The Macmillan Company, New York, 1941), pp. 108-109. President Hancock wrote to Gen. Schuyler that: "What they [the congressional Delegates] expect from your Endeavours is, that the Canadians be induced to accede to an Union with these Colonies...and send Delegates to this Congress..."

[143] Sir George Otto Trevelyan, Bart, <u>The American Revolution, Part I: 1766-1776</u>, (Longmans, Green, and Co., New York, 1899), pp. 381-382.

[144] Jack N. Rakove, <u>The Beginnings of National Politics</u>, (Alfred A. Knopf, New York, 1979), p. 81.

[145] John Keane, <u>Tom Paine: A Political Life</u>, (Bloomsbury, London, 1995), pp. 108-114. "...Paine had succeeded in outflanking the very body that was supposed to be the mouthpiece of the American colonists." Paine's estimate that at least 150,000 copies were sold in America seems credible.

[146] John C. Miller, <u>Triumph of Freedom: 1775-1783</u>, (Little, Brown and Company, Boston, 1948), p. 84.

[147] Merritt Ierley, <u>The Year That Tried Men's Souls: The World of 1776</u>, (A. S. Barnes and Company, London, 1976), pp. 87-88.

[148] Lynn Montross, <u>The Reluctant Rebels</u>, (Harper & Brothers Publishers, New York, 1950), p. 136. Montross argues that "the intention was to clear the way for a decision as to independence..."

[149] John W. Gordon, <u>South Carolina and the American Revolution: A Battlefield History</u>, (University of South Carolina Press, Columbia, SC, 2003), pp. 37-44. The hapless British forces suffered numerous set backs as cannon balls bounced off the palmetto logs of Fort Moultrie, the inlet between Long Island [Isle of Palms] and Sullivan's Island proved to be nearly six feet deeper than had been anticipated, and three British ships ran aground. Four years later Charleston did fall to the British on May 12, 1780.

[150] Edmund Cody Burnett, op. cit., pp. 181-183.

[151] McCllough, op, cit., pp. 128-129.

[152] Donald Barr Chidsey, <u>July 4, 1776: The Dramatic Story of the First Four Days of July, 1776</u>, (Crown Publishers, Inc., New York, 1958), pp. 83-86.

[153] For two centuries, historians believed that the Declaration of Independence was approved

in the afternoon of July 4, based on a comment by Jefferson years later. Researchers have now concluded that it was actually adopted that morning.

[154] Barnet Schecter, The Battle for New York, (Walker & Company, New York, 2002), p. 102.

[155] Schecter, op. cit., pp. 112-113.

[156] Craig L. Symonds, A Battlefield Atlas of the American Revolution, (The Nautical & Aviation Publishing Company of America, Inc., 1986), pp. 26-27. In the dead of night on August 29, 1775, Gen. Washington evacuated his troops from Brooklyn to Manhattan in just six hours.

[157] Symonds, op. cit., pp. 30-31. Contrary to yet another popular myth, the Hessian commander, Col. Johann Gottlieb Rall, was not taken by surprise during a drunken Christmas melee. According to Symonds, the American forces triumphed at Trenton due to superior numbers and having the advantage of the initiative.

[158] Richard M. Ketchum, Saratoga, (Henry Holt and Company, New York, 1997), pp. 355-429. Starting at Freeman's Farm in upstate New York on September 19, 1777, a series of battles took place between British Gen. Johnny Burgoyne and American Gen. Horatio Gates. On October 7, 1777, the action moved to Bemis Heights. On October 13, 1777, negotiations were initiated concerning Burgoyne's surrender. Finally, around Noon on October 17, 1777, at Saratoga, NY, Gen. Burgoyne presented both his sword and his army to Gen. Gates. The two generals had actually known each other since 1745 "when they served together as lieutenants" in the royal army.

[159] David Schoenbrun, Triumph in Paris: The Exploits of Benjamin Franklin, (Harper & Row, Publishers, New York, 1976), pp. 164-170. The news of Burgoyne's surrender reached Franklin on December 4, 1777 while he was in conference with his colleagues, Arthur Lee and Silas Deane. They immediately forwarded the news to French Foreign Minister Vergennes.

Chapter 4

President
HENRY LAURENS
of
SOUTH CAROLINA

The Ultimate Sacrifice

Henry Laurens, one of the wealthiest and most influential merchants of the South, certainly appeared to be the obvious complement to the departing President, John Hancock.

Both were men of the world who knew London first hand. Both were successful and highly respected businessmen who had largely dominated their respective regions. Both had held major political positions in their home states prior to their election to Congress. It was the Stamp Act crisis in the mid-1760s which had nudged each of them toward opposition to British policies despite their affection for their mother country. And, it was the stupidity and greed of British bureaucrats that had driven them into the arms of their more radical colleagues and even transformed them into patriotic heroes.[1] Like many wealthy men of the 18th Century, they even shared the debilitating pain caused by severe bouts of gout. To the casual observer, Henry Laurens, the Fourth President of the Continental Congress, could easily have been described as the Hancock of the South.

Beneath the surface, however, nothing could have been further from the truth. While John Hancock was a natural politician (even before such democratic characteristics were widely appreciated by his peers), Henry Laurens was far too reserved to openly court popular support. Hancock delighted in displays of wealth. He frequently hosted lavish banquets at his Beacon Hill Mansion and he was widely known for his extravagant wardrobe and carriages.[2] Henry, on the other hand, remained a Calvinist at heart and viewed his own mansion in the Ansonborough section of Charleston as the private domain of his large family and as an escape from the demands of the outside world. Hancock preferred to stand aloof from bloody legislative battles. In contrast, Henry was a master of legislative detail who occasionally seemed to take perverse satisfaction in the enemies he made.[3] While their resumes were remarkably similar, their leadership styles were distinctly different.

Unlike Hancock, Henry had not sought membership in the Continental Congress nor election as its leader.[4] He wrote to his son John on February 3, 1777: "I am ordered to the Congress of the United States now sitting at Baltimore in Maryland, many reasons were & more might have been urged in excuse for me, but although among other things I said it would be impossible for me with any propriety to leave this place before the Month of May, the Vote was confirmed, I call it therefore as I feel it, a Command - I go -."[5]

Preparations took longer than anticipated. Henry finally arrived in Philadelphia on July 20, 1777.[6] Two days later he presented his credentials to Congress and joined his fellow delegates from South Carolina: Arthur Middleton (the son of the second President) and Thomas Heyward, Jr.[7] Over the next three months, Henry served on fourteen different congressional committees, several of which he chaired.[8]

After only a month, Henry's devotion to duty and mature judgment were noted by John Adams: "They [South Carolina] have sent Us a new Delegate, whom I greatly admire, Mr. Lawrence [sic], their Lt. Governor, a Gentleman of great Fortune, great Abilities, Modesty and Integrity--and great Experience too. If all the States would send Us such Men, it would be a Pleasure to be here."[9] Henry and Adams worked together on five congressional committees and became personal friends as well as political allies over the months and years ahead.

Another new friend was the Marquis de Lafayette whom Henry assisted in a moment of need. Congress, which had returned to the capital of Philadelphia earlier in the year, was once again forced to flee in mid-September 1777, under the renewed threat of a British invasion. Henry described the scene in his understated style:

"I fled not. Having foreseen from amazing remissness where there ought to have been the utmost attention & vigilance I had sent forward my Baggage, followed it that Evening & next Morning after many thousands had passed by me I made my breakfast, filled my Pipe & soberly entered my Carriage, drove gently on to Bristol, took in the wounded Marquis delafayette & proceeded to Bethleham [where Henry delivered LaFayette to the officers' hospital], thence to Reading & Lancaster."[10]

That Saturday, September 27, 1777, Congress briefly reconvened in Lancaster, but the delegates decided that it would be safer to move their temporary headquarters across the Susquehanna River. Finally, on September 30, Congress did resume its debate on the proposed Articles of Confederation at their new capital in York, Pennsylvania, where they continued to conduct business for the next nine months despite extremely cramped conditions.

It was there, at the end of October, that John Hancock resigned the presidency after two and a half years of unrelenting service. A few months earlier, the wealthy Philadelphia merchant Robert Morris had been urged by his friends to seek the office when Hancock stepped down. Morris, however, refused to consider it due to the demands of his business.[11] Francis Lightfoot Lee of Virginia was also briefly mentioned as a potential presidential candidate,[12] but, on November 1, 1777, all of the delegates, except the victor, cast their votes for Henry Laurens of South Carolina.[13]

Henry's sober devotion to duty, which was both a lifelong personal characteristic as well as a Laurens family trait, had earned him the respect and support of his congressional colleagues His grandfather, Andre Laurens, was a French Huguenot who, in 1682, fled to England with his widowed mother to escape Catholic persecution. There, six years later, Andre Laurens married Marie Lucas, a fellow refugee.[14] The family then emigrated to Ireland for a brief period before sailing on to New York. It was there, in March 1697, that Henry's father, Jean Laurens, was born. During their years in New York, the Laurens family life appears to have centered around the French Church where Jean Laurens and Esther Grasset, another Huguenot descendent, were wed in 1715. That same year, Andre Laurens and his family relocated one final time to Charleston, South Carolina. Many years later, Henry described the family's history after their move to the South:

"My Grand Father died Soon after he arrived in South Carolina, but he had Saved So much Money as enabled him to Set out four Sons & one Daughter with Such portions as put them above low dependence. Some of them retained the French pride of Family, & were content to die poor. My Father was of different Sentiments, he learned a Trade, & by great Industry acquired an Estate with a good Character & Reestablished the Name of his Family."[15]

Jean Laurens began this transformation by casting off pieces of his old-world heritage. He now used the English version of his first name, John, and he chose to join the establishment Church of England, St. Philip's (where he eventually became a warden), rather than the nearby French Huguenot Church (which still stands today at the corner of Church and Queen Streets). As a career, he decided to make and repair saddles and related equipment. It was both a practical and profitable enterprise which eventually led him into real estate, as well. When he died in 1747, John Laurens left a sizable estate.[16]

John Laurens' first son, Henry, was born in Charleston on March 6,

1724. He was the third of six children. As a young child, Henry's closest playmate was Christopher Gadsden, a boy his own age who was also destined to become one of South Carolina's leading patriots. Dr. David Ramsay, Henry's future son-in-law, recorded their intense friendship in *Ramsay's History of South Carolina*:

"[The two boys] were attached in their early youth to each other by the strongest ties of ardent friendship. They made a common cause to support and encourage each other in every virtuous pursuit, to shun every path of vice and folly, to leave company whenever it tended to licentiousness..."[17] Unfortunately, as they grew older and became increasingly active in revolutionary politics, Gadsden's more radical views often clashed with Henry's understated style and their once intimate friendship often turned into bitter opposition.

According to Henry's own recollection, his father gave his children the best education South Carolina had to offer. But, unlike Boston, Charleston's first formal college was not established until later that century. Therefore, in 1744, at the age of 20, Henry was sent to London to serve as an apprentice to James Crokatt, a wealthy Charleston merchant and friend of Henry's father, who had relocated to the British capital a few years earlier. For nearly three years Henry eagerly absorbed all that the older man could teach him concerning international commerce. After Henry completed his internship in early 1747, Crokatt even extended an invitation to him to become a partner in his firm. As tempting as the offer was, Henry decided to return to America. He set sail that April, but "...more than once on my Journey to Portsmouth, & passage to this place I repented me of my resolution to return here & now and then wish'd myself resettled, in the place I had left."[18]

When he arrived in Charleston on June 3, 1747, Henry was devastated to learn that his beloved father had died only four days earlier. As a result, Henry believed that his return to America had once again verified his lifelong motto: Optimum quod evenit (whatever happens, happens for the best).[19] As one of three executors of his father's will, Henry would have to devote months to his father's estate.[20]

A month after his return, Henry received several letters from his old London mentor in which Crokatt renewed the partnership offer, provided that Henry would return to London by April 1748. When even that deadline appeared impossible, Crokatt granted an additional extension. Henry finally left Charleston on September 23, 1748, but did not reach London until November 25. By then, Crokatt had offered the position to another man. Nevertheless, he assured Henry that offers from other merchants were likely to materialize and he urged Henry to remain in England to establish his career.

Henry might have followed that advice; but, before leaving America, he had pledged to establish a partnership in Charleston with George Austin, an experienced businessman, if Crokatt's offer failed to materialize. Since Henry felt an obligation to honor his commitment to Austin, he reluctantly abandoned his dream of attaining success at the center of the Empire. As he wrote to his brother James: "...I shall once more Ship myself to Carolina where, please God I arrive safe, I shall Pitch my Tent."[21]

Before leaving England, Henry spent five months traveling around the country, introducing himself to important businessmen and setting up commercial accounts wherever possible on behalf of his new firm. Finally, on April 20, 1749, Henry set sail once again for America, arriving in Charleston in mid-June. For the next thirteen years, the firm of Austin & Laurens thrived.

Rice, the leading cash crop of South Carolina, was the staple of Henry's enterprise.[22] His markets included England, Spain, Portugal, Germany, Holland, the West Indies and America's Atlantic Coast.[23] As in all things, he took personal responsibility for his business practices. As he explained to one of his commercial customers: "I am very attentive & careful in the purchasing of Rice & perhaps more atentive to the Shipping part than 9 of 10 of my Neighbours..."[24] Henry also exported large quantities of indigo, South Carolina's second major crop, and he traded in naval stores (e.g., pitch, tar and turpentine) as well as deerskins. [25] The firm of Austin & Laurens also handled hundreds of indentured servants from Germany and Ireland.[26]

For both ethical and practical reasons (unlike so many other merchants throughout the colonies) Henry insisted that his firm had to conduct its vast business operations within the legal bounds of the British mercantile system. His letter of appointment to Captain Magnus Watson appears indicative of Henry's *modus operandi*: "Observe as a fundamental article of my instructions that you do not...give any offence against Parliamentary or Provincial Acts or Laws for regulating Trade and commerce in America, but comply faithfully with the terms required in all such Laws."[27]

As a man of his times, Henry also traded in slaves. In fact, from 1751 through 1761, he was one of the most successful and wealthiest of the Charleston slave traders.[28] Austin & Laurens handled slave consignments for important British slave traders in Bristol, Liverpool, Lancaster and London. During that decade, Henry's firm was engaged in sixty slave cargoes for which it usually received a ten percent commission.[29] One historian estimates that Austin & Laurens sold approximately 7,433 slaves during those years, roughly one-third of all slaves imported into Charleston during that decade.[30]

In his correspondence, Henry described the ideal slave: "Gold Coast or Gambia's are best, next to them the Windward Coast are prefer'd to Angola's...Pray observe that our People like tall Slaves best for our business & strong withall....The difference in price between Men & Women here is never less than £3 Sterling per head, sometimes £6...young Lads from 13 to 15 Years of age wont bring so much as Men by 5 or £6 Sterling. At that difference in price they are very Saleable."[31]

By the early 1760s, George Austin's health was failing and Henry was increasingly engaged in public affairs. In August 1762, the partnership was dissolved by mutual agreement. Austin left for England in July 1763. Beyond that point, Henry did continue in business as a sole proprietor, but he drastically reduced his workload and frequently referred old customers to newer firms that he helped to nurture. Nevertheless, Henry complained in early 1768 that "My friends in England you see will force me into Business again..."[32]

That was also true of Henry's involvement in the slave trade. By late 1763, he had resolved to shun the "African Trade" despite the determination of some old customers to throw "further gain into my Lap..."[33] His public stance was that it demanded too much work now that his partner had retired.[34] But, in a letter to his son, Henry's confession is cited by some who describe him as a "Southern Man of Conscience." Whether he deserves such absolution is still intensely debated.[35]

"I abhor Slavery," Henry wrote. "I was born in a Country where Slavery had been established by British Kings & Parliaments as well as by the Laws of that Country Ages before my existence, I found the Christian Religion & Slavery growing under the same authority & cultivation__I nevertheless disliked it...I am not the Man who enslaved them, they are indebted to English Men for that favour, nevertheless I am devising means for manumitting many of them & for cutting off the entail of Slavery__ great powers oppose me, the Laws & Customs of my Country, my own & the avarice of my Country Men...I will do as much as I can in my time & leave the rest to a better hand."[36]

In dealing with his own slaves, Henry's inner turmoil was clear: "I don't know anything that could have been contrived to distress me & embarrass my plantation again more than this unnecessary division of Fathers, Mothers, Husbands, Wives, & Children who tho Slaves are still human Creatures & I cannot be deaf to their cries least a time should come when I should cry & there shall be none to pity me."[37] Despite his anguish, Henry neither freed his slaves nor spoke out publicly.

Another reason that Henry gradually withdrew from his mercantile career was that he had decided to increase his land holdings which rapidly grew to 20,000 acres throughout South Carolina and Georgia. For example, on June 4, 1762, Henry purchased Mepkin Plantation, a 3,000 acre tract along the Cooper River, which eventually became his permanent residence after the Revolution.[38] It was initially a smooth transition since his brother-in-law, John Coming Ball, already served as overseer of Henry's two largest plantations. But, in 1764, Ball died and Henry was forced to assume direct control.[39]

Henry had married Ball's sister, Eleanor, fourteen years earlier on July 6, 1750. They were deeply in love throughout their twenty year marriage. Henry referred to her as "a tender and watchful mother" to their children and "a faithful bosom Friend, a Wife whose constant Study was to make me happy."[40] She bore him twelve children, but only four reached maturity and only three of those survived their father. A daughter named Martha contracted smallpox in 1760 when she was less than one year old and was so ill that she was pronounced dead. While being prepared for burial, however, her doctor discovered that she was still alive. Martha went on to live a very full life.[41]

In the spring of 1764, Henry and his family left their home south of Broad Street and moved to his new mansion in Ansonborough in the northern section of the city at what is today the intersection of Laurens and East Bay Streets. In keeping with Henry's restrained style, the house was a rather "plain...square-built structure" which included a dining room, ballroom, and large library with mahogany bookcases. The large garden was under the care of an English gardener and included "numerous rare and beautiful plants gathered from distant lands."[42] His closest neighbor was none other than his childhood playmate-turned-adversary, Christopher Gadsden.

When the Stamp Act crisis swept across America the next year, Henry found himself at odds with many of his friends and colleagues. Like them, he also opposed Parliament's attempt to trample on colonial rights in order to raise revenue, but Henry believed that petitioning for repeal of the law was the only legitimate course of action.[43] He was repulsed by the militancy demonstrated by Charleston's Sons of Liberty (who were closely identified with Gadsden) and he even refused to vote for delegates to the Stamp Act Congress which met in New York in October, 1765.[44] The issue came to a head on Wednesday, October 23, 1765, when a rumor spread through the streets that the revenue stamps were being secretly stored in Henry's mansion. Around midnight an angry mob assembled at Henry's front door and demanded to search his home. Henry described the scene a few days later:

"Mrs. Laurens's condition & her cries prompted me to open the door...I presently knew several of them under their thickest disguises...& to their great surprise called no less than nine of them by name...they insisted on my taking what they called 'A Bible Oath' that I knew not where the Stamp'd Paper was which I absolutely refused not failing to confirm my denials with Damns of equal weight with their own...they threatened then to carry me away...I replied they might if they would, they had strength enough but I would be glad to have it attempted by any Man alone...they praised me highly & insisted upon giving me three Cheers & then retired with God bless your Honour...A thousand other things you may believe were said & done in an hour & a quarter (the time of their visit)..."[45]

In 1767, after the Stamp Act had been repealed and the Townshend duties on imports were instated, the British were more determined than ever to clamp down on American smuggling.[46] For the first time, the coastal trade, which was the lifeline for inland plantations, was also treated as ocean trade. Charleston's new collector of customs, Daniel Moore, was extremely eager to enforce the stricter standards and higher penalties since he was able to pocket part of the fee. As tensions rose, Henry became a leader of the merchants' resistance.[47] Moore decided to break the back of that resistance by seizing two of Henry's ships under spurious charges.

The trial that followed was held in the Vice Admiralty Court in August 1767. The presiding judge, Egerton Leigh, held various government positions including Attorney General and member of the Commons House of Assembly. Leigh, who was married to Henry's niece, also frequently served as Henry's legal counsel. After hearing the two cases, Leigh attempted to satisfy all parties by ruling against Henry on one count but finding in his favor on the second. Henry was angered by the judge's decision and outraged over the conduct of the customs officials. As he wrote to a friend at the time: "...such Officers are the most likely instruments to effect a disunion between the Mother Country & her American offspring."[48] And, to another, he said: "Such men as that one in Office are the greatest Enemies to Britain of any man in America...[more] than twenty Mouthing Liberty Boys."[49]

Henry was so angry that his characteristic restraint was momentarily broken when he confronted Moore shortly after the trial. As they exchanged insults before a small group, Henry grabbed Moore's nose and twisted it.[50] Of greater consequence, Henry and his fellow merchants were determined to pursue Moore for illegal extortion of fees. At that point, the collector fled to England to escape the merchants' wrath. Henry then turned his fire on George Roupell, Moore's assistant, and sued him for damages. The case was heard in May 1768, with none other than Judge Leigh, now serving as Roupell's attorney. Nevertheless, Henry won a judgment of £1,400. Henry felt vindicated, but Roupell was determined to seek revenge.

A month after the trial, Roupell seized yet another of Henry's ships on completely bogus grounds and then offered to drop the case if Henry would relinquish the judgment he had won earlier. The offer was immediately rejected and the case went to trial with John Rutledge serving as one of Henry's attorneys. Leigh, who was once again on the bench, switched alliances yet again and harshly condemned Roupell's conduct. In contrast, Leigh praised Henry's character and ruled in his favor. But Judge Leigh then used a technicality to prevent Henry from recouping damages from Roupell and ordered both parties to cover their own court costs. Henry was furious with Leigh's conduct and began to prepare a lengthy report on the case, which he eventually circulated throughout America and Britain.[51]

In April 1769, Leigh retaliated with his own pamphlet: *The Man Unmasked*. In it Leigh warned his readers not to be deceived by the almost universal display of affection for Henry throughout Charleston because "the same people perhaps neither regard or respect him...they meet him, 'tis true, with pleasant countenances, because they fear him..."[52] Henry responded with two additional pamphlets attacking Leigh.[53]

This entire affair is of historic significance because it, more than anything else, helped to propel Henry toward the revolutionary cause. As one of his biographers states: "It was for him the birth of a new Americanism."[54] And, by taking such a public leadership role in confronting greedy and corrupt British bureaucrats, Henry, like Hancock, became a popular symbol of resistance to British oppression.[55]

Henry, of course, was far more than just another wealthy Charleston merchant. From 1757 until the opening of the Revolution, he also served continuously in the South Carolina Commons House of Assembly, with only two brief exceptions.[56] It was excellent preparation for what was to come, since the House had a very impressive record of wrenching power from both the Governor's Council and even the Governor himself. In a very real sense, the final confrontation during the American Revolution was only the last act in a much longer drama.[57]

Twice during those years Henry was offered a seat on the Governor's Council and twice he declined. As he wrote to a close friend in 1764, when he turned down the appointment for the first time: "...I cannot attend to the Duty of the Council consistently with my plan of Life & business & I always make a consequence of discharging every trust reposed in me..." He also lamented the fact that the reputation of such an "Honorable Board" had sunk "below contempt" in the eyes of many due to the appointment of so many questionable characters.[58]

On May 22, 1770, Henry's wife died as a result of childbirth. She left him with five children to raise, including their infant daughter Mary Eleanor. Henry was devastated by her death. Four months later he wrote to a friend: "I have not yet got quite out of that dejected State in which from the Death of my Dear Wife and for a long Time after I was overwhelmed... the fatal Blow which took from me, a faithful bosom Friend, a Friend and dear Companion...which took from my Children, a Mother indeed!...a Blow which staggered me almost to the Gates of Death..."[59]

Henry resolved that the care and education of his children were his highest priority. As he wrote to a friend: "We are from the want of a College deprived of the principal Happinesses which we can enjoy in this Life, that of seeing the daily Progress of our Children in Knowledge and Virtue..."[60] To fill that gap, he began preparations to escort his three young sons to Europe for a proper education.

When plans took longer than anticipated, Henry sent his middle son, Harry, ahead of the rest in April 1771. The seven year old boy would study at a school founded in London by a former Charleston friend. Henry and his two other boys finally arrived in England in late October that same year. But, viewing the city as a parent, Henry was shocked by "the fearful wickedness of London."[61] As a result, during the summer of 1772, he enrolled both James and his oldest son John in school in Geneva, a city which still reflected Henry's own Calvinist temperament. A year later, Harry joined them.

During this period, Henry traveled throughout Europe. He had the opportunity to observe both the King and Parliament at close range. As he wrote in September 1772: "You learn from hence, good Sir, that Kings & Princes have Troubles & Perplexities & Passions & Crosses to contend withal, as much as Men have, who move in a more humble Sphere."[62]

While in London, Henry utilized every opportunity to promote American interests and to counter misperceptions of developments in the colonies. News of the Boston Tea Party, however, pushed the British Government over the edge. Even though Henry personally opposed the Tea Party as he did all acts of violence, he wrote to his brother that: "We *are*, I am sure we *are*, upon the main subject in the Right."[63] In March, 1774, he helped to draw up Petitions to the King and both Houses of Parliament. Twenty-nine Americans living in London signed the documents which Henry personally presented to Lord Dartmouth, the Secretary of State for the Colonies.[64]

In April 1774, only a few weeks after the first of the Intolerable

Acts passed Parliament, Henry confided to a close friend: "The present Administration Seem determined, to bring the Colonists into a State of Vassalage. It Seems also to be the King's Will, & the present House of Commons are fit Instruments for their purpose...God forbid that I Should wantonly Suggest any measure for injuring or distressing this Country, but if by the Violence & injustice of the Rulers of this Country we are driven to adopt & pursue measures for the Interest of future Generations, we cannot we shall not be blamed by wise & dispassionate Men."[65]

As tensions mounted, Henry wrote to his brother: "I long to be at home to share the fate whether good or bad with my Country Men."[66] Toward that goal he resettled all three of his boys back in London in order for them to continue with their studies. He then appointed 20 year old John, his oldest, to serve as a surrogate parent. Henry finally set sail for America. He arrived in Charleston Harbor on December 11, 1774, only a month after the South Carolina delegates to the First Continental Congress had returned from Philadelphia.[67]

After an absence of over three years, Henry was delighted to be reunited with his two daughters and his brother James. He also devoted long hours to his business interests. Nevertheless, political developments were an immediate priority. On January 9, 1775, only four weeks after his return, Henry was elected a member of the First Provincial Congress (a new 184 member legislative body which would soon replace the Commons House of Assembly).[68] It met in the Assembly Room of the State House and was, by far, the most representative group in the state's history up to that time.[69] When the Provincial Congress adjourned later that month, it established a General Committee to serve as an interim executive to enforce its decrees. Despite his long absence, Henry was selected as President of that committee.[70]

Through it all, Henry remained a moderating force. His goal was American home rule rather than revolution. Even as he denounced Parliament, he still professed loyalty to the King. In late May 1775, after news of Lexington and Concord had reached Charleston, Henry wrote to his son, John, that "...now is the Critical moment..."[71] On June 1, when the full legislative body reconvened, Henry was elected President of the Provincial Congress.[72] He thus became the highest ranking popularly elected official in South Carolina as the fate of his colony hung in the balance. Through a cruel coincidence, that same day his brother James left for Europe, taking with him Henry's two young daughters for safe keeping. It is impossible to imagine the intense emotions that Henry must have experienced. All those dearest to him would now be an ocean away as he performed the awesome duties of his office seven days a week, "...

Sunday not excepted, never less than eight & sometimes thirteen hours in the day..."[73]

On June 4, the Provincial Congress adopted a document known as the Association which called for meeting force with force. As President, Henry's signature was required for it to go into effect. Before signing, however, he received permission to speak from the chair. Henry pleaded unsuccessfully, even at that late date, to include a declaration of loyalty to the King. He compared the document to his last Will and Testament with the major distinction that "...this is to be signed by my hand & may be Sealed with my Blood ...by signing this I may forfeit my Estate into the hands of my Enemies."[74] Then, to the applause of his fellow delegates, Henry affixed his signature, thereby making the Association official.

Over the next two weeks, Henry tried, with only limited success, to moderate various radical proposals concerning the establishment of a standing military force. The legislators also created a Council of Safety which was granted sweeping powers during the long intervals between congressional sessions. Against his objections, Henry was elected as the President of this powerful new body, as well. As he confided in a letter to his son, John: "...whether they mean it as an additional honour_ or to avail themselves of my diligence in business_ or to keep each one from the post of danger I cannot tell but I am not Satisfied with my elevation_."[75]

While the Provincial Congress was still in session, the last Royal Governor of South Carolina arrived on June 18, 1775. Lord William Campbell was outraged to discover that almost all of his authority had been usurped. But, two days later--due in large measure to Henry's moderating influence--the Provincial Congress presented a surprisingly low-key address to the new governor in which it professed loyalty to the King and asked the governor's help in procuring a reconciliation on constitutional principles.[76] Gov. Campbell foolishly discarded this olive branch and denounced the Provincial Congress as a rebel assembly. One month later, he opened the final session of the Commons House which, to his consternation, reaffirmed the actions of the new legislature. The House then requested permission to adjourn. When the Governor denied its request, the members simply refused to muster a quorum. Tensions continued to mount until Gov. Campbell finally dissolved the Commons House on September 15, 1775, gathered up the seals of government, and retreated to a British warship which was anchored in Charleston Harbor. When this news reached Lord Dartmouth in London, the Secretary of State for the Colonies realized that if South Carolina was in open revolt, then his dream of eventual reconciliation with America had come to an end.[77]

Henry shared Dartmouth's foreboding. He wrote to his son John three days after the governor fled: "Our people here are proceeding by hasty Steps to attempts too mighty for their abilities, & every day convinces me that I was not wrong when I endeavoured to dissuade them from taking the Reins of Government into their hands...I oppose every wrong measure although it is necessary to give motion to many by my Signature...I am ready to cry out, a pox on both their Houses; we are all Mad; all wrong; but if I am to die it Shall be on the right Side, I honestly mean on this Side... Adieu my Dear Son, I commend you to God's protection."[78] Once again, Henry also demanded that John continue with his studies overseas rather than rejoining his father and taking up arms for America as the young man was so eager to do. For the moment, Henry won the argument.

In a letter a month later, Henry described to his son the circumstances of a duel in which he was nearly killed. It apparently took place because Henry had strongly opposed an attempt to make private correspondence subject to inspection. A hotheaded young radical by the name of John Grimke had issued the challenge. Since it was widely known from a few earlier duels that Henry did not aim at an opponent, he was shocked when Grimke shot directly at him. Fortunately, Grimke's gun misfired. After describing the scene in detail, Henry added: "My Dear Son...you know my abhorrence of Duels, I can say no more than this, to dissuade you from such folly such madness as your Father, by the combined Powers of Envy & malice in those who cannot be happy while he is so, has been driven into."[79]

As the moderate leader of an increasingly radical legislature, Henry was more than eager to step down from the presidency of the Provincial Congress. His wish was finally granted on November 1, 1775, when the assembly met again. On November 16, however, that same Congress reappointed Henry as a member of the Council of Safety which then unanimously reelected him to serve as Council President.[80] The Council's work intensified when orders were received from the Continental Congress in Philadelphia "to arrest and secure every person...whose going at large may...endanger the safety of the colony, or the liberties of America."[81]

The year 1776--that fateful year in world history--began for Henry on a profoundly personal note. On January 4, he received the news that his youngest son, James, had died in London in a freak accident.[82] Two days later Henry poured out his soul to his ailing brother James: "Oppressed & sunk down as I am by doubled Woe Mourning & Weeping for the loss of a Dear Son, Mourning & Weeping over my Country in general involved in a bloody Civil War...the Account of my Dear Son's Death at first did shake me, in my anguish I wished that I were with him...but it was not God's

Will that it should be so & my confidence & trust in him has turned me back & I have nothing now to say but__Thy Will be done.__"[83]

Political developments afforded Henry little time to mourn. In 1775, the Continental Congress in Philadelphia had authorized South Carolina to draw up a temporary form of government to replace colonial rule.[84] On February 11, 1776, an eleven-member committee was appointed by South Carolina's Provincial Congress to prepare an interim constitution. It was truly a distinguished commission which included both Henry Middleton, the former President of the Continental Congress, and Henry Laurens, the future President. The committee's work began under intense pressure since, only a few days earlier, Christopher Gadsden had returned from Philadelphia and had introduced to the members of the legislature a copy of Thomas Paine's revolutionary pamphlet, *Common Sense*, which, for the first time, denounced the King as a tyrant. After reading a few passages aloud to the delegates, Gadsden became the first in the colony to formally call for Independence. Even at that late date, most of the members, including Henry, were horrified at the notion of total separation.

On March 26, 1776, the South Carolina Provincial Congress completed its debate on the proposed constitution and became the second colony to officially adopt a new charter. Many anticipated that Henry Middleton, the senior patriot politician of the South, would be elected President of the new General Assembly. The delegates, however, selected a younger and more robust candidate for that post, attorney John Rutledge. Over his repeated objections, Henry Laurens was elected as Vice President. As he wrote to his son, John: "...be assured that I have said & done every thing in my power in order to be excused..."[85]

At this precise moment, British warships appeared off South Carolina's coast. Charlestonians feared that the long anticipated British invasion was at hand. Henry wrote that "...we are now in daily expectation of a visit from General Clinton, Lord Cornwallis or some body else with the friendly suite of 40 Gun Ships...what scenes I am to pass through I know not, God grant me firmn[ess &] Resolution to do my duty...I would most willingly sacrifice my Life, I would most chearfully receive the stroke of Death to bring forward a happy & lasting Peace between Great Britain & these Colonies, but I now begin to fear not only that Peace is at a distance but that reconciliation including filial dependance will never be effected."[86]

The British attack on Charleston finally started on Friday, June 28, 1776, only three days before the debate over Independence began in Philadelphia. To Henry and his colleagues, the price of Independence appeared all too real. Amazingly, their worst fears were not realized. The British cannonballs lodged harmlessly in the spongy palmetto logs of Col.

Moultrie's fort which guarded Charleston Harbor and some of the British soldiers who did land on one of the barrier islands quickly discovered that their route was far more treacherous than anticipated. The attack ended in humiliation for the British and disaster for the deposed Governor who later died of the wounds he suffered when his ship was fired on by the patriots. For the first time, Americans had been able to defeat the British in open combat.[87]

After a taste of victory, it is not surprising that, when a copy of the Declaration of Independence finally reached Charleston a month later, it was greeted with great celebration by the victorious South Carolina patriots. For Henry, however, the event remained bittersweet. As he confided to his son: "...even at this Moment I feel a Tear of affection for the good old Country & for the People in it whom in general I dearly Love...I say even at this Moment my heart is full of the lively sensations of a dutiful Son, thrust by the hand of violence out of a Father's House into the wide World..."[88]

Now that the permanent battle lines had been drawn, Henry reluctantly gave John permission to return home to fight for his new country. When he received his son's response in late October, Henry must have been more than surprised by John's unexpected news: "Will you forgive me Sir for adding a Daughter in Law to your Family without first asking your Consent__" The next line was even more shocking: "...my Wife...promises soon to give you a Grand Child__"[89] John's wife was Martha Manning, the daughter of William Manning, one of Henry's dear friends in London. It was obviously a marriage of necessity. John did not even wait until the birth of their daughter before he left England for France on December 27, 1776. He placed his young pregnant wife in the care of her family. John would never see his daughter, Fanny.[90]

It was in the midst of these tumultuous developments that Henry was elected on January 10, 1777, as one of South Carolina's delegates to the Continental Congress. He cared nothing for the honor associated with his election but he ultimately submitted to the legislature's mandate out of a sense of duty. After arranging his business affairs, and welcoming home his son in mid-April, Henry and John traveled together to Philadelphia where Henry presented his credential to the Continental Congress on July 22, 1777. While Henry was instantly inundated with committee assignments, John made final arrangements to join Gen. Washington's personal staff. When the young man took leave of his father on August 8, Henry confessed to a friend that "my heart was too full at parting..."[91] They were far more than blood relatives. John had become his father's closest confident and dearest friend. Henry saw in his son not only the legacy of all that he had accomplished in his long and eventful life, but also the embodiment of their infant nation as it inspired the world with revolutionary ideals.

Henry also worried constantly about John's safety. His fears were more than justified. The young aide-de-camp received two minor wounds during the Battle of Germantown in October 1777 and quickly developed a reputation for bravery to the point of recklessness on the field of battle.[92] As the Marquis de Lafayette told Henry concerning John's heroism in the earlier Battle of Brandywine: "it was not his fault that he [John] was not killed or wounded he did everything that was necessary to procure one or t'other..."[93]

Meanwhile, on the floor of Congress, Henry waged his own battles with some delegates who, in his judgment, displayed less patriotism than self-interest, and congressional procedures which stretched even minor matters into endless hours of debate. On August 12, he confided to John Rutledge, President of the South Carolina Provincial Congress, that "...I wish ten thousand time [sic] more I had never come as a delegate..."[94] His colleagues, however, obviously disagreed. On November 1, 1777, they unanimously elected him to succeed John Hancock as their fourth President. Even when a serious reoccurrence of gout forced him to remain in bed for weeks in mid-December, Henry continued to handle all of the paperwork associated with his office. On December 27, despite his pain, Henry insisted on being physically carried into the chamber in order to preside over an important debate.[95]

Three days later, Henry described his situation to one of his many correspondents: "I am now sitting, both feet & Legs bound up in a Basket in the room where Congress meets__perhaps two, it may be three, hours after dark I may be permitted to hobble on my Crutches over Ice & frozen Snow or to be carried to such a homely home as I have, where I must sit in Bed one or two or three hours longer at the writing Table, pass the remainder of a tedious night in pain & some anxiety__I hear you reply__ why fait if I was you I would resign the presidentship__ believe me my dear Sir, that was my solid determination on the 2d or 3d day after my present troublesome companion had taken possession of me...[but] Congress were not disposed to grant my request...."[96]

One of the most unsavory problems Henry inherited when he assumed the presidency was a subtle campaign by some military and congressional leaders to replace Washington as Commander-in-Chief of the Continental Army. Gen. Horatio Gates' victory at Saratoga that October (which, in reality, should have been attributed to his deputy, Gen. Benedict Arnold) was repeatedly compared by some to Gen. Washington's string of setbacks and retreats as his army froze that winter at Valley Forge. The very fact that Congress had been driven out of Philadelphia by the British and was forced to meet in York, Pennsylvania was a daily reminder that all was not well on the military front. Both John and Sam Adams freely expressed these sentiments as did Gen. Thomas Mifflin of Pennsylvania, a future President.[97] (The movement to oust Washington, however, is best remembered as the Conway Cabal after yet another military rival, Gen. Thomas Conway.)

Even though Henry was hardly blind to Washington's faults, he used his presidential office, and his son's back channel access, to protect the commander-in-chief from his critics. Henry expressed contempt for the Cabal in a letter to John on January 8, 1778: "...there are prompters & Actors, accomodators, Candle Snuffers, Shifters of Scenes & Mutes __ I have been & am uniformly opposed to all of them__ the motives of your friend [Washington] are pure, he has nothing in view but the happiness of his Country...the rest of them...make patriotism the stalking horse to their private Interests..."[98] Not surprisingly, Washington was very grateful for the President's support: "I cannot sufficiently express the obligation I feel to you for your friendship and politeness upon an occasion in which I am so deeply interested."[99]

Long after the conspiracy had faded, the President and the General remained good friends. They did not agree on every issue, however. In the spring of 1778, Washington urged Congress to grant his officers pensions for life at half-pay in order to stem the resignations which constantly threatened his command. As he wrote to the President in late April of that year: "...it is painful to see men...who have rendered great Services to their [Coun]try, & who are still, and may be most materially wanted, leaving the [Army] on acct. of the distresses of their [fami]ly, and to repair their circumstan[ces] which have been much injured by their zeal..."[100] Henry's response was immediate and unambiguous: "I view the scheme as altogether unjust & unconstitutional in its nature & full of dangerous consequences...a Pension for Officers [would] make them a seperate Body to be provided for by the honest Yeomanry & others of their fellow Citizens many thousands of whom have equal claims upon every ground of Loss of Estate..."[101] Congress ultimately worked out a compromise that both the President and the General reluctantly accepted.[102]

In early 1778, Henry grew deeply depressed over the lack of patriotism, even among some of his fellow delegates, and the widely accepted greed that motivated so many public men: "O Liberty, O Virtue O my Country! upon the base prostitution of these sacred Names__ Knaves & fools are building enormous Estates sapping the foundations of Liberty, Virtue and their Country__ & taxing the honest & undesigning a thousand fold more than the British parliament would or could have done__"[103] To Gov. William Livingston of New Jersey he wrote: "If there be not speedily a Resurrection of able Men & of that Virtue which I thought had been genuine in 1775__ We are gone__ We shall undo ourselves..."[104] Fortunately, Henry's spirits began to brighten later that spring as new delegates arrived from several colonies. He wrote to John Rutledge on May 4, 1778 that "I have resolved to continue here a little longer."[105]

Finally, events took a turn for the better. By late June 1778, the British command abandoned Philadelphia and returned to New York City. As President, Henry had the honor of leading Congress back to the American capital where he "and a number of members met at the State House in Philadelphia on Thursday the 2nd of July..." just in time to mark the second anniversary of the vote on Independence.[106] Later that month, however, Congress was nearly torn apart over a heated dispute between two American diplomats: Silas Deane of New York and Arthur Lee of Virginia.

Both Deane and Lee had been appointed by Congress in 1776 to serve with Benjamin Franklin in Paris. From the start, Lee's dour personality clashed with his two gregarious colleagues. Lee increasingly suspected that both Franklin and Dean were mixing public and private business, and he eagerly shared this concern with his distinguished brother, Richard Henry Lee, who was still serving in Congress. Henry, who also took a sober view of public affairs, had met and befriended Arthur Lee in England prior to the Revolution. In contrast, Henry had earlier confided to his close friend John Lewis Gervais that Deane's "conduct has not given Satisfaction..."[107] When a motion was introduced in Congress in late 1777 to recall Deane to answer Lee's charges, Henry eagerly supported the order.

Silas Deane finally returned to America in July 1778 and testified for the first time before Congress in mid-August. As President, Henry was astonished that Deane had not prepared a detailed rebuttal to the charges of misconduct, and, as a businessman, he was even more outraged that Deane had left most of his financial records behind in Paris. Weeks later, when Deane determined that he was not receiving a fair hearing from Congress, he published his own defense in the *Pennsylvania Packet* on December 5, 1778, along with an attack on the Lee brothers. When Henry read Deane's newspaper report he "found it to contain Articles highly derogatory to the honor and interests of these United States."[108] Henry demanded that Deane be denied any further hearing until a committee could investigate the situation. By now, however, Congress was so divided over the issue that Henry's proposal--which he viewed as a vote of confidence--was rejected.[109]

A few weeks earlier, on the first anniversary of his election as President, Henry had attempted to resign from his office in keeping with the spirit of the one-year term mandated by the new Articles of Confederation which had not yet been ratified by all the States. But, "the House being satisfied with the whole conduct of the President Resolved That it is the unanimous desire of this house that H L Esq continue for some time longer [as pres.]."[110] By early December, however, Henry had grown so disgusted with the petty politics of the Deane Affair that, on December 9, 1778, he once again submitted his resignation. This time, he would not be persuaded to reconsider as he made clear in his resignation speech to the delegates:

"I feel my own honor, and much more forcibly the honor of the Public deeply wounded by Mr. Deanes' address and I am persuaded that it will hold out such encouragement [to] our Enemies to continue their persecution, as will, in its consequences, be more detrimental to [our] Cause than the loss of a Battle...Finally, Gentlemen, from the considerations abovementioned, as I cannot consistently with my own honor, nor with utility to my Country, considering the manner in which Business is transacted here, remain any longer in this Chair, I now resign it."[111]

The next day, the delegates turned to New York and elected John Jay, a close friend and supporter of Silas Deane, as their fifth President.[112] Jay served as President until the following September and Henry remained as an active member of Congress until late 1779.

After his resignation, Henry was appointed a member of the Secret Committee which oversaw some of Congress' most sensitive financial transactions. Henry also engaged in a heated dispute with the North Carolina delegation because he and Richard Henry Lee of Virginia were the only Southern delegates who supported the inclusion of New England fishing rights in the instructions pertaining to peace negotiations. The North Carolina delegates tried everything from persuasion to intimidation in a futile attempt to force Henry to back down from his national perspective. They even recruited Alexander Hamilton, who was then another aide-de-camp to Washington, to use his influence with his close friend and colleague, John Laurens, in order to change Henry's position.[113]

Some even accused Henry of being a pawn of the Lees and Adamses, a charge Henry vigorously denied: "It has been falsely transmitted to Charles Town that I was too closely connected with the Eastern States...I glory in the reproach of being with no Man, with no party longer than he or they steers or steer by the pole Star of reason, Justice, reciprocity, when Men diverge into the Road of self Interestedness, I walk no further with them."[114]

Perhaps Henry's most serious dispute during 1779 was directed at

Charles Thomson, the long-serving Secretary of Congress. The two men had maintained a working relationship during Henry's presidency, but long-simmering animosities finally reached the boiling point on August 31, 1779. As Thomson himself recorded in the official Journal he kept: "Mr. Laurens...having informed Congress, that he had conceived himself treated with disrespect by the Secretary of Congress, Ordered That a committee of three be appointed to enquire into the complaint...and that the committee do at the same time hear the Secretary in his vindication..."[115] The next day, Henry delivered a report to the new committee. After referencing several specific examples of the conduct he found so offensive, Henry concluded his comments by stating: "I consider these affronts of the Secretary though offered to a Delegate, and however Mr. Secretary might have intended them, as abuses of power in Office, and affronts to that Assembly..."[116]

Cooler heads prevailed. Thanks to the intercession of Pennsylvania delegate John Dickinson, the two men pledged to treat each other with greater respect. Under the circumstances, no formal committee report was ever issued.[117]

Henry resumed his regular congressional duties for the next six weeks as he yearned more than ever to return home. On October 21, however, his plans took a dramatic turn when Congress selected him for diplomatic service in The Netherlands. His assignment was to negotiate both a loan and a commercial treaty with the Dutch Government. He left Philadelphia on November 9, 1779, and reached Charleston one month later in order to prepare for his overseas journey. Upon arrival, Henry found his city's morale nearly shattered. Inhabitants feared for their lives due to a smallpox epidemic and the growing threat of a British assault. As in the past, personal business took second place to public affairs. On January 31, 1780, Henry resumed his seat in the General Assembly. But, as events unfolded, Henry, John Rutledge and other South Carolina leaders were forced to flee the city to avoid capture by the British. Charleston finally surrendered on May 12. By then, Henry was working his way north, trying to avoid capture as he sought safe passage across the Atlantic.[118]

Finally, by the end of June, Henry reached Philadelphia where he was reunited with his son, John, who had been captured in the fall of Charleston but was paroled along with most of American Gen. Benjamin Lincoln's staff.[119] From him, Henry learned that his Ansonborough home had been severely damaged and that his beautiful gardens had been destroyed.

On August 13, 1780, Henry set sail from Philadelphia to begin his diplomatic career. John accompanied his father down the Delaware River as far as Fort Penn. These would be the last precious hours they would ever share. Two weeks later, Henry's ship was seized on the high seas by a British frigate and the former President became the highest ranking American prisoner of war. Initially, he was treated well and confided to his secretary that "I shall now be sent to England where I shall be of more real service to my own Country than I could possibly be in any other part of Europe."[120] But, after arriving in London on October 5, he was placed under heavy guard and interrogated by Lord Hillsborough, George Germain and other key parliamentary figures. From there, Henry began a long imprisonment in the dreaded Tower of London.

Not surprisingly, instead of being treated as a former Head of State, Henry was held as a rebel on the suspicion of high treason. Initial attempts by prison officials to intimidate Henry only intensified his determination and even occasionally amused him. When iron bars were added to his window, he wrote in his Journal that "I laughed inwardly because I might have made an escape before I came there [between landing in England and reaching London] had not I detested the Idea."[121] Henry was less amused over the failure of officials to properly attend to his medical needs and the requirement that he had to pay for all the costs related to his imprisonment.

Before long, Henry was able to smuggle out bits of news to the British media. On March 1, 1781, he recorded in his Journal that "At intervals of time I employed my pencil in writing paragraphs of American Intelligence for the Rebel-News papers as they were called, some of these excited jealousy, one of the Secretaries of State, as I was informed, said they smelt strong of the Tower..."[122]

Prison officials used everything from regulating his walks in the courtyard to limiting his visitors in an attempt to break Henry's spirit. Their tactics failed. A few old friends were permitted to meet with him if they agreed to urge Henry to denounce American Independence. On March 7, 1781, Henry responded to one by stating: "Sir I will never subscribe to my own infamy & to the dishonor of my Children...I am afraid of no consequences but such as would flow from dishonorable Acts."[123] In April, when the British learned that Henry's son, John, had arrived in Paris on a diplomatic assignment, they demanded that Henry write to his son to persuade him to abandon his mission in exchange for more lenient treatment. Henry flatly refused. John, for his part, joined with Franklin in entreating the French Court to assist in Henry's release. Serious discussions were held in Philadelphia, Paris and London concerning the prospect of exchanging British Gen. Burgoyne (who surrendered his army at Saratoga in 1777) for the former President, but the plan collapsed when Burgoyne was exchanged for Gen. William Moultrie and several hundred American soldiers.[124]

Finally, on June 23, 1781, feeling abandoned by the Continental Congress and suffering from the sever physical effects of his long confinement, Henry decided to take matters into his own hands. He drew up a petition to the Secretaries of State, meticulously outlining his conduct over the past two decades. He stressed that at every opportunity he had attempted to bridge the gap between Britain and America, and that he had often helped to defend the rights of loyalists from his more radical colleagues. He reminded the officials that he had been "upwards of Eight Months & an half a prisoner in the Tower, great part of that time in very close & painful confinement..." Henry then concluded by requesting pen and ink and more visits with his son, Harry, "together with such further indulgence to the Representer & Petitioner as to Your Lordships Wisdom & Goodness shall seem fitting."[125]

His petition appeared to fall on deaf ears. He received no indication that the ministry ever even saw it. Finally, in early December 1781, Edmund Burke, one of the most respected members of the British House of Commons, attempted to resolve Henry's status and to win his release from the Tower. Burke praised Henry as "one of the most enlightened and liberal men alive."[126] Since Lord Hillsborough insisted that Henry was a State prisoner and not a prisoner of war, he informed Burke that Henry would have to accept a pardon to gain his freedom. Burke replied that "Mr. Laurens will not even connive at a pardon, but expects to be treated as a prisoner of War."[127] Burke was correct. Henry had absolutely no intention of seeking forgiveness for being a patriotic American. Instead, he prepared one final petition, this time it was addressed to the House of Commons. Some American patriots later used it to question Henry's conduct during his incarceration.[128] But, at long last, Henry's imprisonment became the subject of intense interest in Parliament. Once word reached London that Gen. Cornwallis had surrendered his British Army at Yorktown in mid-October, the emphasis shifted from prosecuting the war to pursuing peace.

Despite everything Henry had suffered during his fifteen months in The Tower, British leaders knew that his moderate voice would certainly be put to better use as a diplomat than behind bars. Even though complicated arrangements had been discussed on both sides of the Atlantic concerning the possibility of exchanging President Laurens for Gen. Cornwallis, no public resolution was ever agreed to.[129]

Nevertheless, on December 31, 1781, Henry was placed in a sedan chair (since he was unable to walk because of his gout) and carried to the Inns of Court to appear before Lord Mansfield. As the proceeding began, Henry announced: "...I think it necessary to make this previos declaration, that I hold my self to be a Citizen of the United free & Independent States of North America & I will not do any Act which shall involve me in an acknowledgement of subjection to this Realm..." At the end of the session Henry was released into the custody of two close friends. Henry later described these final moments: "...when the words...'Our Sovereign Lord the King' were repeated I said aloud, 'not my Sovereign Lord.' thus terminated a long & to me an expensive & painful farce. I humbly think Independence is established from this day, my friends here are all of this opinion."[130]

Henry devoted his first weeks of freedom to seeking relief from his gout in the waters at Bath. Upon his return to London, as Lord North's government collapsed that March, Henry began regular conversations with North's replacement, the Marquis of Rockingham, and other members of the new Cabinet. He then traveled to The Netherlands to confer with John Adams concerning peace terms and on to France to visit his ailing brother's family and his own daughters. Back in England, Henry returned to Bath for most of October.

On November 12, 1782, less than a week after Henry had returned to London, he received a letter from John Adams which reconfirmed Henry's assignment as a Peace Commissioner and contained the most painful news he had ever received. Adams enclosed the report that Henry's son, John, had been killed the previous August in a skirmish at Chehaw Neck, South Carolina; he was one of the last American officers to die in the Revolutionary War. Adams wrote: "I feel for you, more than I can or ought to express..."[131] Henry responded: "...the Wound is deep, but I apply to myself the consolation which I administered to the Father, of the Brave Colonel Parker: 'Thank God I had a Son who dared to die in defence of his Country.'"[132]

In typical stoic fashion, Henry struggled to set aside his grief to fulfill his duty. He traveled to Paris in late November where he joined his fellow Peace Commissioners: Benjamin Franklin, John Adams and John Jay (the President who succeed him but was now a member of the diplomatic service). Even one of the British Commissioners, Richard Oswald, was one of Henry's most intimate friends.[133] Though Henry arrived only two days before the document was completed, he did have an impact on the treaty. Henry gave Adams critical support for the inclusion of New England fishing rights. As Adams wrote in his diary: "I was very happy, that Mr. Laurence came...his Judgment [is] as sound, and his heart as firm as ever... the Article which he caused to be inserted at the very last that no Property should be carried off...was worth a longer Journey, if that had been all. But his Name and Weight is added which is of much greater Consequence."

Henry and his colleagues then signed the preliminary Peace Treaty in Paris on November 30, 1782.

Throughout 1783, Henry shuttled between London and Paris, always pressing for the resumption of trade relations between America and Britain and the removal of all British troops from American soil at the earliest possible moment. As his major biographer accurately contends: "Laurens's services during 1782-3-4...entitle him in a very true sense to be considered the first minister of the United States to England."[134] At the same time, Henry continued to attend to family affairs in the south of France where his brother James died early the following January.

Finally, on June 6, 1784, Henry left London for the last time and headed home to America, accompanied by his only surviving son, Harry. Father and son reached New York on August 3, and then traveled to Philadelphia in the hope of reporting directly to Congress. Unfortunately, that body, which had adjourned on June 3, was not scheduled to meet again until late fall. When Congress did reassemble in Trenton, New Jersey on November 1, 1784, only two states were present. Henry met informally with the delegates as they arrived. There was talk of electing him to another term as President, but, by November 16, Henry could wait no longer. He drafted one final letter to Congress and then left the next day for South Carolina. On November 30, while Henry was on his way home, a quorum was finally established and Richard Henry Lee of Virginia was elected as the eleventh President.[135]

Henry and his son Harry reached Charleston on January 14, 1785. City newspapers welcomed the return of his "tried wisdom and patriotism which have been so eminently displayed by this distinguished statesman, in a series of important services to the United States."[136]

Four months later, Henry's two daughters, his widowed sister-in-law and his young grandchild (John's daughter) all arrived. For the first time in thirteen years, all the surviving members of his family were home. Now that Independence had been won, it was time for Henry and his family to rebuild their lives. He retired to Mepkin Plantation, 30 miles up the Cooper River from Charleston, where he personally supervised every detail of the construction of a nine-room house to replace the home the British had destroyed. One historian estimates that "the war had cost him about forty thousand pounds."[137]

In addition to naming a county in Henry's honor, the state legislature repeatedly tried to nudge Henry out of retirement by electing him to various prestigious positions. Each time he firmly declined because of his health. Henry even turned down the honor of being a delegate to the Constitutional Convention in Philadelphia in 1787.[138] Nevertheless, he did briefly reenter public life in May 1788, to cast his vote for the new United States Constitution at the South Carolina Ratification Convention. It is ironic that two centuries later Henry's greatest hesitation concerning the Constitution was that the chief executive's powers might be too limited. Despite that reservation, he found the new charter "infinitely better than our present Confederation."[139] Henry's final appearance on the public stage was as a member of the first Electoral College in 1789. He proudly cast his ballot for George Washington, who's career he once helped to save during the darkest days of the American Revolution.

Like any loving father, Henry's remaining years were primarily devoted to his family. On January 23, 1787, his oldest daughter, Martha (who, as an infant, had once been presumed dead), became the third wife of Dr. David Ramsay, a physician, statesman and historian.[140] They had eleven children of their own, eight of whom survived infancy. They also raised Martha's young niece, Fanny, the child John Laurens never saw. Throughout much of her life, Martha had kept a diary. At her request, her writings were edited into a remarkable memoir by her historian husband after her death in 1811.[141] Today, their home still stands at 92 Broad Street, only a half block from St. Michael's Church where President Henry Middleton once worshiped.

In April 1788, Henry's youngest daughter, Mary Eleanor, married Charles Pinckney III, who was 13 years her senior.[142] He had been a delegate to the Constitutional Convention in Philadelphia the previous year and was elected Governor of South Carolina in 1789. As first lady of the state, it was Mary Eleanor who served as hostess when President Washington made his official visit to Charleston in May 1791. But, after only six years of marriage, she, like her mother, died of complications from childbirth. She left two young children and her infant son, Henry Laurens Pinckney.

Henry's granddaughter, Fanny, eloped in 1795 with Francis Henderson, a Scottish merchant. After they separated, Fanny moved back to Europe where she married again. She died in England on April 25, 1860.[143]

Harry, Henry's only surviving son, married Eliza Rutledge, the daughter of Henry's close friend, John Rutledge, on May 26, 1792. According to family tradition, Henry then turned over the main house at Mepkin to the newlyweds and he moved into a smaller cottage for the remaining six months of his life.[144] Harry, who died in 1821, lived a happy and prosperous life, but he neither sought nor attained the stature that Henry had foreseen for his oldest son, John. Harry and Eliza had nine children.[145]

It was at Mepkin that Martha comforted her father during his final illness. As he slipped into a coma, she sat by his bedside until he quietly passed away on Saturday morning, December 8, 1792. She wrote in her published Memoirs: "At ten o'clock...I closed his venerable eyes."[146] She also made final funeral arrangements according to Henry's clearly stated directive, but she could not bear to witness the event. Because Henry suffered from taphephobia, the fear of being buried alive, he ordered that he be cremated. He thus became the first documented case of an American of European origin to do so in the United States.[147] The ceremony took place at Mepkin three days after his death. His ashes were then buried there in the family plot.

Almost exactly ten years earlier, when his son John died, Henry had expressed his overwhelming grief to his sister-in-law : "My dear Son... dutiful Son, affectionate friend, sensible honest Counsellor, [he] would have fled across the Globe to conduct and to serve his father...he loved his country, he bled and died for it. I shall soon quit this globe and meet him beyond it: happy never more to seperate."[148]

Today, as Henry foretold, father and son rest side by side in the family graveyard along the banks of the Cooper River. Henry was one of only two Presidents to sacrifice a son on the field of battle.[149] For him, it was truly the ultimate sacrifice.[150]

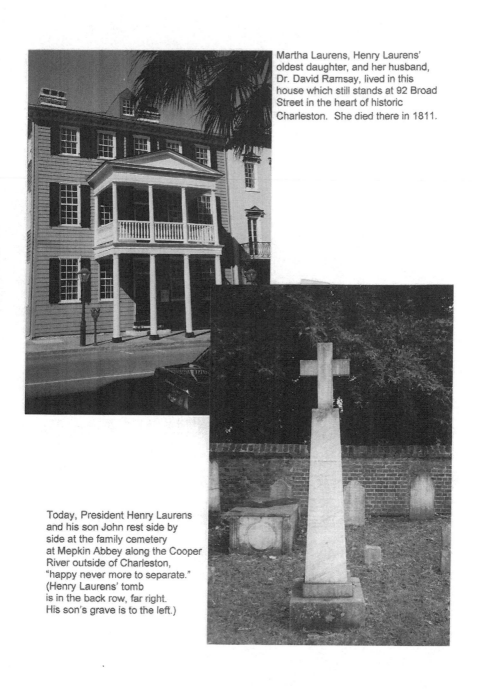

Martha Laurens, Henry Laurens' oldest daughter, and her husband, Dr. David Ramsay, lived in this house which still stands at 92 Broad Street in the heart of historic Charleston. She died there in 1811.

Today, President Henry Laurens and his son John rest side by side at the family cemetery at Mepkin Abbey along the Cooper River outside of Charleston, "happy never more to separate." (Henry Laurens' tomb is in the back row, far right. His son's grave is to the left.)

WHILE HENRY LAURENS
WAS PRESIDENT

November 1777 - December 1778

For most American patriots, the Winter of 1777-78 represented the darkest days of the Revolution. While the Continental Army froze at Valley Forge and the Continental Congress soldiered on in exile, Gen. Howe and 14,700 British troops occupied the American capital.[151] Philadelphia loyalists, such as Joseph Galloway (the former Speaker of the Pennsylvania House), did all in their power to reconcile the local populace to their imperial masters.[152] The elegant balls held in Howe's honor throughout that Winter belied the blood that had already been shed on both sides.

For America, that Winter also marked the turning point in the war. The signs were so subtle that few grasped their full meaning, but the tide was moving in America's favor. On Saturday, November 15, 1777, only two weeks after Henry Laurens had assumed the presidency, the Articles of Confederation were finally adopted by Congress and sent to the States for ratification.[153] It was an essential step in establishing a sense of permanence and national unity, even though several of the provisions contained in the Articles--which were not ratified by all 13 States until 1781--eventually threatened the survival of Congress once the war had been won.[154]

At the end of November, John Adams was drafted into diplomatic service and dispatched to France where he joined Benjamin Franklin and Arthur Lee in a series of delicate European negotiations.[155] In reverse, Baron Frederick von Steuben arrived from France in December 1777, with a letter of introduction from Franklin. Von Steuben, a former officer in the Prussian Army, was named Inspector General and began at once to impose discipline on the ragtag recruits at Valley Forge. More than any other officer, he transformed the starving Continentals into professional soldiers.[156]

On January 23, 1778, Lafayette was assigned to command another invasion of Canada, but the plan collapsed.[157] Exactly two weeks later, the United States and France finally did sign a formal alliance.[158] The British were so distraught by the news that Parliament engaged in a heated debate over the conduct of the war now that it had been transformed into a renewed struggle between Europe's two major powers. It was during that debate in the House of Lords that America's greatest defender, the Earl of Chatham (William Pitt), collapsed while denouncing the war. He died five weeks later.[159]

Back in America, Gen. Howe submitted a new peace proposal in which Britain pledged to capitulate on almost all points of contention except American Independence. Congress formally rejected the plan on June 6, 1778.[160] At his request, Howe was eventually relieved of his command and replaced by Gen. Henry Clinton who then began the withdrawal of British forces from Philadelphia.[161]

In late June, President Henry Laurens led his fellow delegates back to the American capital where it triumphantly reconvened on July 2, 1778, the second anniversary of the vote for Independence.[162] Two days later, along the frontier, Col. George Rogers Clark captured the British outpost of Kaskaskia near the Mississippi River.[163] On July 11, Congress received word that its new ally, the French fleet, had finally arrived in Delaware Bay.[164] Britain would never again dominate the American coast with impunity.

Throughout these thirteen months, Congress devoted countless hours to the ever-present crisis of financing the war. At least $20,000,000 in Continental currency was issued by Congress during that period, while American diplomats overseas desperately sought sizable loans from their new European allies.[165] Henry himself was selected for such a mission only months after he resigned the presidency. He never reached his destination.

Chapter 4

President
HENRY LAURENS
of
SOUTH CAROLINA

Notes

Abbreviation Key

JCC   Journals of the Continental Congress
LDC   Letters of Delegates to Congress
PHL   The Papers of Henry Laurens

[1] See Chapter 3.

[2] See Chapter 3.

[3] Philip M. Hamer, Editor, PHL, (University of South Carolina Press, Columbia, 1968-2003, 16 Volumes), Vol. 5, p. 296. Henry Laurens to James Habersham, September 5, 1767: "I hate lies & oppression & am apt to speak my sentiments without disguise or consideration for the Man. Hence probably it happens, that I sometimes without premeditation draw resentment upon me..."

[4] Chapter 3. John Hancock actually intended to resume the presidency after a few months of rest. But, when he returned to Congress in July 1778, it was clear that President Laurens had no intention of relinquishing the office in deference to his predecessor. The irony is that Hancock, as President, had also declined to step aside when Peyton Randolph, the first President, returned to Congress in September 1775.

[5] PHL, op. cit., Vol. 11, p. 294; Henry Laurens to John Laurens, February 3, 1777. (During his absence, Henry's friend John Lewis Gervais oversaw Henry's affairs at home.)

[6] PHL, op. cit., Vol. 11, p. 404; Henry Laurens to John Lewis Gervais, July 25, 1777.

[7] Worthington Chauncey Ford, Chief, Division of Manuscripts, JCC: 1774-1789, (Library of Congress, Washington, DC, 1904-1937, 34 Volumes), Vol. VIII, p. 570.

[8] David Duncan Wallace, The Life of Henry Laurens, (G. P. Putnam's Sons, New York, 1915), p. 229.

[9] Paul H. Smith, Editor, LDC: 1774-1789, (Library of Congress, Washington, DC, 1976-2000, 26 Volumes), Vol. 7, p. 505; John Adams to Abigail Adams, August 19, 1777.

[10] LDC, op. cit., Vol. 8, p. 149; Henry Laurens to Gen. Robert Howe, October 20, 1777.

[11] T. R. Fehrenbach, <u>Greatness To Sapre</u>, (D. Van Nostrand Company, Inc., Princeton, 1968), p. 100.

[12] LDC, op. cit., Vol. 8, p. 139; John Harvie to Thomas Jefferson, October 18, 1777.

[13] JCC, op. cit., Vol. IX, p. 854.

[14] Wallace, op. cit., p. 4. The family of Andre Laurens' future bride, Marie Lucas, also traveled to England with the Laurens family to escape persecution for their religious beliefs.

[15] PHL, op. cit., Vol. 9, p. 309; Henry Laurens to Messieurs and Madame Laurence, February 25, 1774.

[16] Wallace, op. cit., pp. 7-12.

[17] David Ramsay, <u>Ramsay's History of South Carolina: From Its First Settlement in 1670 to the Year 1808</u>, (W. J. Duffie, Newberry, SC, 1858), Vol. 2, p. 253.

[18] PHL, op. cit., Vol. 1, pp. 22-23; Henry Laurens to William Flower, July 10, 1747.

[19] PHL, op. cit., Vol. 1, pp. 22-23; Henry Laurens to William Flower, July 10, 1747. Henry wrote that "I have often told you that I thought much of my disappointment with Mr. _____ (you know my meaning)..." even though the editors of <u>The Papers</u> identify the unnamed gentleman as Mr. Crokatt, the exact details pertaining to his comment remain unknown.

[20] PHL, op. cit., Vol. 1, pp. 6-7; The Will of John Laurens, recorded June 19, 1747. The other two executors were John Laurens' widow, Elizabeth, and Mr. James Osmond.

[21] PHL, op. cit., Vol. 1, p. 178; Henry Laurens to James Laurens, December 15, 1748.

[22] Warner Oland Moore, Jr., <u>Henry Laurens: A Charleston Merchant in the Eighteenth Century, 1747-1771</u>, Doctoral Dissertation, The University of Alabama, 1974, p. 60.

[23] Moore, op. cit., p. 63.

[24] PHL, op. cit., Vol. 6, p. 427; Henry Laurens to William Cowles & Co., April, 4, 1769; and, Moore, op. cit., p. 239.

[25] Moore, op. cit., pp. 101 & 93.

[26] *South Carolina Gazette*, October 23, 1751.

[27] PHL, op. cit., Vol. 7, p. 232; Henry Laurens to Magnus Watson, February 15, 1770.

[28] Moore, op. cit., p. 154.

[29] Moore, op. cit., p. 158-160.

[30] Moore, op. cit., pp. 185 & 193-194.

[31] PHL, op. cit., Vol. 1, p. 295; Henry Laurens to Smith & Clifton, July 17, 1755.

[32] PHL, op. cit., Vol. 5, p. 571; Henry Laurens to John Moultrie, January 28, 1768.

[33] PHL, op. cit., Vol. 4, p. 96; Henry Laurens to John Knight, December 22, 1763.

[34] Daniel J. McDonough, Christopher Gadsden and Henry Laurens: Two Parallel Lives of Two American Patriots (Associated University Press, Cranbury, NJ, 2000), p. 95.

[35] Joseph P. Kelly, "Henry Laurens: the Southern Man of Conscience in History," *The South Carolina Historical Magazine*, Vol. 107, Number 2 (April 2006), p. 90. Professor Kelly concludes that "It was the son who abhorred slavery, not the father."

[36] PHL, op. cit., Vol. 11, pp. 224-225; Henry Laurens to John Laurens, August 14, 1776. See also: PHL, op. cit., Vol. 16, pp. 762-763; Henry Laurens to David Ramsay, July 7, 1790. Henry notified Dr. Ramsay that Henry's faithful slave, George, should be freed upon Henry's death and that George should receive money and supplies from Henry's estate. (John Laurens shared his father's goal and devised a plan to free his portion of his slave inheritance provided they fight for the American cause and allow him to lead them into battle. Henry eventually endorsed this plan as did the Continental Congress, but the South Carolina legislature repeatedly rejected the idea.)

[37] PHL, op. cit., Vol. 4, p.596; Henry Laurens to Elias Ball, April 1, 1765.

[38] Wallace, op. cit., pp. 130 & 125.

[39] Wallace, op. cit., pp. 131-132. Much like Thomas Jefferson, Henry took delight in constantly improving his agricultural methods and trying new farming techniques.

[40] PHL, op. cit., Vol. 7, p. 300; Henry Laurens to Matthew Robinson, June 1, 1770. It is a great loss to posterity that even though Henry was such a prolific letter writer, none remain that might have been addressed to his devoted wife. The primary reason, however, is that they were so seldom apart during their 20 year marriage.

[41] Joanna Bowen Gillespie, The Life and Times of Martha Laurens Ramsay: 1759-1811, (University of South Carolina Press, Columbia, SC, 2001), p. 22.

[42] Wallace, op. cit., pp. 63-64.

[43] PHL, op. cit., Vol. 5, p.25; Henry Laurens to Joseph Brown, October 11, 1765: "Conclude not hence that I am an advocate for the Stamp Tax. No, by no means. I would give, I would do, a great deal to procure a repeal of the Law which imposes it upon us, but I am sure that nothing but a regular, decent, becoming representation of the inexpediency & inutility of that Law will have the desir'd effect..."

[44] PHL, op. cit., Vol. 15, p.445; Henry Laurens to Secretaries of State, June 23, 1781. This was included in Henry's Petition for release from the Tower of London. See also Introduction, pp. 14-17.

[45] PHL, op. cit., Vol. 5, pp. 29-31; Henry Laurens to Joseph Brown, October 28, 1765.

⁴⁶ Moore, op. cit., p. 268.

⁴⁷ Moore, op. cit., p. 270.

⁴⁸ PHL, op. cit., Vol. 5, p. 298; Henry Laurens to James Habersham, September 5, 1767.

⁴⁹ PHL, op. cit., Vol. 5, p. 669; Henry Laurens to Richard Oswald, April 27, 1768.

⁵⁰ McDonough, op. cit., p. 86.

⁵¹ PHL, op. cit., Vol. 6, pp. 9-49.

⁵² PHL, op. cit., Vol. 6, p. 520. See also: Moore, op. cit., pp. 93-94.

⁵³ In response to *The Man Unmasked*, Henry published a second edition of his earlier pamphlet, *Extracts from the Proceedings of the Court of Vice-Admiralty in Charles-Town, South Carolina*, and another pamphlet entitled *Appendix to the Extracts*. The entire dispute took an even more bizar twist in 1772 when Henry learned that his young niece, Molly Bremar, had given birth to an illegitimate child and that the father was none other than Egerton Leigh, the husband of Molly's older sister.

⁵⁴ Wallace, op. cit., p. 152.

⁵⁵ See Chapter 3.

⁵⁶ Henry did not serve in the South Carolina Commons House of Assembly from January 1762-September 1762. He did return to the House from St. Michael's Parish in the general election which was held in October 1762.

⁵⁷ Professor W. Roy Smith as cited in Wallace, op. cit., p. 43.

⁵⁸ PHL, op. cit., Vol. 4, p. 467; Henry Laurens to Richard Oswald, October 10, 1764.

⁵⁹ PHL, op. cit., Vol. 7, pp. 374-375; Henry Laurens to James Habersham, October 1, 1770.

⁶⁰ PHL, op. cit., Vol. 7, p. 586; Henry Laurens to Benjamin Elliott, September 9, 1771.

⁶¹ Wallace, op. cit., p. 188.

⁶² PHL, op. cit., Vol. 8, pp. 473-474; Henry Laurens to Samuel Wainwright, September 23, 1772.

⁶³ PHL, op. cit., Vol. 9, p. 267; Henry Laurens to his brother James Laurens, February 5, 1774.

⁶⁴ PHL, op. cit., Vol. 15, p. 446; Henry Laurens to the Secretaries of State, June 23, 1781. (Henry discussed the topic in his Petition from the Tower of London.) The Petitions to the House of Commons, House of Lords and to the King can be found in Vol. 9, pp. 368-376.

⁶⁵ PHL, op. cit., Vol. 9, pp. 391 & 393; Henry Laurens to John Lewis Gervais, April 9, 1774. See also Introduction, p. 26.

[66] PHL, op. cit., Vol. 9, p. 354; Henry Laurens to his brother James Laurens, March 16, 1774.

[67] Wallace, op. cit., p. 197.

[68] Wallace, op. cit., p. 199.

[69] McDonough, op. cit., p. 148. The 184 delegates to the First Provincial Congress were chosen from every part of the colony, including 40 of the 48 members of the Commons House of Assembly. Mechanics and the Backcountry were also fairly well represented for the first time in South Carolina's legislative history.

[70] Wallace, op. cit., p. 204.

[71] PHL, op. cit., Vol. 10, p. 155; Henry Laurens to John Laurens, May 27, 1775.

[72] Wallace, op. cit., p. 205.

[73] PHL, op. cit., Vol. 10, p. 162; Henry Laurens to his brother James Laurens, June 7, 1775.

[74] PHL, op. cit., Vol. 10, p. 172; Henry Laurens to John Laurens, June 8, 1775, enclosure (the text of Henry's address to the Provincial Congress in his own hand).

[75] PHL, op. cit., Vol. 10, p. 182; Henry Laurens to John Laurens, June 18, 1775.

[76] McDonough, op. cit., p. 160.

[77] B. D. Bargar, Lord Dartmouth and the American Revolution (The University of South Carolina Press, Columbia, 1965), p. 175.

[78] PHL, op. cit., Vol. 10, pp. 396-397; Henry Laurens to John Laurens, September 18, 1775.

[79] PHL, op. cit., Vol. 10, p. 490; Henry Laurens to John Laurens, October 21, 1775.

[80] McDonough, op. cit., p. 166.

[81] JCC, op. cit., Vol. III, p. 280; October 6, 1775.

[82] Wallace, op. cit., p. 224. James Laurens, Henry's youngest son, died in London in 1776 from a fall. As a result, Henry appeared later that year at the reading of the Declaration of Independence at the Exchange Building in downtown Charleston wearing mourning clothes. Some radicals took offense. Henry responded: "I wept that day as I had done for the melancholy catastrophe which caused me to put on black clothes--the death of a son..."

[83] PHL, op. cit., Vol. 11, p. 4; Henry Laurens to James Laurens, January 6, 1776.

[84] JCC, op. cit., Vol. 3, pp. 326-327; Nov. 4, 1775.

[85] PHL, op. cit., Vol. 11, p. 194; Henry Laurens to John Laurens, March 28, 1776.

[86] PHL, op. cit., Vol. 11, p. 192; Henry Laurens to John Laurens, March 26, 1776.

[87] McDonough, op. cit., pp. 179-180.

[88] PHL, op. cit., Vol. 11, p. 228; Henry Laurens to John Laurens, August 14, 1776.

[89] PHL, op. cit., Vol. 11, p. 277; John Laurens to Henry Laurens, October 26, 1776. John's new wife, Martha Manning, was the daughter of Henry's old and dear friend, William Manning. Their daughter, Frances Eleanor, who was known as Fanny, was baptized on February 18, 1777. She was clearly an unplanned prenuptial pregnancy.

[90] George D. Massey, John Laurens and the American Revolution, (University of South Carolina Press, Columbia, 2000) pp. 66-71.

[91] PHL, op. cit., Vol. 11, p. 428; Henry Laurens to John Lewis Gervais, August 5, 1777 (additional note added on August 9, 1777).

[92] Massey, op. cit., pp. 75-77.

[93] PHL, op. cit., Vol. 11, p. 547; Henry Laurens to John Lewis Gervais, October 8, 1777. The Marquis de Lafayette himself was only 20 years old, two years younger than John Laurens.

[94] PHL, op. cit., Vol. 11, p. 446; Henry Laurens to John Rutledge, August 12, 1777.

[95] Wallace, op. cit., p. 238.

[96] PHL, op. cit., Vol. 12, pp. 220-221; Henry Laurens to John Lewis Gervais, December 30. 1777.

[97] See Chapter 10.

[98] PHL, op. cit., Vol. 12, p. 271; Henry Laurens to John Laurens, January 8, 1778.

[99] PHL, op. cit., Vol. 12, p. 389; George Washington to Henry Laurens, January 31, 1778.

[100] PHL, op. cit., Vol. 13, p. 221; George Washington to Henry Laurens, April 30, 1778.

[101] PHL, op. cit., Vol. 13, p. 257; Henry Laurens to George Washington, May 5, 1778.

[102] Under the compromise, officers who served for the duration would receive half-pay for seven years. Noncommissioned officers and enlisted men received a bonus.

[103] PHL, op. cit., Vol. 12, pp. 345-346; Henry Laurens to Isaac Motte, January 26, 1778.

[104] PHL, op. cit., Vol. 12, p. 358; Henry Laurens to William Livingston, January 27, 1778.

[105] PHL, op. cit., Vol. 13, p. 248; Henry Laurens to John Rutledge, May 4, 1778.

[106] JCC, op. cit., Vol. XI, p. 671; July 2, 1778.

[107] PHL, op. cit., Vol. 11, p. 493; Henry Laurens to John Lewis Gervais, September 5, 1777.

[108] LDC, op. cit., Vol. 11, p. 313.

[109] LDC, op. cit., Vol. 11, p. 316, footnote 1.

[110] LDC, op. cit., Vol. 11, p. 153; Charles Thomson's Draft Resolution of Congress, October 31, 1778.

[111] PHL, op. cit., Vol. 14, pp. 576-577; Henry Laurens: Resignation Speech, December 9, 1778.

[112] LDC, op. cit., Vol. 11, p. 322; James Duane to George Clinton, December 10, 1778. According to James Duane, "Jay was prevailed on to take the chair with a resolution on his part to resign in favor General Schuyler as soon as he attends." It never happened.

[113] The relationship between John Laurens and Alexander Hamilton has become a topic of increased speculation. In his 2000 biography of John Laurens, Gregory D. Massey, op. cit., states on pp. 80-81 that "Hamilton became John's closest friend. The young men expressed themselves in the language of sensibility. 'I wish, my Dear Laurens...to convince you that I love you,' said Hamilton '...you should not have taken advantage of my sensibility to steal into my affections without my consent.'" Massey argues that "Just as American political leaders looked to classical Greece and Rome as republican paradigms, young officers such as Laurens and Hamilton viewed the heroes of that earlier period as examples to be emulated." But, the author then concludes without any evidence that "Their relationship was platonic, a bond formed by their devotion to the Revolution and mutual ambition for fame." In similar fashion, on pp. 133-134, Massey dismisses Hamilton's obvious reference to the size of his penis in a letter addressed to John Laurens as simply an example of the "bawdy humor" common among officers at that time. But, he concludes by saying that "the passage is similar to much of Laurens's surviving correspondence: it raises more questions than it answers." It does indeed.

[114] PHL, op. cit., Vol. 15, p. 171; Henry Laurens to John Laurens, September 21, 1779.

[115] JCC, op. cit., Vol. XIV, p. 1008; Tuesday, August 31, 1779.

[116] PHL, op. cit., Vol. 15, p. 159; Henry Laurens To Committee of Congress, September 1, 1779.

[117] LDC, op. cit., Vol. 13, p. 445, Notes.

[118] PHL, op. cit., Vol. 15, pp. 307-309; Henry Laurens To Committee on Foreign Affairs, July 1, 1780.

[119] Massey, op. cit., pp. 162-163. John Laurens departed Charleston on June 12, 1780 on a troop ship. Under the conditions of his parole, John had pledged on his honor to remain in Pennsylvania until he could be officially exchanged for a British officer.

120 PHL, op. cit., Vol. 15, p. 335; Henry Laurens' *Journal and Narrative of Capture and Confinement in the Tower of London*, August 13, 1780-April 4, 1782.

121 PHL, op. cit., Vol. 15, p. 346; Henry Laurens' *Journal and Narrative of Capture and Confinement in the Tower of London*, August 13, 1780-April 4, 1782.

122 PHL, op. cit., Vol. 15, p. 356; Henry Laurens' *Journal and Narrative of Capture and Confinement in the Tower of London*, August 13, 1780-April 4, 1782.

123 PHL, op. cit., Vol. 15, p. 358; Henry Laurens' *Journal and Narrative of Capture and Confinement in the Tower of London*, August 13, 1780-April 4, 1782.

124 Wallace, op. cit., pp. 386-387.

125 PHL, op. cit., Vol. 15, pp. 443-453; Henry Laurens *Petition To Secretaries of State*, June 23, 1781.

126 Wallace, op. cit., pp. 386-387.

127 PHL, op. cit., Vol. 15, p. 391; Henry Laurens' *Journal and Narrative of Capture and Confinement in the Tower of London*, August 13, 1780-April 4, 1782.

128 Irving Brant, The Fourth President: A Life of James Madison, (The Bobbs-Merrill Company, Inc., Indianapolis, 1970), p. 89. Madison, as quoted by Brant, said on the floor of Congress: "This petition [Henry Laurens to the House of Commons] is stated not as coming from a citizen of the United States but a native of South Carolina. What is this but indirectly relinquishing the claim of independence which we have so solemnly declared and pledged ourselves to maintain at the risk of our lives and fortunes?" The Southern States, however, remained loyal to Henry as did the New England States which knew that he supported their critical fishing rights.

129 Wallace, op. cit., pp. 387-389.

130 PHL, op. cit., Vol. 15, p. 397; Henry Laurens' *Journal and Narrative of Capture and Confinement in the Tower of London*, August 13, 1780-April 4, 1782.

131 PHL, op. cit., Vol. 16, p. 53; John Adams to Henry Laurens, November 6, 1782.

132 PHL, op. cit., Vol. 16, p. 55; Henry Laurens to John Adams, November 12, 1782. The Col. Parker Henry referenced was killed in the siege of Charleston on April 24, 1780.

133 Richard B. Morris, The Peacemakers: The Great Powers and American Independence, (Harper & Row, Publishers, New York, 1965), p. 377.

134 Wallace, op. cit., p. 412.

135 JCC, op. cit., Vol. XXVII, p. 649; November 30, 1784.

136 *SC Gazette and Public Advertiser*, January 15-19, 1785.

137 Wallace, op. cit., p. 424.

138 LDC, op. cit., Vol. 24, p. 303.

[139] PHL, op. cit., Vol. 16, pp. 738 & 739n; Henry Laurens to William Bell, October 11, 1787 and Henry Laurens to Edward Bridgen, October 8, 1787.

[140] Edmund Cody Burnett, The Continental Congress, (The Macmillan Company, New York,1941), p. 640. David Ramsay served for several months as the temporary chairman of the Continental Congress pending the arrival of former President Hancock who had been elected to a new term. Hancock, however, never did return due to his health.

[141] Gillespie, op. cit., pp. 3-4.

[142] It is worth noting that both of Henry's sons-in-law were also original members of the Board of Trustees of the new College of Charleston which Henry so strongly supported. J. H. Easterby, A History of the College of Charleston, (The Scribner Press, 1935) pp. 20-21.

[143] Massey, op. cit., pp. 235-237.

[144] Wallace, op. cit., p. 431. In 1936, Mepkin Plantation was sold to Time Magazine publisher, Henry Luce and his famous wife, The Hon. Clare Boothe Luce. Unlike the Laurens Family, their graves are prominently displayed and cared for due to the trust they established for that purpose. In 1949, the new owners donated a major portion of Mepkin to a Catholic religious order of monks. Today, it is a Cistercian-Trappist Abbey which is open to the public on a daily schedule and also hosts special events such as those related to the annual Piccolo Spoleto Festival in late Spring.

[145] Harry Laurens' legal name was Henry Laurens, Jr., but he was called Harry throughout his life.

[146] David Ramsay, Memoirs of the Life of Martha Laurens Ramsay, (Philadelphia, 1811), pp. 207-210.

[147] PHL, op. cit., Vol. 16, p. 801; Will of Henry Laurens, November 1, 1792. (On December 6, 2002, Al Neuharth, the founder of USA TODAY devoted his daily column to the cremation of President Henry Laurens. Unfortunately, he did get the date wrong. According to Martha Laurens' Memoirs, the actual cremation was performed on Tuesday, December 11, 1792.)

[148] PHL, op. cit., Vol. 16, p. 111; Henry Laurens to his sister-in-law, Mary Laurens, December 30, 1782.

[149] Jacob A. Nelson, John Hanson and the Inseparable Union, (Meador Publishing Company, Boston, 1939), p. 114. In 1776, Lt. Peter Contee Hanson, the son of John Hanson, the eighth President of the Continental Congress (1781-1782), was wounded at Fort Washington in New York and subsequently died of his injuries while being held as a British prisoner of war. Dr. Samuel Hanson, John Hanson's older son, served as a surgeon in Washington's Life Gurads and died in 1781 from illness he contracted in the line of duty. See also: Chapter 8.

[150] Massey, op. cit., p. 227. As Mordecai Gist reported to Gen. Nathanael Greene, John Laurens was originally buried at the Stock Family Plantation near the Combahee River close to where he fell in battle. Harry, John's younger brother, left instructions in his Will in 1821, that John's remains were to be reinterred at Mepkin next to his father. Some

accounts, however, indicate that this was done much earlier. In either case, the tombstones at the Laurens Family Graveyard today include Harry Laurens and his wife Eliza Rutledge Laurens, Henry's youngest daughter, Mary Eleanor Pinckney, and Henry Laurens, the 4th President of the Continental Congress, alongside his son, John.

WHILE HENRY LAURENS
WAS PRESIDENT

Notes

Abbreviation Key

JCC   Journals of the Continental Congress
LDC   Letters of Delegates to Congress
PHL   The Papers of Henry Laurens

[151] Piers Mackesy, The War for America, 1775-1783, (Harvard University Press, Cambridge, 1965), pp. 211-214. According to Mackesy: "The army in the rebel colonies had a strength at that moment [May 1778] of nearly 27,000 rank and file fit for duty: 8,400 at New York, 3,500 at Rhode Island, and 14,700 with the main force in Philadelphia."

[152] Stephen R. Taaffe, The Philadelphia Campaign, 1777-1778, (University Press of Kansas, 2003), pp. 90 & 172. (Taaffe also estimates that the British forces in Philadelphia numbered 16,800 [2,100 more than Mackesy's total]. p. 169.)

[153] Worthington Chauncey Ford, Chief, Division of Manuscripts, JCC, (Library of Congress, Washington, DC, 1907), pp. 906-928. The Articles of Confederation were not ratified for more than three years. They finally went into effect on March 1,1781. See also: Chapter 8.

[154] From 1774-1781, the Continental Congress had maximum flexibility provided that it could convince the States to cooperate. Once the Articles of Confederation went into effect, however, its precise rules and procedures put Congress in a box, seriously limiting both its power and its ability to respond to unforeseen situations. The most fatal flaw was the inability of Congress to raise adequate revenue. The war had served as a common enemy which glued the 13 States together. Once that threat was removed, the Articles became more of a straitjacket than an effective structure of national government.

[155] David McCullough, John Adams, (Simon & Schuster, New York, 2001), pp. 174-177. When the news of his appointment arrived, Adams had already moved back home to Braintree, Massachusetts where he was attempting to resume his private life. His wife Abigail was furious at the latest disruption of her family and the thought of further separation. Their 10 year old son, John Quincy Adams, did accompany his father. It was the first of many overseas assignments for the boy who became one of America's greatest diplomats and the sixth President under the Constitution (1825-1829).

[156] Joseph B. Doyle, Frederick William von Steuben and The American Revolution, (The H. C. Cook Company, Steubenville, Ohio, 1913), pp. 63-64 & 81-93. On December 23, 1783, Washington wrote "...the last letter I shall write while I continue in the service of my

country" to Von Steuben to express "the sense of the obligations the public is under to you for your faithful and meritorious services..." (p. 307). Even though the Baron has long been the hero of German-Americans, he also holds the added distinction of being America's gay Founding Father. In fact, he came to America precisely because his reputation had been challenged in Europe in a letter addressed to the Prince of Hohenzollern-Hechingen on August 13, 1777, in which the unknown author stated that "It has come to me from different sources that M. de Steuben is accused of having taken familiarities with young boys..." See also: John McAuley Palmer, General von Steuben, (Yale University Press, New Haven, 1937), p. 92. Today, the statue which honors Von Steuben on the Northwest corner of Lafayette Square across from The White House captures his personal preference in surprising detail. The sculptor, Albert Jaegers, depicts a young naked soldier stroking his sword in a highly suggestive manner before an older naked officer. See also: George H. Carter (compiled by), *Proceedings Upon the Unveiling of the Statue of Baron von Steuben*, Joint Committee on Printing of the United States Congress, Washington, DC. President William Howard Taft apparently missed the homoerotic significance of the depiction when he dedicated the memorial on December 7, 1910.

[157] Andreas Latzko, Lafayette: A Life, (The Literary Guild, New York, 1936), pp. 63-64.

[158] Benson Bobrick, Angel in the Whirlwind, (Simon & Schuster, New York, 1997), p. 338.

[159] Stanley Ayling, The Elder Pitt, (David McKay Company, Inc., New York, 1976), pp. 424-425. "Chatham, in some turmoil, struggled to raise himself again to answer the Duke [of Richmond], succeeded at last in getting to his feet, but was unable to stay on them, pressed his hand to his heart, swayed alarmingly, sank back, and was prevented from falling to the floor only by the rescuing arms of neighboring peers, one of them Lord Temple." Pitt died on May 11, 1778.

[160] JCC, op. cit., Vol. XI, pp. 574-575; June 6, 1778.

[161] John C. Miller, Triumph of Freedom, 1775-1783, (Little, Brown and Company, Boston, 1948), pp. 228-229. "In the autumn of 1777 Howe decided that the time had come to retire from such an unpropitious struggle."

[162] JCC, op. cit., Vol. XI, p. 671; July 2, 1778.

[163] Craig L. Symonds, A Battlefield Atlas of the American Revolution, (The Nautical & Aviation Publishing Company of America, Inc., 1986), p. 72. Clark then captured Cahokia five days later.

[164] Unfortunately, the French fleet proved to be a serious disappointment to Congress and the Army in its initial engagements, often due to extreme caution or simply bad luck. But, during the siege and surrender of the British Army at Yorktown in October 1781, the French fleet was absolutely essential to victory.

[165] Paul H. Smith, Editor, LDC, (Library of Congress, Washington, DC, 1983), Vol. 10, pp. xiii-xv, July 30, 1778, September 5, 1778 & September 26, 1778; Chronology of Congress.

John Jay

Chapter 5

President
JOHN JAY
of
NEW YORK

Reluctant Revolutionary

When the Continental Congress first met on the morning of Monday, September 5, 1774, one of the least known delegates was an attorney from New York by the name of John Jay. At the age of 28, he was the second youngest member of the assembly and a total neophyte when it came to revolutionary politics. He had been selected by his colony because of his sharp legal mind and his conservative, pro-business connections. John's assignment was to temper his more fiery colleagues and undermine another financially disastrous boycott of British goods. Over the next two months, however, John gradually embraced the moderate wing of the Patriot cause as he learned first hand the details of Parliament's flagrant violation of colonial rights across the continent.

From that first Congress, John's reputation for selfless devotion to duty expanded exponentially. Over the next quarter century he held positions of leadership in all three branches of government at both the state and national levels, a record never again matched by any other American. Two days before his thirty-third birthday he became the youngest President in United States history and, at the end of his distinguished career, he was twice elected Governor of New York. He also served with distinction in both the Continental Congress and the New York Assembly. The Judiciary, however, was always John's first love. He became New York State's first Chief Justice and, a decade later, the first Chief Justice of the United States. But his greatest contribution was as a diplomat. John labored for months as the primary author of the Treaty of Paris which ended the Revolutionary War and forced Britain to recognize American Independence. And, after returning to America, he served as Secretary for Foreign Affairs during the final years of the Continental Congress.

Like his presidential predecessor, Henry Laurens, the journey which led John Jay to his unique American destiny began almost a century earlier in France when King Louis XIV revoked the Edict of Nantes which had provided some legal protection for French Protestants in that intensely Catholic Kingdom. Starting in 1685, French Huguenots were once again declared outlaws who faced discrimination and loss of property rights. Nearly 200,000 fled France in a diaspora which led across Europe and, for some, ultimately to America.[1]

John's great grandfather, Pierre Jay, was a prominent merchant in the village of La Rochelle in Western France when government-sanctioned discrimination was reimposed. He, his wife and his youngest children were eventually able to escape to England where they lived the rest of their lives. His oldest son, Augustus, pursued a different path. Augustus Jay had been out of the country when the rest of the family fled France. His extensive travels eventually led him to America where he married Anna Maria Bayard in 1697. Years later, John commented that his grandfather, because of his marriage, "became encircled with friends who...were disposed to promote his interest as a merchant, and his social happiness as a man..."[2]

The Jays had three daughters, who eventually married into prominent New York families, and one son, born in 1704, whom they named Peter in honor of his grandfather. At the age of 20, Peter Jay joined his father's merchant firm and eventually became a wealthy partner. He also served as an alderman of the City of New York in the 1740s and, despite his Huguenot roots, as an elder of Trinity Church, "the most powerful and fashionable [Anglican] church in the province."[3]

On January 31, 1728, Peter Jay married Mary Van Cortlandt, a member of another of New York's most powerful families. Like her husband, she was also of Huguenot descent. They had ten children. Their eighth child, the future President, was born on the evening of December 12, 1745, at the family home in New York City. As he would occasionally point out in later years, unlike most of his revolutionary colleagues, not one of John Jay's great grandparents had English blood.[4]

Once he secured his fortune, Peter Jay was happy to retire to the life of a country gentleman. He purchased a farm in Rye, on the shores of Long Island Sound (approximately 25 miles from New York City), and relocated his large family to their new country estate in early 1746, only weeks after John's birth. The ease with which he turned his back on the lure of city life for the pastoral joys of his rural retreat was repeated over a half century later when his son, the President, did the same.

Freed from the demands of business, Peter Jay focused his attention on the care and education of his children. He was delighted by John's rapid progress. "Johnny...takes to learning exceedingly well..." the proud father wrote to his older son, James, in 1752. "My Johnny gives me a very pleasing prospect," he told another correspondent a year later, "he seems to be endowed with a very good capacity, is very reserved and quite of his brother James's disposition for books."[5]

At the age of 8, John was sent to a grammar school at New Rochelle, New York to live and study under the tutelage of the Rev. Mr. Stouppe, the pastor of the local French Church. For the next three years he survived spartan conditions on a daily diet of the French language rather then French cuisine. John then returned home to continue his studies under a private tutor before entering the newly established King's College (now Columbia University) in New York City on August 29, 1760.[6] Even though he was only 14, John was by now remarkably self-reliant, thanks, in part, to Pastor Stouppe's conditioning. He was also intensely devoted to his education. He worked tirelessly on correcting a minor speech impediment (difficulty in pronouncing the letter "L") and the habit of speaking too rapidly when reading aloud. The book that had the greatest impact on him was *Plutarch's Lives* and its "idealized picture of the stoical virtues of republican antiquity."[7]

At his graduation on May 22, 1764, John was chosen to deliver an address to a distinguished audience which included Gen. Thomas Gage, Commander-in-Chief of British Forces in North America.[8] John's topic focused on the blessings of peace. Exactly a decade later, these two men would represent opposing sides in the life or death struggle over that same issue.

Ten days after graduation John began his study of the law. He joined Benjamin Kissam's office as an entry level clerk performing repetitious tasks that would have discouraged all but the most determined from pursuing a legal career. As always, John soldiered on as he mastered the legal process, devoured law books and developed a close rapport with his employer and fellow clerks. Years later another of Kissam's employees said of John: "... he was remarkable for strong reasoning powers, comprehensive views, indefatigable application, and uncommon firmness of mind."[9] By 1766, John was responsible for much of the office's routine legal business as well as managing affairs in Kissam's absence. The following year he was awarded a Master of Arts degree from King's College.[10] In October 1768, John was finally admitted to the bar.

What is most surprising about John's internship period is the lack of any significant response from him to the momentous political developments concerning the Stamp Act crisis of 1765-66 or the Townshend Duties the following year. While Peyton Randolph and Henry Middleton were desperately trying to steer Virginia and South Carolina through these crises, and John Hancock and Henry Laurens were wealthy merchants fighting on the front lines, John Jay simply observed developments from the sidelines. In his letters from that period, there is no mention of politics.[11] Unlike his four presidential predecessors, his connection to the crisis was at best secondhand. Since no legal work could be transacted during the crisis, John and his close friend Robert R. Livingston, Jr..decided to take a "New England frolic" rather than join in the protest.[12] As Kissam, his employer, wrote to him in April 1766: "...on the Repeal of the Stamp Act we shall doubtless have a luxuriant harvest of law..."[13]

John's primary focus remained squarely on his new legal career. After completing his internship, John formed a three year partnership with Livingston. In their earlier correspondence, John had described their friendship as "unbounded" and "unlimited"[14] as he presented an extremely rare insight into his personal life by describing the contrast between the two friends: "It appeared to me that you [Livingston] had more vivacity" John wrote. "Bashfulness and pride rendered me more staid. Both equally ambitious but pursuing it in different roads. You flexible, I pertinacious... Both possessed of warm passions, but you of more self-possession...You understood men and women early, I knew them not..."[15]

In November 1770, John joined with 17 other lawyers throughout New York City (including his future father-in-law, William Livingston) in establishing "The Moot," a club that met once a month at a local tavern to debate disputed points of law. He also became a member of the New York Social Club, one of the most fashionable in the city.[16] Through these gatherings, and others, John became well known to many of the most powerful men in the city and gradually acquired social graces while also developing a taste for Madeira, the most popular of colonial wines.

In 1771, John and his close friend decided to disband their legal partnership but not their friendship. Business continued to boom. Over the next three years and eight months John handled approximately 362 cases.[17] As he wrote to his old employer, Samuel Kissam, "With respect to business I am as well circumstanced as I have a right to expect...and upon the whole I have reason to be satisfied with my share of the attention of Providence."[18] During this period, John also had his first taste of public service as the clerk of the New York-New Jersey Boundary Commission where he first met Peyton Randolph, the future President, who was then the Speaker of the Virginia House of Burgesses and a prominent member of the commission.[19]

Unfortunately, John's love life initially proved less successful than his legal career. He courted and eventually proposed to one of the beautiful daughters of Peter de Lancey, head of a politically powerful New York family loyal to the Crown. She rejected John for another. After a proper interval, he then pursued De Lancey's other daughter with the same ego-shattering result.[20] John eventually turned to the Livingston family, the De Lanceys' arch rival, and asked for the hand of Sarah Livingston. Her father, William Livingston, one of the most prominent opponents of British policies, knew John from "The Moot." He was delighted by the match and his daughter readily accepted. On April 28, 1774, John and his "Sally" were married in the great parlor of Liberty Hall, the new Livingston mansion in Elizabeth Town, New Jersey.[21] It was the beginning of a lifelong romance and a powerful political alliance.

Exactly two weeks later, on May 12, colonial politics seized center stage. News reached New York that Parliament had voted to close Boston Harbor in retaliation for the Boston Tea Party the previous December.[22] The message was clear. Britain intended to make an example of Massachusetts in order to intimidate the rest of her American Empire.

New York radicals immediately assembled their Committee of Vigilance and sent a letter pledging total support to their Boston compatriots. At the same time they issued a call for a larger assembly in order to initiate a new boycott. At this point, New York business leaders became more alarmed over popular reaction to the Boston Port Act than the law itself. When the next meeting convened on the evening of May 16, merchants outnumbered radicals. A new "Committee of Fifty-One" was ultimately nominated. Three days later, at yet another public gathering, its membership was ratified. Conservatives, many of whom had known and respected John's father and grandfather, now held the upper hand. Because of his family ties and his reputation as an up-and-coming lawyer, John was elected as a member of this committee's new majority.[23]

The great irony is that John was not even present at this fateful turning point in his life. He had been away on legal business and did not return to the city until May 22.[24] In characteristic fashion, however, he threw himself into his new assignment as a member of a subcommittee which rescinded the blanket pledge of support from the old Committee of Vigilance. Instead, John and his colleagues endorsed the convening of a general Congress in order to ward off an immediate boycott.

The radicals tried unsuccessfully to regain control of developments by calling a "Great Meeting in the Fields" in early July at which 19-year-old Alexander Hamilton launched his political career.[25] But, by the end of the month, the official Committee of Fifty-One won support for a mildly conservative slate of New York delegates to the First Continental Congress, including John.

Over the next four weeks, John worked tirelessly trying to clear his desk before departing for Philadelphia on August 29. He traveled alone to Elizabeth Town where he joined his father-in-law who had been elected a delegate from New Jersey. Once Congress began on September 5, despite his youth and inexperience, John was an active participant from the start. He initially questioned the choice of Carpenter's Hall and challenged the nomination of a non-delegate, Charles Thomson, for the office of secretary.[26] When, on the second day of deliberations, Patrick Henry declared that "Government is dissolved," John immediately rebutted this notion by stating that "The measure of arbitrary power is not full, and I think that it must run over, before we undertake to frame a new constitution..."[27]

During the first week of deliberations, John and James Duane were the two New York delegates selected to serve on the committee to articulate the rights and grievances of the colonies. A month later, John also became the primary author of the Address to the People of Great Britain. Thomas Jefferson later wrote that that Address was "a production certainly of the finest pen in America..."[28] John also expressed strong support for the Galloway Plan which called for the establishment of a provincial American Congress subservient to the Crown.[29]

John's goal throughout this First Continental Congress was reconciliation with the Mother Country, not separation. He was certainly among the majority of delegates who, in the words of one of his earliest biographers, "started back with horror from the abyss of revolution."[30] As John wrote from Philadelphia on September 24, 1774: "God knows how the Contest will end. I sincerely wish it may terminate in a lasting Union with Great Britain."[31]

In the end, like most of his fellow conservatives, John did vote for the Continental Association, the most ambitious boycott ever attempted by the colonies.[32]

He knew that only a united effort on this measure offered any hope of avoiding a far deeper conflict. To him, the alternative was simply unthinkable. As he left Philadelphia in late October, John was no longer an obscure attorney from New York. He had earned the respect and recognition of his peers through his powers of debate as well as his prolific pen.

When the New York delegates returned home, the radicals showered praise on them for approving the continent-wide boycott. Overnight, John and his colleagues were proclaimed Patriot heroes and most of them were elected to a new sixty-member Committee of Inspection, which was charged with the responsibility of enforcing the boycott. In response, some conservative merchants abandoned hope and sided openly with the

Royal Government. Others struggled on, still trying to moderate the mob. Increasingly, John found himself the link between these factions.

The Colonial Assembly of New York met in January 1775, but refused to even recognize the Continental Congress, much less its resolutions. By now, however, the pace of developments rendered the old legislature meaningless and the Assembly adjourned for the last time on April 3.[33] Seventeen days later a new Provincial Convention met in New York City and elected a dozen delegates, including John, to represent New York at the Second Continental Congress.[34]

Then, on Sunday, April 23, the entire city was thrown into turmoil when news of the Battles of Lexington and Concord spread through the streets. In typical New York fashion, yet another, larger Committee of one hundred was chosen on May 1, 1775, to deal with these explosive developments. Once again, John was elected to this newest body but he only attended a few meetings before leaving for Philadelphia and the next session of Congress which opened on May 10.[35]

In stark contrast to his initial arrival in Philadelphia the previous fall, John was now one of the best known congressional delegates. As one biographer described him: "His tall thin figure, with the colorless complexion, the clear penetrating eyes, the aquiline nose and the pointed chin, dressed in black with hair highly powdered, was a familiar sight on the floor and in the committee rooms of the Congress."[36] His first major assignment of the new session was to draft a letter to the inhabitants of Canada in "hopes of your uniting with us in the defence of our common liberty..."[37] Canadians, however, were well aware of the anti-Catholic bias displayed by Congress and were far from convinced that their southern neighbors would be victorious.[38] Canada remained loyal to the Crown.

John also joined forces with John Dickinson of Pennsylvania in urging his colleagues to submit one final petition to the King. John Adams, reminding the delegates that war had already begun, denounced the idea as a "measure of imbecility."[39] To Patrick Henry and Richard Henry Lee it simply confirmed their negative opinion of Mr. Jay. Despite their opposition, on Saturday, June 3, 1775, John introduced the motion for what came to be known as the "Olive Branch Petition."[40] In the end, when it was ignored by the King, that imperial disdain forced even the more reluctant revolutionaries like John to turn toward Independence.

In late June, John was assigned to the Committee to prepare a "Declaration on Taking Up Arms" which would be delivered by the newly appointed Commander-in-Chief, George Washington, upon his arrival in Boston. At the request of his father-in-law, John also authored the "Address to the People of Ireland" which was adopted by Congress on July 28.[41] In late November, John was appointed to the committee to establish secret correspondence with friends in Great Britain, Ireland and throughout the world. During the month of December John's work load was so heavy that he was denied permission by Congress to return home to be with his pregnant wife over Christmas, but he assured her that "nothing but actual Imprisonment will be able to keep me from you" when the time arrived for the delivery of their first child. [42]

John proved true to his word. He was there at Sally's side at her father's New Jersey mansion when she gave birth to Peter Augustus on January 24, 1776, the first of their seven children.[43] Several weeks later he returned to Philadelphia where he served until early May, but the illness of his parents was foremost in his mind. As he told a friend: "The Prospect of being soon deprived of a Father and a Mother whom you know I tenderly love...have occasioned more gloomy Ideas in my mind than it has ever before been the Subject of. Despondency however ill becomes a man...It gives me Consolation...that our great and benevolent Creator will...be my Guide thro this Vale of Tears..."[44] During that period, he was elected a delegate to the State Provincial Congress and summoned back to New York to assist his state in its critical transition.

On May 25 he took his seat in the Third New York Provincial Congress. John concluded that this assembly did not have a popular mandate to decide the issue of independence and therefore joined with those who called for new elections. National developments, however, could not wait for New York. Richard Henry Lee's Virginia Resolution was introduced in the Continental Congress on June 7, 1776, and approved with one abstention (New York) on July 2.[45] Despite his distinguished congressional career since the inception of Congress, John was away trying to resolve New York's dilemma when the Declaration of Independence was adopted two days later and ultimately signed by the delegates in early August.[46] In characteristic fashion he sacrificed the unique title of "Signer" out of a sense of duty to the cause.

When New York's Fourth Provincial Congress finally met at White Plains on July 9, 1776, the members unanimously adopted a resolution, drafted by John, which authorized their delegates in Philadelphia to add New York's name to the Declaration.[47] It was an act of courage and defiance. At that moment, 15,000 British and Hessian forces were pouring into New York as more than 150 British ships plied the coast.[48] New York City was the occupation headquarters, and would remain so until the very end of the war. The legislature, now known as the Convention of the Representatives of the State of New York, had to struggle for survival in the face of such overwhelming military presence while attempting to establish a new form of government. As John wrote to his beloved Sally in late July: "In these days of uncertainty we can be certain only of the present; the future must be the object rather of hope than expectation."[49]

John was again in the eye of the storm. He was appointed to a Secret Committee to secure the Hudson River. He also became a member of the Committee for Detecting Conspiracies which spent the Fall of 1776 attempting to root out Tories and enemy spies. In the process he developed a network of agents throughout the city who kept him remarkably well informed of British troop movements. Despite his herculean tasks at home, his colleagues in Philadelphia pleaded with him to return to the Continental Congress as soon as possible. Robert Morris wrote to John on September 23, 1776, that "...such Men as you, in times like these, shou'd be every where."[50] This momentous year ended when John authored the "Address of the Convention of the State of New York to their Constituents."[51]

Despite his heavy workload, John was an obvious choice for the committee to draft a new State Constitution. Even though he did not chair the committee, he became one of the primary authors of the document which was presented to the Convention on March 12, 1777.[52] Most of the report was well-received, but John's repeated attempts to exclude Catholics from the guarantees of religious freedom if their allegiance to the Pope proved "...inconsistent with the safety of civil society..." was hotly debated.[53] John's conservative beliefs were also reflected in his proposal to limit those eligible to vote for State Senators to men who held property. As William Jay stated in his biography of his father: "...it being a favourite maxim with Mr. Jay, that those who own the country ought to govern it."[54] Where slavery was concerned, however, John pleaded without success that "...in future ages every human being who breathes the air of this State shall enjoy the privileges of a freeman."[55]

When the new state constitution was finally adopted on April 20, 1777, John was once again unable to participate in the signing due to the death of his mother a few days earlier. Despite the haste with which it was drafted, and the failure of several key provisions, New York's first constitution endured for more than forty years.[56]

On May 3, 1777, even though he was still away attending to family business, John was elected as the first Chief Justice of New York.[57] He was also appointed to the new fifteen-member Council of Safety which was charged with managing affairs until elections were held. And, when he did return four days later, John discovered that he was one of four potential candidates for governor. He was determined to discourage such speculation. As he wrote to a colleague: "...my Object in the Course of the present Great Contest has neither been nor will be, either Rank or Money.

I am persuaded that I can be more useful to the State in the office I now hold [Chief Justice], than in the one alluded to, and therefore think it my Duty to continue in it."[58] John ultimately threw his support to Gen. Philip Schuyler but, on July 31, 1777, the more radical faction delighted in the inauguration of Gen. George Clinton who would soon prove to be John's nemesis over the next two decades.

While still serving on the Council of Safety, John opened the first session of the New York Supreme Court at Kingston on September 9, 1777. For the next year he devoted his energy to developing the court system and helping to implement the new state constitution.

But by late 1778, a decade-old dispute over control of the Vermont territory forced John back onto the national stage. As Vermont appealed to the Continental Congress for recognition as the fourteenth state, New York decided to send its brightest legal mind to argue on behalf of its claim to the Vermont territory. Without having to resign his seat on the Court, John returned to Philadelphia on Monday, December 7, 1778.

Even though the issue of Vermont prompted John's return to the Continental Congress (an issue that was not resolved until Vermont won statehood early in the Second Republic) it was the heated debate over Silas Deane's diplomatic service that held center stage upon his arrival in Philadelphia. As described in Chapter 4, Congress had appointed both Silas Deane and Arthur Lee to assist Benjamin Franklin in procuring aid from the French Court prior to a formal alliance. Lee, the brother of Richard Henry Lee, one of the most influential members of Congress, had written from France, charging Deane with corruption. Deane's supporters, including John Jay, strenuously defended their friend. Two days after John's arrival, President Henry Laurens, a Lee supporter, demanded that Deane be further investigated before again being permitted to address Congress. When the delegates narrowly defeated the motion on December 8, Laurens resigned in disgust.[59]

To his amazement, 32-year-old John Jay was elected as the fifth President of Congress the following morning.[60] His friend and fellow delegate Gouverneur Morris described his interpretation of events to Governor Clinton that same day: "The weight of his [Jay"s] personal Character contributed as much to his Election as the Respect for the State which hath done and suffered so much or the Regard for its Delegates which is not inconsiderable."[61] Another New York Delegate, James Duane, viewed developments differently: "A great majority of Congress immediately determined that one of the New York Delegates should succeed in the Chair. We held up General Schuyler, which seemed to be very agreeable. On account of his absence, Mr. Jay was prevailed on to take the chair with a resolution on his part to resign in favor of General Schuyler as soon as he attends."[62] Whatever the exact circumstances, John continued to serve as the youngest American President for the next ten months.

John's amazing elevation to the highest office marked a significant departure from congressional precedent. Unlike Randolph and Middleton, who were selected for their eminence at the end of distinguished careers, John was still a young man just making a name for himself. And, unlike Hancock and Laurens, he was not one of the wealthiest and most powerful men in the new nation. As he would write to a friend a few years later: " I know how to live within the limits of any income, however narrow."[63] John was chosen for his New York connection, sharp legal mind and unblemished reputation for honesty and diligence. His election also prompted Congress to finally appropriate money for a presidential residence complete with servants and carriage, perquisites of the office that continued throughout the First Republic.[64] His young wife, however, lamented the additional separation they would have to endure. "How long am I still to remain in a state of widowhood?" she wrote shortly after hearing the news.[65]

In mid-December 1778, Gen. Washington visited Philadelphia where he held several conferences with the new President. The deplorable state of the economy and its impact on the Army were at the top of their agenda. The urgent need for financial assistance from both France and Spain appeared to them and most members of Congress as the only immediate solution. As John confided to Washington a few months later: "There is as much Intrigue in this State House as in the Vatican, but as little secrecy as in a boarding School."[66]

The French minister, Gerard, and his Spanish counterpart, Don Juan de Mirales, were already in Philadelphia where they apparently misinterpreted John's quiet style of diplomacy. "I have reason to think," John observed with obvious amusement, "that both of them entertained higher opinions of my docility than were well founded."[67] Since the US-French Alliance of February 1778 had again brought the kingdom into direct conflict with Britain, Gerard and his government were eager to draw Spain into the war. To do so, however, Spain demanded recognition from the United States of its claim to Florida and its exclusive navigation rights on the Mississippi River. In effect, "she yearned to transform the Gulf of Mexico into a Spanish lake."[68]

As President, John devoted an increasing amount of time and energy to these critical foreign and financial issues. "It was therefore my opinion," John recorded at the time, "that we should quit all claim to the Floridas, and grant Spain the navigation on her river below our territories, on her giving us a convenient free port on it, under regulations to be specified in a treaty, provided they would acknowledge our Independence, defend it with their arms, and grant us...a proper sum of money..."[69] (As the situation evolved, John ultimately reversed his position and insisted on free navigation of the Mississippi.)

That August, 1779, the Chevalier de la Luzerne arrived in America to replace Minister Gerard. He brought with him news that Spain had declared war on Britain on June 21. The urgent need for parallel developments on the diplomatic front was now obvious. Accordingly, on September 27, Congress appointed John Adams as Peace Commissioner and President John Jay as Minister Plenipotentiary to Spain. The next day, Samuel Huntington of Connecticut was elected to replace John as the sixth President of Congress. And, on October 21, former President Henry Laurens was selected as Minister to The Netherlands in order to secure a major loan and establish a commercial treaty. As described in the previous chapter, Laurens never reached his destination. He was captured by the British on the high seas in September 1780 and eventually confined in the dreaded Tower of London for fifteen months.[70]

John's fate was nearly as torturous, even though his surroundings were far more elegant. His voyage across the Atlantic was fraught with danger and his two-year residence in Spain produced immense frustration. John, his wife and the other six members of his official party finally reached Madrid on April 4, 1780, but, because Spain still had not granted diplomatic recognition to the United States, John was never accorded the courtesy nor the access commiserate with his rank. Nevertheless, season after season, he followed the Spanish Court as it traveled from one region to another.

John's goal was to establish a treaty with Spain and to secure a loan of five million Spanish dollars. Just as a glimmer of hope appeared in July 1780, news of the surrender of Charleston had the effect "...of a hard night's frost on young leaves."[71] In hindsight, it is abundantly clear that Spain's Catholic Monarchy feared rather than favored the new American Republic. King Charles III and his ministers understood all-too-well that a vast Protestant Empire pressed against Spain's foreign domain was hardly in their nation's best interest. Opposition to Great Britain was the only point on which both countries agreed.

In the end, almost nothing was accomplished, but John had learned the hard lessons of European diplomacy which would prove invaluable in his next critical assignment. As he confided to his friend and colleague Gouverneur Morris: "This government [Spain] has little Money, less Wisdom, no Credit, nor any right to it."[72] John's life in Spain was also personally painful in many ways. During their residence in Madrid, his wife gave birth to two daughters, but the first only survived a few weeks.

His official family was also a source of constant heartache. They were completely dysfunctional. Not one of his assistants proved to be either loyal or reliable.[73]

Through it all, "The State of New York is never out of my mind nor heart," he wrote to a friend. Nor was his abhorrence of slavery, as he mentioned in that same letter: "I believe God governs this world, and I believe it to be a maxim in his as in our court, that those who ask for equity ought to do it."[74] In late April 1782, John shared a few concluding thoughts on Spain with his friend Robert Morris: "...I confess that I find little here that resembles, and nothing that can compensate for, the free air, the free conversation, the equal liberty, and the other numerous blessings which God and nature, and the laws of our making, have given and secured to our happier country."[75]

The previous June, Congress had appointed John as a member of the Peace Commission.[76] Four months later, the British surrendered at Yorktown. In March 1782, Lord North's Government collapsed.[77] At long last, the prospects for peace were real. In early May 1782, John received word from Franklin in Paris that "...your constant residence at Madrid is no longer so necessary...Here you are greatly wanted."[78] And then, on June 17, as John and his family were making their difficult journey toward Paris, Parliament passed the Enabling Act which authorized peace with America. It was finally time to assume his new duties at the Peace table along with his colleagues, Franklin, Adams and Laurens.

When John arrived in the French Capital on June 23, he wasted no time in tackling his new assignment. After escorting his family to the Hotel de la Chine, he immediately joined Dr. Franklin, the only other American Commissioner in Paris, at his home on the outskirts of the city. There, America's most experienced diplomat brought John up to date on recent developments. The very next day the two Commissioners called on the French Foreign Minister, the Comte de Vergennes.[79] By the end of the month, however, the entire Jay family came down with the flu that was then epidemic in Paris and John was bedridden for nearly three weeks.[80]

The day after Jay fell ill, the British Government was shaken by the sudden death of the King's First Minister, the Marquis of Rockingham, who had replaced North. Since Parliament was scheduled to adjourn in only ten days, Lord Shelburne, who was selected by George III to form a new Government, knew that he had to complete the Peace negotiations before the legislators returned in early December or else he, too, would be forced from office. To the British negotiators, time was of the essence. This fact proved to be of enormous benefit to the United States.

During John's illness, Franklin drew up a list of American demands and presented them to Richard Oswald, the chief British negotiator, who also happened to be an old friend from Franklin's years as a lobbyist in London. In early August, Oswald's official commission finally reached Paris. He was authorized to treat and conclude peace with the commissioners of "the said colonies or plantations..."[81] Franklin found the document acceptable and was simply glad to proceed with the process. John, however, vehemently objected to the wording. In his opinion, the recognition of American Independence should be clearly acknowledged either by Act of Parliament or Proclamation of the King prior to negotiations. "I told the minister," John said, "that we neither could nor would treat with any nation in the world on any other than an equal footing."[82]

The French Minister sided with Franklin. They argued that as long as the British accepted the authority of Congress to appoint commissioners, then the recognition of American Independence was clearly implied. John was not persuaded. Two long years of Spanish intrigue had made him suspicious of diplomatic assurances. John Adams, who was then in The Hague completing negotiations for a sizable loan, agreed with John on all key points.[83] Their legal minds dismissed the European winks and nods that Franklin had fully mastered. John believed that France and Spain were largely pursing their own clandestine interests and simply using the United States toward that end. As noted historian Richard Morris wrote nearly two centuries later: "The secret documents now available to historians prove that Jay was correct in his appraisal of the situation..."[84]

With the clock ticking, Oswald wrote to Lord Shelburne on August 18, 1782, that "The American commissioners will not move a step until independence is acknowledged..."[85] On September 1, the British Cabinet instructed Oswald to continue to insist that Independence must be incorporated in the final document, and not before. One week later, however, the story took another twist when Dr. Franklin had one of his severe attacks of gout and became incapacitated. The full weight of negotiations now fell squarely on John's shoulders. At the same time, Shelburne and his colleagues realized that America and her European allies were not in complete harmony. They believed that their best chance for completing the treaty was before France and Spain could cause additional complications. When Oswald convinced John to accept a rewording of Oswald's commission from the Crown as acknowl-edgement of American Independence, the impasse was broken.[86]

With obvious satisfaction, John informed Congress that on September 27, Mr. Oswald received his newly-worded commission which unambiguously acknowledged the new nation. Once that issue was resolved, negotiations were resumed with renewed energy. In direct defiance of his original instructions from Congress, John did not consult Vergennes as the final terms of the treaty were debated. Even Lafayette failed to extract the details from his friend. By now, both John Jay and John Adams had lost confidence in French officials. As John stated: "...We shall say to France, the agreement We made with you We shall faithfully perform. But if you have entered into any Separate Measures with other People [i.e., Spain], not included in that Agreement...We shall give ourselves no concern about them."[87]

On October 5, 1782, John handed Oswald a draft of the treaty. Three days later Oswald expressed his approval and forwarded the document to London. Just as final agreement seemed near at hand, news reached London that the British Navy had won a great victory at Gibraltar against America's allies. Under these new circumstances, Lord Shelburne decided to tighten some of the terms in the proposed treaty and sent his Underecretary of State for Foreign Affairs to reopen the negotiations. John responded by urging Adams to join him in Paris at the earliest possible moment. When Adams arrived on October 26, he found John "...in very delicate health, in the midst of great affairs, and without a clerk."[88] Even though Franklin still preferred a more subtle form of diplomacy, he supported his two fiery colleagues in order to present a united front.

As the date for the reopening of Parliament rapidly approached, Shelburne realized that the American peace commissioners were not easily intimidated, and that he was nearly out of time. Therefore, the British Cabinet directed Oswald and his British associates to sign whatever agreement they believed to be most expedient. On Friday, November 29, after his painful confinement in the Tower and his long recuperation, Henry Laurens was finally able to join his colleagues in Paris. At this critical moment he added his voice to Adams' insistence that New England fisheries must have the "liberty" to fish the Northeastern Coast, an article of immense importance to Massachusetts and her neighbors. Laurens also inserted a last-minute provision that prohibited British troops from "carrying off of Negroes or other property of American inhabitants..." an article of equal concern to his own region.[89]

On Saturday, November 30, 1782, the British and American Commissioners gathered at Oswald's lodgings at the Hotel de Moscovie in the heart of Paris. After reviewing the document and correcting minor errors, both sides signed duplicate copies of the preliminary treaty.[90] They then adjourned to Dr. Franklin's home at Passy where they celebrated the completion of the negotiations.

The Comte de Vergenees was not pleased that the Americans had ignored their instructions and had completed the preliminary peace with so little consultation with the French Government. The French Foreign Minister's displeasure, however, could not begin to match the anger George III must have felt as he formally opened Parliament on December 5, 1782. Seated on his throne in the House of Lords, the King declared an end to the offensive war upon the North American Continent and then, for the first time, acknowledged that his former colonies were free and independent States.[91]

In late January 1783, separate preliminary articles of peace were also signed between Great Britain and her two European adversaries: France and Spain. These accomplishments, however, did not save Lord Shelburne. He was replaced on April 2 by a coalition government which attempted without success to renegotiate several key provisions contained in the preliminary agreement. Attempts to negotiate a commercial treaty between Britain and the United States were also abandoned for the moment (John would resume those discussions several years later). On May 21, Governor William Livingston, John's father-in-law, sent words of congratulations concerning the preliminary agreement: "The Treaty is universally applauded; & the American Commissioners who were concerned in making it, have rendered themselves very popular by it."[92]

Throughout 1783, "Almost until the moment of signing, as delay followed delay, mutual suspicions festered."[93] Finally, on the morning of September 3, 1783, the Peace Treaty between Great Britain and the United States was finalized when John and the other representatives of the two countries signed the document in Paris. That same afternoon, the British signed treaties with France and Spain at Versailles. A new chapter in World History had officially begun.

In early October, John left his family in France as he made his maiden voyage to England. For once, his objective was not diplomacy but health. While visiting London, John was joined by John Adams on a truly remarkable tour of Buckingham Palace which, with the King's permission, was conducted by the great American painter, Benjamin West.[94] Unfortunately, John's stay in the capital was interrupted when he became ill with dysentery and acute inflammation of the throat. By late November he was finally well enough to continue his journey to the therapeutic waters at Bath which were already well known to his presidential predecessor, Henry Laurens. John soaked in the springs and dined in the elegant Pump Room where, like all visitors, he drank the 10,000 year old mineral water which was extracted from deep within the Earth. When he returned to Paris in early 1784, John confided to his old friend Gouverneur Morris that "Bath has done me good, for it removed the pain in my breast, which has been almost constant for eighteen months."[95]

During that spring, with renewed stamina and the delicate peace negotiations successfully completed, John and Sally finally had the opportunity to relax in the French countryside and enjoy Parisian culture. According to one biographer: "Mrs. Jay so strikingly resembled Marie Antoinette that once, while entering a theatre with the Lafayettes, the audience, mistaking her for the Queen, rose to its feet."[96] John, however, refused offers from the Continental Congress that he remain in Europe even longer as America's first ambassador to either Britain or France. On May 12, 1784, John performed his last official act as a member of the Peace Commission when he and Dr. Franklin exchanged the formal ratifications of the definitive treaty of peace with the British representative.[97] His objectives now were to return home to New York and to retire from public service. On May 16, he left Paris to pursue that dream.

John did accomplish his first goal. He and his family disembarked in New York Harbor on July 24, 1784. They had been overseas nearly five very long years and their young daughter had never set foot on American soil. Their new nation was now free and secure, thanks in large measure to John's labors, but their beautiful city was in shambles. The last British troops in America had only departed from New York eight months earlier, and everywhere they looked the scars of war were painfully clear.

The country itself was also entering a new "critical" phase. Its common enemy had been defeated and the glue of war which once bound the States together no longer held. Congress was having increasing trouble simply reaching a quorum as one State after another reasserted its own sense of sovereignty. The confederation government was pulling apart just as the United States was becoming part of the family of nations As historian John Fiske entitled his study of this era a century later, the years 1783-1789 were "The Critical Period of American History."[98]

To deal with this crisis, the Continental Congress had appointed John to the office of Secretary for Foreign Affairs even before he left Paris. When he reached New York, the news hit him like a thunderbolt. His cherished dream of retiring to private life was in jeopardy. Secretary Charles Thomson pleaded on behalf of Congress that "your county stands in need of your abilities in that Office."[99] For the first few months, John remained undecided on whether or not to accept the position while he began to rebuild his personal life in the city and the countryside. In early September John wrote to an old friend in England: "I am more contented than I expected. Some things, it is true, are wrong, but more are right. Justice is well administered, offences are rare, and I have never known more public tranquility or private security...The spirit of industry throughout the country was never greater..."[100]

In a familiar pattern, John was again elected as a New York delegate to the Continental Congress which was then meeting at Trenton, New Jersey. He took his seat on December 6, 1784.[101] Before Congress adjourned at the end of that month, the delegates decided that their next home would be New York City. For John, that resolved a major concern about uprooting his family so soon after their return from Europe. Accordingly, he finally accepted the Foreign Affairs portfolio, resigned his seat as a delegate and was sworn into office on December 21.

Under the Articles of Confederation (which had been introduced in 1777 but only ratified in 1781) Congress was slowly being strangled to death. During the war, Congress had a relatively free hand as long as it could persuade the majority of the States to follow its lead. Now, it was in a box. It could neither impose taxes on the States nor force their compliance on other major issues. As John confided to Jefferson, who was now the US Ambassador to France: "It [Congress] certainly is very imperfect, and I fear it will be difficult to remedy its defects, until experience shall render the necessity of doing it more obvious and pressing."[102]

In this weakened condition, the United States was especially vulnerable to foreign encroachments. As one historian described the situation: "Great Britain continued to carry on a commercial war with America" and even "Spain became a dangerous political and commercial rival."[103] These problems, and many more, landed squarely in John's department. At the top of the list was the failure of British compliance with several key provisions of the recent Peace Treaty. The British refused to remove their western posts from American territory. They, in turn, claimed that the United States was in violation of three Articles, including the protection of Loyalists on American soil. On October 13, 1786, John presented a remarkably detailed report to Congress which identified numerous violations on both sides and proposed specific steps to address the crisis. Most importantly, he urged the State Legislatures not to pass "any Act or Acts for interpreting, explaining or construing a National treaty..."[104] In its weakened condition, however, Congress could not impose its will on either Great Britain or the States.

Another major issue which continued to plague John's patience was the renewal of negotiations with Spain. The Spanish Ambassador, Don Diego de Gardoqui, arrived in New York in May 1785. After months of negotiations, a commercial treaty was ready for congressional ratification. Its provisions were very favorable to the United States, but the free navigation of the Mississippi River remained unresolved. Rather than turning the nation's back on desperately needed commerce, John argued that giving up access to the Mississippi during the life of the proposed treaty would cost the country very little, since Spain already excluded the United States from that navigation. The only way to open the river by force would be another war, which the United States was certainly not prepared to fight at that time.

Many denounced John's proposal. James Monroe of Virginia wrote to Jefferson that "I have a conviction in my own mind that Jay has manag'd this negociation [sic] dishonestly."[105] James Madison, another leader of the opposition to the treaty, came to John's defense. "If he [Jay] was mistaken," Madison wrote, "his integrity and probity, more than compensate for the error."[106] The debate actually encompassed more than just the navigation of a major river. It concerned the future development of the Western United States and the impact of that development on the existing States, especially in the South. Some, like Monroe, went so far as to suspect Jay and his supporters of desiring the dismemberment of the union.[107] As the debate raged on, the prospect of any treaty with Spain slipped away. Once again, months of intense negotiations proved useless. In 1788, Congress finally resolved to refer the entire issue to the new federal government which was scheduled to meet the following March.

Generally positive relations with France continued during John's tenure. But attacks on American shipping by the Pirates of the Barbary States off the coast of Africa also occupied John's time during these final years of the Continental Congress.[108] As John confided to President Richard Henry Lee, he actually viewed the Barbary Pirates as a mixed blessing: "This war does not strike me as a great evil. The more we are ill-treated abroad the more we shall unite and consolidate at home."[109] Overall, conducting foreign policy was a thankless task which John performed, as always, with a keen sense of duty. Along with the drudgery, however, came an endless parade of dinner parties for distinguished guests, which he and Mrs. Jay hosted almost every week at their new home on lower Broadway. There were also Tuesday night dinners for the diplomatic corps.[110] The guest list would have impressed even former President Hancock, now the Governor of Massachusetts, who was well known for his lavish banquets on Beacon Hill.

Through these years, John became increasingly convinced that drastic reform of the national government was essential if the union was going to survive. As he wrote to Adams in October 1785: "Our federal government is incompetent to such objects [federal ideas], and as it is in the interest of our country, so it is the duty of her leading characters to co-operate in measures for enlarging and invigorating it."[111] The following year John shared his dark foreboding with his old friend George Washington when he wrote that "I am uneasy and apprehensive; more so than during the war."

But, toward the end of that same letter he told the general that "we shall again recover, and things again go well, I have no doubt."[112]

The New York State Senate, under the tight control of anti-Federalist Gov. Clinton, did not share John's perspective and blocked his election to what became the Constitutional Convention in Philadelphia in 1787. Once again, John was denied the opportunity to affix his signature to a document that he did so much to nurture.[113]

As the ratification campaign began that fall, John eagerly joined with Hamilton and Madison in preparing newspaper articles extolling the benefits of the proposed constitution. Not surprisingly, John's focus was foreign affairs. Even though Gov. Clinton seemed to have a death grip on the debate in upstate New York, John was determined to do all in his power to reverse public sentiment in his home State. From late October 1787 through the following April, John authored five of the 85 articles which appeared under the signature of Publius and are now known as *The Federalist Papers*.[114] He had intended to do more, but poor health afflicted him throughout that Winter. Then, in late spring, John published a pamphlet entitled an *Address to the People of New York* which one of his contemporaries believed "had a most astonishing influence in converting Antifederalists, to a knowledge and belief that the New Constitution was their only political Salvation."[115]

The success of John's *Address* helped to persuade Gov. Clinton to delay action on the proposed constitution until the effect of the pamphlet could wear off. The strategy backfired. By the time the New York State Ratification Convention convened on June 17, 1788, the new constitution was only one state away from the nine required for enactment. Nineteen Federalist delegates, led by John and his colleague Hamilton, prepared to do combat with forty-six Anti-Federalists delegates loyal to Clinton. The odds seemed hopeless. There was even talk of New York City, which was pro-Federalist, breaking off from the State in order to join the new union. Then, on June 25, the Convention received word that New Hampshire, the ninth state, had ratified the constitution.[116] The new federal union was now an established fact. Would mighty New York State stand alone? In the end, the new constitution was ratified by New York on July 26. The vote was 30 to 27. As Hancock had done in Massachusetts,[117] a former President had once again played the pivotal role in turning the tide toward ratification in a key State.

As the final months of the Continental Congress ticked away, it became increasingly difficult for that body to reach a quorum. At the end, on March 2, 1789, only two men who had attended the opening day of Congress in September 1774 were still there to "blow out the candles."

Charles Thomson had been Congress' faithful Secretary for the entire fifteen year period and John Jay, that young political neophyte who began as a delegate and then served as President, had been there for the final four years as Secretary for Foreign Affairs. By then, they had become close colleagues and friends.

When the electoral votes were cast for the first President and Vice President of the Second Republic, John actually came in third place, behind Washington and Adams, with support from New Jersey, Delaware, Connecticut and Rhode Island. His home State of New York did not vote, however, because it could not agree on the selection of electors in time to meet the deadline. Former Presidents John Hancock (4) and Samuel Huntington (2) also recieved votes.[118]

On April 30, 1789, John was also there at Washington's side when the former general took the oath of office as the first President of the Second American Republic. Throughout that summer and fall, the two old revolutionaries spent a great deal of time together. Washington had asked John to stay on as head of foreign affairs until Thomas Jefferson was able to return to America to serve as Secretary of State. At the same time, the new President offered John the position of his choice in the new Federal Government. Madison and others speculated that John might head the Treasury Department. But, John's first love still remained the law. He wanted to be the first Chief Justice of the United States Supreme Court, just as he had held that same title at the State level a decade earlier. Washington readily concurred even though one of the other well qualified candidates for the position was Thomas McKean of Pennsylvania, another past President of Congress.[119]

The first meeting of the United States Supreme Court was held on February 1, 1790, in New York City, the temporary capital. The elegant black silk robe that John wore that morning as he gaveled the Court into existence still hangs today in the Smithsonian Institution in Washington, DC.[120] The next day, John read from the bench the document appointing Edmund Randolph (President Peyton Randolph's adopted son) as the first Attorney-General of the United States. On February 5, John swore in the first three attorneys authorized to appear before the Court, including another former President, Elias Boudinot. Most of the Court's first year was devoted to policy and procedural issues. During these early years, Supreme Court Justices were also assigned to specific Circuits. Each Justice had to ride through his territory joining with District Court Judges in conducting Federal trials. The travel was exhausting and terribly time consuming. The roads were poor and accommodations at taverns along the way consisted of dirty rooms, bed bugs and miserable food. As much as John loved the law, the demands of riding the Circuit took their toll.[121]

The first important case to reach the Supreme Court under John's tenure was *Chisholm v. Georgia* which was argued in 1793. In it, John led the Court in upholding the right of a citizen of one State to bring a law suit against another State. It clearly reflected John's belief that under the new Constitution the States were not sovereign entities but primarily administrative units of the national government. The public uproar that resulted, however, led to the adoption of the Eleventh Amendment to the US Constitution in 1798 which reversed the Court's ruling.[122]

In *Ware v. Hylton* (1793), which was argued by former Gov. Patrick Henry, the Virginia Circuit Court heard a case pertaining to the right of States to supersede the obligations imposed by treaty. John's belief in the supremacy of treaties was outvoted by his two colleagues, including the Virginia District Judge, Cyrus Griffin, who had served as the last President of the Continental Congress. When the case finally reached the Supreme Court, after John had stepped down from the bench, the ruling was overturned and John's position prevailed.[123]

In *Glass v. Sloop Betsy* (1794), one of John's final cases, "his decision did as much as any other single decision of the court to assert the sovereignty and international rights of the United States," according to one biographer.[124] During his tenure, John also established the standard that the Supreme Court does not issue advisory opinions, even if requested to do so by the President. Though John frequently offered his private advice at Washington's request, the Court only addressed those specific cases that came before it. John's most important contribu-tion to the future of the Supreme Court, however, was the foundation he helped to establish for the concept of "judicial review" in *Hayburn's Case* (1792). It proved to be "an early assertion of the power of federal courts to hold statutes enacted by Congress unconstitutional."[125] That concept ultimately established the Judiciary as a truly coequal branch of the national government.

Midway through his four years of service as Chief Justice, John was nominated by his friends and supporters for the office of Governor of New York in 1792. John did not decline the nomination nor did he resign his federal office, but he strictly refused to personally participate in the campaign. The final ballot total gave the election to John; but, Gov. Clinton, the incumbent, controlled the election process and had the results in three Jay-majority counties declared invalid on various technicalities.[126] Despite a massive public outcry, Clinton was then declared the victor. John, who was riding the circuit in New England when he heard the news, shared his thoughts with his dear wife: "The reflection that the majority of the

Electors were for me is a pleasing one; that injustice has taken place does not surprise me, and I hope will not affect you very sensibly...it shall neither discompose my temper, nor postpone my sleep. A few years more will put us all in the dust; and it will then be of more importance to me to have government *myself* than to have governed the *State*."[127] John refused to challenge the results and urged his supporters to accept them, as well.[128]

One of the major issues that did surface during the 1792 campaign was the rumor that, if elected, John would immediately free all slaves in the State of New York. John, who had been actively working to end slavery for years, responded to this accusation in a private letter: "In my opinion, every man of every color and description has a natural right to freedom, and I shall ever acknowledge myself to be an advocate for the manumission of slaves in such way as may be consistent with the justice due to them, with the justice due to their master, and with the regard due to the actual state of society. These considerations unite in convincing me that the abolition of slavery must necessarily be gradual."[129]

While retaining the office of Chief Justice, John was called back into diplomatic service in 1794. Flagrant violations of the Peace Treaty between Britain and America had continued on both sides over the past decade. At the same time, a growing number of United States citizens were openly identifying with the spirit of the French Revolution. The United States was growing dangerously divided. President Washington finally decided to send a special envoy to London to negotiate improved relations with Britain before war became inevitable. His first choice, Alexander Hamilton, could not be confirmed by the Senate. As a result, the President turned to John's proven diplomatic skill even though he headed another branch of government. Knowing the urgency of the situation, John reluctantly agreed. He was confirmed on April 19, 1794, after three days of violent Senate debate during which Sen. James Monroe, Jefferson's loyal lieutenant, led the opposition. Jeffersonians feared that if John was successful, he and the Federalists would become unstoppable in the next presidential election. John saw it very differently. As he wrote to his wife: "No appointment ever operated more unpleasantly upon me; but...to refuse it would be to desert my duty for the sake of my ease and domestic concerns and comforts."[130]

On May 12, John and his oldest son sailed for Europe. They would be gone just over a year. During that period, John met with all the leaders of the British Government, including several audiences with the King. On July 11, he wrote to Hamilton that "I have as yet no reason to complain." And, in keeping with the delicacy of the situation, John added that "I will endeavour to accommodate rather than dispute."[131] Overall, negotiations went well. The British finally set a date certain (June 12, 1796) for surrendering their western forts and agreed to compensate American citizens for losses sustained on the high seas. On behalf of the United States, John withdrew the demand for reimbursement of Negro slaves who were carried off by the British, since they had subsequently been set free. He also assured London that debts owed to British merchants prior to the Revolution would be covered by the new nation. Boundary disputes were to be settled by joint commissions. The Treaty was signed on November 19, 1794.

The commercial articles, especially a prohibition on American trade in the West Indies, received the most intense hostility once the details of the Treaty became known in America in late June 1795. Jeffersonians denounced John and his Treaty at every opportunity, going so far as to repeatedly burn him in effigy. Even Washington came under repeated attacks.[132] John, however, remained resigned to the judgment of history. As he wrote from Paris the day the Treaty was signed: "Should the treaty prove, as I believe it will, beneficial to our country, justice will *finally* be done. If not, be it so--my mind is at ease: I wish I could say as much for my body..."[133] Despite the public outcry, the Jay Treaty, minus the article pertaining to the West Indies, was ratified by the Senate on June 24. As one of John's 19th Century biographers states: "To unprejudiced eyes after the lapse of a hundred years...the treaty seems a very fair one."[134] Above all, war had been averted.

John returned to New York on May 28, 1795.[135] As he disembarked, John learned that he had been nominated for Governor. One week later he was proclaimed the winner. The New York Federalists finally claimed the victory they had been denied in the last election. In this atmosphere, Gov. Clinton had wisely declined renomination in order to avoid the humiliation of defeat. John submitted his resignation as Chief Justice and, once again, postponed his cherished dream of retirement. On July 1, 1795, with the debate over the Treaty swirling around him, John was sworn into office as the second elected Governor of New York.[136]

Only a month after his inauguration a Yellow Fever epidemic swept across the city. Many urged the new Governor to flee, but John and his family refused to leave lest they cause more people to panic. As John dealt with the health crisis as well as the other critical duties of his office, he pledged a nonpartisan administration and refused to fire State employees simply because they had been appointed by his predecessor. His legislative agenda during his first term included promotion of canal navigation, revision of the criminal law and improved prison facilities. He also supported legislative efforts to end slavery throughout the State.

In 1796, as relations with France became more traumatic, John urged President Washington to seek a third term to help calm the storm. Washington refused, but John did follow his own advice in 1798 when he was overwhelmingly reelected as Governor. Ironically, his opponent that year was none other than his old law partner and once intimate friend, Robert R. Livingston. By now, their friendship had split asunder and they had become bitter political enemies. During the next two years, Hamilton tried to rally the Federalists throughout the State as Sen. Aaron Burr mobilized the Jeffersonians. In the election of April 1800, Burr's followers won control of the next State Legislature which would decide New York's twelve electoral votes in the upcoming presidential election. More importantly, New York's votes would determine the next President.

Hamilton, however, devised a desperate strategy to save the national government from what he viewed as Jefferson's radical philosophy. He pleaded with John, as Governor, to call a special session of the old legislature before its mandate expired in order to alter the procedure for selecting the State's electoral votes. Other Federalist leaders, including Secretary of State John Marshall, endorsed Hamilton's plan. John, however, dismissed the proposal as contrary to the clearly expressed popular will in the most recent election. John was a statesman, not a politician. On the back of Hamilton's letter John wrote: "Proposing a measure for *party* purposes, which I think it would not become me to adopt."[137] With that simple stroke of a pen, John almost certainly handed the presidency to his bitter adversary, Jefferson, rather than his old friend and colleague, Adams.

The highlight of John's second term as governor was the adoption of a law that eventually abolished slavery in New York . Henceforth, all children born of slave parents would be free but subject to an apprenticeship (males to the age of twenty-eight and females to the age of twenty-five). This gradual emancipation reflected the approach that John had advocated throughout his public life and during his years as President of the New York Manumission Society. As John explained to an Albany official in November 1798: "I purchase slaves and manumit them at proper ages and when their faithful services shall have afforded a reasonable retribution."[138]

The Federalist Party urged John to seek one final term as Governor. His reply was clear and direct: "The period is now nearly arrived at which I have for many years intended to retire from the cares of public life... not perceiving, after mature consideration, that any duties require me to postpone it, I shall retire accordingly."[139]

But, as always, there was one final twist to the story. In late December 1800, as John prepared to leave the governorship, he received word from recently defeated President Adams that Chief Justice Oliver Ellsworth had resigned and that the President was determined to place a solid Federalist in charge of the Judicial branch. Accordingly, Adams notified John that he had already nominated him for a new term as Chief Justice. The offer caught John by surprise. Of all the positions he had held, the law was still his first love. But, after careful consideration, he wrote to President Adams: "I find that, independent of other considerations, the state of my health removes every doubt, it being clearly and decidedly incompetent to the fatigues incident to the office."[140] Adams then turned to his second choice, Secretary of State John Marshall.

At long last, after 27 years of continuous public service throughout his Nation, his State and three foreign lands, John, like his father before him, gladly turned his back on fame and fortune and retired with his family to Bedford, fifty miles from New York City. There John personally supervised the construction of a new home on 750 acres.[141] Because of poor health, Sally could not join her husband until October 1801. Once she settled into their new home she wrote to a friend: "I can truly say I have never enjoyed so much comfort as I do here."[142] Unfortunately, the one thing they did not have was time. Sarah Livingston Jay passed away on May 28, 1802, surrounded by her family. After her death, John devoted himself to his children and his farm. In 1810, while still mourning the loss of his life-partner, he expressed his relative contentment to a close friend: "I believe that you and I derive more real satisfaction from attending to our vines and fruit-trees, than most conquerors do from cultivating their favourite laurels."[143]

During his retirement, John refused any active role in politics, even though he took great pride in voting in every election. To friends, however, he did denounce President Madison's war in 1812: "In my opinion, the declaration of war was neither necessary, nor expedient, nor seasonable..."[144]

Faith had also played a major role in John's life but, as his son and biographer stated: "Mr. Jay's religion was fervent, but mild and unostentatious."[145] For several years he served as Vice President of the American Bible Society under the leadership of his friend and former presidential colleague, Elias Boudinot. In 1821, when Boudinot died, the Society tried to persuade John to accept the presidency. He initially refused the office because "My health has been declining for twelve years past... such are my maladies that they often confine me to the house, and at times to my chamber..."[146] After assurances that his name alone would further their mission, John did accept and served until 1828 when he became too ill to carry on.

In May 1829, John was stricken by palsy. According to his son William, his speech was slurred but his mind remained sharp as always. "He lingered till noon of Sunday, the 17th, when he expired in the eighty-fourth year of his age."[147] He was buried in the Jay Family Cemetery near his boyhood home in Rye, New York.[148] Of the 43 men who had gathered that cool, damp morning in Philadelphia at the opening of the First Continental Congress so many years earlier, John was the last to die.[149]

Of all his many titles throughout his unique public career--President, Governor, Chief Justice, Secretary for Foreign Affairs--John's greatest legacy will always be that of Peacemaker. John Adams, who was better known for his harsh critique of his colleagues than for his flattery, stated without reservation that "a man and his office were never better united than Mr. Jay and the commission for peace. Had he been detained in Madrid, as I was in Holland...all would have been lost."[150]

The residence of President John Jay's son (above) is built on the site of John Jay's childhood home. It is now part of the Jay Heritage Center in Rye, New York. President Jay's tomb (right) is in the Jay Family Cemetery behind the mansion. Jay descendants are still buried there today.

WHILE JOHN JAY
WAS PRESIDENT

December 1778 - September 1779

Shortly after John Jay became President, the Continental Congress summoned Gen. Washington to return to Philadelphia for consultations. For just over a month, the leaders of the government discussed all aspects of the war. It was decided to abandon another invasion of Canada (which had been advocated by the Marquis de Lafayette). Congress also took steps to improve the administration of the Army and to clarify the authority of the Commander-in-Chief. At Washington's urging, Congress established an across-the-board $200 bounty for anyone who enlisted in the Continental Army for the duration of the war.[151]

The growing financial crisis also continued to devour an increasing amount of congressional time and energy. By late spring 1779, Congress was devoting three days per week to economic issues and still issuing millions of dollars without a comprehensive plan. Finally, on September 1, 1779, the delegates resolved that "on no account whatever" would they authorize emitting bills of credit in excess of $200 million overall (up to that point, $160 million had already been printed).[152] That fall, Congress also decided to redouble its efforts to secure additional loans from Holland, France and Spain.

In the North, American Gen. Benedict Arnold began his treasonous plot with British Gen. Henry Clinton via Clinton's top aide, Maj. John André. Armed with Arnold's intelligence on the status of American forces, Gen. Clinton launched an offensive on the Hudson River in late May and took control of all navigation below West Point.[153] Clinton's goal was to comply with the new strategy devised by Lord Germain and the British Cabinet in London. They were determined to cut off New York from the other colonies in order for the loyalists to reassert control and more effectively engage in their own defense against the rebels.[154]

In the South, despite their humiliating failure three years earlier, the British were once again determined to capture Charleston.[155] During 1779, British forces were deployed throughout Georgia and South Carolina with the conquest of the South Carolina capital as their ultimate goal. In early

May, British Gen. Prevost nearly stumbled into victory months ahead of schedule. At one point, South Carolina Gov. John Rutledge and his Council even offered to pledge the colony's neutrality for the duration of the war if the British would withdraw.[156] Prevost rejected the proposal, but he and his forces were soon forced to retreat when American Gen. Benjamin Lincoln arrived in time to reinforce Gen. William Moultrie.

On the diplomatic front, Spain initially offered to serve as a mediator between Britain and France in exchange for regaining Gibraltar.[157] Not surprisingly, the British declined and Spain then joined with France by declaring war on Great Britain. Unlike France, however, Spain did not recognize American Independence.

Confronted by the alliance of the Bourbon brotherhood, King George III grew increasingly concerned over his own government's lethargy. He tried to rally the Cabinet by summoning its members to an unprecedented meeting at the Queen's House in June 1779. As he wrote to the First Lord of the Admiralty: "If others will not be active, I must drive."[158] In Parliament, Lord Cavendish shared the King's determination but, in contrast to the established policy, Cavendish urged his colleagues to abandon the conflict with America in order to devote all of Britain's resources to the real danger from across the English Channel.[159]

His motion failed.

Chapter 5

President
JOHN JAY
of
NEW YORK

Notes

Abbreviation Key

JCC   Journals of the Continental Congress
LDC   Letters of Delegates to Congress
PHL   The Papers of Henry Laurens

[1] John Butler, The Huguenots in America: A Refugee People in New World Society, (Harvard University Press, Cambridge, 1983), p. 13.

[2] William Jay, The Life of John Jay, (American Foundation Publications, Bridgewater, Virginia, 2000) Vol. I, pp. 1-9. (First published by J. & J. Harper, New York, 1833).

[3] Frank Monaghan, John Jay: Defender of Liberty, (The Bobbs-Merrill Company, New York, 1935), p. 22.

[4] George Pellew, John Jay, (Houghton, Mifflin and Company, Boston, 1899), pp. 6-7.

[5] Pellew, op. cit., pp. 7-8.

[6] Monaghan, op. cit., p. 26.

[7] Monaghan, op. cit., pp. 27-28.

[8] Pellew, op.cit., p. 12.

[9] As cited in Richard B. Morris, John Jay: The Making of a Revolutionary, (Harper & Row, New York, 1975), p. 67. (Elizabeth Frank, editor, Memoirs of the Life and Writings of Lindley Murray, (New York, 1827), p. 34.)

[10] Morris, John Jay, op. cit., Vol. 1, p. 84. The Master of Arts degree "was usually conferred after a perfunctory amount of extra study." John Jay's was awarded on May 19, 1767.

[11] Monaghan, op. cit., p. 35.

[12] As cited in Walter Stahr, John Jay (Hambledon and London, New York, 2005), p. 24.

[13] Henry P. Johnston, Editor, The Correspondence and Public Papers of John Jay: 1763-

<u>1826</u>, (Da Capo Press, New York, 1971), Vol. I, p. 3; Samuel Kissam to John Jay, April 25, 1766;

[14] Morris, <u>John Jay</u>, op. cit., Vol. 1, pp. 74-77; John Jay to Robert R. Livingston, Jr., April 19, 1765.

[15] As cited in Monaghan, op. cit., p. 37; John Jay to Robert R. Livingston, Jr., undated.

[16] Henry Flanders, <u>The Lives and Times of the Chief Justices of the Supreme Court of the United States</u>, (J. B. Lippincott & Company, Philadelphia, 1858), Vol. 1, p. 46. See also: Pellew, op. cit., pp. 17-18.

[17] Monaghan, op. cit., p. 45.

[18] As cited in Pellew, op.cit., pp. 18-19, John Jay to Samuel Kissam, August 27, 1771.

[19] Stahr, op. cit., pp. 25-26.

[20] Monaghan, op. cit., p. 46.

[21] Lois Hobart, <u>Patriot's Lady: The Life of Sarah Livingston Jay</u> (Funk & Wagnalls Company Inc., New York, 1960), p. 47.

[22] For details concerning the Boston Tea Party, see Introduction.

[23] Monaghan, op. cit., pp. 52-53.

[24] Pellew, op.cit., p. 31.

[25] Willard Sterne Randall, <u>Alexander Hamilton: A Life</u>, (Harper Collins Publishers, New York, 2003), pp. 77-78.

[26] L. H. Butterfield, Editor, <u>Diary and Autobiography of John Adams</u> (The Belknap Press, Cambridge, 1961), Vol. 2, p. 123.

[27] Edmund Cody Burnett, <u>The Continental Congress</u>, (The Macmillan Company, New York, 1941), p. 37.

[28] Worthington Chauncey Ford, Editor, <u>JCC: 1774-1789</u>, (Government Printing Office, Washington, DC, 1904), Vol. I, p. 62. Richard Henry Lee prepared the first draft, but it did not win favor with the delegates. William Livingston then submitted the draft prepared by John Jay. It won wide acceptance but, because Jay himself did not initially introduce it, many initially attributed its authorship to his father-in-law. See also: Monaghan, op. cit., p. 61.

[29] For details concerning the Galloway Plan of Union, see Chapter 2.

[30] Flanders, op. cit., Vol. 1., p. 104.

[31] Morris, <u>John Jay</u>, op. cit., Vol. 1, p. 137; John Jay to John Vardill, September 24, 1774.

[32] For details concerning the Continental Association, see Chapter 1.

[33] Pellew, op.cit., p. 39.

[34] Monaghan, op. cit., p. 66.

[35] Stahr, op. cit., p. 45. See also: Monaghan, op. cit., p. 67.

[36] Monaghan, op. cit., p. 68.

[37] JCC, op. cit., Vol. II, p. 70.

[38] Most of the Founding Fathers viewed Catholics as loyal to a foreign power, the Pope, who was at that time also the temporal ruler of the Papal States which covered a large part of Italy. One of the few Catholics welcomed by his congressional colleagues was Charles Carroll of Carrollton who also happened to be one of the wealthiest men in America. See also: Chapter Eight for additional details.

[39] Charles Francis Adams, Editor, The Life and Works of John Adams, (Little, Brown & Company, Boston, 1850-56), Vol. II, p. 415.

[40] Monaghan, op. cit., p. 70.

[41] Jay, op. cit., Vol. I, p. 37. See also: JCC, op. cit., Vol. II, p.212. Since the Irish were also eager to win their Independence from Britain, they were viewed as kindred spirits by many Americans.

[42] Morris, John Jay, op. cit., Vol. 1, p. 212; John Jay to Sarah Jay, December 23, 1775.

[43] Hobart, op. cit., p.60.

[44] Morris, John Jay, op. cit., Vol. 1, p. 232; John Jay to Robert R. Livingston, March 4, 1776.

[45] Jack N. Rakove, The Beginnings of National Politics (Alfred A. Knopf, New York, 1979), p. 100.

[46] Most delegates did not sign the Declaration of Independence until August 2, 1776.

[47] Monaghan, op. cit., pp. 84-85.

[48] Monaghan, op. cit., pp. 83-84: On June 29, 1776, the British fleet under Admiral Shuldam arrived off Sandy Hook, NY. "The British Army, composed of six thousand seasoned soldiers from Halifax, eight thousand veteran troops from Germany, and other detachments from the West Indies, Gibraltar and the British Isles was being disembarked on Staten Island." See also: Morris, op. cit., Vol. 1, p. 295: "...Vice Admiral Viscount Richard Howe (1726-99), who had sailed from England at the head of a fleet whose strength was rumored to be 150 ships with 15,000 British and Hessian soldiers."

[49] Jay, op. cit., Vol. 1, p. 61; John Jay to Sarah Jay, July 29, 1776.

[50] Paul H. Smith, Editor, LDC, (Library of Congress, Washington, DC, 1985), Vol. 5, p. 225; Robert Morris to John Jay, September 23, 1776.

[51] Monaghan, op. cit., p. 92.

[52] Morris, <u>John Jay</u>, op. cit., Vol. 1, pp. 389-394.

[53] As cited in Morris, <u>John Jay</u>, op. cit., Vol. 1, p. 392; *Journals of the Provincial Congress of the State of New York*. During the Revolutionary Era (1760-90), Catholics were more often viewed as agents of a foreign power--the Pope--than as fellow Christians seeking religious freedom. The fact that several key Huguenot descendants, such as John Jay, played such a major role in the Revolution might have been one of the factors prompting anti-Catholic sentiments.

[54] Jay, op. cit., Vol. 1, p. 70.

[55] As cited in Henry Flanders, op. cit., Vol 1, p. 216.

[56] Monaghan, op. cit., p. 97.

[57] Monaghan, op. cit., p. 98.

[58] Morris, <u>John Jay</u>, op. cit., Vol. 1, p. 405; John Jay to Abraham Yates, Jr., May 16, 1777.

[59] See Chapter 4.

[60] <u>JCC</u>, op. cit., Vol. XII, p. 1206.

[61] LDC, op. cit., Vol. 11, p. 328; Gouverneur Morris to George Clinton, December 10, 1778.

[62] <u>LDC</u>, op. cit., Vol. 11, p. 322; James Duane to George Clinton, December 10, 1778.

[63] Jay, op. cit., Vol. II, p. 147; John Jay to Gouverneur Morris, February 10, 1784.

[64] <u>Journal of the Continental Congress</u>, op. cit., Vol. XII, p. 1222; December 16, 1778. The estate of the late President Peyton Randolph and his three successors were also invited "to lay before the Board of Treasury accounts of their expenditures in support of their households while they respectively exercised the office of President, in order to their being adjusted and paid out of the public treasury."

[65] Hobart, op. cit., p. 71.

[66] Morris, <u>John Jay</u>, op. cit., Vol. 1, pp. 587-588; John Jay to George Washington, April 26, 1779.

[67] Jay, op. cit., Vol. I, p. 99; Extracts from *Mr. Jay's History of his Spanish Mission*. William Jay states that "only a few of the first pages of it have been found among his [John Jay's] papers."

[68] Monaghan, op. cit., p. 119.

[69] Jay, op. cit., Vol. I, p. 100.

[70] David R. Chesnutt and C. James Taylor, Editors, <u>PHL</u> (University of South Carolina Press, Columbia, 2000), pp. xxxvi-xxxvii.

[71] As cited in Flanders, op. cit., p. 302; John Jay to Samuel Huntington, July 1780.

72 As cited in Monaghan, op. cit., p. 165; John Jay to Gouverneur Morris, September 28, 1781.

73 Throughout his adult life, John Jay was also repeatedly embarrassed by his older brother, Sir James Jay, who ultimately abandoned his new country and his family for the illusion of influence in Britain. John's most persistent thorn, however, was an ambitious and unprincipled young man by the name of Lewis Littlepage. John initially invited the young man to join his staff in Spain as a favor to a friend, but regretted that decision for years as Littlepage repeatedly harassed John in public and in private.

74 Johnston, op. cit., p. 405; John Jay to Egbert Benson, September 17, 1780.

75 Johnston, op. cit., p. 405; John Jay to Robert Morris, April 25, 1782.

76 Journal of the Continental Congress, op. cit., Vol. XX, p. 636, June 13, 1781. John Adams remained as the original Commissioner. Franklin, Laurens and Jefferson were added the day after Jay, p. 648. Jefferson declined to serve.

77 J. Steven Watson, The Reign of George III (The Clarendon Press, Oxford, 1960), p. 218.

78 Jay, op. cit., Vol. 2, p. 94; Benjamin Franklin to John Jay, April 22, 1782.

79 Pellew, op.cit., p. 132. Thomas Paine, the outspoken revolutionary who authored Common Sense in 1776, considered Vergennes "a despot." Vergennes was, indeed, a very conservative minister in a very conservative government. Nevertheless, his hostility toward Britain proved of enormous benefit to the United States on numerous occasions.

80 Monaghan, op. cit., p.190.

81 As cited in Pellew, op.cit., p. 157.

82 Johnston, op. cit., Vol. II , p. 353; John Jay to Gouveneur Morris, October 13, 1782.

83 David McCullough, John Adams (Simon & Schuster, New York, 2001), pp. 273-275.

84 Richard B. Morris, The Peacemakers, (Harper & Row, Publishers, New York, 1965), p. 309.

85 As cited in Pellew, op.cit., p. 163.

86 Morris, John Jay, op. cit., Vol. II, p. 356; Richard Oswald to Thomas Townshend, September 10, 1782.

87 Morris, John Jay, op. cit., Vol. II, p. 375; Richard Oswald to Thomas Townshend, October 2, 1782.

88 Adams, op. cit., Vol. IX, p. 514; John Adams to Jonathan Jackson, November 17, 1782.

89 Morris, The Peacemakers, op. cit., p. 381.

90 Morris, The Peacemakers, op. cit., p. 382. According to Morris, "...the original [of the

Preliminary Peace Treaty] which went to the Americans has never been found...the single original text [is] in London's Public Record Office."

[91] Morris, The Peacemakers, op. cit., pp. 411-412.

[92] Johnston, op. cit., Vol. III, p. 45; William Livingston to John Jay, May 21, 1783.

[93] Morris, The Peacemakers, op. cit., p. 435.

[94] Morris, John Jay, op. cit., Vol. II, p. 620.

[95] Johnston, op. cit., Vol. III, p. 110; John Jay to Gouverneur Morris, February 10, 1784.

[96] Monaghan, op. cit., p. 217.

[97] Monaghan, op. cit., p. 227.

[98] John Fiske, The Critical Period of American History: 1783-1789, (Riverside Press, Cambridge, 1888).

[99] LDC, op. cit., Vol. 21, p. 694; Charles Thomson to John Jay, June 18, 1784.

[100] Jay, op. cit., Vol. II, p. 158; John Jay to Benjamin Vaughan, September 2, 1784.

[101] John was also elected an honorary member of the Society of the Cincinnati, an elite fraternity of Revolutionary War Officers. John, however, found the organization offensive to the principles of democracy and declined the invitation.

[102] Jay, op. cit., Vol. II, pp. 180-181; John Jay to Thomas Jefferson, January 19, 1786.

[103] Monaghan, op. cit., p. 248.

[104] JCC, op. cit., Vol. XXXI, pp. 781-874.

[105] LDC, op. cit., Vol. 23, p. 404; James Monroe to Thomas Jefferson, July 16, 1786.

[106] James Madison, Writings, Vol. V, p. 182.

[107] Burnett, op, cit., p. 656.

[108] Monaghan, op. cit., pp. 265-266. One development Franco-American relations was almost comical. The Comte de Moustier presented his credentials as the new French Ambassador to the United States in February 1788. At once, he and his sister-in-law scandalized New York society with their arrogance and their peculiar conduct (she took a pet monkey with her wherever she went). Some even suspected an immoral relationship between the two. Moustier went so far as "to boast of having told Griffin, the President of Congress, in the latter's house, that he 'was but a tavern-keeper.'" John Jay, as Secretary of Foreign Affairs, finally demanded that France recall Moustier which it did in October 1789.

[109] Johnston, op. cit., Vol. III, p. 171; John Jay to Richard Henry Lee, October 13, 1785.

[110] Pellew, op. cit., p. 218.

[111] Johnston, op. cit., Vol. III, p. 172; John Jay to John Adams, October 14, 1785.

[112] Johnston, op. cit., Vol. III, p. 204; John Jay to George Washington, June 27, 1786.

[113] John did not sign the Declaration of Independence because he had been called back to New York to help establish the new Provincial Congress. He did not sign New York State's first Constitution, even though he wrote much of it, because he rushed home at the death of his mother. And, even though John helped to lead the battle for a serious revision of the National Government, he did not sign the US Constitution because he was denied election to the Constitutional Convention in 1787 by the Anti-Federalist New York State Senate. The one major document that John Jay did sign was the Treaty of Peace with Great Britain in 1783 which, more than any other individual, he helped to negotiate.

[114] *Federalist Papers* Numbers. 2, 3, 4, 5 & 64 were written by John Jay.

[115] As cited in Monaghan, op. cit., p. 292; Samuel Blatchley Webb to Joseph Barrell, April 1788.

[116] Jack N. Rakove, Original Meanings (Alfred A. Knopf, New York, 1996), p. 125.

[117] Chapter 3.

[118] Margaret Bassett, Profiles and Portraits of American Presidents (David McKay Company, Inc., New York, 1964), p. 255. See also: William A. DeGregerio, The Complete Book of Presidents (Dembnor, New York, 1984), p. 7.

[119] John Jay's nomination as the first Chief Justice of the United States was confirmed by the Senate on September 26, 1789.

[120] Monaghan, op. cit., p. 305.

[121] Monaghan, op. cit., p. 319.

[122] Monaghan, op. cit., p. 311.

[123] Leonard W. Levy, Editor-in-Chief, Encyclopedia of the American Constitution (Macmillan Publishing Company, New York, 1986), Vol. 3, p. 1013.

[124] Monaghan, op. cit., p. 324.

[125] Kermit L. Hall, Editor, The Oxford Companion to the Supreme Court of the United States, (Oxford University Press, New York, 1992), p. 368. Five of the six Justices of the Supreme Court, including Chief Justice John Jay, informed President Washington that the pension law, as written, violated the US Constitution because it abridged the separation of powers.

[126] Flanders, op. cit., Vol. 1, pp. 394-400. John Jay carried the counties of Otsego, Clinton and Tioga in the 1792 race for Governor of New York but the votes in all three counties were disqualified on various technicalities by election officials loyal to incumbent Gov. Clinton. Congress subsequently amended the law.

[127] Johnston, op. cit., Vol. III, p. 435; John Jay to Sarah Jay, June 18, 1792.

[128] Stahr, op. cti., pp. 288-289.

[129] Johnston, op. cit., Vol. III, p. 414; John Jay to J. C. Dongan, February 27, 1792.

[130] Jay, op. cit., Vol. I, p. 311; John Jay to Sarah Jay, April 19, 1794.

[131] Jay, op. cit., Vol. II, p. 228; John Jay to Alexander Hamilton, July 11, 1794.

[132] James Thomas Flexner, <u>George Washington: Anguish and Farewell (1793-1799)</u>, (Little, Brown & Company, Boston, 1972), Vol. 4, p. 245.

[133] Johnston, op. cit., Vol. IV, p. 136; John Jay to Rufus King, November 19, 1794.

[134] Pellew, op. cit., p. 279.

[135] Monaghan, op. cit., p. 387. As always, John Jay suffered from severe seasickness throughout most of the ocean voyage.

[136] John Jay of New York was one of three former Presidents of the Continental Congress who were then serving as Governors, the others were Samuel Huntington of Connecticut and Thomas Mifflin of Pennsylvania. Massachusetts Gov. John Hancock had died a year earlier.

[137] As cited in Monaghan, op. cit., p. 421.

[138] As cited in Pellew, op. cit., p. 294; John Jay to the Albany, NY Assessor, November 8, 1798.

[139] Jay, op. cit., Vol. I, pp. 419-420; John Jay to Richard Hatfield, Chairman of the Federal Meeting, November 8, 1800.

[140] Johnston, op. cit., Vol. IV, p. 286; John Jay to John Adams, January 2, 1801.

[141] The home in Bedford where John Jay died remained in the Jay Family until 1953. Five years later it became the property of the State of New York. Today, the John Jay Homestead is open to the public.

[142] As cited in Monaghan, op. cit., p. 428;; Sarah Jay to a friend, 1801 or 1802; see also Flanders, op. cit., p. 425.

[143] Johnston, op. cit., Vol. IV, p. 329; John Jay to Richard Peters, February 26, 1810.

[144] Jay, op. cit., Vol. I, p. 445; John Jay to a New York Federalist, July 28, 1812.

[145] Jay, op. cit., Vol. I, p. 463. Even though John Jay was the descendant of a French Huguenot family, he was a lifelong member of the Episcopal Church.

[146] Jay, op. cit., Vol. I, p. 454; John Jay to The Rev. S. S. Wodhull, Secretary of the American Bible Society, December 7, 1821.

[147] Jay, op. cit., Vol. I, p. 459.

[148] John Jay's grave is located in a private family cemetery in Rye, New York behind the

home built by his oldest son, Peter Augustus Jay, on the same spot where John grew up. In 1992, the house became part of the non-profit Jay Heritage Center which is open to the public.

[149] Chapter 1.

[150] Adams, op. cit., Vol. IX, p. 516; John Adams to Jonathan Jackson, November 17, 1782. See also: Jay, op. cit., Vol. I, p. 418; John Adams to John Jay, November 24, 1800.

WHILE JOHN JAY
WAS PRESIDENT

Notes

Abbreviation Key

JCC   Journals of the Continental Congress
LDC   Letters of Delegates to Congress
PHL   The Papers of Henry Laurens

[151] Edmund Cody Burnett, The Continental Congress, The Macmillan Company, New York, 1941), pp. 386-389.

[152] Worthington Chauncey Ford, JCC, (Government Printing Office, Washington, DC, 1909), Vol. XIV, p. 1013.

[153] Barnet Schecter, The Battle for New York, (Walker & Company, New Your, 2002), p. 324; see also pp. 337-338.

[154] Two centuries later President Richard Nixon would call a similar plan "Vietnamization" and it would prove equally delusional.

[155] See Chapter 3.

[156] Henry Flanders, The Lives and Times of The Chief Justices of the Supreme Court of the United States, (J. B. Lippincott & Co., Philadelphia, 1858), Vol. I, p. 562.

[157] Richard B. Morris, The Peacemakers, (Harper & Row, New York, 1965), p. 14.

[158] King George III to Lord Sandwich, First Lord of the Admiralty, 1779; as cited in John Brooke, King George II, (McGraw-Hill Book Company, New York, 1972), p. 200.

[159] L. Edward Purcell and David F. Burg, (The World Almanac of the American Revolution, (Pharos Books, New York, 1992), pp. 208-209.

Sam.ᵈ Huntington

Chapter 6

President
SAMUEL HUNTINGTON
of
CONNECTICUT

Uncommon Sense

The election of the sixth President of the Continental Congress reflected a clear pattern during the early years of the First Republic. Like a political Noah's Ark, congressional leadership seemed to come in pairs. Randolph and Middleton, the first two Presidents, had been father figures who helped to guide their largely younger and less experienced colleagues through uncharted waters. Their immediate successors, Hancock and Laurens, had brought energy and arrogance to the increasing demands of the office after the war began. But, by the time Laurens resigned in a fiery farewell at the end of 1778, years of executive prodding had taken their toll. The delegates yearned for competent yet understated leadership. Jay, a brilliant New York attorney with the patience of Job, fit the bill perfectly. When his tenure was cut short by a critical overseas assignment, it is hardly surprising that Congress selected another distinguished northern attorney who had demonstrated those same virtues while serving as a delegate. Samuel Huntington of Connecticut was their unanimous choice.

Samuel Huntington, like Jay, had been a complete unknown outside of his home State before he joined the Continental Congress. In fact, his journey to Philadelphia in May 1776 was the first time in his 44 years that he had crossed the Connecticut border.[1] What he and his predecessor did share were sharp legal minds that had brought distinction to both men at home. They were also known for resolving crises through reason rather than rhetoric. They were admired for their moderation in times of extreme provocation. In Congress, both men demonstrated a calming influence even when events seemed on the verge of spinning out of control.

Despite their personal similarities, the states they represented were nearly polar opposites. While New York, the headquarters of the British military occupation, was notorious for the number of loyalists in its population,[2] Connecticut was second to none in its commitment to the cause of liberty. At every step throughout the American Revolution, Connecticut was there to do its part. Yankee independence was bred into the citizens of Connecticut from birth.

The Huntington Family was certainly no exception. They arrived in America in 1633. Samuel's great-great-grandfather, Simon Huntington, died of smallpox on that voyage and was buried at sea, but his wife and three young children somehow survived. In 1660, two of their sons were among the first settlers of Norwich, Connecticut. Simon, the younger, served as a deacon of his church and a representative of Norwich in the General Court at Hartford. Simon Huntington's son Joseph grew up and married in Norwich but shortly after the birth of his son Nathaniel in September 1691, Joseph Huntington and his young family moved to the nearby town of Windham where he, like his father, served as a church deacon.

Nathaniel Huntington, the President's father, lived in Windham all his life and died there in 1767. He was a prosperous farmer and clothier who carried on the family tradition of service to his church. He also held the position of Justice of the Peace for over a quarter of a century. In February 1723, Nathaniel Huntington married Mehetable Thurston from Bristol, Rhode Island. She was nine years his junior. She not only gave birth to ten children during their 45 years of marriage, but she lived to the remarkable age of 81. Samuel's mother helped to instill in her family a special spirit after their long hours in the fields were finished. As the editor of the *History of Windham County* has described the Huntington household, it was "the favorite gathering place of the young people of the parish, who were drawn thither by the attraction of music, for which the family was famed, and for the wit and good cheer which always abounded."[3]

It was a remarkable family in many ways. Four of Nathaniel & Mehetable's seven sons became Congregational ministers, three of whom attended Yale. In 1762, Enoch Huntington, their eighth child, delivered the Master's Valedictory Address at Yale's commencement ceremony while his brother Joseph gave the Bachelor's Salutatory Address. Their youngest daughter, Sibel, also married a minister. Eliphalet, the fifth son, followed in his father's footsteps and eventually took over the family farm. Only the youngest boy died in childhood.

Samuel, the second oldest son and future president, was born in Windham on July 3, 1731.[4] The two-story house in which he and his siblings grew up still stands along State Highway 14, but today it is located in the town of Scotland which officially separated from Windham in 1857. Some sources state that, in order to learn a trade, Samuel was apprenticed to a cooper between the ages of 16 to 21, but there is no known confirmation of this claim.[5] In fact, in the sermon preached at Samuel's funeral, his friend and pastor, the Rev. Joseph Strong, stated that "his juvenile occupations were chiefly of the agricultural kind."[6]

What is known is that Samuel, unlike most of his brothers, was "a reticent, retiring individual" who, despite his lack of a formal education, did share their thirst for knowledge.[7] In her *History of Norwich*, Frances M. Caulkins quotes a long-time friend of the family who stated, "I never heard a frivolous observation from him; his conversation ever turned to something of a practical nature; he was moderate and circumspect in all his movements, and delivered his sentiments in few but weighty words."[8]

Thanks to the generosity of his Windham minister, the Rev. Ebenezer Devotion, Samuel freely borrowed from his pastor's library and gradually taught himself Latin. He then moved on to the study of law. Once again, through the encouragement of two prominent local attorneys, Eliphalet Dyer and Jedediah Elderkin, he had access to their law books. Even though the record is sketchy, Samuel most likely followed the custom of the day and served an apprenticeship with one or both of his legal patrons. Whatever the circumstances, he was admitted to the Bar in March 1754 and soon opened his first law office in Windham.[9] An old biographical sketch described the young attorney as having been "distinguished by a strict integrity...and strong common sense..." as well as punctuality.[10]

In 1760, to expand his law practice, Samuel moved to Norwich, the second largest town in the colony. In doing so, he was also returning to his Huntington Family roots. In April of the following year he wed Martha Devotion, the daughter of the man who had been his friend and pastor for years. Even though Samuel and Martha began to attend services at the First Church in Norwich soon after their marriage, they did not officially transfer their church membership from the Scotland Congregational Church in Windham until after his father-in-law's death a decade later. An intensely religious man, Samuel became a pillar of First Church and "occasionally the people's mouth to God" whenever he was called upon to deliver the sermon in the absence of ordained clergy.[11]

Samuel and Martha were viewed as "uncommonly happy" in their relationship, but they were unable to conceive children.[12] Ten years after their marriage they finally became foster parents. They assumed guardianship over the son and daughter of Samuel's brother, the Rev. Joseph Huntington, when his wife (who was also Martha's sister) died. Six-year-old Samuel and his two-year-old sister Frances (known throughout her life as Fanny) brought tremendous joy to Samuel and Martha and remained devoted to their new family for the rest of their lives. For several years, they also raised Martha's younger stepbrother, Mason Cogswell.

An early 20th Century study of the Governors of Connecticut states that upon Samuel's arrival in Norwich "his uncommon ability was recognized at once, and honors heaped upon him."[13] The fact that both he and his wife had deep family roots in the community certainly made the transition much smoother.[14] The town's economically progressive yet socially conservative character also fit Samuel well.[15] Shortly after he arrived, he became the principal attorney for the town. The majority of his private practice, however, concerned the collection of debts owed to prominent merchants throughout New England. As one biographer states: "There is no evidence that he ever handled a criminal case in his entire career...and [he] apparently never argued before a jury."[16] Not surprisingly, Samuel's careful, meticulous style impressed many of the most distinguished members of the community who eventually encouraged him to seek public office. Even though he continued to practice law whenever possible, the rest of his life would be devoted to public service.

Samuel's public life began in 1764 when he was elected for one year to represent Norwich in the Connecticut General Assembly. The following year, that same General Assembly appointed Samuel to serve as a Justice of the Peace for New London County, an office he held for nearly a decade. But the most important development in 1765 was Parliament's adoption of the Stamp Act.[17] In response, the Norwich Town Clerk, Benjamin Huntington (Samuel's second cousin) called a Town Meeting to ascertain whether or not the local citizens wanted him to abide by the new law. It was Samuel who introduced a resolution that directed "that the clerk shall proceed in his office as usual, and the town will save him harmless from all damage that he may sustain thereby."[18]

Despite his forthright opposition to an Act of Parliament, Samuel still considered himself a loyal subject of the British Crown. What is most amazing is that he was appointed King's Attorney for Connecticut that same year.[19]

Shortly after the Stamp Act was passed, all colonial governors were ordered by the King to take an oath of loyalty pertaining to enactment of that legislation. Connecticut's popular governor, Thomas Fitch--who had tried in vain to derail the Act before its adoption--finally submitted to the oath on October 29, 1765, two days before the Act went into effect. The people were outraged. Since Connecticut, unlike most other colonies, enjoyed the right of electing its own chief executive, popular displeasure with Gov. Fitch was demonstrated at the polls the following May when he was defeated for reelection by his Lt. Governor, William Pitkin, who had been one of the earliest opponents of that measure.[20] Pitkin's election represented a major turning point in Connecticut politics. From the day he assumed the governorship in 1766, Connecticut never again hesitated to speak out on behalf of American liberty.

John Adams characterized Connecticut politics as having "always been governed by an aristocracy, more decisively than the empire of Great Britain is. Half a dozen, or, at most, a dozen families, have controlled that country when a colony, as well as since it has been a state."[21] Samuel was now a member of that elite body, but he kept a low political profile as he continued his law practice and carried out his public duties.

When Gov. Pitkin died in 1769, Lt. Gov. Jonathan Trumbull succeeded him. Gov. Trumbull served his state with dedication and distinction for the next fourteen tumultuous years.[22] During that period, as one of the Governor's closest allies and most devoted friends, Samuel became part of the inner sanctum of the Trumbull Administration.

On the brink of the Revolution, Samuel took on additional public responsibilities. He was elected tax collector for Norwich in 1773. That spring he was also selected by the General Assembly to fill a vacancy on the Superior Court. One year later, as news of the Intolerable Acts spread across America,[23] a special Norwich Town Meeting was called for June 6, 1774. At that gathering, Samuel was chosen to head a nine-member committee which drafted the town's response to the Anglo-American crisis: "VOTED: that we will to the utmost of our abilities assert and defend the Liberties and Immunities of British America, and that we will cooperate with our Brethren in this and the other Colonies in such reasonable measures as shall in General Congress or otherwise be judged most proper to relieve us from Burthens which we now feel, and secure us from greater evils we fear will follow from the principles adopted by the British Parliament respecting the town of Boston."[24]

Two years later, while retaining his seat on the Court, Samuel was again chosen as a deputy for the Connecticut House of Representatives but he resigned his seat when he was elected as one of the twelve Assistants on the Governor's Council which collectively served as the upper chamber of the legislature. Membership in this self-perpetuating oligarchy was second only to the chief executive itself.[25] Not surprisingly, as his patriot responsibilities intensified, Samuel severed his official link to the Crown by resigning his commission as King's Attorney in 1774.[26]

Three months after shots were first fired at Lexington and Concord, Samuel represented Connecticut's Upper Chamber on the joint legislative committee which designed an emergency military preparedness program for the colony. Of even greater importance, he was appointed to the nine-member Council of Safety (initially known as the Committee of War) which was created by the General Assembly to assist Gov. Trumbull in managing colonial affairs whenever the legislature was not in session.[27] The fact that three of the nine Council members were named Huntington is a clear indication of the importance of Samuel's family ties.[28] From June through December 1775 Samuel played an active role as a member of that Council.

That October, the General Assembly elected Connecticut's delegates to the next session of the Continental Congress. Two incumbents, Roger Sherman and Titus Hosmer, were reelected, but their controversial colleagues, Silas Deane and Eliphalet Dyer, were replaced. In a rare moment of insight, Deane reflected on his defeat in a letter to his wife that November: "I have greater reason to wonder how I ever became popular at all."[29] Oliver Wolcott, William Williams and Samuel Huntington were elected to replace them. Since Sherman, Wolcott and Huntington received the most votes, they were designated as Connecticut's official congressional delegates for the new year while Hosmer and Williams were alternates.[30]

At the start of 1776 Samuel and his colleague, Oliver Wolcott, set out for Congress. Their lives were about to intersect with one of the most momentous years in modern history. The two delegates arrived in Philadelphia on Monday, January 15 and took their seats the following day. While Wolcott's first letter home mentioned the hardships of traveling in the dead of winter, Samuel simply stated that "I arrived at this place the last Monday Morning after a Comfortable Journey Considering the Season."[31] His understated style quickly proved popular with his fellow delegates who had grown weary of Silas Deane's confrontational attitude.

As with all delegates, Samuel was deluged with committee assignments from the start. Initially he served on Ad Hoc Committees which dealt with short-term assignments. But, as his diligence to duty became obvious, his work load continued to increase. Only two weeks after his arrival, however, Samuel was stricken with smallpox and confined to his bed until the third week of February when he was well enough to return to Congress. Once back, he took the seat previously held by Silas Deane on the powerful Marine Committee; and, in early September he became one of the five members of the Board of War. Samuel also joined young Thomas Jefferson on the Committee on Indian Affairs and held membership on the Post Office Committee. In all, he served on a total of fifteen committees during that period, two of which were central to the conduct of the war.[32]

In late March 1776, Samuel shared his initial thoughts on life in Philadelphia with the Rev. James Cogswell, his wife's stepfather. It began with a humorous account of one of his first experiences in a big city. "On

Sunday morning the 17th Inst my attention from my Chamber window was Suddenly called to behold a mighty Cavalcade of Plebeians marching thro' the Street with drums beating..." He went on to describe that "I was apprehensive Some outrage was about to be Committed, but Soon perceived my mistaken apprehentions & that it was a Religious exercise of the Sons of Saint Patrick, it being the anniversary of that Saint..."

After a good laugh, Samuel went on to describe life as a member of Congress. "My Business is very arduous as well as Important. We commonly Set from Ten in the morning until between four & five in the afternoon Intent on business without any refreshment. It was very tedious at first but by usage is become Tolerable." Samuel then added a brief comment which expressed his Calvinist philosophy: "It is disagreable to be So long removed from my family & Friends, however I must chearfully obey the calls & dictates of Providence with out refuising." [33]

Beyond its daily routine, the primary focus of this Congressional session was the debate over Independence. It began only days before Samuel arrived in the Capital when Thomas Paine's revolutionary pamphlet, Common Sense, started to circulate throughout the colonies. No longer was the king himself exempt from public ridicule. On June 10, Richard Henry Lee of Virginia introduced the Virginia Resolution which finally called for Independence. Five days later, the Connecticut General Assembly instructed its delegates to support independence. Samuel did exactly that on July 2, the day before his forty-fifth birthday. He and his fellow delegate, Roger Sherman, cast Connecticut's vote for Independence and then, two days later, endorsed the Declaration which announced that fateful step to all the world. On August 2, when all the delegates were invited to affix their signatures to the document, Samuel and his Connecticut colleagues signed on the lower right-hand side. He is one of six Presidents whose signatures appear on the Declaration: four from the First American Republic---Hancock, Huntington, Lee and McKean--and two from the Second Republic--Adams and Jefferson.. [34]

In late August and again in early September, Samuel shared his thoughts with his political associates back home. He described the conflict as "Contending for our Just rights on the Defensive" and fretted over "the disagreable Intelligence of our Troops Evacuating Long Island." He dismissed Lord Howe's last-minute peace initiative as an attempt on Howe's part "to Create a belief in the people that he is desirous for peace & we desire to protract the war." And, on a personal note, Samuel added that "I have enjoyed as much health as could be expected with the fatigue of business during the Sultry Season in the Stagnate air of this City." He concluded his August letter by wistfully stating that "Sometimes [I] pant for the purer Air of my native land."[35]

At the same time, Samuel's congressional colleague, William Williams, was urging members of the Connecticut legislature to "rechose" both Sherman and Huntington for another year's service. "I must say," Williams wrote in late September 1776, "that Mr Sherman...has acquired much Respect & is an exceeding valuable Member, & so is Mr Huntington & truly judicious, upright & worthy..."[36]

On October 10, 1776, Samuel was overwhelmingly reelected by the Connecticut General Assembly to continue his service as a congressional delegate. In fact, Samuel's vote total was second only to Roger Sherman who by then had become a congressional institution. But the demands of that extraordinary year had taken their toll on Samuel's health. He returned home to Norwich in early November to regain his strength and to inhale its "purer" air.[37] Back in Philadelphia, Samuel's dedication and broad national view were sorely missed by his colleagues. Over two decades later Pennsylvania Delegate Benjamin Rush reflected on those critical days when he described Samuel Huntington as "a sensible, candid and worthy man, and wholly free from State prejudices."[38]

Samuel's homecoming, however, was anything but restful. Less than a week after he returned, he traveled to a meeting of the Council of Safety in Lebanon and then went on to Hartford for a special session of the General Assembly on November 19. At the end of the month he and his fellow members of the Governor's Council met with Gov. Trumbull. Finally, in early December, Samuel did return home for two glorious weeks during which he attended to private business and family affairs. But he was off again for a special legislative session in Middletown on December 18, and yet another meeting of the Governor's Council ten days later.[39] It was, to say the least, an exhausting yet exhilarating year for the mild-mannered attorney.

Despite his reelection as a congressional delegate, Samuel's other political duties kept him in New England throughout 1777. He was once again reelected as a member of the Governor's Council and reappointed as an assistant judge of the Superior Court. During the regular General Assembly session from May 8 through June 7 he served as the Council's representative on a number of joint committees, including several which pertained to military affairs. On July 18, the Council of Safety then appointed him as a member of Connecticut's delegation to meet in Springfield, Massachusetts with representatives of New York and other New England States to discuss the current economic crisis. Two years earlier, Congress had begun to issue paper currency, but public confidence in the new "Continentals" had always been lukewarm, at best. That conference ended on August 6 without any clear solution in sight.[40] Both Samuel and Congress continued to wrestle with the crisis for years.

Exactly one week after the Springfield Conference, Samuel was back in Hartford for a special legislative session on August 13, 1777. He returned in early October for the regular fall session of the General Assembly where he was again elected to represent Connecticut in Congress.[41] Most of January 1778 he spent preparing for another long absence from home and on February 16, 1778, Samuel resumed his seat in Congress after an absence of fifteen months. By now, however, the Continental Congress was meeting in York, Pennsylvania since Philadelphia had been occupied by Lord Howe and the British Army the previous October.

Other major developments during Samuel's absence included John Hancock's resignation as President because of poor health. Henry Laurens of South Carolina, "the Hancock of the South," had been elected to replace him. In addition, the Articles of Confederation had been adopted in November 1777. The Articles, which were designed to serve as the basic structure for the new national government, did not become operative for over three more years since all thirteen States still had to ratify them.

Samuel was again appointed to serve on the Marine Committee along with a litany of other important assignments, several of which dealt with the sorry state of the economy. As a highly respected "hard money" man who strenuously opposed inflationary currency, Samuel later confided to fellow delegate Oliver Wolcott that "in my Opinion the most Essential thing for giving any Stability to the Currency is to Stop the press."[42]

Like President Henry Laurens, Samuel and his Connecticut colleagues demonstrated intense opposition to Gen. Washington's proposal to provide half-pay for life to officers in the Continental Army if they agreed to serve for the duration of the war. To Washington, "the salvation of the cause depends upon it..."[43] But Samuel was one of nine members of what Professor James Henderson describes as the "radical center" who strenuously objected to the economic, military and social implications of Washington's plan.[44] A letter to Gov. Trumbull from the Connecticut Delegation on May 18, written by Samuel, described the plan as "the most painfull & disagreable question that hath ever been Agitated in Congress."[45]

On May 15 an amendment was moved to limit the half-pay pension to only seven years for commissioned officers and to add a bonus of $80 for non-commissioned staff and soldiers. Samuel, President Laurens and five other members of the radical center reluctantly voted for the congressional compromise "so as to answer the necessities of the Army & preserve harmony & unanimity in all the States."[46]

At approximately the same time, Samuel split with President Laurens and many of his colleagues on another critical topic. On April 20, 1778, word reached Congress that Lord North was prepared to offer fresh terms for opening peace talks with the American colonies. Two days later, in the hope of ending the war, Samuel risked alienating some of his best friends when he introduced the first motion of his congressional career:

> "Resolved, That notwithstanding the Unmeritted, Injurious & Cruel Treatment the United States of America have receivd from the hands of Great Brittain, they are ever willing & desirous to put an end to the Calamities of War; & not averse from entering into a Treaty for Peace and Commerce between the two Countries for the mutual Interest & Benefit of both, Upon Terms not Inconsistant with the Freedom, Sovereignty & Independence of these States..."[47]

President Laurens argued against Samuel's Resolution. "I am averse," he said. "The whole World must know we are disposed to treat of Peace & to conclude one upon honorable terms. To Publish therefore is unnecessary--it would be a dangerous Act, encourage our Enemies & alarm our friends."[48] The debate, however, was cut short on May 2, 1778, when the delegates were called back into a rare Saturday night session. News had just arrived from Paris that a Franco-American Alliance had finally been reached.[49] The following Monday that Alliance was unanimously ratified by Congress. And, on June 17, Congress unanimously rejected the British peace proposal but made clear that it would still be willing to discuss such a motion "when the king of Great Britain shall demonstrate a sincere disposition for that purpose." Congress went on to clarify that "The only solid proof of this disposition, will be, an explicit acknowledgement of the independence of these states, or the withdrawing his fleets and armies."[50]

Throughout these critical days Samuel continued to battle poor health. Both he and his colleague Oliver Wolcott suffered from the "Lime water" common to York which, according to Delegate James Lovell, "tears your Countryman's Bowels out..."[51] Personal finances were also a source of constant concern. Unlike the wealthy members of Congress, Samuel's income was negligible during his months of congressional service. Both his law practice and his lands suffered from his long absences. Nevertheless, he remained in Congress long enough to mark the withdrawal of British forces from Philadelphia in June and the triumphant reentry of Congress in time to celebrate the second anniversary of American Independence in early July.

On July 9, only hours before his departure, Samuel joined his Connecticut colleagues in signing the engrossed parchment copy of the Articles of Confederation.[52] Nine days later he arrived home in Connecticut where he would devote his energy to personal and State business for the rest of the year.

When Samuel finally did return to Congress on Friday, May 21, 1779, he was about to enter the most important phase of his life. By now, he was widely recognized by his congressional colleagues as a humble, yet seasoned legislator who preferred to lead by example. Between May and September he introduced six motions and served on twenty committees, including reappointment to the Marine Committee. But his most important responsibility that summer was as a member of the five-person committee which drafted the instructions for the soon-to-be-appointed American peace negotiator. The significance of that appointment is reflected in the fact that three of the five committee members--Laurens, Huntington and McKean--also served as President of Congress during the Revolution.[53]

Despite the economic crisis and endless congressional bickering, Samuel became increasingly hopeful as the summer wore on. He drew special encouragement from Spain's declaration of war on Britain in mid-June. "The Aspects of public afairs in Europe at present are very favourable" he told Gov. Trumbull. "There Seems great probability that dire necessity will Soon bring Great Brittain in Spite of themselves to reasonable terms of peace with us."[54]

Through it all, Samuel still detested life in Philadelphia and confided to a friend that summer that "I heartily wish that Congress were removed from this City.."[55] At the very least, Samuel hoped to head home "as soon as public business will permit." Accordingly, on September 9, he wrote to Gov. Trumbull asking permission "to retire and Attend to my private concerns."[56]

Fate, however, imposed a very different agenda. Through a series of intricate negotiations, President John Jay was selected to serve as Minister Plenipotentiary to Spain on September 28, 1779.[57] The following day, Samuel Huntington was unanimously elected to replace Jay as the sixth President of Congress. By the time he relinquished the office 21 months later, Samuel's presidential term would be second only to John Hancock's in length of service during the First Republic.

How did this self-educated small town Yankee lawyer reach the highest office in his new nation ? He did not yet dominate his home state the way Randolph and Middleton did when they were elected nor was Samuel even close to the economic status of Hancock and Laurens. Like Jay, however, Samuel had consistently exhibited a commitment to a national rather than regional perspective, and he had demonstrated uncommon sense in an assembly better known for oversized egos and heated rhetoric. At this critical stage of the war, Samuel Huntington was, in the eyes of his peers, the obvious choice as demonstrated by his unanimous election in 1779 and his reelection one year later.

Now that he was President, one of Samuel's first official duties was to prepare a circular letter to the Governors of all thirteen States, trying to convince them of "the necessity of the punctual payment of their respective Quotas on which...the existence of their Army, and the support of their Liberties so greatly depend."[58] It was among the first of scores of official letters her would write throughout his presidency. It was an arduous and exhausting task as his predecessors knew all too well.

Samuel's presidential duties also required that he preside over Congress during its endless hours of discussion and debate. True to character, he took his responsibility so seriously that he only missed four out of 242 roll call votes during his tenure. The fact that he was only in the minority on 23 of those votes further indicates how closely his views mirrored the sentiment of the body.[59] It also reflected his personal philosophy concerning public service. "I find one Consolation very necessary in public life," he confided to a friend in early 1780, "that is to believe or at least act as if I did fully believe there are many wise men who can Judge better than myself on Important Subjects, & I have the happiness generally to unite in promoting their determinations, as far as duty requires in any Sphere I am called to act in..."[60]

The presidency had a significant impact on Samuel's personal life. For the first time, his wife Martha joined him in Philadelphia in late 1779. The Marquis de Chastellux, who occasionally dined at the President's house during his travels in America, described his host: "We found him in his cabinet, lighted by a single candle...Mr. Huntington," he wrote, "is an upright man, and exposes no party." The Marquis added that "Mrs. Huntington [is] a stout, rather good-looking woman, but no longer young."[61]

In March 1780, Congress rented the Joseph Pemberton House, one of the finest in the city, as the President's official residence.[62] Located only two blocks from the State House where Congress met, it was noted for its beautiful gardens. A carriage, horses and servants were also provided. Unfortunately, the presidential salary was inadequate to meet the financial demands of his new office which included receiving "the Company of all Forreigners of Distinction Especially the Foreign Minister."[63] Whenever possible, he and Martha maintained their simple republican lifestyle out of necessity as well as choice. Over breakfast one morning, while conversing with Pierre DuPonceau, Baron von Steuben's young French secretary, the President asked: "What now, Mr. Duponceau, would the princes of Europe say, could they see the first magistrate of this great country at his frugal repast?"[64]

As the bills mounted Samuel's Yankee soul must have cast a deep sigh when he was forced to turn to his home State for support. He wrote to Gov. Trumbull on January 17, 1780, that "I am under the disagreable necessity of Requesting that two thousand dollars may be advanced to me or my order out of the public Treasury for which I will be Accountable...I am unwill[ing] to request any Advancement from the Continental Treasury, which would be rather out of Character."[65] The Connecticut Legislature came to his rescue.

Ridicule from the British Press was another irritant that came with the office. On November 6, 1779, *The Royal Gazette*, published in occupied New York, featured a poem entitled *The Congratulations*:

Joy to great Congress, joy an hundred fold,
The grand cajolers are themselves cajol'd,
The farce of empire will be finish'd soon,
And each mock-monarch dwindle to a loon,
Mock-money and mock-states shall melt away,
And the mock troops disband for want of pay.
E'en now decisive ruin is prepar'd,
E'en now the heart of Huntington is scar'd.[66]

Unfortunately, the condition of the Army during the harsh winter of 1779-80 was even worse than *The Gazette* depicted. As President, it was Samuel's job to plead with the States to meet their obligations. He confided to Gov. Trumbull that "I am distressed on account of Supplies for the Army, I fear they will not be fed thro' the winter without vigorous Exertions by the Several States." He attributed this dire situation to the fact that "Individuals Seem to have laid aside all thoughts of danger, and are pursuing their private gains in Opposition to the public."[67]

Of even greater importance was the continuous struggle all Revolutionary War Presidents faced in urging the States to meet their troop quotas. In his Circular letter to the Governors in February 1780, Samuel underscored that "It is recommended to each State respectively in the strongest Terms punctually to comply with this requisition by furnishing their respective Quotas of Men compleat without loss of Time." He concluded his letter by stating that "Vigorous exertions and a respectable Army in the field are the most sure means...to crown it [the spring campaign] with the desired success and put a period to the Contest upon honourable Terms."[68]

As if the profound problems facing the military were not enough, the nation's fiscal crisis also came to a head that same spring. The exchange rate for Continental currency had dropped to $167.50 per Spanish milled dollar. On March 18, with a stroke of his pen, Samuel signed legislation which decreed that Continentals would henceforth be redeemable at one-fortieth their face value. The new bills to be issued would be redeemable in specie after six years at six percent interest.[69] In forwarding the Resolution to the States, Samuel described the new monetary policy as "the result of much Labour and Deliberation" and he assured the Governors that it was "the happiest Expedient that could be adopted to extricate these States from the Embarrassments of a fluctuating Medium and at the same time in some Measure afford the necessary Means for supporting the ensuing Campaign."[70]

These drastic economic measures did help, but they fell short of the Army's basic needs. Washington was unable to mount a spring campaign. Despite these developments, spirits temporarily lifted when word arrived that Comte de Rochambeau had sailed from France with 5,000 men. Samuel's optimism was obvious when he wrote to Gen. Benjamin Lincoln on May 17, 1780, informing him that "we may daily expect the Arrival of a considerable Armament of Naval & Land Forces from France to act in Conjunction with our Forces which gives us great Reason to hope we may be able to expell our Enemies from all their Posts in the United States." In a cruel twist of fate, he added, "I am unable to judge in what Situation this Leter may find you but make no Doubt if you are able to defend the Town [Charleston] but a little longer the Enemy will be obliged to raise their Siege or become Prisoners."[71]

What Samuel did not know as he penned those words was that Gen. Lincoln was already a prisoner. Five days earlier he had been forced to surrender the city of Charleston and his entire army to Gen. Clinton, the British commander. As Gen. Clinton later described his victory: "... there fell into our hands seven generals and a multitude of other officers, belonging to ten Continental regiments and three battlions of artillery, which, with the militia and sailors doing duty in the siege, amounted to about six thousand men in arms."[72] It was America's greatest military defeat of the entire war. It's impact on Patriot morale and international confidence was devastating.

Samuel worked tirelessly to counteract the impact of depressing military developments on America's allies by showering the French, in particular, with attention and praise. He took every opportunity to nurture a strong bond with the French Minister, the Chevalier de La Luzerne. Typical of his approach was his letter to the Minister on May 24, 1780: "Permit me Sir to express the Pleasure and Satisfaction which I have received from the active Zeal and Ardour which the Minister of France hath manifested on all Occasions, and especially the present, to promote the Interest, and aid the Exertions of these United States."[73] These sentiments were reciprocated by the French. The Marquis de Barbe-Marbois, a member of the French Delegation to the United States, described President Huntington to the French Foreign Minister, Vergennes, as a man "whose conduct we have always found worthy of praise...[a] straightforward and unpretentious man, one of the finest citizens of America."[74]

By late July events in Europe gave Samuel renewed hope that developments overseas would work to America's favor. "We have lately received Intelligence," he wrote to a friend, "that the United Netherlands with Denmark, Sweeden & the Empress of Russia at their head have determind to maintain a Neutrality & protect their Trade." He described it as "an important Stroke & all that America would wish for on the Subject..." More surprisingly, Samuel stated that "great Harmony & Unanimity continues in Congress. Notwithstanding the many Embarassments & difficulties they have to go through..."[75]

There was no doubt, however, that the Continental Army was still in desperate need of recruits and supplies. Once again, some Members of Congress seriously proposed giving Washington dictatorial powers to force the States to support the troops.[76] On August 1, 1780, Rhode Island Delegate Ezekiel Cornell wrote to Gov. William Greene: "The Necessity of appointing General Washington, sole Dictator of America, is again talked of as the only means under God by which we can be saved..."[77] James Lovell of Massachusetts described the idea as "a most scandalous Motion" and "the product of Camp Education of some of our Members..." But he admitted that "if we have not a Supply of Money from the States, we must expect frequent Maggets about creating Omnipotencies."[78]

Inside Congress, the Delegates voted to establish "civil executive departments" as the foundation of a permanent national government. Previously, all executive tasks had been performed by congressional committees or by either the President or Secretary. On January 10, 1781, Congress approved a new Department of Foreign Affairs and one month later it created the Departments of War, Finance and Marine.[79] Robert Morris of Pennsylvania, the first Superintendent of Finance, then persuaded the delegates, including President Huntington, to authorize a National Bank.[80]

After the Articles of Confederation went into effect on March 1, 1781,

Congress further refined its operating procedures by adopting twenty-eight revised rules for the conduct of congressional business.[81]

Less than two months later Congress and the country were shaken by news of Gen. Benedict Arnold's defection to the British Army. Samuel was doubly disturbed by "the Black & infamous Conduct of Arnold" because the general was also a native of Samuel's home town of Norwich.[82] Not only had Arnold been one of the most brilliant officers in the Continental Army, but his change of allegiance near the end of such a disastrous year also implied that he had given up hope of American victory.[83]

In this intense atmosphere, Samuel prepared for retirement. Even though the Articles of Confederation had not yet been ratified by all thirteen States, he made clear his intention to honor the provision in Article IX which mandated a one year presidential term.[84] He wrote to Gov. Trumbull in early September that "The Period that confines me to my present painful Situation is almost expired and I have been long absent from any private Affairs & my health somewhat impaired with the Burthen & Fatigue of Business, I hope to obtain Leave of Absence in about a Month and wish a Gentleman from Connecticut better qualified may come forward to relieve me."[85] His congressional colleagues, however, felt otherwise. On Thursday, September 28, 1780, they voted unanimously to waive the term limit in order for Samuel to remain in office for up to one additional year.[86]

Delegate John Mathews of South Carolina did vote for the motion but his private correspondence spewed forth a hatred of the President that stands in stark contrast to almost every other opinion ever recorded. He wrote that "I think of all the men of ambition I have ever met with in the course of my peregrinations...S. H. bears away the prize in tryumph...an elevated station had made a man forget himself, who from being a very modest one, had so strongly inbibed the sweets of power, as to become a very conceited, & ambitious one." But Mathews also objected to the process itself: "Could Old Randolph have risen from the Dead, & been in the chair, I wou'd have opposed his continuance, with the same activity & spirit, I did the present person, on the principles of true Republicanism..."[87]

Delegate Thomas Rodney of Delaware offered a far more popular view: "His Excellency Samuel Huntington President is a Man of a Mild, Steady & firm Conduct and of Sound & Methodical Judgment tho not a Man of Many Words or very Shining abilities. But upon the Whole is better Suted to Preside than any other Member Now in Congress." Rodney added that "In his Dress & Manners, he is very plain, very gentlemanly and Truely republican."[88]

As Samuel began his second year in office, Congress developed yet another plan to reorganize the Army. The lack of adequate support for the troops grew increasingly critical month after month. In mid-September 1780, Samuel confided to Gov. Trumbull that "should either of the States fail substantially to comply with this requisition it is more than probable the Army must disband, or supply themselves at the Point of the Bayonet, and the most fatal Consequences must insue."[89]

While the never-ending debate over military affairs and finances continued to grip Congress, the logjam over ratification of the Articles of Confederation finally came to an end in late February 1781 when Maryland Delegate John Hanson, a future President, signed the document and thereby made adoption unanimous.[90] According to noted historian Edmund Cody Burnett it "roused the majority of its members to a pitch of enthusiasm greater probably than they had known since the news of the French treaty."[91] America's first constitution went into effect at Noon on Thursday, March 1, 1781.

Thomas Rodney captured that historic day in his diary: "At Two OClock the members of Congress, The members of the General Assembly of Pensylvania, the President and Council of that State, the officers of the Army in Town, the officers of State and a great number of Gentlemen waited on the President of Congress To Congratulate him on this occasion; And partook of a Collation preparired at his House for that purpose...In the evening there was a grand exhibition of fireworks at the State House, & also on board Paul Jones Frigate in the Harbour..."[92]

Samuel informed the Governors of the adoption of the Articles in his typical understated style: "We are happy to congratulate our Constituents on this important Event, desired by our Friends but dreaded by our Enemies."[93] During the next few months Samuel devoted his energy to implementing the Articles while overseeing the daily work of Congress.[94] The weight of his responsibilities, however, forced him to confide to Gov. Trumbull in late March 1781 that "I cannot think of enduring the Burden & Confinement of my present Situation another Summer."[95]

On May 8 Samuel asked for an official leave of absence but when Congress held an election on May 10 to replace him, no candidate had more than two votes. According to Delegate John Witherspoon of New Jersey, "we requested the President to continue..."[96] Samuel did so for another two months but in early July, in his farewell letter to Gen. Washington, Samuel stated that "My Health is so much impaired by long Confinement & Application as compels me to retire from Congress." But, ever the optimist, he added that "It also gives me much Satisfaction on retiring, to see our public Affairs, in many Respects wear a more promising Aspect than heretofore."[97]

On Monday, July 9, 1781, Congress accepted Samuel Huntington's resignation and elected Samuel Johnston of North Carolina to replace him. But the next day, as the Journal records, "Mr. [Samuel] Johnston having decline to accept the office of President, and offered such reasons as were satisfactory, the House proceeded to another election; and, the ballots being taken, the hon. Thomas McKean was elected."[98] Unlike Hancock and Laurens, it is hardly surprising that Samuel did not presume to offer his colleagues a formal farewell address. He simply told them "I entertain the highest sense of the honor they have done me."[99] By resolution, Congress expressed its thanks to the departing President "in testimony of their approbation of his conduct in the chair and in the execution of public business."[100]

Samuel carried his strong nationalist views with him as he returned to Connecticut. He reached Norwich on the evening of July 25, 1781, where he was saluted by thirteen cannon and a flood of friends and family.[101] Three months later, Cornwallis surrendered at Yorktown and the ultimate outcome of the war finally came into focus. As the British troops gradually withdrew from America, Samuel rebuilt his legal practice and resumed an active role in State Government as a member of the Governor's Council and a Judge of the Superior Court. Even though he was again elected to Congress in May 1782, he did not attend. But, when he was reelected a year later, Samuel did return to Congress which was then meeting in Princeton. Elias Boudinot of New Jersey was serving as President. On July 29, 1783, Samuel resumed his congressional duties one last time.

The major topic under debate was how to disband the Continental Army. Gen. Washington appeared before Congress in late August to help to devise such a plan. Samuel invited the General "to breakfast at my lodgings in the morning of the Same day..."[102] Finally, on November 4, Congress authorized the discharge of the Continental troops "except 500 men, with proper officers." It was Samuel's last recorded vote as a Member of the Continental Congress. On his motion, the assembly adjourned that same day and reconvened several weeks later in Annapolis.[103] By then, Samuel was home for good, ready to assume leadership of his State during the critical postwar years.

Because of his calm demeanor and his long absences while serving in Congress, Samuel had been able to avoid most of the partisan conflicts which engulfed Connecticut politics at the end of the war. As a result, when Gov. Trumbull retired in 1784, Samuel had the unusual distinction of becoming the candidate for Lt. Governor of both major factions. Rhode Island Delegate William Ellery best described the situation in a letter to Samuel that June: "Your natural disposition, and knowledge of mankind concurr in enabling you to steer your bark with wonderful facility and without offense through the storms of contending parties."[104] Even though the elderly Matthew Griswold was elected Governor after 15 years as Trumbull's deputy "more as a reward for past service,"[105] it became increasingly clear that Samuel would soon succeed him as the State's chief executive. As Lt. Governor, Samuel also became Chief Justice of the State Superior Court on which he had served for eleven years as an Associate Judge.

In 1785, Samuel uncharacteristically challenged Gov. Griswold's reelection but he was narrowly defeated by the incumbent. The following year none of the gubernatorial candidates received a majority. Under the Connecticut Constitution, the General Assembly then cast the final vote. It overwhelmingly elected 54-year-old Samuel Huntington as Connecticut's third Governor since Independence.[106] He served with distinction in that office for the remaining ten years of his life.

In keeping with his self-effacing philosophy, Samuel left most legislative matters to the General Assembly even though he did urge various progressive reforms such as abolishing whipping and death as punishments for burglary.[107] Samuel devoted most of his efforts to his administrative duties as Governor, which he usually conducted from his home in Norwich since Connecticut did not provide a Governor's Mansion. Each year, however, he traveled to Hartford in May and New Haven in October to preside over the Legislature and to confer with the Council.[108]

From his unique perspective as a former President, Samuel, now Governor, gave critical support to the call for a national convention to propose amendments to the Articles of Confederation. Through his insistence, the General Assembly made the election of delegates to that convention (which became the Constitutional Convention) its first legislative priority when it met in Hartford in May 1787. The following January, during Connecticut's Ratification Convention, Samuel spoke out strongly in support of the new Constitution. He argued from personal experience "that the great council of the union must have a controlling power with respect to national concerns" and he reminded the delegates that they were participating in "a new event in the history of mankind."[109] On January 9, 1788, by a vote of more than three to one, Connecticut became the fourth State to ratify the document.[110]

One year later, Connecticut selected Samuel as a member of the first Electoral College. Like his presidential predecessors Hancock and Jay, Samuel even received a few home-state votes for Vice President in that year's election.[111] That fall, as Governor of the State, Samuel officially welcomed President Washington to New Haven during his official tour of New England.[112]

After 33 years of marriage, Samuel's devoted wife Martha died on June 3, 1794. Fortunately, his two foster children were there to care for him during his final months until he, too, passed away at home on Tuesday, January 5, 1796 at the age of 64. Funeral services with full honors were held at the First Church of Norwich. The text of Pastor Joseph Strong's laudatory sermon is still widely available.[113] And then Gov. Samuel Huntington of Connecticut--the sixth President of the Continental Congress--was laid to rest in Old Norwichtown Burial Ground. His plain red brick grave still stands in the shadow of his home at 34 East Town Street.

Less than five months after her foster father's death, Fanny married the Rev. E. D. Griffin of Boston who later became the President of Williams College. Her older brother Samuel, a lawyer, followed in the President's footsteps. He moved west to Ohio in 1801 where he enjoyed an active public life, which included serving as Chief Justice of the State Supreme Court and ultimately winning election as the third Governor of Ohio.

Today, only the county and town of Huntington, Indiana are still named in honor of President Samuel Huntington. Even the Connecticut village that once shared that distinction was rededicated years later to commemorate a local businessman.[114] Like his thirteen distinguished colleagues, Samuel's remarkable life and critical contribution to the founding of the United States are now all but forgotten. And yet, for nearly two years, during some of the darkest days of the Revolution, Samuel devoted all his energy and jeopardized his fragile health as his new nation's Head of State.

In many respects, Samuel Huntington served as a model for some of the great men who followed him as President during the Second Republic. Like Jefferson, he practiced simple republican virtues both publicly and privately. Like Coolidge, he proved that a soft-spoken Yankee could win the respect and support of his peers nationwide. And like Truman, Samuel demonstrated that, in a democracy, a self-educated man of humble origins could indeed lead his nation through war and renewal.

WHILE SAMUEL HUNTINGTON WAS PRESIDENT

September 1779 - July 1781

Battles throughout the South became the focus of the War during President Samuel Huntington's twenty-one months in office. On September 23, 1779, the United States under Gen. Benjamin Lincoln joined with Admiral d'Estaing's French fleet to begin a siege of British forces at Savannah. On October 9, they launched a full scale attack but met fierce British resistance.[115] The French and Americans suffered heavy casualties, including the death of Gen. Pulaski, before they were finally forced to withdraw.[116]

The following spring witnessed America's greatest military defeat of the war. On May 12, 1780, at the urging of local political leaders who wanted to spare the city further devastation, Gen. Lincoln was forced to surrender Charleston and his entire Army.[117]

Without consulting the Commander-in-Chief, Congress appointed Gen. Horatio Gates to replace Lincoln as they began to assemble a new Southern Army. Gates, the hero of Saratoga three years earlier had also been deeply implicated in the Conway Cabal that tried to topple Washington. Gates arrived in North Carolina in late July to join forces with Gen. Baron de Kalb.[118] As Gates marched south, British Gen. Cornwallis headed north from Charleston to intercept him. Their armies collided outside of Camden on August 16, 1780. Gates' Militia forces collapsed under fire and Gen. De Kalb died of his wounds. Only seven hundred Americans out of a force of four thousand escaped, including Gen. Gates, who lost his command in disgrace after fleeing from the battle.[119]

Having annihilated Gates' Army, Cornwallis marched on to Charlotte, North Carolina. In the process, he assigned Major Patrick Ferguson to lead a flanking operation in the surrounding countryside. At dawn on October 7, 1780, Ferguson's British forces encountered nearly 1,000 Patriots at King's Mountain along the North and South Carolina border. The Americans withstood repeated bayonet charges as they cut down the British troops. Ferguson was killed and his remaining 600 British soldiers surrendered. As Jefferson said later: "That glorious victory was the joyful annunciation of that turn in the tide of success which terminated the Revolutionary War."[120]

After the debacle with Gates, Congress did consult Washington on the appointment of yet another new Commander for the Southern Army, the third in less than a year. The honor went to Washington's favorite, Gen. Nathanael Greene, who assumed his new command in early December. When Greene sent 600 of his troops to the west under Gen. Daniel Morgan, Cornwallis responded by assigning the ruthless Lt. Col. Banastre Tarleton to lead his cavalry in pursuit. On January 17, 1781, Morgan, a crusty old veteran who had risen through the ranks, defeated Tarleton at the Battle of Cowpens in what some have called "a military masterpiece."[121]

Cornwallis was so infuriated by news of Cowpens that he burned his own supply wagons in order to expedite his unsuccessful pursuit of Morgan.[122] But by early March 1781, Morgan's troops had rejoined Greene along with additional forces that brought the American Army to 4,400 men. On March 15, 1781, Greene decided to face Cornwallis head on at Guilford Court House. After an intense battle, Cornwallis claimed victory even though more than a quarter of his British troops lay dead or wounded.[123] In Parliament, opposition leader Charles James Fox sarcastically charged that "Another such victory would ruin the British army."[124]

Cornwallis led the rest of his forces to Wilmington, North Carolina while Gen. Greene and his American troops eventually looped back into South Carolina. On April 25, 1781, Greene was forced to fall back from Hobkirk's Hill near Camden, but the British troops under Lord Rawdon soon withdrew all the way to Charleston.[125] It was the beginning of the end of the British military occupation of South Carolina's back country. Cornwallis' dream of decisively destroying the American Army had been denied.

Across the Atlantic, news of Clinton's occupation of Charleston in 1780 and Cronwallis' victory at Camden "even encouraged the transitory delusion that America might after all be militarily subjugated."[126] In early June the North Administration received an additional boost from the anti-Catholic riots that broke out in London. As the mob grew violent, 458 people were killed or wounded.[127] Even the opposition was forced to turn to North's government to stabilize the situation, thereby strengthening his overall position.

By 1781, however, reports of British losses at King's Mountain, Cowpens and Guilford Court House dampened any hopes of a quick end to the rebellion. Instead, as the situation in Europe grew worse, the British Government became increasingly eager to redeploy as many of its forces as possible. By now, the hostility of France, Spain and The Netherlands was of paramount importance to North and his Cabinet since "Britain was still, as she had been since 1763, without a friend in Europe." France was not only aiding the United States, but it was trying to recapture the West Indies and even India. Spain's major objective, as always, was the reconquest of Gibraltar. And The Netherlands and other European Powers were eager to share the spoils if Britain faltered.[128]

As historian W. E. Lunt states in his History of England, "Great Britain was vulnerable through the very extent of her empire, and the necessity of defense elsewhere weakened her offensive in America." As early as 1779, Lord North desired to resign rather than continue to prosecute the war against the American colonies. He remained only at the insistence of the King "who knew that the loss of North would [also] end his personal power" since royal interference in Parliament was clearly unconstitutional. As the Whig Party had repeatedly warned, the success of His Majesty's policy in American could result in the establishment of a tyranny at home. But even George III's determination "could not survive the news of Yorktown."[129]

President SAMUEL HUNTINGTON is buried at the Old Norwichtown
Burial Ground in Norwich, Connecticut only a short distance from his
Home at 34 East Town Street where he lived while serving as Governor
during the final decade of his life. (Photo of Samuel Huntington's home
by Jeffrey Leonard.)

Chapter 6

President
SAMUEL HUNTINGTON
of
CONNECTICUT

Notes

Abbreviation Key

JCC   Journals of the Continental Congress
LDC   Letters of Delegates to Congress
PHL   The Papers of Henry Laurens

[1] Larry R. Gerlach, Connecticut Congressman: Samuel Huntington, 1731-1796, (The American Revolution Bicentennial Commission of Connecticut, Hartford, 1976), p. 32.

[2] Barnet Schecter, The Battle for New York (Walker & Company, New York, 2002), p. 3.

[3] Ellen Douglas Larned, editor, History of Windham County, Connecticut (New York, C. Hamilton, 1874-1880), pp. 228 & 230.

[4] Albert. E. Waugh, Samuel Huntington and His Family, (The Pequot Press, Inc., Stonington, CT, 1968), pp. 5-6. There is an unresolved dispute over Samuel Huntington's exact birth date due to the condition of the pertinent document in the Windham Vital Records office. Biographers debate whether is was July 3 or July 5, old style, but all agree that he was born in 1731.

[5] Waugh, op. cit., p. 11. Waugh states that Samuel Huntington was apprenticed to a cooper but this point is persuasively contradicted by Gerlach, op. cit., pp. 15-16. See also: Charles A. Goodrich, Lives of the Signers to the Declaration of Independence, (R. G. H. Huntington & Philip D. Webb, Hartford, 1841), p. 170. Goodrich states: "...at the age of twenty-two he relinquished the labours of the field, for the more agreeable study of the law..."

[6] Joseph Strong, *A Sermon Delivered at the Funeral of His Excellency Samuel Huntington, Governor of the State of Connecticut* (Hudson & Goodwin, Hartford, 1796), p. 14.

[7] Gerlach, op. cit., p. 12.

[8] Frances M. Caulkins, History of Norwich (Hartford, 1866), p. 518.

[9] Gerlach, op. cit., p. 18. According to some sources, the date Samuel Huntington was admitted to the Bar is listed as 1758.

[10] Goodrich, op. cit., p. 170.

[11] Strong, op. cit., p. 15.

[12] Strong, op. cit., p. 16.

[13] Frederick Calvin Norton, The Governors of Connecticut (The Connecticut Magazine Company, Hartford, 1905), p. 114.

[14] Gerlach, op. cit., pp. 20-21. Samuel's second cousin, Benjamin Huntington (1736-1801), who became the first mayor of Norwich in 1784, quickly became his close friend and political ally. On the other hand, Martha Huntington was a member of the influential Lathrop family of Norwich. "Her grandfather, Col. Simon Lathrop, was a pillar of the community."

[15] Gerlach, op. cit., p. 20.

[16] Gerlach, op. cit., p. 19.

[17] See Introduction.

[18] Waugh, op. cit., p. 18.

[19] Waugh, op. cit., p. 19.

[20] Norton, op. cit., pp. 87-95.

[21] As cited in Waugh, op. cit., p. 24.

[22] James Grant Wilson and John Fiske, Appletons' Cyclopaedia of American Biography (D. Appleton & Company, New York, 1889), Vol. 6, p. 168.

[23] See Introduction.

[24] Waugh, op. cit., p. 22.

[25] Gerlach, op. cit., p. 25.

[26] Waugh, op. cit., p. 19.

[27] Christopher Collier, Roger Sherman's Connecticut: Yankee Politics and the American Revolution, (Wesleyan University Press, Middletown, Connecticut, 1971), footnote p. 88.

[28] Susan D. Huntington, "Samuel Huntington," *Connecticut Magazine*, Vol. 6, No. 4, 1900, p. 248. The three Huntingtons who served on the nine-member Council of Safety in 1775 were Samuel, Benjamin and Jabez, a former Speaker of the Connecticut General Assembly, all from Norwich.

[29] Paul H. Smith, Editor, LDC, (Library of Congress, Washington, DC, 1977), Vol. 2, p. 392; Silas Deane to Elizabeth Deane, November 26, 1775.

[30] Worthington Chauncey Ford, Editor, JCC 1774-1789, (Government Printing Office,

Washington, DC, 1906), Vol. IV, pp. 57-58. The official instructions stated that "...Roger Sherman, Oliver Wolcott, and Samuel Huntington, Esqrs. do attend said Congress, and on the failure of either of the said Gentlemen, by sickness, or otherwise, then the said Titus Hosmer, or William Williams, Esqrs. are to supply the place or places of any or either of the said three Gentlemen first named, in such manner, that three of said Delegates, and three only, do attend said Congress at any one Time..."

[31] LDC, op. cit., Vol. 3, p. 113.

[32] Gerlach, op. cit., pp. 33-34.

[33] LDC, op. cit., Vol. 3, p. 465; Samuel Huntington to James Cogswell, March 30, 1776.

[34] George Kelsey Dreher, Longer Than Expected, (Iron Horse Free Press, Midland, TX, 1996), pp. 1-2. Biographer George Kelsey Dreher also contends that Samuel Huntington is clearly visible in the center of the famous painting "The Declaration of Independence" by his friend Jonathan Trumbull, Jr. According to Dreher, Huntington is seated to Charles Thomson's right. To view the painting, see Dumas Malone, The Story of the Declaration of Independence, (Oxford University Press, New York, 1954), p. 91.

[35] LDC, op. cit.,Vol. 5, p. 119; Samuel Huntington to Matthew Griswold, Eliphalet Dyer and William Pitkin, August 30, 1776 and September 7, 1776.

[36] LDC, op. cit., Vol. 5, p. 267; William Williams to Jabez Huntington, September 30, 1776. Even though Williams stressed in his letter that he did not desire to be reelected as a delegate to Congress, he was reappointed along with Sherman, Huntington and Wolcott and Eliphalet Dyer and Richard Law were also added to the Connecticut delegation. See also: Vol. 5, p. 269.

[37] LDC, op. cit., Vol. 5, p. 449. In his claim for compensation for services rendered as a delegate to Congress, which clearly included travel time between Connecticut and Philadelphia, Samuel's request lists November 7, 1776, as the last date of his service for that year.

[38] George W. Corner, Editor, The Autobiography of Benjamin Rush (Greenwood Press, Westport, CT, 1948), p. 146.

[39] Gerlach, op. cit., pp. 37-38.

[40] Gerlach, op. cit., pp. 38-39.

[41] LDC, op. cit., Vol. 26, p. vi.

[42] LDC, op. cit., Vol. 13, p. 159; Samuel Huntington to Oliver Wolcott, July 7, 1779.

[43] John C. Fitzpatrick, Editor, The Writings of George Washington, (Government Printing Office, Washington, DC, 1934), Vol. 11, pp. 237.

[44] H. James Henderson, Party Politics in the Continental Congress, (McGraw-Hill Book Company, New York, 1974), pp. 120-124.

[45] LDC, op. cit., Vol. 9, pp. 707-709; Connecticut Delegates to Jonathan Trumbull, Sr. (The editor states that this letter was "Written by Huntington and signed by Huntington, Sherman, and Wolcott.")

[46] Ibid., p. 708.

[47] LDC, op. cit., Vol. 9, p. 468; Samuel Huntington's Proposed Resolution, April 22-23?, 1778.

[48] LDC, op. cit., Vol. 9, p. 514; Henry Laurens to John Laurens, April 28, 1778.

[49] Edmund Cody Burnett, The Continental Congress, (The Macmillan Company, New York, 1941), p. 332.

[50] JCC, op. cit., Vol. XI, p. 615.

[51] LDC, op. cit., Vol. 9, p. 407; James Lovell to Joseph Trumbull, April 13, 1778.

[52] JCC, op. cit., Vol. XI, p. 677.

[53] JCC, op. cit., Vol. XIV, p. 922.

[54] LDC, op. cit., Vol. 13, p. 487; Samuel Huntington to Jonathan Trumbull, Sr., September 9, 1779.

[55] LDC, op. cit., Vol. 13, p. 283; Samuel Huntington to Jeremiah Wadsworth, July 22, 1779.

[56] LDC, op. cit., Vol. 13, p. 487; Samuel Huntington to Jonathan Trumbull, Sr., September 9, 1779.

[57] For more detail on John Jay's selection as Minister to Spain, see Chapter 5.

[58] LDC, op. cit., Vol. 14, p. 52; Samuel Huntington to the States, October 9, 1779.

[59] Gerlach, op. cit., p. 54.

[60] LDC, op. cit., Vol. 14, pp. 314-315; Samuel Huntington to Jonathan Trumbull, Jr., January 3, 1780.

[61] Marquis de Chastellux, Travels in North America in the Years 1780, 1781 and 1782, (The University of North Carolina Press, Chapel Hill, 1963), Vol. 1, p. 160. See also: Benson J. Lossing, The Pictorial Field-Book of the Revolution, (Charles E. Tuttle Company, Rutland, Vermont, 1972), Vol. II, pp. 106-107, footnote 5.

[62] JCC, op. cit., Vol. XVI, p. 235. The Joseph Pemberton House, also known as "Clarke Hall" was located on the southwest corner of Third and Chestnut Streets.

[63] LDC, op. cit., Vol. 14, pp. 348-349; Samuel Huntington to John Lawrence, January 18, 1780.

[64] Lossing, op. cit., Vol. II, p. 107, footnote 5.

65 LDC, op. cit., Vol. 14, p. 347; Samuel Huntington to Jonathan Trumbull, Sr., January 17, 1780. See also: Vol. 14, p. 390; Samuel Huntington to Jonathan Trumbull, Sr., February 7, 1780. Samuel Huntington acknowledged that the money he requested had been appropriated.

66 As cited in Dreher, op. cit., p. 54; James Rivington, *Royal Gazette*, November 6, 1779.

67 LDC, op. cit., Vol. 14, p. 284; Samuel Huntington to Jonathan Trumbull, Sr., December 20, 1779.

68 LDC, op. cit., Vol. 14, p. 406; Samuel Huntington to the States, Circular Letter, February 10, 1780.

69 JCC, op. cit., Vol. XVI, pp. 262-267. See also: Gerlach, op. cit., pp. 62-63.

70 LDC, op. cit., Vol. 14, p. 52; Samuel Huntington to the States, Circular Letter, March 20, 1780.

71 LDC, op. cit., Vol. 15, pp. 144-145; Samuel Huntington to Benjamin Lincoln, May 17, 1780.

72 Henry Clinton, The American Rebellion, (Yale University Press, New Haven, 1954), p. 171.

73 LDC, op. cit., Vol. 15, p. 185; Samuel Huntington to the Chevalier de La Luzerne, May 24, 1780.

74 Quoted in Stinchcombe, French Alliance, p. 63, Marquis de Barbe-Marbois to Foreign Minister Vergennes, July 11, 1781, as cited in Gerlach, op. cit., pp. 66-68.

75 LDC, op. cit., Vol. 15, pp. 485-486; Samuel Huntington to James Cogswell, July 22, 1780.

76 LDC, op. cit., Vol. 15, p. 70, Footnote 2; John Mathews to George Washington. "Mathews proposed that Congress give Washington near dictatorial powers to raise, supply, and feed an army of 25,000 for the duration of the war, to call state militia into service, and 'to do all such other matters & things as shall appear to him necessary to promote the Welfare of these united states'."

77 LDC, op. cit., Vol. 15, pp. 527-528; Ezekiel Cornell to Rhode Island Governor William Greene, August 1, 1780.

78 LDC, op. cit., Vol. 15, pp. 20-21; James Lovell to Elbridge Gerry, September 5, 1780.

79 Gaillard Hunt, Editor, JCC, 1774-1789, (Government Printing Office, Washington, DC, 1912), Vol. XIX, pp. 42-44; January 10, 1781; and, pp. 125-128, February 7, 1781.

80 JCC, op. cit., Vol. XX, pp. 545-548, May 26, 1781.

81 JCC, op. cit., Vol. XX, pp. 476-482, May 4, 1781.

82 LDC, op. cit., Vol. 16, p. 117; Samuel Huntington to Nathanael Greene, September 27, 1780.

[83] John C. Miller, Triumph of Freedom 1775-1783, (Little, Brown and Company, Boston, 1948), p. 536.

[84] Henry Steele Commager, Documents of American History, Seventh Edition, (Meredith Publishing Company, New York, 1963), p. 114. Article IX states, in part: "The united states in congress assembled shall have authority...to appoint one of their number to preside, provided that no person be allowed to serve in the office of president more than one year in any term of three years..."

[85] LDC, op. cit., Vol. 16, p. 17; Samuel Huntington to Jonathan Trumbull, Sr., September 4, 1780.

[86] JCC, op. cit., Vol. XVIII, pp. 869-871, September 28, 1780.

[87] LDC, op. cit., Vol. 16, p.143; John Mathews to Nathaniel Peabody, October 3, 1780.

[88] LDC, op. cit., Vol. 17, pp. 36-37; Thomas Rodney's Notes, March 8, 1781.

[89] LDC, op. cit., Vol. 16, p.67; Samuel Huntington to Jonathan Trumbull, Sr., September 15, 1780.

[90] Burnett, op. cit., p. 341. Maryland refused to ratify the Articles of Confederation because of its objection to the claim of several States that their boundaries extended to the Mississippi River or beyond. When one by one those States relinquished such claims, Maryland finally voted ratification in February 1781.

[91] Burnett, op. cit., p. 493.

[92] LDC, op. cit., Vol. 17, p. 3; Thomas Rodney's Diary, March 1, 1781.

[93] LDC, op. cit., Vol. 17, p. 5; Samuel Huntington to the States (Circular Letter), March 2, 1781.

[94] Since Samuel's presidential tenure continued once the Articles went into effect, some have argued that he thus became the first President of the United States. Others reserve that distinction for various reasons for his two immediate successors, McKean and Hanson. The fact is that since the Continental Congress first opened on September 5, 1774, American self-government has continued without interruption to the present day. Therefore, Peyton Randolph was this new nation's first President even though the full scope of Congress and the nation had not yet been defined.

[95] LDC, op. cit., Vol. 17, p. 85; Samuel Huntington to Jonathan Trumbull, Sr., March 24, 1781.

[96] LDC, op. cit., Vol. 17, p. 252; John Witherspoon to Richard Henry Lee, May 19, 1781.

[97] LDC, op. cit., Vol. 17, p. 391; Samuel Huntington to George Washington, July 10, 1781. Dreher, op. cit., p. 5. In his biography of Samuel Huntington, George Kelsey Dreher points out the frequency of Samuel's use of the word "hope."

[98] JCC, op. cit., Vol. XX, pp. 332-333. See also: LDC, op. cit., Vol. 17, p. 394; Thomas

Rodney to Caesar Rodney. According to Delegate Thomas Rodney, Johnston's excuse was "his Bad state of health."

[99] John P. Butler, Editor, The Papers of the Continental Congress, (US Government Printing Office, Washington, DC, 1978), 78, 12:159; Samuel Huntington to the President of Congress, July 11, 1781.

[100] JCC, op. cit., Vol. XX, p. 737; July 10, 1781.

[101] *Norwich Packet*, July 26, 1781, as cited in Gerlach, op. cit., p. 74.

[102] LDC, op. cit., Vol. 20, p. xv. There is no record as to whether or not the General accepted the invitation. See also: Vol. 20, p. 699; Committee of Congress to George Washington, September 22, 1783.

[103] JCC, op. cit., Vol. XXV, pp. 803-807; November 4, 1783.

[104] Frederic R. Kirkland, Editor, Letters on the American Revolution, (Private Printing, Philadelphia, 1941-1952), Vol. II, p. 97; William Ellery to Samuel Huntington, June 27, 1784.

[105] Gerlach, op. cit., p. 85.

[106] Gerlach, op. cit., p. 87. The vote of the Connecticut General Assembly for Governor in 1786 was: Samuel Huntington, 94; Oliver Wolcott, 39; and, incumbent Matthew Griswold, 10.

[107] Waugh, op. cit., p. 36.

[108] Gerlach, op. cit., p. 103.

[109] Dreher, op. cit., p. 185; Samuel Huntington's Address to the Connecticut Ratification Convention, January 4, 1788. See also: Gerlach, op. cit., p. 99.

[110] Gerlach, op. cit., pp. 99-100. While Samuel Huntington pointed out that the Convention "would have preferred some Alterations & Amendments rather than the present form...it must be left to the wisdom & virtue of the States to make Amendments in the future."

[111] Margaret Bassett, Profiles and Portraits of American Presidents, (David McKay Company, New York, 1977), p. 255. In the 1789 election for President and Vice President--the first under the Second Republic--John Jay received 9 Electoral Votes, John Hancock received 4 and Samuel Huntington received 2. George Washington received exactly half, 69, and John Adams received 34. Seven other individuals also received between one and six votes each.

[112] Governor Huntington's welcome of President Washington in New Haven was free of the drama that characterized Washington's arrival in Boston and Governor Hancock's reception during that same New England tour. For details, see Chapter 3, p. 108.

[113] Joseph Strong, *A Sermon Delivered at the Funeral of His Excellency Samuel Huntington, Governor of the State of Connecticut*, (Hudson and Goodwin, Hartford, 1796), 19 pages.

[114] Gerlach, op. cit., p. 106.

WHILE SAMUEL HUNTINGTON WAS PRESIDENT

Notes

Abbreviation Key

JCC   Journals of the Continental Congress
LDC   Letters of Delegates to Congress
PHL   The Papers of Henry Laurens

[115] Robert E. Lee, Editor,The American Revolution in the South by Henry (Light Horse Harry) Lee, (Arno Press, 1969), pp. 138-142.

[116] James Grant Wilson, Editor, Appletons' Cyclopaedia of American Biography, (D. Appleton & Company, New York, 1888), Vol. 5, pp. 133-134. Gen. Casimir Pulaski, born in Poland, joined the Continental Army in 1777. He died on October 11, 1779, two days after being wounded in the Siege of Savannah. His statue now stands in the northeast corner of Lafayette Park (opposite The White House, in Washington, DC). It is one of four honoring foreign military leaders who fought in the American Revolution. The others are Generals Layayette (southeast corner), Rochambeau (southwest corner) and Steuben (northwest corner).

[117] Lee, op. cit., p. 157.

[118] Mark M. Boatner III, Editor, Encyclopedia of the American Revolution, (David McKay Company, New York, 1974), pp. 570-571. General Baron de Kalb, the son of Bavarian peasants, arrived in America in 1777. He suffered eleven wounds during the Battle of Camden and died three days later, on August 19, 1780.

[119] Don Cook, The Long Fuse: How England Lost the American Colonies, (The Atlantic Monthly Press, New York, 1995), p. 331.

[120] As cited in Benson Bobrick, Angel in the Whirlwind, (Simon & Schuster, New York, 1997), p. 427.

[121] Boatner, op. cit., p. 1088.

[122] Craig L. Symonds, A Battlefield Atlas of the American Revolution, (The Nautical & Aviation Publishing Company of America, 1986), p. 93.

[123] John C. Miller, Triumph of Freedom 1775-1783, (Little, Brown & Company, Boston, 1948), p. 551. Miller records: "Of the three thousand men with whom Cornwallis had

entered North Carolina, barely seven hundred remained; two thirds of his troops had been lost by battle, disease, and desertion."

[124] As cited in Symonds, op. cit., p. 93.

[125] Boatner, op. cit., pp. 918-919. Lord Rawdon began his military career in America in 1775 at the Battle of Bunker [Breed's] Hill "where he took command of the company after his captain was hit and led it forward with conspicuous gallantry."

[126] John Sainsbury, Disaffected Patriots: London Supporters of Revolutionary America 1769-1782, (McGill-Queen's University Press, Kingston, 1987), p. 159.

[127] J. Steven Watson, The Reign of George III, 1760-1815, (The Clarendon Press, Oxford, 1960), pp. 236-242. The "Gordon Riots" were prompted by the false impression that Roman Catholics were in the process of increasing their influence in Parliament. Lord George Gordon and some of the members of the London City Council fanned the flames of popular unrest for their own purposes. The situation quickly got out of hand. Surprisingly, John Wilkes, the champion of British and American Liberties, tried to calm the disturbance while Lord North used force to end the riots.

[128] Watson, op. cit., pp. 236-242.

[129] W. E. Lunt, History of England, (Harper & Brothers, New York, 1947), pp. 561-562.

Chapter 7

President
THOMAS McKEAN
of
DELAWARE & PENNSYLVANIA

Double Distinction

Thomas McKean. For nearly a half century, no one served longer nor struggled harder to establish the American Republic.

One year before Peyton Randolph was elected Speaker of the Virginia House of Burgesses, Thomas McKean had already taken his seat as the second youngest delegate at the Stamp Act Congress of 1765 (the only one of the fourteen Presidents of the Continental Congress who was there). In 1808, thirty-two years after the signing of the Declaration of Independence, Thomas McKean finally withdrew from public life at the completion of his third term as Governor of Pennsylvania. By then, most of his revolutionary contemporaries had either died or had long since retired.[1]

During his illustrious career, Thomas had the double distinction of having led not one but two states. In 1762, he was elected to the Delaware House of Assembly, serving as Speaker of that legislature for three of the next seventeen years. When the British invasion threatened that state's government, he also briefly assumed the office of President [i.e., Governor] of Delaware. During that same period, Thomas was also appointed as the first Chief Justice of the Supreme Court of Pennsylvania, a position he exercised with undaunted determination for over two decades.

At the national level, Thomas' tenure was equally exceptional. He was elected as a delegate from Delaware to the First Continental Congress in 1774 and reelected to that position with only one year's absence throughout the entire Revolutionary War. Of the 344 delegates to Congress during its fifteen year history, only Roger Sherman of Connecticut served longer.[2] On July 10, 1781, as the Continental Army mobilized its forces for the decisive assault at Yorktown, it was Thomas McKean, the Delegate from Delaware and Chief Justice of Pennsylvania, who was elected as the seventh

President of the Continental Congress. Late that October, as Head of State, Thomas reviewed the victorious French troops as they marched through Philadelphia.[3]

Thomas reached this pinnacle of power through personal dedication and intense determination. His father William was born in Ireland in 1707, the child of a poor Scotch-Irish family that emigrated to America in the 1720s. The earliest records indicate that Thomas' grandmother, Susannah McCain (as Thomas and his family apparently pronounced their name), claimed a 300 acre tract of land in New London Township in Chester County, Pennsylvania in 1725.[4] When she died there six years later, her two oldest sons inherited her farm. Later, in 1731, William McKean, the eldest, married Letitia Finney, daughter of another nearby Scotch-Irish family. They settled into a house on his mother's property and began to raise their family. Letitia gave birth to their first child, Robert, in 1732, and on March 19, 1734, their second son, the future president, was born. Two more children were added to the family before they moved to Chatham, Pennsylvania in 1741.

In Chatham, Thomas' father began a new career as a tavern-keeper. After only a year, however, their young family was torn apart by Letitia's death at the age of thirty-three. This tragedy led to one of the most fortuitous events of Thomas' life. Since his father was unable to care for four young children, he made arrangements in 1743 for his two oldest boys to attend the Presbyterian academy recently established by the Rev. Francis Alison in New London. Years later, in his *Autobiographical Sketch*, Thomas described the school as "the most celebrated in the province."[5] Thomas and his brother lived and studied there for nearly seven years. Rev. Alison was a strict disciplinarian who educated the young men under his charge to be the leaders of their new land. "Liberty," he insisted, "is a most tender plant that thrives in a very few soils; neglected it soon withers and is lost; but is scarce ever recovered."[6] In addition to President McKean, other distinguished leaders of the American Revolution who were graduates of his academy included Charles Thomson (who served as Secretary of Congress for its entire fifteen-year history), three other Signers of the Declaration of Independence, and Hugh Williamson (a Delegate to the Constitutional Convention).[7]

Unlike his father's family, Thomas' maternal relatives, the Finneys, were well established. Therefore, at the age of 16, after completing his course of studies at Rev. Alison's Academy, Thomas moved to New Castle in the Lower Counties (Delaware) to study law under the supervision of his cousin, David Finney. In characteristic fashion, Thomas pursued his new career with avidity. He devoted endless hours to the theory of law by devouring the books that lined his cousin's office and he grasped every opportunity to master legal practice by working his way through various clerkships in the local courts. Gradually, Thomas took over more of the routine legal work.

In 1754, as the French and Indian War broke out along the American frontier, Thomas was admitted as an attorney in the Courts of Common Pleas and the Supreme Court of the Lower Counties. The following year, as he turned twenty-one, he was also accepted to practice in the City and County of Philadelphia. The Attorney General of Pennsylvania and the Lower Counties even appointed Thomas as his deputy prosecutor in Sussex County, a position he held for the next two years. In April 1758, Thomas was admitted to the Bar of the Pennsylvania Supreme Court, a court he would dominate two decades later. At the same time, Thomas was clearly interested in attending the Middle Temple of the Inns of Court in London, the most prestigious law school in the Empire. For some reason, even though a number of his contemporaries studied there, Thomas ultimately decided to remain in America instead.[8] In fact, unlike Randolph, Hancock, Laurens and Jay, Thomas never did set foot on European soil.

Throughout his life, Thomas demonstrated a nearly unrivaled command of the law. He also understood how to use legal theatrics on behalf of his clients. In one particular case in which his defendant was being sued for slander, Thomas did not even attempt to refute the facts as presented by the prosecutor, he simply called witness after witness to demonstrate that his client "was such a notorious liar" that no man in the county believed anything he [the defendant] said and "therefore no damage could possibly have been sustained by the plaintiff." Thomas won the case.[9]

During these early days, Thomas struck a lifelong friendship with another young Pennsylvania lawyer, John Dickinson. Over the years, through close collaboration as well as heated disagreements, their friendship lasted for a lifetime. Another early friendship with profound significance was Thomas' relationship with Caesar Rodney, a leader of the Lower Counties. Together, they played the pivotal role in helping to create the State of Delaware and lead it through the darkest days of the Revolutionary War.

The relationship between Pennsylvania and the Lower Counties was unique. In 1682, William Penn first landed in America and established a basic frame of government for what became Pennsylvania. When he rewrote that charter a year later, he succeeded in adding to his proprietorship the Three Lower Counties--Newcastle, Kent and Sussex--which he had just purchased from the Duke of York. His new assembly, however, proved unworkable and the counselors from the Lower Counties withdrew in 1691 to form a separate body. Finally, in 1703, the first General Assembly of the Lower Counties met at New Castle where it continued until the State of Delaware was proclaimed in 1777. Throughout that period, William Penn and his descendants continued to serve as governor of both colonies.

The Lower Counties enjoyed certain advantages as a result of salutary neglect. Without a resident Governor, their legislature exercised greater autonomy than most other colonies. The most amazing development was that not one piece of legislation passed by the Lower Counties was ever rejected by the Privy Council since their legislation was simply never submitted. Several leading politicians of that era, most especially Thomas, held offices simultaneously in both colonies.[10]

In 1763, as the French finally ceded most of North America to the victorious British, Thomas extended his influence further north into New Jersey when he married the beautiful nineteen year old Mary Borden, the eldest daughter of Joseph Borden, a wealthy and influential colonial politician. Over the next decade they had two sons and four daughters; all but one lived well into maturity. Mary, however, was not as blessed. She died at the age of twenty-nine on March 12, 1773, only two weeks after giving birth.

Thomas launched his political career a year before his marriage when he was elected from New Castle County to the eighteen-member House of Assembly. In the brief *Autobiographical Sketch* he wrote a half century later he stated that for the first time he "ventured on the stormy sea of politics, which he encountered and stemmed afterwards for forty-six years."[11] From the start, Thomas exhibited the energy and exuberance that characterized his entire career.

In October 1764, Thomas chaired a three-member Committee of Correspondence which "drew up a petition to the King asking redress from the arbitrary tactics employed in enforcing the acts of trade and navigation."[12] He also made known his strong opposition to the Stamp Act which had been proposed in Parliament. By the time the Act became law in 1765, Thomas had added Justice of the Court of Common Pleas of New Castle County to his growing list of governmental duties. In that capacity, he ordered that legal business before his court should continue uninterrupted on unstamped paper. He proudly, but inaccurately, stated in his *Autobiography* that his was the only colonial court to take such a firm stand.[13]

Opposition to the proposed Stamp Act took center stage in June 1765. The Massachusetts General Assembly voted to take unprecedented action by issuing a call to its sister colonies to meet that fall in New York City. The goal was to coordinate a continent-wide response to the legislation which was scheduled to go into effect on November 1. Since the circular letter from Boston reached the Lower Counties after its Assembly had adjourned, three delegates--Thomas McKean, Caesar Rodney and Speaker Jacob Kollock--were chosen through an unconventional process which was later approved by the legislature. Speaker Kollock was unable to attend but his two colleagues arrived in New York City on September 30, 1765.

Despite the recent Stamp Act riots which had led to violence in Boston and New York, the members of the Stamp Act Congress pledged their loyalty to the king while urging him to intervene on their behalf. As Robert R. Livingston of New York confided to an associate in London that December: "...if I really wished to see America in a state of independence I should desire as one of the most effectual means to that end that the stamp act should be inforced. This would unite the whole colony in disaffection, etc."[14]

At the age of 31, Thomas was the second youngest representative to attend the session.[15] The 27 delegates from 9 colonies included Thomas' good friend, John Dickinson of Pennsylvania, and Thomas' father-in-law, Joseph Borden of New Jersey. Caesar Rodney characterized the gathering as "an Assembly of the greatest Ability I ever yet saw."[16] Gen. Thomas Gage, the commander of British forces in America, wrote to his superior in London that "...the Spirit of Democracy is strong amongst them..."[17] Indeed it was. Four of these men went on to sign the Declaration of Independence.

The Stamp Act Congress opened on October 7, 1765. Thomas played a leadership role from the start as he strenuously supported the election of James Otis as President. To his regret, Otis, "the godfather of American liberty," lost by one vote to his fellow Massachusetts delegate, Timothy Ruggles, a British loyalist. Despite his disappointment, Thomas did win the pivotal debate which allocated only one vote to each state. Years later he wrote that " ...a vote by States was by me made a *sine qua non* in the first Congress held at New York in 1765..."[18] It was absolutely critical for Delaware's Lower Counties with a population of only 25,000 (one-tenth the size of Massachusetts) and the other small colonies. It also set the precedent for the Continental Congress eleven years later.

After nearly two weeks of debate, the Stamp Act Congress adopted a *Declaration of the Rights and Grievances of the Colonists* which was based on the guarantees accorded all Englishmen rather than specific provisions outlined in their various charters. Article Three of that document cut to the heart of the debate: "...it is the Undoubted Right of Englishmen, that no Taxes be imposed on them, but with their own Consent, given personally or by their Representatives."[19] Congress then ordered that separate petitions be prepared for the King, Lords and Commons.

Thomas joined Otis and Thomas Lynch of South Carolina in drafting the document to be submitted to the House of Commons. In addition to the legal points outlined in all three petitions, their proposal also "incorporated strong economic arguments that had been advanced by the merchant delegates."[20] It was read and adopted on Wednesday, October 23.

As Congress completed its work over the next two days, only six of the nine colonies were able to sign the documents since the delegates from New York, Connecticut and South Carolina were not authorized to act without prior approval from their respective legislatures. In addition, the Speaker of the New Jersey House, Robert Ogden, and the President of the Stamp Act Congress, Timothy Ruggles, also refused to sign. When Thomas demanded to know why the presiding officer suddenly decided to withhold his approval, a heated argument ensued during which Ruggles challenged Thomas to a duel. Thomas readily accepted, but the confrontation never took place. Ruggles left early the next morning prior to final adjournment.[21] Ruggles was later reprimanded by the Massachusetts House, and Ogden was removed as Speaker after he returned to New Jersey. Years later, Thomas reflected on his fellow delegates in a letter to John Adams: "There was less fortitude in that Body than in the succeeding congress of 1774: indeed some of the members appeared as timid as if engaged in a traitorous conspiracy."[22]

In truth, the American boycott of British goods and the fear it instilled in the hearts of British merchants had far more to do with Parliament's repeal of the Stamp Act in March 1766 than did the documents so carefully crafted by the delegates in New York. The real importance of the Stamp Act Congress was the precedent it established when the next great crisis arose a decade later and the impact it had on men like Thomas McKean who would lead the revolution. For the rest of his life this earliest independent assembly would set Thomas apart from most of the Founding Fathers, including his presidential colleagues. As John Adams later wrote: "Your Name among the Members of Congress in New York in October 1765, is and has long been a singular distinction."[23]

The following June, the legislature of the Lower Counties selected Thomas along with Caesar Rodney and George Read as the colony's official Committee of Correspondence with both its sister colonies and colonial lobbyists in London. This "Delaware Triumvirate" dominated local politics for most of the next two decades.[24]

Tension mounted once again in June 1767 when Parliament enacted the Townshend Acts, yet another shortsighted attempted to raise revenue in the colonies.[25] Even worse, the legislation included suspension of the New York Assembly for its failure to comply with the demand of the Lords and Commons that New York quarter British troops. For the first time, the sole prerogative of the Crown to veto acts of colonial legislatures had been usurped by Parliament. Thomas witnessed these developments first hand since he was living in New York that summer while on special assignment from the Delaware legislature.[26] A decade later, he reflected on the crisis in his instructions to a grand jury: "A standing army in time of profound peace without the consent of our legislatures, and above the controul [sic] of all civil authority, were then quartered in America, to dragoon us into a submission to these tyrannical measures..."[27]

While a new boycott of British goods gradually took hold in response to the Townshend Acts (a boycott Thomas joined in August 1769),[28] the Delaware Triumvirate were instructed by their legislature to prepare yet another humiliating petition to the King: "...permit us, Royal Sir...to prostrate ourselvs at your Royal Feet, and humbly to implore your gracious Attention..."[29] Thomas' true feelings were once again expressed a decade later: "...absolute domination took possession of [the King's] soul; he by the advice and assistance of a corrupt, profligate and abandoned ministry meditated a plan of subjugating and enslaving his subjects abroad..."[30]

During this period, Thomas continued to expand his influence. In 1766, he was licensed to practice law throughout Pennsylvania and New Jersey and in 1769 he was appointed a Justice of the Peace in Pennsylvania. He did not, however, neglect his home base. In October 1772, Thomas was unanimously elected Speaker of the Delaware Assembly and reelected in 1773 and 1777.

As one biographer asserts, by the 1770s, friends and foes alike had learned "that the key to dealing with McKean was to restrain his excesses while allowing free reign to his talents."[31] Another maintains that Thomas' "mind was clear and steady, but the emotions were unpredictable."[32] "Always a powerful and persuasive speaker," he was not a man to be trifled with nor could he be ignored. He was "a complex and even enigmatic man..."[33] A third biographer describes him as "not a political theorist" but rather a "man of practical affairs..."[34] And, like his presidential colleague Henry Laurens, he often seemed to take perverse pleasure in the enemies he made. He was a large man with an oversized ego and a brilliant mind who preferred to intimidate those foolish enough to oppose him.

The year 1774 marked several major turning points in Thomas' life. Even though he continued his public service in the Lower Counties, in May he took lodgings in Philadelphia where he became a member of the powerful City Committee. Not only did the city help to expand his already prosperous law practice, but, as he told John Dickinson years later, his "most valuable and valued acquaintances & friends resided there."[35] That September, after seventeen months as a widower (and only two days before the opening of Congress), Thomas married Sarah (Sally) Armitage of New Castle. Unlike his first wife, who was a Catholic, Sally shared Thomas' Presbyterian faith. She proved to be a good mother to his six children and a wise, loving and intelligent companion for the next 43 years.[36]

Politics, of course, dominated 1774. In response to the Intolerable Acts and the closure of Boston Harbor, Massachusetts sent an urgent appeal to her sister colonies to initiate a new boycott and to meet that fall to coordinate a continent-wide response to British oppression.[37] In early August, fifteen members of the Delaware Assembly met in New Castle to support the call for a Congress and, not surprisingly, elected the members of the Triumvirate (i.e., Read, Rodney and McKean) as the delegates from the Lower Counties. According to historian Edmund Cody Burnett, Thomas was "among the first to extend the welcoming hand to the Massachusetts delegation" when it arrived in Philadelphia later that month.[38]

Almost immediately, Thomas found a kindred spirit in John Adams. They were both men of action who exhibited little patience for their more indecisive colleagues. Their dinners together prior to the opening of Congress built the foundation for a life-long friendship. Decades later Adams wrote that from the start Thomas McKean, Caesar Rodney and Patrick Henry appeared to him "to see more clearly to the end of the business than any others of the whole body."[39] The fact that Adams served with Thomas on the committee to proclaim the rights of the colonies gave them the opportunity to closely collaborate. As one biographer insightfully observes: "Congress eventually proved to be the vehicle by which McKean's latent radicalism was liberated."[40]

As in 1765, Thomas helped to persuade his fellow delegates to allot only one vote per colony despite strong opposition from Patrick Henry. He also vigorously opposed Joseph Galloway's Plan of Union which was "anathema" to Adams and the more radical members, including Thomas. Since both Adams and McKean served on the committee to revise the official journal they made certain that any mention of the Plan was expunged from the record, as ordered by Congress.[41] Thomas also gave his wholehearted support to the adoption of the comprehensive boycott of British goods known as the Continental Association.[42]

On Wednesday, October 26, 1774, Thomas joined his colleagues in signing the official Petition to the King as Congress prepared to adjourn. That evening "all the Congress and several Gentlemen of the Town" gathered together for one final dinner at City Tavern on Second Street.

Even though they had voted to reconvene the following May, if necessary, some, like John Adams, thought that "It is not very likely that I shall ever see this Part of the World again..."[43] For once, Adams proved a poor prophet.

On January 28, 1775, William Pitt (now elevated to the House of Lords as the Earl of Chatham) demanded the immediate withdrawal of British troops from North America. Despite Pitt's plea, British policy continued to shift away from reconciliation toward brute force. When Gen. Thomas Gage, military governor of Massachusetts, was ordered to suppress the rebellion and arrest the ringleaders, his orders to seize munitions at Concord led to the opening shots of the Revolutionary War on Lexington Green.

Three weeks later, Congress reconvened on May 10, 1775. It now met at the Pennsylvania State House since Joseph Galloway, the former Speaker who had exhibited loyalist sympathies the previous fall, was no longer a delegate. Instead, Galloway remained in seclusion at his residence outside the city.[44] Thomas, reelected as a delegate from Delaware, welcomed several important new congressional colleagues including Benjamin Franklin (who had just returned from London), John Hancock (soon to be elected President) and, a few weeks later, Thomas Jefferson. Over the next thirteen months, despite the death of his first child by his second marriage, Thomas McKean served on 38 committees, five of which he chaired.[45] Since the Continental Congress served as a plural executive as well as a unicameral legislature, many of these committees functioned in an executive capacity with full authority to implement the will of Congress.

One of Thomas' most important assignments was as a member of the Secret Committee which handled the procurement of arms and ammunition for the Continental Army.[46] He also served on the committee to "prepare the bonds for the continental treasurer to execute."[47] For one of the few times in his life, Thomas confessed that "I am almost wore down...owing to the multiplicity of business."[48]

As chairman of the Committee on Prisoners, Thomas dealt sternly with British captives. As one inmate recounted in his journal: "...the violent raging rebel McKean, introduced himself by abusing, in the grossest terms, the King, Parliament and Ministry..."[49] But his committee recommended to Congress "that the allowance to each prisoner be punctually paid..." and he inquired of Gen. Philip Schuyler if some captured forces "may, consistent with the public safety, be permitted to return to their respective homes on their parole."[50]

Throughout 1775-76, as Thomas increasingly became one of the leaders of Philadelphia's Committee of Observation and Inspection, he "was in the peculiar position of representing the Lower Counties in Congress, and informally representing Congress in Pennsylvania." As one biographer described that period: "McKean was wearing so many hats...and rushing from one meeting to another with such split-second timing, that his role was blurred, and almost no one could define it."[51]

Finally, starting on May 10, 1776, the disparate pieces of the puzzle began to fall into place when Congress adopted a motion by John Adams which authorized each colony, where necessary, "to adopt such government as shall...best conduce to the happiness and safety of their constituents in particular, and America in general."[52] Even John Dickinson supported the motion since he thought Pennsylvania was exempt from its provisions. Five days later, after Dickinson had retired to his country estate, Adams and Richard Henry Lee of Virginia successfully added a preamble which transformed the original motion into a direct challenge to British rule: "... it is necessary that the exercise of every kind of authority under the said crown should be totally suppressed, and all the powers of government exerted, under the authority of the people of the colonies..."[53]

Thomas strongly supported both the motion as well as the preamble. "There are now," he said, "two governments in direct opposition to each other...I do think we shall lose our liberties, properties, and lives too, if we do not take this step."[54] Armed with this congressional directive, Thomas redoubled his efforts to prod both Pennsylvania and Delaware toward a reversal of their opposition to Independence. The fact that both goals were accomplished in only seven weeks still defies imagination.

Thomas began immediately by chairing a special meeting in Philadelphia only hours after the Preamble had been approved. This led to a mass meeting of approximately four-thousand citizens on Monday morning, May 20. Since the conservative Pennsylvania Assembly had refused to respond to the will of Congress, it was resolved that "a Provincial Convention ought to be chosen, by the People, for the express purpose of carrying the said Resolution of Congress into Execution."[55] Thomas served as President of that Pennsylvania Provincial Congress on June 24, 1776. The final declaration made clear that they met for the purpose of "suppressing all authority in this province, derived from the crown of Great Britain..." and that they "unanimously declare our willingness to concur in a vote of the congress, declaring the United Colonies free and independent states..."[56]

While orchestrating events in Pennsylvania, Thomas, still a member of the Delaware Assembly, rushed back to New Castle on Friday, June 14, to urge his colleagues there to support the congressional resolution. With the help of Caesar Rodney and others, the legislature of the Lower Counties voted unanimously the following afternoon to suspend government under the crown and issued new instructions to its delegates in Congress, permitting them to support Independence.[57]

Both colonies had now authorized a vote for Independence but the final determination was left to their elected delegates. On Monday, July 1, 1776, the Committee of the Whole House took its first test vote on Independence at the end of a tense day of debate. Despite Thomas' tireless efforts, only nine colonies voted in the affirmative. New York abstained while waiting for instructions from its legislature and Ned Rutledge, concerned over the growing influence of New England and its potential impact on his state's slave economy, cast a negative vote on behalf of South Carolina. He indicated, however, that his state might vote aye if that would make the motion unanimous.[58] In the end, the question of American Independence came down to Pennsylvania (where a four-to-three majority of the delegates still opposed Independence) and Delaware (where Thomas McKean and George Read split on the issue).

The next day, John Dickinson and Robert Morris, two of the dissenting voices in the Pennsylvania Delegation, withdrew from Congress rather than stand in the way of the will of the majority.[59] Pennsylvania then switched to the affirmative on a vote of three-to-two. The tie in Delaware was broken because of Thomas' quick action the night before when he sent an express rider 80 miles to Dover to urge the third member of the triumvirate, Caesar Rodney, to come to Philadelphia immediately. Rodney, "tho detained by thunder and Rain," arrived exhausted at the State House door on Tuesday morning, just in time to join Thomas in breaking Delaware's tie in favor of Independence. Rodney's historic journey (at great risk to his delicate health) is now depicted on the back of the Delaware commemorative Quarter.[60] Thus, on the morning of July 2, 1776 (despite popular misperception concerning the date), the independence of the United States was adopted by a vote of twelve-to-zero, with New York abstaining.[61]

For the next two days the delegates debated the formal Declaration which, after many revisions, was finally approved on July 4. Not until one month later, August 2, 1776, was the engrossed parchment placed on the table for the delegates to sign.[62] By then, however, Thomas was away on military duty. In fact, he and John Dickinson "were the only two members of Congress who took up arms in defense of their country" during 1776.[63]

On July 15, as a colonel in the Philadelphia Associators (a local militia), Thomas led his 4th Battalion to New Jersey in response to that State's urgent request for protection until the arrival of the Continental Army.

Eleven days later, Thomas wrote a long letter to his wife describing his first contact with the enemy: "...about twenty Cannon balls flew close to me sometimes on one side sometimes on the other and some just over my head...I confess I was not a little alarmed myself (being the first time that I had ever heard a cannon ball) but clapped spurs to my horse and rode on amidst the balls... thro' God's favor I escaped unhurt..."[64] He wrote again on August 7 and told her that he "wished to be rid of all public employments..." but then quickly added that "nothing is too great a sacrifice to preserve the liberties of my country. My life shall follow the loss of them."

By Sunday, August 25, Thomas and his Battalion had returned safely to Philadelphia. On November 30 he resigned his commission, thereby ending his brief military career. Thomas was not enamored with army life and he found the recruits "impudent, lazy, dirty fellows..."[65]

During his absence, Thomas had missed the opportunity to sign the Declaration of Independence. As a result, in January 1777, when Congress directed that authenticated copies of the Declaration should be sent to the states, Thomas' name was not listed.[66] However, the published document did include seven new delegates who had not been there on July 4, and even a new member from New Hampshire who was permitted to sign in November 1776. Sometime after 1777, Thomas McKean--who had voted for Independence on July 4--was finally able to add his signature. He was the last to sign.[67]

Thomas also missed the Pennsylvania Constitutional Convention which opened on July 15. Even though he had done as much as any man to initiate this gathering, his decision to trade his gavel for gunpowder at that precise moment was one of the colossal mistakes of his long public career. Thomas' legal knowledge and extensive legislative experience would have been invaluable in drafting Pennsylvania's first constitution. Instead, as Charles Thomson lamented, the affair was thrown "into the hands of men totally unequal to them."[68] The same radicals that Thomas had helped to unleash a few months earlier in his determination to hasten Independence had now gone on to dictate the new State Constitution, but Thomas was no longer there to temper their views. Benjamin Rush, a congressional delegate, spoke for many when he described the final document as "rather too much upon the democratical Order, for liberty is as apt to degenerate into licensiousness, as power is to become arbitrary."[69] The new Constitution, which contained such unusual provisions as a dominant unicameral legislature and a plural executive (similar in some respects to the Continental Congress itself), was proclaimed by the Convention on September 28, 1776, without a vote of the people.[70]

To ward off a similar disaster in Delaware, Thomas hurried to New

Castle in time for the opening of that State's Convention on Tuesday, August 27. This time, however, the challenge came from the conservative side of the aisle. After only three days, Thomas was called away to the bedside of his dying sister, Dorothea, and his twelve year old son, Joseph, who gradually recovered from his illness. Thomas returned to the Convention on September 6, grief-stricken but determined. He was immediately appointed to the committee to prepare a declaration of rights and then to the committee to design the structure of state government. By the time the Convention completed its work on Saturday, September 21, Thomas was reasonably satisfied with the new Delaware Constitution despite the opposition he encountered on several key points.[71]

For the next two months, Thomas shuttled back and forth between New Castle and Philadelphia while also attending to congressional business. As one biographer observed, "He was in the odd position of being almost-too-radical in Delaware, and almost-too-conservative in Pennsylvania."[72] In Philadelphia, on the evening of October 21, at a mass meeting which drew approximately 1,500 people, both Thomas and John Dickinson spoke out in strong opposition to Pennsylvania's new Constitution. Despite their efforts and the opposition of most prominent Philadelphians, Radicals won control of the first Assembly under the new constitution, thanks to support from rural voters.

Back in Delaware, Thomas was reelected to the State Assembly (even though his close colleague Caesar Rodney was not), but in November 1776 neither he nor Rodney were reappointed as delegates to the Continental Congress. It was the only time between 1774-83 that Thomas was not a member of the national government. Despite that defeat, the Delaware Assembly did elect Thomas to serve a third term as Speaker in January 1777. As a result, he remained in Delaware during the first half of the year. It was there, in July, that his wife delivered their second child, Sara Maria, who, through marriage, later become a member of the Spanish nobility.[73]

In Pennsylvania, despite the growing threat that the capital might soon be captured, the radical new government was continuing to encounter substantial opposition from many of the most prominent leaders of the city. In late July, in an attempt at solidarity in the face of the enemy, the State Supreme Executive Council offered Thomas the position of Chief Justice. Without retracting his earlier opposition to the new Constitution, he accepted. Some attributed his action to unbridled ambition, but to Thomas the struggle for Independence superseded all other considerations. Only a unified government could resist British tyranny.[74]

On September 1, 1777, Thomas McKean was sworn into office as the first Chief Justice of the State of Pennsylvania. For the next twenty-two years he dominated that Court as he carefully crafted the Judicial branch of State government despite repeated attacks from Radical opponents. One of his earliest biographers reported that "the Chief Justice when on the bench wore an immense cocked-hat, and was dressed in a scarlet gown."[75] Despite his authoritarian demeanor, Thomas expressed his core legal philosophy in the case of Respublica v. Samuel Chapman (1781) when he instructed the jury that "...at all events, it is better to err on the side of mercy, than of strict justice."[76] But Thomas would not tolerate interference with his official pronouncements as Gen. Greene discovered when he tried to squash a warrant that was issued to one of Greene's deputies. In response, Thomas stated that "...what attracks my attention most is your observation, that you cannot without great necessity consent to his being absent. As to that, Sir, I shall not ask your consent, nor that of any person in or out of the army, whether my Precept shall be obeyed or not in Pennsylvania."[77]

Less than two weeks after Thomas assumed his judicial office, Gen. Howe and his British troops invaded Delaware and captured President John McKinly, the Governor. Thomas, who was now Chief Justice of Pennsylvania, was still Speaker of the neighboring state's Assembly and was thereby required to rush back to Delaware to become Acting Governor for the next month.[78] "The consequence," he later wrote to John Adams, "was to be hunted like a fox by the enemy...I was obliged to remove my family five times in a few months...but safety was not to be found...for they were soon obliged to remove again, occasioned by the incursions of the Indians."[79]

By the time Thomas returned to Pennsylvania later that fall, the British had already occupied Philadelphia, the Continental Army was in winter camp at Valley Forge and Congress had fled to York, Pennsylvania. On December 17, 1777, both Thomas and Caesar Rodney were reelected as congressional delegates from Delaware after their one year absence. Henry Laurens, then serving as President, was obviously pleased when he described Thomas' return as "a valuable acquisition in Congress."[80] For the next six months Thomas divided his time between his congressional duties in York and his judicial obligations to the State. That April he boasted to Rodney that "I have worked double tides (as the Sailors say) all the last week, being every day in Court, and also in Congress..."[81] In mid-June, Thomas wrote to Rodney again concerning the latest British peace proposal. "Be upon your guard with regard to Letters from the Enemy," he warned, "they intend to seduce, corrupt & bribe by every method possible...warn the people to double their vigilance..."[82]

After Congress returned to Philadelphia in July 1778, Thomas initially rented a house but he ultimately purchased the magnificent mansion at the corner of Third and Pine Streets which had been confiscated from the Rev. Jacob Duché who had fled with the British.[83] Inspired by the design of Lambeth Palace, the residence of the Archbishop of Canterbury, it included a coach house and stables.[84] For the rest of his life, the Duché Mansion would be Thomas' primary residence. Henceforth, Pennsylvania politics would take center stage in his career as his ties to Delaware gradually faded.

As Chief Justice, Thomas was also an ex officio member of the Board of Trustees of the College of Philadelphia and on June 4, 1778, he was elected President of the Board. He served in that capacity for many years and remained a member of the Board for the rest of his life.[85] In 1780, Thomas also joined with other leaders of the city in helping to finance the Bank of Pennsylvania to assist in supplying the Army with provisions. Thomas personally invested £2000.[86]

Thomas did continue as a member of the Delaware Assembly until the fall of 1779, but seldom attended its sessions. On October 1 of that year he returned to New Castle on election day to urge his loyal constituents, after seventeen years, to select his replacement. One month later, his namesake, Thomas McKean, Jr., was born. But, despite the personal and political demands on him in Pennsylvania, Thomas continued to represent Delaware in Congress for another four years. In that capacity, Thomas signed the Articles of Confederation on behalf of the State of Delaware in February 1779.[87] Two years later, when the Articles finally went into effect on March 1, 1781, Thomas proudly proclaimed: "Our Enemies can no longer say, we are but a rope of sand. Our whole Government is now established, but it will require considerable improvements to bring it to perfection...I flatter myself its Inhabitants will yet be as happy as any society of people under the Heavens."[88]

On July 10, 1781, Thomas reached the pinnacle of national office when he was elected as the seventh President of the Continental Congress.[89] He thus became the first President to be chosen under the Articles of Confederation.[90] No one could have brought greater experience or dedication to that office. As he had confided to John Dickinson the previous Christmas: "...what I undertake to perform, I do with all my might..."[91] He made clear, however, that because of his previous commitment he could only serve until the opening of the fall session of the Pennsylvania Supreme Court. When he was attacked in the press for again holding multiple offices, he dismissed his media critics by stating that while "it is natural for puppies to bark at any great or new object; it is not for men of glass to throw stones."[92]

Four months before Thomas' election as President, Thomas Rodney,

Caesar's brother, confided to his private diary that "Mr. McKean...is a Man of Talents--of great Vanity, extremely fond of power & entirely goverened by passions, ever pursuing the Object present With Warm enthusiastic Zeal Without Much reflection or forecast."[93] If Rodney was correct, then Thomas must have delighted in the ceremonial aspects of his office at the precise moment of victory. On Sunday, September 2, 1781, the Continental Army passed through Philadelphia on its march toward destiny at Yorktown. As President, Thomas reviewed the troops with Generals Washington and Rochambeau on his left and the French Minister, M. de Luzerne, on his right.[94] Seven and a half weeks later an express rider from Washington's camp pounded on the front door of the President's mansion at midnight to inform him of Cornwallis' surrender. For days the capital city exploded in celebration as leaders of Congress and other dignitaries called on President McKean. Early in November the British colors captured from Cornwallis were brought to Philadelphia and formally presented to the President.[95]

In the midst of those momentous events Thomas wrote to Secretary Charles Thomson on October 23, reminding him that "before I assumed the Chair, I informed them that as Chief-Justice of Pennsylvania I should be under the necessity of attending the Supreme Court of that State the latter end of September or at farthest in October...I must therefore request that they will be pleased to proceed to the choice of another President."[96] The next day, however, Congress unanimously requested that Thomas "act as President till the First Monday in November..." which was the day prescribed under the Articles of Confederation for the beginning of the next session.[97] Thomas agreed to the request and continued to serve until Monday, November 5, 1781. His successor, John Hanson of Maryland, wrote to him a few days later, forwarding the resolution of appreciation from Congress and thanking Thomas for his "...great abilities...exemplary patience and Unequalled skill..."[98]

Thomas continued as a Delegate from Delaware throughout 1782. One of his primary committee assignments during that year concerned "the reestablishment of national credit..." He remained optimistic. In a letter to Sam Adams on August 6, 1782, he stated that "Congress is at present composed of virtuous men, and were it not for some diversity of opinions respecting the Fisheries and Western Lands there would be more harmony in that Body than I have heretofore observed." He also agreed with Adams that "...every thing seems...to demand an immediate attempt to establish [an American Navy]."[99] Finally, on February 1, 1783, Thomas' long and distinguished congressional career came to an end. By then, he had already switched his primary focus to Pennsylvania politics as the demands of nation-building replaced the urgency of war.

A perennial problem facing the Chief Justice was the unique position of Pennsylvania Quakers throughout the State. They not only avoided military service on religious grounds but also exercised a considerable amount of political resistance to some of the provisions of the new government. Thomas "spoke sharply against them, as being obstinately disaffected & that he supposed they wanted or expected to have a leaf in the book of Sufferings."[100] Warren Mifflin, one of Thomas' longtime Quaker friends, chided the Chief Justice: "You have made a just stir in this land about liberty, and we can not help taking notice as I lately have of the kind that is brought forth, the tree being...known by its fruits." Mifflin cut even deeper when he added that "I am more concerned for you under whom my friends suffer than I am for them."[101]

Thomas also exhibited little sympathy for slaves. He personally owned "black servants" and often sided with those seeking to reclaim runaway slaves. In the case of Respublica v. Negro Betsy (1786) one biographer claims that Thomas "not only supported the institution of slavery but expressed personal reservations about the free negro's ability to function in a free, white society."[102] He was, however, remarkably progressive on the issue of prison reform. Thomas advocated ideas that are still under debate two centuries later when he wrote that "a wise and frugal government is more bent upon preventing than punishing crime...a penitentiary prison is a bad school for teaching good morals."[103] He advocated the elimination of the death penalty for robbery and burglary and, in a debate hauntingly familiar in the post-9/11 world of the 21st Century, he denounced torture.

Throughout his twenty-two years as Chief Justice, Thomas persisted in his goal of a truly independent judiciary firmly established on respect for the rule of law. As one biographer states: "The foundations of an independent judiciary so painstakingly prepared by McKean during the war years were buttressed after 1784 by the ultimate acceptance and explicit acknowledgement--however grudging--of the Court's powers on the part of the Council and Assembly."[104]

By 1787, the desperate need for structural reform in the national government led to what is now known as the Constitutional Convention which met in Philadelphia from May to September. Thomas was not elected as a delegate, but he dined with members of the Convention so frequently that he once complained that "I am tired feasting with them."[105] When the Pennsylvania Ratification Convention opened that November, Thomas, a representative from Philadelphia, lost the presidency of the Convention to Frederick Muhlenberg by only one vote. Nevertheless,

Thomas joined fellow attorney James Wilson in leading the successful battle for endorsement. Thomas concluded his final speech to the Convention by stating that "The law has been my study from my infancy...and from all my study, observation and experience, I must declare, that...it [the Constitution] appears to me the best the world has yet seen."[106]

In typical fashion, Thomas occasionally lost his temper during the lengthy debates, once dismissing the opposition's arguments as "a sound...a mere sound, like the working of small beer."[107] To those who demanded the inclusion of a Bill of Rights, Thomas replied that "...it is unnecessary, for the power of congress...being therein enumerated and positively granted, can be no other than what this positive grant conveys."[108] How history has betrayed him!

On July 4, 1788, a great "Federal Procession" was staged in Philadelphia to celebrate the ratification of the Constitution by ten States, one more than required for adoption. Elaborate floats were drawn by pairs of horses through the main streets of the city. On one carriage there was a replica of the federal eagle over thirteen feet high and at its base sat the silver-haired, scarlet-clad Chief Justice, "reminiscent of an old Roman senator...his hand upon a staff bearing a replica of the Constitution."[109]

On March 2, 1789, the First American Republic receded into history as the Continental Congress was replaced by the new federal Constitution. Both Thomas and his colleague James Wilson made clear to President-elect Washington their interest in heading the new United States Supreme Court. Both were deeply disappointed when former President John Jay was ultimately accorded that honor. Wilson was forced to settle for the position of Associate Justice and Thomas, who was in so many ways the precursor of John Marshall, remained as Chief Justice of Pennsylvania.[110] The experience weakened Thomas' affection for the Federalist faction and helped to plant the seeds for his eventual alliance with Thomas Jefferson.

On November 25, 1789, the long-awaited Pennsylvania Constitutional Convention convened. For thirteen years Thomas and many other prominent leaders had eagerly anticipated rewriting the State's radical charter; this was their chance. Thomas was elected Chairman of the Committee of the Whole as the delegates began their debate.[111] While he unsuccessfully sought to tie the right to vote to strict property qualifications, Thomas was able to win approval for free education for poor children throughout the State. Benjamin Franklin, at the end of his glorious career, was less successful. He argued in vain to retain the old Constitution's unicameral legislature and plural executive. Early that September the new Constitution was adopted with a bicameral legislature and a single executive.[112]

Despite being out of step with the leaders of the Convention, Franklin's funeral on April 17, 1790, produced a massive outpouring of grief. The major pallbearers included Gov. Thomas Mifflin and Chief Justice Thomas McKean, both former Presidents under the First Republic.

By 1792, the Federalists dominated Pennsylvania politics but the opposition Republicans increasingly challenged their leadership. Late that July Thomas was named chairman of a massive Republican meeting in Philadelphia. Convincing Thomas to take center stage was, as one biographer points out, "effective bait in luring moderate Federalists into opposition."[113] Foreign policy also played a major role in Thomas' political conversion. As always, he distrusted the British and resented what he and many others viewed as the Washington Administration's anti-French bias. Thomas even became President of the Society of Friends of the French Revolution. Like many other political leaders he denounced the Jay Treaty in 1795 and unsuccessfully urged President Washington to renegotiate its provisions.[114]

The 1796 presidential election marked a painful rupture in Thomas' friendship with John Adams, the Federalist candidate. In Thomas' opinion, Adams' long association with Washington and Hamilton had tarnished his republican credentials. As a result, the Chief Justice headed the ticket of presidential electors pledged to Thomas Jefferson. Two years later his worst fears were realized with the passage of the infamous Alien and Sedition Acts. Thomas considered these measures grossly unconstitutional as well as "unnecessary, nay injurious and provoking..."[115]

By 1799, Pennsylvania Republicans urged Thomas to run for Governor. As one biographer states: " No one in Pennsylvania could claim more general experience on the executive, legislative, and judicial levels than the chief justice, or claim to have participated in more crucial conventions or decision-making bodies responsible for the destiny of the state."[116] William Duane, the editor of the Republican newspaper Aurora, threw his full support behind Thomas' campaign. William Cobbett, editor of Porcupine's Gazette, worked equally hard to denounce Thomas as a "political weathercock" who switched sides simply to advance his own career.[117]

Thomas won the election. On December 17, 1799 (three days after Washing-ton's death), sixty-five year old Thomas McKean was inaugurated as Governor of Pennsylvania, following former President Thomas Mifflin's three consecutive terms as their State's chief executive.[118] Six months later he boastfully confided to Dickinson that "I have never had greater employment for body & mind, than from the last six months, unless when I was president of Congress."[119] Even though Republicans also took control of the House of Representatives, the Pennsylvania Senate retained its

Federalist majority. Nevertheless, Thomas reassured his wife that "As to the tempests & irritation in public station I have been so long habituated to them that they now make a weak impression upon me: the oldest sailor cannot bear the buffetings of the waves with more sang-froid than I can."[120]

One year later, after a prolonged battle, Thomas Jefferson was elected President. As leaders of the Republican Party, the newly elected Governor and President developed a close correspondence. Thomas reminded Jefferson to be leery of their enemies. "From long and attentive experience," he told Jefferson, "no measure your Excellency or myself can adopt will ever obtain their cordial approbation and that whenever a favorable opportunity shall occur they will exhibit their accustomed enmity."[121] He also told Jefferson that he wished he had replaced even more Federalist office holders "for it is not right to put a dagger in the hands of an assassin."[122]

Even though some Republicans leaders, especially the editor of the *Aurora*, were disappointed that they had not received more patronage during Thomas' first term as Governor, they realized that his reelection was assured. They were correct. In the 1802 contest Thomas carried thirty-three out of thirty-six counties.[123] In reflecting on the election, Thomas magnanimously shared the credit with the President. "The last general election in Pennsylvania," he told Jefferson, "...cannot be attributed merely to...good management; but permit me to say, in no small degree to the President of the United States, and his patriotic and wise measures..."[124]

As the 1804 presidential election rapidly approached, Thomas was frequently mentioned as a potential vice presidential candidate. His response was unequivocal: "I am much obliged to the kind sentiments of my friends...but most absolutely decline that honor...[I] am satisfied with my share of honors; that of President of the United States in Congress Assembled in the year 1781...equalled any merit or pretensions of mine, and cannot now be increased by the office of Vice-President."[125] His response disappointed some local Republican leaders such as Duane who supported the proposal in the hope of removing Thomas from state politics.

Not only did Duane and his associates hope to control Pennsylvania without interference, but the Governor's increasing attacks on "the unparallelled licentiousness of the press in publishing seditious and infamous libels" pitted the two most powerful men in Pennsylvania against each other.[126] The cracks in the state Republican Party eventually led to the formation of a new group, loyal to the Governor, that Duane branded as the "Quids." In February 1805, in one of his last letters to President Jefferson, Thomas blamed the schism on "Mr. Duane...He affects to consider his importance, as an Editor of a News-Paper, to be superior to the Governor of a State, or even of the President of the United States."[127] When Duane and his allies pushed for a State Constitutional Convention to streamline the Judiciary, Thomas exclaimed: "shall a set of clodpoles and ignoramuses, overthrow it? No; it shall not be! I will firmly resist it: I will use my utmost exertions, to prevent the danger and the mischief..."[128]

Not surprisingly, the Republican caucus at Lancaster in 1805 denied Thomas his party's nomination for a third term as Governor. In response, Thomas defiantly told his son that a person "who has not been affected by the roaring of the British Lion, cannot possibly be affrighted by the braying of Asses."[129] Those loyal to the Governor, both Quids and a growing number of Federalists, then joined together to nominate Thomas under the banner of Constitutionalists. Duane's Aurora, which was once the backbone of Thomas' successful campaign in 1799, now led the opposition to what it termed "the monster aristocracy."[130]

At the end of that bitter campaign, Thomas was again victorious. His fragile coalition, however, did not survive. Neither did his friendship with President Jefferson. They never corresponded again after March 1805.[131] To Dickinson, Thomas confided his extreme frustration, describing his enemy's tactics as a "conspiracy...hatched in hell and propagated by the imps of darkness."[132] His enemies returned the animus at every opportunity.

By August 1806, Thomas had had enough. He filed a libel suit against Duane and the Aurora. That December he told the State Assembly that "Libeling (gross and malignant libellings) have become the crying sin of the nation and the times!"[133] On January 12, 1807, Duane responded in the Aurora by demanding the Governor's impeachment. Duane's allies in the legislature then initiated the process which led to formal charges, but the Assembly postponed the final debate until after that fall's election in which the friends of the Governor picked up a few crucial seats in the House.[134]

At the start of the new session Thomas responded by confessing that "I may have erred in judgment...but no act of my public life was ever done, from a corrupt motive, [or] without a deliberate opinion that the act was lawful and proper in itself."[135] None of the six bogus impeachment charges held up under Thomas' detailed defense. By February 1808 the drama had played out and attention shifted to the election of Thomas' successor since he had reached the three term limit mandated by the State Constitution. Without Thomas to head the ticket, the Quids and Federalist coalition disintegrated as most Quids returned to their Republican roots.

In December 1808, Thomas retired to his Philadelphia mansion at the completion of forty-six years of continuous public service. He withdrew from active politics even though he followed developments closely and continued to enjoy good health. During the War of 1812 he briefly reappeared at a town meeting to prepare Philadelphia's defenses in case of a British invasion. At the age of 80 he was persuaded to preside as chairman, and did so with characteristic dignity.[136]

As elder statesmen, Thomas and John Adams did resume their old friendship which had been suspended by their disagreement over the French Revolution. On June 13, 1812, Thomas wrote to Adams that "I thank God, the faculties of my mind are as yet little, if anything impaired, and...I do assure you that I venerate our early friendship, and am happy in a continuance of it."[137] In July 1815, Thomas again wrote to Adams: "We have been spectators of such wonderful scenes within the last fifty years of our lives as perhaps were never seen before in the same space of time..."[138]

By the spring of 1817, Thomas' health had failed. On the afternoon of June 24, at the age of 83, he died quietly at home. His devoted wife and eight of his eleven children survived him.[139] Today, his final resting place is marked by a beautiful white marble tomb in historic Laurel Hill Cemetery in the heart of Philadelphia, the city he loved.

For nearly a half century, no one served longer nor struggled harder to establish the American Republic than Thomas McKean.

President Thomas McKean's grave at Laurel Hill Cemetery
Philadelphia, Pennsylvania.

WHILE THOMAS MCKEAN
WAS PRESIDENT

July - November 1781

Congress continued its endless debate over finances throughout Thomas McKean's presidency. It also began the process of restructuring the national government now that the Articles of Confederation had gone into effect.[140] On July 11, 1781, Robert Morris, the Superintendent of Finance, was authorized to negotiate loans with Spain and Portugal. On August 10, Robert Livingston of New York was appointed as the first Secretary for Foreign Affairs.[141] Six days later, John Adams, who was already in Europe on congressional business, was instructed to negotiate an alliance with the Dutch. In October, salaries were set for the Secretaries of War and Marine and the Department of the Post Office was reformed. At the end of the month, General Benjamin Lincoln became the first Secretary at War.[142]

British and American armies in the Carolinas clashed for the last time on September 8, 1781, at Eutaw Springs, fifty miles northwest of Charleston. Lt. Col. Alexander Stewart commanded 2,300 British forces when his camp was attacked by American Gen. Nathanael Greene's 2,200 men, many of whom were militia. Just as Greene's Army was on the verge of a decisive victory, discipline broke down when his men began to loot the British camp.[143] As one historian has described the scene: "Row upon row of canvas tents...supplies, food, and even spirits lay there for the taking."[144] Greene was forced to withdraw and the British reclaimed the field. Both sides suffered very heavy losses.[145] Despite his victory, Stewart retreated to the safety of British-occupied Charleston where his army remained for the duration of the war.

By the fall of 1781, Britain was not only waging war with America, France and Spain but it was also facing the imminent declaration of war by The Netherlands. In New York, General Clinton was calling for huge reinforcements. But, as historian Piers Mackesy states, "the harvest of recruits was drying up...To find the men the bounty was raised, and raised again. Physical requirements were lowered, and age limits widened."[146]

The dominant development of Thomas McKean's presidency was clearly the British surrender at Yorktown.

Only days after Thomas was elected President in July 1781, French General Rochambeau consulted with General Washington on the possibility of a full-scale siege against the British Headquarters in New York. However, when it became obvious that British General Cornwallis had selected Yorktown as his new headquarters,[147] American attention shifted to Virginia. Congress immediately began to review plans for a Southern Campaign.[148]

On August 21, Washington and Rochambeau started their march south. After stops in Philadelphia and Williamsburg they reached Yorktown on September 28 and began the bombardment of British forces eleven days later as the French fleet blockaded the coast. General Cornwallis was finally forced to surrender his 7,000 British troops on October 19, 1781.[149]

In his memoirs, Sir Henry Clinton, Commanding General of British Forces in North America, attempted to refute the charge that he was to blame for the defeat at Yorktown by stating that "I had very early represented to His Majesty's Ministers the danger to which operations in the Chesapeake were likely to be exposed unless we had a fleet there sufficiently strong to cover them..." If such an armada had been provided by the Lords of the Admiralty, Clinton argued, then "Lord Cornwallis' army could not have been lost, and the United States of America would in all probability have composed a part of the British Empire at this hour."[150]

Clinton's lame attempt at personal exoneration could not negate the fact that, as one observer noted, Lord North received news of the British defeat at Yorktown "like a ball in the breast."[151]

Chapter 7

President
THOMAS McKEAN
of
DELAWARE & PENNSYLVANIA

Notes

Abbreviation Key

JCC Journals of the Continental Congress
LDC Letters of Delegates to Congress
PHL The Papers of Henry Laurens

[1] Roberdeau Buchanan, <u>Genealogy of the McKean Family of Pennsylvania</u>, (Inquire Printing Company, Lancaster, Pennsylvania, 1890), p. 113. When President McKean eventually died in 1817, only five of the Signers of the Declaration of Independence were still alive: William Ellery, William Floyd, John Adams, Thomas Jefferson and Charles Carroll of Carrollton.

[2] John M. Coleman, <u>Thomas McKean: Forgotten Leader of the Revolution</u>, (American Faculty Press, Rockaway, New Jersey, 1975), p. 117. See also: Ronald M. Gephart and Paul H. Smith, Editors, <u>LDC: 1774-1789</u>, (Library of Congress, Washington, DC, 2000), Vol. 26, p. v. According to the Library of Congress, 435 delegates were selected by the colonies/states between 1774-1789, but the record indicates that only 344 delegates actually served in the Continental Congress.

[3] G. S. Rowe, <u>Thomas McKean: The Shaping of an American Republicanism</u>, (Colorado Associated University Press, Boulder, 1978), p. 163.

[4] Buchanan, op. cit., p. 8. Even though Thomas McKean's grandmother spelled her name "McCain," Thomas and his immediate relatives spelled it "McKean." Most biographers agree, however, that he probably pronounced his last name "McCain." Satirical rhymes published in several newspapers during Thomas McKean's life are contradictory, but at least one 21st Century branch of the family maintains that it has always been pronounced "McCain."

[5] Thomas McKean, *Autobiographical Sketch*, Historical Society of Pennsylvania.

[6] As cited in Rowe, <u>Thomas McKean: The Shaping of an American Republicanism</u>, op. cit., p. 7.

[7] Lewis R. Harley, <u>The Life of Charles Thomson</u> (George W. Jacobs & Co., Philadelphia, 1900), p. 29.

[8] Rowe, Thomas McKean: The Shaping of an American Republicanism, op. cit., pp. 20-21.

[9] As cited in James Hedley Peeling, The Public Life of Thomas McKean, Ph.D. Dissertation, The University of Chicago, Chicago, 1929, p. 9.

[10] Coleman, op. cit., p. 25.

[11] McKean, op. cit., p. 3.

[12] Peeling, op. cit., p. 14.

[13] McKean, op. cit., p. 10.

[14] Livingston Papers, Bancroft Transcripts, New York Public Library; Robert R. Livingston to New York's special agent in London, John Sergeant, December 20, 1765.

[15] The youngest delegate to attend the Stamp Act Congress was John Rutledge, 26, of South Carolina who, like Thomas McKean, continued to play a major role throughout the American Revolution. He died in Charleston in 1800.

[16] As cited in C. A. Weslager, The Stamp Act Congress, (University of Delaware Press, Newark, 1976), p. 111.

[17] Clarence Edwin Carter, Editor, The Correspondence of Major General Thomas Gage, (New Haven, Connecticut,1931, Vol. 1, pp. 69-70; Gen. Thomas Gage to Gen. Henry S. Conway, Secretary of State for the Southern Department, October 12, 1765.

[18] McKean Papers, Historical Society of Pennsylvania; Thomas McKean to Timothy Pickering, January 13, 1804.

[19] Weslager, op. cit., p. 201.

[20] Weslager, op. cit., p. 146.

[21] McKean Papers, op. cit., p. 8.

[22] McKean Papers, op. cit., Vol. IV, p. 25; Thomas McKean to John Adams, August 20, 1813. See also: Weslager, op. cit., pp. 169-178. John Adams wrote to Thomas McKean in search of a copy of the Journal of the Stamp Act Congress. Even though the original has been lost for over two centuries, McKean was eventually able to track down one incomplete copy for Adams. The fascinating reconstruction of the complete Journal is recounted in detail in The Stamp Act Congress thanks to the dedication of that book's author.

[23] McKean Papers, op. cit.; John Adams to Thomas McKean, June 21, 1812.

[24] Coleman, op. cit., pp. 80-81.

[25] For additional background on the Townshend Acts, see Introduction, pp. 19-23.

[26] Coleman, op. cit., pp. 81-84. On behalf of the Assembly of the Lower Counties, Thomas McKean went to New York in the summer of 1767 to copy and compile all land records pertaining to his home colony prior to 1682 which were not available elsewhere.

[27] As cited in Coleman, op. cit., p. 84; *Charge Delivered by The Hon. Thomas McKean to the Grand Jury*, Lancaster, 1778.

[28] G. S. Rowe, <u>Thomas McKean, The Shaping of an American Republicanism</u>, (Colorado Associated University Press, Boulder, 1978), p. 45. Thomas McKean joined the boycott on August 26, 1769.

[29] *Minutes of the House of Representatives of the Government of the Counties of New Castle, Kent and Sussex upon Delaware at Sessions held at New Castle in the Years, 1765-1770*, (Dover, 1931), pp. 167-168.

[30] *Charge Delivered by The Hon. Thomas McKean to the Grand Jury*, Lancaser, 1778; as cited in Coleman, op. cit., p. 84.

[31] Rowe, op. cit., p. 46.

[32] Coleman, op. cit., pp. 96-97.

[33] G. S. Rowe, "Thomas McKean and the Coming of the Revolution," *Pennsylvania Magazine of History and Biography*, Vol. XCVI, Number 1, January, 1972, p. 23.

[34] Peeling, op. cit., p. 28.

[35] "Narrative," p. 77; *Dickinson Papers*, R. R. Logan Collection, Box 5, HSP; Thomas McKean to John Dickinson, September 14, 1801.

[36] Coleman, op. cit., p. 107. Sarah Armitage McKean's oldest sister was the second wife of Dr. Francis Alison who had been Thomas' mentor, tutor and friend since childhood.

[37] For additional background on the Intolerable Acts and Boston's response, see Introduction, pp. 26-28.

[38] Edmund Cody Burnett, <u>The Continental Congress</u>, (The Macmillan Company, New York, 1941), p. 28.

[39] Charles Francis Adams, <u>The Life and Works of John Adams</u>, (Little, Brown and Company, Boston, 1850-1856), Vol. X, p. 269; Microfiche Collection, LAC 20283-92; John Adams to John M. Jackson, December 30, 1817.

[40] Rowe, *Thomas McKean and the Coming of the Revolution*, op. cit., p. 27.

[41] For details on the Galloway Plan, see Chapter 2, pp. 58-60.

[42] For additional background on the Continental Association, see Chapter 1, pp. 47-48.

[43] L. H. Butterfield, Editor, <u>Diary and Autobiography of John Adams</u>, (The Belknap Press, Cambridge, 1961), Vol. 2, p. 157.

[44] John E. Ferling, <u>The Loyalist Mind</u> (The Pennsylvania University Press, University Park, 1977), p. 34.

[45] Buchanan, op. cit., p. 124. Thomas McKean's second wife, Sally, gave birth to their first child, a boy, on November 1, 1775. The infant died that same day.

[46] Worthington Chauncey Ford, Chief, Division of Manuscripts, <u>JCC: 1774-1789</u>, (Government Printing Office, Washington, DC, 1905), Vol. II, pp. 253-255.

[47] JCC, op. cit., Vol. II, p. 212.

[48] LDC, Vol. 3, p. 115; Thomas McKean to George Read, January 19, 1776.

[49] "Narrative Journal of Captain Smythe, Queen's Rangers," *Pennsylvania Magazine of History & Biography*, Vol. XXXIX, pp. 143-169.

[50] JCC, op. cit., Vol. IV, p. 26. See also: <u>LDC</u>, op. cit., Vol. 3, p. 518; Thomas McKean to Philip Schuyler, April 13, 1776.

[51] Coleman, op. cit., pp. 144-145.

[52] JCC, op. cit., Vol. IV, p. 342.

[53] JCC, op. cit., Vol. IV, p. 358.

[54] JCC, op. cit., Vol. IV, p. 1075; John Adams, *Notes of Debates*.

[55] As cited in Coleman, op. cit., p. 158.

[56] Alden T. Vaughan, Editor, <u>Chronicles of the American Revolution</u>, (Grosset & Dunlap, New York, 1965), pp. 240-241.

[57] LDC, op. cit., Vol. 4, p. 210; John Adams to Samuel Chase, June 14 [?], 1776. See also: Burnett, op. cit., p. 178.

[58] LDC, op. cit., Vol. 4, pp. 337-338; Edward Rutledge to John Jay, June 29, 1776. See also: James Haw, <u>John & Edward Rutledge of South Carolina</u>, (The University of Georgia Press, Athens, 1997), pp. 92-94.

[59] Jack N. Rakove, <u>The Beginnings of National Politics</u>, (Alfred A. Knopf, New York, 1979), p. 100.

[60] LDC, op. cit., Vol. 4, p. 388; Caesar Rodney to Thomas Rodney, July 4, 1776.

[61] JCC, op. cit., Vol. V, pp. 506-507.

[62] JCC, op. cit., Vol. V, p. 626.

[63] Coleman, op. cit., p. 201.

[64] McKean Papers, op. cit.; Thomas McKean to Sally McKean, July 26, 1776.

[65] LDC, op. cit., Vol. 15, p. 634; Thomas McKean to Joseph Reed, August 29, 1780.

[66] JCC, op. cit., Vol. VII, p. 48.

[67] Buchanan, op. cit., pp. 31-49. According to Buchanan's account, of the 70 delegates who were accredited to Congress in early July 1776, only 51 were in attendance at that time. Of that number, only 47 were present in Congress on August 2, 1776, when the engrossed

copy of the Declaration was signed. Seven new members, who were not delegates on July 4, also signed on August 2. Matthew Thornton, a new delegate from New Hampshire, was permitted to sign that November. Thomas McKean, who cast his vote for Independence on July 2 and for the Declaration on July 4, was away on military service in early August 1776. He became the last person to sign sometime after January 1777. The exact date remains unresolved.

[68] LDC, op. cit., Vol. 5, p. 10; Charles Thomson to John Dickinson, August 16, 1776.

[69] LDC, op. cit., Vol. 5, p. 235; Benjamin Rush to Anthony Wayne, September 24, 1776.

[70] Stephen E. Lucas, Portents of Rebellion, (Temple University Press, Philadelphia, 1976), p. 246.

[71] Peeling, op. cit., pp. 65-68. See also: Rowe, Thomas McKean, The Shaping of an American Republicanism, pp. 88-90. In a letter to Caesar A. Rodney (the Signer's nephew) dated September 22, 1813, Thomas recounted from memory that he "...joined the Convention for forming a constitution for the future government of the State of Delaware...which I wrote in a tavern, without a book or any assistance." His biographers, however, attribute his claim to the faulty recollection of an elderly man who had been constantly engaged in public service during the period in question.

[72] Coleman, op. cit., p. 203.

[73] Sarah Maria Theresa McKean was married on April 10, 1798 to Senor Don Carlos Martinez de Yrujo in Philadelphia. In 1803, when her husband was elevated to Marquis de Casa Yrujo, Sarah became the Marchioness de Casa Yrujo. She died in Madrid on January 4, 1841. She was survived by one son and one daughter. Buchanan, op. cit., pp. 133-138.

[74] Rowe, Thomas McKean, The Shaping of an American Republicanism, op. cit., pp. 99-100. See also Peeling, op. cit., p. 124. Joseph Reed was initially offered the office of Chief Justice, but he declined.

[75] Buchanan, op. cit., p. 61.

[76] As cited in Coleman, op. cit., p. 220.

[77] LDC, op. cit., Vol. 10, p. 57; Thomas McKean to Nathanael Greene, June 9, 1778.

[78] Peeling, op. cit., p. 70. When President [Governor] McKinly was captured, the next in line of succession was George Read, the Speaker of the Council. He, however, pleaded ill health and took refuge in a relative's home in Maryland.

[79] LDC, op. cit., Vol. 14, p. 162; Thomas McKean to John Adams, November 8, 1779.

[80] LDC, op. cit., Vol. 8, p. 691; Henry Laurens to George Read, January 30, 1778.

[81] LDC, op. cit., Vol. 9, p. 521; Thomas McKean to Caesar Rodney, April 28, 1778.

[82] LDC, op. cit., Vol. 10, p. 130; Thomas McKean to Caesar Rodney, June 18, 1778.

[83] As cited in Burnett, op. cit., p. 40. Rev. Duché was at first the darling of the Continental

Congress. He was the first minister invited to offer a prayer at the opening of its third day on Wednesday, September 7, 1774. Even John Adams remarked that "Mr. Duché...struck out into an extemporary prayer...as pertinent, as affectionate, as sublime, as devout, as I ever heard offered up to Heaven."

[84] Coleman, op. cit., p. 232.

[85] Coleman, op. cit., p. 234.

[86] Buchanan, op. cit., p. 69.

[87] Buchanan, op. cit., pp. 64-67.

[88] LDC, op. cit., Vol. 16, p. 666; Thomas McKean to Thomas Collins, February 3, 1781.

[89] JCC, op. cit., Vol. XX, pp. 724-733. Samuel Johnston of North Carolina had initially been elected on July 9, 1781, to replace retiring President Samuel Huntington of Connecticut, but he declined the position and withdrew from Congress on July 13, 1781. On July 10, 1781, a new election was held and Thomas McKean of Delaware was elected.

[90] For over two centuries Maryland has claimed that its native son, John Hanson, was really the first President of the United States since he was the first to be elected under the Articles of Confederation who served a full presidential term (see Chapter Eight). But Thomas McKean was undisputedly the first to be elected under the Articles and Samuel Huntington was serving as President on March 1, 1781, when the Articles went into effect. The honor of being America's first President, however, belongs to Peyton Randolph who was elected at the opening of the Continental Congress on September 5, 1774.

[91] LDC, op. cit., Vol. 16,.p. 481; Thomas McKean to John Dickinson, December 25, 1780.

[92] LDC, op. cit., Vol. 17, p. 431; Thomas McKean to Francis Bailey, July 23, 1781.

[93] LDC, op. cit., Vol. 17, p. 38; Thomas Rodney's Notes, March 8, 1781.

[94] Buchanan, op. cit., p. 71.

[95] As cited in Peeling, op. cit., p. 111. *Pennsylvania Magazine of History & Biography*, Vol. XVI, pp. 103-104 and p. 160.

[96] LDC, op. cit., Vol. 18, pp. 160-161; Thomas McKean to Charles Thomson, October 23, 1781.

[97] JCC, op. cit., Vol. XXI, p. 1071. See also: LDC, op. cit., Vol. 18, p. 161, footnote.

[98] LDC, op. cit., Vol. 18, p. 189; John Hanson to Thomas McKean, November 10, 1781.

[99] LDC, op. cit., Vol. 19, pp. 27-28; Thomas McKean to Samuel Adams, August 6,1782.

[100] As cited in Rowe, Thomas McKean, The Shaping of an American Republicanism, op. cit., p. 130.; Journal of Samuel Rowland Fisher, pp. 279-280.

[101] Cox-Parrish-Wharton Collection, Vol. 11, p. 79, Historical Society of Pennsylvania, Philadelphia; Warren Mifflin to Thomas McKean, May 11, 1781.

[102] Rowe, Thomas McKean, The Shaping of an American Republicanism, op. cit., pp. 230-235.

[103] As cited in Rowe, Thomas McKean, The Shaping of an American Republicanism, op. cit., p. 235; Thomas McKean to Paul Hamilton, September 1, 1800.

[104] Rowe, Thomas McKean, The Shaping of an American Republicanism, op. cit., p. 226.

[105] As cited in Rowe, Thomas McKean, The Shaping of an American Republicanism, op. cit., p. 243; Thomas McKean to William Atlee, August 16, 1787; and, October 22, 1787. Atlee Manuscripts, Library of Congress.

[106] Thomas Lloyd, Debates of the Convention of the State of Pennsylvania on the Constitution Proposed for the Government of the United States, (Joseph James, Printer, Philadelphia, 1788), Vol. I, p.

[107] John B. McMaster & Frederick D. Stone, Editors, Pennsylvania and the Federal Constitution, 1787-1788, (Philadelphia, 1888), p. 378.

[108] Lloyd, op. cit., pp. 145-146.

[109] Rowe, Thomas McKean, The Shaping of an American Republicanism, op. cit., p. 252.

[110] If the more assertive Thomas McKean had been appointed instead of John Jay, the US Supreme Court might well have enforced its coequal status a decade before John Marshal arrived.

[111] Thomas Mifflin, the tenth President of the Continental Congress, was elected as President of the Pennsylvania Constitutional Convention in November 1789.

[112] Allan Nevins, The American States During and After the Revolution, (The Macmillan Company, New York, 1927), p. 199.

[113] Rowe, Thomas McKean, The Shaping of an American Republicanism, op. cit., p. 268.

[114] For background on the Jay Treaty of 1795, see Chapter Five, pp. 166-168.

[115] Robert R. Logan Collection, Historical Society of Pennsylvania, Philadelphia, Vol. 12, p. 79.; Thomas McKean to John Dickinson, July 30, 1798.

[116] Rowe, Thomas McKean, The Shaping of an American Republicanism, op. cit., p. 304.

[117] As cited in Rowe, Thomas McKean, The Shaping of an American Republicanism, op. cit., p. 308.

[118] Rowe, <u>Thomas McKean, The Shaping of an American Republicanism</u>, op. cit., p. 313.

[119] McKean Papers, op. cit.; Thomas McKean to John Dickinson, June 23, 1800.

[120] McKean Papers, op. cit.; Thomas McKean to Mrs. McKean, December 30, 1801.

[121] Thomas Jefferson, Presidential Papers; Thomas McKean to Thomas Jefferson, August 10,1801.

[122] McKean Papers, op. cit.; Thomas McKean to Thomas Jefferson, January 10,1801. Throughout his nine years as Governor of Pennsylvania, Thomas was repeatedly criticized for the number of relatives he appointed to public office including two sons and a nephew. See Also: Buchanan, op. cit., p. 97, for a complete list.

[123] Peeling, op. cit., p. 230.

[124] McKean Papers, op. cit.; Thomas McKean to Thomas Jefferson, February 7, 1803.

[125] Henry Adams, <u>The Life of Albert Gallatin</u>, pp. 312-313, Microform, LAC 11368; Thomas McKean to A. J. Dallas, October 16, 1803.

[126] As cited in Peeling, op. cit., p. 249.

[127] McKean Papers, op. cit.; Thomas McKean to Thomas Jefferson, February 16, 1805.

[128] As cited in Peeling, op. cit., p. 256. See also: Rowe, <u>Thomas McKean, The Shaping of an American Republicanism</u>, op. cit., p. 351.

[129] McKean Papers, op. cit.; Thomas McKean to Thomas McKean, Jr., April 7, 1805.

[130] William Duane, Editor, *Aurora*, June 6, 1805.

[131] Rowe, <u>Thomas McKean, The Shaping of an American Republicanism</u>, op. cit., p. 360.

[132] McKean Papers, op. cit.; Thomas McKean to John Dickinson, November 28, 1805.

[133] *Journal of the House of Representatives of the Commonwealth of Pennsylvania, 1806-1807*, pp. 15-16; December 4,1806.

[134] In some interesting respects, the blatant political move for Gov. McKean's impeachment paralleled the impeachment of President Bill Clinton two centuries later. Just as Speaker Newt Gingrich"s resignation resulted from the 1999 event which he so carefully orchestrated, so too did Editor William Duane fail miserably in his bid for a seat in the Pennsylvania Senate in 1807. Both seriously miscalculated the public's pulse and paid a heavy price for their own vindictiveness.

[135] *Journal of the House of Representatives of the Commonwealth of Pennsylvania, 1807-1808*, pp. 428-429.

[136] Peeling, op. cit., p. 303. The meeting was held on August 26,1814.

[137] Adams, op. cit., Vol. X, pp. 14-15; Thomas McKean to John Adams, June 13, 1812.

[138] McKean Papers, op. cit.; Thomas McKean to John Adams, July 1, 1815.

[139] Buchanan, op. cit., p. 124.

WHILE THOMAS MCKEAN
WAS PRESIDENT

Notes

Abbreviation Key

JCC   Journals of the Continental Congress
LDC   Letters of Delegates to Congress
PHL   The Papers of Henry Laurens

140 Edmund Cody Burnett, The Continental Congress, (The Macmillan Company, New York, 1941), p. 500. The thirteenth State, Maryland, finally signed the Articles of Confederation on February 24, 1781. They went into effect on March 1, 1781, at high noon.

141 Gaillard Hunt, Chief, Division of Manuscripts, JCC: 1774-1789, (Government Printing Office, Washington, DC, 1912), Vol. XXI, pp. 851-52.

142 JCC, op. cit., p. 1087.

143 Theodore P. Savas and J. David Dameron, A guide to the Battles of the American Revolution (Savas Beatie, New York, 2010), pp. 324-328.

144 Craig L. Symonds, A Battlefield Atlas of the American Revolution, (The Nautical & Aviation Publishing Company of America, 1986), p. 97.

145 Savas, op. cit., p. 329.

146 Piers Mackesy, The War for America: 1775-1783, (Harvard University Press, Cambridge, 1965), p.368.

147 L. Edward Purcell and David F. Burg, Editors, World Almanac of the American Revolution, (World Almanac, New York, 1992), p. 281.

148 Paul H. Smith, Editor, LDC: 1774-1789, (Library of Congress, Washington, DC, 1991), p. xi.

149 Purcell, op. cit., pp. 282-291.

150 Henry Clinton, The American Rebellion, (Yale University Press, New Haven, 1954), pp. 333-334.

151 Alden T. Vaughan, Chronicles of the American Revolution, (Grosset & Dunlap, New York, 1965), The British Government Reacts to the Defeat [Extracts from the Memoirs of N. W. Wraxall], pp. 303-304.

Chapter 8

President
JOHN HANSON
of
MARYLAND

Mistaken Identity

In this country, the highest honor that a state and the nation can bestow on one of its own is to have a statue placed in the United States Capitol. John Hanson of Maryland, the eighth President of the Continental Congress, has been accorded that exceptional recognition.

This custom began in 1864, by Act of Congress, when each state was invited to present to the nation life-size images of its two most distinguished citizens. On December 15, 1902, the Governor of Maryland informed Congress that his state had completed its selection and that Maryland's two favorite sons--John Hanson, President of the Continental Congress, and Charles Carroll of Carrollton, Signer of the Declaration of Independence--stood ready for admission. On Saturday afternoon, January 31, 1903, bronze statues of Hanson and Carroll (both sculpted by Richard E. Brooks of Boston) were unveiled in Statuary Hall, the old chamber of the House of Representatives, America's Pantheon.[1]

At that dedication, Congressman George Alexander Pearre of Maryland recounted the critical role that both Hanson and Carroll played in the American Revolution when "the leaven of liberty" transformed a colonial outpost into a magnificent new nation.[2] Senator Jonathan Dolliver of Iowa proclaimed that "in the case of...John Hanson [Maryland] has done a tardy act of justice to a man whose eminence in the public service had been almost lost in the waste of time; a man who in a peculiarly appropriate sense was the representative of the national ideal throughout the Revolutionary struggle."[3]

In his remarks, Maryland Congressman Charles Schirm praised President Hanson for "having done more than any other one man in the colony to destroy the supremacy of Great Britain." He credited Hanson as "the leading spirit among a band of determined patriots during the transition of Maryland from a dependent, proprietary province into a sovereign State." Schirm concluded his address by describing Hanson as "one of those modest, unassuming great men who seek no glory for themselves, but find their highest reward in the good that accrues from their efforts to the great body of the people."[4]

Senator Louis McComas of Maryland proclaimed that "John Hanson's name will be associated forever with laying the corner stone of our great nation..." and by his "election to the Presidency of Congress John Hanson became in a political sense the foremost person in the United States, and represented its dignity."[5] It is for that reason, Senator McComas said, Maryland "bestows upon his name the highest honor whereby an American State can commemorate an illustrious citizen."[6]

It is hardly surprising that this mark of distinction was bestowed upon a patriot of John Hanson's stature. What is shocking is that only one of his equally-deserving presidential colleagues from the First Republic--John Hancock--stands with him today in the Capitol.

Despite his prominence, several of the major details pertaining to John Hanson's life remain subject to scrutiny over two centuries later. Even his birth, death and burial are open to conjecture. Two Hanson biographers as well as the official Congressional Directory list 1715 as the year of John's birth.[7] The Library of Congress and the Maryland Historical Society, however, supported by more recent and persuasive research, place the year at 1721.[8] The exact date of John's death is also in dispute. In fact, John's passing was first reported eight months before he died. In similar fashion, the debate over John's burial site remains unresolved. While all sources agree that he died while visiting his nephew at Oxon Hill, Maryland in 1783, John's final resting place has not yet been determined with absolute certainty.[9]

Even John's ancestry is open to interpretation. He is unquestionably the most prominent Founding Father of Swedish descent. In fact, John Hanson and John Jay were two Presidents of the First Republic who did not claim direct British ancestry.[10] The arrival of the Hanson family in America, however, is shrouded in myth. The most popular version claims that during the Thirty Years War John's great-grandfather fought alongside King Gustavus II Adolphus of Sweden, "the military champion of the Protestant cause in Europe." According to this tale, both Col. Hanson and his sovereign were killed in the Battle of Lützen in Saxony in November 1632. A decade later, the Colonel's four sons (Andrew, Randolph, William and John; ranging in age from 24 to 12) supposedly arrived in America and settled in the recently established colony of New Sweden along the banks of the Delaware River. When the Swedish colony fell to the Dutch in

1656,[11] the Hanson brothers along with many of their fellow Scandinavians followed the Elk River Trail to Maryland. It was there that the youngest son, John Hanson (the President's grandfather), became one of the earliest settlers of the new Charles County which was founded in May 1658.[12]

A Maryland genealogist, however, concludes that "the records which have been preserved in Maryland somehow seem to contradict the narrative" above. In Charles County Gentry (1940), Harry Wright Newman suggests that the President's grandfather might actually have been related to Sir Robert Hanson, the Lord Mayor of London. Whether or not the family had celebrity connections, Newman insists that "the first reference to [grandfather] John Hanson in Charles County was of June 1672..." It was there that Grandfather Hanson eventually wed his wife Mary who bore him seven children; and, it was there that the old man died in late 1713, at what one historian speculates was the age of eighty-three.[13]

The most historically significant debate over President John Hanson, however, concerns his public life. Since John was the first Head of State elected for a full one-year term after the ratification of the Articles of Confederation, several biographers have mistakenly identified John Hanson as the first President of the United States. The most passionate support for this hypothesis came from Seymour Wemyss Smith in his 1932 biography: John Hanson, Our First President. Smith and other advocates overlook the fact that John was actually the third President to serve under the Articles. When that new charter finally went into effect on March 1, 1781, Samuel Huntington, the sixth President of the Continental Congress, continued as Head of State for another three months without interruption. Thomas McKean of Delaware then became the first person to actually be elected under the Articles when he replaced Huntington in July 1781.[14] Of even greater importance is the fact that the office of President had been handed down without interruption since the election of the very first President, Peyton Randolph of Virginia, in September 1774.[15] Even though the adoption of the Articles of Confederation did play a significant role in restructuring the work of Congress (e.g., establishing administrative offices pertaining to finance and foreign affairs), the President continued to function as Head of State as he had done for the past seven years.

Irving Brant, the author of the definitive six-volume biography of James Madison, described Smith's thesis as a "Maryland publicity hoax" and a "yarn...first told by the Chamber of Commerce boys and is retold by their dupes." According to Brant, "the title, 'President of the United States in Congress Assembled' [the official designation under the Articles], was merely a new name for the President of the Continental Congress..."[16] Even the State Department got caught up in the debate over Smith's book. In response to public inquiries, the Department's historical advisor, Hunter Miller, simply dismissed all of the Presidents of the Continental Congress and ruled that "George Washington was the first President of the United States of America."[17] Once again, the First American Republic was banished to an historic Black Hole.

Despite the contention over his birth, death, burial, ancestry and mistaken identity, John Hanson was nevertheless a very real patriot who helped to change the course of history for his state and his nation.

His father, Samuel, was born around 1684 in Port Tobacco Hundred, Charles County, Maryland. At the age of 22, Samuel Hanson married Elizabeth Story Warren, a recent widow. She was a truly remarkable woman who not only gave birth to ten children but also survived her husband by twenty-four years. Their youngest son, the future President, was born at Mulberry Grove, Port Tobacco Parish on April 3, 1721.[18]

In 1716 and again in 1728, Samuel Hanson represented Charles County in the Maryland State Legislature. He also succeeded his oldest brother Robert as High Sheriff of Charles County in 1719 and later became the county's Deputy Commissary. By the time of Samuel Hanson's death in October 1740, he had acquired at least 1,031 acres of land. In distributing his estate, Samuel Hanson willed Hereford Plantation to his son John.[19] Throughout his life, however, John was identified with the family's homestead, Mulberry Grove.

In 1743, John married fifteen-year-old Jane Contee who was a descendant of a French Huguenot family from La Rochelle, the same village in the south of France that had been home to President John Jay's ancestors.[20] John Hanson and his wife had eight children, but three died very young and two others gave their lives during military service: Dr. Samuel Hanson died in 1781 from illness he contracted while serving as a surgeon in Washington's Life Guards; and, Lt. Peter Hanson, who was wounded at Ft. Washington, died in 1776 while being held as a prisoner of war. (John Hanson and Henry Laurens were the only Presidents who lost sons in the Revolutionary War.)[21] John's grown daughter, Jane Contee Thomas, also died in 1781. Only two of his children--Catherine Contee Alexander and Alexander Contee Hanson--survived their father's death in 1783.[22]

Like his father and uncle before him, John became Sheriff of Charles County in 1750. Seven years later he was elected to the House of Delegates where he represented Charles County over the next twelve years.[23] According to Professor Ralph B. Levering, during John's service in Annapolis, he became one of the leaders of the powerful political caucus known as the "country party" which was opposed to "the system of proprietary privilege and taxation which enriched the Calvert Family." Levering contends that "...the American Revolution in Maryland was both a revolt against proprietary rule and a process of abandoning allegiance to Great Britain."[24]

As a member of the General Assembly, John took a forceful stand against the Stamp Act that the British tried to impose on the American Colonies in 1765. John strongly supported the convening of a continent-wide congress to form a united front against Parliament. He was chosen to serve on the legislative committee which drew up instructions for the Maryland delegates and John wholeheartedly supported the boycott mandated by the Stamp Act Congress.[25] When the Act was rescinded by the House of Commons in early 1766, John's sense of relief was cut short by the introduction of the Townshend Acts the following year. According to biographer Jacob Nelson, John "was one of the most spirited opponents of the new bill."[26] His leadership contributed significantly to Maryland's adoption of the Non-Importation Resolution which John signed on June 22, 1769.[27] The following October, when a British merchant ship landed in Charles County and attempted to unload its cargo in violation of the boycott, John, "leading a group of colonists in broad daylight, and without fear of detection or prosecution, compelled the captain of the vessel to re-ship the goods to England."[28]

Throughout these prerevolutionary years, John also developed a close friendship with his Virginia neighbors George and Martha Washington who lived just across the Potomac River from Mulberry Grove. John occasionally stayed overnight at Mount Vernon as Washington recorded in his diary for April 20-22, 1772.[29]

John left the legislature in the fall of 1769 to become deputy surveyor of Frederick County which, at that time, covered the entire western one-third of the colony.[30] During the next three years, once the Townshend Acts had been repealed (except for the tax on tea), a lull settled over American-British relations with only an occasional crisis to stir the waters. It was in 1773, during that period of relative calm, that John took the surprising step of moving his family and fortune to the colony's newest and western-most county of Frederick which he knew so well from his extensive survey work No clear motive has ever been established for why such a well-established man would be willing to uproot his family and relocate at the age of fifty-two. Was his motive personal, political or financial; or perhaps a mix of all three? Whatever the case, John was again elected to the General Assembly from 1777-1780, but this time as the delegate from Frederick County.[31] On the eve of the American Revolution John was the elder statesman on Maryland's western frontier.

Later that year, while John and his family were still settling into their new home, the arrival of British ships, eager to unload East India tea at American ports, lit the fuse that quickly exploded into full-scale revolution. Following the Boston Tea Party that December, Parliament passed the draconian Intolerable Acts which suspended Massachusetts self-government and closed Boston Harbor.[32] In response to Boston's plea for support, a meeting was held at the new Frederick County Court House on June 20, 1774. John was elected to preside. Resolutions were adopted calling for an end to "all commercial intercourse with Great Britain" and demanding that "every other act oppressive to American liberty, be repealed" in order to preserve American "rights, liberties and privileges."[33]

Before adjourning, John was elected to head a delegation from Frederick which met with representatives from across Maryland. At that "general congress" at Annapolis, June 22-25, 1774, delegates were selected to represent Maryland at the upcoming Continental Congress. The citizens of Frederick County gathered again on November 18, 1774, reelected John as chairman, endorsed the resolutions adopted in Philadelphia and voted to organize a militia while declaring that the Governor's authority had ended.[34] John was also elected to serve on the county's Committee of Correspondence and he remained Chairman of the Frederick Committee of Observation on which his 26 year-old son Alexander also served. It was, in effect, the county government.

For the rest of the Revolution, Frederick County, under John's leadership, would prove second to none in urging Maryland's full support for an end to British rule.[35] For example, on February 17, 1775, the committee wrote to Sam Adams in Boston informing him that "We...have this day forwarded £1200...for the relief of the poor of your place." It was signed by "John Hanson, President."[36]

On June 21, 1775, John added the office of County Treasurer to his already hectic schedule. Following news of the Battle of Bunker [Breed's] Hill, John also played a major role in organizing two companies of riflemen from Western Maryland who arrived at Washington's Headquarters in Boston on August 9. They were among the first southern troops to reach New England.[37]

At the same time, John, his son and his son-in-law, Dr. Philip Thomas, were reelected as county delegates to Maryland's fifth Provincial Convention which met at Annapolis in late July.[38] In reflecting on that session, Hanson biographer Jacob Nelson states that even though John was "not a fiery orator like Patrick Henry...[John] could also rise to the occasion and speak in bold and fearless words, as he did at the Maryland Convention, July 26, 1775." Nelson describes John at that session as "one of the most vigorous and aggressive men at the meeting, urging that Maryland take a definite stand for the cause of freedom." By adopting the "Association of Freemen of Maryland," which approved the use of arms to repel British troops, the Convention did precisely that.[39]

As political authority rapidly shifted to the American patriots, rumors spread that Virginia Gov. Dunmore and British Gen. Gage were desperately attempting to incite Indian uprisings along the frontier. Speculation turned to alarm when four suspicious strangers were captured near Hagerstown, Maryland in mid-November 1775. After conducting an intense interrogation, John wrote to John Hancock, the President of the Continental Congress, on November 24, 1775:

"Sir: - I am directed by the Committee of this County to transmit to you copies of the examination of Allan Cameron, John Smith, John Connoly, and a letter to one Gibson, from Connoly, and Lord Dunmore's speech to White Eyes, and a proposal by Connolly to General Gage for raising an army for the destruction of the liberties of the Colonies. Any orders relative to the prisoners will be strictly observed; the committee and the inhabitants of this County being determined to pursue every measure which the Congress may recommend to them as necessary for the preservation of these Colonies, at this time of imminent danger. I am, very respectfully sir, your most humble servant, John Hanson, Chairman."[40]

President Hancock immediately forwarded confirmation of the Dunmore Conspiracy to Gen. Washington when he wrote on December 2, 1775, that "Yesterday we Rec'd Advice by an Express from the Committee of Frederic in Maryland, that Conolly & three associates were taken prisoners and are now in Confinement in that County."[41] Six days later President Hancock informed John and the Frederick County Committee that "the Congress highly approve your Conduct and Vigilance in seizing Cameron, Smith and Conally...and I am directed to desire you...to send the Prisoners under Guard to Philada."[42]

In June 1776, Frederick County adopted a powerful resolution which pledged "that what may be recommended by a majority of the Congress equally delegated by the people of the United Colonies, we will, at the hazard of our lives and fortunes, support and maintain..."[43] Throughout that winter and spring the state delegates debated the steady drumbeat toward total separation from Britain. Finally, in June 1776, resolutions were introduced on the floor of Maryland's Convention to instruct her congressional delegates to vote in favor of Independence. John concluded that fateful debate by stating that "these resolutions ought to be passed and it is high time."[44] On July 2, 1776, with Maryland's full support, that moment finally arrived as the Continental Congress voted for Independence.

In October 1776, John was appointed to a committee to reorganize the Maryland militia. He and members of that committee traveled to the camp of the Maryland troops in New Jersey "with power to appoint officers and to encourage the reenlistment of the Maryland militia."[45]

The following month John served as a delegate to the Convention which adopted the first State Constitution, including a Bill of Rights. On February 13, 1777, the new government of the State of Maryland officially came into existence with his close friend and colleague, Thomas Johnson of Frederick, serving as its first governor.[46] Despite the awesome challenges ahead, John believed that "we will win the war with George Washington in the field, if we do our share at home. In the end we will establish an Inseparable Union, and ultimately it will become the greatest nation in the world."[47]

In order to accomplish this lofty goal, however, both John Hanson and the state of Maryland insisted that extravagant land claims on the part of several states had to be resolved in favor of the new nation. The crisis had begun nearly two centuries earlier when King James I issued the Second Charter of Virginia in May 1609. He expanded the territory along the Atlantic Coast which he had originally granted to the Virginia Company in 1607, and then added the incomprehensible phrase "from Sea to Sea, West, and Northwest..."[48] In just seven words the British Sovereign had disposed of much of North America. Over the next century several other colonies were also granted vague western boundaries, but none as egregious as Virginia's.[49]

With such a vast empire at stake, greed quickly flourished. Powerful land trusts such as The Ohio Company petitioned the Crown for vast territorial tracks, some as large of 2,500,000 acres. Lawrence and George Washington and Benjamin Franklin were among many Americans who joined with prominent British politicians such as Lt. Gov. Dinwiddie of Virginia, the Duke of Bedford and London banker Thomas Walpole in search of unrivaled wealth.[50] The Walpole Company, for example, was able to enhance its prospects "by spreading around ownership shares to an array of top ministers, including the lord chancellor..."[51] These often conflicting corporate claims further complicated the critical issue of westward expansion.

Maryland did not enjoy such open-ended territorial claims, nor were its most prominent men engaged in these massive real estate ventures. Its boundaries were set. Therefore, in 1777, when the Articles of Confederation were reported to Congress for debate and adoption, Maryland insisted that all state lines had to be clearly delineated before the new nation's first charter could be approved. On October 15, 1777, the Maryland congressional delegation introduced the following Resolution:

"That, in order to render the present union and confederacy firm and perpetual, it is essential that the limits of each respective territorial jurisdiction should be ascertained by the articles of confederation; and, therefore, it is recommended to the legislatures of every State to lay before Congress a description of the territorial lands of each of their respective states, and a summary of the grants, treaties, and proofs upon which they are claimed or established."[52] Only New York joined Maryland in support of this Resolution. Undaunted, Maryland then introduced an even more controversial proposal:

"That the United States, in Congress assembled, shall have the sole and exclusive right and power to ascertain and fix the western boundary of such states as claim to the Mississippi or South Sea, and lay out the land beyond the boundary, so ascertained, into separate and independent states, from time to time, as the numbers and circumstances of the people thereof may require." On this Resolution, Maryland stood alone.[53]

On Saturday, November 15, 1777, the Articles of Confederation were adopted by the Continental Congress despite Maryland's concerns. The debate, however, was far from over. In order for the new charter to become law, each of the thirteen states had to ratify the document. Unanimous consent was required. Virginia, New York and Massachusetts were eager to give their approval. Even smaller states such as Rhode Island, New Jersey and Delaware were willing to put aside their concerns in order to solidify the country in the midst of war. By February 1779, twelve states had ratified the Articles.[54]

Only Maryland stood in the way of formal confederation. On May 21, 1779, John and his colleagues in the Maryland General Assembly clearly articulated what they viewed as the righteousness of their position: "We are convinced, policy and justice require, that a country unsettled at the commencement of this war, claimed by the British crown, and ceded to it by the treaty of Paris, if wrested from the common enemy by the blood and treasure of the thirteen States, should be considered as a common property, subject to be parceled out by Congress into free, convenient and independent governments, in such manner and at such times as the wisdom of that assembly shall hereafter direct."[55]

Out of frustration, some delegates began to debate "whether we shall send to all the States for their consent to a Confederation of twelve, or wait for Maryland to consider better of it, and accede..."[56] On April 24, 1779, Richard Henry Lee wrote to John Adams that "The Assembly of Virginia have directed their Delegates to move Congress to fix a day for closing this great Compact between such of the States as have consented...We shall shortly move Congress for this purpose."[57] One disgusted congressman exclaimed that "There now only remains Maryland who has seldom done anything with a good Grace...she has always been a forward hussy."[58]

Despite the growing impatience of its sister states, Maryland held firm. As noted historian John C. Miller described the situation: "In Maryland's conduct there was something more than met the eye...the fate of the American West was at stake and, whatever their motives, the leaders of Maryland were upholding the cause of nationalism in the West. Their fight against the Articles of Confederation was a filibuster designed to break the grip of the great landed states upon what ultimately became the national domain of the United States."[59] Throughout the battle over western lands, "John Hanson was the dominant influence in Maryland politics" wrote one of his biographers, "and he was backed to the limit by Daniel Carroll and Charles Carroll...and by the several distinguished delegates who represented the State in Congress at that time."[60]

Virginia was just as adamant. It "denied that Congress--'a foreign tribunal'--had any authority to limit the western boundaries of the states and refused to submit to such 'intolerable despotism'...but Virginia's bid for empire had aroused the jealousy and apprehension of other states, including some that also claimed Western lands."[61] The tide was starting to turn as the focus of public pressure began to shift from Maryland to Virginia. At the Annapolis Capitol, John and his colleagues had stood their ground against overwhelming congressional opposition. Now, as the issue came to a head, John was elected as a delegate to Congress on December 22, 1779. The following February, New York started to unravel the deadlock by relinquishing to Congress part of its Western lands.[62] Connecticut eventually withdrew its claims, as well. Virginia, however, remained adamant.

During the ongoing debate over the western lands, the American military situation grew far more precarious when the great port city of Charleston fell to the British on May 12, 1780. Gen. Benjamin Lincoln's entire Southern Army of 5,500 Continentals was lost.[63] Despite this devastating development, John somehow retained his optimism. In a letter from Philadelphia on July 1, 1780, John wrote to Maryland Gov. Thomas Sim Lee: "Our affairs it is true have of late worn but an unfavorable Aspect, but we are far from being in the last Ditch, as some are dastardly enough to immagine. Our resources are great, And we are now roused I hope to A proper exertion."[64] New Jersey Delegate William Churchill Houston clearly shared John's sentiments: "Considering the Disaster we have met with on a general Scale, we are not in the least dejected by it...Nothing but a better Supply of Money is wanting to give decisive vigour to the War..."[65]

John's optimism was underscored when he wrote to Charles Carroll of Carrollton in late July that "We have official Accounts of the Arrival of the french fleet at Rhode Island...with 5000 land forces."[66] John was even more hopeful a week later in his next letter to Carroll when he confidently stated "that the Issue of the present Campaign will be glorious for the united States of America; nothing will prevent it, but the want of money-- little or none in the Continental Treasury, and the States pay in very Slow indeed."[67] "Our Magnanimous Aly is making most noble Exertions in our favour," John wrote, "and it will be degrading indeed Should we fail in doing our part. The want of money is very Embarrassing..." Even John's home state did not escape his wrath: "Of the one million two hundred and odd thousand Dollrs. required of Maryland, 200,000 only has been Sent in, And the other States are equally Deficient."[68] John was just as blunt in pointing out to Gov. Lee that "The Treasury Board who has had the direction of this Business, has been most Shamefully negligent."[69]

John also lamented that "Reinforcements Come in very Slowly every State greatly deficient in their Quotas of men, much therefore must depend upon the Militia of New England, New York, Jersey and Pensylvania. We are told by the Delegates from those states that men will not be Wanting, I wish it may turn out so."[70] By mid-August 1780, John was "persuaded there will be no want of men to Carry on the Expedition...but the feeding them is the difficulty."[71]

In the midst of managing a war, John and his congressional colleagues were bombarded with requests for personal favors from friends and officials back home. Almost as soon as he arrived in Philadelphia, John began the tedious process of commissioning a new coach for his friend, Gov. Lee. The negotiations dragged out for months before a suitable carriage at an acceptable price was finally agreed upon by all parties.[72] In mid-October 1780, John was able to inform the governor that "Your Carriage is now painting and will be ready by the first Week in November."[73] At the end of November, John finally reported that "Your Carriage is finished and the man is impatient for his money."[74] Even the day before the final ratification of the Articles of Confederation John was distracted from official business when, in response to a request from his daughter, he described to his son-in-law "The Extravagant price of Goods here especially White Broad Cloth..."[75] Replying to yet another request, John wrote to Gov. Lee: "I will give directions to have a hat immediately made for you tho' my finances are very low."[76]

The delegates also tried as best they could to oversee family matters, as well as their business interests, through detailed correspondence. John's son-in-law, Dr. Philip Thomas, was his primary confident and correspondent. Repeatedly John would enquire about "the State of [his daughter] Janeys health" and he would just as frequently report on his wife's delicate condition.[77] John also fretted over developments pertaining to his estate, especially one particular slave named George who kept running away. In the conflicted ethical climate of that era, John advised his son-in-law that it would be better to sell George "at allmost Any price than exercise the Cruelty which would be necessary to oblige him to Stay with you."[78]

Throughout their congressional service, the Maryland Delegation was also forced to repeatedly plead with their governor and legislature back in Annapolis for their salary. On August 15, 1780, John wrote to Gov. Lee that "My finances begin to run low and I believe my Colleagues are not much better--pray Save in Some Cash..."[79] Two weeks later he reminded the governor that "Our Embarrassments for want of money daily increases."[80] Fellow delegate George Plater repeated their plea in mid-November when he wrote to Gov. Lee that "we must put you to the Trouble of forwarding...the Money for our Support, of which we stand in great Need." Finally, on November 18, 1780, the Maryland Council ordered £3,000 to be forwarded to each of its congressional delegates.[81] The following March, Maryland Delegate Daniel Carroll took up the same theme when he told Gov. Lee that "...my finances are very low, & that I cannot take any measures for living in a manner I think I ought to do until I receive a supply." Despite their need, Gov. Lee informed the delegates on March 23, 1781, that "an 'exhausted' treasury prevented the state from sending them money immediately." Nevertheless, the Council "was able to remit $1,500 each to Hanson and Carroll by the end of April."[82] But by mid-July 1781, Maryland Delegate Richard Potts reported to the Governor that "The Necessity of being obliged to have Recourse to our friends has been the Lot of us all and it is unnecessary to comment on so humiliating a State."[83]

Letters from family and friends were one of John's greatest sources of joy and consolation during his two-and-a-half years in Congress. To Charles Carroll--with whom John would one day share Statuary Hall in the United States Capitol--he wrote that "It always gives me much pleasure when I receive a line from you."[84]

During the first two weeks of September 1780, John was "so unwell... that I was not able to Write." But he reassured his friend Carroll that "I am now on the recovery, and hope to be able to attend Congress in a day or two." In the same letter his characteristic optimism began to fade as he expressed his growing distress over the lack of adequate provisions for the soldiers and the fact that in New Jersey the army was "Stripping that part of the Country of the remainder of its Cattle."[85] Despite this outrage, John told his son-in-law a few days later that "Our Army is Still much distressed for want of meat. They get one meal only in three days, and how long that Scanty allowance will Continue is uncertain."[86]

John lamented that "This manner of procuring is very distressing and attended With ruin to the morals and discipline of the Army..." and that "enormous excesses were Committed." John feared that all of this led to an even deeper concern: "It has been no inconsiderable Support to our Cause to have had it in our power to Contrast the Conduct of our Army With that of the Enemy, and to Convince the Inhabitants, that While their rights were Wantonly Violated by the British Troops, by ours they were respected. This distinction must now unhapily Cease, and we must assume the Odious Character of the plunderers instead of the protectors of the people..." If allowed to continue, John predicted disaster: "...in short, if this method of procuring provisions for the Army is not very speedily prevented, by an exertion of the States in Sending forward Supplies the Army must disband, and we are undone."[87]

In September 1780, John confided to his son-in-law that "...there Seems to be a fatality attending every measure that has been adopted to put our finances into order--the most probable Schemes have, by Some means or other been rendered ineffectual...Our present Situation is truly Alarming--the Army in want of every thing--no money in the Treasury, And our Credit Exausted. God grant us a Speedy, Safe and Honourable Peace."[88] Three days later, John joined his state's delegation (Daniel of St. Thomas Jenifer and John Henry) in forwarding to Annapolis "A Resolve of Congress, recommending to the State of Maryland, to furnish five hundred head of Cattle, for the immediate use of the Army." It was, they assured their political colleagues back home, "...a measure absolutely necessary to be Complied with..."[89]

By early October 1780, John's focus shifted from the troops to their officers. He wrote to Dr. Thomas that Gen. Gates had arrogantly requested to be removed from command rather than be held accountable for his shameful conduct at the Battle of Camden two months earlier. John, who well remembered that in 1778 Gates had been accused of scheming with Gen. Conway and others to replace Washington,[90] commented with obvious satisfaction, "How is the mighty fallen and the proud humbled." John then switched his focus to "the most horrid plot that ever was Conceived by the heart of man," the treason of Gen. Benedict Arnold. John wrote that "...had it Succeeded [it] would have been a most fatal Stroke to the liberties of America. The fort at West point was not only to have been delivered up to the Enemy, but our worthy General [Washington] was also to have been put into their hands." As John concluded his lengthy letter late that fall night, he shared one final bit of bad news: "The french fleet is not Arrived And as the Season is so far Advanced, it is not probable I think they Will Come at all."[91] Gone were the high hopes of earlier that summer when the French were first sighted off the Rhode Island coast.

To Charles Carroll, John predicted that "All the [European] powers will find it difficult to procure money to Carry on the War. France hath allready begun to Tax..." John also reported the disturbing news that "Mr. Laurence [Laurens] was taken on his passage to Holland and Conveyed to London, And is Committed to the Tower on a Charge of High Treason." In a postscript, John urged his friend to accept his recent election to Congress, saying that "It would give me great pleasure to see you here." Unfortunately for John, Carroll officially declined the position.[92] To Gov. Lee, John expressed his deep regret "that the principal end of the assemblys being Called together, has not yet been under their Consideration, I mean the raising men And Supplies for the Army." He also touched on two well-worn topics when he told the governor that "I hope you will have it in your power to send me 10000 Dollars by the next post, my Finances are lowe indeed," and John delicately pointed out that "You desire me to pay the money inclosed to the Coachmaker, but none was inclosed."[93]

On October 10, 1780, attention shifted back to the Western boundaries as Congress debated a Resolution introduced by Virginia which, on the surface, sounded fairly conciliatory: "That the unappropriated lands that may be ceded or relinquished to the United State, by any particular states, pursuant to the recommendation of Congress...shall be disposed of for the common benefit of the United States and be settled and formed into distinct republican states which shall become members of the federal union..." Even though the Virginia Resolution was an important step forward, John was clearly not satisfied since his no vote resulted in a tie of five states in favor and five opposed, with two states split.[94]

Finally, on January 2, 1781, the Virginia State Assembly moved from generalities to specifics when it passed an act ceding to the United States all land claims north of the Ohio River.[95] For years thereafter, it was widely assumed that this was the development that tipped the scales and led directly to Maryland's ratification of the Articles. In his definitive study of the Continental Congress, however, Edmund Cody Burnett argued that the deciding factor was actually "a word of admonition from the French minister, Luzerne" that convinced Maryland that the time had come to complete the Confederation. The Minister implied that Maryland's request for French assistance in defending Chesapeake Bay against the British had a much greater chance of success once the formal union of the thirteen states had been completed. The Maryland General Assembly responded by accepting the concessions of the larger states, despite some lingering reservations, and instructing its congressional representatives to sign the document.[96]

On February 12, 1781, Maryland's newest delegate, Daniel Carroll, entered Congress prepared to affix his signature to the waiting parchment. He informed Gov. Lee that "On the first day of my appearing in Congress, I delivered the Act empowering the Deligates of Maryland to Subscribe the Articles of Confederation...it was read, & entered on the Journals. The presence of another Delegate is only wanting to compleat this important business [two signatures were required from each state]."[97] Several days later, John returned to Philadelphia where, with the stroke of his pen, the Articles of Confederation finally came into effect at noon on March 1, 1781.[98]

As recorded in the Journals of the Continental Congress: "According to the order of the day, the honble John Hanson and Daniel Carroll, two of the delegates for the State of Maryland, in pursuance of the act of the legislature of that State...did...sign and ratify the said articles, by which act the Confederation of the United States of America was completed..." The process had begun on June 8, 1776, when Richard Henry Lee first introduced the Virginia Resolution for Independence, Confederation and Foreign Alliances. Now, five years later, all three components of that Resolution had been accomplished. Among those who signed the Articles were six of the Presidents of Congress: Hancock, Laurens, Huntington, McKean, Hanson and Lee.[99]

Thomas Rodney, a delegate from Delaware, described that historic day's celebration in his Diary: "...The Completion of this grand Union & Confederaton was anounced by Fireing thirteen Cannon on the Hill And the same number on board Captn. Paul Jones Frigate in the Harbour. At Two OClock the members of Congress, The members of the General Assembly of Pensylvania, the President and Council of that State, the officers of the Army in Town, the officers of State and a great number of Gentlemen waited on the President of Congress [Samuel Huntington] To Congratulate him on this occasion...In the evening there was a grand exhibition of fireworks at the State House, & also on board Paul Jones Frigate in the Harbour--And all the Vessels in the Harbour were Decorated and Illuminated..."[100]

The Pennsylvania Packet recorded that: "Thursday, the first of March, will be a day memorable in the annals of America to the latest posterity..."[101] Even though the decisive victory at Yorktown was still eight months into the future, the United States of America was at long last able to celebrate formal confederation. And, thanks to the tenacity of John Hanson and the State of Maryland, that new nation would be able to expand into a dynamic matrix of states "from Sea to Sea."

In the midst of this celebration, little thought was given to those Native Americans who repeatedly protested the wholesale thievery of their ancestral lands. Most white men dismissed Indian claims just as easily as one western frontiersman who wrote at the time: "I am so far from thinking the Indians have a right to the soil that, not having made a better use of it for many hundred years, I conceive they have forfeited all pretense to claim and ought to be driven from it." And, in response to what was repeatedly termed "Indian atrocities" by those colonists who often dispensed the same "frontier justice," the writer went on to say that "They [Native Americans] have the shapes of men and may be of the human species, but certainly in their present state they approach nearer the character of devils."[102] Thus were the rights and property of the indigenous people of America sacrificed by those revolutionaries who so self-righteously proclaimed their own "inalienable rights" to "life, liberty and the pursuit of happiness."

Furthermore, despite the hopefulness of the occasion, the ratification of the Articles of Confederation actually marked the beginning of the end for the Continental Congress. Until the process of confederation was completed, Congress had been fluid enough to adapt to circumstances provided it could retain support from the states. There simply were no hard and fast rules. Congress operated as a pragmatic parliament free to function as the demands of the day dictated. The Articles limited rather than enhanced congressional power and, in effect, put the national government in a box. Henceforth, Congress' relation to the States would be strictly structured and, worst of all, its ability to raise funds from the States diminished even further. While the Articles had first been drafted during the early days of the war when the parameters of the job were unknown, they came into effect only months before the glue that had held the new nation together (i.e., the war against a common powerful enemy) began to loose its adhesive power.

Psychologically and diplomatically, however, the ratification of the Articles was, at that moment, a shot in the arm for the government, its troops and its allies. Because of France's sizable investment in the new nation, it was especially relieved to see the process of confederation completed. Within weeks the French Minister to the United States, the Chevalier de La Luzerne, requested a conference with members of Congress "to discuss Franklin's proposal for establishing a line of credit in France in return for the delivery of provisions to French agents in America." On

March 24, a select committee was appointed for this purpose consisting of Sam Adams, Thomas Burke, John Hanson, Joseph Jones, Thomas McKean and James Madison. The committee subsequently "recommended that the United States 'take every measure in their power' to implement the scheme." Congress concurred.[103]

Even though John's days were completely engulfed in critical affairs of state, his heart remained with his family as they suffered through the frequent illnesses so common to 18th Century life. On April 10, 1781, John confessed his conflicted sense of duty to his son-in-law: "Janey and Tammys State of health and the distressed and perplexed Situation Mrs. Hanson is in left alone a prey to Melancholly and despair destroys my peace of mind and renders me truly Misserable. Should have left this place last week but since the ratification of the Confederation 9 States are required to make a Congress. 4 are unrepreseented And my withdrawing would leave a number insufficient to transact Business, which at this Critical Conjuncture would perhaps be thought unpardonable however I hope to get Away by Thursday next." John was able to return home later that month in time to be with his daughter when she died.[104] His sorrow was compounded when he also lost his son, Dr. Samuel Hanson, that same fateful year.[105]

Despite his profound grief, John returned to Congress by September 24, 1781, for what would become the most intense and important phase of his life. In early October he reported to Gov. Lee that the British had "Suffered greatly in their late Engagement with Count de Grasse" and he correctly predicted that "The Defeat of the British fleet is a most Glorious and fortunate Event, as it will Effectually prevent Any Succors being Sent to Cornwallis, whose fate from present Appearances I think is inevitable-- God grant the Business may be Speedily Effected."[106] One week later John wrote again to the governor to report that "The Enemy remain on Staten Island altogether inactive." Unaware of what fate held in store for him, John also mentioned that "My Stay here is uncertain, it depends upon the next Election of Delegates to Congress, and in these Cases you Know, no great reliance is to be put in popular assemblies..."[107]

On October 16, John wrote to his son-in-law that "I am very Sorry Mr Johnson is left out of the Delegation." And, in his typical understated style, John added that "I wish with all my heart he had been in my place. Conscious of his Superior Abilities to Serve the public in general and our Country in Particular."[108] John later expressed the same sentiments to Gov. Lee: "I am very desirous of haveing Mr Johnson in our assembly and if I am informed that there is a probability of his being Elected in Case of a vacancy, I shall immediately resigned my Seat."[109]

In mid-October, John's latest letter to Gov. Lee expressed alarm over recent reports that the British fleet had been reinforced and that it was attempting to relieve Cornwallis. "...As so much depends upon the Issue of their enterprize," John wrote, "I must Confess my fears are some what Excited--but hope for the best."[110] Just one week later, John expressed tremendous relief to his son-in-law that his hopes had indeed been realized. "The Capture of Cornwallis," John said, "...is a most Capital Stroke and will tend more towards obtaining peace and to the security of our Independance than the best managed negotiations."[111] On October 27, John added that "The advantages which must result from the Capture of that Army are more than Can be Conceived."[112] Even more inconceivable to John would have been the fact that in only nine days he would be thrust into the highest office in the land.

On Monday, November 5, 1781, "Congress proceeded to the election of a President; and the ballots being taken, the honble John Hanson was elected."[113] The humble patriot from Maryland, the man who helped to open a vast area of the west to the formation of new states, was elected as the eighth President of the Continental Congress for what was now set by the Articles of Confederation as a one-year term. At the age of 60, John was also the oldest man to be chosen Head of State throughout the First American Republic.

One of John's first official acts was to resign his seat in the Maryland State Legislature.[114] He then extended appreciation to his immediate presidential predecessor, Thomas McKean. "It is with inexpressible satisfaction," John wrote, "that I present you the thanks of the United States in Congress assembled, in testimony of their approbation of your conduct in the Chair..." In characteristic fashion John then added that "altho' I cannot equal the bright example that is recently set me, yet it shall be my unremitting study to imitate it as far as possible; and...I shall invariably pursue the sacred path of Virtue, which alone ought to preserve me free from censure."[115]

That same day John wrote to his old friend and former neighbor, George Washington, who was now basking in his glorious victory over Cornwallis. John pledged that "Any intelligence worth communicating, which first reaches me, shall be related with unreserved freedom, candor & punctuality--And permit me to hope for a similar treatment from your Excellency." John, who knew Washington on a personal basis better than any of his presidential predecessors, quickly added that "Already my knowledge of your Character leads me to anticipate infinite satisfaction." John further mentioned that "the present Aspect of our Public Affairs is particularly pleasing..." And, in his simple, direct style, he expressed the hope that "...we shall not relapse into our former state of imbecility and distress." In closing John stated that "The events of the present Campaign will, no doubt, fill the most brilliant pages in the history of America. May Heaven still continue to smile on our efforts!"[116] Washington responded by congratulating "your Execellency on your appointment to fill the most important seat in the United States."[117]

By November 13, however, John expressed serious misgivings over his new office to his wife and his son-in-law: "The load of Business which I have very unwillingly And very imprudently taken on me I am afraid will be more than my Constitution will be able to bear, And the form and Ceremony necessary to be observed by a President of Congress is to me Extremely irksome, moreover I find my health declining and the Situation of my family requires my being at home." Under these circumstances, John said that "I Shall therefore take the first opportunity of applying for leave of Absence." Fortunately, John's friends in Congress were able to convince him that it would be extremely difficult for them to select a replacement so quickly since only seven states were currently represented.[118] Out of duty, John decided to stay at his post, and three days later he wrote again to his wife, urging her to "immediately prepare to Come up, if your State of health will permit it." He assured her that "You will have very little trouble in Housekeeping, a Steward, a House Keeper, And necessary Servants Are found as are also a Coach and Horses."[119]

On November 27, Gen. Washington arrived in Philadelphia. According to one biographer: "...it is kown that the General both dined and lodged at the President's House that night."[120] The following afternoon the Commander-in-Chief made a triumphal appearance in Congress. John, in his official capacity as President, welcomed his old friend: "Sir: Congress, at all times happy in seeing your Excellency, feel particular pleasure in your presence at this time, after the glorious success of the allied arms in Virginia." Washington replied: "Mr. President: I feel very sensibly the favorable declaration of Congress expressed by your Excellency."[121] At the request of Congress, Washington stayed in the city for several weeks for consultations.

Over the course of John's presidency, because of his age and declining health, he was able to deflect some of the tedious tasks that most of his predecessors had performed. The fact that the new structure of government under the Articles distributed certain responsibilities to specific departments (e.g., Foreign Affairs and Finance) also helped to ease the level of correspondence required of the President. According to the Library of Congress, "the volume of presidential correspondence had crested at slightly over 50 letters per month during the presidency of Henry Laurens, remained relatively constant at about 40 letters per month during the terms of his successors John Jay and Samuel Huntington, and dropped off to about 30 letters per month with President Thomas McKean." It was even lower under John.[122] Finally, on January 28, 1782, a Congressional Resolution transferred primary responsibility for communicating congressional policy from the President to Secretary Charles Thomson "In order that the President may be relieved from the business with which he is unnecessarily incumbered."[123] Former President John Hancock, who viewed his extensive correspondence as one of the most important responsibilities of his office, would have been shocked.

Within weeks of his election in November 1781, John was forced to write to the Governors of Connecticut, Delaware, New Hampshire, New Jersey, New York and North Carolina "respecting the deficiency of a Representation from your State." He stated that "the most important powers vested in Congress by the Confederation lie dormant at this time by reason of the impunctuality of the Delegates" and that he hoped "that your Excellency's influence will be exerted to prevail upon your State to send forward and keep up a full Representation in future."[124]

On a happier note, John wrote to the Marquis de Lafayette on November 24, 1781, forwarding to him an Act of Congress which granted him permission to return to France and expressed its profound gratitude for "your distinguished and zealous attachment to the cause of America..." The Marquis was also requested to personally present a letter of appreciation to the French monarch, "the greatest and best of Kings" (a special designation so often repeated in earlier years on petitions to the British Sovereign)."[125]

Despite the favorable turn in recent events, John's enthusiasm was tempered by his growing concern that the new nation might foolishly lose its focus. The day after Washington arrived in Philadelphia, John warned Gov. Lee of the importance of the moment: "Let us not entertain the Sentiment that our late Extraordinary Successes have Superseded the necessity of any further Extraordinary Exertions, as has been too often the Case, but on the Contrary let us Strain every nerve to drive the Enemy from every part of our Country...until that is done, there Can be but little hopes of peace."[126] In a similar vein, John sent a circular letter to all the States on December 12, calling upon "the Legislature of each State, in the most pressing manner, to compleat the Quota of troops assigned to them." He also enclosed a copy of an Act of Congress "recommending" that each State "ascertain, as soon as practicable, their number of white Inhabitants."[127] It was America's first national census.

That December, John was directed by Congress to inform Washington that he should "proceed to the exchange of Officers that are on parole, for an equal number of our Officers who are Prisoners of War, Rank for Rank," with the exception of Cornwallis. By the end of the month, however, John received word that Gen. Clinton, the British Commander in America, "refused 'to proceed in the exchange of Officers except Lord Cornwallis is included.'"[128]

Even as President, John's precious time and fragile health were still being taxed by outside issues. At the start of the new year, as a personal favor to Gov. Lee, John was once again engaged in the purchase of yet another carriage, this time for a close friend of the governor. "I went immediately to a Coach maker," John reported, "...the man Shewed me one he had just finished I think the most Elegant thing I ever Saw of the Kind, Price £225." In return, John was forced yet again to "beg" for his salary: "I wrote you Some time ago mentioning the sums I had recd of Mr Mollehon on Account of the State, And requesting a further Supply as Soon as possible--which I hope will be Complyed With." In closing, John underscored the urgency of his request when he added that "I have not ten pounds by me."[129]

To his son-in-law, John expressed his true feelings concerning "the tardiness of our Executive, in Supplyg me with my allowance (Scanty as it is) as a Delegate in Congress..." He also urged Dr. Thomas to retrieve yet another runaway slave that had recently been captured and to "let him Know, that his pardon depends upon his future behavour--that if he behaves well, and endeavours to make Amends for his past Conduct, I will when I return home purchase his wife, if her master will Sell at a reasonable price." John's own wife had arrived in Philadelphia by January 1782, where she immediately fell ill for the first few weeks but, as John informed Dr. Thomas, "She begins to be better reconciled to the place and intends to begin...to return Visits."[130]

In his next two letters to Dr. Thomas, John sadly reported that his wife was still "not very well, nor do I expect She will be perfectly recovered, until the weather is such as to permit her to Exercise frequently." And, as usual, he lamented his "want of Cash." In reference to his runaway slave, John offered several more suggestions but revealed his growing frustration when he told his son-in-law to "do...as you please." John's letter of February 14 did express "great hopes, if we act with Vigor the next Campaign to improve the Advantages we have gained over the Enemy in the last, our Independence will in the Course of a few months be Acknowledged by both Spain & Holland." But, by February 23, John sadly concluded that there is no prospect of peace "takeing place dureing this year--nor Shall we have peace in my Opinion untill we Can drive the Enemy from N york & Charles Town."[131]

On March 20, 1782, John sent a circular letter to the States enclosing a congressional Proclamation of the previous day which "set apart the last Thursday in April next, as a day of fasting, humiliation and prayer."[132] Six days later, John warned Gov. Lee of Maryland that the British might still be determined to defeat the United States. "If the Enemy should take this Step," John predicted, "it is probable the mode of Carrying on the War is to be changed, they will prosecute it more by Sea And endeavour to distress us as much as possible by intercepting our trade."[133]

On April 10, John reported to Dr. Thomas that "I am a little unwell with a Cold." Unfortunately, his condition worsened over the next two weeks as his absence from Congress indicated. When he wrote again to his son-in-law on April 27, John stated that "I have lately had a most Severe fit of Sickness, but thank God am so far recovered as to be able to ride out..." But two days later John confessed that "I Am not yet perfectly recovered, am Generally feverish--began this morning to take the Bark, which with the help of Exercise I am hopes I shall in a few days be restored to my former health." Finally, on May 8, John reported that "We are now, I thank God, all pretty well."[134] John's recovery came just in time for him to host the French Minister at a formal ceremony and state dinner on May 13, 1782, which marked the victory of the Franco-Ameican alliance.[135]

On May 28, however, more mundane responsibilities resurfaced as John was forced yet again to plead with the States "to keep up a constant representation" and once more he had to plead with Connecticut, Delaware, New Hampshire, New Jersey, New York and North Carolina to send delegates immediately "inasmuch as business of the greatest consequence is often delayed or retarded for want of a sufficient representation."[136] Of even greater urgency was the desperate need for additional funding. John wrote on June 11 that "The Continental Treasury is very low indeed, nothing paid in by Any of the States." Yet another pressing concern was the fate of the French fleet in the West Indies. The fact that "They have lost six ships in the late engagement" John wrote, "is a fact I fear too well Confirmed, but I Console myself in the hope that the British have Suffered equal damage."[137] In late June, Gen. Washington added to this litany of woe when he expressed his distress "at the Languor and Inertion of the several States in sending on the Recruits to the Army, which have been requested."[138]

On the sixth anniversary of the vote for Independence (July 2, 1782), President John Hanson's official correspondence with Maryland Governor Thomas Sim Lee did not focus on the momentous nature of the occasion but, once again, centered on the real world and John's desperate financial plight!. John informed the Governor that "I have received but fifty pounds Since March. I have now due to me near £200...I assure you Sir--that I am distressed for want of money and hope your Excellency and the Honorable Council will furnish me with two hundred pounds as soon as possible."[139] While the first four Presidents--Randolph, Middleton, Hancock and Laurens--were independently wealthy, their successors paid a tremendous financial price when they were required to take long absences from their professions and plantations.

Finally, on July 20, there was glorious news. John was able to inform all the Governors that "...it is beyound a doubt that the States General of the United Provinces [Holland] have received Mr. Adams in his public Character and acknowledged our Independence, on which important & very interesting event, I most sincerely congratulate you."[140] When John shared this report with his son-in-law three days later, he speculated that "The naval Force of the united Provinces added to those of France and Spain must give them a decided Superiority and dispose the British (Vain and Haughty as they are) to offer reasonable terms for a general peace..." In closing, John mentioned that Washington was in town. "Our Gen. is in high health and looks better than ever I see him." And then, with the affection of an old colleague and friend, John added: "God protect him."[141]

More good news reached Philadelphia early the next month. On August 5, Gen. Washington forwarded to Congress a conciliatory letter sent to him by the new British Commander, Gen. Guy Carleton, in which Gen. Carleton announced "that negociations for a general Peace have already commenced at Paris."[142] In response, John wrote to his son-in-law: "We are amused here with peace...The British may be Sincere in what is given out but I Confess I Cant help Suspecting that it is Calculated to deceive however if the Opinion Should generaly prevail Among the people that peace is near at hand, it will be an Excellent opportunity of recruiting the Army during the War so that what they may have intended as An Injury may turn out to our Advantage. We must have patience," John cautioned, "a little time will discover their real intentions."[143]

Four days later John again expressed his doubts to Dr. Thomas: "When the Enemy withdraw their forces from the Continent I Shall believe they are in Earnest about peace but not till then."[144] On August 21, 1782, despite British rumors, John confessed to his son-in-law that "We have had no intelligence from either of our Ministers abroad for upwards of four months which at a time so Critical is very distressing." He again added that " I hope for the best but I cant help Suspecting the designs of our Rascally Enemy, which may be to Effect by deceit, and Acts of Kindness, what they could not Accomplish by force."[145]

Whatever the case, John took obvious relief in the fact that his presidential term was nearing its end: "We Shall I hope be at home about the middle of November."[146] And by "home" John clearly meant retirement from public affairs. "As to my serving as a Delegate in our assembly next year I hope my friends will Excuse me. I think the public Can have no further Claim to my services. I have," John asserted, "performed my Tour of Duty and they must give me a discharge, retirement to people of my age must be most desireable and I hope I shall enjoy it in future without being Censured for withdrawing from the public Service."[147]

During his final weeks as President, however, John presided over two acts of Congress of special note. His Swedish ancestors would have taken enormous pride in the "PLAN OF A TREATY OF AMITY AND COMMERCE BETWEEN THE UNITED STATES AND THE KING OF SWEDEN" which was adopted by Congress on Saturday, September 28, 1782. Article One stated: "There shall be a firm, inviolable and universal peace and sincere friendship between the King of Sweden...and the United States of America..." It was witnessed by "His Excellency John Hanson, Esq. President of the United States in Congress assembled."[148]

And, on October 11, 1782, Congress commanded "the observation of Thursday, the 28 day of November next, as a day of solemn thanksgiving to God for all his mercies..." It was the continuation of a sacred American tradition (incorrectly attributed to Washington's Administration) which had been initiated a year earlier when his predecessor, President McKean, had issued the first Proclamation.[149]

On Monday, November 4, 1782, John's presidential term came to an end as a new congressional year began. Following the election of Elias Boudinot as the ninth President, it was resolved "That the thanks of Congress be given to the Hon. John Hanson, late President of Congress, in testimony of their approbation of his conduct in the chair, and in the execution of public business."[150] John then took his leave of Congress as he completed over three decades of continuous public service.

John returned home to Frederick, Maryland to begin what he knew would be the final phase of his life. A popular newspaper, The Pennsylvania Packet, almost "brought down the curtain" prematurely. On March 29, 1783, it incorrectly reported John's death. Two weeks later, President Boudinot wrote to John that "we having had your Death announced in the public news Papers, concluded with the Children, that what was printed must be true...Permit me Sir to rejoice with your other friends on the agreeable mistake, and to wish you long to enjoy the Blessings of that Peace you have so long struggled for." President Boudinot then shared with John the news America had eagerly waited to hear for so long: "Yesterday Sr. Guy Carleton sent by Express the King of Englands Proclamation for the Cessation of all Hostilties, and this morning we recd from France...the official Information of the same Circumstance on our part by a separate Instrument of accession." The President then added that we "shall proclaim a Cessation of all Hostilities on the part of America tomorrow."[151] The Revolutionary War was finally over. Against all the odds, the American patriots had triumphed over the greatest empire on Earth. John had lived just long enough to hear the news.

During his all-too-brief retirement, John journeyed across his beloved Maryland when his health permitted, delighting in visits with old friends and family. In the late fall, John's travels brought him to Oxon Hill Manor (just south of today's national capital).[152] His favorite nephew, Thomas Hawkins Hanson, and Thomas' wife, Rebecca (the widow of Thomas Addison), were managing that estate until her young son, Walter Dulany Addison, the true inheritor, came of age. It was at Oxon Hill, on Saturday, November 15, 1783, that John died.[153]

While it has been assumed for two centuries that John was also buried at Oxon Hill, a detailed report from the Oxon Hill Manor Project in 1986 stated: "Members of the John Hanson Society have explored the possibility that Hanson was buried at Oxon Hill, either in the Addison cemetery or in a mausoleum near the house...This has not been determined."[154] According to 18th Century custom, prominent individuals who died away from home during the winter were often buried on the spot but their bodies were returned home at a later date. That was precisely what had happened to Peyton Randolph, the first President, when he died unexpectedly in Philadelphia in late 1775.[155] One fact, however, argues against that tradition in this instance. John's wife, Jane Contee Hanson (who survived her husband by 29 years), was the great-granddaughter of Col. John Addison, the father of the founder of Oxon Hill. Since John's wife had even closer family ties to the actual owners of the estate, she might well have approved of Oxon Hill as John's final resting place, under the circumstances.[156] No credible evidence has ever been uncovered to the contrary.

Oxon Hill Manor was destroyed by fire in 1895, and the family plot was desecrated sometime after that. Today, the burial site is completely overgrown by weeds on a fenced-off hill overlooking the Potomac River in the middle of a large construction site. Nearby, a small stone monument to President John Hanson now stands along side the new Oxon Hill Manor which was built by Sumner Welles prior to has appointment as Under Secretary of State in the 1930s.[157] President Franklin Roosevelt, who had known Welles for many years, occasionally sought refuge there.[158]

John's only surviving son, Alexander Contee Hanson, was a delegate to Maryland's Ratification Convention for the new United States Constitution in April 1788; and, in October of the following year, he was appointed Chancellor of Maryland, a position he held until his death in 1806. His son and namesake, Alexander Contee Hanson II (John's grandson) was elected to Congress in 1812 and later served in the United States Senate from 1817 to 1819.[159]

Several members of John's extended family were also distinguished public servants. His sister Elizabeth's son, Daniel of St. Thomas Jenifer, signed the United States Constitution.[160] That same sister's grandson, Thomas Stone, was a signer of the Declaration of Independence; and, another of her grandsons, John Stone, was elected Governor of Maryland (1794-1797). Her third grandson, Michael Stone, was a member of the First Federal Congress (1789-1791). Two of President Hanson's younger relatives--Frederick Stone and Daniel Jenifer--were also elected to Congress later in the 19th Century. Few families can match that record of government service.[161]

Of all of John Hanson's significant achievements throughout his long and distinguished public life, the nurturing of new states will always remain his primary legacy. Six years after the territorial claims of Virginia were resolved and the Articles of Confederation were finally ratified by John's signature, Congress passed the Northwest Ordinance of 1787, which divided part of that newly acquired national territory into what eventually became the states of Ohio, Michigan, Indiana, Illinois and Wisconsin. In the opinion of noted historian Richard B. Morris: "Of all the legislation adopted by the Congress of the Confederation, the Great Ordinance proved to be that body's most seminal achievement."[162] Without John's dream and determination, those new states, and others that followed, might never have been possible. In the words of the former President of the National Geographic Society: "To the illustrious Marylanders, John Hanson particularly...belong the credit of suggesting and successfully urging the policy that has changed the whole map of the United States and the whole course of our national life."[163]

John Hanson did, indeed, lay the cornerstone for his new nation.

President John Hanson died on November 15, 1783 while visiting his favorite nephew Thomas Hawkins Hanson at Oxon Hill, Maryland. He was buried there in the Addison Family Cemetery which was later desecrated after Oxon Hill Manor was destroyed by fire in 1895.

Today, the burial site is overgrown by weeds on a fenced-off hill overlooking the Potomac River in the middle of a construction zone. The memorial stone (right) is located nearby at the new Oxon Hill Manor.

JOHN HANSON

Honored Patriot of the American Revolution

WHILE JOHN HANSON
WAS PRESIDENT

November 1781 - November 1782

President John Hanson presided over a significant transition in his new nation's government. Only days before he took office, news of Cornwallis' surrender at Yorktown gave Congress and the country their first real glimpse of victory after seven long years of war. At the same time, the first full year under the Articles of Confederation ushered in new procedures and customs, many of which continue to this day.

During John's presidency the Great Seal of the United States was adopted by Congress on June 20, 1782.[164] It was first used the following September when it was impressed on the commission to Gen. Washington pertaining to the exchange of prisoners.[165] The Great Seal reflected the newly ratified Confederation by employing the now familiar motto: "E Pluribus Unum."

Additional developments pertained to the nation's economy. Robert Morris, who had been appointed Superintendent of Finance prior to John's election, proposed the establishment of a national bank as a means of stabilizing the country's currency. Thanks to his persistence, Congress adopted "The ordinance for incorporating the subscribers to the Bank of North America" on New Year's Eve 1781. It officially opened early the next month.[166] At the same time, Morris proposed "the establishment of a decimal system and the use of the Spanish dollar... as the basis for his monetary system."[167] They remain the standard today.

In mid-October, Congress also extensively revamped the postal system when it approved "An Ordinance for Regulating the Post Office of the United States of America." As part of that revision it established what is now known as the "Franking Privilege" whereby "...letters...to and from the members and secretary of Congress...shall be free of postage."[168]

John's term in office also witnessed a debate over the admission of two new states. In Kentucky, nearly 700 inhabitants had "signed a memorial to Congress asking it to form them into a separate State."[169] Vermont went even further when it sent two "delegates" to Congress who unsuccessfully sought recognition.[170]

Across the Atlantic, momentous developments were rapidly unfolding. On Sunday, November 25, 1781, the first report of the British surrender at Yorktown was delivered to Lord Germain (the Secretary of State for the American Department) at his home in London.[171] Based on the memoirs of a close confidant, Lord Germain, after consulting with three of his colleagues, "determined to lay it themselves, in person before lord North. He [North] had not received any intimation of the event when they arrived at his door, in Downing Street, between 1 and 2 o'clock." On hearing the news, Lord North "opened his arms, exclaiming wildly...'Oh God! it is all over!"[172]

According to British historian Piers Mackesy, the King's response was to reject any talk of defeat since he believed that "a separation from America would be the end of Britain as a Great Power..." When Parliament opened just two days later, "The leaders of the Opposition were quite unprepared to exploit the disaster" "Nevertheless," in Mackesy's judgment, "the opening success of the Ministry in the new session concealed only momentarily the gravity of the political crisis."[173]

By early spring, that crisis had forced North's Government from power. As Mackesy described the scene: "Never had there been such a massacre. The new rulers were numerous and vengeful..." On March 27, 1782, the Marquis of Rockingham was chosen to head a new Cabinet which was "dedicated to the liquidation of the American War and the making of peace" despite the King's displeasure. British envoys were immediately sent to Paris to begin negotiations with America and her allies. On July 1, however, the government shifted yet again when Rockingham suddenly died and Lord Shelburne, who enjoyed the King's confidence, took control."[174]

Not surprisingly, a new military commander was also sent to America to replace Sir Henry Clinton who was only too eager to resign.[175] Sir Guy Carleton arrived in New York in May 1782, as the last Commander-in-Chief of the 31,000 British forces still stationed in North America.[176]

Thus, during John Hanson's presidency, Congress faced three very different British Governments in the space of just one year. The King himself remained the only constant as his American policy collapsed around him.

Chapter 8

President
JOHN HANSON
of
MARYLAND

Notes

Abbreviation Key

JCC   Journals of the Continental Congress
LDC   Letters of Delegates to Congress
PHL   The Papers of Henry Laurens

[1] Proceedings in the Senate and House of Representatives upon the Reception and Acceptance from the State of Maryland of the Statues of Charles Carroll of Carrollton and of John Hanson, January 31, 1903, pp. 5-6. Charles Carroll of Carrollton was one of the few Catholics accepted as an equal by the Founding Fathers who were, on the whole, rabidly anti-Catholic (they viewed the Pope, who was then a temporal as well as a spiritual leader, as a foreign power). The fact that Carroll was probably the richest man in America seemed to make it easier for his peers to overlook his religious affiliation. In 1832, at the age of 95, he was the last of the Signers of the Declaration of Independence to die. By then he was also a founder of the B&O Railroad and still one of the wealthiest man in the new nation he helped to create.

[2] Ibid, p. 80.

[3] Ibid, p. 30.

[4] Ibid, pp. 106 & 110.

[5] Ibid, p. 14.

[6] Ibid, p. 15.

[7] Seymour Wemyss Smith, John Hanson, Our First President, (Brewer, Warren & Putnam, New York, 1932), p. 14. See also: J. Bruce Kremer, John Hanson of Mulberry Grove, (Albert & Charles Boni, Inc., New York, 1938), p. 84. Biographical Directory of the American Congress 1774-1961, (Government Printing Office, Washington, DC, 1961), p. 1004.

[8] Paul H. Smith, Editor, LDC: 1774-1789, (Library of Congress, Washington, DC, 1991), Vol. 18, p. xxv. Both the History of Charles County Maryland by Margaret Brown Klapthor and Paul Dennis Brown, (Charles County Tercentenary, Inc., LaPlata, MD, 1958), and Charles County Gentry by Harry Wright Newman, (Clearfield, Baltimore,

1997), support the later date as did Nancy G. Boles, former Curator of Manuscripts of the Maryland Historical Society, *Maryland Historical Magazine*, Vol. 65, p. 304. Most persuasive is the 1783 obituary published in the *Maryland Journal* and cited by Newman. It states that John Hanson died "in the 63 year of his age" which firmly places the year of his birth at 1721.

[9] Herbert J. Stoeckel, The Strange Story of John Hanson, First President of the United States, (Hanson House, Hartford, CT, 1956), p. 19. Stoeckel states that the Addison burying ground at Oxen Hill, Maryland is "the site of President Hanson's grave." However, the 1986 Oxon Hill Manor Archaeological Site Mitigation Project (Patrick H. Garrow and Thomas R. Wheaton, Jr., Editors) does not confirm the location of John Hanson's grave since the Project did not examine the family graves at the old Addison Cemetery.

[10] Richard B. Morris, The Forging of the Union, 1781-1789, (Harper & Row, Publishers, New York, 1987), pp. 107-108.

[11] Kremer, op. cit., pp..23-26 & 51. The colony of New Sweden was established in March 1638 at Fort Christina, what is today the city of Wilmington, Delaware. After only eighteen years New Sweden fell to the Dutch under the command of Peter Stuyvesant and became part of New Amsterdam. Eight years later the British took over the territory and it eventually became the three Lower Counties of William Penn's Proprietorship, the present-day Delaware.

[12] Jacob A. Nelson, John Hanson and the Inseparable Union, (Meador Publishing Company, Boston, 1939), pp. 25-26. See also: William L. Langer, An Encyclopedia of World History, Houghton-Mifflin Company, Boston, 1968), 5th Edition, pp. 434-435; and, Klapthor, op. cit., pp. 9 & 47.

[13] Newman, op. cit., pp. 219-223; and, Kremer, op. cit., Family Chart following p. 40.

[14] Edmund Cody Burnett, The Continental Congress, (The Macmillan Company, New York, 1941), p. 524.

[15] Morris, op. cit., pp. 107-108.

[16] Irving Brant, *The Great Hanson Hoax*, Letters to the Editor, *The New York Times*, February 17, 1959, p. A12.

[17] *Washington is Accepted as First President; Hanson and McKean Officially Ruled Out*, Special to the *New York Times*, May 10, 1932, p. 1.

[18] Newman, op. cit., p. 226 & pp. 231-233.

[19] Smith, op. cit., p. 14. See also: Newman, op. cit., p. 232.

[20] See Chapter 5.

[21] Kremer, op. cit., p; 176; see also: Chapter 4, pp. 137-138 & 140.

[22] Nelson, op. cit., pp. 43-44.

[23] J. Thomas Scharf, *Essay on John Hanson, 1892*, Miscellaneous Manuscripts Collection, Library of Congress, mm79002184, p. 18.

[24] Ralph B. Levering, John Hanson Public Servant, *Maryland Historical Magazine*, Vol. 71, No. 2, p. 115.

[25] Nelson, op. cit., p. 60.

[26] Nelson, op. cit., p. 62. For additional background on both the Stamp Act and the Townshend Acts, see Introduction.

[27] Scharf, op. cit., p. 18.

[28] Nelson, op. cit., p. 65.

[29] John C. Fitzpatrick, Editor, The Diaries of George Washington, 1748-1799, (Houghton Mifflin Company, Boston, 1925), Vol. II, p. 61.

[30] Levering, op. cit., pp. 114-115.

[31] Kremer, op. cit., pp. 89-92; and, Scharf, op. cit., p. 18.

[32] For background on the Boston Tea Party and the Intolerable Acts, see Introduction.

[33] As cited in Levering, op. cit., p. 119.

[34] Kremer, op. cit., pp. 97-99.

[35] Levering, op. cit., p. 120.

[36] Ibid.

[37] Levering, op. cit., p. 121.

[38] Kremer, op. cit., pp. 102-103.

[39] Nelson, op. cit., pp. 79-80 & 83.

[40] Kremer, op. cit., p. 104.

[41] LDC, op. cit., Vol. 2, pp. 423-424; John Hancock to George Washington, December 2, 1775. See also: Worthington Chauncey Ford, Chief, Division of Manuscripts, JCC, (Government Printing Office, Washington, DC, 1905), Vol. III, p. 394.

[42] LDC, op. cit., Vol. 2, pp. 454-455; John Hancock to the Frederick County Committee of Inspection, December 8, 1775. See also: JCC, op. cit., Vol. III, p. 415.

[43] Levering, op. cit., p. 124.

[44] Kremer, op. cit., p. 107.

[45] James Grant Wilson and John Fiske, Editors, Appletons' Cyclopaedia of American Biography, (D. Appleton and Company, New York, 1888), Vol. III, p. 75.

[46] Scharf, op. cit., pp. 8-9.

[47] As cited in Nelson, op. cit., p. 82.

[48] Henry Steele Commager, Editor, <u>Documents of American History</u>, (Appleton-Century-Crofts, New York, 1958), 7th Edition, p. 11.

[49] Smith, op. cit., p. 43.

[50] James Thomas Flexner, <u>George Washington, The Forge of Experience (1732-1775)</u>, (Little, Brown and Company, Boston, 1965), p. 47.

[51] Walter Isaacson, <u>Benjamin Franklin, An American Life</u>, (Simon & Schuster, New York, 2003), p. 270.

[52] <u>JCC</u>, op. cit., Vol. IX, p. 806.

[53] Ibid., pp. 807-808.

[54] <u>LDC</u>, op. cit., Vol. 12, p. 51; Connecticut Delegates to Jonathan Trumbull, Sr., February 11, 1779.

[55] Gilbert Grosvenor, President of the National Geographic Society, A Maryland Pilgrimage, *National Geographic Magazine*, Vol. LI, No. 2, February 1927, p. 171.

[56] <u>LDC</u>, op. cit., Vol. 12, p. 51; Connecticut Delegates to Jonathan Trumbull, Sr., February 11, 1779.

[57] <u>LDC</u>, op. cit., Vol. 11, p. 491.

[58] As cited in John C. Miller, <u>Triumph of Freedom, 1775-1783</u>, (Little, Brown and Company, Boston, 1948), p. 652.

[59] Miller, op. cit., p. 652.

[60] Smith, op. cit., p. 46.

[61] Miller, op. cit., p.655.

[62] Jack P. Greene and J. R. Pole, Editors, <u>The Blackwell Encyclopedia of the American Revolution</u>, (Blackwell, Cambridge, 1991), pp. 349-351.

[63] See Chapter 2 for additional details pertaining to the surrender of Charleston.

[64] <u>LDC</u>, op. cit., Vol. 15, p. 397; John Hanson to Thomas Sim Lee, July 1, 1780.

[65] <u>LDC</u>, op. cit., Vol. 15, p. 430; William Churchill Houston to John Adams, July 11, 1780.

[66] <u>LDC</u>, op. cit., Vol. 15, pp. 502-503; John Hanson to Charles Carroll of Carrollton, July 25, 1780.

[67] LDC, op. cit., Vol. 15, p. 555; John Hanson to Charles Carroll of Carrollton, August 7, 1780.

[68] LDC, op. cit., Vol. 15, pp. 502-503; John Hanson to Charles Carroll of Carrollton, July 25, 1780.

[69] LDC, op. cit., Vol. 15, p. 557; John Hanson to Thomas Sim Lee, August 7, 1780.

[70] LDC, op. cit., Vol. 15, p. 511; John Hanson to Philip Thomas, July 26, 1780.

[71] LDC, op. cit., Vol. 15, p. 581; John Hanson to Charles Carroll of Carrollton, August 15, 1780.

[72] LDC, op. cit., Vol. 15, pp. 437, 503, 628,

[73] LDC, op. cit., Vol. 16, p. 206; John Hanson to Thomas Sim Lee, October 16, 1780.

[74] LDC, op. cit., Vol. 16, p 395; John Hanson to Thomas Sim Lee, November 28, 1780.

[75] LDC, op. cit., Vol. 16, p. 755; John Hanson to Philip Thomas, February 28, 1781.

[76] LDC, op. cit., Vol. 19, p. 216; John Hanson to Thomas Sim Lee, October 1, 1782.

[77] LDC, op. cit., Vol. 15, p. 511; Vol. 16, p. 91,

[78] LDC, op. cit., Vol. 16, p. 183; John Hanson to Philip Thomas, October 10, 1780.

[79] LDC, op. cit., Vol. 15, p. 582; John Hanson to Thomas Sim Lee, August 15, 1780.

[80] LDC, op. cit., Vol. 15, p. 628; John Hanson to Thomas Sim Lee, August 28, 1780.

[81] LDC, op. cit., Vol. 16, p. 331; George Plater to Thomas Sim Lee, November 13, 1780.

[82] LDC, op. cit., Vol. 17, p. 53; Daniel Carroll to Thomas Sim Lee, March 12, 1781; and, p. 58; Maryland Delegates to Thomas Sim Lee, March 13, 1781; footnote #1.

[83] LDC, op. cit., Vol. 17, p. 417; Richard Potts to Thomas Sim Lee, July 17, 1781.

[84] LDC, op. cit., Vol. 15, p. 631; John Hanson to Charles Carroll of Carrollton, August 29, 1780.

[85] LDC, op. cit., Vol. 16, p. 78; John Hanson to Thomas Sim Lee, September 18, 1780; and, pp.49-50; John Hanson to Charles Carroll of Carrollton, September 11, 1780.

[86] LDC, op. cit., Vol. 16, p. 91; John Hanson to Philip Thomas, September 19, 1780.

[87] LDC, op. cit., Vol. 16, pp.49-50; John Hanson to Charles Carroll of Carrollton, September 11, 1780.

[88] LDC, op. cit., Vol. 16, pp.91-92; John Hanson to Philip Thomas, September 19, 1780.

[89] LDC, op. cit., Vol. 16, pp. 102-103; Maryland Delegates to the Maryland Council, September 22, 1780. Maryland's Council did respond to Congress' urgent appeal for 500 head of cattle but when they were delivered to the Continental receiving depot in

Maryland, the Continental agents "refused to receive and forward the Cattle to the Army alleging it to be no part of the Business of their respective Departments." LDC, op. cit., Vol. 16, p. 419; Maryland Delegates to the Maryland Council, December 6, 1780; footnote number 2.

[90] Alexander Hamilton's response to the flight of Gen. Gates underscores its importance: "Was there ever such an instance of a general running away...from his whole army? And was there ever so precipitous a flight?" Craig L. Symonds, A Battlefield Atlas of the American Revolution, (The Nautical & Aviation Publishing Company of America, Inc., 1986), p. 87. For additional information on the Conway Cabal, see Chapter 4, pp. 130-131.

[91] LDC, op. cit., Vol. 16, p. 124; John Hanson to Philip Thomas, October 2, 1780.

[92] LDC, op. cit., Vol. 16, pp. 430-431; John Hanson to Charles Carroll of Carrollton, December 11, 1780.

[93] LDC, op. cit., Vol. 16, pp. 432-433; John Hanson to Thomas Sim Lee, December 11, 1780.

[94] JCC, op. cit., Vol. XVIII, pp. 915-916.

[95] *Virginia's Cession of Western Lands*, The Annals of America, (Encyclopaedia Britannica, Inc., Chicago, 1976), Vol. 2, p. 580. Virginia's "land cession [January 2, 1781] was burdened with too many conditions for Congress to accept it...Virginia's offer of December 20, 1783, was approved, and the deed for the land was signed on March 1, 1784." See also Greene, op. cit., pp. 349-351.

[96] Burnett, op. cit., pp. 499-500.

[97] LDC, op. cit., Vol. 16, pp. 721-722; Daniel Carroll to Thomas Sim Lee, February 20, 1781.

[98] JCC, op. cit., Vol. XIX, pp. 213-223.

[99] JCC, op. cit., Vol. XIX, pp. 213-214 and 222-223.

[100] LDC, op. cit., Vol. 17, p.3; Thomas Rodney's Diary, March 1, 1783.

[101] As cited in Burnett, op. cit., pp. 500-501.

[102] Hugh H. Brackenridge, *A Negative View of Indian Rights*, The Annals of America, (Encyclopaedia Britannica, Inc., Chicago, 1976), Vol. 2, pp. 580-583.

[103] LDC, op. cit., Vol. 17, p. 104-105; Committee of Congress to the Chevalier de La Luzerne, March 29, 1781.

[104] LDC, op. cit., Vol. 17, pp. 140-141; John Hanson to Philip Thomas, April 10, 1781; and, p. 164; Daniel Carroll to Thomas Sim Lee, April 17, 1781.

[105] See Chapter 8.

[106] LDC, op. cit., Vol. 18, p. 98; John Hanson to Thomas Sim Lee, October 2, 1781.

[107] LDC, op. cit., Vol. 18, p. 117; John Hanson to Thomas Sim Lee, October 9, 1781.

[108] LDC, op. cit., Vol. 18, p. 141; John Hanson to Philip Thomas, October 16, 1781.

[109] LDC, op. cit., Vol. 18, p. 167; John Hanson to Thomas Sim Lee, October 30, 1781.

[110] LDC, op. cit., Vol. 18, p. 140; John Hanson to Thomas Sim Lee, October 16, 1781.

[111] LDC, op. cit., Vol. 18, p. 160; John Hanson to Philip Thomas, October 23, 1781.

[112] LDC, op. cit., Vol. 18, p. 166; John Hanson to Philip Thomas, October 27, 1781.

[113] JCC, op. cit., Vol. XXI, p. 1100.

[114] LDC, op. cit., Vol. 18, p. 181; John Hanson to Philip Thomas, November 6, 1781.

[115] LDC, op. cit., Vol. 18, p. 189; John Hanson to Thomas McKean, November 10, 1781.

[116] LDC, op. cit., Vol. 18, pp. 190-191; John Hanson to George Washington, November 10, 1781.

[117] George Washington to John Hanson, November 30, 1781, as cited in Kremer, op. cit., p. 157.

[118] LDC, op. cit., Vol. 18, p. 191; John Hanson to Philip Thomas, November 13, 1781.

[119] LDC, op. cit., Vol. 18, pp. 200-201; John Hanson to Jane Hanson, November 16, 1781.

[120] Nelson, op. cit., p. 119.

[121] JCC, op. cit., Vol. XXI, pp. 1143-1144.

[122] LDC, op. cit., Vol. 18, p. 190; John Hanson to Thomas McKean, November 10, 1781, Footnote.

[123] JCC, op. cit., Vol. XXII, p. 55-57.

[124] LDC, op. cit., Vol. 18, p. 200; John Hanson to Certain States, November 15, 1781.

[125] JCC, op. cit., Vol. XXI, p. 1134; and, LDC, op. cit., Vol. 18, p. 212; John Hanson to the Marquis de Lafayette, November 24, 1781.

[126] LDC, op. cit., Vol. 18, p. 214; John Hanson to Thomas Sim Lee, November 27, 1781.

[127] LDC, op. cit., Vol. 18, p. 244; John Hanson to the States, December 12, 1781.

[128] LDC, op. cit., Vol. 18, p. 233; John Hanson to George Washington, December 5, 1781.

[129] LDC, op. cit., Vol. 18, p. 279; John Hanson to Thomas Sim Lee, January 9, 1782.

[130] LDC, op. cit., Vol. 18, p. 283; John Hanson to Philip Thomas, January 14, 1782; and, pp. 313-314; John Hanson to Philip Thomas, January 29, 1782.

[131] LDC, op. cit., Vol. 18, pp. 336-338; John Hanson to Philip Thomas, February 14, 1782; and, pp. 354-355; John Hanson to Philip Thomas, February 23, 1782.

[132] LDC, op. cit., Vol. 18, p. 415; John Hanson to the States, March 20, 1782; and, JCC, op. cit., Vol. XXII, pp. 137-138.

[133] LDC, op. cit., Vol. 18, p. 420; John Hanson to Thomas Sim Lee, March 26, 1782.

[134] LDC, op. cit., Vol. 18, p. 450; John Hanson to Philip Thomas, April 10, 1782; p. 473; John Hanson to Philip Thomas, April 27, 1782; p. 478; John Hanson to Philip Thomas, April 30, 1782; and, p. 501; John Hanson to Philip Thomas, May 8, 1782.

[135] Levering, op. cit., p.129.

[136] LDC, op. cit., Vol. 18, pp. 533-534; John Hanson to the States, May 28, 1782; and, JCC, op. cit., Vol. XXII, p. 301.

[137] LDC, op. cit., Vol. 18, p. 575; John Hanson to John Hall, June 11, 1782.

[138] LDC, op. cit., Vol. 18, p. 610; John Hanson to George Washington, June 27, 1782, footnote.

[139] LDC, op. cit., Vol. 18, pp. 617-618; John Hanson to Thomas Sim Lee, July 2, 1782.

[140] LDC, op. cit., Vol. 18, p. 652; John Hanson to the States, July 20, 1782.

[141] LDC, op. cit., Vol. 18, p. 660; John Hanson to Philip Thomas, July 23, 1782.

[142] LDC, op. cit., Vol. 19, p. 58; John Hanson to George Washington, August 13, 1782.

[143] LDC, op. cit., Vol. 19, p. 52; John Hanson to Philip Thomas, August 10, 1782.

[144] LDC, op. cit., Vol. 19, p. 64; John Hanson to Philip Thomas, August 14, 1782.

[145] LDC, op. cit., Vol. 19, p. 88; John Hanson to Philip Thomas, August 21, 1782.

[146] Ibid.

[147] LDC, op. cit., Vol. 19, p. 126; John Hanson to Philip Thomas, September 4, 1782.

[148] JCC, op. cit., Vol. XXIII, pp. 610-622.

[149] JCC, op. cit., Vol. XXI, pp. 1074-1076.

[150] JCC, op. cit., Vol. XXIII, p. 710.

[151] LDC, op. cit., Vol. 20, p. 160; Elias Boudinot to John Hanson, April 10, 1783.

[152] From 1927-1953, a New Oxon Hill Manor was constructed on the property by Sumner Welles, President Franklin Roosevelt's Under Secretary of State. During his first term,

"Roosevelt had spent a summer Sunday at Oxon Hill" as Welles' guest. Irwin F. Gellman, Secret Affairs, (The Johns Hopkins University Press, Baltimore, 1995), p. 158.

153 Patrick H. Garrow and Thomas R. Wheaton, Jr., Editors, *Oxon Hill Manor Archaeological Site Mitigation Project*, (Maryland Department of Transportation, State Highway Administration, 1986), Contract No. P.878 255 512, pp. 653 and 79. Even though this report lists the date of John Hanson's death as November 15, 1783, numerous sources such as the Dictionary of American Biography, (Charles Scribner's Sons, New York, 1943), Vol. VIII, p. 231, set the date at November 22. Nelson's biography of John Hanson, op. cit., helps to resolve the dispute. It includes a reproduction of the *Maryland Gazette* of November 21, 1783, which states: 'On Saturday last departed...in the sixty-third year of his age, the honourable JOHN HANSON, Esq.'" "Saturday last," would have been November 15, not November 22.

154 Ibid., p. 79.

155 See Chapter 1.

156 Garrow, op. cit., p. 79.

157 George Price, Maryland Historian, telephone interview, December 1994.

158 Oxon Hill Manor brochure printed by the Maryland-National Capital Park & Planning Commission, 2007. See also: Irwin F. Gellman, Secret Affairs (The Johns Hopkins University Press, Baltimore, 1995), pp. 69, 306 & 397. In many respects, Oxon Hill Manor (which is only a few miles south of the White House) might well have reminded Roosevelt of his own estate at Hyde Park, New York. Secretary Welles, who was ultimately forced out of office because of his secret gay affairs despite three marriages, had known FDR most of his life. Roosevelt once described Welles as "one of my very old friends." Welles' boss, Secretary of State Cordell Hull, deeply resented the fact that his chief deputy and the President were close social friends. In 1994, after Oxon Hill Manor had been taken over by the State of Maryland, the Democratic National Committee rented the facility to host President Bill Clinton's birthday celebration.

159 Dictionary of American Biography, op. cit., Vol. VIII, pp. 230-232.

160 Dictionary of American Biography, op. cit., Vol. X, pp. 42-43.

161 Kremer, op. cit., Family Tree following p. 40.

162 Morris, op. cit., p.229.

163 Grosvenor, op. cit., p. 171.

WHILE JOHN HANSON WAS PRESIDENT

Notes

Abbreviation Key

JCC   Journals of the Continental Congress
LDC   Letters of Delegates to Congress
PHL   The Papers of Henry Laurens

164 Gaillard Hunt, Chief, Division of Manuscripts, JCC, (Government Printing Office, Washington, DC, 1914), Vol. XXII, pp. 338-340.

165 JCC, op. cit., Vol. XXIII, p.581; see also, Jacob A. Nelson, John Hanson and the Inseparable Union, (Meador Publishing Company, Boston, 1939), p. 130.

166 JCC, op. cit., Vol. XXI, p. 1186; and, Edmund Cody Burnett, The Continental Congress, (The Macmillan Company, 1941), pp. 515-516.

167 Seymour Wemyss Smith, John Hanson, Our First President, (Brewer, Warren & Putnam, New York, 1932), pp. 94-95. The Report from the Superintendent of Finance was issued on January 15, 1782.

168 JCC, op. cit., Vol. XXIII, pp. 670 & 678.

169 Allan Nevins, The American States During and After the Revolution, 1775-1789, (The Macmillan Company, New York, 1927), p. 669.

170 Paul H. Smith, Editor, LDC, 1774-1789, (Library of Congress, Washington, DC, 1991), Vol. 18, p. 326. "Ira Allen and Jonas Fay had presented their credentials as Vermont 'delegates' to Congress in a January 30 [1782] letter to President John Hanson, which had been read in Congress on February 1."

171 Lord Germain, who shared the King's distaste for failure, was elderly and experienced but disliked by most of his Cabinet colleagues. "His unpopularity in some quarters was inflamed by the belief that he was a homosexual." Piers Mackesy, The War for American, 1775-1783, (Harvard University Press, Cambridge, 1965), p. 51.

172 Alden T. Vaughan, Chronicles of the American Revolution, (Grosset & Dunlap, New York, 1965), The British Government Reacts to the Defeat [Extracts from the Memoirs of N. W. Wraxall], pp.303-304.

173 Mackesy, op. cit., pp. 460-470.

[174] Ibid., pp. 471-473.

[175] Sir Henry Clinton, The American Rebellion, (Yale University Press, New Haven, 1954), p. 595; Lord George Germain to Sir Henry Clinton, February 6, 1782; see also, William Seymour, The Price of Folly, (Brassey's, London, 1995), p. 240.

[176] Benson Bobrick, Angel in the Whirlwind, (Simon & Schuster, New York, 1997), p. 472; see also, Seymour, op. cit., p. 236.

Chapter 9

President
ELIAS BOUDINOT
of
NEW JERSEY

Battles & Bibles

As the Revolutionary War inched toward victory after eight brutal and bloody years, the structure of the national government slowly evolved under the Articles of Confederation.

For the first time, Presidents served clearly defined one-year terms. On November 4, 1782, John Hanson of Maryland reached that milepost as he eagerly relinquished the responsibilities of his office to the new Head of State: Elias Boudinot of New Jersey. Unlike Laurens or McKean, both Hanson and Boudinot were quiet, understated men who led by example rather than intimidation. For Hanson, the Swedish-American founding father, the burden and the glory of the presidency came at the end of life. For Boudinot, the third President of French Huguenot descent, the office marked the midpoint of an extremely active and eclectic career.

Elias Boudinot was also one of only two of the fourteen presidents to serve in Congress under both the First and Second Republics.[1] His four years in the Continental Congress were matched by another six in the House of Representatives. In fact, when the revamped government was initially organized in the spring of 1789 in New York City, Elias, as a former President, secretly aspired to serve as the first Speaker of the House but he was far too modest to publicly seek the position. In the end, big state politics determined the selection when Pennsylvania, the most powerful of the middle states, was given that honor.[2] Nevertheless, despite his denial, Elias' disappointment in the election's outcome seeps through in the letter he wrote to his wife on April 2, 1789:

"The first thing we did was to choose a Speaker, which fell on Mr. Muhlenburgh [of Pennsylvania] without any dissension--I feel myself very happy that I am clear of it--I am sensible that the honor is great but then the confinement is what I never could have submitted to without having you in the city...I believe I should not have refused it had it been offered...but I am much better pleased without it, and consider it as a kind Providence towards us--This is between ourselves, for such is the rage for office, that no one will believe the Sentiment, as they suppose it impossible to be so dead to the honors of this World--I bless God I feel not the least desire after them..."[3]

True to his word, Elias' long life of public service was devoted to substance rather than showmanship unlike many of his contemporaries. Through it all, however, he never lost sight of his family's financial security. He excelled at both. As George Adams Boyd, his biographer, states: "Elias...had inherited the two outstanding characteristics of the Huguenot bourgeoisie--piety and an acquisitive instinct."[4]

Those Huguenot roots can be traced back to his great-great grandfather who lived only eleven miles from La Rochelle in western France, the ancestral home of Presidents Henry Laurens and John Jay. All three Protestant families eventually fled to London in the face of Catholic persecution. From there, Elias Boudinot (the President's great-grandfather) and his family emigrated to New York in 1687. His 25 year old son, Elias II, was married there in 1699, and his grandson, Elias III (the President's father), was born in New York in 1706.[5] Only fourteen years later the young boy was orphaned and thereby forced to seek a seven-year apprenticeship with a local silversmith in order to survive.

By the time Elias III completed his indenture, he had grown into a 21 year old man who eagerly accepted the invitation of his late uncle's widow and headed to the island of Antigua in the Caribbean. Elias III lived there for nearly a decade, surviving his first wife, Susannah Le Roo, and later marrying Catharine Williams. When the young couple returned to the mainland in 1736, they eventually settled in Philadelphia, next door to the print shop and residence of one of the city's best known citizens, Benjamin Franklin.[6] It was there, above his father's silversmith shop, that Elias IV, the future President, was born on April 21, 1740. He was the fourth of ten children, three of whom died in infancy.

In 1750, the Boudinot family moved to New Jersey where Elias III founded a company to explore newly discovered copper deposits near the town of New Brunswick. They initially lived in the village of Rocky Hill, but eventually moved to Princeton where they rented a home from the Rev. Aaron Burr, the second president of the College of New Jersey (now Princeton University) and the father of Thomas Jefferson's notorious Vice President.[7] Another of the most prominent families in Princeton, the Stocktons, became deeply entwined with the Boudinots in 1755 when Richard Stockton married Annis Boudinot, Elias III's oldest daughter. Two years later the Stockton estate (which Annis renamed "Morvan") passed to the newlyweds when Richard's father died.[8] By 1758, a second family romance had blossomed between Annis' brother, 18 year old Elias IV (the future President), and Richard's 22 year old sister, Hannah. They playfully referred to each other as "Narcissus" and "Eugenia" as they initiated a romantic intimacy that grew ever stronger throughout their long lives.[9]

Even though Elias IV had hoped to enter the ministry, family finances barred his admission to the college in Princeton, which stood directly across from the Boudinot's newest home. At this critical moment, Elias received help from his future brother-in-law, Richard Stockton, who invited Elias to work in his law office. Elias eagerly accepted the offer and, as would be true throughout his life, devoted his considerable talent and energy to the task at hand. On November 9, 1760--only two weeks after George III acceded to the throne--Elias was licensed to practice law. Shortly thereafter Elias IV relocated to Elizabeth Town, New Jersey to begin his legal career. He also began a lifelong process of investing in land whenever his finances permitted.[10] Over the years, those investments made Elias a very wealthy man.

Absence, however, made his heart grow even fonder for his "Eugenia." Despite her concerns over the difference in their ages and his awareness of the gap in their social status, Elias' persistence won her heart. He shared the news of their engagement with his parents on December 23, 1761.[11] The following February Elias informed Hannah that he had found their first home. Two months later, on Elias' twenty-second birthday, they were married at Morvan, the bride's home.[12]

Because of his father's poor health, the leadership of the Boudinot family now shifted to Elias IV, the young married attorney. His parents and youngest siblings even moved to Elizabeth Town where, several years later, Elias confided to a friend that "My Father has been for many Years afflicted with the dead Palsy and been entirely supported by my Industry...."[13] At the same time his first daughter, Susanne, was born on December 21, 1764. She remained forever the apple of her devoted father's eye.[14] Elias' mother died a year later on November 1, 1765, the day that the dreaded Stamp Act went into effect.[15] In response to the legislation, Elias wrote a letter from "A Jersey Lawyer" to the publisher of the New-York Mercury.[16] It was Elias' first known public opposition to British rule. Five years later, Elias' father passed away on July 4, 1770.

In April 1772, a second daughter, Anna Maria, was born, but she she lived only two and a half years. That October Elias managed to pool his resources--including part of Hannah's inheritance from her father's estate--in order to buy the mansion known as Boxwood Hall which had been the home of Elizabeth Town's late mayor. It still stands today. That same year Elias was elected to serve on the Board of Trustees of the College of New Jersey. Over the next half century, he helped to transform that small institution into one of America's premier universities.

Elias also served on the board of Elizabeth Town Academy which helped to prepare promising young students for college. In that capacity Elias became almost a surrogate father to one of the brightest young stars of the American Revolution.

In November 1772, after recently arriving in America from St. Croix in the Caribbean, 15 year old Alexander Hamilton was in search of the most expedient path to attaining a college education. Toward that goal, Hamilton traveled to Elizabeth Town with letters of introduction. There he met William Livingston, the master of Liberty Hall and one of the wealthiest men in America, and Elias Boudinot, Livingston's close friend, colleague and fellow trustee at both the college and the academy. As a leading Hamilton biographer states, the "most enduring tie formed by Hamilton [in Elizabeth Town] was with Elias Boudinot...As a regular visitor to Boudinot's mansion, Boxwood Hall, Hamilton was exposed to a refined world of books, political debate, and high culture."[17]

Another prominent Hamilton biographer describes Elias as a "portly philanthropist..." and a "deeply yet bearably spiritual man" who "could not help making money and friends." The author adds that "In long evenings at Boxwood Hall, a few minutes' walk over from the academy, Hamilton gave and received affection for the first time in many years."[18] Throughout the military and political battles ahead, Hamilton never forgot Elias' friendship and fatherly concern during his early years, and Elias never wavered in his affection for this brilliant and remarkable young man.

By the summer of 1774, news of the Intolerable Acts had spread across America as Massachusetts pleaded with its fellow colonies to boycott British goods and join in a continent-wide assembly.[19] The inhabitants of Essex County, New Jersey, met on Saturday afternoon, June 11 "to consult and deliberate, and firmly resolve upon the most prudent and salutary measures to secure and maintain the constitutional rights of his Majesty's subjects in America."[20] The meeting agreed that a Continental Congress should be called "to form a general plan of union," and it appointed a nine member Committee of Correspondence for Essex county, which included both William Livingston and Elias Boudinot.

Similar meetings were held in every county. Those local committees then came together at New Brunswick on July 21-23, 1774, where five delegates were elected to represent New Jersey at the upcoming Continental Congress. Elias was unable to attend the New Brunswick convention because he was on a special mission to Canada to encourage its residents to join with the 13 colonies in a show of solidarity.[21] Despite his absence, Elias was selected as one of twelve members of a new Committee of Correspondence which was established for the entire colony.

The pace of developments quickened as one colony after another selected delegates for the new Congress. But in the midst of these momentous events, Elias faced one of the greatest losses of his life. On September 3, 1774, only two days before the opening of the Continental Congress, Elias' precious two-and-a-half year old daughter, Anna Maria, died after a brief illness. By then, the bond between Elias and Hamilton had grown so intimate that "Hamilton kept a vigil by the sickly child and composed an affecting elegy after she died."[22]

By early 1775, Elias' leadership role in the revolution was well known to New Jersey's last Royal Governor, William Franklin, the illegitimate and estranged son of Benjamin Franklin. In a letter dated March 12, Gov. Franklin complained that both Boudinot and Livingston "had caballed among the members" [of the legislature] in seeking approval of the delegates to the Continental Congress.[23] Six weeks later, while serving as Chairman of the Committee of Safety, Elias was one of the first to receive the official report from Massachusetts describing the battles at Lexington and Concord.[24] Sensing the momentous importance of the times, Elias began a personal Journal that April (1775) which he kept for the next fourteen years. In it he recorded "A great many interesting anecdotes, that happened during the American Revolutionary War...likely to be lost to Posterity by the negligence of the parties concerned...I shall therefore...set down those I have had any acquaintance with..."[25]

Early the next month, Elias and his colleagues on the Committee of Correspondence met in New Brunswick to formulate a response to the alarming news from New England. The members condemned New Jersey's colonial government and called for a new assembly to meet in Trenton on May 23. At that first Provincial Congress, Elias and William Peartree Smith were sent to Philadelphia to seek guidance from the Continental Congress. They arrived just as John Hancock began his long tenure as President. Congress, however, had not yet formulated a specific plan for reforming colonial government. As a result, the New Jersey men returned to Trenton on May 30 empty-handed.

Out of necessity, New Jersey's Provincial Congress took matters into its own hands during the summer of 1775. Legislation was passed providing for the enlistment and funding of several militia units and elections were called for a Second Provincial Congress to meet that October. Elias, however, did not attend the October meeting. He was trying to refocus for a few months on putting his professional and financial house in order. Nevertheless, when Gen. Washington, the newly appointed Commander-in-Chief, issued a desperate plea for gun powder,[26] Elias immediately responded. He later described the circumstances in his Journal: "I was the chairman of the Committee of safety at Elizabeth Town, and had about Six or Seven Quarter Casks of Powder...which were sent to Boston..."[27] New Jersey was, in fact, the first colony to respond.

Earlier that summer Elias had also sent a letter of recommendation to Washington on behalf of young Aaron Burr, the only son of the college's late president. It is ironic that Elias nurtured the careers of both Hamilton and Burr, two of the most promising sons of the Revolution, whose lives would be tragically entwined over the next twenty-nine years until their fatal duel at Weehawken, New Jersey.

Despite the escalation of hostilities, Elias, like many, still clung to the hope that a peaceful solution could be found. As late as April 1776, he debated the college's new president, Dr. John Witherspoon, over the issue of independence. "...I rose, and in a speech of about half an hour or better, stated...That we had chosen a Continental Congress, to whom we had resigned the Consideration of our public affairs...In short, that they were the only proper Judges of the measures to be pursued..." When the resolution was finally put to a vote, 32 of the 36 attendees supported Elias' position. But, at the end of this Journal entry, Elias added that when the Continental Congress did proclaim Independence two months later, "...no part of the Union were more trusty than the State of New Jersey."[28]

That November, Elias moved his family from their exposed location in Elizabeth Town to a farm he had previously purchased in Baskinridge. The fear of a surprise British assault, however, was ever present as painfully demonstrated that December when Elias' wealthy brother-in-law and mentor, Richard Stockton, was captured and condemned to such harsh treatment in prison that he never recovered his health.[29]

By the spring of 1777, after two years of war, the plight of American prisoners and the logistics pertaining to captured British and Hessian soldiers had reached crisis proportions. Washington was desperate to find a "Commissary of Prisoners" who could lift this additional burden from his shoulders. (According to one source, there were approximately 5,000 Americans prisoners at the end of 1776, and America held nearly 3,000 of the enemy who were scattered along the East Coast and confined in various states.[30]) Not surprisingly, ambitious men did not covet the appointment. The General's first choice, Col. Cornelius Cox, turned down the offer because it was "unconnected with any Corps & out of all Line of Honor & Distinction."[31] Finally, Washington's newest aide-de-camp, Lt. Col.

Alexander Hamilton, strongly recommended his friend and mentor as an ideal candidate. Washington wrote to Elias on April 1, 1777, urging him to accept the position and adding yet "...another duty to this Office, and that is, the procuring of Intelligence."[32]

Elias responded to Washington's offer in person. "I waited on him and politely declined the task urging the wants of the Prisoners & having nothing to supply them..." Washington lamented that "if Men of Character & Influence would not come forward & join him in his Exertions all would be lost--Affected by this address, and supposing that I could be of some service to the Prisoners...I consented to accept the Commission..." In his Journal, Elias added that the position would also permit him to keep "an Eye on the Military Power & prevent its Incroachment, on Civil Authority..."[33]

As the new Commissary General of Prisoners with the rank of Colonel, Elias recorded his first encounter with his new reality. "Soon after I had entered on my department, the applications of the [American] Prisoners were so numerous and their distress so urgent, that I exerted every nerve to obtain Supplies but invain--Excepting £600...I could not by any means get a farthing more, except in Continental Money, which was of no avail in New York" where most American prisoners were being held. In desperation, Elias told Washington that "I knew of no means in my Power but to take what Monies I had of my own, & to borrow from my friends in New York, to accomplish the desirable purpose." Washington encouraged Elias to do precisely that and he pledged to split the losses if Congress failed to reimburse him.[34]

In October 1777, the glorious news of Gen. Burgoyne's surrender at Saratoga conveyed a very different message to Elias. In addition to his already overwhelming responsibilities, he would eventually have to feed and quarter an additional 5,790 British troops. In early December, Elias was permitted to enter Philadelphia, which was now under enemy control, to meet with his British counterpart. Repeated attempts at prisoner exchanges, however, proved unsuccessful.

Three days before Christmas 1777, as Americans established their Winter Quarters at Valley Forge, Elias shared his profound frustration with his wife: "I dare not think of Home. The Ideas of past Happiness, that follow of Course, form too great a Contrast for even Patriotism to resist. The loss of...domestic Happiness...added to the sinking our little Property, sometimes make such formidable attacks, that it requires very strong Intrenchments of publick Virtue & love of Posterity to resist." But then, drawing upon his bedrock of faith, he added: "But blessed be God, the way of Duty is the way of Safety..."[35]

Life quickly became even more complicated when Elias learned that in late November the New Jersey legislature had elected him as a member of Congress.[36] On January 4, 1778, he sought his wife's guidance: "I know not what to say to it, am exceedingly puzzled to determine what is my Duty, and at all Events, shall not attempt it, till I see & consult you...You know my Heart, that I have never aimed at any publick Employment, nor ever had a desire of entering into political Consequence...I was called to my present Employment, not from any desire of increasing either my Wealth or Importance, but from an abhorrence of being an Idle Spectator of my Country's Distress, and a passionate Fondness for obliging our worthy General..."[37]

For the time being, thoughts of congressional service were swept aside by the demands of his current office. At Washington's insistence, Elias finally received permission to personally inspect the treatment of American prisoners in New York City. On February 3, 1778, he entered the city under guard and met with the British Commandant, Gen. Robertson, "who I had formerly known." In his Journal, Elias recorded that "I wore a uniform & sword by my side. The General rec'd me with great politeness and appeared as friendly & sociable as he had used to do before the War." General Robertson assured Elias that rumors of prisoner abuse were "a parcel of damned lies..." But, when Elias met with 30 American Officers who were incarcerated he learned the true facts.

In one case, an American Officer was thrown into the dungeon for ten weeks without having his leg wound bandaged. There, he and the other inmates were only fed "4 lb hard spoiled Biscuit & 2 lb Pork per week; which they were obliged to Eat raw..." Elias also toured two hospitals full of sick prisoners. Based on his interviews and observations, Elias delivered a stinging report to his British host. "I then stated to him the facts, and assured him that they turned out worse than anything we had heard..." Elias' report apparently produced desperately needed improvements. "From every account I received, I found that their treatment had been greatly changed for the better, within a few months past., except at the Provost."[38]

On Gen. Robertson's part, humanitarian concerns were clearly secondary to his larger agenda. "One Day Calling on Genl Robertson he asked me if I had any objection against a free private political Conversation." As Elias recorded in his Journal, the General then stated that "...he was authorized to assure me that if any one would step forward & heal the unhappy difference, that he should be rewarded in any manner he should ask, even to a Pension of Ten Thousand Pounds Sterling.." Elias dismissed this clumsy attempt at bribery and stated that "...the Americans were desirous of Peace, and would eagerly seize every opportunity of embracing it, but the proposition from the nature of the thing must come from them [the British]."[39]

During his 13 days in the city Elias "...proceeded to borrow Money or take Goods in New York on my own Credit.--Thus I furnished 300 Officers with a handsome Suit of Cloathes each, and 1100 Men with a plain Suit, found them Blankets, Shirts &c. and added to their provisions found by the British a full half ration of Bread & Beef per Day for upwards of 15 months...I was near Thirty thousand Dollars in advance for the Prisoners..."[40] Receiving reimbursement from his government proved nearly as difficult as the assignment that triggered it. Since Elias had already been elected to Congress, Washington urged him to take his seat as soon as possible in order to argue his case in person. Accordingly, Elias resigned his military commission on May 11, 1778, but last minute negotiations with the British over the release of prisoners kept him in uniform until June.

As always, Elias longed for Hannah's companionship and wrote to her frequently to keep her spirit near. After leaving New York, while struggling to catch up with the correspondence that had accumulated during his absence, Elias shared with her that "Since I have eat my Breakfast, have I been driving the Quill as hard as I possibly can, and now it is near 8 oClock in the Evening..."[41] A few weeks later he sent her a humorous observation concerning his time behind enemy lines: "...I long to see you. I know you will laugh at me as an old Fashioned Fellow with a bald Pate & grey Head, but I can't help it...I have been so long with the gay, accomplished, proud English men, that I ought to be a foot higher than I used to be, therefore prepare yourself accordingly."[42] By June 28, they were briefly reunited at their Baskinridge home; but, all too soon, he had to rush to Philadelphia and his newest assignment.

Elias finally arrived in the recently liberated capital in early July 1778, just as President Laurens and the Continental Congress returned from their exile in York, Pennsylvania. On July 7, Elias officially entered Congress.[43] The next day he responded to a private letter from his protégée, Hamilton, who had been with Washington during the American victory at Monmouth Court House ten days earlier. "...The General I allways revered & loved ever since I knew him..." Reflecting on his own situation, Elias added that "...I am afraid I shall have my Hands full here and am not greatly elated at the Prospect."[44]

His first attempt at financial compensation received wide support from his colleagues but fell victim to determined opposition from two of the delegates.[45] As a result, Elias was forced to close his account in New York. But, when he received a response "painting the destitution of the

Prisoners in so striking a manner..." Elias "rose with tears in my eyes...to read the letter...a unanimous vote immediately passed for a warrant in my favour £10,000 in specie, which was immediately sent to New York."[46] (Full restitution was not completed until thirteen years later, in November 1791, when Elias was a member of the new House of Representatives.[47])

Elias' initial impression of America's largest city was clearly negative. Shortly after he arrived he wrote to his wife that "It is so hot that I cannot sleep...This City is enough to kill a horse..." A month later, he took a more philosophical view: "My desire is to be useful & as my Gracious God has in his all wise Providence been pleased to favour me beyond the common Lott of the children of men..so I would endeavour at the risque of every earthly comfort & enjoyment to do his Will under any circumstances of Life...My ambition is satisfied and when it pleases Him whose I am & ever wish to be, a return to my original obscurity will be acknowledged with gratitude & Praise..."[48]

While serving in Congress during the summer of 1778, Elias kept in close contact with Hamilton who occasionally used his old mentor as a valuable back channel between Headquarters and Congress. For example, when the highly-regarded German officer, Baron von Steuben, threatened to leave America's service over a question of rank, Elias served on a three member committee that temporarily resolved the issue.[49] In early August, he also attended the lavish European-style ceremony that officially welcomed the first French Minister, M. Gerard, to America. Later that month, Elias completed his initial term in Congress and eagerly returned home to New Jersey.[50]

On October 14, 1778, Elias attended his brother Elisha's marriage to Catharine Smith. (While local lore maintains that both Washington and Hamilton were in attendance, the historic record proves otherwise.) Even though Elias devoted most of the next two years to the safety of his family and the security of his estate, he continued to keep in close contact with Washington. In a letter dated May 3, 1779, Washington urged Elias to tap his sources in New York City: "It is a matter of great Importance to have early and good intelligence of the Enemy's strength and motions and, as far as possible, designs..."[51] Elias passed on to the General any information he received, and over time a close personal--as well as professional--correspondence developed.

In March 1779, while in Philadelphia on business, Elias also expressed his growing optimism concerning the international aspects of the war in a letter to Hannah: "The Powers of Europe are all in our favour. The Burgomasters of Amsterdam have acknowledged our Independency. The Court of Spain, is beyond a doubt on our side. The King of the Two Sicilys the Court of Sweden the Barbary Powers are also declaring for us...In short we seem to be aided from every quarter except from ourselves -- but alas all publick virtue is flown..."[52]

Despite the encouraging developments overseas, Elias feared that America might still snatch defeat from the jaws of victory. During the brutal winter of 1779-80, Washington established his headquarters at Morristown, not far from Elias' home in Baskinridge. Since part of the Army was actually camped on his property, Elias saw first hand the tremendous hardship the soldiers were suffering. He wrote to Timothy Pickering at the War Office that "the Continual sight of these half starved Beings keeps me in perpetual misery...it is impossible for a delicate Mind, to see his fellow Creatures and those who have fought & bled for his Safety, perishing for want of Food, while he has a Mouthful left...I have fed many of them this Day who could not see the Victuals without discovering Sensations enough to break your Heart...can nothing be done to save our sinking Cause."[53]

The human cost of the war is also painfully illustrated by the tragic story of the Rev. James Caldwell, the pastor of the First Presbyterian Church of Elizabeth Town, and a fellow Huguenot and close friend of Elias. Because Rev. Caldwell was an ardent patriot, his church was burned by the British in July 1780. The following June his wife, the mother of his nine children, was shot dead by the enemy while at prayer. And then, on November 24, 1781, the Pastor himself was murdered. At the end of the memorial service, Elias gathered the nine orphan children around their father's coffin and pleaded with his friends to open their hearts and their homes to these young souls. All were eventually adopted, including one young boy who went to live with Lafayette in France where he became a distinguished editor and philanthropist; and another, named Elias, who was welcomed home by Elias and Hannah.[54]

During the summer of 1781, Elias received word that the New Jersey Legislature once again intended to elect him as a delegate to Congress. His initial response was that "I have but just begun...to retrieve the great losses I have met with..." But he then added that "My determination always had been to sacrifice everything for the Publick Service while my Country was in distress & wanted aid--But I had taken it for granted that that period was past and there were no want of Solicitors for offices of every kind. I therefore had no Idea of every engaging again in political Life." In conclusion he stated that "I have determined to make the sacrifice tho' to the great distress & anxiety of my family...to God & my country I am willing to yield my every Service..."[55] On June 12, 1781, the Legislature made Elias' election official.[56]

Elias began his new term as a Delegate on Monday, July 23, 1781. He was immediately thrust into familiar territory when he received a letter from American prisoners aboard a British prison ship. On July 30, Elias moved "That a committee of three be appointed to take into consideration the state of the American prisoners in the power of the enemy..."[57] When the committee made its initial report on August 3, Congress resolved "That no circumstances of the enemy's particular situation can justify this outrage on humanity, it being contrary to the usage and custom of civilized nations..."[58] Both the committee and Washington were directed to look into the issue.

To his wife, Elias wrote in late July that "The City is so filled with the distressed Georgia & Carolina Refugees, that I was afraid that I should be prevented getting any quarters out of a Tavern." He finally did find a room "with very disagreeable company" on the third floor of a house at the Corner of Chestnut & Front Streets." Elias pledged to Hannah that "while I remain in this important Station, [I] will make up by Integrity & Application my want of those other qualifications necessary for the important trust."[59]

Elias was also thrust into critical boundary disputes. He chaired the committee concerning Vermont's ongoing demand to be admitted as the 14th State over the strenuous objections of New Hampshire and New York. An even tougher assignment was his appointment as chair of a five-member committee that tried to settle the cessions of Virginia, New York and Connecticut territory that Maryland had demanded as the price for unanimous ratification of the Articles of Confederation the previous February.[60] Since Elias was well known and respected as a successful land speculator, James Madison of Virginia found the committee's conduct "objectionable" and did not trust Elias' impartiality.[61] Unaccustomed to criticism, Elias shared his feelings with his daughter Susan: "I am sorry, even the meanest, Person of my Acquaintance should think evil of me, I hope I do not deserve it from them. I pity them and am confident in the End, they will see their Error." He then added his oft-repeated spiritual mantra: "God governs the World and all things must be right at last..."[62]

When news of Cornwallis' surrender at Yorktown reached Philadelphia on October 22, 1781, congressional spirits brightened, but this event also underscored how financially desperate Congress was. Elias recorded that "When the messenger brought the News...it was necessary to furnish him with hard money for his Expenses -- There was not a sufficiency in the Treasury to do it and the Members of Congress of which I was one, each paid a Dollar to accomplish it."[63]

Since Elias' tenure was set to expire less than two weeks later, he eagerly anticipated turning over a greatly improved military situation to his successor. But on Saturday, November 3, Elias' life took another direction. He received word that both he and his colleague had been reelected by their State Legislature for another one-year term as delegates. In his response to a member of the legislature, Elias complained that "The Monstrous expense attending a residence in this city, must soon take away the ready Cash of any fortune among us..." But, as a good soldier, he then added that "as there were only Mr. Clark & myself here and our Presence absolutely necessary to form a Congress in this important Conjuncture, We took our seats this Day [November 5, 1781]...Never was there Time which required a full Representation of the States more than the present as Matters of the Utmost future consequence to this Empire, are and must be the subjects of constant discussion..."[64]

One of the first issues to arise was a debate in Congress calling for the execution of Gen. Cornwallis in retaliation for his cruelty to the citizens of South Carolina, which was still under British occupation. Leading the charge was Arthur Middleton, the eldest son of Henry Middleton, the second President of the Continental Congress. Elias headed the opposition, as he described in his Journal: "Mr. Duane & myself opposed it with all our Powers as contrary to all good faith, having entered into a Capitulation with him [Cornwallis]...The Debate continued several Days and with great Difficulty we succeeded in putting a Negative on it by a small Majority."[65] Elias then led the effort to exchange Gen. Cornwallis, the highest ranking British prisoner, for former President Henry Laurens who had been captured at sea while on a diplomatic mission to The Netherlands and was being held in the Tower of London.[66] Ultimately that proposal failed, as well.

By late February 1782, the dream of a quick peace had faded. Elias told his brother Elisha that "There is not the least prospect of Peace or scarcely a probability of it--on the other hand every measure is adopting in England to send over a large body of Hanoverians & some English Regulars early in the Spring. The Comr in chief expects the next campaign is to be the most important of any that has been or will be in America this war--Alas! we are distressed with the languor & Inactivity of the States--All that can be done by Congress, has been, to rouse them from their Lethargy..." Elias then added that "My cash is all gone--I most earnestly wish you could get some for me...I can get none from the State."[67]

On June 25, 1782, Congress voted to adopt The Great Seal of the United States. While Secretary Charles Thomson had the distinction of designing one side of the Seal, William Barton, in consultation with Elias and Arthur Lee, created the image on the reverse side which featured "an all-seeing eye" over an unfinished pyramid. That image is still depicted today on the one dollar bill.[68]

By late October, Elias was resigned to the likelihood of his reelection to Congress, but he was also determined to return home for a few months while his fellow New Jersey delegates represented the interests of their State. As he wrote to an associate: "I am decided on my not attending in Congress this winter unless something very unexpected & extraordinary relating to Peace should turn up."[69] Two weeks later, something "very unexpected & extraordinary" did indeed turn up as he explained to this wife on November 4, 1782: "The things of this World are as uncertain as the Wind...I have been pleasing myself with the approaching Enjoyment of my dear Wife & Family in domestic Retirement during the coming Winter -- But Providence has otherwise determined for us -- This moment I have accepted the President's chair of Congress, not without a trembling hand..."[70] Elias received the votes of seven States (New Hampshire, Rhode Island, Connecticut, New Jersey, Pennsylvania, Delaware and Maryland). Massachusetts, having only one delegate present, could not vote. George was absent. Elias's most notable opponent was John Rutledge of Charleston who received the support of North Carolina. Not surprisingly, James Madison and Theodorick Bland of Virginia voted against Elias.[71]

Two days after his election Elias wrote a lengthy letter to his wife, filled with instructions on household tasks prior to her departure for Philadelphia. But, above all, Elias urged her to hurry. "Suffice it to say, that every day will appear a Week till you arrive here." Ever the romantic, Elias then promised to "send the Coach...to transport you to the most welcome Place you will meet with in this World, I mean the Arms & Heart of your affectionate Husband."[72]

As Elias settled into his new position, Washington sent congratulations from his headquarters in Newburgh, New York.[73] Despite the afterglow of Yorktown, however, the first four months of Elias' tenure as Head of State were extremely stressful. Washington fretted over the very real prospect of planning yet another military campaign as his officers and troops grew increasingly impatient over their back pay. None other than Gen. Henry Knox, the bedrock of the American Army, was among those who signed a memorial which was presented to Congress on January 7, 1783: "...We have borne all that men can bear--our property is expended--our private resources are at an end, and our friends are wearied out and disgusted with our incessant applications. We, therefore, most seriously and earnestly beg, that a supply of money may be forwarded to the army as soon as possible. The uneasiness of the soldiers, for want of pay, is great and dangerous; and further experiments on their patience may have fatal effects."[74]

As critical as the military situation was, it underscored an even more profound financial crisis. When Congress desperately turned for guidance to the Superintendent of Finance, Robert Morris, he informed them on January 9, that he had already overdrawn the known funds in Europe to the amount of three and a half million dollars.[75] On the other hand, most of the States, as usual, were deeply in arrears in meeting their allotted contributions to the national government. For all practical purposes, Congress was totally bankrupt.

On Monday, February 24, Elias, as President, sent a circular letter to all of the States which included a Resolution of Congress "founded on reasons of the utmost importance to the United States."[76] The Resolution pleaded with all of the States to meet their financial obligations to the nation and urged Delaware, Maryland and Georgia to immediately send delegates. Hamilton, now a delegate from New York, viewed the crisis as yet another demonstration of the structural flaws in the Articles of Confederation. In a letter to New York Governor George Clinton, Hamilton argued that "The only possible way then of making them [the States] contribute to the general expence in an equal proportion to their means is by general taxes imposed under Continental authority."[77] At the same time, North Carolina Delegate Hugh Williamson confided to a friend that "The cloud of public ceditors, including the army, are gathering about us; the prospect thickens. Believe me, that I would rather take the field in the hardest military service I ever saw, than face the difficulties that await us in Congress within a few months."[78]

Everything now hinged on reaching a formal peace agreement with Britain before the new nation's government imploded. And yet, month after month, there was simply no news from the American Peace Commissioners in Paris. Thus began Elias' term as President.

And then, on March 12, 1783, Captain Joshua Barney arrived in Philadelphia with news that a preliminary peace treaty had been signed between Britain and the United States the previous November. Elias immediately shared the glorious news with Washington. But exactly one week later the euphoria of the moment was nearly washed away by news from the Commander-in-Chief that some of his Officers were more determined than ever to force Congress to meet the Army's financial demands. Added to this was the fact that the French were outraged that the American Peace Commissioners had ignored their instructions and had negotiated a separate peace with Britain without consulting France. Furthermore, Robert Morris was threatening to resign his position as Superintendent of Finance.[79] In reviewing these rapidly unfolding developments in mid-March, James Madison came to the conclusion that they "...oppressed the minds of Congs. with an anxiety & distress which had been scarcely felt in any period of the revolution."[80]

Once again, as victory was being snatched away, news from overseas saved the day. On Sunday, March 23, 1783, Congress received word that France had also signed a preliminary peace treaty with Britain two months earlier. Since the American treaty was contingent upon this agreement, peace was finally at hand. Elias forwarded the news to Washington at 9 pm that same evening: "These are not official dispatches, but as there can be no doubt of the event I thought it of the highest consequence to give your Excellency and my fellow Citizens of the Army the earliest notice of this glorious end of all their trials and labours."[81]

It is of special interest that the very next day Elias also wrote to Gen. James Robertson, the last Royal Governor of New York (1780-83) who had been his friend prior to the revolution and with whom Elias had earlier negotiated the care of American prisoners: "I have the honor to congratulate you, Sir, on a general peace between all the beligerent powers in Europe and that we are once more Friends."[82] One week later, in response to a congratulatory note from a friend, Elias' deep religious belief led him to write: "God almighty grant that hereafter Peace may reign on Earth & good will to Men, and may they by this Means be led to give glory to God in the highest." And then, with remarkable clarity, he added that "The Contemplation of this Epocha, almost overcomes me at times. It opens a new Scene to Mankind, and I believe is big with inconcievable Effects in the political & I hope in the moral world."[83]

In early April, Gen. Sir Guy Carleton (the last of the British commanders in North America) sent the King's Proclamation for the cessation of all hostilities to President Boudinot. On April 10, in a letter to his predecessor, John Hanson, Elias shared this information and mentioned that "...this morning we received from France...the official Information of the same circumstances..." Elias then added that Congress "shall proclaim a Cessation of all Hostilities on the part of America tomorrow..."[84] Elias also shared his joy in a letter to the Marquis de Lafayette: "The glorious struggle, blessed be God, is now over..."[85]

On Tuesday, April 15, 1783, "...the United States in Congress assembled... ratified and confirmed...the said articles, and every part, article and clause thereof, on our part...In testimony whereof, [we have caused our seal to be hereunto affixed. Witness his Excellency Elias Boudinot, President..]"[86] And with that stroke of his quill pen, Elias Boudinot, the ninth President of the Continental Congress, brought the American Revolutionary War to the threshold of peace.

As the nation celebrated, news of the treaty actually intensified the strains within the military. Not only did officers and enlisted men continue to press for the money owed them, but now that the fighting was over many were eager to return to civilian life. As the founding fathers had always feared, a large standing army, kept idle, was indeed a potential threat to liberty. Even though Washington and Congress hesitated to disband the army before the final peace treaty was in hand, Congress gave the Commander-in-Chief permission to grant generous furloughs or even early discharges starting as early as late April.[87]

In May, Elias was again forced to write a Circular Letter to all of the States, once more pleading with them to meet their financial obligations to Congress and urging them to send delegates as quickly as possible.[88] On June 4, Elias' responsibilities were further expanded when Robert Livingston resigned his position as Secretary for Foreign Affairs to become Chancellor of New York. Even though Secretary Thomson was directed to secure that office during its vacancy, Elias had to assume even more international correspondence.[89] For example, on June 18, in his first letter to Franklin since Livingston's departure, Elias pointed out that "We have not heard from any of our Commissioners since February, tho' our anxiety and expectations have been wound up to the highest pitch."[90]

On June 19, growing concerns over the military resurfaced. Congress received two letters warning that "a detachment of about Eighty mutineers are on their way from Lancaster to this place [Philadelphia]..."[91] On June 21, Elias sent an urgent letter to Washington describing the situation: "They entered this City yesterday morning...and took possession of the Barracks, and with those Troops then quartered there make up about five hundred men...the Mutineers, joined by those at the Barracks...very unexpectedly appeared before, and surrounded, the State House, with fixed Bayonets." Elias went on to describe how the mutineers had seized the public Magazine later that afternoon and he expressed his fear "that the worst is not yet come."[92]

Throughout the weekend, while Maj. Gen. Arthur St. Clair (a future President) tried to convince the rebel troops to stand down, Hamilton negotiated with city and state officials, trying to persuade them to protect Congress. But on Tuesday, June 24, he had to report to Elias that no help would be forthcoming. Accordingly, as previously authorized by the delegates, Elias announced that Congress would immediately adjourn to Princeton where his home State of New Jersey would guarantee their safety.[93]

The following Monday, June 30, Congress resumed its work at Princeton and soon moved into Nassau Hall on the campus of the College of New Jersey where Elias still served as a trustee. In celebration of American

Independence, Elias hosted a banquet for Congress and other dignitaries on July 4 at Morvan, his sister's estate where Elias lived.[94] Finally, by July 29, a quorum of nine states had arrived and official business could resume.[95] The small size of the town, however, and the lack of adequate facilities made Princeton less than adequate as a national capital. Elias described the members of Congress as "grumbling & dissatisfied."[96] Since the city only consisted of 75 houses, even James Madison had to share a bed with fellow delegate Joseph Jones.[97]

Under these cramped conditions, debate concerning a permanent site for the national government began in earnest. Philadelphia was now eager to welcome Congress back. Elias wrote to Washington: "I believe the Citizens of Philadelphia begin to reflect on their Conduct towards the foederal Government, in a very different point of View, than that in which they first considered it."[98] The delegates finally decided on two sites in order to keep a regional balance: one in the vicinity of Trenton, New Jersey and the second near Georgetown, Maryland. But, until then, Congress would divide its time between Trenton and Annapolis.[99] Elias summed up the situation for Robert Livingston by stating that "we are to be...wandering Stars..."[100]

At Elias' invitation, Gen. Washington attended Congress on Tuesday, August 26, 1783. In his welcoming remarks, the President stated: "Hostilities have now ceased, but your country still needs your services. She wishes to avail herself of your talents in forming the arrangements which will be necessary for her in the time of peace. For this reason your atendance at Congress has been requested." In his reply, the General thanked Congress for "...the honorable reception I have now experienced" and for "...the great and uniform support I have received in every vicissitude of fortune" during the "course of the war."[101] Washington remained in Princeton for nearly two months.

While anxiously waiting for news of the final Peace Treaty, Congress also conducted several pieces of critical business. On October 18, Elias officially issued the Proclamation to disband most of the Continental Army, effective November 4, 1783.[102] State Militias would again serve as the primary line of defense except during war.[103] In addition, the soldiers who were scheduled to be executed for leading the mutiny in Philadelphia were pardoned by Congress at the last minute.[104]

And then, on Friday, October 31, as Congress prepared to officially welcome the Minister Plenipotentiary from "their High Mightinesses the States General" of the United Netherlands, news reached Princeton that the definitive peace treaty had been signed in Paris on September 3.[105] What a joyful occasion for Elias' last public ceremony as Head of State. In his official welcome, Elias underscored the unique bond which linked their two nations: "Goverened by the same ardent love of freedom...we pesuade ourselves that the most friendly and beneficial connection between the two republics, will be preserved inviolate to the latest ages."[106] And so it has for over two centuries. That evening Elias Boudinot, the President of a free and independent nation, presided over a state banquet for more than fifty distinguished guests.[107]

Three days later, on Monday, November 3, 1783, as a new Congress began, Elias eagerly relinquished the presidency to Thomas Mifflin of Pennsylvania. As one delegate recorded: "Our president was cheered, members of the Congress rising as he left the Chair." The next day, Thomas Jefferson returned as a delegate (after having served two disastrous years as Governor of Virginia). That same afternoon Congress voted to adjourn to Annapolis where it reconvened on Saturday, December 13, 1783.[108]

Elias took leave of the Continental Congress with a sense of accomplishment that "...My Presidentship has also been honored by the signature of both Preliminary articles & Definitive Treaty, which has greatly compensated for all my other Sacrifices-" At the age of 43 he eagerly looked forward to private life "under the blessings of so glorious a Peace..."[109] In a farewell note to John Adams, Elias expressed the sentiments of all his congressional colleagues when he wrote that "I rejoice to have seen the end of all our labours so happily accomplished."[110]

Before he left Princeton, Elias received word that, because of his service as Commissary of Prisoners during the war, he had been elected an honorary member of the New Jersey Chapter of the Society of the Cincinnati, the fraternity of former Continental Army Officers that many aspired to and others feared. Elias was delighted by the "high sense I entertain of the honor done me by this unsolicited mark of...respect and attention..."[111]

On November 21, Elias and Hannah finally returned to their home in Elizabeth Town, New Jersey. He wrote to a friend that "The seventh anniversary of our Expulsion from our happy Cottage, was the very day of my Return..."[112] That same day he forwarded to his successor, President Thomas Mifflin, the Peace Treaty which had been delivered to Elias by mistake and he informed Congress that "The British have at last evacuated New York..."[113]

In early January 1784, after Washington had officially resigned his commission as Commander-in-Chief and retired to Mount Vernon, Elias sent him a heartfelt message of congratulations: "It is with the warmest affection & attachment, that we join the United Voice of your Country, in Congratulating your & our Dr Mrs. Washington on this happy &

interesting Event...I shall ever esteem it one of the greatest Honors of my Life that I have served my Country in conjunction with & under the Direction of Gen Washington..."[114] Washington responded one month later: "The private congratulations of friendship...are received with more pleasure when they are known to flow from a source which has always been the same. The affectionate terms therefore, in which your Letter is expressed, could not fail to affect all my sensibility and to call for a return of my warmest thanks, these I offer most sincerely."[115]

On September 28, 1784, Elias gave his only daughter's hand in marriage to William Bradford, a brilliant man with a bright political future. Family and Faith remained uppermost in Elias' soul. Whenever he was forced to part from Hannah because of professional or political affairs, Elias would write frequently "To tell you I love you...an old story you have heard a thousand Times. To say I wish you to be always with me--no more than what you know by twenty odd years experience..."[116]

Even the young orphan that Lafayette had taken to France at Elias' urging remained near to his heart. A few years later, as the boy was growing into manhood, he shared with Elias that he felt called to the Roman Catholic faith, a religion deeply unpopular with most of the Founding Fathers due to the Pope's temporal power. Elias, however, did not scold the youth or threaten him with damnation. Instead, he told him that "I am satisfied that the grace of God is not confined to Sect or Party..."[117]

As Elias rebuilt his law practice, he also intensified his speculation in land, especially in the west. He was one of twenty-four investors in the Ohio Company which was established in 1786. Its initial goal was to purchase two million acres between the Great and Little Miami Rivers. Along the way, Elias was also "instrumental in founding the state of Ohio and the city of Cincinnati."[118] Even though his major business partner in this venture, John Cleves Symmes, proved to be erratic and vengeful, Elias grew increasingly wealthy during the late 1780s.

Business affairs, however, diverted Elias from any direct role in the creation or ratification of the new US Constitution. Nevertheless, Elias was pleased with the work of the Constitutional Convention. He told his son-in-law that the proposed Constitution was better than he had expected, considering "the difficulty of reconciling thirteen Jarring Interests..." Elias also predicted that "It will not meet with any Opposition in this State as it gives universal Satisfaction as far as I can judge."[119] Elias' prediction came true on December 18, 1787, when the Constitution was unanimously approved by the New Jersey Ratification Convention.

In February 1789, Elias returned to public service when he was elected as one of four members of the new House of Representatives from the State of New Jersey.[120] This development was anticipated by William Bradford the previous December when he wrote to his father-in-law: "By all the information I receive from West Jersey, I find the people there are so determined upon running you for a member of Congress, that I am not surprised at your acquiescence. There are occasions where a person appears to be so particulary called on that it seems like an indifference to public opinion to refuse..."[121]

As the Second Republic began on March 4, 1789, one thing that did not change was the difficulty in establishing a quorum. Over the next four weeks the new Congressmen and Senators slowly trickled into New York, the temporary capital. Elias and the New Jersey Delegation did not arrive until March 18. Finally, on Wednesday, April 1, 1789, the House of Representatives was able to convene.

Despite Elias' disappointment in the election for Speaker (as described earlier), he totally committed himself to his new congressional duties. Elias' first assignment was to chair the eleven member committee that developed the rules and procedures for the House. He presented the committee's report one week later; a remarkable achievement.

As Elias reported to his wife, congressional life under the new Constitution was still hard work: "I am up at 7 o'clock or a little after, spend an half hour in my Room -- Dress & Breakfast by half past eight, in Committee at 9 -- from thence immediately to the House -- adjourn at 3 o'clock --In Committee again at 6 -- return at 8 and write till 12 at night... except when I dine out, which to me is harder Service..."[122]

On April 23, as Washington, accompanied by Secretary Charles Thomson, journeyed from Mount Vernon to Elizabeth Town, he met Elias, who was leading a five member congressional delegation, and other dignitaries who would escort the President-elect on a fifteen mile sail past Staten Island to the tip of Manhattan.[123] First, however, they proceeded to Boxwood Hall where Elias hosted an elegant luncheon in Washington's honor.[124] The next day, Elias tried to describe the rest of the journey to Hannah even though he assured her that "I cannot do it justice..." "Boat after Boat & Sloop after Sloop added to our Train," he wrote. "We now discovered the Shores crowded with thousands of People...Nay I may venture to say Tens of Thousands..."[125] Once their barge landed, Washington was met by New York Governor George Clinton-- who had fought against ratification of the Constitution--and another wave of government officials who escorted Washington "to the house formerly occupied by the President of Congress."[126] Exactly one week later George Washington was sworn into office as the first President of the United States under the Second Republic.[127]

In mid-August, Elias--who often served as Chair of the Committee of the Whole--was presiding when Madison introduced the Bill of Rights. By late September all twelve proposed amendments to the Constitution were adopted by Congress and sent to the States which eventually ratified only ten.[128]

Of Elias' many committee assignments and legislative battles during his six years in the House, his most important and passionate pertained to his beloved Hamilton. On May 19, 1789, Elias led the fight for the creation of the Department of the Treasury. Despite the objections of many who favored establishing a Board rather than a single executive to head the office, Elias won the debate when the legislation he favored was finally approved by both the House and Senate on September 2, 1789. Nine days later Alexander Hamilton was sworn in as the first Treasury Secretary.[129]

On September 29, the House adjourned for a three month recess. During its absence, Secretary Hamilton prepared a series of reports concerning the Public Credit. The most controversial document proposed that the national government should assume all outstanding State debts estimated at $25,000,000. Hamilton's bold fiscal policy, which was initially introduced on February 8, 1790, produced months of heated debate. Once again, Elias spoke forcefully on Hamilton's behalf. He reminded his congressional colleagues that "...we are bound by every principle of honor, justice, and policy, to fund the debt of the United States, which has been one great means, under heaven, of securing to us our independence."[130] Hamilton's proposal passed the Committee of the Whole on April 9, 1790, but his victory was reversed three days later when the North Carolina Delegation finally arrived.

On April 15, Elias expressed his extreme frustration in a letter to his son-in-law: "...all the evils I have so long foretold, are taking place. The harmony of our House is broken up...In short, I fear the worse...we are all at Bay."[131] Old-fashioned politics ultimately resolved the impasse on July 26 when Hamilton and Jefferson (the new Secretary of State) and Madison agreed to locate the permanent capital along the Potomac River, as the South favored, in exchange for enough votes to enact Hamilton's financial plan.[132] And thus, the District of Columbia was born.

On February 5, 1790, Elias became the first attorney admitted to practice before the newly established Supreme Court.[133] That December, Congress moved home to Philadelphia while the permanent seat of government was under construction along the Potomac. During that congressional session Elias moved in with his daughter and her husband on Market Street, opposite the President's Mansion, only one block from the capitol.[134] The First Congress of the Second Republic came to a dramatic end two months later when Hamilton's bill to establish a privately financed Bank of the United States was approved by the House on a vote of 39-20. In support of Hamilton, Elias successfully argued against the strict constructionists that Congress' power to create such an institution was clearly implied in the Constitution.[135]

When the Second Congress opened in Philadelphia on October 27, 1791, Elias was the only one of New Jersey's four original representatives to have been reelected. Again, Elias took an active role in House debates. When Congress called for vengeance against the Indians who defeated Gen. Arthur St. Clair's campaign along the frontier,[136] Elias articulated his deep concern for Native Americans: "The Indians are with difficulty to be reduced by the sword, but may easily be gained by justice and moderation."[137] (Years later Elias wrote a book, *A Star in the West*, in which he theorized that American Indians were actually the direct descendants of the lost ten tribes of Israel.[138])

Elias and his brother Elisha were also known for their strong opposition to slavery. In 1790, for example, the Pennsylvania Society for Promoting the Abolition of Slavery sent "their sincere Thanks" to Elias "for thy humane and spirited Exertions in the cause of the Negro Silas, before the Supreme Court of New Jersey."[139] Elias believed that "Emancipation should be gradual, and by the provisions of laws, and under the protection of civil government." But, as a lawyer, he also argued that the Constitution's provision that prohibited Congress from ending the slave trade before 1808 must be respected, no matter how odious the institution might be.[140]

Despite his compassion, Elias was frugal with public funds. On January 14, 1793, he made what one biographer refers to as "one of his longest and most impressive speeches" concerning the claims of Revolutionary War veterans for deficiency pay.[141] Elias argued that all government creditors should be dealt with on an equal basis and that Congress was "...not sent here to show their generosity; it was to do justice..."[142] His' House colleagues agreed and the request was rejected.

Less than two weeks later, Elias was again engaged in a parliamentary battle concerning the Secretary of the Treasury. On January 23, Congressman Giles of Virginia--at the urging of Jefferson and Madison--demanded that Hamilton account for his handling of public funds. By early February, Hamilton submitted a detailed report in response to the initial charges. In response, Giles introduced nine very specific Resolutions that had been prepared by Jefferson. On the floor of the Committee of the Whole, Madison led the charge. Elias fought back with facts and figures on behalf of his "adopted" son. Days later, at the end of the debate, Elias concluded that "...this prosecution has been rashly brought forward...I consider the conduct of the officer concerned in this transaction not only wholly cleared up, but the measures he has pursued as stamped with wisdom and official knowledge...I think him deserving of the thankful approbation of his country for his economy and strict attention to the true interests and credit of the United States."[143] Once again, the House concurred. All the Resolutions against Hamilton were easily defeated.[144]

Elias began his third and final term when the new Congress convened on December 2, 1793. The French Revolution increasingly dominated American political debate as popular opinion split between the British and the French. Nearly all were shocked the previous April when Louis XVI was beheaded. In response, President Washington had issued a proclamation of neutrality which angered many on both sides of the argument. Once again, Elias sided with Hamilton who not only feared French excess but fervently desired a commercial treaty with Britain. Madison and Jefferson again led the opposition. When legislation which could have easily escalated into war between the US and Britain was introduced on March 27, 1794, Elias pleaded with his colleagues to consider how many lives might be sacrificed: "...did not the measure threaten a sudden transition from a state of profound peace and happiness...into a state of war and bloodshed, without taking those previous and prudent measures that might probably lead to an avoidance of this national evil..."[145] This time, Elias was in the minority when the House passed the Resolution. In the Senate, however, Vice President Adams broke a tie and thereby defeated the measure. Shortly thereafter Chief Justice John Jay (who had served as both President and Secretary for Foreign Affairs during the First Republic) was dispatched to London to calm the crisis.

During his final term in Congress, Elias delivered the annual Independence Day Oration to the Society of the Cincinnati in New Jersey. It was a truly remarkable and prophetic speech. "The eyes of the nations of the earth are fast opening," he said, "and the inhabitants of this globe...are but just beginning to discover their brotherhood to each other, and that all men, however different with regard to nation or color, have an essential interest in each other's welfare." Then, seriously underestimating the pace of progress, he added: "The Rights of Women are no longer strange sounds to an American ear...I devoutly hope that the day is not far distant when we shall find them dignifying...the jurisprudence of the several States in the Union."[146]

In December 1794, Elias took on a new challenge which occupied his attention for most of the rest of his life. Because Congress was dissatisfied with the initial performance of the new US Mint, a three-member committee was established to look into the issue. Elias was named chairman. Since Elias had previously made known his intention not to seek reelection, his committee report on February 9, 1795, was one of his last official acts as a Member of Congress.

In August 1795, Elias' son-in-law, William Bradford (who had become Washington's second Attorney General only a year earlier) died very suddenly of Yellow Fever. The entire Boudinot family was distraught. Elias wrote to a close friend that "My white hairs are going down with sorrow to the grave and nothing but having a God to go to could support my hopes."[147]

One month later President Washington asked Elias to become the new Director of the Mint. On October 28, 1795, it became official. Some close friends speculated that Elias accepted the thankless task in order to combat his grief.[148] In typical fashion, he threw himself into the challenge. By early November he had prepared a 36 page report entitled "Orders and Directions for Conducting the Mint of the United States." The following May, Elias wrote to a friend that "The only disagreeable consequence attending it, is confinement to Philadelphia, as every day brings some thing that cannot be done but by the Director alone."[149] Elias held an even lower opinion of the new Congress: "It has done but little--Indeed they have been the most miserable Representatives the Nation has ever had... The great difficulty has been to prevent them from doing evil..."[150]

For the next ten years Elias and his family lived at Rose Hill, three miles from downtown Philadelphia, as he devoted his remarkable energy and administrative skills to managing the Mint.[151] Half way through his latest career the political winds shifted to the new Democratic-Republican Party. When the outcome of the 1800 Election resulted in a tie between Jefferson and Burr, Elias expressed his true feelings in remarkably blunt terms: "We are indeed in a critical & alarming Situation to be confined to a choice between two such great evils. Alas! for my Country!"[152] He even suggested to the outgoing Federalist President that Adams appoint himself Chief Justice before leaving office.[153] Nevertheless, despite his intense dislike for the new Administration, Elias continued his work at the Government Mint into Jefferson's second term.

When he did leave office in July 1805, Elias relocated to Western New Jersey which had long been his political base. Prior to the move he had built a mansion along the Delaware River in the heart of Burlington.[154] It was there in their "delightful paradise"[155] that the 65 year old "Narcissus" and his beloved "Eugenia" shared their final three years until Hannah's death on October 28, 1808. On her birthday two years earlier, Elias had expressed his feelings for the woman who was the love of his life:

O Hannah! how I love to think
On all the blessings we've enjoy'd.
How does my heart, tho at life's brink,
Bless God, that you became my Bride.[156]

Even before leaving the Mint, Elias had written a book entitled *The Age of Revelation* in rebuttal to Thomas Paine's *Age of Reason*.[157] Now, in retirement, Elias prepared a biography of his friend, the Rev. William Tennent; and, a 577 page study of the French Revolution from a religious perspective, *The Second Advent of the Messiah*, which included a description of Napoleon as the biblical antichrist. His final book was the study of Native Americans described earlier. Because of his religious convictions and his concern for American Indians, Elias also contributed generously to the Institution for Instructing and Educating the Heathen in Cornwall, Connecticut. A young Cherokee attending that school was so impressed with his patron that he adopted the former President's first and last name. Elias' namesake later translated part of the New Testament into Cherokee and became a leader of his tribe.[158]

Elias also continued his half century of service on the Board of Directors of the College of New Jersey. Religion, however, became the dominant focus of Elias' life during his final years. He was always a deeply spiritual man. Now, in retirement, Elias devoted much of his time to overseeing the distribution of Bibles throughout the country and along the frontier as well as writing scholarly commentary on biblical passages.[159] In 1816, he became the founding President of the American Bible Society. It was, he wrote, "... the greatest honour that could have been conferred on me this side of the grave."[160] His former colleague from the First Republic, John Jay of New York, was elected Vice President and later succeeded him at the helm.

On October 17, 1819, Elias' younger brother Elisha died. A close friend described the scene at the funeral: "The Venerable Dr. Boudinot seated in a chair near the Minister, looked like a Patriarch & endured the solemn scene like a Christian philosopher."[161] And yet, despite his pain, Elias continued to focus on the issues that stirred his soul. Only a month after his brother's funeral, Elias wrote to Elisha's only surviving son--Elias E. Boudinot--condemning the spread of slavery to the Missouri Territory: "...if it should take place there is an end to the happiness of the United States..." And, on December 15, 1819, Elias told his nephew that "It is the most important question ever before Congress..."[162]

Elias made his last public appearance in May 1821, at the annual meeting of the American Bible Society in New York City. That July he wrote his final Will, leaving his sizable fortune to a wide variety of charitable organizations as well as individuals, especially his only surviving daughter, Susan Boudinot Bradford. By the fall, he knew his days were numbered. On Friday, October 12, at 6 o'clock in the morning, Elias wrote a final note to Susan which was later found in the family Bible: "I am prepared to go."[163] Four days later he slipped into a coma until the morning of Wednesday, October 24, 1821, when Elias quietly died at the age of eighty-one.[164]

Burial took place that Friday at St. Mary's Episcopal Churchyard in Burlington, only a brief walk from Elias' home.[165] Today a short stone obelisk stands guard over the graves of Elias and Hannah who are now joined together for eternity.

Throughout his life, Elias expressed confidence in the future of the nation he loved and served so faithfully. "Who knows" he once said, "but the country for which we have fought and bled may hereafter become a theatre of greater events than yet have been known to mankind."[166]

The small stone obelisk that guards the graves of Hannah and Elias Boudinot at St. Mary's Episcopal Churchyard in Burlington, New Jersey.

HERE LIE THE REMAINS OF THE HONORABLE.
ELIAS BOUDINOT, L.L.D.
BORN ON THE 2ND OF MAY 1740
HE DIED ON THE 24TH OF OCT 1821

HIS LIFE WAS AN EXHIBITION
OF FERVENT PIETY OF USEFUL TALENT
AND OF EXTENSIVE BENEVOLENCE.

The original St. Mary's Episcopal Church, founded in 1703, where Elias Boudinot worshiped during the final 16 years of his life.

WHILE ELIAS BOUDINOT WAS PRESIDENT

November 1782 - November 1783

On January 23, 1783, while Elias was President, Congress ratified the Treaty with the United Provinces of the Netherlands that had been negotiated by John Adams.[167] Then, in mid-March, it finally received the preliminary Treaty of Peace from the American Commissioners in Paris. After careful examination and debate, Congress adopted a cease-fire proclamation on April 11, 1783 and then ratified the preliminary Treaty four days later. Surprisingly, the first direct impact of the Treaty was that Congress, on April 17, order the sale of Continental Army horses. Six days later it also authorized Gen. Washington to start discharging Continental troops.

With the end of the war finally in sight, Congress moved quickly to normalize relations with a number of other nations. On May 1, the American Ministers at the Peace Conference in Paris were instructed to negotiate a treaty of commerce with Great Britain as soon as peace negotiations were concluded. (Unfortunately, that task proved elusive for years.) Three weeks later Francis Dana was directed to negotiate a treaty with Russia. On July 29, the Treaty of Amity and Commerce with Sweden was ratified. During this period Congress appointed Oliver Pollock as its commercial agent to Cuba.[168] And, on October 31, 1783, it officially received the first Dutch minister to the United States.[169]

Throughout this period, Congress devoted days of debate to issues pertaining to the public credit and pleaded with the States for authority to levy revenue duties.[170] What Congress discovered yet again were the pitfalls embedded in the Articles of Confederation which made it extremely difficult for the national government to raise the revenues essential for the success of the First Republic.

Midway through Elias' term of office Congress was confronted by angry Continental troops seeking back pay who threatened the Delegates assembled in Philadelphia. In response, Elias led the government to Princeton for the duration of his presidency where the State of New Jersey, unlike Pennsylvania, promised to protect its members.[171]

Across the Atlantic, revolving-door ministries were again the rule rather than the exception in the wake of Britain's loss of its American Empire. The Earl of Shelburne, who enjoyed the King's support, was completing his fourth month as head of government when Elias became President of the United States in November 1782. Shelburne's ministry collapsed the following April and was briefly replaced by the team of Charles James Fox, the Foreign Minister (who then led the "old Whigs" who had remained loyal to Chatham and Rockingham), and, once again, Lord North, whom the King now considered a "traitor" to their former friendship. They, in turn, were pushed aside that December by William Pitt the Younger, the second son of the late Earl of Chatham.[172]

In the shadow of Britain's defeat in the American Revolution, Ireland also took another major step toward its total Independence when the Renunciation Act of 1783 was passed by Parliament which confirmed the complete legislative and judicial independence of Ireland, an important step in its long struggle for liberty.[173]

In France, Foreign Minister Vergennes delighted in America's victory over France's historic enemy and was well-satisfied by the treaty signed between Britain and France. He was, however, outraged that the American Peace Commissioners had ignored their instructions and had failed to consult France during the negotiations. As Vergennes confided to his ambassador in America: "If we can judge the future by what we have just seen, we shall be poorly repaid for what we have done for the United States of America."[174] When Benjamin Franklin was instructed by Congress to seek yet an additional loan from France, the Foreign Minister initially responded that "...When you can solve my doubts on this subject [the failure of the Americans to consult France], I will ask his Majesty to satisfy your demands."[175] Nevertheless, the Minister did intervene with the French King and part of the funds the Americans requested were granted at five percent interest even though the French Government itself was, at the same time, paying seven percent on the money it borrowed.[176] All too soon France would pay dearly for its poor financial management and the example of a popular revolution which it had so lavishly supported.

Chapter 9

President
ELIAS BOUDINOT
of
NEW JERSEY

Notes

Abbreviation Key

JCC   Journals of the Continental Congress
LDC   Letters of Delegates to Congress
PHL   The Papers of Henry Laurens

[1] Elias Boudinot was elected as a three-term congressman from New Jersey at the start of the Second American Republic. Richard Henry Lee was selected by the Virginia legislature as one of its first two United States Senators.

[2] Frederick Muhlenberg (1750-1801) was a Lutheran clergyman and politician from Pennsylvania. His election as the first Speaker of the US House of Representatives (1789) was "...undoubtedly influenced by the consideration that, since the President came from the South and the Vice-President from New England, it was desirable to select the Speaker from the most powerful of the middle states." Dumas Malone, Editor, Dictionary of American Biography, (Charles Scribner's Sons, New York, 1934). Vol. XIII, p. 307.

[3] J. J. Boudinot, Editor, The Life, Public Services, Addresses and Letters of ELIAS BOUDINOT, LL.D., President of the Continental Congress, Vol. II, pp. 37-38.

[4] George Adams Boyd, Elias Boudinot: Patriot and Statesman, (Princeton University Press, Princeton, 1952), p. 3.

[5] Barbara Louise Clark, E. B.: The Story of Elias Boudinot IV, His Family, His Friends, and His Country, (Dorrance & Company, Philadelphia, 1977), pp. 3-4.

[6] Boyd, op. cit., p. 7.

[7] James Grant Wilson & John Fiske, Editors, Appletons' Cyclopaedia of American Biography, (D. Appleton & Co., New York, 1887), Vol. 1, p. 465. The College of New Jersey was founded in Newark in 1748 and was officially transfered to Princeton on November 13, 1756. Today, six of the early university presidents are buried next to the Rev. Aaron Burr in Princeton.

[8] Clark, op. cit., p. 16.

[9] Boyd, op. cit., p. 13.

[10] Clark, op. cit., p. 23.

[11] Boyd, op. cit., p. 17.

[12] Boyd, op. cit., p. 16.

[13] As quoted in Boyd, op. cit., p. 17; Elias Boudinot to Ezekial Goldthwaite, September 16, 1769;

[14] Clark, op. cit., p. 22.

[15] See Introduction for details pertaining to the Stamp Act.

[16] As cited in Boyd, op. cit., p. 17.

[17] Ron Chernow, <u>Alexander Hamilton</u>, (The Penguin Press, New York, 2004).

[18] Willard Sterne Randall, <u>Alexander Hamilton: A Life</u>, (Harper-Collins Publishers, New York, 2003), p. 54.

[19] See Introduction for details pertaining to the Intolerable Acts.

[20] Boyd, op. cit., p. 22.

[21] As cited in Boyd, op. cit., p. 22; Elias Boudinot to Hannah Boudinot, July 21, 1774.

[22] Chernow, op. cit., p. 45.

[23] As cited in Boudinot, Vol. I, p. 6; William Franklin to Joseph Galloway, March 12, 1775.

[24] Boyd, op. cit., p. 24.

[25] Elias Boudinot, <u>Journal of Historical Recollections of American Events During The Revolutionary War</u>, (Arno Press, 1968), [copied from His Own Original Manuscript and first published by Frederick Bourquin, Philadelphia, 1894], pp. 2-3.

[26] One Boudinot biographer records that Washington even stopped in Elizabeth Town, New Jersey on his way to Boston to meet with the local Committee of Safety and that "A room in the Boudinot mansion is pointed out as a place where Washington slept." More recent sources do not repeat this story which seems extremely unlikely due to the urgency of Washington's journey. And yet, it could explain why Boudinot was the first to send gun powder to Boston only a few weeks later. Clark, op. cit., p. 39.

[27] Boudinot Journal, op. cit., p. 72.

[28] Boudinot Journal, op. cit., pp.7-8.

[29] Boyd, op. cit., p. 31.

[30] Boyd, op. cit., p. 34

[31] As cited in Boyd, op. cit., p. 35.

[32] John C. Fitzpatrick, Editor, The Writings of George Washington, (US Government Printing Office, Washington, DC, 1932), Vol. VII, p. 343; George Washington to Elias Boudinot, April 1, 1777.

[33] Boudinot Journal, op. cit., p. 9.

[34] Boudinot Journal, op. cit., pp. 9-10.

[35] As cited in Boyd, op. cit., p. 48; Elias Boudinot to Hannah Boudinot, December 22, 1777.

[36] Paul H. Smith, Editor, LDC 1774-1789, (Library of Congress, Washington, DC, 1981), Vol. 8, p. xix.

[37] As cited in Boyd, op. cit., pp. 49-50; Elias Boudinot to Hannah Boudinot, January 4, 1778.

[38] Boudinot Journal, op. cit., pp. 11-18.

[39] Boudinot Journal, op. cit., pp. 19-23.

[40] J. J. Boudinot, op. cit., Vol. I, p. 159.

[41] As cited in Clark, op. cit., p. 107; Elias Boudinot to Hannah Boudinot, March 29, 1778.

[42] As cited in Boyd, op. cit., p. 62; Elias Boudinot to Hannah Boudinot, April 17, 1778.

[43] Worthington Chauncey Ford, Editor, JCC: 1774-1789, (Government Printing Office, Washington, DC, 1908), Vol. XI, p. 672.

[44] As cited in Boyd, op. cit., pp. 68-69; Elias Boudinot to Alexander Hamilton, July 8, 1778.

[45] Boudinot Journal, op. cit., p. 70.

[46] Boudinot Journal, op. cit., pp. 70-71.

[47] Boyd, op. cit., p. 80.

[48] J. J. Boudinot, op. cit., Vol. I, p. 155; Elias Boudinot to Hannah Boudinot, August 13, 1778.

[49] For additional information on the unique role of Baron von Steuben in the American Revolution, see Chapter 4, endnote #6.

[50] LDC, op. cit., Vol. 26, p. xxii.

[51] J. J. Boudinot, op. cit., Vol. I, p. 180; George Washington to Elias Boudinot, May 3, 1779.

[52] J. J. Boudinot, op. cit., Vol. I, pp. 177-178; Elias Boudinot to Hannah Boudinot, March 5, 1779.

[53] As cited in Boyd, op. cit., p. 82; Elias Boudinot to Timothy Pickering, January 7, 1780.

[54] J. J. Boudinot, op. cit., Vol. I, pp. 187-189.

[55] J. J. Boudinot, op. cit., Vol. I, p. 217; Elias Boudinot to Nathaniel Scudder, June 18, 1781.

[56] LDC, op. cit., Vol. 26, p. xxii.

[57] JCC, op. cit., Vol. XXI, p. 815.

[58] Ibid. pp. 829-830.

[59] J. J. Boudinot, op. cit., Vol. I, pp. 223-225.

[60] For additional information on the cessions of Virginia, New York and Connecticut territory see Chapter 8, pp. xxx.

[61] Boyd, op. cit., pp. 92-93.

[62] As cited in Boyd, op. cit., p. 94; Elias Boudinot to Susan Boudinot, October 22, 1781.

[63] J. J. Boudinot, op. cit., Vol. I, p. 235.

[64] J. J. Boudinot, op. cit., Vol. I, pp. 228-229; Elias Boudinot to John Stevens, November 5, 1781.

[65] J. J. Boudinot, op. cit., Vol. I, pp. 242-243.

[66] JCC, op. cit., Vol. XXII, p. 95. See also: Chapter 4, pp. XXXX.

[67] J. J. Boudinot, op. cit., Vol. I, p. 244; Elias Boudinot to Elisha Boudinot, February 20, 1782.

[68] J. Edwin Hendricks, Charles Thomson and the Making of a New Nation, (Associated University Presses, Inc., Cranbury, NJ, 1979), p. 136. See also: Boyd, op. cit., p. 101.

[69] LDC, op. cit., Vol. 19, p. 284; Elias Boudinot to Lewis Pintard, October 22, 1782.

[70] J. J. Boudinot, op. cit., Vol. I, p. 263; Elias Boudinot to Hannah Boudinot, November 4, 1782.

[71] Boyd, op. cit., p. 106.

[72] LDC, op. cit., Vol. 19, pp. 354-355; Elias Boudinot to Hannah Boudinot, November 6, 1782.

[73] Fitzpatrick, op. cit., Vol. 25, p. 350; George Washington to Elias Boudinot, November 1782.

[74] JCC, op. cit., Vol. XXIV, p. 291.

[75] Edmund Cody Burnett, <u>The Continental Congress</u>, (The Macmillan Company, New York, 1941), p. 555.

[76] LDC, op. cit., Vol. 19, p. 724; Elias Boudinot to the States; February 24, 1783.

[77] LDC, op. cit., Vol. 19, p. 725; Alexander Hamilton to George Clinton, February 24, 1783.

[78] LDC, op. cit., Vol. 19, p. 699; Hugh Williamson to James Iredell, February 17, 1783.

[79] Burnett, op. cit., p. 573.

[80] LDC, op. cit., Vol. 20, p. 39; James Madison's Notes of Debates, March 17, 1783.

[81] LDC, op. cit., Vol. 20, p. 74; Elias Boudinot to George Washington, March 23, 1783.

[82] LDC, op. cit., Vol. 20, p. 81; Elias Boudinot to James Robertson, March 24, 1783.

[83] LDC, op. cit., Vol. 20, pp. 125-126; Elias Boudinot to James Searle, April 1, 1783.

[84] LDC, op. cit., Vol. 20, p. 314; Elias Boudinot to John Hanson, April 10, 1783. See also: JCC, op. cit., Vol. XXIV, pp. 238-241. The Proclamation declaring the cessation of hostilities was proclaimed by Congress on April 11, 1783.

[85] LDC, op. cit., Vol. 20, p. 169; Elias Boudinot to Marquis de Lafayette, April, 12, 1783.

[86] JCC, op. cit., Vol. XXIV, p. 251.

[87] Burnett, op. cit., p. 574.

[88] LDC, op. cit., Vol. 20, p. 240; Elias Boudinot to the States, May 9, 1783.

[89] JCC, op. cit., Vol. XXIV, p. 382.

[90] J. J. Boudinot, op. cit., Vol. I, p. 326.

[91] LDC, op. cit., Vol. 20, p. 344; Committee of Congress to William Jackson, June 19, 1783.

[92] LDC, op. cit., Vol. 20, pp. 349-350; Elias Boudinot to George Washington, June 21, 1783, 4 O'Clock P.M.

[93] JCC, op. cit., Vol. XXIV, p. 410.

[94] Clark, op. cit., p. 248.

[95] Burnett, op. cit., p. 580.

[96] LDC, op. cit., Vol. 20, p. 675; Elias Boudinot to Robert R. Livingston, September 16, 1783.

[97] LDC, op. cit., Vol. 20, p. 606; James Madison to James Madison, Sr., August 30, 1783.

[98] LDC, op. cit., Vol. 20, p. 398; Elias Boudinot to George Washington, July 5, 1783.

[99] Burnett, op. cit., pp. 586-587.

[100] LDC, op. cit., Vol. 21, p. 94; Elias Boudinot to Robert R. Livingston, October 23, 1783.

[101] JCC, op. cit., Vol.XXIV, pp. 521-523.

[102] JCC, op. cit., Vol. XXV, p. 703.

[103] The Founding Fathers fear of standing armies--roost recently reinforced by Congress' need to flee Philadelphia--was the clear rationale for what became the Second Amendment to the US Constitution contrary to the message espoused by some 20th Century organizations.

[104] LDC, op. cit., Vol. 21, p. 120; Elias Boudinot to the Ministers Plenipotentiary, October 27, 1783.

[105] J. J. Boudinot, op. cit., Vol. I, pp, 362-363; John Adams to Elias Boudinot, September 5, 1783: "On Wednesday the third of this Month the American Ministers met the British Minister at his Lodgings at the Hotel de York, and signed sealed and delivered the Definitive Treaty of Peace between the United States of America and the King of Great Britain."

[106] JCC, op. cit., Vol. XXV, pp. 785-786.

[107] Boyd, op. cit., p. 136.

[108] LDC, op. cit., Vol. 21, p. 145. See also: JCC, op. cit., Vol. XXV, p. 799 & pp. 803-809.

[109] LDC, op. cit., Vol. 21, p. 120; Elias Boudinot to the Ministers Plenipotentiary, October 27, 1783.

[110] LDC, op. cit., Vol. 21, p. 130; Elias Boudinot to John Adams, November 1, 1783.

[111] J. J. Boudinot, op. cit., Vol. II, p. 16; Elias Boudinot to Elias Dayton, November 6, 1783.

[112] As cited in Boyd, p. 138; Elias Boudinot to Elizabeth Ferguson, January 2, 1784.

[113] LDC, op. cit., Vol. 21, p. 157; Elias Boudinot to Thomas Mifflin, November 21, 1783.

[114] J. J. Boudinot, op. cit., Vol. II, pp. 18-19; Elias Boudinot to George Washington, January 11, 1784.

[115] Fitzpatrick, op. cit., Vol. 27; p. 336; George Washington to Elias Boudinot, February 18, 1784.

[116] J. J. Boudinot, op. cit., Vol. II, p. 24; Elias Boudinot to Hannah Boudinot, December 12, 1785.

117 As cited in Boyd, op. cit., p. 146; Elias Boudinot to John Caldwell, May 2, 1790.

118 Donald W. Whisenhunt, <u>Elias Boudinot</u>, (New Jersey Historical Commission, Trenton, 1975), p. 27. See also: William Benton, Publisher, Encyclopaedia Britannica, (Encyclopaedia Britannica, Inc., Chicago, 1966), Vol. 16, p. 895. This was actually the second land trust to be named The Ohio Company. The first was prior to July 1776.

119 As cited in Boyd, op. cti., p. 146; Elias Boudinot to William Bradford, September 28, 1787.

120 Clark, op. cit., pp. 332-333. The election of all four of New Jersey's first congressmen was challenged by a petition presented to Congress, but the issue was ultimately resolved by the House in favor of Elias and his congressional colleagues on September 2, 1789.

121 As cited in Boyd, op. cit., pp. 154-155; William Bradford to Elias Boudinot, December 23, 1788; (Wallace Papers, Historical Society of Pennsylvania).

122 J. J. Boudinot, op. cit., Vol. II, p. 39; Elias Boudinot to Hannah Boudinot, April 14, 1789.

123 James Thomas Flexner, <u>George Washington and the New Nation</u>, (Little, Brown and Company, Boston, 1970), p. 178.

124 Clark, op. cit., pp. 311-319.

125 J. J. Boudinot, op. cit., Vol. II, pp. 40-44; Elias Boudinot to Hannah Boudinot, April 24, 1789.

126 J. J. Boudinot, op. cit., Vol. II, p. 179.

127 Clark, op. cit., p. 324. Before Washington's swearing in it was discovered that there was no Bible at Federal Hall. Robert Livingston urgently sent out for the Bible at nearby St. John's Masonic Lodge of which he was Grand Master.

128 One of Madison's missing amendments, concerning congressional salaries, eventually resurfaced two centuries later and was ratified by three-fourths of the States in 1992.

129 Randall, op. cit., p. 369.

130 <u>Annals</u>, 1st Congress, 2nd Session, p. 1137.

131 J. J. Boudinot, op. cit., Vol. II, pp. 61-62; Elias Boudinot to William Bradford, April 15, 1790.

132 Chernow, op. cit., pp. 328-331. Madison never did vote for Hamilton's bill, but he persuaded two congressmen from Virginia and two from Maryland to switch their votes in order to win approval.

133 J. J. Boudinot, op. cit., Vol. II, pp. 355.

134 The Bradford home, where Elias lived during the congressional session of 1790, stood on the north side of Market Street between 5th and 6th Streets. The former residence of Colonial Gov. Penn, on the opposite side of Market which was then owned by Robert

Morris, was used as the new Presidential Mansion from 1790-1800. The brick Court House building that served as the interim capitol was one block south along 6th Street, next to Independence Hall.

[135] J. J. Boudinot, op. cit., Vol. II, pp. 229-248.

[136] For additional information concerning St. Clair's defeat, see Chapter 13.

[137] Annals, 2nd Congress, 1st Session, p. 144.

[138] Elias Boudinot, A Star in the West, (Books for Libraries Press, Freeport, NY), Reprinted 1970.

[139] J. J. Boudinot, op. cit., Vol. II, pp. 69-70; James Pemerton to Elias Boudinot, November 8, 1790.

[140] Annals, 1st Congress, 2nd Session, p. 1470.

[141] Boyd, op. cit., p. 202.

[142] Annals, 2nd Congress, 2nd Session, p. 822.

[143] Annals, 2nd Congress, 2nd Session, pp. 954-955.

[144] On the nine Resolutions against Hamilton, 41 congressmen voted. The total cast in opposition to Hamilton ranged from a low of 7 to a high of 15.

[145] Annals, 2nd Congress, 2nd Session, pp. 571-575.

[146] J. J. Boudinot, op. cit., Vol. II, pp. 363 & 374-375; July 4, 1793.

[147] J. J. Boudinot, op. cit., Vol. II, p. 104; Elias Boudinot to Samuel Bayard, August 25, 1795.

[148] J. J. Boudinot, op. cit., Vol. II, p. 115; Rachel Bradford to a friend; November 26, 1795.

[149] J. J. Boudinot, op. cit., Vol. II, p. 109; Elias Boudinot, May 11, 1796.

[150] J. J. Boudinot, op. cit., Vol. II, p. 123; Elias Boudinot to Samuel Bayard, March 9, 1797.

[151] Clark, op. cit., p. 291.

[152] As cited in Boyd, op. cit., p. 239.

[153] Charles Francis Adams, Editor, The Works of John Adams, (Little, Brown & Co., Boston, 1854), Vol. IX, p. 93n.

[154] As cited in Clark, op. cit., p. 289. As early as January 7, 1784, Elias had written to Richard Morris that "I once thought that I was settled for life, but the late glorious Revolution in our political World and the necessary War & Confusion attending it have so deranged my affairs and so entirely altered my connections in this Place, that, after a

Seven Years' Expulsion from my House & Estate here, I find my attachment in Elizth Town grealy [sic] weakened...I know not where I shall Determine my future abode...."

[155] As cited in Clark, op. cit., p. 416; John Pintard to his daughter, October 17, 1816.

[156] As cited in Boyd, op. cit., p. 276; Stimson Deposit, Princeton University Library.

[157] Clark, op. cit., p. 431. During his yeas at the Mint Elias had also written *The Saviour and His Work*, which he described as "merely old truths condensed..."

[158] Unfortunately, Elias Boudinot, the Cherokee leader, made powerful enemies within his tribe and was ultimately assassinated in 1839.

[159] Clark, op. cit., p. 431.

[160] As cited in Clark, op. cit., p. 438; Elias Boudinot to Rev. Dr. Romeyn, June 5, 1816.

[161] Dorothy C. Barck, Editor, Letters from John Pinard to His Daughter, (New York, 1940), Vol. 1, p. 238; as cited in Boyd, op. cit., p. 289. The title "Dr. Boudinot" stems from the honorary doctoral degree that Elias received from Yale University in 1790.

[162] J. J. Boudinot, op. cit., Vol. II, pp. 172-173; Elias Boudinot to Elias E. Boudinot, November 27, 1819 and December 15, 1819.

[163] As cited in Boyd, op. cit., p. 292; Stimson Deposit, Princeton University Library.

[164] As cited in Clarke, op. cit., p. 460; John Pintard to his daughter, October 25, 1821.

[165] Even though Elias was a lifelong Presbyterian, and President of the General Assembly of the Presbyterian Church at the time of his death, he and Hannah joined St. Mary's Episcopal Church in Burlington--the oldest Episcopal Church in New Jersey, built in 1703--because there were not enough members of his own faith in the city to organize a separate congregation.

[166] J. J. Boudinot, op. cit., Vol. II, p. 378; Elias Boudinot's Independence Day Oration to the New Jersey Society of the Cincinnati, July 4, 1793.

WHILE ELIAS BOUDINOT
WAS PRESIDENT

Notes

Abbreviation Key

JCC   Journals of the Continental Congress
LDC   Letters of Delegates to Congress
PHL   The Papers of Henry Laurens

[167] Paul H. Smith, Editor, LDC: 1774-1789, (Library of Congress, Washington, DC, 1992), Vol. 19, p. xvi.

[168] LDC: 1774-1789, op. cit., Vol. 20, pp. xii-xiii.

[169] LDC: 1774-1789, op. cit., Vol. 21, p. xii.

[170] Edmund Cody Burnett, The Continental Congress, (The Macmillan Company, New York, 1941), pp. 570-571.

[171] Burnett, op. cit., p. 578.

[172] W. E. Lunt, History of England, (Harper & Brothers, New York, 1945), pp. 563-565.

[173] Chris Cook & John Stevenson, British Historical Facts 1760-1830, (Archon Books, Hamden, Connecticut, 1980), p. 117.

[174] As cited in James Breck Perkins, France in the American Revolution, (Corner House Publishers, Williamstown, Massachusetts, 1970), p. 487; Comte de Vergennes to M. La Luzerne.

[175] As cited in Perkins, op. cit., p. 490; Comte de Vergennes to Benjamin Franklin.

[176] Perkins, op. cit., p. 491.

President
THOMAS MIFFLIN
of
PENNSYLVANIA

Breaking with History

The most dramatic moment of the American Revolution took place over two years after the British surrendered at Yorktown.

The State House in Annapolis, which still serves today as Maryland's Capitol, was then the temporary seat of the new nation. It was there at noon on Tuesday, December 23, 1783 (exactly a decade after the Boston Tea Party) that Gen. George Washington, Commander-in-Chief of the Continental Army, surrendered his military commission to President Thomas Mifflin. It was the precise moment that separated the American Revolution from most of recorded history. Unlike Caesar, Cromwell or Napoleon, the conquering American commander freely submitted to civilian authority and retired to private life. It was Washington's greatest moment and America's most triumphant victory.[1]

As recorded in the Journals of the Continental Congress: "...his Excellency the Commander in Chief was admitted to a public audience... the President, after a pause, informed him, that the United States in Congress assembled, were prepeared to receive his communications; Whereupon, he [Washington] arose and addressed Congress...*He then advanced and delivered to the President his commission*...the President returned him the following answer: ...You have persevered, till these United States... have been enabled, under a just Providence, to close the war in freedom, safety and independence; on which happy event we sincerely join you in congratulations."[2]

The fact that George Washington relinquished his commission to Thomas Mifflin added even greater poignancy to this historic event. These two outstanding patriots, who originally met as delegates at the opening of the First Continental Congress in 1774, had had an intense and complex relationship throughout the war. When Washington rode out of

Philadelphia on June 23, 1775, to take command of his new army, at his side was Major Thomas Mifflin, his first Aide-de-Camp. One year later Thomas was promoted to the critical position of Quartermaster General. In time, however, Thomas grew uncertain of Washington's leadership and speculated about a replacement in what became known as the Conway Cabal. When Thomas was later appointed to the Board of War, which oversaw the military, their relationship further deteriorated; especially when some of Washington's defenders tried to disparage Thomas' character. But, by late 1783, they had set aside their mutual distrust and had largely repaired their professional relationship. In the future, they would even join together again to write their nation's new Constitution.

Like his revolutionary colleagues, Thomas Mifflin could never have imagined where destiny would lead him. He was born in Philadelphia on January 10, 1744, the eldest son of John Mifflin, a prosperous merchant who held various local political offices, and his wife Elizabeth. John Mifflin was a descendant of a prominent Quaker family that had emigrated from Warminster, England sometime before 1680. As a child, Thomas attended a Quaker school and, in May 1760, at the age of 16, he graduated from the College of Philadelphia where his father served as a trustee.[3] For the next four years Thomas worked for William Coleman, a wealthy Philadelphia merchant who was a close friend of Benjamin Franklin."[4]

To further his mercantile ambitions, Thomas sailed for Europe at the age of 21. He reached Falmouth on March 16, 1764, after suffering severe seasickness. His travels for the rest of the year were largely devoted to France, a country he came to love and clearly favored during political battles later in life. By late that fall, Thomas had settled in England for his final few months before sailing for home. Despite Europe's obvious enticements, Thomas wrote from London on November 23, 1764, that "I find myself as great a patriot for America as when I first left it."[5]

After returning to Philadelphia in 1765, Thomas went into business with his younger brother, George. Building on their father's reputation, their store at the corner of Front and Chestnut proved highly successful. Two years later, when Thomas' career appeared firmly established and his income seemed secure, Thomas proposed to his cousin, Sarah Morris, who was three years his junior. They were married in Philadelphia on March 4, 1767. John Adams once described her as "a charming Quaker girl."[6] Silas Deane of Connecticut said that she was "a most agreeable lady..."[7] Even though she is otherwise lost to history, as are far too many women of the Revolution, her image is preserved in a painting of the couple by the distinguished American artist, John Singleton Copley. Together, Thomas and Sarah shared 23 happy but childless years until her death in 1790.[8]

One year after his wedding, Thomas further enhanced his public profile when he became a member of the American Philosophical Society, the revival of a group that had been founded by Benjamin Franklin nearly a quarter of a century earlier. Through the Society Thomas came to know many of the most prominent men of Philadelphia including Franklin, John Dickinson and Charles Thomson. Together, these four men would soon play a pivotal role in the founding of their new nation.[9]

Thomas, who was short, well-built and handsome, was one of the youngest and clearly one of the most ambitious of this elite group.[10] What also set him apart from many of his older colleagues was his exceptional oratory. As one biographer states: "He was through life noted for his fervid eloquence...his tongue was often unloosed, and never without instant and electric effect."[11] By the early 1770s, Thomas decided to merge his natural talents and impressive contacts by seeking public office. Like John Hancock, Thomas proved to be a natural politician long before the profession was fully appreciated. In 1772, he won his first of four consecutive elections to the Pennsylvania Assembly, one of only two members from the city of Philadelphia. His popularity steadily increased.

To avoid the summer heat, many prominent Philadelphia families sought refuge along the New England coast. In July 1773, while the Mifflins were vacationing at Newport, Rhode Island, Thomas attended his maternal grandfather's funeral in Boston. He took the opportunity to introduce himself to several local politicians. After their meeting on July 15, John Adams described Thomas as "a very sensible and agreable Man...an easy Speaker--and a very correct Speaker."[12] Those brief social encounters provided the foundation for productive working relationships in the months and years ahead. For example, when news of the Boston Tea Party reached Philadelphia, Thomas sent Sam Adams a letter of congratulations on December 27, 1773, in which he described their own success in forcing the tea ships out of Philadelphia.

When Britain unleashed its wrath on Massachusetts by imposing the Intolerable Acts,[13] Thomas, Charles Thomson, John Dickinson and Joseph Reed took the lead in organizing Philadelphia's response. Despite sizable public support, they could not persuade most merchants to engage in yet another disastrous boycott of British goods. Thomas broke the news to Sam Adams on May 21, 1774, explaining the impasse and urging that a continent-wide congress be called first. "When we are thus united in Councils what Measure prudent & salutary may we not effect..."[14] Thomas' argument ultimately prevailed and Virginia took the lead in calling for a Continental Congress to meet in Philadelphia early that fall.

After overcoming enormous opposition from Governor Penn and

Speaker Galloway, the State Assembly finally met on July 22, 1774. Thomas was the youngest of the six members of the Pennsylvania legislature who were initially selected as delegates to the First Continental Congress.[15] Since the meetings were to be held only a few blocks from his home, Thomas wasted no time in greeting the distinguished visitors when they arrived. On Monday evening, August 29, 1774, he and several other delegates, including Thomas McKean, drove five miles out of town to meet the Massachusetts delegation, including his old friends, John and Sam Adams. In his diary, John Adams remembered the event as being "most cordially wellcomed to Philadelphia."[16]

Thomas also hosted both large and small dinner parties in honor of the delegates. Again, like Hancock, Thomas was truly in his element when presiding over lavish banquets at his Philadelphia mansion. As John Adams recorded in his diary on his first full day in Philadelphia (Tuesday, August 30, 1774), we "call'd at Mr. Mifflins--a grand, spacious, and elegant House. Here We had much Conversation with Mr. Charles Thompson [Thomson]..." Two days later Thomas hosted Adams, Thomson and Robert Treat Paine for breakfast, and the following day (Friday, September 2), Adams recorded that he "Dined at Mr. Thom. Mifflins with Mr. Lynch, Mr. Middleton, and the two Rutledges with their Ladies...We were very sociable, and happy. After Coffee We went to the Tavern, where we were introduced to Peyton Randolph Esqr., Speaker of Virginia..."[17]

On Saturday, Adams again "Spent the Evening at Mr. Mifflins with Lee and Harrison from Virginia, the two Rutledges, Dr. Witherspoon, Dr. Shippen, Dr. Steptoe and another Gentleman. An elegant Supper, and We drank Sentiments till 11 O Clock. Lee and Harrison were very high..." By Monday morning, when the Continental Congress officially opened, Thomas was well known to most of his colleagues, especially those from Massachusetts, Virginia and South Carolina.

Throughout the next two months, Thomas continued to entertain his fellow delegates. George Washington, for example, "Dined at Mr. Thos. Mifflin's" on September 13 and again "spent the Evening at Mr. Mifflin's" on October 17.[18] Others, including Silas Deane of Connecticut, recorded similar engagements.[19]

From the moment the delegates assembled at Smith's City Tavern and marched to Carpenter's Hall, Thomas, one of the youngest members, clearly identified with the more "radical" faction.[20] As a merchant and patriot, he took a leading role in helping to create the Continental Association, the comprehensive boycott of imported British goods that would later extend to a prohibition on American exports, as well.[21]

On October 3, 1774, in the midst of congressional deliberations,

Thomas was overwhelmingly reelected for a fourth term to the Pennsylvania Assembly. John Adams shared the good news with his wife: "The Spirit and Principles of Liberty, here, are greatly cherished...The Elections of the last Week in this City, prove this...The Broadbrims [Quakers] began an opposition to your Friend Mr. Mifflin, because he was too warm in the Cause. This instantly alarmed the Friends of Liberty and ended in the Election of Mr. Mifflin, by Eleven hundred Votes out of Thirteen, and in the Election of our Secretary Mr. Charles Thompson to be a Burgess with him. This is considered here as a most compleat and decisive Victory in favour of the American Cause."[22] Thomas Cushing, another Massachusetts delegate, wrote that the election of Mifflin and Thomson was "A good sign that the people are hearty in the Cause of Liberty."[23]

As a result of the election, conservative Delegate Joseph Galloway was soon ousted as Speaker of the Pennsylvania Assembly and his influence in Congress was further diminished.[24] In contrast, Thomas' stature in both Congress and his state had never been greater despite the growing divide between his aggressive policies and the Quaker community.

The Continental Association was approved in its final form on October 18, and signed by the delegates, including six current or future Presidents of Congress--Randolph, Middleton, Jay, McKean, Mifflin & Lee--on October 20.[25] Thomas had played a critical role in its creation. During the next week, Congress approved an Address to the People of Great Britain, a Memorial to the Inhabitants of the British Colonies, an Address to the Inhabitants of Quebec and a Petition to the King. Congress then adjourned on Saturday, October 22, 1774.

Thomas immediately shifted his attention to local developments. On December 10, the Pennsylvania Assembly unanimously approved the proceedings of the First Continental Congress, the first colonial legislature to do so. The Assembly also reelected most of its delegates, including Thomas, to the Second Continental Congress which was scheduled to convene in May. After the Assembly adjourned, the more radical Philadelphia Committee issued a call for another provincial convention, similar to one that had been held the previous year.

The Second Pennsylvania Convention (January 23-28, 1775) also endorsed the work of Congress and resolved to support the Association's boycott. One month later, the Assembly reconvened and was forced to deal with Governor Penn's proposal that Pennsylvania petition the King for a redress of grievances, independent of Congress. Thomas and his fellow radicals were able to defeat the combined forces of Galloway and the Governor and the Assembly rejected the motion prior to adjournment on March 18.[26] Writing to a fellow delegate in Pennsylvania, Charles Lee of

Virginia described developments from his perspective: "The damn'd slow, heavy quakering Nag, your province...If it had not been for the smart whip of my friend Mifflin, I believe she never would have advanced a single inch."[27]

Events took a dramatic turn on April 19, 1775, as the first shots of the American Revolution were fired on Lexington Green. News of the carnage reached Philadelphia on Monday, April 24. The next day nearly 8,000 citizens turned out for a massive Town Meeting. Of all the speakers, Thomas issued the clearest challenge to the crowd: "Let us not be bold in declarations, and afterwards cold in action. Let not the patriotic feelings of to-day be forgotten to-morrow, nor have it said of Philadelphia, that she passed noble resolutions, slept upon them, and afterwards neglected them."[28]

True to his word, Thomas immediately helped to organize a militia, including some fellow Quakers, who became known as "The Quaker Blues." His initial rank was "Major" but, as John Adams commented at the time, he "ought to have been a general" because he served as the "animating soul" of the movement.[29] In just over a year, he was. The Quaker elders, however, were not as impressed by Thomas' military ardor. Three months later they declared that Thomas "hath separated himself from religious fellowship with us."[30] It was a price he was clearly willing to pay.

When the Second Continental Congress assembled on Wednesday, May 10, 1775, the focus had shifted from politics to the military situation rapidly unfolding in Boston. Steps were taken to create a Continental Army and, thanks largely to John Adams' instigation, a former Virginia militiaman and fellow delegate, George Washington, was unanimously selected on June 15 as America's first Commander-in-Chief.[31] Prior to his departure, Gen. Washington selected Thomas as his Aid-de-Camp. On June 21, John Adams described the eager new officer to an old friend in Massachusetts: "Major Mifflin goes in the Character of Aid-de-Camp to General Washington. I wish You to be acquainted with him, because, he has great Spirit Activity, and Abilities, both in civil and military Life. He is a gentleman of Education, Family and Fortune."[32]

The next day, Sam Adams wrote home to James Warren to inform him that Major General Charles Lee and Major Thomas Mifflin would be accompanying General Washington to Boston. Adams added that it was "A Triumvirate you will be pleasd with."[33] That same day Silas Deane penned a glowing report to his wife in Connecticut: "Mr. Mifflin of whom I have often spoke is...Aid de Camp as I hear to the General. He is my particular Friend, & am happy in the Thought that you will be able to return some of the many Civilities I have received from him in this City.

If ever there was true Spirit & patriotism in Man he possesses them."[34] Even cantankerous old Roger Sherman of Connecticut described Thomas as "...a very Useful member of this Congress...an upright, firm, Spirited and Active Friend in the Cause of Liberty."[35]

And thus, on June 23, 1775, John Adams described the historic tableau that morning as Washington rode off to glory: "The Three Generals [Washington, Lee and Schuyler] were all mounted, on Horse back, accompanied by Major Mifflin...Such is the Pride and Pomp of War." Adams then indulged in one of his periodic bouts of self-pity: "I, poor Creature, worn out with scribbling, for my Bread and my Liberty, low in Spirits and weak in Health, must leave others to wear the Lawrells which I have sown; others, to eat the Bread which I have earned.--A Common Cause."[36]

In Boston, Thomas longed for military glory but his critical role at Washington's right hand made such assignments unlikely. Once, however, Thomas did persuade his chief to appoint him to head a small band of militia to ward off a detachment of British soldiers who were scavenging for cattle. William Rawle, Thomas' first biographer (1829), recorded that General Craig had told him directly that Craig "never saw a greater display of personal bravery, than was exhibited on this occasion in the cool and intrepid conduct of Colonel Mifflin."[37] Thomas was also popular with the ladies. Abigail Adams confided, tongue-in-cheek, that "I do not know whether her [Mrs. Mifflin] husband is safe here...You hear nothing from the ladies but about Major Mifflin's easy address, politeness, complaisance, etc. 'Tis well he has so agreable a lady at Philadelphia."[38]

On July 4, 1775, Washington reorganized important components of the Army, including the establishment of a Quartermaster General to oversee the purchase of military supplies. Even though he was under intense pressure to appoint a Massachusetts man, Washington selected Thomas for this nearly impossible and thankless task.[39] Once again, Thomas' battlefield dreams would be deferred for the good of the cause. Like Elias Boudinot (Commissary of Prisoners), Thomas accepted duty over honor.[40] Richard Henry Lee heartily approved of the selection as he confided to Washington that September: "I think you could not possibly have appointed a better Man to his present Office than Mr. Mifflin. He is a singular Man, and you certainly will meet with the applause and support of all good men by promoting and countenancing real Merit and public virtue, in opposition to all private interests..."[41] Months later, Sam Adams explained to a friend that "Mr. M[ifflin]s Character stood so high that no Gentleman could hesitate to put him into a place which was understood to be vacant & which he was so well qualified to fill."[42]

In late December, President Hancock informed Washington that Congress had promoted Thomas to the rank of Colonel."[43] At the same time, Thomas grew deeply concerned over some of the business dealings of his relatives as they impacted his office. To his cousin Jonathan he wrote: "I hope and pray that you will not leave me by your new project under the Necessity of quitting a Service in which I trust I am of some Consequence... your proposition has alarmd me exceedingly."[44] Three months later, however, rumors started to circulate and Washington confided to Joseph Reed that "I have taken occasion to hint to a certain gentleman in this camp, without introducing names, my apprehensions of his being concerned in trade. He protests most solemnly that he is not, directly nor indirectly, and derives no other profit than the Congress allows him for defraying the expenses, to wit, 5 per cent, on the goods purchased."[45] Despite Thomas' best efforts, the bond between the two men was beginning to unravel.

Earlier, as winter approached and the guns grew silent, Mrs. Washington, Mrs. Mifflin and several of the other wives arrived in Boston. Despite the circumstances, Thomas and his wife hosted some of the most memorable parties of the season. In January 1776, as John Adams was preparing to return to Philadelphia, he first "dined at C[olonel] Mifflins at Cambridge with G. Washington, and Gates and their Ladies, and half a Dozen Sachems and Warriours of the french Cocknowaga Tribe, with their Wives and Children...It was a Savage feast...Yet they were wondrous polite."[46]

On March 17, 1776, after Gen. Washington had successfully utilized cannons that had been captured earlier at Forth Ticonderoga, the British evacuated Boston. Their ships, however, stood just out of cannon range beyond the harbor for another ten days. Finally, on March 27, the enemy set sail for Halifax.[47] Boston would never again be attacked.

Washington left for New York on April 4, ordering Thomas to provide barracks and, "in short, every necessary Article for the public Service, and which, your Experience in the last Campaign convinces you, will be wanted for that now approaching."[48] At the same time, in a letter to Gen. Putnam, Washington set aside his concerns when he referred to Thomas as a man of "excellent Talents."[49] As preparations continued for the New York Campaign, Washington, Gates and Mifflin were summoned to Philadelphia to consult with Congress. While there, Gates was promoted to Major General and Thomas was elected Brigadier General on May 16.[50] Seven weeks later, Congress proclaimed Independence.

Gen. Nathanael Greene, Joseph Ward and other New Englanders were disgruntled by the fact that so few military promotions were going to Northerners. It was only the opening salvo in a protracted battle between

Greene and Mifflin. In response, John Adams reported to Greene that: "Mifflin was a Gentleman of Family and Fortune in his Country, of the best Education and Abilities, of great Knowledge of the World, and remarkable Activity. Besides this, the Rank he had held as a Member of the Legislature of this Province, and a Member of Congress...and especially his activity and Success in infusing into this Province a martial Spirit and ambition which it never felt before, were thought Sufficient Causes for his Advancement."[51]

Before leaving Philadelphia on June 5, Thomas resigned his office of Quartermaster General in the hope of playing a more exciting role in the upcoming battle for New York. Finally, on June 29, he was placed in charge of two Pennsylvania battalions which General Heath later described as "the best disciplined of any troops that I have yet seen in the army."[52]

In late August, when Washington was forced to evacuate 9,500 troops from Long Island to Manhattan in the dead of night, Thomas was ordered to use his men to cover the withdrawal lest the British discover their retreat. In mid course, Thomas received verbal orders to join in the escape. When Thomas met up with the Commander-in-Chief, Washington cried out: "Good God ! General Mifflin ! I am afraid you have ruined us by so unseasonably withdrawing the troops from the lines." Thomas heatedly replied that "I do so by your order." "It cannot be !" exclaimed Washington. "By G--, I did !...I had orders through him [Seammel, Washington's aide de camp]." "it is a dreadful mistake," rejoined Washington. Thomas and his men hurried back to their post and later that night were among the last to cross the East River, but the memory of his confrontation with Washington made a lasting impression on him as did the humiliating retreat.[53]

Throughout September 1776, Washington's army was gradually forced to withdraw from New York under massive British pressure. As a result, the Commander-in-Chief made a number of staff changes. Since the new Quartermaster General proved unsuited to the task, Washington prevailed on Thomas to resume his former position, "confident that there was not another man in the army who could carry on the business upon the present large plan." With deep reluctance, Thomas accepted.[54] On October 1, Congress made the reappointment official.

Response from individual members of Congress was overwhelmingly positive. William Ellery of Rhode Island wrote that "The Quarter Master General Moylan was persuaded by the Committee to resign and Brigadier Genl. Mifflin to accept that office with the Rank and Pay of Brigadier General. This Appointment will give great Satisfaction to the Army; for Gen. Mifflin is not only well acquainted with the Business of the Office, but he hat Spirit and Activity to execute it in the proper Manner."[55] Sam

Adams told a friend that "We have an excellent Commissary & Quarter Master General, officers of great Importance. Mifflin, who servd so much to our Advantage in the latter of these Employments, has condescended to take it again though he had been promoted to the Rank & Pay of a Brigadier General."[56]

By October 10, Thomas had returned to Washington's temporary headquarters at Harlem Heights just above New York City. In the face of the growing British threat, the Americans retreated further to White Plains where they were attacked by Gen. Howe, the British Commander, on October 28. Washington, in accordance with the wishes of Congress, then divided his already inferior forces as he led part of his army across the Hudson to Hackensack, New Jersey. Many of the troops left behind failed to hold their positions and were captured. According to military historian Craig L. Symonds: "All in all it had been a disastrous campaign. Washington lost New York City and over 4,000 men to the enemy." [57]

For the Quartermaster General it was hell. Not only did Thomas try desperately to meet the urgent needs of his fleeing comrades, but large quantities of "Artillery, Cannon, Stores, Provisions and their Baggage" were lost when the British overran forts in New York and New Jersey.[58] From the center of the storm, Thomas shared his doubts and frustration in a letter to Robert Morris: "The bad policy of attempting to make a stand at Mt Washington is now evident. I...was never more surprised or shagrined than when I heard that post was reinforced instead of being dismantled and abandon'd...the unhappy affair of Mount Washington has totally changed the Face of the Campaign and may probably encourage the Enemy to push forward until they are rebuff'd...The situation of Philad^a is in my opinion critical."[59]

Congress shared Thomas' deep concern over Philadelphia's safety. On November 14, the Board of War informed Gen. Washington that "...judging that immediate Steps were necessary to be taken for the preservation and Defence of this City...As Genl. Mifflin has a considerable Influence in this place, the Board judge it for the Interest of the Service that he be immediately order'd to this City, where his Exertions we doubt not will turn out to the Advantage of our Cause."[60]

On Sunday evening, November 24, Thomas arrived in Philadelphia to join with Gen. Putnam in taking command of its defenses. President Hancock informed Gen. Washington two days later that "The Congress have ordered General Mifflin to stay in this City until you shall require his Attendance at Head Quarters..."[61] Delegate William Hooper of North Carolina poured out his despair to a friend: "Washington again and again has asked the Militia from this. Not a man moves...Mifflin...is now here...

to rouse them from their Lethargy--but it is a torper from which they never will awake but in bondage. We do not deserve to be saved...Heaven they say fights for them, well that it does for they attempt nothing for themselves."[62] On December 6, George Read of Delaware sounded a slightly more encouraging note when he reported that "The Delegates of Maryland with Genl Mifflin harangued a great Number perhaps 6 or 700 of them [soldiers who had served out their enlistment] in the State House Yard yesterday with Success and it is expected a great part will return for a Month."[63]

With so few troops at his command, Thomas reluctantly urged Congress to adjourn to Baltimore lest the British take them by surprise. Delegate Oliver Wolcott shared this alarming news with his wife in a priceless example of 18th Century understatement: "...upon the advice of Genl. Putman and Mifflin...it was judged that the Council of America ought not to Sit in a place liable to be interrupted by the rude Disorder of Arms."[64] While Congress fled to safety in mid-December,[65] Thomas briefly returned to Washington's headquarters in New Jersey with 1,500 new militia.[66] He then went back to Pennsylvania to continue his recruitment efforts as far west as Lancaster. The sense of desperation was dramatically underscored in Washington's December 18 letter in which he told his brother that if replacements could not be found, "I think the game is pretty near up."[67] Against all odds, however, Thomas did find them. Robert Morris reported to President Hancock in late December, that Thomas' efforts to raise more troops had proven to be "a Successful excursion."[68] On Christmas Day, the Americans crossed the Delaware River and surprised the British at Trenton. That fateful year ended with renewed hope against almost insurmountable obstacles.

While raising critically needed new recruits[69] Thomas also continued his heavy responsibilities as Quartermaster General. But on February 4, 1777, Robert Morris informed President Hancock that Congress "has not a farthing to give him [Mifflin], therefore his whole operations must be at a stand until he can be supplied."[70] The only thing Congress could grant him was one final military promotion. Thomas' superhuman efforts were gratefully acknowledged on February 19, 1777, when he was named Major General.[71]

More than ever, Thomas hoped to transform his new rank into a battlefield command since he felt that his bifurcated responsibilities were increasingly impossible to maintain. In mid-March Thomas informed Congress that "In the last Campaign my Time was divided between the Command of a Brigade, and the Duties of the Qr Mr Genls Department...I will always strive to execute with Success every Command of Congress--At the same time I hope that some One Line will be marked out for me..."[72] In reality, neither Congress nor Washington could spare Thomas from either of his major duties. As President Hancock wrote to Gen. Washington that April, Congress decided "to detain Genl. Mifflin in this City for some Time knowing his Popularity and Influence to be very great..."[73]

The British finally did conquer the American Capital in October 1777. Congress fled to Lancaster and then on to York, Pennsylvania as Thomas joined his wife in Reading. Totally exhausted and deeply discouraged, Thomas threw his career into reverse when he wrote to Congress on October 8, 1777, that "My Health is so much impaired...that I consider myself as a very useless Officer: & think it my Duty to return to Congress their commission to me of Major & Quarter Master General...I am still warmly attached to the Cause of my Country and determined to exert myself in its Defence as far as my Health and Situation will permit...and hope in all Things to prove myself a sincere Patriot."[74]

Because Congress could find no one remotely qualified and willing to assume the duties of Quartermaster General through that bitter Valley Forge Winter it requested that Thomas continue in that thankless post which he had already held for a total of 26 months (in late December, however, it assigned that responsibility to an ineffective ad hoc committee of Congress).[75] It also refused to accept Thomas' resignation as a Major General. Instead, on November 7, Congress appointed Thomas to be a member of a newly created Board of War[76] where he urged that his friend, Gen. Horatio Gates, the hero of that fall's American victory at Saratoga, should be named the Board's President.[77] As one delegate wrote: "It is deemd of very great importance, as You will readily perceive by the members appointed."[78]

It was during these turbulent times that Gen. Conway shared with Thomas his deep concerns over the military's deplorable situation. Conway denounced what he termed "childish schemes" to attack the British in Philadelphia and argued that "saving the shattered remains of this naked army, which is melting every day..." should be the highest priority.[79] Many both in and out of Congress shared Conway's concerns about Washington's ability to turn the tide,[80] but others, such as President Henry Laurens, Hancock's successor, stood solidly behind the Commander-in-Chief and denounced those who sowed dissent.[81]

For two centuries, historians have argued over the depth of Thomas' direct involvement in what became known as the "Conway Cabal." John Laurens, the President's son who served as Washington's latest Aide-de-Camp, never doubted that Thomas was "at the head" of the click.[82] Researchers at the Library of Congress finally resolved this critical question in 1981 when they were able to identify Thomas Mifflin as the author of the following letter to Gen. Gates (November 17, 1777): "You have savd our Northern Hemisphere, and in Spite of our consummate & repeated Blundering you have changed the Constitution of the Southern Campaign on the part of the Enemy from Offensive to Defensive...Repeated Slights & unjustifiable Arrogance combind with other Causes to drive form the Army those who would not worship the Image & pay an undeservd Tribute of Praise & Flattery to the great & powerful...We have had a noble Army melted down by illjudgd Marches--Marches that disgrace their Authors & Directors--& which have occasiond the severest & most just Sarcasm & Contempt of our Enemies. How much are you to be envied my dear General? How different your Conduct & your Fortune!"[83]

As word of the Cabal reached Washington, Thomas' relationship with the commander further deteriorated. Gen. Nathanael Greene had by now become Washington's favorite and Thomas' political rival. James Lovell predicted as early as October 1777 that "By the Winter the middle Army will be divided into Greanites & Mifflineans, if Things do not take a great Turn from their present Situation."[84] Thomas, who knew Washington well, did not view his comments as personal attacks but rather as desperately needed constructive criticism at a moment of crisis. "...I have spoken my sentiments on public maters with decency and firmness," Thomas stated, "But I have seen...that General Washington's judgment in military points was frequently counteracted by what I believed a dangerous influence." That "dangerous influence" was, in Thomas' opinion, Gen. Greene.[85]

The cauldron continued to bubble over in late January 1778, when Congress ordered Thomas to turn over all records and receipts pertaining to the Quartermaster General's office. Five weeks later, Gen. Greene was named as Thomas' successor.

Thomas devoted most of that spring to preparing the materials requested. On May 15, 1778, he informed Congress that the accounts under his direct supervision were ready for review. The Auditor-General, however, insisted that the report must include a detailed account of all funds transmitted to his deputies, as well. On June 11, after a heated four hour debate, Congress voted to conduct a full military inquiry into the Quartermaster's department and, if necessary, a court martial. The two factions were now in open warfare as Thomas urged the military, and ultimately Congress, to begin the inquiry as quickly as possible in order to clear his name.

On August 10, 1778, Thomas informed President Laurens that "I am prepared to Defend my own Conduct as Quarter Master General; and that the Officers who acted under me in that department, are ready to answer any Charges which may be made against them--"[86] One week later Thomas took matters into his own hands when he informed the President that "I have borne for a long time the most bitter Calumny; and have suffered the most abusive Lies, against my Character...I consider an immediate, public, unbiassed Enquiry into the causes of the Army's distresses last winter [Valley Forge] absolutely necessary...I now enclose my Commission of Major General, which I request you to present to Congress, with my most respectful resignation of the same...I do not mean to fly from any Enquiry... On the Contrary, I shall...most cheerfully appear before any Committee appointed by them for that purpose--"[87] Thomas then printed his recent correspondence with Congress in the August 20 issue of the *Pennsylvania Packet* and publicly demanded that Congress afford him the opportunity to clear his name.[88]

Despite the doubts planted by his enemies, that September Congress appropriated another million dollars for Thomas to use in order to settle any outstanding accounts. And yet, Congress still refused to schedule an inquiry and Washington dismissed the notion of a court martial since Thomas had already resigned his commission. No formal hearing was ever held as the political nature of the charges eventually played themselves out.[89] Benjamin Rush summed up the unhappy saga in a letter to David Ramsay in November 1778: "We destroy *reputation* which is dearer to a military man than life itself, CONWAY--MIFFLIN & [Charles] Lee were sacrificed to the excessive influence & popularity of *One Man*...Where is the republican Spirit of our country?"[90] It is also ironic that Gen. Greene, the new Quartermaster General who eagerly fanned the flames in 1778, also resigned the Quartermaster position two years later claiming, like Thomas, that it was "injurious to my health, harassing to my mind, and opposed to my military pursuits."[91]

By the summer of 1779, the storm clouds of the Conway Cabal had largely blown over. Henry Laurens, no long President, even referenced Thomas in a letter that July without any hint of his earlier animosity.[92] On January 24, 1780, President Samuel Huntington informed Thomas that he, Gen. Schuyler and Col. Pickering had been appointed by Congress to serve as Commissioners 'to enquire into the expences of the staff departments."[93] The Commissioners had the authority "to call in any of the Officers thereof for Information, to discharge all persons therein that are supernumerary or delinquent...& to adopt a general Reformation of the Departments."[94] Schuyler declined the appointment, but Mifflin and Pickering submitted a lengthy report on March 27, 1780.[95]

Throughout most of 1779-1782, however, Thomas focused on the Pennsylvania State Assembly which was bitterly divided between westerners who supported the populist constitution of 1776 (which included a plural executive), and wealthy easterners, like Thomas, who fought for a more conventional form of government.

When he was attacked in the press for supposedly profiting during his service as Quartermaster General, Thomas vigorously responded in an open letter in the Pennsylvania *Gazette* on February 6, 1782. He pointed out that he had previously "inherited & had acquired some degree of independence both of fortune and spirit." Thomas went on to demonstrate that his pay during that period brought him no wealth. He concluded by reminding his fellow citizens that "My pen (when unknown to you) and my voice have roused many of you into action in the beginning of the controversy, before you saw the impending danger."[96]

Once Thomas and his political allies were back in power in the State Assembly, he was reelected to Congress on November 12, 1782. Eight days later Thomas presented his credentials to the newly elected President, Elias Boudinot.[97]

Despite progress at the Paris Peace Conference, many delegates still shared Alexander Hamilton's fear that "In all probability the war will not end here and to carry it on we require absolutely more solid arrangements of finance."[98] To supply that desperately needed revenue--and thereby reassure foreign nations that America could repay its loans--Congress had established a duty on imported goods. Rhode Island refused to participate. Thomas' first assignment now that he had returned to Congress was as a member of a three-person congressional delegation to persuade the Rhode Island legislature to meet its obligation.[99] Just as they left Philadelphia for Providence on December 22, Thomas and his colleagues received word that Virginia had rescinded its approval. The mission was suspended and the financial crisis continued.[100] Thomas was also appointed to a committee to begin "collecting every book & tract which related to American Antiquities and the affairs of the U. S. since many of the most valuable of these were every day becoming extinct." When that motion was voted down, it was proposed that at least the most essential books should be acquired. That, too, was defeated because of Congress' financial plight.[101]

On October 31, 1783, as Congress prepared to welcome the first Dutch Minister to America's temporary capital in Princeton, word arrived that the definitive peace treaty had been signed in Paris early that September.[102] The following Monday, November 3, marked the start of the new congressional year. Even though he was not present, Thomas was elected that morning as the 10th President of the Continental Congress. Thomas Jefferson described the selection a few days later: "The rule of rotation had reduced the choice of a President to Pennsylvania, Rhode Island and N. Carolina.

The choice fell pretty unanimously on General Mifflin." To another friend, Jefferson noted that Pennsylvania "being displeased with the departure of Congress it was thought this choice would be soothing to them."[103] Congress then voted to reconvene in Annapolis in December.

During the interim, Thomas received word from his predecessor that the final Peace Treaty had arrived and that it must be ratified and returned to Europe by March 3, 1784. Since it took a minimum of two delegates from nine States to constitute a quorum, Thomas immediately wrote to the Governors, urging them to stress to their members "the necessity of their attending in Congress as soon as possible."[104]

When the Continental Congress did reassemble in the Maryland Capitol on December 13, 1783, only seven States were fully represented with one additional delegate each from New Hampshire and South Carolina.[105] On the evening of December 22, during that hopeful yet intensely frustrating period, two hundred attended "an elegant public dinner" in Gen. Washington's honor, followed by a ball at the State House.[106] The next day, at noon, the General surrendered his military commission to President Mifflin. As a delegate from Maryland recorded: "The spectators all wept, and there was hardly a member of Congress who did not drop tears. The General's hand which held the address shook as he read it."[107]

Following Washington's departure, Thomas returned to his office that same day to pen yet another desperate message to the missing States, reminding them that "the ratification of the definitive Treaty and several other matters of great national concern are now pending before Congress which require the utmost dispatch and to which the assent of at least nine States is necessary."[108] The next day Thomas wrote again to the Governors of New Jersey and Connecticut.[109] He also informed the Governor of Delaware that one of his delegates was threatening to leave to attend to personal business.[110] Early in January 1784, Thomas even sent his private secretary, Col. Josiah Harmar, to meet with Governor Livingston of New Jersey in a desperate attempt to rally new delegates.[111] At one point, delegates from the States already in attendance even debated the possibility of ratifying the Treaty with only seven votes, but the idea was quickly rejected.[112]

A quorum of nine States was finally established on Wednesday, January 14, 1784, and the definitive Treaty of Peace between the United States of America and his Britannic Majesty was unanimously ratified by the Continental Congress that same morning. (Thomas was the only one of the fourteen Presidents of the First American Republic who actually cast a ballot on this seminal document.) Following the vote, Thomas signed a formal Proclamation "enjoining the strict and faithful observance thereof and published an earnest recommendation to the several States in the very words of the fifth Article [pertaining to the restitution of all confiscated property belonging to British subjects]."[113] As President, Thomas also wrote to the Governors (including his presidential predecessor, Governor John Hancock of Massachusetts), the Peace Commissioners (including his predecessors John Jay and Henry Laurens), and the French Minister, enclosing copies of the Treaty and Proclamation.

Since there were only seven weeks left before the newly approved Treaty had to be exchanged with the British Government, Col. Harmar was again called into service with instructions to deliver the Treaty to the American Peace Commissioners in Paris with all possible speed.[114] Because of the uncertainty of sea travel, two additional copies were also dispatched on other vessels. Like Thomas Jefferson, many feared that Britain "might hope for some favorable opportunity of changing the face of the treaty. And if the ratifications are not there by the day she will have too much ground for objection to the validity of the treaty..." In the end, none of the three messengers reached Paris by the March 3 deadline.[115] The British, however, did not use the delay as a pretense for reopening negotiations even though Congress did not receive this news for several months. The ratified Peace Treaties were ultimately exchanged in Paris on May 12, 1784. The War was truly over and Independence had been won.[116]

In a profound sense, the ratification of the Peace Treaty in early 1784 also marked the beginning of the end of the Continental Congress. Historian John Fiske described the five years that followed as "The Critical Period of American History."[117] Now that the common enemy had been defeated and the imminent threat of execution removed, many of the revolutionary leaders and their respective States began to drift apart through self-interest. The glue that had bound the confederacy through nearly impossible challenges no longer held. Three days after the Treaty was ratified, Congress again lost its quorum and was unable to officially reconvene until March 1. During that period, Delegate James Tilton of Delaware confided that "the situation of Congress is truly alarming; the most important business pending and not states enough to take it up; whilst those present are fatigued into resentment and almost despair, with loitering away their time, to little purpose, while waiting for others to come."[118] As President, Thomas faced the daunting challenge of holding his new nation together now that it had won its Independence.

The delegates who remained in Annapolis next turned their attention to the many unresolved issues pertaining to relations with the Native Americans. On February 10, those present approved a Resolution, instructing Gen. Schuyler to inform the Six Indian Nations that they "may be assured of the protection of the United States, so long as they continue in the peaceable disposition which they now manifest" and that Congress "will hold a meeting, for settling a general treaty with the Indian nations" as soon as circumstances permit.[119]

Unfortunately, without a quorum, congressional prerogative was extremely limited. Once again, Thomas was forced to plead with the Governors of New Hampshire, New York, New Jersey, Delaware, Maryland, North Carolina and Georgia: "I think it a duty I owe to the office I am honoured with, as well as to the Union, to inform your Excellency... that the great business of the United States is at a stand, for want of a representation agreeable to the Articles of Confederation...there are many matters of the highest importance to the safety, honour, and happiness of the United States, which require immediate Attention. Among these I need only mention the establishing a general peace with the Indians, and settling the western territory, the arranging our foreign Affairs, and taking measures for securing our frontiers, preserving our stores and Magazines; making requisitions for the expences of the current year and for satisfying the public Creditors...and, that the Members present... are very impatient under their situation."[120]

A quorum was finally established on Monday, March 1, 1784. Jonathan Blanchard, the new Delegate from New Hampshire, wrote that evening: "To day I have attended Congress & had the honour of dining with the President...there are 9 States now Represented in Congress."[121] The first order of business was the appointment of Indian Commissioners. On March 6, Thomas immediately notified those who had been selected, including his former nemesis, Nathanael Greene, who subsequently declined the appointment.[122] Unfortunately, Thomas was ill from March 9 through 13.[123] At first, Congress adjourned from day to day, but, on Friday, March 12, Congress decided to proceed with debate in the President's absence and elected Thomas Jefferson of Virginia to serve as temporary chairman.[124] (It was the only time in United States history that a President of the Second American Republic presided over the Continental Congress.) On Monday, March 15, President Mifflin resumed the chair as the debate over Indian negotiations continued.[125]

By April 1, congressional finances had reclaimed top priority as Thomas sent a circular letter to the States concerning "the most urgent necessity." He informed the Governors that "The State of our finances is such as to require the united efforts of Congress and of the several States for obtaining immediately a supply of money, to prevent the loss of public credit....Congress think it their duty to communicate the matter confidentially to the Supreme Executive of each State; and to request in the most pressing terms their influence and exertion to furnish with all possible dispatch, on requisitions unsatisfied, their respective quotas of the sum mentioned..."[126]

The financial crisis also had major international implications. The Minister of France wrote to Congress on April 9 "requesting to know what measures had been taken by the United States, relative to the payments of the principal and interest of the loan[s]...furnished [and guaranteed] by his Most Christian Majesty..."[127] In response, Thomas tried to assure him that "supplementary requisitions on the States will be adopted to provide for the interest of the loans aforesaid for the present year, and that the greatest care will be taken by subsequent measures for the punctual payment of the principle and interest as they may respectively become due..."[128]

Implementation of the terms of the Peace Treaty was also high on the congressional agenda. In mid-May, Thomas wrote to Gen. Henry Knox concerning the removal of British Posts "within the Territories of the United States" which were still occupied by foreign troops.[129] At the same time, the British repeatedly complained about America's reluctance to compensate British subjects for their confiscated property. On May 11, Congress also adopted instructions for negotiation of commercial treaties. Not surprisingly, European powers demanded to know if they were dealing with thirteen seperate governments, or just one.[130]

Exhausted after almost continuous service since 1775, Congress decided in late April to invoke Title X of the Articles of Confederation which permitted a "Committee of the States" to oversee national affairs during a congressional recess.[131]

On May 29, the powers of that committee were enumerated and on Thursday, June 3, 1784, the Delegates officially Resolved "That the thanks of Congress be given to his Excellency Thomas Mifflin, for his able and faithful discharge of the duties of President..."[132] The Continental Congress adjourned late that night until the fall. The Committee of the States (which, like Congress, needed nine States to constitute a quorum, but, unlike Congress, required only one member from each State) met the next day and elected Samuel Hardy of Virginia to serve as its Chairman. It then adjourned until July and ultimately disbanded in mid-August, for lack of a quorum.[133]

Before heading home, Thomas traveled to Mount Vernon to pay his respects to the Washingtons.[134] He then briefly returned to Annapolis before plunging back into the rough and tumble of Pennsylvania politics. The local Republican faction with which Thomas identified did so poorly in that fall's elections even he lost his campaign for the State Assembly and thereby any prospect of returning to Congress to complete his presidential term. One year later, however, the voters did return Thomas to the Assembly where he was elected Speaker in October 1785. For the rest of his life, Thomas was continuously elected to State office.[135] Again, like Hancock, his secret to success was to stand above the legislative fray.

By the end of 1786, as the crisis of national leadership continued to intensify, most of the States had agreed to send representatives back to Philadelphia in order to amend the Articles of Confederation. As Speaker, it is hardly surprising that Thomas was tied for the most votes of the seven delegates elected by the Pennsylvania Assembly.[136] Thomas was also one of only two Presidents of the First Republic (the other being Nathaniel Gorham of Massachusetts) who served on what came to be known as the Constitutional Convention.

The Pennsylvania Delegation (which soon expanded to eight members) was immensely impressive. Serving with Thomas were Robert Morris (whose financial magic had somehow kept the Congress and the Army alive through their darkest days), Gouverneur Morris and James Wilson (who would leave their indelible mark on the final document), and that quintessential American, Benjamin Franklin.

On Sunday afternoon, May 13, 1787, "Generals Mifflin, Knox and Varnum--splendid on their mounts, swords at their sides, in their old blue-and-buff uniforms--rode to Chester, Pennsylvania to personally escort Gen. Washington's coach to Philadelphia."[137] The Convention, however, did not open until Friday, May 25, 1784; late, of course, for lack of a quorum. The following Monday Thomas and Franklin presented their credentials.[138] William Pierce, a Georgia Delegate, recorded this brief sketch of his colleague: "General Mifflin is well known for the activity of his mind, and the brillancy of his parts. He is well informed and a graceful Speaker. The General is about 40 years of age [actually 43], and a very handsome man."[139]

Thomas attended the daily sessions which stretched into mid-September and he no doubt entertained many of his fellow delegates, as always; but, his oratorical powers were better suited to motivating large gatherings rather than the minutia of constitutional construction. According to James Madison's journal, Thomas spoke only once when he seconded a Motion by Charles Pinckney of South Carolina that "the members of each House shall be incapable of holding any office under the U. S. for which they or any...others for their benefit receive any salary, fees, or emoluments of any kind--and the acceptance of such office shall vacate their seats respectively."[140] According to Professor Forrest McDonald's analysis of this debate, Thomas was thereby intellectually and politically aligned with

Alexander Hamilton, Nathaniel Gorham, and his fellow Pennsylvanians, James Wilson and Gouverneur Morris.[141]

Another author describes an anecdote in which Thomas helped to reinforce the Convention's strict secrecy rule. One morning, as he was entering the State House, Thomas found a handwritten copy of the Virginia Plan which had apparently fallen out of a fellow delegate's pocket. Thomas privately presented the document to Washington, who was serving as President of the Convention. At the end of that day's session, Washington scolded the members for their carelessness as he "flung the paper down on a desk..." The "culprit" was never identified.[142]

On Monday morning, September 17, 1787, the delegates to the Convention met one last time. The engrossed constitution was read to the members and one final amendment was unanimously approved. Benjamin Franklin then rose to urge its adoption despite his own hesitations on several points. "...the older I grow," Franklin said, "the more apt I am to doubt my own Judgment, and to pay more Respect to the Judgment of others."[143] Edmund Randolph, the Governor of Virginia, then addressed his colleagues with regret because, unlike Franklin, he could not support the document. Randolph, the favorite nephew and "adopted son" of the first President, was one of only three that day who withheld consent. One by one, 37 Delegates, including Thomas, then came forward to sign the proposed constitution.[144]

That document was then sent to the Continental Congress (which was still meeting in New York City) with the request that copies be forwarded to each of the States for special ratification conventions. Most of the Delegates then adjourned to City Tavern where Thomas Mifflin, George Washington and their old colleagues had gathered just over thirteen years earlier on the opening day of the First Continental Congress.[145]

On September 28, 1787, after a heated debate, Congress did as requested and forwarded copies of the proposed constitution to the thirteen States without any recommendation. On December 7, by a unanimous vote, Delaware became the first to ratify. In Pennsylvania, the perpetual political battles denied Thomas and most of his fellow national delegates seats at the State Ratification Convention. Nevertheless, on December 12, 1787, Pennsylvania also approved the Constitution by a vote of 46 to 23 along strict Federalist/Anti-Federalist lines. New Hampshire's approval on June 21 of the next year gave the Constitution the nine States required for activation.[146] (Rhode Island, which had not attended the Convention, became the last State to ratify when it approved the Constitution on May 29, 1790, by only two votes.)

By October 1788, Thomas was back in the majority when the voters of Philadelphia County elected him as one of the three members of the

Supreme Executive Council, the plural executive under Pennsylvania's peculiar State Constitution. At that time, Benjamin Franklin had been serving as President of that Council and thereby de facto Governor. When Franklin stepped down because of age, Thomas was elected to replace him as President of Pennsylvania on November 8, 1788, and reelected to that position in October 1789.[147] One month later, the Pennsylvania Constitutional Convention opened and Thomas Mifflin was elected President of that body, as well. (Thomas McKean, the seventh President of the Continental Congress and Chief Justice of Pennsylvania, served as Chair of the Convention's Committee of the Whole.) As the debate over a new State Constitution continued, the nation suffered a tremendous loss when Benjamin Franklin died on April 17, 1790. That summer, Thomas also lost his dear wife, Sarah, after 23 years of marriage.[148] By the time the new Pennsylvania Constitution was signed on September 2, 1790, Thomas embarked on the final decade of his life, more popular than ever, but alone.

In typical Pennsylvania fashion, political winds shifted again during the brief campaign for Governor under the new 1790 State Constitution. Several of Thomas' allies, including Robert Morris and Benjamin Rush, threw their support to Major General Arthur St. Clair (another former President of the Continental Congress). At the same time, a speech by Colonel Jacob Morgan in support of Thomas (which was reported in the *Pennsylvania Gazette* on September 22, 1790) underscored Thomas' popularity: "...as a servant of the Union, he has fought her battles, and presided in her councils--while, as a citizen of Pennsylvania, he has introduced system and accuracy into the Legislature, and order and energy into the Executive Department of the Government..." In the end, the election wasn't even close. Thomas carried every county in the State and won the city of Philadelphia by a vote of 1,761 to 96.[149]

For the next nine years, Thomas served three consecutive three-year terms as Governor of Pennsylvania. Combined with his two previous years as President of the State, Thomas still has the record for having been Pennsylvania's Chief Executive longer than any person since Independence. When the national government returned to Philadelphia in 1790, awaiting the construction of its permanent home on the Potomac, Thomas, as Governor, lived most of that decade only a short stroll from both his presidential predecessor, Elias Boudinot (a member of the new Congress), as well as President Washington.

Now a widower, Thomas' public stature was tempered by his mounting financial problems. Contrary to earlier baseless charges, Thomas was not one of those officials who, in the words of Henry Laurens, "make patriotism the stalking horse to their private Interests."[150] Instead, like Jefferson after him, Thomas demonstrated an unholy disregard for the almighty dollar. Benjamin Rush noted in his diary that Thomas "lived beyond his income, and was much in debt." Charles Biddle, who often served as Thomas' financial lifeline, confirmed that Thomas was "frequently embarrassed for money, of which he was extravagant and thoughtless."[151] (Again, he bore a remarkable resemblance to John Hancock, except for the fact that only Hancock could afford such a lavish lifestyle.) It was also widely rumored that Thomas had a drinking problem. Secretary of the Treasury Oliver Wolcott, in a letter to his predecessor, Alexander Hamilton, reported that "The governor is a habitual drunkard. Every day, and not unfrequently in the forenoon, he is unable to articulate distinctly."[152] If this was true, his exceptionally talented and dedicated young executive secretary, Alexander James Dallas, carefully covered for his mentor whenever possible.[153]

During his first term as Governor, finances were at the top of the State's agenda. Thomas was extremely fortunate that his legislative partner on this issue was State Representative Albert Gallatin, a brilliant man who later served as United States Secretary of the Treasury.[154] Just months prior to his reelection in 1793, however, Philadelphia was plagued by two new crises. The first began in triumph. On May 16, 1793, Citizen Genet, the Minister of the First French Republic, received a tremendous welcome to America's Capital. As Governor and a lifelong Francophile, Thomas presided over a number of banquets in honor of the French Revolution. In response, Genet overplayed his hand and ultimately alienated the Washington Administration and forced Thomas to reevaluate his public support, as well.

And then, in August 1793, as Thomas began his reelection campaign, Philadelphia was hit by a severe Yellow Fever epidemic. Public officials as well as average citizens fled the city. Despite Thomas' aggressive efforts to curtail the epidemic and his support for measures advocated by the College of Physicians, only the onset of cold weather brought the disease to an end. By mid-October, the city's population had been reduced by nearly ten percent but the citizens of the State remained loyal to their Governor. Thomas won an overwhelming vote, loosing only two counties.[155]

Thomas' second term was dominated by the Whiskey Rebellion in Western Pennsylvania which was triggered by the National Government's new tax on distilled spirits which hit that region's economy especially hard. Beneath the surface, it represented a delicate balance between State and National authority in the new Federal system, once again straining relations between the Governor and the President. On August 2, 1794, President Washington called a conference at his Market Street mansion which included both Thomas Mifflin and his Chief Justice, Thomas McKean, as well as Alexander Hamilton. As a noted Washington biographer described the two key players, Thomas "was as old a fox as Washington..."[156] It is, therefore, not surprising that the meeting ended in stalemate. Thomas urged the President to let State Courts continue to take the lead before employing the militia. Washington urged quicker action. Their disagreement prompted a series of letters between the two executives, but Thomas assured the President that if the judiciary proved unable to handle the crisis, then he would support "the most vigorous co-operation of the whole force which the constitution and Laws of the State entrust to me for the purpose of compelling a due obedience to the Government."

When the Courts failed to force compliance, Thomas did join with the Governors of Virginia and Maryland in calling out their State Militias.[157] Their combined forces totaled nearly 15,000 men. As they marched west toward Allegheny County under President Washington's orders, the insurrection collapsed. At the opening of the Pennsylvania Assembly on December 6, 1794, Thomas announced that "Law, order and tranquility have been restored in the western Counties of the State..."[158]

Only a few months after the rebellion had been suppressed, Foreign Policy reemerged as the primary issue facing the Nation and the States. In March 1795, Chief Justice John Jay returned from his difficult negotiations with the British concerning implementation of the Peace Treaty as well as commercial interests. Popular response to the Jay Treaty was overwhelmingly negative, especially in cities such as Philadelphia which still favored their former French allies. Thomas vocally opposed the Treaty, but suffered no serious consequences when Washington gave it his support. The Treaty was finally ratified by the Senate on June 24, 1795.[159]

Following the pattern of their lives, Mifflin and Washington once again shared the stage the next year when Thomas, who had served several terms as President of the Pennsylvania Chapter of the Society of the Cincinnati, was elected by its members as Vice President of the national Society under Washington, the Society President.[160]

In October 1796, Thomas ran uncontested for his third and final term as Governor. One month later, his support for Jefferson also helped to win Pennsylvania for the new Democratic-Republican Party. But, on December 20, 1796, the date of Thomas' inauguration, "a severe indisposition" prevented him from attending his own swearing-in ceremony. A delegation was hurriedly sent to his mansion to deliver the oath of office. One week later the Philadelphia *Gazette* attributed the Governor's sudden illness to his mounting financial problems. Charles Biddle, who once again came to Thomas' rescue, pointed out that it wasn't just the Governor's lavish lifestyle, but that "he could not refuse it to any of his friends who called to borrow."[161]

Most of the Governor's final months in office were largely devoted to combating the recurring outbreaks of Yellow Fever in 1797 and 1798, and to implementing a series of improvements pertaining to the public's health. In his final address to the State Assembly on December 7, 1799, Thomas spoke from the new State Capital in Lancaster, congratulating Philadelphia's health officials for their dedicated service and the legislators for their critical support. He then acknowledged "with heartfelt gratitude, the public kindness, confidence, and support, which I have uninterruptedly enjoyed for the greater portion of an active and anxious life."[162]

Because of his own poor health, Thomas turned down several offers to seek election to the Federal Congress which would soon reconvene in the new national capital but, out of financial necessity as well as his love of public service, Thomas did accept nomination to the Pennsylvania State House where he had begun his political career nearly three decades earlier. On December 17, 1799 (three days after Washington's death), Thomas relinquished the Governor's office to his friend and former presidential colleague, Thomas McKean, as he himself took up his new duties in the State House of Representatives.

After only four weeks in the Assembly, however, Thomas fell ill and, early on Monday, January 20, 1800, he died. At noon the following Wednesday, Thomas was buried at Trinity Lutheran Church in the heart of the new capital of Lancaster. His faded white tombstone is still imbedded in the side of the church just to the left of the main entrance. Beneath it now stands a bronze plaque placed there in 1987 by the Daughters of the American Revolution to commemorate the Signers of the United States Constitution.

Perhaps the best description of Thomas Mifflin, the man and the patriot, flowed from the pen of John Adams during the early days of the Revolution: "You Speak of a General Mifflin who was young in Experience, and in the service. I wish our Massachusets Collonels, old as they are, had as much Activity and as extensive Capacities and accomplishments as that young General...He has the utmost Spirit and Activity, and the best Education and Abilities. He is of one of the best Families and has an handsome Fortune in his Country. He has been long a Member of the Legislature here, and of Congress. He was long the most indefatigable and successful Supporter of the American Cause in his Province...and has infused a martial Spirit into a People who never felt any Thing like it before. You can Scarcely name a Man any where who has more Signal Merit."[163]

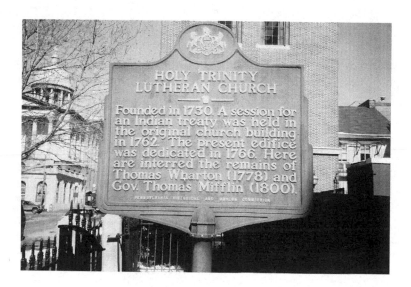

The German Lutheran Church in Lancaster, Pennsylvania where President Thomas Mifflin was laid to rest on January 22, 1800. (Neither marker even mentions that he served as President of his new nation.)

WHILE THOMAS MIFFLIN WAS PRESIDENT

November 1783 - June 1784

On November 4, 1783, the day after Thomas Mifflin was elected President, the Continental Congress discharged most of the Continental Army, "except 500 men, with proper officers."[164] It then adjourned as the delegates eagerly withdrew from their cramped quarters in Princeton. The following June, meeting in Annapolis, Congress completed the process when it dismissed the remaining Continental troops "except 25 privates to guard the stores at Fort Pitt, and 55 to guard the stores at West Point."[165] Philosophically, the Founding Fathers still feared the potential threat of standing armies. Realistically, there were simply no funds to cover the cost.

On January 8, 1784, Congress debated a petition from the Quakers which called for the suppression of the slave trade. The committee report resolved that "this address from so respectable a part of the people...[is] a testimony of their sincere concern for the rights of mankind, and of their respect for those with whom the powers of Government are entrusted." Congress then sidestepped its own responsibility by recommending "to the legislature of the several States to enact such laws as to their wisdom may appear best calculated" to conform to Article 2 of the Continental Association of October 1774 (the original boycott which had pledged to "wholly discontinue the slave trade").[166]

Congress also grappled over the critical position of Secretary for Foreign Affairs, an office that had been vacant for a year during which time the work load had been divided between the President and Secretary Thomson. On May 7, 1784, former President John Jay, one of the American Peace Commissioners still in Paris, was elected to undertake that assignment.[167] It was months before Jay even learned of his selection and not until late December that he was sworn into office.

Despite the ongoing struggle to establish and maintain a quorum, the Articles of Confederation forced Congress to reject the credentials of the delegates from Delaware who had exceeded their three-year term limit.[168] It was yet another example of how the adoption of the Articles, ratified in February 1781, actually threatened the effectiveness of Congress.

The delegates from Rhode Island would also have faced the same fate if Congress had not recessed during the summer.[169]

British politics was equally chaotic during this transition period. The coalition ministry of Lord North and Charles James Fox, who were bitter opponents, only survived for a year before William Pitt the Younger (son of "The Great Commoner") swept them from power in a landslide election in March 1784. Pitt's triumph was rooted in his image as a patriot rather than merely a politician (not unlike his famous father's early success as a populist before he sacrificed his reputation for the title Earl of Chatham). Since Fox was known for his opposition to the King, Pitt's victory also marked the momentary resurgence of George III despite the loss of his American Empire.[170] Once again, politics made very strange bedfellows.

In this tumultuous atmosphere, Britain and America began to quarrel over the implementation of the Peace Treaty's terms before the ink had dried. The United States repeatedly charged that the British were not honoring their commitment to evacuate their frontier forts "with all convenient speed."[171] In response, Parliament demanded that Congress must fulfill its obligation to urge the States to restore confiscated estates to British subjects.[172] The debate raged on for another decade and seriously hindered America's goal of renewing pre-Independence commercial relations with the United Kingdom.

Franco-American relations had also shifted with the signing of the Treaty. As prominent historian Richard B. Morris reported, the French archives "confirm the impression...that France was unenthusiastic about seeing a strong and viable new nation emerge across the Atlantic."[173] For example, in the dispute between the United States and Spain over free access to the Mississippi River, France clearly sided with its European neighbor. In the end, of course, the French monarchy paid the ultimate price for its calculated and costly support of the Americans when revolutionary fever spread to Paris less than five years later.

Chapter 10

President
THOMAS MIFFLIN
of
PENNSYLVANIA

Notes

Abbreviation Key

JCC   Journals of the Continental Congress
LDC   Letters of Delegates to Congress
PHL   The Papers of Henry Laurens

[1] L. H. Butterfield, Editor, Diary and Autobiography of John Adams, (The Belknap Press, Cambridge, 1961), Vol. 3, pp. 321-325. The fact that Washington returned his commission to civilian authority and retired to public life also confirmed John Adams' rationale in personally orchestrating Washington's selection as Commander-in-Chief in June 1775.

[2] Gaillard Hunt, Editor, JCC: 1774-1789, (Government Printing Office, Washington, DC, 1922), Vol. XXV, p. 838.

[3] Dumas Malone, Editor, Dictionary of American Biography, (Charles Scribner's Sons, New York, 1943), Vol. XII, p. 606.

[4] As cited in William Rawle, Sketch of the Life of Thomas Mifflin, Memoirs of the Historical Society of Pennsylvania, Vol. II, Part II, (E. Litell, Philadelphia, 1830), p. 108.

[5] As cited in Malone, op. cit., p. 606.

[6] Paul H. Smith, Editor, LDC: 1774-1789, (Library of Congress, Washington, DC, 1976), Vol. 1, p. 155; John Adams to Abigail Adams, October 7, 1774.

[7] Silas Deane to Elizabeth Deane, September 1775; as cited in Kenneth R. Rossman, Thomas Mifflin and the Politics of the American Revolution, (The University of North Carolina Press, Chapel Hill, 1952), p.44.

[8] Rossman, op. cit., pp. 8-9.

[9] Benjamin Franklin was not only the dominant politician of Philadelphia but also the best known American in Europe because of his 15 years in London as the lobbyist for several American colonies. John Dickinson had just acquired continent wide fame as the author of the "Letters from a Pennsylvania Farmer" which denounced the British Government's repeated attempts to imposed taxes on the colonies. Charles Thomson

would soon be referred to as the "Sam Adams of Philadelphia." During the upcoming period of the Continental Congress, he served as its only Secretary for its entire 15 year history (see Chapter 15).

[10] Rossman, op. cit., p. 11.

[11] William C. Armor, Lives of the Governors of Pennsylvania: 1609-1873, (T. H. Davis & Co., Norwich, CT, 1874), p. 275.

[12] Butterfield, op. cit., Vol. 2, p. 84. Thomas' maternal grandfather is refered to as "Mr. Bagnall of this Town."

[13] See Introduction for details pertaining to the Intolerable Acts.

[14] Thomas Mifflin to Sam Adams, May 21, 1774; Sam Adams Papers, as cited in Rossman, op. cit., p. 21.

[15] LDC, Vol. 1, pp. xxx-xxxi.

[16] Butterfield, op. cit., Vol. 2, p. 114.

[17] Butterfield, op. cit., Vol. 2, pp. 118-119. See also LDC, Robert Treat Paine's Diary, Vol. 1, p. 13.

[18] John C. Fitzpatrick, Editor, The Diaries of George Washington: 1748-1799, (Houghton Mifflin Company, Boston, 1925), Vol. II, pp. 164-168.

[19] LDC, Vol. 1, p. 139.

[20] Ned Rutledge, 25, from South Carolina was the youngest delegate. John Jay of New York was next in line at the age of 28. Thomas Mifflin was 30.

[21] JCC, op. cit., Vol. 1, pp. 75-81.

[22] LDC, Vol. 1, p. 155; John Adams to Abigail Adams, October 7, 1774.

[23] LDC, Vol. 1, p. 142; Thomas Cushing to Deborah Cushing, October 4, 1774.

[24] LDC, Vol. 1, p. 156. Galloway's dream of being elected the first President of Congress was crushed on opening day when Peyton Randolph of Virginia was selected. That same day, Charles Thomson, Galloway's political nemesis, was elected to serve as Secretary of Congress. See Chapter 1.

[25] JCC, op. cit., Vol. 1, pp. 75-81.

[26] Rossman, op. cit., pp. 38-39.

[27] Charles Lee to Robert Morris, January 27, 1775; as cited in Rossman, op. cit., p. 38.

[28] Rawle, op. cit., pp. 110-111.

[29] As cited in Malone, op. cit., p. 607.

[30] As cited in Rossman, op. cit., p. 41; the Quaker comdenmation was issued on July 28, 1775.

[31] JCC, op. cit., Vol. II, p. 91. Knowing he was personally unpopular, John Adams often orchestrated major events behind the screen as in the selection of Washington. He convinced Thomas Johnson of Maryland to make the formal nomination. See also: Butterfield, op. cit., Vol 3, pp. 322-323.

[32] LDC, Vol. 1, p. 529; John Adams to Cotton Tufts, June 21, 1775.

[33] LDC, Vol. 1, p. 531; Sam Adams to James Warren, June 22, 1775.

[34] LDC, Vol. 1, p. 532; Silas Deane to Elizabeth Deane, June 22, 1775.

[35] LDC, Vol. 1, p. 599; Roger Sherman to Joseph Trumbull, July 6, 1775.

[36] LDC, Vol. 1, pp. 536-537; John Adams to Abigail Adams, June 23, 1775. Thanks to David McCullough's majestic biography of John Adams, the "Atlas of the Revolution" is finally receiving at least some of the glory that he has so richly deserved for over two centuries.

[37] Rawle, op. cit., p. 111.

[38] Abigail Adams to John Adams; as cited in Rossman, op. cit., p. 44.

[39] James Thomas Flexner, George Washington: In the American Revolution (1775-1783), (Little, Brown and Company, Boston, 1968), Vol. 2, p. 37.

[40] See Chapter 9.

[41] LDC, Vol. 2, p. 66; Richard Henry Lee to George Washington, September 26, 1775.

[42] LDC, Vol. 3, p. 474; Samuel Adams to Joseph Palmer, April 2, 1776.

[43] LDC, Vol. 2, p. 509; John Hancock to George Washington, December 22, 1775.

[44] As cited in Rossman, op. cit., p.48; Thomas Mifflin to Jonathan Mifflin, December 20, 1775.

[45] John C. Fitzpatrick, Editor, The Writings of Washington, Vol. VII, p. 301; George Washington to Joseph Reed, March 25, 1776.

[46] Butterfield, op. cit., Vol. 2, pp. 226-227.

[47] Flexner, op. cit., Vol. 2, p. 83.

[48] The Writings of Washington, Vol. IV, pp. 429-430; George Washington to Thomas Mifflin, March 24, 1776.

[49] The Writings of Washington, Vol. IV, p. 443; George Washington to Israel Putnam, March 29, 1776.

[50] JCC, op. cit., Vol. IV, p. 359.

[51] LDC, Vol. 4, pp. 620-621; John Adams to Nahanael Greene, August 4, 1776.

[52] As cited in Washington Irving, Life of George Washington, (G. P. Putnam & Co., New York, 1855), Vol. II, p. 308.

[53] Irving, op. cit., p. 333.

[54] LDC, Vol. 5, p. 294; Caesar Rodney to Thomas Rodney, October 2, 1776.

[55] LDC, Vol. 5, p. 308; William Ellery to Nicholas Cooke, October 5, 1776.

[56] LDC, Vol. 5, p. 390; Samuel Adams to Samuel Mather, October 26, 1776.

[57] Craig L. Symonds, A Battlefield Atlas of the American Revolution, (The Nautical & Aviation Publishing Company of America, Inc., 1986), p. 29.

[58] LDC, Vol. 5, p. 529; Samuel Chase to the Maryland Council of Safety, November 23, 1776.

[59] As cited in Rossman, op. cit., p. 68; Thomas Mifflin to Robert Morris, November 21, 1776.

[60] LDC, Vol. 5, p. 483; Board of War to George Washington, November 14, 1776.

[61] LDC, Vol. 5, p. 546; John Hancock to George Washington, November 26, 1776.

[62] LDC, Vol. 5, p. 553; William Hooper to Joseph Hewes, November 29, 1776.

[63] LDC, Vol. 5, pp. 582-583; George Read to Gertrude Read, December 6, 1776.

[64] LDC, Vol. 5, p. 606; Oliver Wolcott to Laura Wolcott, December 13, 1776.

[65] JCC, op. cit., Vol. VI, p. 1027.

[66] The Writings of Washington, Vol. VI, p. 352.

[67] The Writings of Washington, Vol. VI, p. xxx; George Washington to XXX Washington, December 18, 1776.

[68] LDC, Vol. 5, p. 682; Robert Morris to John Hancock, December 27, 1776.

[69] LDC, Vol. 7, p. 194; John Adams to Abigail Adams, June 14, 1777: "Mifflin made an Harrangue...The Citizens by loud shous and Huzzas, promised him to turn out, and accordingly, they met him in great Numbers Yesterday."

[70] LDC, Vol. 6, p. 214; Executive Committee to John Hancock, February 4, 1777.

[71] JCC, op. cit., Vol. VII, p. 133. Arthur St. Clair of Pennsylvania, the 13th President of the Continental Congress, was also promoted to Major General at the same time.

[72] The Papers of the Continental Congress: 1774-1789, M247, r179, i161, p. 8; Thomas Mifflin to John Hancock, March 12, 1777.

[73] LDC, Vol. 6, p. 651; John Hancock to George Washington, April 25, 1777.

[74] The Papers of the Continental Congress: 1774-1789, M247, r179, i161, p. 16; Thomas Mifflin to John Hancock, October 8, 1777.

[75] JCC, op. cit., Vol. IX, p. 1065. See also: LDC, Vol. 10, p. 75, Footnote No. 1. Thomas Mifflin served as Quartermaster General from August 1775 to June 1776, and again from September 1776 to November 1777, for a total of 26 months.

[76] LDC, Vol. 8, pp. 244-245; Henry Laurens to Thomas Mifflin, November 8, 1777 (two letters of the same date).

[77] LDC, Vol. 8, p. 313.

[78] LDC, Vol. 8, p. 341; William Williams to Johathan Trumbull, Sr. The Board of War initially consisted of Horatio Gates, Thomas Mifflin, Timothy Pickering, Joseph Trumbull & Richard Peters.

[79] As cited in Rossman, op. cit., p. 92; Thomas Conway to Thomas Mifflin, October 13, 1777.

[80] LDC, Vol. 8, pp. 329-331; James Lovel to Horatio Gates, November 27, 1777. See also: Vol. 9, p. 265, Footnote No. 2.

[81] See Chapter 4.

[82] LDC, Vol. 8, p. 549, Footnote No. 6; John Laurens to Henry Laurens, January 3, 1778.

[83] LDC, Vol. 8, pp. 314-315 Footnote; Thomas Mifflin to Horatio Gates, November 17, 1777. It provides the "firm proof of [Mifflin's] active direction of the campaign to displace Washington..."

[84] LDC, Vol. 8, pp. 57-58; James Lovell to Horatio Gates, October 5, 1777.

[85] Thomas Mifflin to Colonel Delany, February 1, 1778; as cited in Armor, op. cit., p. 283.

[86] The Papers of the Continental Congress: 1774-1789, M247, r179, i161, p. 40; Thomas Mifflin to Henry Laurens, August 10, 1778.

[87] The Papers of the Continental Congress: 1774-1789, M247, r179, i161, p. 52; Thomas Mifflin to Henry Laurens, August 17, 1778.

[88] LDC, Vol. 10, p. 447, Footnote No. 1.

[89] LDC, Vol. 10. p. 75, Footnote No. 1; Henry Laurens to George Washington, June 11. 1778.

[90] Benjamin Rush to David Ramsay, November 1, 1778.

[91] Rossman, op. cit., p. 160.

[92] LDC, Vol. 13, p. 315; Henry Laurens to John Laurens, July 31, 1779.

[93] LDC, Vol. 14, pp. 367-368; Samuel Huntington to Thomas Mifflin, January 24, 1780.

[94] LDC, Vol. 14, p. 371; Elbridge Gerry to James Warren, January 25, 1780.

[95] JCC, op. cit., Vol. XVI, pp. 293-311.

[96] *Pennsylvania Gazette*, February 6, 1782; as cited in Rossman, op. cit., p. 174.

[97] JCC, op. cit., Vol. XXIII, p. 739.

[98] LDC, Vol. 19, p. 481; Alexander Hamilton to John Laurence, December 12, 1782.

[99] JCC, op. cit., Vol. XXIII, p. 772.

[100] LDC, Vol. 19, p. 510, Footnote No. 2.

[101] LDC, Vol. 19, pp. 603-604; James Madison's Notes of Debates, January 24, 1783.

[102] See Chapter 5.

[103] LDC, Vol. 21, pp. 150-151; Thomas Jefferson to Francis Eppes, November 10, 1783 and Thomas Jefferson to Isaac Zane, November 8, 1783.

[104] LDC, Vol. 21, p. 162; Thomas Mifflin to Certain States, Novembe 23, 1783.

[105] LDC, Vol. 21, p. 222. The States represented by at least two delegates on December 13, 1783 were: Massachusetts, Rhode Island, Pennsylvania, Delaware, Maryland, Virginia & North Carolina.

[106] Edmund Cody Burnett, The Continental Congress, (The Macmillan company, New York, 1941), pp. 590-591.

[107] LDC, Vol. 21, p. 221; James McHenry to Margaret Caldwell, December 23, 1783.

[108] LDC, Vol. 21, p. 222; Thomas Mifflin to Certain States, December 23, 1783.

[109] LDC, Vol. 21, pp. 230-231; Thomas Mifflin to Certain States, December 24, 1783.

[110] LDC, Vol. 21, p. 231; Thomas Mifflin to Nicholas Van Dyke, December 24, 1783.

[111] LDC, Vol. 21, p. 258; Thomas Mifflin to William Livingston, January 4, 1784.

[112] LDC, Vol. 21, p. 243; Pennsylvania Delegates to john Dickinson, December 30, 1783.

[113] JCC, op. cit., Vol. XXVI, p. 30. See also: LDC, Vol. 21, p. 275; Thomas Mifflin to the Chevalier de La Luzerne, January 14, 1784.

[114] JCC, op. cit., Vol. XXVI, pp. 22-29. The nine States eligible to vote were: Massachusetts, Rhode Island, Connecticut, Pennsylvania, Delaware, Maryland, Virginia, North Carolina and South Carolina. New Hampshire and New Jersey were only represented by one delegate each and therefore ineligible to vote. New York and Georgia were not in attendance.

[115] LDC, op. cit., Vol. 21, p. 763, Footnote No. 1. Josiah Harmar finally delivered the original ratified Peace Treaty to Benjamin Franklin in Paris on March 29, 1784;

[116] Burnett, op. cit., pp. 593-594.

[117] John Fiske, The Critical Period of American History: 1783-1789, (Riverside Press, Cambridge, 1898).

[118] As cited in Burnett, op. cit., pp. 595-596; James Tilton to Nicholas Van Dyke, February 16, 1784.

[119] JCC, op. cit., Vol. XXVI, pp. 73-74.

[120] LDC, Vol. 21, pp. 371-372; Thomas Mifflin to Certain States, February 20, 1784.

[121] LDC, Vol. 21, p. 395; Jonahan Blanchard to Josiah Bartlett, March 1, 1784.

[122] LDC, Vol. 21, p. 422; Thomas Mifflin to the Indian Commissioners, March 6, 1784.

[123] LDC, Vol. 21, p. 426; New Hampshire Delegates to Meshech Weare, March 11, 1784.

[124] JCC, op. cit., Vol. XXVI, p. 133.

[125] LDC, Vol. 21, p. 450, Footnote No. 2. "Appropriation of Indian lands was justified, according to official policy, because the Indians had been, as some of them acknowledge, agressors in the war without even a pretense of provocation, a view so widely shared that it seems to have escaped critical examinaiton."

[126] LDC, Vol. 21, p. 469; Thomas Mifflin to the States, April 1, 1784.

[127] LDC, Vol. 21, p. 535, Footnote No. 2.

[128] LDC, Vol. 21, p. 534; Thomas Mifflin to the Chevalier de La Luzerne, April 21, 1784.

[129] LDC, Vol. 21, p. 619; Thomas Mifflin to Henry Knox, May 15, 1784.

[130] Fiske, op. cit., p. 160.

[131] Henry Steele Commager, Editor, Documents of American History, (Appleton-Century-Crofts, New York, 1963), p. 115.

[132] JCC, op. cit., Vol. XXVII, pp. 505 & 553. On June 1, 1784, Congress resolved "that on the adjournment of the present Congress, the duties of their President cease; and that when the United States assemble pursuant to such adjournment, or in consequence of a call from the Committee of the states, his Excellency Thomas Mifflin, do resume the chair."

[133] Burnett, op. cit., pp. 607-609. See also: JCC, op. cit., Vol. XXVII, pp. 636-638.

[134] LDC, Vol. 21, p. 679; Samuel Hardy to Charles Thomson, June 11, 1784.

[135] Rossman, op. cit., p. 183.

[136] Rossman, op. cit., pp. 185-186.

[137] Charles L. Mee, Jr., The Genius of the People, (Harper & Row, Publishers, New York, 1987), p. 42. See also, Irving, op. cit., Vol. IV, pp. 494-495.

[138] Gaillard Hunt and James Brown Scott, Editors, The Debates in the Federal Convention of 1787 Which Framed the Constitution of the United States of America: Reported by James Madison, (Prometheus Books, Buffalo, 1987), Vol. 1, pp. 17-18.

[139] Arthur Taylor Prescott, Editor, Drafting the Federal Constitution, (Louisiana State University Press, 1941), p. 28.

[140] Hunt, op. cit., Vol. 2, pp. 395-396.

[141] Forrest McDonald, Novus Ordo Seclorum: The Intellectual Origins of the Constitution, (University Press of Kansas, Lawrence, 1985), pp. 199-200.

[142] Christopher Collier and James Lincoln Collier, Decision in Philadelphia, (Random House, New York, 1986), p. 84.

[143] Bernard Bailyn, Editor, The Debate on the Constitution, Part One, (The Library of America, New York, 1993), p. 3.

[144] Mee, op. cit., pp. 277-283. The final amendment, which was introduced by Nathanier Gorham, increased the number of members in the new House of Representatives. In addition to Edmund Randolph, George Mason of Virginia and Elbridge Gerry of Massachusetts also refused to sign. Only 37 Delegates were actually present to sign the Constitution on September 17, 1787. John Dickinson's signature was added that same day by George Read at Dickinson's request since he had left Philadelphia the preceeding weekend.

[145] See Chapter 1.

[146] Saul K. Padover, To Secure These Blessings, (A Washiington Square Press/Ridge Press Book, New York, 1962), p. 43.

[147] Albert S. Bolles, Pennsylvania: Province and State, (Burt Franklin Press, New York, 1970), Vol. 2, p. 112.

[148] Rossman, op. cit., pp. 190-191.

[149] Rossman, op. cit., pp. 194-196.

[150] Laurens, op. cit., Vol. 12, p. 271, Henry Laurens to John Laurens, January 8, 1778.

[151] As cited in Rossman, op. cit., p. 194. Charles Biddle was the father of Nicholas Biddle, the founder of the Bank of the United States and arch-enemy of President Andrew Jackson a generation later.

[152] Oliver Wolcott to Alexander Hamilton, as cited in Rossman, op. cit., p. 300.

[153] James Grant Wilson and John Fiske, Editors, Appletons' Cyclopaedia of American Biography, (D. Appleton and Company, New York, 1887), Vol. II, p. 58. In 1814, President

James Madison appointed Alexander James Dallas as his Secretary of the Treasury. See also, Rossman, op. cit., p. 207-208.

[154] Malone, op. cit., Vol. VII, p. 105.

[155] Rossman, op. cit., pp. 215-231.

[156] Flexner, op. cit., Vol. 4, p. 166.

[157] Irving, op. cit., Vol. V, p. 214.

[158] Rossman, op. cit., pp. 265-266.

[159] Commager, op. cit., p. 165.

[160] Rossman, op. cit., pp. 200-201. The Society of the Cincinnati was an organization of former Revolutionary War Officers. It was a very prestigious group that was, at the same time, denounced by other powerful men who saw it as an attempt to create a class system in America similar to the strict social divisions in Britain.

[161] Rossman, op. cit., pp. 276-279.

[162] Rossman, op. cit., pp. 305-306.

[163] <u>LDC</u>, Vol. 5, pp. 28-29; John Adams to Joseph Ward, August 20, 1776.

WHILE THOMAS MIFFLIN WAS PRESIDENT

Notes

Abbreviation Key

JCC   Journals of the Continental Congress
LDC   Letters of Delegates to Congress
PHL   The Papers of Henry Laurens

[164] Gaillard Hunt, Editor, JCC: 1774-1789, (Government Printing Office, Washington, DC, 1922), Vol. XXV, p. 806.

[165] Paul H. Smith, Editor, LDC: 1774-1789, (Library of Congress, Washington, DC, 1994), Vol. 21, p. xvi.

[166] JCC, op. cit., Vol. XXVI, pp. 13-14 & Vol. I, p. 77.

[167] JCC, op. cit., Vol. XXVI, p. 355.

[168] LDC, op. cit., Vol. 21, p. xiv.

[169] LDC, op. cit., Vol. 21, p. 509; William Ellery to Jabez Bowen, April 10, 1784.

[170] J. Steven Watson, The Reign of George III: 1760-1815, (University Press, Oxford, 1960), pp. 271-274.

[171] Henry Steele Commager, Documents of American History, (Appleton-Century-Crofts, New York, 1963), Seventh Edition, p. 119.

[172] Forrest McDonald, E Pluribus Unum: The Formation of the American Republic, 1776-1790, (Liberty Press, Indianapolis, 1979), pp. 132-133.

[173] Richard B. Morris, The Forging of the Union: 1781-1789, Harper & Row, Publishers, New York, 1987), p. 209.

Richard Henry Lee

Chapter 11

President
RICHARD HENRY LEE
of
VIRGINIA

"We Cannot Do Without You"[1]

It is impossible to imagine the early history of the United States without Richard Henry Lee. The scion of one of America's greatest families, he was a born revolution-ary long before the Randolphs and the Washingtons were converted to the cause. For five decades, he cast a giant shadow over the birth of his new nation. A "young Turk" in Virginia's House of Burgesses in the late 1750s, he became a leading colonial voice for American rights in the 1760s. It was Richard Henry Lee who introduced the Resolution for Independence in the Continental Congress in 1776 and, in the mid-1780s, served as its President. Even as the Second Republic took shape during the 1790s, Richard Henry fought for the adoption of a Bill of Rights as a founding member of the new United States Senate.

Richard Henry Lee was not only a remarkable patriot, but, unlike his presidential peers, his efforts were magnified many times over by the closely-knit political family he led. The Sons of Stratford--Richard Henry, Thomas Ludwell, Francis Lightfoot, William and Arthur--worked tirelessly throughout the Revolution as a unique political band of brothers at the state, national and international levels. At several points, Richard Henry and Francis Lightfoot served in the Continental Congress while Thomas Ludwell was a member of the Virginia Assembly and William and Arthur held important diplomatic missions overseas. These siblings even developed their own secret Lee Family cipher for international correspondence.[2] Given their history, it is hardly surprising that Richard Henry and Francis Lightfoot were also the only set of brothers who signed the Declaration of Independence.

Even John Adams spoke in glowing terms of these remarkable siblings when he wrote to a friend in 1779 that "I am no Idolater of that Family or any other: but I believe their greatest fault is having more Men of {*exalted*}

Merit in it, than any other Family. And if that Family fails the American Cause, or grows unpopular among their fellow Citizens, I know not what Family or what Person, will stand the Test."[3] Remarkable praise from the leader of New England's most distinguished clan.

The Lee Family's good fortune took hold the moment Richard Henry's great-grandfather (Richard I) arrived in Jamestown, Virginia in early 1640. The twenty-one year old emigrant was extremely fortunate to have made the Atlantic crossing with the newly appointed governor, Sir Francis Wyatt.[4] During their long voyage the two men obviously bonded and, upon arrival, Richard I was appointed to a position in the secretary of state's office. Shortly thereafter, he further enhanced his prospects by marrying another of his traveling companions, Ann Constable, a member of the Governor's household.[5]

Richard I rose rapidly through colonial government as he easily adapted to Wyatt's successor, Governor William Berkeley. He became Attorney General in 1643 and later Secretary of State. He was also elected to the House of Burgesses and then served for seven years as a member of the Governor's Council, a position in rank second only to the Governor himself. Despite political upheaval throughout the empire during Cromwell's Protectorate, both Gov. Berkeley and Richard I returned to power stronger than ever when King Charles II reclaimed the throne in 1660.[6]

During his career, Richard I placed even greater emphasis on securing his family's financial future. He purchased enormous tracks of land throughout Virginia and Maryland and, according to biographer Paul C. Nagel, he "was among the planters who led in importing Africans as chattel."[7] He also made several trips back to England where he established an estate near London and made arrangements for the education of his sons. In 1662, Richard I returned to America. It was there in Virginia that he died in March 1664, survived by his wife and eight of their ten children. Historian Oliver Perry Chitwood estimates that at the time of his death, Richard I "was probably the richest man in Virginia."[8]

In keeping with his late father's wishes, the eldest son, John, returned to America to execute his father's will. Nine years later, when John died without leaving an heir, Richard II (known as "The Scholar" because of his Oxford education) became head of the family and carried on his father's political legacy. In 1674, Richard the Scholar married Laetitia Corbin, who's family could trace their lineage back to the Norman Conquest in 1066.[9] They had seven children, six of whom survived their father.

Unlike his grandson a century later, Richard the Scholar was conservative by temperament and slow to adapt to the political winds. In time, however, he did accept the reign of William and Mary and regained his family's political standing within the colony.[10] His first love, however, remained his extensive library. This Richard preferred acquiring books to purchasing land. His Potomac River home, known as Machodoc, housed one of the finest libraries in the colonies. In 1715, he died there and was buried at the family graveyard near his home.

Richard the Scholar's fourth son, 25 year old Thomas, received a relatively modest portion of his father's inheritance, but through wit and determination he came to play the dominant role in the next generation of his increasingly well-connected Virginia family. Shortly before his father died, Thomas Lee had been appointed as the interim agent for part of the vast landholdings of the Fairfax family. This assignment afforded him a lucrative income and made it possible for him to purchase choice parcels of land. In 1722, he married Hannah Ludwell, who's mother was part of the distinguished Harrison clan that included President Peyton Randolph's wife.[11]

Thomas and Hannah Lee first lived at Machodoc until their home and his father's library were destroyed by fire in 1729. All that remains today is the family cemetery now known as "Burnt House Field."[12] Thomas Lee ultimately chose a spot about twenty miles upriver as the site for his new plantation. There he built a nearly self-contained community, including more than two hundred slaves and indentured servants, which he named Stratford. The Great House, which still stands today, is a brilliant reflection of Virginia's Planter aristocracy. It is in the shape of an "H" with two clusters of chimneys from which platforms provide majestic views of the Potomac River. Completed around 1738, Stratford was the boyhood home of Thomas and Hannah's six sons and two daughters, including President Richard Henry Lee. (Civil War buffs also know it as the birthplace of Confederate General Robert E. Lee.)[13]

Thomas Lee eagerly assumed his rightful place in colonial politics. Following in his father and grandfather's footsteps, he was elected to the House of Burgesses and later took his seat on the Governor's Council, the third generation of Lees to hold both high offices.[14] Biographer Burton J. Hendrick maintains that Thomas Lee was "the foremost Virginian of his day...in his influence on American history."[15] That was especially true in 1744 when he headed a delegation that negotiated the Lancaster Treaty with the Six Nations of the Iroquois Federation. In exchange for cash and various supplies, the Indians relinquished most of the land between the Ohio and upper Mississippi Rivers which was later known as the Northwest Territory.[16]

Building on his diplomatic success with "these extraordinary people," as Thomas Lee respectfully referred to Native Americans, he next founded the Ohio Company and served as its first president. Membership eventually included four of his sons, several members of the Washington family and other distinguished Virginians who collectively sought to buy vast amounts of the newly "acquired" territory. Other land speculators, such as Lt. Gov. Gooch and Speaker John Robinson, quickly formed rival enterprises which planted the seeds of intense competition that spilled over into the House of Burgesses for decades afterwards. On an even larger scale, the westward expansion which Thomas Lee helped to spark led directly to resistance from Quebec fur traders and the start of the French and Indian War (1754-1763).[17]

Thomas Lee did not live long enough to fully embrace the western empire he so clearly envisioned. He died in 1750 while serving as "The President of Virginia," the title he chose to describe his one year tenure as acting governor. After his death, Philip, his eldest son and primary heir who had spent years of study overseas at Eaton and the Inns of Court, returned to America to settle his father's estate and eventually assume the Lee Family's seat on the Council. As the executor, however, Philip Lee became seriously estranged from most of his siblings.[18] Their political differences were also severe. While five of the sons of Stratford actively opposed Britain's authoritarian policies, Philip remained loyal to the Crown.[19] His death in February 1775, at the start of the Revolution, spared his family enormous turmoil.[20]

Richard Henry, the only Stratford Son who remained close to his brother Philip, had been studying at Wakefield Academy in England for over five years when their father died. He returned to Stratford the following year at the age of 19 and lived there with Philip for the next six years.[21] Even though he had inherited 4,200 acres in Prince William County, Richard Henry preferred Westmoreland County where he eventually rented 500 acres from Philip, three miles down river from Stratford. There he established his permanent home: Chantilly.[22]

In 1757, Richard Henry and his older brother, Thomas Ludwell, married their neighbors Anne and Mary Aylett.[23] Richard Henry, who was born on January 20, 1732 (a month before his fellow Virginian, George Washington), was 25 at the time and eager to make his mark on the world.[24] He and Anne enjoyed eleven years of married life at Chantilly where they raised two sons and two daughters.[25]

The year after his marriage, Richard Henry was elected to the Virginia House of Burgesses for the first time, along with his brothers Thomas Ludwell and Francis Lightfoot. Two of their cousins--Richard Lee and Henry Lee--were also selected from various counties. Since Philip, was then serving on the Governor's Council, the Lee Family's impact on government in 1758 was unmistakable.[26] For the remainder of Virginia's colonial history, one or more Lees remained in the legislature.

Exhibiting more courage than judgment, Richard Henry embarked on his new career in the Burgesses by attacking its most powerful member, Speaker John Robinson, who also held the lucrative office of Treasurer. Richard Henry demanded that these positions be separated and later charged that there was an "enormous deficiency" in the treasury."[27] Battle lines were immediately drawn, based partially on the earlier rivalry over land between Richard Henry's late father and the Speaker. Ultimately, Richard Henry's charges were confirmed in 1766 when Robinson died and an audit uncovered a £109,000 deficit.[28] As a result, the two powerful positions were finally separated, but Robinson's associates never forgave Richard Henry for upsetting the established order of the House. Time and again, these old animosities were revived throughout Richard Henry's long political career.

In 1759, the "young Turk" from Westmoreland County made a frontal assault on yet another sacred institution: the slave trade. According to his grandson's Memoir of the Life of Richard Henry Lee, he proposed "to lay so heavy a duty on the importation of slaves, as effectually to put an end to that iniquitous and disgraceful traffic within the colony of Virginia." His motives were not purely altruistic. "...the importation of slaves into this colony has been," he argued, "and will be attended with effects, dangerous, both of our political and moral interests. When it is observed that some of our neighbouring colonies, though much later than ourselves in point of settlement, are now far before us in improvement...The reason seems to be this: *that with their whites they import arts and agriculture, whilst we, with our blacks, exclude both.*" He did, however, challenge the morality of "...our cruel trade to Africa..." when he pointed out that "...we *Christians*..." carry on such commerce in order that Virginians "...may be furnished with our *fellow-creatures*, who are no longer to be considered as created in the image of God..."[29] Several other prominent colonial leaders such as George Mason shared Richard Henry's convictions.[30]

Richard Henry was also acknowledged as an exceptional speaker. St. George Tucker, a contemporary Virginia lawyer and professor at the College of William and Mary, declared that Richard Henry Lee's "eloquence approach'd more nearly to that of Cicero...than any other I ever heard."[31] In the tumultuous years ahead, Patrick Henry would be acclaimed as the Demosthenes of the Revolution, but Richard Henry would retain his title as Cicero for his less bombastic, classically crafted oratory.[32]

Upon their first introduction, John Adams described Richard Henry as "a tall, spare man." Adams was especially impressed by his new friend's assertion that it was time for the opposition to make "vigorous Exertions."[33] As one biographer asserts: "Timidity was totally foreign to his character..."[34] St. George Tucker wrote that "His aquiline nose and Roman profile struck me...forcibly."[35] Throughout his life, however, Richard Henry's fragile health failed to match his resolute spirit. He suffered from various physical ailments, including epilepsy, asthma and especially gout. A hunting accident in 1768 added to his maladies when the four fingers of his left hand were severed. Thereafter, this lanky redheaded classicist always wore a large black silk bandage which he learned to use effectively when gesturing during debate.[36]

Like his future presidential colleague, John Hancock, Richard Henry was also a natural politician long before the profession was truly acknowledged. But, unlike Hancock, he did not have a fortune to support his lifestyle.[37] As his family grew and his public responsibilities increased, Richard Henry frequently fretted over finances. More than once, these financial pressures nearly toppled his political ambitions.

Despite his strong stance on abolishing the slave trade (even though he maintained approximately 43 slaves at his Chantilly estate), at one point, out of financial need, Richard Henry unsuccessfully explored the possibility of becoming a slave trader himself. He told his brother William that "As the Planters are nearly out of debt and Negroes are become valuable here, I should be extremely glad to be employed on reasonable terms..."[38] When William warned his brother that it could impair his image, Richard Henry replied: "You know in general I have always thought the Trade bad; but since it will be carried on, I do not see how I could in justice to my family refuse any advantage that might arise from the selling of them."[39]

The most damaging example of how finances occasionally clouded his political judgment developed as a result of the Stamp Act which the British Parliament tried to impose on the American colonies in 1765.[40] In Virginia, Richard Henry had publicly and privately denounced such legislation. In 1764, for example, he wrote to a friend in London that " '...the right to be governed by laws made by our representatives, and the illegality of taxation without consent,' are such essential principles of the British constitution, that it is a matter of wonder how men, who have almost imbibed them in their mother's milk...should be of opinion that the people of America were to be taxed without consulting their representatives!"[41]

Only six months later, however, Richard Henry eagerly sought appointment to the lucrative office of Stamp Collector for Virginia. At first, his interest in the position was not widely known. In September 1765, he even led a boisterous public protest in Westmoreland County against George Mercer, the obstinate fool who did receive the appointment and refused to resign. In retaliation, Mercer's brother wrote a series of letters to the *Virginia Gazette* in order to expose Richard Henry's "Hypocrisy."[42] Desperate to save his reputation, Richard Henry published a rebuttal in the same paper in 1766. In it, he acknowledged having made a "hasty application" but contended that "It was but a few days after my letters were sent away...the impropriety of an American being concerned in such an affair struck me in the strongest manner..." Seeking forgiveness, he argued that "...to err is certainly the portion of humanity, but that it was the business of an honest Man to recede from error as soon as he discovered it..."[43]

To underscore his condemnation of the Stamp Act and also retain faith with his constituents, Richard Henry authored one of the most radical documents prior to the Revolution. The 1766 Westmoreland Articles of Association was a truly remarkable manifesto which one historian has characterized as "far more seditious" than the Declaration of Independence a decade later.[44] It did acknowledge "all due allegiance to our lawful sovereign," but only "...so far as is consistent with the preservation of our constitution, our rights, and liberty..." . Richard Henry's signature led the list of 115 prominent men, including three of his brothers as well as several of George Washington's siblings. They pledged "at every hazard, and paying no regard to danger or to death, to exert every faculty to prevent the execution of the said stamp act."[45]

In a separate "Letter to the Good People of Virginia," Richard Henry proclaimed that "Now is the time, my countrymen, by nipping in the bud this wicked design, to show the world that you determine to hand down to your children, the liberty given you by your fathers..."[46] From this point on, he never wavered. As he later wrote: "...I cannot go along with those who would derive security from submission."[47]

When Speaker Robinson died in May 1766, in the midst of the Stamp Act crisis, the financial scandal that Richard Henry had long predicted, combined with the debate over colonial rights, led to a major power shift within the House of Burgesses. Even though the establishment candidate, Peyton Randolph (who later became America's first President), was able to withstand the threat of a challenge by Richard Henry for the Speakership, the Treasurer's office was assigned elsewhere. Thus, by the end of 1766, the Lee Family, Patrick Henry and their allies, including the young Thomas Jefferson, enjoyed enhanced prestige as the final decade of colonial rule unfolded.[48]

News of Parliament's repeal of the Stamp Act reached Virginia in mid-1766. Colonial leaders briefly basked in the glow of victory. One year later, however, reality came crashing down as Charles Townshend, Chancellor of the Exchequer, developed a new set of "external" taxes on goods the colonists had to import.[49]

At this time, Arthur Lee, Richard Henry's youngest brother who often worked in London as an agent for Massachusetts, had a remarkably wide circle of friends, including the most prominent British champion of Liberty, John Wilkes.[50] Even more surprising, Richard Henry's second youngest brother, William, was elected as a London Alderman prior to the Revolution. The Lee Family was indeed well connected. As soon as the Townshend Acts went into effect in November 1767, those family ties proved valuable yet again. When a leading Philadelphia politician, John Dickinson, began a series of "Letters From a Pennsylvania Farmer" which were widely reprinted, Arthur Lee urged Richard Henry to contact Dickinson and provided an introduction. In July 1768, Richard Henry did write to Dickinson in the hope that "...a private correspondence should be conducted between the lovers of liberty in every province." In addition, Richard Henry was among the first to urge that "select committees should be appointed..." in order to develop a "union of counsel and action among all the colonies..."[51]

While recovering from his shooting accident in 1768, Richard Henry continued to devote much of his time to extensive correspondence. Toward the end of that year, personal tragedy struck once again. On the evening of December 8, Richard Henry shared his deep distress with a friend: "--Poor Mrs. Lee and my two sons [are] laboring under a severe Pleurisy and now so ill that I know not what may be the issue of this night --"[52] Fortunately, his boys did recover, but his beloved wife, Anne Aylett Lee, died four days later, leaving him with four young children to raise.

By the following May, Richard Henry's health permitted his return to Williamsburg in time to welcome the new Governor, the Baron de Botetourt, whom he described as possessing "good sense, affability, and politeness."[53] As the first Royal Governor to actually live in Virginia since 1705 (his predecessors in Williamsburg had been Lieutenant Governors), Botetourt was exceptionally popular.[54] But even he could not undue the damage caused by the Townshend Acts. After only eleven days, the opposition of the Burgesses toward the new taxes forced the governor to dissolve the House. Rather than disbanding, however, 89 of the elected members, led by Speaker Randolph, adjourned to Raleigh's Tavern, only a brief walk from the Capitol, where they formed an association to once again boycott British goods as they had done during the Stamp Act crisis.[55]

In describing these developments to his brother Arthur in London, Richard Henry stated: "The flame of liberty burns bright and clear, nor can its light and luster be impair'd by any Ministerial art or delusion. The

Americans, from one end of the Continent to the other, appear too wise, too brave, and much too honest, to be either talked, terrified, or bribed from the assertion of just, equitable, and long possessed rights--It is clear beyond question, that nothing but just honest, and friendly measures, can secure to Great Britain, the obedience and love of America."[56]

Not everyone agreed. Since the direct impact of the Townshend taxes was less onerous than Parliament's earlier attempt at raising a stamp revenue, continentwide support for a boycott was anemic from the start. Then, in November 1769, when the Burgesses reconvened, Gov. Botetourt informed them that the Townshend taxes were going to be repealed the following year, except for the tax on tea. While many celebrated what they perceived as yet another victory, Richard Henry and a number of his colleagues denounced Parliament's determination to impose any tax and renewed their call for resistance.[57] In June 1770, the House appointed a committee chaired by Richard Henry to prepare yet another useless petition to the King.[58]

As the new decade began, most Americans did not yet share Richard Henry's depth of commitment to the cause. Once the majority of the taxes were rescinded, colonial legislatures and merchants rapidly lost interest. Gov. Botetourt reported to London that "the Spirt of Association' seemed to be 'cooling every day'."[59] The end of the crisis actually produced a respite in the conflict between Britain and her colonies.

Despite his deep disappointment over the failure of the tea boycott, Richard Henry desperately needed to devote more time to his new and rapidly expanding family. During the summer of 1769, the father of four had taken a new bride, Anne Pinckard, a "pretty little widow," who brought life and love back to Chantilly. Together, they had another five children. Their happiness, however, also led to growing financial pressures. At one point, Richard Henry wrote: "Five children already, another far advanced in the stocks, with a teeming little wife are circumstances sufficiently alarming." Nevertheless, he was well known as a devoted husband and father who, later in life, took special joy in his grandchildren. His sister's son, Tommy Shippen, remembered how Uncle Richard was often "... very fond of promoting mirth..."[60]

In reflecting on the early 1770s, historian John C. Miller concluded that "the era of good feelings proved to be merely a breathing spell in the contest" between Britain and her American colonies. In 1772, that calm was shattered when the British schooner *Gsapee* ran aground off the coast of Rhode Island while hunting down smugglers. Irate local residents set the ship on fire. Outraged, the British Government ordered that the perpetrators would be sent to London for trial in order to guarantee conviction.[61] In February 1773, in order to learn the exact details of the case, Richard Henry initiated a correspondence with yet another giant of colonial politics, Sam Adams of Boston. Richard Henry denounced the "fatal precedent, of removing Americans beyond the water" for such a trial. "This is so unreasonable," he wrote, "and so unconstitutional a stretch of power, that I hope it will never be permitted to take place, while a spark of virtue, or one manly sentiment remains in America."[62]

In his response that April, Sam Adams assured Richard Henry that his letter was received "with singular pleasure...because I had frequently heard of your character and merit, as a warm advocate of virtue and liberty." It was the beginning of an intense lifelong friendship which soon included John Adams, Sam's younger cousin. Over the next decade, these three men-- the "Lee-Adams Junto"--dominated American politics. At every turn, the alliance they formed between their respective states of Massachusetts and Virginia led the way in the struggle for Independence.

Richard Henry's 1768 proposal for a "union of counsel and action among all the colonies" also came to fruition in the spring of 1773.[63] Thomas Jefferson descried it best in his brief Autobiography: "Not thinking our old & leading members up to the point of forwardness & zeal which the times required, Mr. Henry, R. H. Lee, Francis L. Lee, Mr. Carr & myself agreed to meet...to consult on the state of things...We were all sensible that the most urgent of all measures was that of coming to an understanding with all the other colonies to consider the British claims as a common cause to all, & to produce an unity of action: and for this purpose that a comm[itt]ee of correspondence in each colony would be the best instrument for intercommunication: and that their first measure would probably be to propose a meeting of deputies from every colony at some central place, who would be charged with the direction of the measures which should be taken by all."[64]

Their proposal to establish a Committee of Correspondence with their sister colonies was formally adopted by the Virginia House of Burgesses on Friday, March 12, 1773. Richard Henry, Speaker Randolph, Patrick Henry and Thomas Jefferson were among the eleven Burgesses appointed to this body. The Speaker was further directed to transmit this information to "the Speakers of the different Assemblys of the British Colonies..." and to "request them to appoint some Person or Persons, of their respective Bodies, to communicate...with the said Committee."[65]

Over the next year, most of the other colonies adopted Virginia's proposal. By the time the dispute over tea and taxes reached its dramatic climax in Boston Harbor that December, the American colonies, and many of their leaders, were no longer strangers.[66] When Parliament retaliated against Boston in the spring of 1774 by adopting the Intolerable Acts, thereby closing its harbor and suspending self-government, Massachusetts sent out an urgent call "that a meeting of Committees from the several Colonies on this Continent is highly expedient and necessary, & that they propose that such Meeting be at the City of Philadelphia on the first day of September next..."[67]

Even before the Massachusetts plea was received, Richard Henry had prepared seven Resolutions in support of New England. He and his allies even called for a Day of fasting in solidarity with Boston. On May 26, 1774, in response to these developments, Virginia's new governor, Lord Dunmore, dissolved the House.[68] Once again, the Burgesses reconvened at Raleigh Tavern where they adopted a stronger boycott of British goods. The Virginia Committee of Correspondence then wrote to the other colonies on May 28, urging "the Propriety of appointing Deputies from the several Colonies of British America to meet annually in general Congress...."[69] A few days later, Speaker Randolph and two dozen of his fellow legislators issued a call for a convention to meet in Williamsburg.

The First Virginia Convention opened on August 1, 1774. After six days of debate and resolutions, it elected seven of its members as delegates to the First Continental Congress which was scheduled to convene on September 5. Speaker Randolph, who presided at the Convention, led the list of electees with 104 votes, followed by Richard Henry with 100 and George Washington with 98. The delegation included Patrick Henry, Richard Bland, Benjamin Harrison and Edmund Pendleton.[70]

Richard Henry, Speaker Randolph and two of their Virginia colleagues arrived in Philadelphia on Friday, September 2. They met John Adams for the first time that same evening at City Tavern. Adams was uncharacteristically impressed. He recorded in his diary that "These Gentlemen from Virginia appear to be the most spirited and consistent, of any." The next morning, Adams again joined Richard Henry for breakfast at the home of Richard Henry's younger sister, Alice, and her husband, Dr. William Shippen, where Richard Henry was staying. That afternoon, Richard Henry spent several hours drinking burgundy at the country estate of John Dickinson who was by then an old friend even though the two had never met. Later that day, Richard Henry again joined Adams and other distinguished guests for a lavish banquet at the home of Pennsylvania Delegate Thomas Mifflin (who would later become Richard Henry's presidential predecessor). According to Adams, "We drank sentiments 'till eleven O Clock. Lee and Harrison were very high."[71]

When the First Continental Congress opened the following Monday morning, September 5, 1774, Richard Henry's credentials were presented, but he was unable to attend.[72] The Madeira had apparently taken its toll on his delicate health. By Tuesday, however, he had recovered in time to hear his colleague, Patrick Henry, declare that "Government is dissolved... We are in a State of Nature."[73] After some debate, Congress voted "That a Committee be appointed to State the rights of the Colonies...and the means most proper to be pursued for obtaining a restoration of them." Two members from each colony were appointed to this new committee (including future Presidents Jay of New York and McKean of Delaware). Richard Henry and Edmund Pendleton represented Virginia.[74]

As John Adams recorded at the first meeting of that committee, Richard Henry opened several weeks of debate by stating that American rights "are built on a fourfold foundation--on Nature, on the british Constitution, on Charters, and on immemorial Usage." He went on to argue that the colonists should "lay our Rights upon the broadest Bottom, the Ground of Nature. Our Ancestors found here no Government."[75]

Two weeks later, Congress received and approved a copy of the Suffolk County Resolutions which had been adopted by Boston-area residents in response to a false rumor that six of their fellow citizens had been killed. The document stated that "the late acts of the British parliament...are gross infractions of those rights to which we are justly entitled...that they be rejected as the attempts of a wicked administration to enslave America." In response, Richard Henry introduced a resolution: "That this assembly deeply feels the suffering of their countrymen in the Massachusetts-Bay, under the operation of the late unjust, cruel and oppressive acts of the British Parliament," and that "contributions from all the colonies for supplying the necessities, and alleviating the distresses of our brethren at Boston, ought to be continued..."[76]

That evening, John Adams recorded in his diary that "This was one of the happiest Days of my Life. In Congress We had generous, noble Sentiments, and manly Eloquence. This Day convinced me that America will support the Massachusetts or perish with her."[77] Richard Henry shared that optimism: "we have great hopes that their vigor and unanimity will prove the ruin of our Ministerial Enemies and the salvation of American Liberty." He added that the citizens of Massachusetts "are most firmly resolved to dye rather than submit to the change of their Government. In this too they will have the concurring support of the other Colonies..."[78]

On September 27, Richard Henry successfully introduced a motion to establish a boycott of British imports starting on December 1. The next day, Pennsylvania Speaker Joseph Galloway took the opposite approach when he proposed a "Plan of Union" that would establish an American "President-General" and a permanent "Grand Council...an inferior and distinct branch of the British Legislature." Richard Henry led the attack on the Galloway Plan. That same evening he and Washington privately consulted with John Adams.[79] After two more days of intense debate, Congress voted six to five (with Rhode Island split and Georgia not yet in attendance) to table the Plan. (The following month, through shrewd maneuvering on the part of Galloway's opponents, the Plan never came up for a final vote.)[80]

Richard Henry continued to cast a large shadow throughout the First Congress. When the delegates voted on September 30 to add non-exportation of American goods to its boycott, Richard Henry was appointed as one of five members of the committee responsible for developing such a plan. When Congress voted the following day to submit a Petition to the King, Richard Henry was appointed chairman of that committee. In similar fashion, when Congress decided to prepare an Address to the People of Great Britain, a Memorial to the people of British America and an Address to the People of Quebec (urging them to join the new confederation), Richard Henry was appointed to serve on all three committees.[81]

On Tuesday, October 18, Congress gave final approval to a comprehensive boycott, known as the "Continental Association." which called for non-importation, non-consumption and ultimately non-exportation with Great Britain. One week later, having completed all other business, it approved the Petition to the King and then adjourned.[82] Years later, reflecting on the reports he had heard concerning that First Congress, Thomas Jefferson wrote that Patrick Henry and Richard Henry Lee "took at once the lead in that assembly, & by the high style of their eloquence, were, in the first days of the session, looked up to as the primi inter pares."[83] John Adams, who was there, confided to his diary that "Lee, Henry, and Hooper [are] the orators."[84] During that historic two month session, Richard Henry had served on six of Congress' nine committees and had been chairman of three.[85]

The following spring, news reached America that the King had denounced Congress' "unwarrantable attempts...to obstruct the commerce of this kingdom, by unlawful combinations."[86] Nevertheless, when the second Virginia Convention met in Richmond, it endorsed the policies of the First Congress. It was there on March 23, 1775, that Patrick Henry delivered his fiery appeal for "Liberty or Death."[87] According to delegate Edmund Randolph, Richard Henry then "fanned and refreshed with a gale of pleasure" as he reminded the assembly that "'the race is not to the swift, nor the battle to the strong...' I will say with our immortal bard: 'Thrice is he armed, who hath his quarrel just!'"[88]

The following month, the extensive Lee Family connections once again proved invaluable. On April 10, 1775, the Lord Mayor and aldermen of London sent an Address to the King in support of the American cause. Richard Henry's younger brother William was then one of the Aldermen and their youngest brother, Arthur, had actually written the document.[89]

On May 3, Richard Henry spent the night with fellow delegate George Washington at Mount Vernon before setting out for Philadelphia the next day.[90] By the time the Second Continental Congress opened on May 10, 1775, the focus had shifted from theoretical debate to military defense. The murder of American patriots at Lexington Green less than three weeks earlier had, in a bizarre twist of fate, trans-formed Congress into a government in exile. Peyton Randolph was again selected to preside, but he soon had to return to Virginia to safeguard the colony from Gov. Dunmore's treachery.[91] In his place, John Hancock of Boston, the newest and richest delegate, was elected President. Benjamin Franklin and Thomas Jefferson also joined Congress over the next few months.

The previous October, Richard Henry had failed to convince Congress to "recommend it to the several Colonies that a Militia be forthwith appointed and well disciplined." In March, however, he and Patrick Henry had persuaded their own colony to adopt such a plan.[92] Now, after Lexington, the entire Congress understood the necessity for action. On May 16, Richard Henry introduced a proposal for raising a Continental Army.[93] This time Congress agreed to establish such a force and, on June 15, voted to appoint George Washington as its Commander-in-Chief.[94] By July, Richard Henry reported to a friend that "we have 15,000 men under command..."[95]

Over the vigorous opposition of John Adams, Congress also devoted part of the summer of 1775 to one final round of pleadings with the King and his English subjects. On July 5, at John Dickinson's insistence, the "Olive Branch Petition" to George III was adopted. Three days later, the committee chaired by Richard Henry presented a revised Address to the People of Great Britain which was also adopted.[96] (These last-ditch efforts at reconciliation were ignored in London where, on August 23, 1775, the King proclaimed the colonies in open rebellion.)[97]

The future of Canada was another topic of intense interest to the delegates, especially Richard Henry Lee, during the early years of the Continental Congress. As previously seen, the Address to the People of Quebec in 1774 had invited them to join the confederation. On June 27, 1775, Congress tried the opposite tactic, calling for an invasion. Four months later, Richard Henry shared his concerns with Washington: "Ministerial dependance on Canada is so great, that no object can be of greater importance to North America than to defeat them [the British] there.[98] Richard Henry had convinced himself that "the far greater part of the Canadians are surely on our side." He firmly believed "that this Congress will be shortly joined by Delegates from Canada..."[99] But his dreams of conquest were dashed on December 31, 1775, when the American forces were repelled at Quebec. The obsession with Canada's inclusion in the confederation, however, continued for years.[100]

During a short congressional recess in August 1775, Richard Henry went directly to the Virginia Convention in Richmond. There, he strongly supported plans to raise a state militia. As his enemy, Gov. Dunmore, later reported to Lord Dartmouth in London: "Richard Henry Lee one of the most daring and at the same time the most popular of the Convention, informed them of the resolutions of the Congress in a very long & artful speech."[101] When Virginia's new representatives to Congress were then selected, not only was Richard Henry reelected, but his younger brother Francis Lightfoot, a member of the Convention, was added to the congressional delegation.

After a brief visit to his family at Chantilly (his wife was six months pregnant), Richard Henry returned to Congress on Monday, September 25.[102] He was immediately assigned to work with John Adams in preparing an official response to Gen. Washington's latest correspondence.[103] Early the next month, in one of Richard Henry's many private letters to his old friend, George Washington, during the Revolutionary War, he told the General: "May heaven preserve you, and give your Army success in the most glorious cause that was ever contended for by human nature." A few weeks later he tried to comfort Washington's frustration with Congress by reminding him that "Great bodies...move slow...We must be content however to take human nature as we find it, and endeavor to draw good out of evil." The next morning he added a sad footnote: "our good old Speaker Peyton Randolph" had died the previous evening.[104]

At the end of October, Richard Henry was appointed to the recently created Naval Committee (later renamed the Marine Committee).[105] He took great pride in this endeavor: "America may not at first be in condition to meet the force of G. Britain, yet as Hercules was once in his Cradle, so, time and attention will, under the fostering hand of Liberty, make great changes [in] this matter."[106] That fall, Richard Henry was also one of the strongest advocates for opening American ports to foreign commerce; a step that sounded too much like Independence to conservative delegates.[107]

In early 1776, Richard Henry divided his time between attending Virginia's Fourth Convention in Williamsburg and his home at Chantilly, where his wife, who had just delivered another daughter, was recovering from a serious illness. Despite these conflicting obligations, he was back in Congress by March 11, only two weeks after news had arrived from London that Parliament had removed the American colonies from the King's protection. He expressed his outrage to a friend by stating that "the Court by one bold Act of Parliament, and by a conduct the most extensively hostile, have already put the two Countries asunder..." And yet, he wrote in disgust, "people here are disputing and hesitating about independancy..."[108]

Fortunately, some good news finally broke through when word reached Philadelphia on March 19 that the British troops had deserted Boston Harbor.[109] Taking renewed heart from America's victory, Richard Henry pleaded with Congress to immediately dispatch four battalions to forcibly annex Canada. The expedition, however, soon ended in total chaos when "not a Mouthful of food" or other supplies were adequately provided. Richard Henry's response represents one of the great understatements of the war: "Our affairs in that Country begin to wear an unfavorable aspect..."[110] By now, however, Richard Henry placed even greater emphasis on foreign alliances.

On April 20, 1776, as Virginia's Fifth Convention was preparing to open in Williamsburg, Richard Henry wrote to several colleagues, including Patrick Henry, explaining why he could not take time away form his duties in Congress; but, he urged them to procure a resolution from the State Convention calling for Independence: "Ages yet unborn, and millions existing at present, may rue or bless that Assembly, on which their happiness or misery will so eminently depend. Virginia has hitherto taken the lead in great affairs, and many now look to her with anxious expectation, hoping that the spirit, wisdom, and energy of her councils, will rouse America..." He went on to argue that "no State in Europe will either Treat or Trade with us so long as we consider ourselves Subjects of G. B...until we take rank as an independent people." Richard Henry then captured the moment: "This I take to be the time & thing meant by Shakespeare when he says 'There is a Tide in the Affairs of Men which taken at the Flood leads on to fortune--That omitted, we are ever after bound in Shallows.'"[111]

On May 15, the Virginia Convention did, indeed, adopt his proposal and on Friday, June 7, 1776, Richard Henry Lee rose on the floor of Congress to introduce the Virginia Resolution for Independence, Foreign Alliances and Confederation.[112]

After three days of debate in the Committee of the Whole, Congress decided to postpone a final vote on Independence until July 1; but, "in case the Congress agree thereto," it also created a five member committee to prepare a formal declaration.[113] For years, historians have speculated on sinister motives to explain why Richard Henry was not appointed to head that committee and thereby afforded the opportunity to author the Declaration of Independence. The record, however, easily dispels such theories. On May 18, 1776, George Mason pleaded with Richard Henry to hurry back to Virginia to assist in crafting a new state constitution: "I need not tell you how much you will be wanted here on this Occasion... We can not do without you--"[114] As early as May 28, Richard Henry had informed his brother, Thomas Ludwell, that he intended to "sett out for Virginia..." in order to "attend the Convention at Williamsburg." On June 2, he mentioned to Landon Carter that "I hope to be in Virga. in 10 or 12 days..."[115]

Knowing that Virginia's congressional vote for Independence was secure, Richard Henry left Philadelphia on June 13, six days after he had introduced the Resolution.[116] When Independence was finally adopted on July 2 and Jefferson's Declaration was approved two days later, Richard Henry, having launched that debate, was back in Virginia helping to complete his state's new Constitution. On July 6 he wrote to Sam Adams from Williamsburg: "A fortnights stay here has enabled me to assist my Countrymen in finishing our form of Government --The mighty work is now done..."[117] In a very real sense, he was able to be in two places at once.

Francis Lightfoot Lee signed the Declaration of Independence on August 2, 1776, along with most of his congressional colleagues. After returning to Congress in late August, Richard Henry Lee proudly added his signature in the space that his Virginia colleagues had reserved for him just above Jefferson.[118]

Three months after Independence had been declared, Richard Henry still hoped that Britain, which he now referred to as the "Devils of despotism" would come to its senses and cease its attack on America. He wrote to his brother William early in October that "I do realy think, that if a great Statesman with proper powers were to arise in England, he would endeavor to save his Country by immediately acknowledging the independence of North America and forming with these States an advantageous Treaty of Commerce. Shortly it may be too late."[119] Richard Henry also anticipated that "a general war in Europe is not far off."[120]

Over the next three years, Richard Henry continued his congressional labors during the darkest days of the war. Of all the challenges he faced, the dispute between his youngest brother Arthur and former Connecticut Delegate Silas Deane was certainly the most wrenching. In the Fall of 1776, both men, along with Benjamin Franklin, had been appointed as "commissioners to the court of France."[121] To complicate matters further,

William Lee had also been designated as a commercial agent in Europe.[122] Franklin's informal style of diplomacy appealed to Deane and their French hosts. Arthur and William, however, were appalled by their colleagues' conduct. Arthur Lee eventually charged Deane with embezzling public funds.[123]

When Henry Laurens, the consummate businessman, became President in November 1777, he shared Arthur Lee's outrage over Deane's questionable conduct. Richard Henry, of course, sided with the President and his brothers against Deane's powerful allies in Congress, including John Jay and financier Robert Morris. On November 21, Richard Henry successfully introduced a motion to recall Deane in the hope of resolving the conflict.[124] He later stated that Deane's "{recall} which I now rejoice at will prevent all future {machinations} from him, at least in {Europe}." He urged his brother to "Persevere in {honest patriotism} and all will be well."[125]

Throughout 1778, the Lee-Deane Affair grew as a cancer throughout Congress while critical time and energy were diverted from the demands of the Revolution. Old animosities were revived and new enemies were created. As historian Edmund Cody Burnett stated in his seminal study of the Continental Congress: "Congress had already split into two factions on the subject...Unless this rift could be closed there was the most serious danger that the whole American structure would come down in irretrievable ruin."[126] When Deane finally did testify before Congress on August 15, 17 and 21, 1778, little was resolved since he had failed to bring his account books with him.[127] President Laurens was outraged. Cyrus Griffin of Virginia, destined to become the last President of Congress, wrote to Jefferson in the Fall that "We are plagued to death with quarrels and recriminations relative to our Commissioners abroad; these men will involve the Continent in perdition."[128]

The Lee Family was also tarred by the charges being hurled in all directions. While Richard Henry claimed that "I look with indifference on the malice of my enemies,"[129] he was always a fierce defender of his family's honor. He even speculated to Arthur that their eminent colleague, Benjamin Franklin, was involved in the affair. "The {Doctor} is as I always thought him, I am not in the least disappointed or informed by any thing {immoral} that I hear of him. We do not know he has {written} any thing against {you} but I strongly {suspect} it from the conduct of some Men."[130]

On September 14, 1778, Congress attempted to resolve the crisis by eliminating the commission system and appointing Franklin as the sole Minister Plenipotentiary to the French Court.[131] The uproar, however, did not subside. Unable to get another hearing before Congress, Deane published his defense in the *Pennsylvania Packet* early that December, hurling counter charges at Arthur Lee. It was, in the opinion of Sam Adams, "filled with Insinuations and Assertions without any Evidence to support them."[132] When President Laurens failed to convince Congress to discipline Deane for his indiscretion, the President's response on December 9 shocked friends and foes alike: "I feel my own honor, and much more forcibly the honor of the Public deeply wounded by Mr. Deanes' address and I am persuaded that it will hold out such encouragement [to] our Enemies to continue their persecution, as will, in its consequences, be more detrimental to [our] Cause than the loss of a Battle...as I cannot consistently with my own honor, nor with utility to my Country, considering the manner in which Business is transacted here, remain any longer in this Chair, I now resign it."[133]

John Jay of New York, one of Deane's strongest supporters, was elected as the Fifth President of Congress the following day.[134] Laurens and the Lees had suffered a serious defeat. By Christmas Day 1778, even Francis Lightfoot Lee, the most even-tempered of the brothers, sent a sarcastic report to Richard Henry who had already left Philadelphia in disgust: "Mr. Deane produced to Congress his written narrative of his transactions & accusations. The first the most pompous bloated thing that ever was on paper. The only charges against Doctr. [Arthur] Lee are that he is suspicious, jealous, affrontive to every body he has any business with, & very disgusting to the whole french Nation...Mr. W. Lee is mean, & goes shares with the Agents he appointed. The whole is the most grossly abuseve of both of them."[135]

In the end, Deane paid the highest price. His reputation ruined, he died in poverty in England in 1789.[136] The bitter feelings in Congress, however, lasted far longer than the sordid details that had initially prompted the debate.

Both Sam and John Adams never wavered in their support for the Lees. In early 1779, Sam Adams wrote: "They are a Family, who have been as early, as uniform, as persevering and perhaps as able American Patriots as any in the United States."[137] The feeling was clearly mutual. A few years later, Richard Henry confided to Sam Adams that "You have certainly done me justice when you have taken me for an *Unchanging Friend*. I endeavor not to take up friendships lightly, and therefore I am not capable of lightly laying them down."[138]

Arthur Lee returned to America in 1780, and later served as a Virginia Delegate to Congress from 1782-84; the third of the Sons of Stratford elected to that high office.[139] Francis Lightfoot, however, had had enough. He left Congress for good on April 16, 1779. As he wrote four days later:

"I am determined to retire being fully convinced, that at present, the post of honor, is a private station."[140] On May 4, 1779, even Richard Henry sent his letter of resignation to the Virginia House of Delegates: "A long, laborious, and almost unremitting attendance on public business...compels me humbly to request that the honorable house of Delegates will accept the resignation of my appointment as a Member of Congress..." But he made clear that "I do not desire totally to withdraw from the public service..."[141] Richard Henry finally left Congress on May 24, 1779, exhausted and disillusioned.

Richard Henry returned to Virginia just as the British literally arrived at his back door. That June, enemy ships were moving up the Potomac River toward Chantilly and Westmoreland County. Once again, personal affairs and his fragile health had to be set aside to confront the growing crisis. As a longstanding colonel in the Virginia Militia, Richard Henry "used every possible means to get the militia of Westmoreland well armed" as he took on the uncharacteristic role of field commander rather than legislator.[142] One British officer paid him a high compliment when he wrote: "I never set my foot upon Westmoreland that the militia are not upon me directly."[143]

During that same summer, Richard Henry also kept abreast of the latest charges being hurled by Deane at his brother Arthur. Starting on August 10 (using the pseudonym "Rowland"), Richard Henry wrote a series of essays in Arthur's defense which appeared in the *Pennsylvania Packet*.[144] At the same time, friends such as Pennsylvania Delegate James Searle, expressed support. Searle referred to Richard Henry as "a Gentleman to whom (as a grateful American) I look up with Veneration & high respect for the many, the important services he has done my County."[145]

Richard Henry clearly felt adrift during the fall of 1779. Even though his family was the embodiment of everything southern, he confessed in a remarkably candid letter to John Adams: "I feel myself interested in the establishment of a wise and free republican government in Massachusetts, where yet I hope to finish the remainder of my days. The hasty, unpersevering, aristocratic genius of the south suits not my disposition, and is inconsistent with my views of what must constitute social happiness and security."[146] The surprisingly tender words Henry Laurens penned to him a few weeks later must have been doubly appreciated: "God bless you my Dear Sir, have patience & all things will work together in support of honesty & truth."[147]

In the Spring of 1780, Richard Henry found some comfort by rejoining Virginia's House of Delegates as it opened its first session in the new state capital of Richmond. He even fulfilled the goal of his early legislative career when he was elected Speaker of the House for the short session that lasted from March 2-22, 1781. Military defense still dominated Virginia's agenda. Richard Henry painfully described the situation in a letter to his brother Arthur on June 4, 1781: "...we have received next to no assistance from our Sister States or from our Ally...The people...find themselves abandoned."[148] In a letter to Washington, he desperately pleaded for help: "Our country [Virginia] is truly Sir in a deplorable way, and if relief comes not from you it will probably come not at all..." Somehow, Virginia did manager to hang on just long enough for Cornwallis' surrender at Yorktown that October.

By the fall of 1782, enemies of the Lee Family struck again when Richard Henry, Sam Adams and Henry Laurens were accused of leading a pro-British party. The Virginia House unanimously agreed that the charges were completely unfounded and that "on the contrary this Committee do bear testimony to the World that the uniform rectitude of his [Richard Henry Lee's] public conduct entitles him to the fullest confidence and warmest approbation of his country."[149]

In May 1783, despite their warm sentiments, Richard Henry lost his next race for Speaker.[150] Late that year he also suffered "a long continued, severe illness, that had nearly ended my days."[151] The following June, after he had regained his health, the House of Delegates once again elected him to represent Virginia in the Continental Congress. Richard Henry, now 52, and his 26 year old colleague, James Monroe, arrived at the temporary capital of Trenton, New Jersey on November 1, 1784.[152] While those present anxiously awaited the ever elusive quorum, Richard Henry reflected on the lessons he had learned in a letter to his old comrade Sam Adams: "I remember when once I detested the moderate character. At this moment I think that moderation, wisdom, firmness, and attention, are the principles proper for our adoption; and highly becoming the dignity of our successful situation."[153]

He also wrote to James Madison, sharing an idea that would eventually transform their new nation: "It is by many here suggested as a very necessary Step for Congress to take--The calling upon the States to form a Convention for the Sole purpose of revising the Confederation so far as to enable Congress to execute with more energy, effect, & vigor the powers assigned it..."[154]

Finally, on November 30, 1784, enough delegates had arrived to proceed to the election of their eleventh President. Richard Henry Lee of Virginia, by now recognized by friend and foe alike as an elder statesman, was chosen to take the chair.[155] Since Trenton was simply not large enough to meet their needs, the delegates also decided to adjourn on December 24 and reconvene in New York City the following month.[156]

When President Lee called Congress into session in New York on

Tuesday, January 11, 1785--the city that had been the British headquarters throughout the Revolution--it marked both the start of the postwar era and the final phase of the Continental Congress.[157] Historian John Fiske referred to it as the "Critical Period of American History," because this unique American experiment stood at the crossroads between success and failure; between one great nation or a cluster of minor, warring states waiting to be devoured by mighty European powers.[158]

Historian Merrill Jensen took note of the fact that five years after Richard Henry had left Congress in disgust, "by 1785 Congress was back in the hands of the Lee-Adams junto, with Richard Henry Lee himself as president." In addition, his bitter opponent, financier Robert Morris was gone, and in his place now stood a three member Treasury Board which included Richard Henry's brother, Arthur Lee.[159] The new Foreign Affairs Secretary, however, was none other than Richard Henry's old nemesis, John Jay.[160] In addition, another perceived enemy, Secretary Charles Thomson, still held firm to his office despite powerful opponents, including the Lees.

For Richard Henry, this was the national recognition he had long craved and much deserved. One of his first orders of business was to lease "a very elegant House" appropriate to his status as Head of State. The mansion he selected at No. 3 Cherry Street (paid for by Congress, as was customary) belonged to the widow of New York merchant Walter Franklin. It served as the chief executive's home throughout the final years of Congress and was then occupied by Washington at the start of the Second Republic.[161] The President's wardrobe was also of interest. Richard Henry employed a tailor recommended by his nephew, Tommy Shippen. On January 17, the President reported to Shippen that "Mr. Barthold has by this time I suppose rigged me out in such a manner as to convert the old President into a young Beau. Very well, if for the good of my Country I must be a Beau, why I will be a Beau."[162]

One of the first crises to reach Congress as it settled into New York was the urgency of raising enough revenue to meet interest payments on French and Dutch loans. As President, Richard Henry sent a circular letter to the State Governors, urging them to meet their financial obligations.[163] In regard to diplomatic representation, Congress selected John Adams to serve as America's first ambassador to the Court of St. James. The following month it appointed Thomas Jefferson to replace Franklin at the Court of Versailles.[164] In other developments, in July 1785, Congress adopted the Dollar as the official monetary unit for the United States.[165]

Despite Congress' many shortcomings during the postwar period, scholars point with pride to its redistribution of land northwest of the

Ohio River. In the opinion of noted historian Richard B. Morris, Congress "scored its greatest success in its arrangements for the public domain and its statesmanlike provisions for the settlement and the admission of new states."[166] On May 20, 1785, Congress took an important step toward that goal when it adopted the "Ordinance for assertaining the mode of disposing of Lands in the Western Territory."[167] As Richard Henry pointed out: sale of the land will "discharge the oppressive public debt created by the war."[168]

Mrs. Lee remained at Chantilly with their young brood during her husband's year-long residence at the "Presidents House." Richard Henry deeply missed the company of his family, but he obviously enjoyed his unique status in New York's society, as well. As President, he frequently hosted banquets and receptions. He told his nephew that "the Champaign, Claret, Madeira & Muscat are good." He even admitted to having developed a taste for "Havanna Segars."[169] His health, however, always remained a concern. On August 17, Richard Henry was forced to take a leave of absence from Congress in order to recuperate at his sister's home in Philadelphia. Delegate Samuel Holten of Massachusetts, "sensible of the high honor done me by the united States in Congress assembled," was selected to preside as "chairman" until the President resumed his position on September 29.[170]

President Lee returned from the Chalybeate Springs outside of Philadelphia "with a Stock of health that I hope will be sufficient at least to carry me triumphantly thro my Presidential year." Having tasted freedom from his daily legislative grind, Richard Henry was starting to anticipate the end of his presidency. "On the 8th of next month I shall return to Virga. after thirteen months absence from my family."[171] Already, he was receiving a list of items he had to purchase prior to his return. He wrote to his nephew, Tommy Shippen, on October 14 that "Mrs. Lee writes me that she must & will have a handsome Bread Tray...also a Basket proper for holding clean plates...I must again put your friendship to Work to find these out..."[172]

On November 4, 1785, Richard Henry completed his one year presidential term. In the opinion of historian Morris, "Richard Henry Lee of Virginia, both a renowned libertarian and a jealous advocate of states' rights, stands out as the most distinguished incumbent of the congressional presidency during the years of the Confederation [1781-89]."[173]

On his way home, Richard Henry and his son Ludwell spent the night of Wednesday, November 16, with the Washingtons at Mount Vernon.[174] As he finally reached Chantilly, months of unattended family and state business occupied Richard Henry's time throughout the following year. Nevertheless, his congressional responsibilities were not over. In November 1786, the State legislature once again elected him as a delegate to Congress.[175]

In March 1787, Richard Henry was also selected as one of Virginia's delegates to the upcoming Philadelphia Convention that would recommend amendments to the Articles of Confederation. It was the type of assembly that he had proposed to Madison over two years earlier. Despite his deep interest in the process and his unique perspective as a former president, Richard Henry turned down the appointment. He shared his reasoning with John Adams: "...being a member of Congress where the plan of Convention must be approved, there appeard an inconsistency for members...[to] pass judgement at New York upon their opinion at Philadelphia."[176] (Ten other congressional delegates who did participate in the Philadelphia Convention obviously did not share his scruples.)[177]

Instead, on July 9, 1787, Richard Henry returned to Congress in New York. Four days later, he and his fellow delegates approved the Northwest Ordinance which "combined a structure of territorial government and a schedule of admission to statehood..." Richard Morris described it as Congress' "most seminal achievement" during the postwar period.[178] Later that month, while the Convention delegates were still meeting, Richard Henry expressed confidence that "It seems probable that they will propose a government of much more Tone than that which at present attempts to rule the Confederacy."[179]

When the finished document, an entirely new Constitution, was finally read in Congress on September 20, Richard Henry led a vigorous opposition on three key points: 1) Congress should do its duty by amending and voting on the document before sending it to the States; 2) the document's provision for approval by only nine States was in violation of the "unanimous" standard set by the Articles of Confederation which were still the operative law; and, 3) the document was simply unacceptable without a comprehensive Bill of Rights to protect the people from their government.[180]

Despite Richard Henry's impassioned plea, Congress voted on September 28, 1787, to forward the new Constitution directly to the States as the Convention had directed.[181] Undaunted, he began a strenuous campaign the following day to win support at the state level by widely distributing detailed copies of his proposed amendments, including the establishment of "a Council of State or Privy Council...to advise and assist in the arduous business assigned to the Executive power"; and, the creation of a "Bill of Rights, clearly and precisely stating the principles upon which this Social Compact is founded..."[182] For nearly two centuries, Richard Henry was also widely believed to have been the author of the influential, anti-Federalist *Letters from the Federal Farmer*. Today, however, Library of Congress researchers agree that historian Gordon S. Wood has "thoroughly refuted" that claim.[183]

As the Ratification Conventions began at the State level, Richard Henry's voice grew louder. He wrote to George Mason on October 1: "The greatness of the powers given, & the multitude of Places to be created, produces a coalition of Monarchy men, Military men, Aristocrats, and Drones whose noise, imprudence & zeal exceeds all before...In this state of things, the Patriot voice is raised in vain for such changes and securities as Reason and Experience prove to be necessary against the encroachments of power upon the indispensable rights of human nature." Richard Henry added, however, that "This constitution has a great many excellent Regulations in it, and if it could be reasonably amended would be a fine System."[184]

To his brother-in-law, William Shippen, Richard Henry wrote "that in its present State, unamended, the adoption of it will put Civil Liberty and the happiness of the people at the mercy of rulers who may possess the great unguarded powers given."[185] To Sam Adams he argued that the American Patriots had "contended for free government in the fullest, clearest, and strongest sense. That they had no idea of being brought under despotic rule under the notion of 'Strong government'...Chains being still Chains, whether made of gold or iron."[186] Other powerful Virginians shared many of Richard Henry's concerns. Both Gov. Edmund Randolph (the late Presi-dent's favorite nephew) and George Mason had refused to sign the document in Philadelphia.

When Virginia's ratification debate finally began in Richmond on June 2, 1788, Patrick Henry's great oratorical powers led the attack against soft-spoken James Madison.[187] Richard Henry Lee was not there. After leading the opposition for months, he chose not to seek election as a delegate. It was a remarkable development which historians have debated for over two centuries. His stated excuse, as so often, was his health: "Repeated expereience having shown me that I could not be at Richmond and be in health, prevented me from attempting to be a member of our State Convention; but," he added, "I have omitted no occasion of enforcing, to the utmost of my power, the propriety of so stating amendments as to secure their adoption..."[188] The fact that both his brother Francis Lightfoot Lee and his cousin Henry Lee were attending as delegates supporting ratification might also have been a significant factor. Whatever the reason, Virginia did vote to ratify: 89-79.[189]

To those who were genuinely distraught over the rush to ratification, only one clear course remained. Since United States Senators in the Second

Republic were originally elected by State Legislatures rather than the people, Richard Henry mobilized his lifetime of political connections on November 8, 1788, to be elected as one of Virginia's first two Senators. The following spring, on his way to New York, he again visited Washington at Mount Vernon.[190] A few weeks later, on April 30, 1789, United States Senator Richard Henry Lee of Virginia, as co-chair of the Joint Congressional Committee on the Inauguration, had the honor of introducing President-elect George Washington to the Senate prior to his inauguration.[191]

As always, Richard Henry took an active part in major legislation; he even chaired the committee that wrote the Judiciary Act of 1789. But it was his commitment "to secure civil liberty," he told Patrick Henry, "the wish to do which, was, I assure you, the sole reason that could have influenced me to come here, for I agree perfectly with you, that your time of life and mine, after the turbulence we have passed through, renders repose necessary to our declining years." He also reiterated his firm belief that "the liberties of the people are not so safe under the gracious manner of government, as by the limitation of power."[192]

As Madison introduced his set of proposed amendments in the House, Richard Henry outlined a much bolder approach in the Senate. When the House version ultimately came up for a vote in September 1789, Richard Henry shared his grave concerns with his brother, Francis Lightfoot: "I have been absorbed about the Amendments to the Constitution. They have at length passed the Senate, with difficulty, after being much mutilated and enfeebled...What with design in some, and fear of Anarchy in others, it is very clear, I think, that a government very different from a free one will take place eer many years are passed...The love of liberty has fled from hence to France..."[193]

In May 1790, severe sickness rapidly spread throughout the government. Richard Henry informed his nephew that "I have had a most dangerous attack of the Influenza in my Lungs & Head which has nearly destroyed me..." Ten days later he again wrote to Tommy Shippen that "I am informed by some of the Physicians who attended the President, he has been dangerously ill, but...his recovery is not now doubted." In a postscript he added that "Mr. Jefferson...too has been extremely ill..."[194]

By June, still weak and eager to abandon illness-plagued New York, Richard Henry threw himself into the great debate over Hamilton's fiscal plan. He wrote to Patrick Henry that "every thing met with in my former life is mere triffling, compared with this, and you know that I have been in very stormy legislative scenes." He feared that "a vast monied interest is to be created, that will forever be warring against the landed interest, to the destruction of the latter..."[195] The one bright spot came the following month when the Senate voted that Congress should transfer to Philadelphia for ten years and that a new capital should be constructed along the Potomac.[196]

Richard Henry reached Chantilly by the end of August 1790. While there for over a year to regain his strength, he bared his soul to his nephew concerning the French Revolution: "How are the Mighty fallen, indeed? It is not easy for a Mind of sensibility not to feel for the King & Queen of France--for the latter especially...I am not yet so *hardened* with politicks as to have lost humanity. Nor am I ashamed to own that I begin to be heartily sick of politicks & politicians. I think that generally speaking, the former may be called the Science of fraud--and the latter, the Professors of that Science."[197]

In December 1791, he journeyed to Philadelphia where he was elected as the Senate's President *Pro Tempore* the following April. By October 1792, however, he was forced to write to the Speaker of the Virginia House: "It is not in my power to convey to you an adequate idea of the regret I feel at being compelled by the feeble state of my health to retire from the service of my Country."[198]

In February 1794, too weak to write, he dictated a letter to his nephew in which he again discussed the French Revolution: "I too love Liberty, but it is a regulated Liberty, so that the ends & principles of society may not be disturbed by the fury of a Mob or by the art, cunning, and industry of wicked, vicious & avaricious Men."[199] One month later, in his last surviving letter, Richard Henry wrote to President Washington, applauding his neutrality stance: "Fortunately, very fortunately for these States, the Wisdom and Patriotism, firmness & vigilance of our Government hath frustrated the destructive design." He then concluded his life of public service with one final word of advice: "The success & happiness of the United States is our care, and if the nations of Europe approve War, we surely may be permitted to cultivate the arts of peace."[200]

Richard Henry Lee died on June 19, 1794,[201] at Chantilly, survived by his second wife, his nine children--including two under the age of 16--and the last two surviving Sons of Stratford: Francis Lightfoot and William Lee.[202] Like his father and grandfather, Richard Henry and his two wives were buried at Burnt House Field which is now a brick-enclosed graveyard in the middle of open farm land just off of Route 612, outside of Hague, Virginia.

Inscribed on Richard Henry's tomb are the words that George Mason penned to him during one of the many critical moments in their young nation's history. They rang true from the very earliest days of the Revolution throughout the founding of the United States: "We cannot do without you."[203]

President Richard Henry Lee lived at Stratford (above) during his childhood and after he returned from studying in England. In 1794, he was buried at the Lee Family graveyard (below) known as Burnt House Field.

Here was Buried
RICHARD HENRY LEE
of Virginia
1732   1794
Author of the
Westmoreland Resolutions
of
Mover of the Resolution
for Independence
Signer of the
Declaration of Independence
President of the
Continental Congress
United States Senator
from Virginia

"We cannot do without you."

WHILE RICHARD HENRY LEE WAS PRESIDENT

November 1784 - November 1785

Richard Henry Lee's presidency marked the beginning of America's postwar era. No event underscored that transition more dramatically than the appointment of John Adams as the first United States Minister to Great Britain. In London, on the afternoon of Wednesday, June 1, 1785, the "Atlas of American Independence" entered St. James' Palace to formally present his credentials to His Majesty, King George III.[204] In a brief speech, Adams said: "I shall esteem my self the happiest of men if I can be instrumental in...restoring an entire esteem, confidence, and affection... between people who, though separated by an ocean and under different governments, have the same language, a similar religion, and kindred blood."[205]

In his response, as Adams reported, the King stated that: "I was the last to consent to separation; but the separation having been made, and having become inevitable, I have always said, as I say now, that I would be the first to meet the friendship of the United States as an independent power."[206] It was a solid first step at the end of a bloody war despite the diplomatic tangles and military clashes still ahead. Not until the end of the War of 1812, with America's new capital in flames, would true peace finally be restored. But 1785 clearly marked the start of what eventually became--and still remains--America's strongest bilateral alliance.

Heading the British Government at that time was William Pitt the Younger, the son of America's deceased champion. Implementation of the Peace Treaty and establishment of a commercial treaty between the two countries were by then the primary points of interest. Progress was slow on both fronts. As Adams reported to Foreign Secretary John Jay that August: "Britain has ventured to begin commercial hostilities...A jealousy of our naval power, is the true motive...they consider the United States as their rival..."[207] In October 1785, relying on Adams as his source, President Richard Henry Lee informed retired Gen. George Washington that Britain had been "so engrossed with Irish affairs" that little progress had been made thus far on American issues.[208]

At the same time, leaders of the Church of England in America met in General Convention in Philadelphia where the fledgling Episcopal Church of the United States sent an address to the Bishops of England, requesting the consecration of an American Bishop. President Lee, on their behalf, asked Adams to assist them in this endeavor "which is of very great importance to those whom it concerns..." It is ironic that today the relationship of the Episcopal Church to the Anglican Communion is once again headline news over two centuries later.[209]

Another international topic of contemporary interest also plagued the United States during its post-war period. In October 1785, President Lee wrote to James Monroe concerning the threat of Algerian pirates who "have declared war against our Commerce. These pirates having lately made a profitable peace with Spain, they have now (to the shame of Europe be it said) almost the whole of Europe their Tributaries..."[210] Today, the scene has shifted to the Indian Ocean, but the threat of armed piracy once again threatens international commerce.

At the same time, in response to a letter from the Marquis de Lafayette, President Lee applauded the French monarch in glowing terms that were eerily similar to President Jimmy Carter's effusive support for the Shah of Iran just prior to that 20th Century Revolution. President Lee wrote to the Marquis that the reign of King Louis XVI "has been so eminent for promoting the good of mankind, whilst sovereigns in general, employ their power to increase the miseries of human nature!"[211] The outbreak of the French Revolution four years later made a mockery of Richard Henry's diplomatic praise.

Perhaps the most surprising international development during Richard Henry's year-long presidency was America's first encounter with China. He described it in a letter to Thomas Jefferson who was then United States Minister to France: "The first attempt made by these States for the trade of the East Indies was from this City [New York]. A Ship has gone to, and returned from Canton in fourteen months with a valuable Cargo, and met with the most friendly treatment from the Chinese."[212] In correspondence with James Madison, he added that "The Chinese were ...glad to see a new Source of Commerce opened to them from a *New People*, as they called us."[213] The United States was beginning to find its way on the World stage.

Chapter 11

President
RICHARD HENRY LEE
of
VIRGINIA

Notes

Abbreviation Key

JCC   Journals of the Continental Congress
LDC   Letters of Delegates to Congress
PHL   The Papers of Henry Laurens

[1] Robert A. Rutland, Editor, The Papers of George Mason (1725-1792), (The University of North Carolina Press, Chapel Hill, 1970), Vol. 1, p. 271; George Mason to Richard Henry Lee, May 18, 1776.

[2] Paul Chadwick Bowers, Jr., Richard Henry Lee and the Continental Congress: 1774-1779 (Ph.D. Dissertation, Duke University, 1965), pp. 295-296. "The Lees used four codes altogether."

[3] Gregg L. Lint, Editor, Papers of John Adams, (The Belknap Press, Cambridge, 1989), Vol. 7, p. 432; John Adams to Samuel Cooper, February 28, 1779.

[4] Sir Francis Wyatt had served as Virginia's first Royal Governor 20 years before his return in 1640.

[5] Paul C. Nagel, The Lees of Virginia: Seven Generations of an American Family, (Oxford University Press, New York, 1990), pp, 8-10.

[6] Mary Elizabeth Virginia, Richard Henry Lee of Virginia: A Biography (Ph.D. Dissertation, State University of New York at Buffalo, 1992), pp. 57-62.

[7] Nagel, op. cit., p. 14.

[8] Oliver Perry Chitwood, Richard Henry Lee: Statesman of the Revolution, (McClain Printing Company, Parsons, WV, 1967), p. 2.

[9] Nagel, op. cit., p. 22.

[10] Burton J. Hendrick, The Lees of Virginia: Biography of a Family, (Little, Brow, and Company, Boston, 1935), pp. 37-41.

[11] See Chapter 1.

[12] Alonzo T. Dill and Mary Tyler Cheek, <u>A Visit to Stratford and the Story of the Lees</u>, (The W.M. Brown and Son Printing Company, Richmond, 1986), p. 41. The Lee Family's Machodoc home was destroyed by arson on January 29, 1729. Indentured servants ultimately confessed to the crime. The "Brunt House Field," which now stands in an open field surrounded by a brick wall, is the final resting place of Richard Henry Lee and his two wives.

[13] Dill, op. cit., p. 15. (See also the correction notice attached to the booklet in September 1988 which updated the estimate of the date of Stratford's completion.)

[14] Anita Grimm Taylor, <u>Richard Henry Lee, Rhetoric and Rebellion</u> (Ph.D. Dissertation, University of Missouri-Columbia, 1971), pp. 78-79.

[15] Hendrick, op. cit., p. 52.

[16] Hendrick, op. cit., pp. 63-65.

[17] Virginia, op. cit., pp. 77-82.

[18] Nagel, op. cit., pp. 65-67. After marrying his wealthy neighbor, Elizabeth Steptoe, in 1763, Philip Lee carried Stratford and his personal lifestyle to new heights. According to Nagel, when Philip traveled, he even had trumpeters "seated atop the lumbering Stratford coach, making triumphal noises to announce Phil's arrival."

[19] Nagel, op. cit., pp. 54-64. Richard Henry Lee's two sisters were also exceptional. His older sister, Hannah (who, like her grandfather, loved books), was married to Gawin Corbin for nearly 12 years. They had one daughter. After her husband's death, she invited her physician, Richard Hall, to live with her, but, due to the details of her inheritance, they never married. The couple, who gave birth to a son and daughter, further scandalized Virginia society when they converted to the Baptist faith. Richard Henry Lee's younger sister, Alice, emigrated to England as a young woman, where she met and fell in love with William Shippen who was just completing his medical studies with her brother, Arthur Lee. The Shippens returned to Philadelphia, Dr. Shippen's home, raised a family (including Richard Henry's favorite nephew, Tommy Shippen), and played an active part throughout the Revolution. Alice housed her brother, Richard Henry, during his long congressional visits and hosted numerous banquets for nearly all the congressional leaders. In 1780, Dr. Shippen was forced to face a Court Martial concerning his conduct in office as Director General of the Medical Department of the Continental Army. <u>LDC</u>, op. cit., Vol. 14, p. 504, footnote 1.

[20] James Curtis Ballagh, editor., <u>The Letters of Richard Henry Lee</u> (New York: The Macmillan Company, 1911), Vol. 1, p. 131; Richard Henry Lee to Arthur Lee, February 24, 1775.

[21] Virginia, op. cit., p. 102. While earlier biographers maintained that Richard Henry Lee toured the European continent before returning to Startford, Dr. Virginia's research could find no evidence to support that statement.

[22] Chitwood, op. cit., pp. 7-9. Chitwood even speculates that the head of Wakefield during richard Henry's residence, the Rev. Benjamin Wilson, might have been the clergyman made famous in Goldsmith's famous novel, "The Vicar of Wakefield."

23 Nagel, op. cit., p. 69 & p. 79. In that closely-knitt colony, the Aylett sisters also happened to be the stepsisters of their brother Philip's new wife, Elizabeth Steptoe.

24 John Carter Matthews, Richard Henry Lee (Virginia Independence Bicentennial Commission, Williamsburg, 1978), p. 2. While most sources, including the Library of Congress (LDC, Vol. 22, p. xxviii) list 1732 at the date of Richard Henry Lee's birth, biographer Oliver Perry Chitwood, op., cit., maintains that according to "the record in the Lee family Bible, 1733 is the correct date."

25 Richard Henry's children by his first marriage were: Thomas, Ludwell, Mary and Hannah. He had five more children by his second wife, Anne Pinckard Lee.

26 Matthews, op. cit., p. 2.

27 As cited in Bowers, op. cit., p.10; Speech delivered by Richard Henry Lee in the House of Burgesses in May 1763.

28 Lucille Griffith, The Virginia House of Burgesses: 1750-1774 (The University of Alabama Press, University, AL, 1970), Revised Edition, p. 149.

29 Richard Henry Lee (grandson), Memoir of the Life of Richard Henry Lee and His Correspondence (William Brown, Printer, Philadelphia, 1825), Kessinger Publishing's Rare Reprints, Vol. 1, pp. 17-19.

30 Rutland, op. cit., Vol. 1, p. 61; George Mason to George William Fairfax and George Washington, December 23, 1765.

31 As cited in Virginia, op. cit., p. 144.

32 L. H. Butterfield, Editor, Diary and Autobiography of John Adams (The Belknap Press, Cambridge, 1961), Vol. 2, p. 113; John Adams Diary entry, August 28, 1774. See also: Paul H. Smith, Editor, LDC: 1774-1789 (Library of Congress, Washington, DC, 1976), Vol. 1, p. 62; Silas Deane to Elizabeth Deane, September 10-11, 1774. See also: William N. Brigance, Editor, A History & Criticism of American Public Address (Russell & Russell, New York, Reprint 1960), Chapter 1: *The Colonial Period* by George V. Bohman, p. 38: "For quality of speaking...a recapitulation of the criticisms leaves Patrick Henry and Richard Henry Lee the foremost speakers [of the Continental Congress]."

33 Butterfield, op. cit., Vol. 2, p. 120; September 2, 1774; and, Saturday, September 3, 1774.

34 Taylor, op. cit., p. 194.

35 As cited in Virginia, op. cit., p. 146. In this physical characteristic, Richard Henry Lee must have born a remarkable resemblance to his presidential colleague, John Jay (see Chapter 5).

36 Virginia, op. cit., p. 146.

37 See Chapter 3.

38 Ballagh, op. cit., p. 75-76, Richard Henry Lee to William Lee, July 12, 1772.

[39] As cited in Chitwood, op. cit., p. 21; Richard Henry Lee to William Lee, May 13, 1773.

[40] See Introduction.

[41] Ballagh, op. cit., Vol. 1, p. 6.; Letter to a gentleman in London, May 31, 1764.

[42] Taylor, op. cit., p. 159. The title of James Mercer's letter was: "An Enemy to Hypocrisy."

[43] Ballagh, op. cit., Vol. 1, pp. 16-18; Letter to the Editor of the Virginia Gazette, July 25, 1766.

[44] Hendrick, op. cit., p. 134.

[45] Lee, op. cit., pp. 34-35.

[46] Lee, op. cit., pp. 37-39.

[47] Lee, op. cit., p. 68; Richard Henry Lee to John Dickinson, November 26, 1768.

[48] Griffith, op. cit., p. 149. See also: Matthews, op. cit., p. 11. Even though Richard Henry Lee considered Peyton Randolph a defender of the established power structure in 1766, when Randolph died nearly a decade later, Richard Henry referred to Randolph as "our good old Speaker" and wrote that "Thus has American liberty lost a powerful Advocate, and human nature a sincere friend." See also: Ballagh, op. cit., pp. 153-154; Richard Henry Lee to George Washington, October 22, 1775.

[49] See Introduction.

[50] Lee, op. cit., p. 56 & pp. 61-65.

[51] Ballagh, op. cit., p. 29; Richard Henry Lee to John Dickinson, July 25, 1768.

[52] Ballagh, op. cit., p. 32; Richard Henry Lee to Landon Carter, December 8, 1768.

[53] Ballagh, op. cit., p. 30; Richard Henry Lee to John Dickinson, November 26, 1768.

[54] Griffith, op. cit., p. 47.

[55] Chitwood, op. cit., pp. 48-49.

[56] Ballagh, op. cit., p. 34; Richard Henry Lee to Arthur Lee, May 19, 1769.

[57] Allen Johnson, Editor, Dictionary of American Biography (Charles Scribner's Sons, New York, 1943), Vol. 2, p. 468.

[58] Chitwood, op. cit., p. 51.

[59] As cited in Virginia, op. cit., p. 226; Gov. Botetourt to the Board of Trade, December 19, 1769. (In the dissertation, the date is incorrectly listed as 1770, but Gov. Botetourt actually died on October 15, 1770; Johnson, op. cit., p. 468.)

[60] As cited in Nagel, op. cit., p.78 & p. 140.

[61] John C. Miller, <u>Origins of the American Revolution</u> (Little, Brown and Company, Boston, 1943), pp. 325-330.

[62] Lee, op. cit., p. 87; Richard Henry Lee to Samuel Adams, February 4, 1773.

[63] Ballagh, op. cit., p. 29; Richard Henry Lee to John Dickinson, July 25, 1768.

[64] Thomas Jefferson, <u>Thomas Jefferson Writings</u> (The Library of America, New York, 1984), pp. 6-7.

[65] John Pendleton Kennedy, Editor, <u>Journals of the House of Burgesses of Virginia: 1773-1776</u> (Heritage Books, Inc., Bowie, MD, 1996), p. 28.

[66] For details on the Boston Tea Party, see Introduction.

[67] Kennedy, op. cit., p. 156.

[68] Matthews, op. cit., p. 20. Richard Henry Lee's low opinion of Gov. Dunmore is best illustrated in his letter to Mrs. Catherine McCaulay, November 29, 1775: "If Administration had searched thro the world for a person the best fetted to ruin their cause, and procure union and success for these Colonies, hey could not have found a more complete Agent than Lord Dunmore--" See also: Ballagh, op. cit., p. 162.

[69] Kennedy, op. cit., p. 138.

[70] Matthews, op. cit., pp. 21-22.

[71] Butterfield, op. cit., Vol. 2, pp. 119-121.

[72] Worthington Chauncey Ford, Editor, <u>JCC: 1774-1789</u> (Government Printing Office, Washington, DC, 1904), Vol. 1, p. 14 & p. 25.

[73] Butterfield, op. cit., Vol. 2, p. 124.

[74] <u>JCC</u>, op. cit., Vol. 1, pp. 27-29.

[75] Butterfield, op. cit., Vol. 2, p. 128.

[76] <u>JCC</u>, op. cit., Vol. 1, pp. 31-40. (In a rare mistake, the Journals list the date of the congressional resolution as "Saturday, September 18" when that Saturday was actually September 17). See also: Lee, op. cit., pp. 109-110, The footnote states: "Taken from the original manuscripts of Mr. Lee."

[77] Butterfield, op. cit., Vol. 2, pp. 134-135.

[78] <u>LDC</u>, op. cit., Vol. 1, pp. 87-88; Richard Henry Lee to William Lee, September 20, 1774.

[79] Butterfield, op. cit., Vol. 2, pp. 140-141; Wednesday, September 28, 1774. This was apparently "the first intimate contact" between John Adams and George Washington.

[80] Bowers, op. cit., p. 80. See also Chapter 2, pp. 54-55.

[81] JCC, op. cit., Vol. 1, pp. 62, 101 & 111-112. See also Bowers, op. cit., pp. 85-86.

[82] JCC, op. cit., Vol. 1, pp. 75 & 104.

[83] As cited in Bowers, op. cit., p. 86. Thomas Jefferson did not attend Congress until 1775.

[84] LDC, op. cit., Vol. 1, p. 168; October 10, 1774. The third delegate Adams mentioned is William Hooper from North Carolina.

[85] Matthews, op. cit., p. 29.

[86] LDC, op. cit., Vol. 1, p. 315: footnote #1.

[87] David J. Brewer, Editor, The World's Best Orations (Fred P. Kaiser, St. Louis, 1899), Vol. VII, pp. 2475-2477. See also: Matthews, op. cit., p. 31. Henrico Paris Church in Richmond, where that historic Convention was held, is now known as St. John's.

[88] Chitwood, op. cit., pp. 78-79.

[89] Bowers, op. cit., p. 116. See also: LDC, op. cit., Vol. 1, p. 615, Footnote #2.

[90] John C. Fitzpatrick, Editor, The Diaries of George Washington (Houghton Mifflin Company, Boston, 1925), Vol. II, p. 194. See also: Chitwood, op. cit., p. 82.

[91] LDC, op. cit., Vol. 1, p. 366; Richard Henry Lee to Francis Lightfoot Lee, May 21, 1775.

[92] LDC, op. cit., Vol. 1, p. 140; Richard Henry Lee's Proposed Resolution, October 3, 1774. See also: Bowers, op. cit., pp. 103-104.

[93] LDC, op. cit., Vol. 1, p. 351; Silas Deane's Diary, May 16, 1775.

[94] JCC, op. cit., Vol. II, pp. 85-91.

[95] LDC, op. cit., Vol. 1, p. 569; Richard Henry Lee to Robert Carter, July 1, 1775.

[96] JCC, op. cit., Vol. II, p. 127. See also: LDC, op. cit., Vol. 1, p. 551; Footnote #1.

[97] Don Cook, The Long Fuse: How England Lost the American Colonies, 1760-1785 (The Atlantic Monthly Press, New York, 1995), p. 230.

[98] JCC, op. cit., Vol. II, pp. 109-110. See also: LDC, op. cit., Vol. 1, p. 558; Richard Henry Lee to George Washington, June 29, 1775; Vol. 2, p. 146 Footnote #4; and, Vol. 2, p. 229; Richard Henry Lee to George Washington, October 22, 1775.

[99] LDC, op. cit., Vol. 2, p. 395; Richard Henry Lee to George Washington, November 26, 1775. See also: p. 405; Richard Henry Lee to Catherine Macaulay, November 29, 1775.

[100] LDC, op. cit., Vol. 9, p. 665; Committee for Foreign Affairs to William Lee, May 14, 1778. "Nova Scotia has long ago expressed its wishes to be adopted by Us...Canada will

be greatly affected by the news of our alliance with its former parent state." See also: Vol. 11, p. 130: October 27, 1778. Once again Congress was planning yet another invasion of Canada that never took place.

101 As cited in Bowers, op. cit., pp. 125-126; Gov. Dunmore to Lord Dartmouth, October 22, 1775.

102 Matthews, op. cit., p. 38.

103 JCC, op. cit., Vol. III, p. 261.

104 LDC, op. cit., Vol. 2, p. 144 & p. 229; Richard Henry Lee to George Washington, October 8, 1775 & October 22, 1775.

105 JCC, op. cit., Vol. III, p. 312.

106 LDC, op. cit., Vol. 2, p. 405; Richard Henry Lee to Catherine Macaulay, November 29, 1775.

107 Bowers, op. cit., pp. 138-141.

108 LDC, op. cit., Vol. 3, p. 470; Richard Henry Lee to Landon Carter, April 1, 1776.

109 JCC, op. cit., Vol. IV, p. 215; March 19, 1776.

110 LDC, op. cit., Vol. 3, p. 439; Richard Henry Lee to Charles Lee, March 25, 1776. See also: Vol. 3, p. Richard Smith's Diary, March 25, 1776; and, Vol. 4, p. 21; Samuel Chase to Richard Henry Lee, May 17, 1776; and, Vol. 4, p. 36; Richard Henry Lee to Charles Lee, May 18, 1776. According to John Adams, "...the Small Pox, which infected every Man we Sent there [Canada] compleated our Ruin, and have compell'd us to evacuate that important Province. We must however regain it, sometime or other." Vol. 4, p. 345; John Adams to Archibald Bulloch, July 1, 1776.

111 LDC, op. cit., Vol. 3, pp. 563-565; Richard Henry Lee to Patrick Henry, April 20, 1776. Richard Henry Lee also wrote to other Virginia Convention delegates, including Edmund Pendleton, who served as President of that Convention; pp. 667-668; Richard Henry Lee to Edmound Pendleton, May 12, 1776.

112 JCC, op. cit., Vol. V, p. 425. See also: LDC, op. cit., Vol. 4, p. xxiii.

113 JCC, op. cit., Vol. V, pp. 428-431.

114 Rutland, op. cit., Vol. 1, p. 271; George Mason to Richard Henry Lee, May 18, 1776.

115 LDC, op. cit., Vol. 4, p. 90; Richard Henry Lee to Thomas Ludwell Lee, May 28, 1776. See also: p. 118; Richard Henry Lee to Landon Carter, June 2, 1776. On July 8, 1776, Jefferson even sent Richard Henry Lee a friendly letter, enclosing a copy of the Declaration of Independence. Richard Henry responded with equal friendliness on July 21. Clearly no rift had developed between the two Virginians as a result of Jefferson's authorship. See also: Vol. 4, p. 412.

116 LDC, op. cit., Vol. 4, p. 207; Richard Henry Lee to George Washington, June 13, 1776.

[117] Ballagh, op. cit., Vol. 1, p. 207; Richard Henry Lee to Samuel Adams, July 6, 1776.

[118] JCC, op. cit., Vol. V, p. 626. See also: Chitwood, op. cit., p. 98.

[119] LDC, op. cit., Vol. 5, p. 293; Richard Henry Lee to William Lee, October 2, 1776. See also: p. 411; Richard Henry Lee to George Washington, October 27, 1776.

[120] LDC, op. cit., Vol. 5, p. 365; Richard Henry Lee to Unknown, October 22, 1776.

[121] JCC, op. cit., Vol. V, p. 827 & Vol. VI, p. 897. Thomas Jefferson was originally selected as the third commissioner, but when he refused the assignment, Arthur Lee was added in his place.

[122] LDC, op. cit., Vol. 6, p. 102; Secret Committee to Robert Morris, January 13, 1777.

[123] Edmund Cody Burnett, The Continental Congress (The Macmillan Company, New York, 1941), pp. 360-361.

[124] JCC, op. cit., Vol. IX, p. 946.

[125] LDC, op. cit., Vol. 9, p. 653; Richard Henry Lee to Arthur Lee, May 12, 1778. (The words enclosed in {braces} were translated from the Lee Family cipher by Edmund Cody Burnett. See footnote #2.) See also: p. 720; Richard Henry Lee to Arthur Lee, May 19, 1778.

[126] Burnett, op. cit., p. 361.

[127] LDC, op. cit., Vol. 10, p. 448; Richard Henry Lee's Notes on Silas Deane's Testimony, August 15-21, 1778, footnote #1.

[128] LDC, op. cit., Vol. 11, p. 33; Cyrus Griffin to Thomas Jefferson, October 6, 1778.

[129] LDC, op. cit., Vol. 7, p. 121; Richard Henry Lee to Patrick Henry, May 26, 1777.

[130] LDC, op. cit., Vol. 10, p. 652; Richard Henry Lee to Arthur Lee, September 16, 1778.

[131] JCC, op. cit., Vol. XII, p. 908.

[132] LDC, op. cit., Vol. 11, p. 334; Samuel Adams to Elizabeth Adams, December 13, 1778.

[133] Philip M. Hamer, Editor, PHL, (University of South Carolina Press, Columbia, 1968-2003, 16 Volumes), Vol. 14, pp. 576-577, Henry Laurens: Resignation Speech, December 9, 1778. See also: LDC, op. cit., Vol. 11, p. 321; Nathaniel Scudder to Richard Henry Lee, December 9, 1778. (In October 1781, Scudder became "the only delegate to Congress to fall in Battle during the American Revolution." See also: LDC, op. cit., Vol. 14, p. xxvi.)

[134] See Chapter 5.

[135] LDC, op. cit., Vol. 11, p. 383; Francis Lightfoot Lee to Richard Henry Lee, December 25, 1778.

[136] James Grant Wilson and John Fiske, Editors, Appletons' Cyclopaedia of American Biography (D. Appleton and Company, New York, 1887), Vol. II, p. 116. In 1842, Congress revisited the case and vindicated Deane's honor.

[137] LDC, op. cit., Vol. 11, p. 421; Samuel Adams to James Warren, January 6, 1779. See also: Lint, op. cit., Vol. 7, p. 432; John Adams to Samuel Cooper, February 28, 1779.

[138] LDC, op. cit., Vol. 22, p. 314; Richard Henry Lee to Samuel Adams, April 7, 1785.

[139] LDC, op. cit., Vol. 20, pp. xxviii-xxix.

[140] LDC, op. cit., Vol. 12, p. 369; Francis Lightfoot Lee to Arthur Lee, April 22, 1779.

[141] LDC, op. cit., Vol. 11, p. 428; Richard Henry Lee to the Virginia House of Delegates, May 4, 1779.

[142] Ballagh, op. cit., Vol. 2, pp. 263-264; Richard Henry Lee to Gov. Thomas Nelson, October 28, 1781.

[143] As cited in Matthews, op. cit., pp. 74-75.

[144] LDC, op. cit., Vol. 13, p. 382; footnote #3.

[145] LDC, op. cit., Vol. 13, p. 192; James Searle to Richard Henry Lee, July 10, 1779.

[146] Lee, op. cit., p. 226; Richard Henry Lee to John Adams, October 7, 1779.

[147] LDC, op. cit., Vol. 14; Henry Laurens to Richard Henry Lee, October 12, 1779.

[148] Ballagh, op. cit., Vol. 2, p. 230; Richard Henry Lee to Arthur Lee, June 4, 1781.

[149] Ballagh, op. cit., Vol. 2, p. 277; Richard Henry Lee to William Shippen, January 7, 1783.

[150] Chitwood, op. cit., pp. 143-147. The candidate who won the Speakership in 1783 was John Tyler, the father of President John Tyler during the Second Republic.

[151] LDC, op. cit., Vol. 22. p. 21; Richard Henry Lee to Samuel Adams, November 18, 1784.

[152] LDC, op. cit., Vol. 21, p. 393; James Monroe to Richard Henry Lee, February 1784. Even before they served together in Congress, Monroe made clear his respect for RHL's age and experience (RHL was twice Monroe's age.)

[153] LDC, op. cit., Vol. 22, p. 22; Richard Henry Lee to Samuel Adams, November 18, 1784.

[154] Ballagh, op. cit., Vol. 2, p. 307; Richard Henry Lee to James Madison, November 26, 1784.

[155] LDC, op. cit., Vol. 21, p. 791, footnote #4. Arthur Lee had predicted Richard Henry's election as President of Congress in a letter to him on September 8, 1784. The election was hotly contested. It took at least eight ballots.

[156] JCC, op. cit., Vol. XXVII, p. 710; December 24, 1784.

[157] JCC, op. cit., Vol. XXVIII, p. 1.

[158] John Fiske, The Critical Period of American History: 1783-1789 (Riverside Press, Cambridge, 1888), pp. ix-xi.

[159] Merrill Jensen, The New Nation (Alfred A. Knopf, New York, 1950), p. 83.

[160] Walter Stahr, John Jay (Hambledon and London, New York, 2005), pp. 197-198.

[161] Douglas Southall Freeman, Washington (An Abridgment by Richard Harwell), (Charles Scribner's Sons, New York, 1968), p. 563.

[162] LDC, op. cit., Vol. 22, p. 123; footnotes #1 & #2.

[163] LDC, op. cit., Vol. 22, p. 125; Richard Henry Lee to the States, January 21, 1785.

[164] LDC, op. cit., Vol. 22, p. 336; Richard Henry Lee to George Washington, April 18, 1785.

[165] JCC, op. cit., Vol. XXIX, p. 500.

[166] Richard B. Morris, The Forging of the Union: 1781-1789 (Harper & Row Publishers, New York, 1987), p. 226.

[167] JCC, op. cit., Vol. XXVIII, pp. 375-381.

[168] LDC, op. cit., Vol. 22, p. 397; Richard Henry Lee to Samuel Adams, May 20, 1785.

[169] LDC, op. cit., Vol. 22, p. 519; Richard Henry Lee to John Jay, July 19, 1785. See also: p. 432; Richard Henry Lee to Thomas Lee Shippen, June 4, 1785.

[170] LDC, op. cit., Vol. 22, p. 582; Samuel Holton to Israel Hutchinson, August 22, 1785; and, p. 565: footnote #1.

[171] LDC, op. cit., Vol. 22, pp. 676-677; Richard Henry Lee to Unknown, October 10, 1785.

[172] LDC, op. cit., Vol. 22, p. 685; Richard Henry Lee to Thomas Lee Shippen, October 14, 1785.

[173] Morris, op. cit., p. 106.

[174] Fitzpatrick, op. cit., Vol. II, p. 442.

[175] LDC, op. cit., Vol. 26, p. xlvi.

[176] LDC, op. cit., Vol. 24, p. 423; Richard Henry Lee to John Adams, September 3, 1787.

[177] LDC, op. cit., Vol. 24, p. 254; Edward Carrington to Thomas Jefferson, April 24, 1787. See also: Vol. 24, p. 276; footnote #1.

[178] Morris, op. cit., p. 231 & p. 229.

[179] LDC, op. cit., Vol. 24, p. 381; Richard Henry Lee to William Lee, July 30, 1787.

[180] Julius Goebel, Jr., Melancton Smith's Minutes of Debates on the New Constitution, September 1787. Columbia Law Review, Vol. 64, No. 1 (Jan. 1964), pp. 26-43.

[181] JCC, op. cit., Vol. XXXIII, p. 549.

[182] LDC, op. cit., Vol. 24, pp. 450-454; Richard Henry Lee to Elbridge Gerry, September 29, 1787.

[183] LDC, op. cit., Vol. 24, p. 454, footnote #1.

[184] LDC, op. cit., Vol. 24, pp. 458-459; Richard Henry Lee to George Mason, October 1, 1787.

[185] LDC, op. cit., Vol. 24, p. 461; Richard Henry Lee to William Shippen, Jr., October 2, 1787.

[186] LDC, op. cit., Vol. 24, p. p. 465; Richard Henry Lee to Samuel Adams, October 5,1787.

[187] LDC, op. cit., Vol. 24, p. 493; Edward Carrington to Thomas Jefferson, October 23, 1787; and, p. 550; William Grayson to William Short, November 10, 1787.

[188] Ballagh, op. cit., Vol. II, p. 475; Richard Henry Lee to John Lamb, June 27, 1788.

[189] Matthews, op. cit., p. 81.

[190] Ballagh, op. cit., Vol. II, p. 482; Richard Henry Lee to George Washington, April 6, 1789.

[191] Chitwood, op. cit., pp. 183-185. Richard Henry Lee received 98 votes and William Grayson, another anti-Federalist, received 86. They defeated James Madison, the "Father of the Constitution," who received only 77 votes but went on to be elected by the people as a founding member of the US House of Representatives. See also: Boyd Stanley Schlenther, Charles Thomson (Associated University Presses, London, 1990), p. 190.

[192] Ballagh, op. cit., Vol. II, pp. 487-488; Richard Henry Lee to Patrick Henry, May 28, 1789.

[193] Ballagh, op. cit., Vol. II, pp. 500-501; Richard Henry Lee to Francis Lightfoot Lee, September 13, 1789.

[194] Ballagh, op. cit., Vol. II, p. 510; Richard Henry Lee to Thomas Lee Shippen, May 8, 1790; and, p. 516; Richard Henry Lee to Thomas Lee Shippen, May 18, 1790.

[195] Ballagh, op. cit., Vol. II, p. 524; Richard Henry Lee to Patrick Henry, June 10, 1790.

[196] Ballagh, op. cit., Vol. II, p. 531; Richard Henry Lee to Thomas Lee Shippen, July 1, 1790.

[197] Ballagh, op. cit., Vol. II, p. 544; Richard Henry Lee to Thomas Lee Shippen, September 21, 1791.

[198] Ballagh, op. cit., Vol. II, p. 550; Richard Henry Lee to the Speaker of the House of Delegates of Virginia, October 8, 1792.

[199] Ballagh, op. cit., Vol. II, p. 570; Richard Henry Lee to Thomas Lee Shippen, February 12, 1794.

[200] Ballagh, op. cit., Vol. II, pp. 582-583; Richard Henry Lee to George Washington, March 8, 1794.

[201] Biographical Directory of the American Congress: 1774-1961 (Government Printing Office, Washington, DC, 1961). p. 1206. While a few sources list June 14, 1794 as the date of Richard Henry Lee's death, the vast majority agree with the official congressional directory which lists June 19, 1794.

[202] Nagel, op. cit., pp. 140-141. Two of Richard Henry Lee's daughters--Mary and Hannah--married into the Washington family: John Augustine Washington and Corbin Washington, respectively. Nancy and Sarah married brothers who were also their cousins: Charles Lee and Edmund Jennings Lee. Ludwell, the second oldest son married Flora, the younger daughter of Richard Henry's oldest brother, Philip. His brother Thomas Ludwell Lee had died in 1778; Arthur Lee died in 1792.

[203] Rutland, op. cit., Vol. 1, p. 271. The inscription on Richard Henry Lee's grave presents "cannot" as one word, unlike George Mason's spelling in his letter of May 18, 1776.

WHILE RICHARD HENRY LEE WAS PRESIDENT

Notes

Abbreviation Key

JCC   Journals of the Continental Congress
LDC   Letters of Delegates to Congress
PHL   The Papers of Henry Laurens

[204] L. H. Butterfield, Editor, Diary and Autobiography of John Adams (The Belknap Press, Cambridge, 1961), Vol. 4, p. 265. Richard Stockton, Delegate from New Jersey, refered to John Adams as the "Atlas of American Independence." See also: Charles Francis Adams, Editor, The Works of John Adams, Vol. III, p. 56.

[205] David McCullough, John Adams (Simon & Schuster, New York, 2001), pp. 335-336.

[206] As cited in David McCullough, John Adams (Simon & Schuster, New York, 2001), p. 336.

[207] Ruhl J. Bartlett, Editor, The Record of American Diplomacy (Alfred A. Knopf, New York, 1950), p. 51; John Adams to John Jay, August 6, 1785.

[208] Paul H. Smith, Editor, LDC: 1774-1789 (Library of Congress, Washington, DC, 1976), Vol. 22, p. 679; Richard Henry Lee to George Washington, October 11, 1785.

[209] LDC, op. cit., Vol. 22, pp. 700-701; Richard Henry Lee to John Adams, October 24, 1785. In 2003, following the election of New Hampshire's openly gay Bishop, Gene Robinson, and his subsequent consecration by the Episcopal hierarchy, some conservative churches and diocese in the United States began to separate from the US denomination and petitioned direct alignment with the Worldwide Anglican Church.

[210] LDC, op. cit., Vol. 22, p. 693; Richard Henry Lee to James Monroe, October 17, 1785.

[211] LDC, op. cit., Vol. 22, p. 712; Richard Henry Lee to the Marquis de Lafayette, October 30, 1785.

[212] LDC, op. cit., Vol. 22, p. 393; Richard Henry Lee to Thomas Jefferson, May 16, 1785.

[213] LDC, op. cit., Vol. 22, p. 418; Richard Henry Lee to James Madison, May 30, 1785.

Nath Gorham

Chapter 12

President
NATHANIEL GORHAM
of
MASSACHUSETTS

Unrequited Honor

Nathaniel Gorham, the Speaker of the Massachusetts General Assembly, was elected by his legislative colleagues in 1782 to serve as a Delegate to the Continental Congress. Four years later he was chosen by that body to become America's Twelfth President.[1] In 1787, following the completion of his term as Head of State, Nathaniel was again elected to represent Massachusetts at the Philadelphia conclave that became known as the Constitutional Convention. There, he was unanimously selected to serve as Chairman of the Committee of the Whole, presiding over weeks of historic debates as he and his fellow delegates wrote their country's new charter. And then, in 1788, the citizens of Charlestown, Massachusetts entrusted Nathaniel with the responsibility of representing them at their State's Ratification Convention where he played a critical role in securing "the consent of the governed" for the new United States Constitution.[2]

Despite this repeated recognition at the highest levels of both his state and his nation, Nathaniel Gorham's grave at Phipps Street Burying Ground in Charlestown (only a few blocks from the Bunker Hill Monument), went unmarked for nearly two centuries. Even more shocking, this distinguished patriot has never been accorded a full-scale biography nor even been the subject of a doctoral dissertation.[3] In fact, this brief chapter marks the longest biographical sketch that has ever been devoted to his life.

Beyond his remarkable role in the Revolution, Nathaniel Gorham was also the only one of the fourteen Presidents of the First Republic who could trace his lineage to the arrival of the Mayflower in 1620. His ancestor, John Gorham, who emigrated to America shortly after the Pilgrims arrived, was married to Desire Howland in 1643.[4] She was the daughter of John Howland and Elizabeth Tillie, both of whom had made that historic voyage. Her father, one of the most colorful members of that expedition, was nearly lost at sea even before he reached America. According to <u>Bradford's History of Plimoth Plantation</u>, "...in a mighty storme, a lustie yonge man (called John Howland) coming upon some occasion above yͤ grattings, was, with a seele of yͤ shipe throwne into [yͤ] sea; but it pleased God yͤ had caught hould of yͤ top-saile halliards... yet he held his hould (though he was sundrie fadomes under water) till he was hald up...and then with a boat hooke & other means got into yͤ shipe againe, & his life saved."[5] Having ferociously clung to life, John Howland proved to be equally tenacious in matrimonial affairs. Despite the harsh conditions the Pilgrims encountered, John and Elizabeth Howland gave birth to ten children who, in turn, blessed them and their young colony with eighty-eight grandchildren.[6]

Nathaniel's father, who was referred to as Captain Nathaniel Gorham, was a merchant and respected member of Charlestown, Massachusetts.[7] He died there in the early 1760s. Nathaniel's mother, Mary Soley, who married Captain Gorham in February 1737, not only outlived her husband but also survived her oldest son by four years. She died in Boston on May 12, 1800.[8]

Nathaniel, the future President, was the eldest of their five children.[9] While the Biographical Directory of the American Congress lists his birth date as May 27, 1738, the Dictionary of American Biography states that Nathaniel was baptized at the First Christian Church in Charlestown on May 21, 1738, six days earlier.[10] At least all available sources agree on the month and year (unlike the eighth President, John Hanson, for whom there is a six year discrepancy in the reports pertaining to his birth.)[11] Nathaniel had two sisters (Mary and Elizabeth) and two brothers (John and Stephen). Years later, when Nathaniel was a member of the Continental Congress, Stephen was employed by Congress as the Commissioner on Continental Accounts for the State of New Hampshire.[12]

According to the publication "The Genealogies and Estates of Charlestown," Nathaniel Gorham, the President, was "one of the most eminent men ever resident in town."[13] In 1763, at the age of 25, Nathaniel married Rebecca Call who was five years his junior. Like her mother-in-law, Rebecca also outlived her husband despite the fact that she gave birth to nine children. She died on November 18, 1812. Their oldest child, a son also named Nathaniel, was born less than two months after they married. He would inherit his father's passion for opening up his nation's western frontier; but, unlike his father, young Nathaniel would one day live west of the Alleghenies. Next came a daughter, Rebecca, who was named for her mother. Two more daughters, Mary and Elizabeth, followed. Their fifth child, Ann (also known as Nancy), became the wife of Peter Chardon Brooks who, at the time of his death in 1849, was reputed to be the wealthiest man in New England. She bore him thirteen children, one of whom married Charles Francis Adams, the grandson of her father's revolutionary compatriot, John Adams.[14]

Nathaniel and Rebecca's sixth child, John, remains largely a mystery. Their seventh, Benjamin, was born in February 1775, two months before the opening shots of the American Revolution not far from their home. He graduated from Harvard College in 1795 and, like his father, he went on to a distinguished political career in the Massachusetts State Legislature. In 1819, Benjamin Gorham was first elected to Congress where he served for most of the next fifteen years, including 1827, when he was chosen to fill the vacancy created by the resignation of Daniel Webster (who had been elected to the Senate). When Benjamin died in 1855, he was buried at Phipps Street Cemetery, not far from his father's unmarked grave.[15] Their eighth child, Stephen, never married. He was a successful merchant who helped to found the Second Congregational (Unitarian) Society in 1816.[16] Lydia, their ninth and last child, was the grandmother of Phillips Brooks, one of the first Episcopal bishops in the United States.[17]

What little is known of Nathaniel's early years was handed down to us in the Eulogy that was delivered in his honor on June 29, 1796, by Dr. Thomas Welsh at the request of the Selectmen and citizens of Charlestown, Massachusetts. It is shamefully ironic that Dr. Welsh's soliloquy began with the following sentence: "It has been the laudable practice in all ages, to perpetuate the memory of their illustrious dead, either by erecting to their fame, monuments of the most durable materials; or immortalizing their names in the faithful pages of history."[18] Despite Dr. Welsh's oratorical flourish, at the start of the 21st Century, neither of those honors has yet been bestowed on President Nathaniel Gorham.

Dr. Welsh tells us that as a boy, Nathaniel was taught writing, arithmetic, reading and "instruction in the latin and greek languages, by which he was qualified for admission into the university." There is, however, no mention of attending Harvard. Instead, Nathaniel began an apprenticeship with a merchant by the name of Nathaniel Coffin in New London, Connecticut. In 1759, when he completed his apprenticeship, Nathaniel "took a tour of Canada" during the final phase of the French & Indian War. It was the furthest he ever traveled.[19]

At the age of 21, Nathaniel returned to Charlestown to open his own business "which appears to have prospered early..."[20] Welsh informs us, however, that even as a merchant, Nathaniel "indulged his prevailing and favorite inclination in the reading of History...he made himself, in a great degree, master of the History of England, as well as that of his own country. By these means, his mind was stored with a fund of historical facts, which were of great use afterwards, in the course of his public business."[21] Welsh also described Nathaniel as "Possessed of a mind clear and discerning, and of a temper mild and conciliating, accompanied with patience and prudence..." According to Welsh, Nathaniel had "a natural propensity to sympathy... and as a neighbour, [he was] sociable and friendly.."[22]

In public affairs, Nathaniel "was early elected selectman of the town [Charlestown], and served many years in that office."[23] From 1771-75, he was also a member of the colonial legislature during its final days. Nathaniel was there in Salem early on the morning of June 17, 1774, when he and his colleagues cleared the galleries, ordered that the doors be locked and proceeded to elect delegates to the Congress that was scheduled to meet in Philadelphia that September. Having heard of their plan, Gov. Thomas Gage, the commander of British troops in North America, immediately sent word that the legislature was dissolved. His messenger, however, was only admitted after their business had been completed.[24]

That Fall, while John Adams, Sam Adams, Thomas Cushing and Robert Treat Paine were away in Philadelphia at the First Continental Congress, Gov. Gage issued a call for the Massachusetts legislature to reassemble once again in Salem. As the representatives arrived, however, they received news that the governor had changed his mind due to the "unhappy state of the province..." The ninety representatives who had already gathered, including Nathaniel, decided to take matters into their own hands. On Thursday, October 6, 1774, they organized themselves into a convention. John Hancock, the future President, was elected chairman; Benjamin Lincoln, who later became a Major General in the American Revolution, was chosen as Secretary. The following day the members of the Convention notified the Governor that they had resolved themselves into a Provincial Congress. Over 200 delegates, including Nathaniel, then reconvened on Tuesday, October 11, 1774, at Concord, on the outskirts of Boston.[25]

On Thursday, October 13, 1774, the Provincial Congress informed Gov. Gage that his hostile attitude threatened "to involve us in all the confusion and horrors of a civil war." The next day the delegates decided that henceforth taxes would be paid directly to the colony rather than into the King's treasury. The following Monday, Nathaniel and his colleagues again ignored the Governor's orders by moving their meeting to Cambridge, across the Charles River from Boston. Most surprising of all, their "Thanksgiving Proclamation" on October 22, omitted the words: "God Save the King." The Governor's response to these incendiary developments grew increasingly firm. He warned the members of the Provincial Congress "to desist from such illegal and unconstitutional proceedings." [26]

As political argument erupted into military confrontation in the Spring of 1775, the little town of Charlestown found itself at the epicenter of revolution. Gen. Gage sent for Nathaniel, one of the leading politicians of Charlestown, to inform him "that in case the Americans approached Boston on that side he would be under the necessity of ordering that town to be burned; and that he could not be justifi[ed] by the laws of war to suffer it to stand to cover the approach of the Enemy.[27] After Nathaniel shared Gage's warning with the American militia and his fellow residents, most of the town's residents fled as the battle on Breed's Hill (mistakenly known to history as the battle of Bunker Hill) shattered their homes and shops. Nathaniel led his wife and their seven small children to the town of Lunenburg, in the county of Worcester, where his family remained while he returned to his public duties.[28]

Once the British fleet was driven from Boston in the Spring of 1776, the devastation left behind was extreme. On November 28, 1776, the Selectmen of Charlestown adopted a petition requesting £163,405 in financial assistance from the Continental Congress in order to rebuild their town.[29] Nathaniel and his colleague Thomas Russell were commissioned to travel to Philadelphia in order to plead their case directly to Congress. On May 21,1777, the Congressional Delegates from Massachusetts-- including John Hancock and both John and Sam Adams--reported back to their State Assembly that "the Gentlemen who presented the Petition have urged every Motive which could either show the Justice & Policy of granting the Request, or which could move the Humanity & Charity of those who heard it." Nevertheless, their Petition was denied "on Account of the present Condition of the Finances of the United States..."[30] In private correspondence with his wife, John Adams informed her that "Mr. Gorham and Mr. Russell are here with a Petition...It grieves me that they are to return without success."[31]

In October 1778, Nathaniel assumed yet another critical role when he was appointed by the Massachusetts Assembly as a member of the Board of War. He served in that capacity until the Board was dissolved three years later. Finally, in 1779, Nathaniel's family was able to return to Charlestown. That same year he was again elected to the State Assembly and, later that year, to the Massachusetts Constitutional Convention which, thanks largely to the brilliance of John Adams, produced what many still consider the best state constitution of the Revolutionary Era.[32] (Nathaniel's experience on this body proved invaluable eight years later when he played a pivotal role in drafting the new United States Constitution.)

Nathaniel was elected to the State Senate in 1780, but the following year he returned to the Assembly where he was selected by his legislative colleagues to serve as their Speaker in 1781, 1782 and 1785. When a rebellion arose in the Springfield area in 1782, Nathaniel was appointed by the Legislature along with Sam Adams and Artemas Ward to meet with the leaders of the uprising that August. Their negotiations were successful and bloodshed was averted. In July 1785, he was also appointed Judge of the Middlesex County Court of Common Pleas. Toward the end of that decade (1788-89) Nathaniel also served on the prestigious Governor's Council. Through it all, however, Nathaniel remained active in business and a true friend to his fellow merchants. He was a pragmatic man, far more interested in results than political theory.[33] He spoke with conviction rather than spellbinding oratory; closer in style to John Hancock than Richard Henry Lee.

During this already-intense period, the Massachusetts Legislature designated Nathaniel as the newest member of its Congressional Delegation. He was first elected on May 2, 1782, but he declined the honor because of the press of public and private responsibilities at home.[34] Nevertheless, Nathaniel kept current on congressional affairs through correspondence with John Lowell and other delegates.[35] That October he was again elected to represent Massachusetts and this time he did accept. On Thursday, December 12, 1782, Nathaniel submitted his certification to President Elias Boudinot and assumed his seat in his State's Delegation.[36] Less than two weeks later, however, Nathaniel suffered a bout of sickness that kept him confined for ten or twelve days, but he was reported "growing better" by the beginning of the new year.[37]

From the start, Nathaniel made a strong impression on some of his new colleagues. In early January 1783, Dr. David Ramsay of South Carolina (a noted historian and physician) commented to a friend from Massachusetts that "Your speaker Mr. Gorham has the esteem of Congress & is reckoned a man of abilities & integrity."[38] Not surprisingly, as a leading New England merchant, Nathaniel quickly acquired committee assignments pertaining to public finance. In mid-January he was selected as one of three members of a new congressional committee "to consider the expediency of making further applications for loans in Europe, & to confer with the Superintdt. of Finance on the subject."[39] Later that month, when the Superintendent of Finance, Robert Morris, informed Congress of his desire to resign from his office after years of service, Nathaniel expressed "extreme regret" and observed that "the Administration of Mr. M[orris] had inspired great confidence and expectation in his State [Massachusetts]." The delegates finally decided to keep Morris' intentions secret for the moment and Morris agreed to continue in his position for the time being.[40]

As Congress wrestled with administrative details that winter, the delegates anxiously awaited word from their Peace Commissioners in Paris. On January 29, 1783, Nathaniel shared his nagging doubts with his friend John Lowell in Massachusetts: "I observe that the publications in the Boston news papers indicate a speedy peace...but I conceive those publications are in some respects made in much stronger terms than advices received will justify, and in consequence there of the people & perhaps the Government may fall into a secure and lethargic state, which at this time would be peculiarly unhappy and perhaps destructive." Nathaniel explained that there was "No prospect at present of further foreign loans..." and that only $400,000 had been received from the States out of the $8,000,000 that Congress had requisitioned. He lamented that the Army had not been paid in two years and that "public creditors here are violently clamorous for their interest money." He warned his friend that "If the warr continues another year the distress of Congress must be in the extream their embarresments being now very great."[41]

Despite his affability, Nathaniel did not hesitate to speak his mind during debate. He vigorously challenged Virginia's right to withhold funding that Congress had requisitioned.[42] In another debate he corrected New York Delegate Alexander Hamilton's misperception of how taxes were collected in Massachusetts.[43] He clashed with John Rutledge of South Carolina over an interpretation of the rules pertaining to voting and later over the process of establishing the value of lands and buildings in each State.[44] On the issue of public credit he argued against Richard Henry Lee's position on redemption of certificates.[45]

After a day of debate, however, most of the delegates would socialize in the evenings either at the ever-popular City Tavern on North Second Street (five blocks from the State House) or at private lodgings. For example, after arguing the details of public finance that winter, Nathaniel would join Hamilton, Madison and several of their colleagues at the home of Thomas FitzSimons of Pennsylvania.[46] Thomas Mifflin, another Pennsylvania Delegate who would soon be elected President, was also well known for his lavish hospitality.[47]

The new nation, however, stood at a crossroads which could not always be bridged by a late night bottle of Madeira. As noted historian Merrill Jensen pointed out in his history of the United States during the Confederation, Adam Smith's *Wealth of Nations* [published in London in 1776] soon made its way to the United States where it was bought and read and where parts of it were printed in newspapers. People who accepted its views believed that governments should not meddle with economic life and particularly with trade."[48] And yet, only Congress could take the lead. H. James Henderson, in his remarkable analysis of congressional politics during that period, classifies Nathaniel as an independent, clearly leaning toward the Nationalist point of view. But, when James Wilson of Pennsylvania introduced a proposal for raising desperately needed funds, "Even Nathaniel Gorham of Massachusetts, who sympathized with the Nationalists, disliked the looseness of Wilson's original motion for general funds. He preferred that the taxes be specified before approving the resolution."[49]

The congressional debate on Friday, February 21, 1783, underscored how dangerous the problem could become if not resolved. As Madison recorded in his Notes of Debates: "Mr. Ghorum adverted with some warmth to the doctrines advanced by Mr. Lee & Mercer concerning the loan office Creditors. He said the Union could never be maintained on any other ground than that of Justice; that some States had suffered greatly from the deficiencies of others already; that if Justice was not to be obtained through the foederal system & this system was to fail as would necessarily follow, it was time this should be known that some of the States might be forming other confederacies adequate to the purposes of their safety."[50]

Four days later, in a letter to Edmund Randolph, his friend and fellow Virginian, Madison made clear how seriously he took Nathaniel's warning: "However erroneous these ideas may be, do they not {merit serious attention?} Unless some amicable & adequate arrangements be speedily taken for adjusting all the subsisting accounts and discharging the public engagements, a {dissolution of the union} will be {inevitable}. Will not in that event the {S{outhern} S{tates} which at sea} will be {opulent & } weak, be an {easy prey to the eastern} which {will be powerful and rapacious? &} particularly if supposed {claims of justice} are {on the side of the latter} will they not be a {ready pretext for reprisals?} The consequences of such a situation would probably be that {at alliances} would be {sought...&} this {country} be {made subservi[ent] to the wars & politics of Europe}.[51]

Nathaniel's fear and frustration over federal finances and what he perceived as his State's leadership in trying to raise the desperately needed taxes is perhaps best illustrated in his letter to Caleb Davis, his successor as Speaker of the State House: "...the powers of Congress are not adequate to the means of doing justice between the States--and that while the States continue so jealous of Congress they cannot be made so." He added that "I am more & more convinced that those States which have beene forward [like Massachusetts] will never obtain justice until funds are established-- and Unless such establishments are made or some alteration in the articles of confederation take place the union must ere long dissolve." Nathaniel pointed out that Virginia, the largest state, had only contributed $35,000 of the $8,000,000 that had been requisitioned from all the States. But he stressed to Davis that "I write this in confidence as some people would say from those sentiments that my head was turned that I was intoxicated with power &c. not considering that in a few months I should be as much under the power of Congress as any man whatever--but let such people be some time in Congress & they will alter their opinion."[52]

In a desperate attempt to resolve this crisis, Nathaniel was appointed to a congressional committee which also included Hamilton, Madison, Rutledge and FitzSimons. Their task was "to consider further the means of restoring and supporting public credit, and of obtaining from the states substantial funds for funding the whole debt of the United States..."[53] On March 6, 1783, this committee's report included the following: "That it be recommended to the several States, as indispensably necessary to the restoration of public credit, and the punctual and honorable discharge of the public debts, to vest in the United States in Congress assembled, a power to levy for the use of the United States, a duty of five per centum ad valorem, at the time and place of importation, upon all goods, wares and merchandizes of foreign growth and manufactures, which may be imported into any of the said States, from any foreign port...except arms, ammunition, clothing and other articles imported on account of the United States, or any of them, and except wool cards, cotton cards, and wire for making them, and also except salt during the war..."

The resolution then went into excruciating detail on various items. Finally, in an attempt to win support from the States, the motion also stated that "...with a view to a more amicable and complete adjustment of all accounts between the United States and individual states, all reasonable expences which shall have been incurred by the states separately without the sanction of Congress, in their defence against, or attacks upon British or savage enemies...and which shall be supported by satisfactory proofs, shall be considered as part of the common charges incident to this present war." Toward that goal, the report also called for amending Article Eight of the Articles of Confederation, a process that demanded unanimous consent of all 13 States. After much debate, the Committee's Report, as amended, was approved by Congress on Friday, April 18, 1783. Only Rhode Island voted no.[54] Delegate Stephen Higginson of Massachusetts described it as "a strange, though artful, plan of finance, in which are combined a heterogeneous mixture of imperceptible and visible, constitutional and unconstitutional taxes."[55]

In order to bring the issue to a head, Nathaniel informed Congress in early April that "A call had been issued by Massachusetts to the New England states and New York to send commissioners to a convention at Hartford on April 30 to consider 'such General & uniform system of

Taxation by import & excise as may be thought advantageous to the Said States.'" According to Madison's Notes, he and Hamilton "disapproved of these partial conventions..." Hamilton then stated that "he wished instead of them to see a general Convention take place & that he sd. soon in pursuance of instructions from his Constituents, propose to Congs. a plan for that purpose." Higginson said that no Gentleman need be alarmed at any rate for it was pretty certain that the [Hartford] Convention would not take place."[56] Higginson's prediction proved correct.

On June 4, 1783, Nathaniel informed Caleb Davis that Congress had devised a plan to help pay off the war debt by urging the States to cede their vacant lands to the national government. He also expressed the hope that "Congress will adjourn for three or four months...This place is exceedingly expensive and will undoubtedly encrease in that way--as foreign ministers increas. The Dutch minister...wrote to Mr. Livingston [Secretary for Foreign Affairs] desiring him to hire for use the best house in Town--& to buy him the most elegant carriage & six of the best carriage horses that can be bought--& if the dutchman rides with six horses the ministers of France England &c. will not chuse to ride with less."[57]

On Saturday, June 21, 1783, Congress confronted yet another crisis when mutinous soldiers from the Pennsylvania Line marched on the State House demanding their back pay. Nathaniel, who had earlier called for discharging all enlisted men as a cost-saving device, met with Robert Morris to discuss the implications of this confrontation.[58] Later that day, when Pennsylvania officials refused to call out the State Militia to protect the Delegates, President Boudinot issued the order that Congress, for its own safety, should adjourn to New Jersey.[59] When Congress did reconvene in Princeton nine days later, Nathaniel was not in attendance. His State Legislature, which did not favor generous pensions for army officers, refused to reappoint him because he had voted the previous March to alter the terms of the existing pension plan for the Continental Army.[60]

Mystery still surrounds Nathaniel's journey back to Boston. In a letter he received in early August from Stephen Higginson, his former congressional colleague, Higginson stated that "I fear you have expressed yourself too freely in New York [which was still occupied by the British], tho' I agree with you that proper communications may be useful. You must take care not to commit me nor yourself in too great a degree. If I return through New York, I should have no objection to a conversation with Sir Guy [Carleton, the last commander of British troops in North America]..." but he told Nathaniel that he would be adverse to the hurdles it would require until the definitive peace treaty arrived. What neither man knew was that Gen. Carleton had obtained a copy of Higginson's long and remarkably candid letter and had forwarded it to Lord North in London. Researchers at the Library of Congress have concluded that "No other information about the nature of Higginson's and Gorham's contacts with Sir Guy Carleton in New York has been found."[61]

Back home in Massachusetts, Nathaniel attended to his long-neglected family and financial affairs. As the political winds shifted, he was reelected to Congress on November 3, 1784, and again on June 16, 1785, but he chose to remain in Massachusetts instead.[62] There he resumed his duties as Speaker of the State House of Representatives. In addition to his legislative responsibilities, he was appointed that July as Judge of the Middlesex County Court of Common Pleas, a position he held until a few days before he died.[63] During 1785, Nathaniel also joined with then former Governor John Hancock and his recent congressional colleague John Lowell as incorporators of the Charles River Bridge, a major construction project that was the first to link Charlestown to Boston by land. Hancock served as President and Nathaniel as Vice President of the Corporation.[64]

As always, Hancock was much in demand, In November 1785, Congress once again elected the former President (1775-1777), to reprise his role as Head of State. Hancock accepted, but his health prevented him from traveling to New York City where Congress was then meeting. In his absence, David Ramsay of South Carolina was chosen to serve as Chairman, pending the new President's arrival.[65] At the same time, Congress was having even more difficulty than usual establishing a quorum in order to conduct business. Edmund Cody Burnett, the author of one of the most authoritative studies of the Continental Congress, described the Delegates as "exasperated" as the new year began.[66] It was in the midst of these developments that Nathaniel finally resumed his own congressional career on January 17, 1786.[67]

Despite Nathaniel's twenty month absence, the urgency pertaining to public credit still remained Congress' most pressing crisis. He wrote to Caleb Davis in February 1786 that "Our foreign creditors begin to be very serious in their applications respecting the provisions necessary for their reimbursement & the prospect of gaining the impost of any other permanent system of revenue to answer those demands appears to be distant...The failure of a compliance with the requisitions you will easily se[e] works a dissolution of the federal Government & with that an end to all our National importance & happiness." In the hope of setting an example and thereby avoiding such a catastrophe, Nathaniel urged his State to once again lead the way: "I hope you will therefore take care and procure a compliance on the part of Massachusetts with the present requisition."[68]

Toward the end of that letter, Nathaniel mentioned to Davis that "The State of Virginia...have appointed a Committee to meet the other States" to resolve problems related to trade. That meeting, which was held in Annapolis in September 1786, attracted only five States (but it lit the fuse that led directly to the Constitutional Convention the following May).[69] In his next letter to Davis (March 1, 1786), Nathaniel expressed his strong support for such a gathering: "I wish Massts could se[e] their way clear to request Congress to call a Convention--it would very much strengthen the hands of Congress..." More than most, Nathaniel clearly understood how constrain-ing the Articles of Confederation had become. While Congress had led with a relatively free hand from 1774-1781--operating as it deemed necessary as long as it could persuade a majority of the States to follow-- the Articles, which finally went into effect on March 1, 1781, had clearly placed Congress in a box. Tenure and procedures were formalized, powers were expressly limited, and raising revenue became even more torturous. Written in 1777, very early in its existence, the Articles of Confederation proved to be the death knell of the Continental Congress by the mid-1780s. As a Delegate, Nathaniel repeatedly challenged his colleagues to correct Congress' structural defects and strengthen the national government.

Too often, Nathaniel's admonitions fell on deaf ears. He attributed part of the problem to the rule which allotted only one vote to each State, regardless of size. "It is indeed a great inconvenience to the Union that the smallest States have equal weight in Congress with the largest...Congress is but the shadow of a Government." he told Davis.[70] In a letter to James Warren he argued that "There is no reason that RI, Delr. & Georgia should have equal weight in the federal councils with Massa., Penna. & Virginia- -and if the representation had been apportiond according to numbers or property--and a suitable quorum established & the major vote to determine questions--this inattention would not exist. But as unanimity is now necessary upon the most trivial questions we feel all the inconveniencies of the liberum Veto of a Polish Diet."[71]

The most immediate example was the New Jersey Legislature which had just declared "they will not pass a Tax Law in consequence of & in conformity to the last requistions of Congress..." until the State of New York stopped imposing an Impost tax on New Jersey.[72] Nathaniel warned James Warren that "however NJ may suffer by her paying taxes for N York her refusal to comply with the requisition is unjus[ti]fiable-- and unless she re[s]cinds her resolution must work the end of all federal Government."[73] In this instance, the members of Congress clearly shared Nathaniel's forebodings. On March 7, 1786, Congress appointed a three-member committee consisting of Nathaniel Gorham, William Grayson of

Virginia and Charles Pinckney of South Carolina. Their assignment was to travel to Trenton to inform the New Jersey Legislature "in the strongest terms, the fatal Consequences that must inevitably result to the said State, as well as to the rest of the Union, from their refusal to comply with the requisition of Congress..."[74]

On March 13, 1786, the three congressional Delegates individually addressed the New Jersey Assembly. As reported in the *New Jersey Gazette* one week later, Grayson, the Delegate from Virginia, was remarkably blunt. He warned the Assembly that if the present union was dissolved and an attempt was made to create a new national government in its place, "it could be supposed the lesser states [like New Jersey] would not be allowed to confederate upon equal terms with the more important." In its official response the following day, the New Jersey Legislature made clear that it was "desirous of promoting among all the states a lasting union, established upon prrinciples of justice and equality" and that it was "ready to accede to any measures founded on such a basis." The Assembly then attempted to save face by justifying its February Resolution, but it ultimately voted to preserve the union by rescinding its earlier Resolution, even though the members had no intention of reversing their underlying policy.[75] Under the circumstances, the illusion of compliance was the best attainable option. How long that delusion could be maintained was the fundamental question.

On Monday, May 15, 1786, Nathaniel's life continued to intersect with the history of his young nation when he was elected to replace David Ramsay as Chairman of the Continental Congress which was still awaiting the arrival of its President, John Hancock.[76] On June 5, however, word finally arrived from Boston. Benjamin Hichborn, on behalf of John Hancock, informed Congress that Hancock was "still confined to his bed, and unable to write himself..." Therefore, because of "the total uncertainty of his future health," Hancock felt obligated "to request their acceptance of his resignation of the Office of President..."[77] The following day, Tuesday, June 6, 1786, Chairman Nathaniel Gorham was elected as the twelfth President of the Continental Congress and the only Massachusetts Delegate other than Hancock to serve as Head of State during the First American Republic.[78]

As President, Nathaniel, like his predecessors, had to confront Congress' most persistent problem: the lack of a quorum. He wrote to Caleb Davis ten days after his election that "The business of Congress is excessively retarded by the delinquency of the States in their representation and what has heretofore been unusual this delinquency is principally with the Eastern States--NH., RI. & Cont. being unrepresented & have been so for some time past--RI ever since November last. The interest of the Union suffers extreamly by this conduct--many important subjects now before Congress cannot be passed on for want of nine States."[79]

The following day, Nathaniel wrote to Massachusetts Gov. James Bowdoin, who had been elected after Hancock suddenly resigned on January 29, 1785, because of poor health.[80] As President, Nathaniel pointed out to the new Governor that even Massachusetts was now in arrears on the money it owed Congress. Nathaniel warned that "Unless the States make great exertion the very appearance of the federal Government must cease--the civil list being without their pay for almost two quarters." He added that " Exertion is the more necessary as the collection of the outstanding taxes is the only dependence for every purpose." Later in the letter, Nathaniel switched emphasis to point out to his Massachusetts colleague that "Yesterday & the day before N York sold a large quantity of Land at auction being part of that claimed by Massachusetts..."[81] A long-running dispute over the exact boundary between the two States had been a source of friction between New York and Massachusetts for several years. As the issue came closer to a resolution, tensions also tended to escalate. (Later, after he retired from public life, this territory became the primary focus of Nathaniel's life.)

On June 27, 1786, the Massachusetts General Assembly held its annual election of Delegates to Congress. Not surprisingly, Nathaniel received by far the largest majority: 134 votes. None of his three colleagues--Nathan Dane, Samuel Holton and Rufus King--received more than eighty.[82] With John Hancock in temporary retirement and John Adams still serving as Minister to Great Britain, Nathaniel Gorham, the President of Congress, was now the most powerful politician from Massachusetts.

As was customary, Nathaniel hosted a glorious 4th of July celebration at his presidential mansion at No. 3 Cherry Street in New York City.[83] From the hours of twelve to two, the President held a public levee which included congressional Delegates, members of the Diplomatic Corps, the Secretary at War, the Commissioners of the Board of Treasury, the Commissioners for Indian Affairs, the Governor of New York, the Mayor of New York City and other dignitaries.[84] As Head of State, ceremonial functions have always been the prerogative of the President.

Like many of his distinguished predecessors, such lavish celebrations cut deeply into Nathaniel's limited resources during his term as President. That Fall, he was forced to write to Thomas Ivers, the Treasurer of Massachusetts: "I have been under the necessity of borrowing some money of a Friend in this place for which I have given him a Bill on your for 300 dollars... I must intreat your exertions that it may be paid as I cannot leave this place without the negotiation of that sum at least...I shall be much [obligated] to you for your assistance."[85]

Perhaps the strangest yet least-known development of the entire Revolutionary Era occurred in the Fall of 1786, during Nathaniel's presidency. Researchers at the Library of Congress who compiled and edited the 26 volume Letters of Delegates to Congress have written that "Historians were once fascinated with the idea of monarchical tendencies in the United States, seizing upon a number of statements and rhetorical flourishes gleaned from the correspondence of several founding fathers... [Rufus] King and his colleague Nathaniel Gorham had been linked with such sentiments..."[86]

In September 1786, Rufus King wrote a remarkable letter to his congressional predecessor, Jonathan Jackson: "What can be done is the Question--the answer is various. Some say, and the opinion is extensive, infuse a new portion of Strength into the confederation and all will be well...Others, and by no means the least respectable, answer, that nothing can be done in our present Form; that the Error lies in the original plan... they tell you that a League or confederation between so many small, and unequal, Sovereignities never did, or can, answer the views of its Patrons--they illustrate, by affirming that the Greek Republics were finally melted down, and united, under one Head--that in France and Spain...the People did not find their Happiness in...small Divisions, but sought it under their present form..." King immediately added that "It must not be understood that these Remarks authorize an Opinion that a monarch would promote the Happiness of the people of America--far, very far, from it. But they show this; if wise & prudent men discerning the Imperfections of the present Governments, do not in Season and without Fear, propose suitable Remedies, the causes which changed the Governments alluded to may, and probably will, change those of America."[87]

Edmund Cody Burnett, who was also the first historian to publish a collection of congressional letters, has written that there were "many indications that the idea of establishing a monarchy in America was in circulation at that time, although perhaps only in whispers." As evidence, he cited an article by Richard Krauel that was published in 1911 in the American Historical Review.[88] In "Prince Henry of Prussia and the Regency of the United States, 1786," Krauel quoted a memorandum written by Rufus King on May 10, 1824: "Col. Miller this evening said to me, speaking of Mr. Pr[esident] Monroe, that he had told him that Mr. Gorham, formerly President of Congress, had written a letter to Prince Henry, brother of the great Frederic, desiring him to come to the U. S. to be their king, and that the Prince had declined by informing Mr. Gorham that the Americans had shown so much determination agt. their old King, that they wd. not readily submit to a new one..." According to Krauel, both John Quincy Adams and Henry Clay gave the story enough credence to make further inquires, but neither found any corroborating evidence.[89]

Such evidence, however, was finally uncovered nearly a century later by Krauel. He discovered the draft of a letter from Prince Henry in the Prussian archives in Charlottenburg, Germany. It was in response to a November 1786 letter from the Prince's old companion, the Baron von Steuben, who, after faithfully serving Prince Henry through many campaigns, had emigrated to America in search of a steady income. Von Steuben served as a Major General and as Inspector General during the American Revolution.[90] Even though Prince Henry's letter is undated, Krauel convincingly reconstructs the date as early April 1787, the time frame appropriate for a response to a letter that would have been sent by ship the previous Fall. The text of the letter, composed in French (as was all of Prince Henry's correspondence), is friendly yet intentionally vague since it was not written in code. The Prince implied that von Steuben had enclosed "the letter from one of your friends" with his own. The closest the Prince came to acknowledging the presumed topic is when he wrote that "I would never believe that one could resolve to change the government principles which the USA has established for itself, but if the entire nation were to be in agreement to establish there (in the USA) another government, and were to choose for its model the constitution of England, then, in my opinion I would believe that it (the English Const.) among all the constitutions which I know, seems to me to be the most perfect."[91]

By 1786, Nathaniel's profound anxiety over the existing congressional government had become painfully clear. Whether, as President, he went even further by exploring the possibility of establishing an American monarchy still remains conjecture. Madison, however, was well aware of such undercurrents. In a letter to a friend on February 24, 1787, he stated: "The late turbulent scenes in Massts. [Shay's Rebellion] & infamous ones in Rhode Island, have done inexpressible injury to the republican characer in that part of the U. States; and a propensity towards Monarchy is said to have been produced by it in some leading minds."[92] The issue arose once again while Nathaniel was attending the Constitutional Convention in Philadelphia. According to an article published in the Mississippi Valley Historical Review in 1938, The Rev. Manasseh Cutler claimed that he had sat up "'till half after one that morning of July 13 [1787] in deep speech with Nathaniel Gorham, the brains of the monarchical party in the United States."[93] What was undisputed during this early stage in the country's history was that, having won the war for independence, the United States was on the verge of imploding. As described in detail by historian John Fiske, it was, indeed, "The Critical Period of American History."[94]

Nathaniel's presidential service (the final six months of John Hancock's second, but unattended, term) was scheduled to end on Monday, November 6, 1786, when the new congressional session was supposed to begin. Two weeks later, he left New York, most likely headed for Connecticut to attend the Hartford Convention "which met November 30 to December 16 to settle Massachusetts' claims to lands in western New York..." As a Massachusetts politician and businessman, Nathaniel was deeply concerned over the final agreement reached between the two States.[95]

In Congress, however, the lack of a quorum postponed the selection of Nathaniel's successor--Major General Arthur St. Clair--until Friday, February 2, 1787.[96] By February 21, Congress was finally ready to review the letter written by John Dickinson the previous Fall on behalf of the five States--Virginia, Delaware, Pennsylvania, New Jersey and New York--that had assembled at Annapolis in September 1786. It urged Congress to call a new convention. In response, Congress approved the following Motion: "Resolved that in the opinion of Congress, it is expedient that on the second Monday in May next a Convention of delegates who shall have been appointed by the several States be held at Philadelphia for the sole and express purpose of revising the Articles of Confederation and reporting to Congress and the several legislatures such alterations and provisions therein as shall when agreed to in Congress and confirmed by the States render the federal Constitution adequate to the exigencies of Government and the preservation of the Union."[97]

The Massachusetts Assembly elected Nathaniel Gorham, Rufus King, Nathan Dane, Elbridge Gerry and Caleb Strong as its representatives to the Philadelphia Convention (Dane, however, chose to remain in Congress).[98] Of the four Massachusetts Delegates who did participate in the Convention, Nathaniel was the only one who had not attended Harvard.[99] On March 18, James Madison reported to George Washington that "The appointments for the Convention go on very successfully."[100] The next day, he informed Jefferson (who was serving as United States Minister to France) that "I just learn from the Governor of Virginia that Mr. Henry has resigned his place in the deputation from that State..."[101] Since Patrick Henry was already well known as an opponent of a stronger central government, Madison probably greeted the news with some momentary relief.

While awaiting the opening of the Philadelphia Convention, Nathaniel returned to his congressional duties in New York on April 21.[102] According to Madison's Notes, the following Monday Congress debated the ongoing struggle with Spain over access to the Mississippi River. Nathaniel "avowed his opinion that the Shutting the Mississippi would be advantageous to the Atlantic States, and wished to see it shut."[103] Many of his congressional colleagues strongly disagreed.

On May 3, Madison left New York for Philadelphia. In total, ten current Members of Congress participated in the Convention while two others--Richard Henry Lee of Virginia and Abraham Clark of New Jersey--had also been elected to both but felt that their primary responsibility was to Congress.[104] Nathaniel briefly remained in New York to help Congress attain a quorum. But, on May 22, he informed Caleb Davis that "...as Congress cannot be kept up at present I shall set of[f] for Phia tomorrow or next day in hopes that some of the other Gentm will soon be after me. The Business of the convention is of the last importance for if the meeting or its doings should proved abortive, The present phantom of a Government must soon expire..."[105] Changes were underway back in Boston, as well. One hundred fifty-six new members had been elected to the Massachusetts House of Representatives (out of 216) and the ailing John Hancock had recovered both his physical and political health in time to reclaim the governorship on May 30, 1787.[106]

At the Philadelphia Convention, which officially opened on a rainy Friday morning, May 25, 1787, George Washington was elected as the presiding officer. Nathaniel arrived the following Monday.[107] The General's duties as President, however, were largely symbolic. Only once during the five month session did Washington ask permission to speak directly to an issue prior to a vote. For weeks, the real day-to-day debate took place in the Committee of the Whole where the rules and procedures provided a less restrained environment in which all the delegates could freely express themselves. Nathaniel, having successfully presided over Congress the previous year, was elected on Wednesday, May 30, to chair that critical committee.[108] As historian Charles L. Mee, Jr. stated in his study of the Convention, Nathaniel's "selection as chairman placed in that highly visible presiding officer's chair a self-made man, a man whose very presence argued, if not for democracy, at least against aristocracy."[109]

One of the Delegates from Georgia, William Pierce, sketched brief yet insightful profiles of some of his colleagues as the Convention's work began. He described Nathaniel as "a Merchant in Boston, high in reputation, and much in the esteem of his Countrymen. He is a Man of very good sense, but not much improved in his education. He is eloquent and easy in public debate, but has nothing fashionable or elegant in his style;--all he aims at is to convince, and where he fails it never is from his auditory not understanding him, for no Man is more perspicuous and full. He has been President of Congress, and three years a Member of that Body. Mr. Gorham is about 46 years of age [he had actually just turned 49], rather lusty, and has an agreable and pleasing manner."[110]

Nathaniel lodged at the popular Indian Queen Tavern at the corner of Market and North Fourth Street, only two and a half blocks from the State House. Hamilton, Madison, George Mason of Virginia, Charles Pinckney and John Rutledge of South Carolina and several other delegates were also housed there.[111] Such close proximity afforded endless opportunities for "out-of-doors" conversations among that remarkable and diverse group.

On May 29, Edmund Randolph, now Governor, introduced "The Virginia Plan" which had been largely drafted by James Madison.[112] Starting the following morning, the Committee of the Whole, under Nathaniel's leadership, devoted two full weeks to Randolph's proposal which included the establishment of two branches of the national legislature, the first of which would be elected by the people of each State and the other to be chosen by the first branch. It also called for the national executive to be chosen by the national legislature and for a national judiciary. This "Plan of Union," as Randolph called it, also made provisions for the introduction of future amendments and the admission of new states. It clearly called for the dissolution of the existing Congress--even though it anticipated Congress' vote of "approbation"--and it mandated that the States would be "bound by oath to support the Articles of Union."[113]

Then, on June 15, William Patterson of New Jersey spoke out on behalf of his own State--as well as the smaller States, in general--when he introduced the "New Jersey Plan" which was designed to amend the existing Articles of Confederation (as clearly mandated by Congress) rather than replacing the Continental Congress with an entirely new national government.[114] Rhode Island, one of the smallest States, boycotted the entire Convention.

In mid-June, as the initial debate over the Virginia Plan was drawing to a close, Nathaniel shared a few of his observations with his friend Theophilus Parsons, who later became Chief Justice of the Massachusetts Supreme Judicial Court: "...The present Federal Government seems near its exit; and whether we shall in the Convention be able to agree upon mending it, or forming and recommending a new one, is not certain. All agree, however, that much greater powers are necessary to be given, under some form or other. But the large States think the representation ought to be more in proportion to the magnitude of the States, and consequently more like a national government, while the smaller ones are for adhering to the present mode...all agree the legislative and executive ought to be separate, and that there should be a national judiciary."[115]

One week later, a plaintive message from Nathan Dane, who was still attending Congress in New York, added even more drama to an already tense situation. "I assure you," Dane said, "the present State of Congress has a very disagreeable effect in the Eastern States. The people hear of a Convention in Philada. and that Congress is done sitting, &c. Many of them are told, it seems, that Congress will never meet again probably... these things have a pernicious effect on the industry, peace, & habits of the people...if we mean to avoid convulsions those appearances which to the unthinking look so much like abandoning the established Government ought not to be suffered to take place."[116]

In addition to chairing the Convention's key committee, Nathaniel was also actively engaged in the debate. When John Mercer of Maryland argued that permitting the average citizen to elect the House of Representatives was foolish because "The people cannot know and judge of the characters of candidates..." Nathaniel forcefully replied that "He had never seen any inconvenience from allowing such as were not freeholders to vote...The elections in Philadelphia, New York, and Boston, where the merchants and mechanics vote, are at least as good as those made by freeholders only." Nathaniel added that "The people have been long accustomed to this right in various parts of America, and will never allow it to be abridged. We must consult their rooted prejudices if we expect their concurrence in our propositions."[117]

When the debate shifted to the newly proposed Senate, several suggestions were offered concerning the length of a senator's service. On June 26, Nathaniel introduced a motion to set the term at six years, and that the rotation be triennial. Wilson of Pennsylvania seconded and a majority of the Delegates approved.[118]

A much tougher debate revolved around the Virginia Plan's proposal that members of the Senate should be elected by the US House of Representatives, "out of persons nominated by the State Legislatures."[119] Even though such a proposal could have benefited his home State because of its size, Nathaniel "thought there was some weight in the objections of the small states."[120] Once that notion was defeated, an even more acrimonious debate revolved around whether or not the number of senators from each State should be based on a proportional standard, as would be true in the new House of Representatives; or, on an equal basis, as had been the rule in Congress over the previous thirteen years. According to the authors of Decision in Philadelphia, a detailed analysis of the 1787 Convention, this was "without question the single most critical moment at the Convention."[121] With only ten States present on that fateful day, five States voted to give the smaller States equal representation while four of the largest States voted against it. If Massachusetts had sided with the largest States, its natural allies, the motion would have died with a tie vote. But, its delegation was split and therefore its vote didn't count. Nathaniel and King did, indeed, support proportional representation, but Gerry and Strong backed Delaware and the smaller States. Thus, the new United States Senate would, in effect, continue the tradition of the Continental Congress and afford each State, large or small, equal representation.[122] As originally designed, those senators were to be elected by the State Legislatures (this method of election was eventually changed to a popular election by the adoption of the 17th Amendment in 1913).

In the midst of their deliberations, the Convention Delegates voted to establish a Committee of Detail which would attempt to sketch the first draft of a constitution based upon the decisions that had been reached up to that point. The members of that powerful committee included John Rutledge and Edmund Randolph (Peyton Randolph's favorite nephew) who were selected to represent the Southern States; James Wilson of Pennsylvania, chosen on behalf of the middle States; and, Oliver Ellsworth of Connecticut and Nathaniel Gorham to represent New England. These five members began their delicate task on July 27, working steadily over the next ten days as their more fortunate colleagues enjoyed a desperately needed break.[123]

The Report their committee issued on Monday, August 6, went far beyond the language that had already been approved by the Delegates. That was especially true pertaining to the issue of slavery. Even though the five members had been chosen, in part, for geographic balance, James Wilson, the middle-States representative, was a business ally of John Rutledge and had housed Rutledge at his Philadelphia home for the first three weeks of the Convention.[124] Oliver Ellsworth's position was to "Let every state import what it pleases. The morality or wisdom of slavery are considerations belonging to the states themselves."[125] Nathaniel was the only member of the committee who had repeatedly opposed slavery but, as a successful businessman, he understood Rutledge's economic arguments; and, as a pragmatic politician, he took very seriously Delegate Charles Pinckney's contention that "South Carolina can never receive the plan if it prohibits the slave trade."[126] Pinckney argued that if slavery was wrong, it was nevertheless "justified by the example of all the world."[127] At one point, however, Nathaniel did argue against the South's demand to count a slave as a full person when calculating the size of a State's delegation in the House of Representatives. He successfully pointed out that the three-fifths ratio, which "was fixed by Congress as a rule of taxation," should continue to be the applicable standard.[128] But, on August 24, for reasons that remain unclear, Nathaniel seconded the motion introduced by Charles Cotesworth Pinckney of South Carolina, to extend the date for limiting the importation of slaves from 1800 to 1808.[129]

When the debate shifted to the election of federal judges, many of the delegates initially favored having them nominated and elected by Congress. Nathaniel strongly disagreed. Drawing upon the 140 year procedure common to Massachusetts, Nathaniel introduced a motion that "the judges be nominated and appointed by the executive, by and with the advice and consent of the second branch [senate]..."[130] His approach prevailed.

Nathaniel was exceptionally blunt concerning Article VII, Section 6 of the draft introduced by his own committee. It stated that "No navigation act shall be passed without the assent of two thirds of the members present in each house."[131] As a leading merchant who relied heavily on overseas trade, he "Did not see the propriety of it." He demanded to know if it was meant "to require a greater proportion of votes? He desired it to be remembered that the eastern states had no motive to union but a commercial one. They were able to protect themselves. They were not afraid of external danger, and did not need the aid of the southern states."[132] Once again, Nathaniel won the debate.

One specific item that repeatedly bedeviled the delegates concerned the number of citizens who should be represented by each member of the House. Madison objected to the ratio of one for every forty thousand inhabitants as a perpetual rule because he anticipated that the potential growth of the new nation would eventually make the size of that body ungovernable. Nathaniel responded that "It is not to be supposed that the government will last so long as to produce this effect. Can it be supposed," he argued, "that this vast country, including the western territory, will, one hundred and fifty years hence, remain one nation?"[133]

At long last, the Convention's work was completed, or so the Delegates thought. They met for the last time on Monday morning, September 17, 1787. Just as they were ready to sign the document, Nathaniel rose to address his colleagues yet again on the issue of representation. "If it was not too late," he said, "he could wish, for the purpose of lessening objection to the Constitution, that the clause, declaring that 'the number of Representatives shall not exceed one for every forty thousand,' which had produced so much discussion, might yet be reconsidered..." He proposed lowering the number to thirty thousand in order to guarantee more popular participation in the House. And then, for the first and only time during the entire Convention, President Washington rose to speak in favor of the motion. It was agreed to unanimously.[134]

Of the 39 signatures that were affixed to the new Constitution that afternoon, Nathaniel and his colleague Rufus King were the only two delegates from Massachusetts to do so. Caleb Strong, who supported it, had already left Philadelphia and Elbridge Gerry refused to endorse the final document.[135] Nathaniel was also one of only two Presidents of Congress to sign the Constitution. The other, Thomas Mifflin, played only a minor role during the formal deliberations but his well-earned reputation for hospitality certainly contributed significantly to the ongoing dialogue.

Nathaniel returned to Congress on Thursday, September 20, 1787, just as the proposed Constitution was being submitted. Even though the original Congressional Resolution the preceding February which authorized the Convention stated clearly that its "sole and express purpose" was to revise the Articles of Confederation and that the final document would then have to be "agreed to in Congress," the Members of Congress reluctantly adopted the Convention's proposal and simply passed it on to the States without a congressional vote.[136]

On October 12, Nathaniel finally headed home to Charlestown after seven grueling yet historic months. Eager to attend to his political base after years of national service, he was delighted when the Massachusetts Assembly placed his name in nomination for Lt. Governor, to serve under Gov. Hancock. When the votes were counted in the Senate, however, Nathaniel lost the election to Thomas Cushing, Hanckock's closest political ally.[137]

But, as Nathaniel well knew, a much bigger battle over ratification of the new Constitution was just ahead. By one estimate, "over 55 percent of the members of the General Court [State Legislature] came from towns opposed to the Constitution." To make matters worse, Gerry, who had opposed the document in Philadelphia, made available to the 329 State Delegates his list of specific objections.[138] Nathaniel pleaded with King to hurry back to Boston in time for the Convention. He told King that "You can have no idea how much depends on your presence."[139] According to one source, they even prepared "an elaborate refutation of Gerry's objections" but decided not to distribute it lest they give their opponent's views even greater credence.[140]

In his analysis of the Massachusetts Ratification Convention, historian Jack N. Rakove states that "In no other state did the division between the parties rest more on differences of social class than on specific objections to the Constitution, leaving Federalists puzzled as to how to allay the diffuse fears their opponents voiced."[141] As King wrote to Madison: "... their opposition seems to arise from an Opinion, that is immovable, that some injury is plotted against them..."[142] It is therefore ironic that Elbridge Gerry became the champion of the "lower classes" even though he was the only Massachusetts Delegate to the Constitutional Convention who "did not like the election by the people" for membership in the new House of Representatives. In Philadelphia, Gerry had even argued that "The evils we experience flow from the excess of democracy."[143]

Nathaniel also realized that "we cannot gain the question without some amendments."[144] Since Hancock once again dominated State politics, Nathaniel and his fellow Federalists wisely followed the old political precept that you can accomplish anything if you don't care who gets the credit. He therefore asked the Governor to take the lead in recommending any necessary changes that could be introduced during the first session of the new Federal Congress.

Having served as both President and Governor, Hancock viewed the process from a unique perspective. He also knew that he was the prime candidate for the soon-to-be-enhanced presidency if Virginia failed to ratify and Washington thereby became ineligible for the office.[145]

After being elected as the presiding officer of the Massachusetts Ratification Convention on January 9, 1788, Hancock withdrew to his Beacon Hill mansion supposedly to nurse his latest case of gout; but, in his time-honored tradition, his medical condition also provided the perfect opportunity for him to observe the political landscape before declaring his own position. Meanwhile, at the Convention, Nathaniel repeatedly responded to critics who feared that the new system would jeopardize their liberties. He stressed the importance of the separation of powers and the checks and balances that had been placed on the three branches of the new government. Nathaniel even obtained a copy of Benjamin Franklin's final speech at the Philadelphia Convention in support of the Constitution which he eagerly shared with his fellow delegates in Boston.[146]

Finally, on January 31, Gov. Hancock was carried into the Convention, propped up against the podium, and delivered his speech in support of the new Constitution, urging that nine specific amendments be added as soon as the new Congress convened. [147] Six days later, Massachusetts ratified the Constitution by a vote of 187-168.[148] The importance of that victory cannot be overstated.

From the first hint of American Independence in February 1761, when James Otis argued the Writs of Assistance case, Massachusetts had consistently taken the lead in the struggle for liberty.[149] Without its support for the new Constitution at that critical crossroads, Virginia and New York would almost certainly have rejected the document, as well. The new Federal Government would have been stillborn and with it, defeat would have been snatched from the jaws of victory. How different the 21st

Century would be had not Hancock, Gorham and King given their all at that fateful moment in their nation's history!

At the local level, political change was also in the air. After the annual elections for the Massachusetts General Assembly in May 1788, Samuel A. Otis (James Otis' younger brother) shared his surprise at the outcome with Caleb Davis: "The rejection of Mr Warren at Milton, Mr Reed, and especially Mr Gorham, is very unaccountable. I thot the latter had the fee simple of the Charlestown Seat."[150] Nevertheless, on June 6, Nathaniel was reelected by the newly seated legislature to represent his State one final time in the Continental Congress as the First American Republic gradually faded from the scene. According to the official Journal, he presented his credentials on Monday, January 26, 1789.[151] The expense account he later submitted indicated that he stayed in New York until the conclusion of the Continental Congress in early March.[152] During this period, Nathaniel still held the office of Judge in Middlesex County and, from 1788-89, he was also a member of the prestigious Governor's Council.[153]

Once nine States had ratified the new Constitution by June 1788, the transition to the Second Republic began.[154] On December 18, 1788, Nathaniel's name was placed in nomination for election to the first House of Representatives. In that initial round of balloting in the Middlesex District, he led with 37 percent of the vote compared to 26 percent for Elbridge Gerry, who had refused to sign the Constitution. Before the final election, however, word spread among Nathaniel's friends that he "gave out publicly and in the most positive manner before he set out for New York that he would not accept if chosen." As a result, Gerry was elected in January 1789.[155] By early April, the new Congress had finally established a quorum and on April 30, 1789, George Washington was inaugurated at Federal Hall in New York City as the first President of the Second American Republic.[156]

After more than two decades of uninterrupted public service at all levels of government, Nathaniel decided to shift his emphasis back to business affairs now that his new nation was secure. The land ceded by New York State in December 1786, as part of the settlement of its boundary dispute with Massachusetts, presented an extremely tempting target.[157] In 1788, Nathaniel joined forces with another prominent patriot, Oliver Phelps, who had stood at Lexington Green as the "shot heard round the world" was fired in April 1775. Together, they created a syndicate that purchased nearly 6,000,000 acres which became known as the "Phelps and Gorham's Purchase" of the Genesee Country. The $1,000.000 price was to be repaid to the State of Massachusetts in three annual installments in "the public paper of the commonwealth." Phelps, the "general agent," even settled part-time on the land in 1789 after successfully negotiating a clear title to over a third of the territory in direct negotiations with various Indian tribes. Nathaniel concentrated on negotiations with New York State.[158]

Their grand scheme began to unravel in 1789 when they "found themselves unable to fulfill the engagements they had made for the payment of the purchase money. They had predicated payment upon the supposition, that they could purchase the public paper of Massachusetts, at its then market value, which was but about fifty cents on the dollar. In the interval, before pay day arrived, the prospect of success in the formation of a Federal government, and a consequent funding of the debts of the States, the paper they had stipulated to make payment in, had nearly a par value in market.."[159] It is painfully ironic that Nathaniel's determination to save the national government resulted in his own financial ruin.

Other prominent Americans also suffered a similar fate. The rush toward land speculation or equally risky investments eventually led ten Convention Delegates to "excruciatingly difficult financial times" or even bankruptcy.[160] Robert Morris, the wealthy Philadelphia financier who had devoted so much of his energy and income to repeatedly rescuing both Congress and the Continental Army, not only lost his fortune but even suffered the added indignity of three and a half years in debtors prison.[161]

Nathaniel and his partner Phelps were able to avoid the humiliation of incarceration, but neither of them ever recovered financially nor emotionally from the collapse of their empire. Their eldest sons, however, did not give up on their fathers' dream. Both Nathaniel Gorham, Jr. and Oliver Leicester Phelps eventually settled on the land that had brought ruin to their elders. In time, both younger men even became leaders of that emerging frontier territory.[162]

Nathaniel's health, however, steadily declined. "Despondent over his financial losses," he died of apoplexy at his home in Charlestown on June 11, 1796.[163]

Because his estate could not even afford a separate burial plot, his remains were interned with his mother's family. It was only in 1987, in celebration of the bicentennial of the United States Constitution, that the Daughters of the American Revolution placed special markers on the burial sites of most of the Signers.[164] For the first time in nearly two centuries, President Nathaniel Gorham's grave finally bore his name.

Because of financial losses during the final years of his life,
President Nathaniel Gorham was buried in the plot belonging
to his Mother's family at Phipps Street Burying Ground in Charlestown,
Massachusetts. His name did not appear on his grave until 1987.

WHILE NATHANIEL GORHAM
WAS PRESIDENT

June 1786 - November 1786

Just as Richard Henry Lee had been called upon in 1784 in the hope of rejuvenating Congress during its awkward transition to peace, another senior statesman was elected to replace Lee on November 23, 1785.[165] John Hancock, who had already served as President for over two years during the early days of the Revolution, was summoned once again to take the helm of the national government.[166] Hancock, who had most recently served as Governor of Massachusetts, was clearly flattered, but cautious. During the new post-war period, Congress no longer dominated the American agenda. In fact, under the Articles of Confederation (which had not gone into effect until three and a half years after Hancock had left the presidency), the powers and prerogatives of Congress had been significantly curtailed.

Whenever in doubt, Hancock relied on his painful bouts of gout to remain aloof long enough to test the political winds. He therefore accepted his election as President, but notified Congress that his arrival would be delayed until his health improved.[167] In Hancock's absence, Delegate David Ramsay--a medical doctor and distinguished patriot from Charleston, South Carolina--agreed to preside over debate on those rare occasions when a quorum could be reached. (Ramsay, who was also an American historian, would marry former President Henry Laurens' eldest daughter the following year.)[168] He held the title of Chairman of the Continental Congress from November 23, 1785 until May 15, 1786, when his term as a Delegate expired.[169]

Since there was still no word from Boston, Congress immediately proceeded to the selection of another Chairman, pending Hancock's arrival. Nathaniel Gorham, another distinguished Massachusetts Delegate who had worked closely with Hancock on a wide range of public issues and had served as Speaker of his State's House, was unanimously elected.[170] He held the chairmanship for three weeks until Hancock finally submitted his resignation. Nathaniel was then elected to complete the final six months of the presidential term.[171]

During 1786, the rebellion in Western Massachusetts captured the nation's attention. Daniel Shays, who had served in the Continental Army at Bunker Hill and Saratoga, led an uprising of farmers and retired military who faced financial ruin during the depression that followed the end of the Revolutionary War.[172] The insurgents attributed their defiance to several major causes, including "The present expensive mode of collecting debts, which by reason of the great scarcity of cash will of necessity fill our jails with unhappy debtors, and thereby a reputable body of people [will be] rendered incapable of being serviceable either to themselves or the community."[173]

As President, Nathaniel wrote to Massachusetts Gov. Bowdoin that "The affairs of the Western Country are in such a state as to induce Congress to propose an augmentation of the Troops--a considerable number of which are assigned to Massachusetts..."[174] Congress did authorize the recruitment of an additional 1,340 "noncommissioned Officers and privates" to meet the crisis.[175] Beyond its military impact, the rebellion scared many prominent merchants and community leaders into supporting a stronger central government.

Shays Rebellion also raised deep-seated concerns over how much democracy the people could handle. On August 1, 1786, Washington wrote from Mount Vernon that "We have errors to correct. We have probably had too good an opinion of human nature in forming our confederation. Experience has taught us that men will not adopt and carry into execution measures the best calculated for their own good without the intervention of a coercive power." Toward the end of that same letter, Washington commented that "I am told that even respectable characters speak of a monarchical form of government without horror."[176]

In contrast, the role of the British Monarch was gradually being undermined by his chief minister, William Pitt the Younger (the son of America's late, great defender). Pitt was building the foundation for the system known today as Cabinet Government with himself, rather than the King, at the center of the decision-making process. The Oxford History of England states that "respect for his [Pitt's] political acumen and fear of thwarting so powerful a figure increased year by year."[177] Eventually, that process evolved into the modern concept of the British Prime Minister as Head of Government.

Chapter 12

President
NATHANIEL GORHAM
of
MASSACHUSETTS

Notes

Abbreviation Key

JCC   Journals of the Continental Congress
LDC   Letters of Delegates to Congress
PHL   The Papers of Henry Laurens

[1] John C. Fitzpatrick, Editor, JCC: 1774-1789, (Government Printing Office, Washington, DC, 1904), Vol. XXX, p. 330.

[2] The Declaration of Independence: "Governments are instituted among Men, deriving their just powers from the consent of the governed."

[3] Rosanne Atwood-Humes, Project Supervisor, *Historic Burial Grounds Inventory Project* (Phipps Street Burial Ground, Charlestown, MA, 1984), p. 2.

[4] Allen Johnson & Dumas Malone, Dictionary of American Biography (Charles Scribner's Sons, New York, 1931), Vol. VII, p. 433.

[5] William Bradford, Bradford's History "Of Plimoth Plantation" (From the Original Manuscript), (Wright & Potter Printing Co., Boston, 1900), pp. 92-92; 531 & 534. John Howland was one of two manservants to John Carver, the first Governor of Plymouth Colony.

[6] Nathaniel Philbrick, Mayflower, (Viking, New York, 2006), p. 33.

[7] Thomas Welsh, *An Eulogy Delivered June 29, 1796* (Samuel Hall Printer, Boston, 1796), p. 5.

[8] Thomas Bellows Wyman, The Genealogies and Estates of Charlestown...1629-1818 (David Clapp and Son, Boston, 1879), p. 423.

[9] Wyman, op. cit., pp. 423-424.

[10] Biographical Directory of the American Congress: 1774-1961 (Government Printing Office, Washington, DC, 1961), p. 961; see also Johnson, op. cit., p. 433.

[11] See Chapter 8.

[12] Paul H. Smith, Editor, <u>LDC: 1774-1789</u> (Library of Congress, Washington, DC, 1992), Vol. 19, p. 572; Phillips White to Josiah Bartlett, January 9, 1783.

[13] Wyman, op. cit., p. 424.

[14] Johnson, op. cit., Vol. 3, p. 83.

[15] <u>Biographical Directory of the American Congress: 1774-1961</u>, op. cit., pp. 961 & 107.

[16] Wyman, op. cit., pp. 424-425.

[17] Johnson, op. cit., Vol. 3, pp. 83-84. See also: Vol. 7, p. 434.

[18] Welsh, op. cit., p. 3.

[19] Welsh, op. cit., p. 5.

[20] Johnson, op. cit., p. 433.

[21] Welsh, op. cit., p. 6.

[22] Welsh, op. cit., pp. 12 & 14.

[23] Welsh, op. cit., p. 6.

[24] L. H. Butterfield, Editor-in-Chief, <u>The Diary and Autobiography of John Adams</u> (The Belknap Press, Cambridge, 1961), Vol. 2, pp. 96-97. Gov. Gage had moved the legislature to Salem, Massachusetts to try to diminish resistance to royal authority. The five delegates elected to the Continental Congress that morning were John Adams, Samuel Adams, Thomas Cushing, Robert Treat Paine and James Bowdoin. Only the first four actually attended.

[25] Paul D. Brandes, <u>John Hancock's Life and Speeches</u> (The Scarecrow Press, Inc., Lanham, MD, 1996), pp. 131-132. See also: Chapter 3.

[26] Brandes, op. cit., pp. 132-134.

[27] <u>LDC</u>, op. cit., Vol. 23, p. 624; Charles Thomson to David Ramsay, November 4, 1786. Thomas shared this information with Ramsay who was then compiling his *History of the American Revolution* which was published in two volumes in 1789. See also: p. 633, footnote 2.

[28] Welsh, op. cit., p. 9.

[29] <u>LDC</u> op. cit., Vol. 7, p. 89, footnote 1.

[30] <u>LDC</u>, op. cit., Vol. 7, pp. 99-101; Massachusetts Delegates to the Massachusetts Assembly, May 21, 1777. The Petition was read in Congress on May 14, 1777 and rejected two days later.

[31] <u>LDC</u>, op. cit., Vol. 7, p. 88; John Adams to Abigail Adams, May 17, 1777.

[32] David McCullough, <u>John Adams</u> (Simon & Schuster, New York, 2001), p. 225.

[33] Charles W. Meister, The Founding Fathers (McFarland & Company, Inc., Jefferson, NC, 1987), pp. 96-97.

[34] LDC, op. cit., Vol. 18, p. xix.

[35] LDC, op. cit., Vol. 18, p. 593; John Lowell to Rebecca Lowell.

[36] JCC, op. cit., Vol. XXIII, p. 786.

[37] LDC, op. cit., Vol. 19, p. 529; Samuel Osgood to Benjamin Lincoln, January 1, 1783.

[38] LDC, op. cit., Vol. 19, p. 531; David Ramsay to John Eliot, January 2, 1783.

[39] LDC, op. cit., Vol. 19, p. 578, James Madison's Notes of Debates, January 13, 1783.

[40] LDC, op. cit., Vol. 19, p. 610, James Madison's Notes of Debates, January 24, 1783. On February 26, 1783, however, Congress reversed itself at Morris' request and "annulled... the injunction of secrecy." See also: LDC, op. cit., Vol. 19, p. 743, footnote 7. On April 28, 1783, a committee of Congress conferred with Morris, declaring "that Congress are of opinion that public service requires his continuance in office." See also: LDC, op. cit., Vol. 19, p. 763, footnote 8.

[41] LDC, op. cit., Vol. 19, p. 637; Nathaniel Gorham to John Lowell, January 29, 1783.

[42] LDC, op. cit., Vol. 19, p. 637; Nathaniel Gorham to John Lowell, January 23, 1783.

[43] LDC, op. cit., Vol. 19, p. 620; James Madison's Notes of Debates, January 27, 1783.

[44] LDC, op. cit., Vol. 19, p. 654; James Madison's Notes of Debates, February 4, 1783. See also: Vol. 19, p. 672; James Madison's Notes of Debates, February 11, 1783.

[45] LDC, op. cit., Vol. 19, p. 718; James Madison's Notes of Debates, February 20, 1783.

[46] LDC, op. cit., Vol. 19, p. 718; James Madison's Notes of Debates, February 20, 1783.

[47] See Chapter 10.

[48] Merrill Jensen, The New Nation: A History of the United States During the Confederation, 1781-1789 (Alfred A. Knopf, Publisher, New York, 1950), p. 282.

[49] H. James Henderson, Party Politics in the Continental Congress (McGraw-Hill, New York, 1974), PP. 320 & 329.

[50] LDC, op. cit., Vol. 19, p. 722; James Madison's Notes of Debates; February 21, 1783.

[51] LDC, op. cit., Vol. 19, p. 734; James Madison to Edmund Randolph, February 25, 1783.

[52] LDC, op. cit., Vol. 19, pp. 736-737; Nathaniel Gorham to Caleb Davis, February 26, 1783.

[53] JCC, op. cit., Vol. XXIV, p. 144.

[54] JCC, op. cit., Vol. XXIV, pp. 170-174 & 257-261.

[55] LDC, op. cit., Vol. 20, p. 141; Stephen Higginson to Theophilus Parsons, April 7-10. 1783.

[56] LDC, op. cit., Vol. 20, pp. 127-128; James Madison's Notes of Debates, April 1, 1783.

[57] LDC, op. cit., Vol. 20, p. 304; Nathaniel Gorham to Caleb Davis, June 4, 1783.

[58] LDC, op. cit., Vol. 20, p. 277; James Madison's Notes of Debates, May 23, 1783; and, p. 378, footnote 2.

[59] LDC, op. cit., Vol. 20, p. xiv.

[60] LDC, op. cit., Vol. 20, p. 493, footnote 4. See also: Henderson, op. cit., p. 335. Like Madison, Gorham believed that the change from half-pension for life to a five year plan would actually save the country money, but the nuances of the new plan were lost on his Massachusetts colleagues back home.

[61] LDC, op. cit., Vol. 20, pp. 525-526; Stephen Higginson to Nathaniel Gorham, August 5, 1783; and, p. 527, footnote 8.

[62] LDC, op. cit., Vol. 22, p. xxi.

[63] Johnson, op. cit., Vol. 7, p. 434. See also Welsh, op. cit., p. 11.

[64] Charles River Bridge Company...At a Meeting of the Proprietors...A Committee to Prepare Rules and Regulations... (Boston, 1785) pp. 1 & 14. See also: William M. Fowler, Jr., The Baron of Beacon Hill (Houghton Mifflin Company, Boston, 1980), p. 262.

[65] Edmund Cody Burnett, The Continental Congress (The Macmillan Company, New York, 1941), p. 640.

[66] Burnett, op. cit., p. 640.

[67] JCC, op. cit., Vol. XXX, p. 20. According to a letter Nathaniel Gorham wrote to Dr. Richard Price on December 26, 1785, Nathaniel originally intended to "set off tomorrow [December 27, 1785] with Mr. Hancock the President to take my Seat in Congress." Hancock's inability to make the trip apparently delayed Nathaniel's departure. See also: LDC, op. cit., Vol. 23, p. 112, footnote 1.

[68] LDC, op. cit., Vol. 23, pp. 160-161; Nathaniel Gorham to Caleb Davis, February 23, 1786.

[69] LDC, op. cit., Vol. 23, pp. 161-162; Nathaniel Gorham to Caleb Davis, February 23, 1786; see footnote 4.

[70] LDC, op. cit., Vol. 23, pp. 166-167; Nathaniel Gorham to Caleb Davis, March 1, 1786.

[71] LDC, op. cit., Vol. 23, pp. 180-181; Nathaniel Gorham to James Warren, March 6, 1786. A "liberum veto" is a veto exercised by a single member of a legislative body

under rules requiring unanimous consent. See also: <u>Webster's Third New International Dictionary</u> (Encyclopaedia Britannica, Inc., Chicago, 1966), p. 1304.

[72] <u>LDC</u>, op. cit., Vol. 23, pp. 166-167; Nathaniel Gorham to Caleb Davis, March 1, 1786. The New Jersey Resolution was passed on February 20, 1786; Vol. 23, p. 184; Committee of Congress to William Livingston, March 12, 1786.

[73] <u>LDC</u>, op. cit., Vol. 23, pp. 180; Nathaniel Gorham to James Warren, March 6, 1786.

[74] <u>JCC</u>, op. cit., Vol. XXX, p. 97.

[75] <u>LDC</u>, op. cit., Vol. 23, pp. 187-196, See especially footnote 8; Charles Pinckney's Speech to the New Jersey Assembly, March 13, 1786. William Grayson later reported to Richard Henry Lee that some of the New Jersey legislators "wish for annihilation & that E. Jersey might be joined to N. York & W. Jersey to Pensylvany." See also: Vol. 23, p. 201: William Grayson to Richard Henry Lee, March 22, 1786.

[76] <u>JCC</u>, op. cit., Vol. XXX, p. 264.

[77] <u>JCC</u>, op. cit., Vol. XXX, p. 328.

[78] <u>JCC</u>, op. cit., Vol. XXX, p. 330.

[79] <u>LDC</u>, op. cit., Vol. 23, p. 358; Nathaniel Gorham to Caleb Davis, June 16, 1786.

[80] Chapter 1.

[81] <u>LDC</u>, op. cit., Vol. 23, p. 362; Nathaniel Gorham to James Bowdoin, June 17, 1786.

[82] <u>LDC</u>, op. cit., Vol. 23, p. 381, footnote 2.

[83] See Chapter 11.

[84] <u>LDC</u>, op. cit., Vol. 23, p. 375; Charles Thomson to John Jay, June 29, 1786.

[85] <u>LDC</u>, op. cit., Vol. 23, pp. 619-620, footnote 2.

[86] <u>LDC</u>, op. cit., Vol. 23, p. 543, footnote 1.

[87] <u>LDC</u>, op. cit., Vol. 23, pp. 542-543; Rufus King to Jonathan Jackson, September 3, 1786.

[88] Edmund Cody Burnett, <u>Letters of Members of the Continental Congress</u> (Carnegie Institute of Washington, Washington, DC 1921-36), Vol. 8, p. 459, footnote 3.

[89] Richard Krauel, "Prince Henry of Prussia and the Regency of the United States, 1786," *The American Historical Review*, Vol. 17, No. 1 (October 1911), p. 46. The topic of monarchy was addressed directly by the Delegates of the Constitutional Convention on August 19, 1787. As cited in Carl Van Doren, <u>The Great Rehearsal</u> (The Viking Press, New York, 1948), p. 145. The Convention briefly broke its rule of silence to issue the following statement in the *Pennsylvania Herald*: "We are well informed that many letters have been written...that it is intended to establish a monarchical government, to send for the Bishop of Osnaburgh...to which it has been uniformly answered, 'tho' we cannot, affirmativly,

tell you what we are doing; we can, negatively, tell you what we are not doing--we never once thought of a king."

[90] LDC, op. cit., Vol. 23, p.544, footnote 1. The Baron von Steuben's letter to Prince Henry was dated November 2, 1786. The Baron, who entered America's military service during the darkest days at Valley Forge, is universally credited with transforming the Continental Army into a disciplined fighting force. See also: John C. Fitzpatrick, Editor, The Writings of George Washington (Government Printing Office, Washington, DC 1958), Vol. 27, p. 283; George Washington to Baron von Steuben, Annapolis, December 23, 1783. At the end of the war, in his very last official letter as Commander-in -Chief, Washington wrote to Von Steuben: "...I wish to make use of this last Moment of my public Life, to Signify in the strongest terms, my intire Approbabtion of your Conduct, and to express my Sense of the Obligations the public is under to you for your faithful and Meritorious Services..." Today, the Baron von Steuben is honored by both his fellow German-Americans and by Gay Americans who recognize him as the nation's "Gay Founding Father."

[91] Krauel, op. cit., pp. 47-48. (Translation provided by Paul A. Garcia, Ph.D., Past President, American Council on the Teaching of Foreign Languages, 2000.)

[92] LDC, op. cit., Vol. 24, p. 117; James Madison to Edmund Pendleton, February 27, 1787.

[93] Theodore C. Pease, The Ordinance of 1787, *Mississippi Valley Historical Review*, Vol. 25, p. 171; September 1938.

[94] John Fiske, The Critical Period of American History: 1783-1789 (Riverside Press, Cambridge, 1898).

[95] LDC, op. cit., Vol. 24, p. 33, footnote 1.

[96] JCC, op. cit., Vol. XXXII, p. 11.

[97] JCC, op. cit., Vol. XXXII, p. 74.

[98] LDC, op. cit., Vol. 24, p. 139; James Madison to Edmund Randolph, March 11, 1787.

[99] Christopher Collier and James Lincoln Collier, Decision in Philadelphia (Random House, New York, 1986), p. 77.

[100] LDC, op. cit., Vol. 24, p. 149; James Madison to George Washington, March 18, 1787.

[101] LDC, op. cit., Vol. 24, p. 151; James Madison to Thomas Jefferson, March 19, 1787.

[102] JCC, op. cit., Vol. XXXII, p. 226.

[103] LDC, op. cit., Vol. 24, p. 248; James Madison's Notes of Debates, April 23, 1787.

[104] LDC, op. cit., Vol. 24, pp. 275-276; James Madison to William Irvine; May 5, 1787; footnote 1. The ten Congressional Delegates who also served as Members of the Constitutional Convention in the summer of 1787 were: Gorham and King (MA);

Madison (VA); Blount (NC); Butler (SC); Few & Pierce (GA); Gilman & Langdon (NH); and, Johnson (CT).

105 LDC, op. cit., Vol. 24, p. 286; Nathaniel Gorham to Caleb Davis, May 22, 1787.

106 LDC, op. cit., Vol. 24, p. 296; Nathan Dane to James Bowdoin, May 31, 1787. See also: p. 302; Nathan Dane to Nathaniel Gorham, June 6, 1787.

107 Arthur Taylor Prescott, Drafting the Federal Constitution (Louisiana State University Press, University, Louisiana, 1941), pp. 37-38 & 20. See also Van Doren, op. cit., p. 23.

108 Van Doren, op. cit., p. 32.

109 Charles L. Mee, Jr., The Genius of the People (Harper & Row Publishers, New York, 1987), p. 94.

110 As cited in Prescott, op. cit., pp. 23-24.

111 Meister, op. cit., p. 100.

112 Van Doren, op. cit., pp. 30-31.

113 Prescott, op. cit., pp. 46-51.

114 Van Doren, op. cit., pp. 84-89. See also: Forrest McDonald, Novus Ordo Seclorum: The Intellectual Origins of the Constitution (University Press of Kansas, Lawrence, 1985), p. 227.

115 LDC, op. cit., Vol. 24, p. 332; Nathaniel Gorham to Theophilus Parsons, June 18, 1787.

116 LDC, op. cit., Vol. 24, p. 339; Nathan Dane to Nathaniel Gorham, June 22, 1787.

117 Prescott, op. cit., pp. 217-218.

118 Prescott, op. cit., p. 259.

119 E. H. Scott, Editor, Journal of the Federal Convention Kept by James Madison (Scott, Foresman and Company, Chicago, 1898), p. 81.

120 Prescott, op. cit., p. 254.

121 Collier, op. cit., p. 128.

122 Collier, op. cit., p. 131. See also: James H. Charleton, Framers of the Constitution (National Archives and Records Administration, Washington, DC, 1986), p. 47. Rhode Island never attended the Convention and New York was absent at this time. New Hampshire's delegation didn't arrive until July 23, 1787.

123 Collier, op. cit., pp. 168-169. During this ten day break, Washington traveled back to Valley Forge, the location of that bitter winter's encampment ten years earlier. Van Dorn, op. cit., pp. 138-139.

[124] Collier, op. cit., p. 168.

[125] Prescott, op. cit., p. 697.

[126] As cited in Van Dorn, op. cit., p. 152.

[127] As cited in Van Dorn, op. cit., p. 153.

[128] Prescott, op. cit., p. 350.

[129] Prescott, op. cit., p. 703.

[130] Prescott, op. cit., p. 692.

[131] Senate Document No. 728, <u>Secret Proceedings and Debates of the Convention Assembled at Philadelphia, in the Year 1787, for the Purpose of Forming The Constitution of the United States of America</u> (Government Printing Office, Washington, DC, 1909), p. 163.

[132] Prescott, op. cit., p. 710.

[133] Prescott, op. cit., p. 389.

[134] E. H. Scott, <u>Journal of the Federal Convention Kept by James Madison</u> (Scott, Foresman and Company, Chicago, 1898), pp. 743-744.

[135] Meister, op. cit., p. 107. See also: Charleton, op. cit., p. 73. Only 38 individuals actually signed the new Constitution in person on the afternoon of September 17, 1787. George Read of Delaware also signed John Dickinson's name at Dickinson's request since he had left the Convention early due to illness. It is interesting to note that John Dickinson, the author of the "Olive Branch Petition," had refused to sign the Declaration of Independence in 1776 because he felt that it was premature.

[136] JCC, op. cit., Vol. XXXII, p. 74; and, Vol. XXXIII, p.549.

[137] Meister, op. cit., p. 107.

[138] Meister, op. cit., pp. 107-108. See also: Robert Ernst, <u>Rufus King: American Federalist</u> (The University of North Carolina Press, Chapel Hill, 1968), p. 121.

[139] As cited in Ernst, op. cit., p. 119; Nathaniel Gorham to Rufus King, December 12, 1787.

[140] Jack N. Rakove, <u>Original Meanings: Politics and Ideas in the Making of the Constitution</u> (Alfred A. Knapf, New York, 1996), p. 138.

[141] Rakove, op. cit., p. 119.

[142] William t. Hutchinson, William M. E. Rachal, Robert Rutland, et. al., Editors, <u>The Papers of James Madison</u> (Chicago and Charlottesville, 1962-91), Vol. XI, pp. 436-437; Rufus King to James Madison, January 27, 1788.

[143] Scott, op. cit., pp. 78-80.

[144] Van Beck Hall, Politics Without Parties: Massachusetts, 1780-1791 (University of Pittsburgh Press, Pittsburgh, 1972), p. 285.

[145] The only two men who had a larger national following were Benjamin Franklin, who was too old to seek the office, and George Washington, who would be ineligible if his home State of Virginia did not join the new Union which, at that moment, seemed very possible due, in part, to the strong opposition of then Gov. Patrick Henry.

[146] Meister, op. cit., p. 108. See also: Scott, op. cit., p. 743. Franklin told the Delegates during the final moments of the Convention that "I cannot help expressing a wish that every member of the Convention who may still have objections to it, would with me... doubt a little of his own infalibility, and...put his name to this instrument."

[147] See Chapter 3.

[148] Meister, op. cit., p. 109.

[149] See Introduction.

[150] LDC, op. cit., Vol. 25, p. 120; Samuel A. Otis to Caleb Davis, May 27, 1788.

[151] JCC, op. cit., Vol. XXXIV, p. 605.

[152] LDC, op. cit., Vol. 25, p. 477, footnote 2.

[153] M. E. Bradford, A Worthy Company (Plymouth Rock Foundation, 1982), p. 20.

[154] Sol Bloom, History of the Formation of the Union Under the Constitution (US Constitution Sesquicentennial Commission, Government Printing Office, 1943), p. 60. On June 21, 1788, when New Hampshire became the ninth State to ratify the US Constitution, the Second American Republic was officially launched. Virginia then ratified it five days later by a vote of 89 to 79; and, on July 26, 1788, New York reluctantly joined the new Union by a vote of 30 to 27. North Carolina did not join until November 1789 and Rhode Island, which had boycotted the Constitutional Convention, finally reunited with its sister states on May 29, 1790, by a vote of 34 -32.

[155] Margaret C. S. Christman, The First Federal Congress: 1789-1791 (Smithsonian Institution Press, Washington, DC, 1989), pp. 45-52.

[156] Bloom, op. cit., pp. 238-239 & 275-277.

[157] LDC, op. cit., Vol. 25, p. 77, footnote 2.

[158] O. Turner, History of the Pioneer Settlement of Phelps and Gorham's Purchase and Morris' Reserve (William Alling, New York, 1851), pp. 135-142. See also: LDC, op. cit., Vol. 23, p. xxxi.

[159] Turner, op. cit., p. 142.

[160] Mee, op. cit., p. 152.

[161] Johnson, op. cit., Vol. XIII, pp. 219-223. Robert Morris of Pennsylvania was one of only two men (the other was Roger Sherman of Connecticut) who signed the three major

documents of the First American Republic: The Declaration of Independence, the Articles of Confederation and the US Constitution.

[162] Turner, op. cit., pp. 149-151.

[163] Meister, op. cit., p. 111.

[164] Telephone interview with Kathy Kottaridis of the Boston Parks & Recreation Department who was then in charge of the Phipps Street Burying Ground, December 28, 1993. See also: A Self-Guiding Bicycle Tour of Boston's Historic Burying Grounds, Second Edition, published by the Boston Parks & Recreation Department, p. 38: "This is the final resting place of John Harvard, who founded the college that bears his name. Also buried here (at an unmarked spot) is Nahtaniel Gorham, president of the Continental Congress and a signer of the U. S. Constitution."

WHILE NATHANIEL GORHAM
WAS PRESIDENT

Notes

Abbreviation Key

JCC   Journals of the Continental Congress
LDC   Letters of Delegates to Congress
PHL   The Papers of Henry Laurens

165 John C. Fitzpatrick, Editor, JCC: 1774-1789 (Government Printing Office, Washington, DC, 1933), Vol. XXIX, p. 883.

166 Chapter 3.

167 Paul H. Smith, Editor, LDC: 1774-1789 (Library of Congress, Washington, DC, 1995), Vol. 23, pp. 52-53. See also: Herbert S. Allan, John Hancock: Patriot in Purple (The Macmillan Company, New York, 1948), pp. 320-321.

168 Arthur H. Shaffer, To Be an American: David Ramsay and the Making of the American Consciousness (University of South Carolina Press, Columbia, SC, 1991), pp. 73-77.

169 LDC, Vol. 23, pp. 82-83; David Ramsay to William Moultrie, December 31, 1785. Ramsay requested that he be "left out of the delegation" for the coming year because "an absence from my business a second Year would be very inconvenient."

170 JCC, op. cit., Vol. XXX, p. 264.

171 JCC, op. cit., Vol. XXX, pp. 328 & 330.

172 William Benton, Publisher, Encyclopaedia Britannica (Encyclopaedia Britannica, Inc., Chicago, 1966), Vol. 20, p. 481.

173 The Annals of America (Encyclopaedia Britannica, Inc., Chicago, 1976), Vol. 3, p. 61; The Causes of Shays's Rebellion by Daniel Gray.

174 LDC, Vol. 23, p. 610; Nathaniel Gorham to James Bowdoin, October 22, 1786.

175 LDC, Vol. 23, p. 610; Charles Thomson to the States, October 21, 1786.

176 The Annals of America, op. cit., Vol. 3, pp. 64-65; George Washington to John Jay, August 1, 1786.

177 J. Steven Watson, The Reign of George III: 1760-1815 (The Clarendon Press, Oxford, 1960), The Oxford History of England, p. 300.

Engraved by E. Wellmore from a drawing by J.B. Longacre after the original Portrait by C.W. Peale.

MAJOR GENERAL ARTHUR St. CLAIR.

Chapter 13

President
ARTHUR ST. CLAIR
of
PENNSYLVANIA

TRIUMPH & TRAGEDY

Of the tens of thousands of courageous patriots who served as soldiers or statesmen during the American Revolution, Major General Arthur St. Clair earned several unique distinctions. He was the only individual born outside the United States who has held, or will ever hold, the title of President.[1] He was also the only officer, except Washington, who served in uniform throughout the entire Revolutionary War and then went on to become Head of State of his new Nation. Later, after he left the Continental Congress, Arthur St. Clair labored for fifteen years as the first and only Governor of the vast Northwest Territory (which now encompasses five midwestern states).[2] And, of all the Founding Fathers who debated and dreamed of western expansion, only Arthur St. Clair actually reached the banks of the mighty Mississippi.[3]

Unlike Hancock or Mifflin, Arthur was definitely not a politician; nor was he primarily a legislator like Huntington or Lee. Arthur St. Clair was a soldier. His selection as the thirteenth President of the Continental Congress was itself a most unusual step, justified by his reputation for public service and his devotion to duty. Throughout his career, both in and out of uniform, Arthur St. Clair consistently took what he perceived to be the noble course even at great personal cost to his family, his career and his fortune. His sense of right and wrong was as firmly rooted in his soul as his proud Scottish heritage.

While all sources agree that Arthur was born in Thurso, the most northerly town on the mainland of Scotland,[4] there is a major discrepancy in the year of his birth. The *Biographical Directory of the American Congress* as well as his two biographers list the date as 1734.[5] A more recent publication by the Library of Congress, however, and the *Dictionary of American Biography* both set his birth two years later.[6] Most sources do agree that

Arthur was born on March 23 (old style)[7] and that he was related to the "Lordly Line of High St. Clair," as Sir Walter Scott once described them,[8] but that Arthur's father, William, was a simple merchant who provided well for his family but died at an early age. After his father's death, Arthur's mother, Elizabeth, enrolled him in the University of Edinburgh. He was later indentured to Dr. William Hunter, a "celebrated anatomist of London,"[9] but, upon his mother's death, Arthur decided to pursue his true ambition, the military.[10]

In 1757, Arthur was commissioned as an Ensign in the Royal American Regiment of Foot, an elite unit which had been organized by the Duke of Cumberland when the French & Indian War reached the shores of Europe.[11] One year later, on May 28, 1758, Arthur and his Regiment arrived in America where they served under Gen. Jeffrey Amherst during the final weeks of the siege of Louisburg, a strategic French fortress. In 1759, Arthur was promoted to Lieutenant and reassigned to serve under Gen. James Wolfe at the battle of the Plains of Abraham where "his battalion was joined with other light troops under the command of Colonel Howe"[12] (who would later became Commander-in-Chief of British forces during the American Revolution). The British victory that September led to the surrender of Quebec and ultimately to the defeat of the French in North America.[13] Having had the opportunity to participate in such historic battles so early in his career, Arthur had already become a seasoned junior officer by the age of 24.

Years later, Arthur himself best described his military career: "At a very early time of life I took up the profession of arms and served through the whole war of 1756 under some of the first generals in the world. I had the honor to serve under and to be trusted by a Wolfe, a Moncton and a Murray. I served again through the whole of the last war (Revolution). I had joined theory to practice by an attentive perusal of the best military books, in most languages, and had myself acquainted with the engineer's branch, as far at least as it concerns fortification..."[14]

Both of Arthur's biographers speculate that during his military service he had occasionally traveled to Boston either on official business or to visit his cousin, Gen. Thomas Gage (who would serve as Commander-in-Chief of the British Army in North America at the outbreak of the Revolution). Whatever the circumstances, Arthur had somehow met the beautiful Phoebe Bayard, the daughter of Balthazar and Mary Bayard and the niece of Massachusetts Governor James Bowdoin. After the victory at Quebec, Arthur obtained a furlough and returned to Boston where he and Phoebe were married on May 14, 1760, in the chapel of Trinity Church. Arthur's 19th Century biographer described the bride as "throughly educated, of amiable disposition and agreeable manners." As for the groom, he was "tall, graceful, dignified, with chestnut hair, handsome blue-gray eyes, and blonde complexion."[15]

Through marriage, Arthur also took charge of a £14,000 bequest that Phoebe had inherited. Combined with his savings from the military and his own small family inheritance, the new couple were well positioned financially when he decided to retire from the British Army in April 1762.[16] For the next two years, they stayed close to her parents in Boston where their first two sons--Daniel (1762) and John Murray (1764)--were born. Eventually, their family grew to seven children with the births of Elizabeth (1768), Arthur, Jr. (1770), Louisa (1773), Jane (1774) and Margaret (1781).[17]

In 1764, Arthur set out alone for Western Pennsylvania, an area already favored by Scottish immigrants, to claim land granted by the King to those who had served in the military. He combined that royal largesse with the purchase of an additional 4,000 acres in the valley near Fort Ligonier.[18] By the time his first daughter was born in 1768, Arthur's wife and two young sons had already joined him in the wilderness.[19] For Phoebe, it was a wrenching departure from the elegant lifestyle she had known.

Starting in 1770, as "the largest resident property owner in Pennsylvania west of the mountains,"[20] Arthur was appointed by Lt. Gov. Penn to a number of important local offices in Cumberland County, Bedford County and ultimately Westmoreland County when it was carved out of Bedford in 1773.[21] In the words of one historian, Arthur had become the *"ex officio governor"* of the region.[22]

Early in 1774, the long-standing boundary dispute between Virginia and Pennsylvania took an ominous turn when Lord Dunmore, the last Royal Governor of Virginia, attempted to assert his land claims by taking possession of Fort Pitt which had been abandoned by the British. Located approximately fifty miles from Fort Ligonier and within his official jurisdiction, Arthur, ever the soldier at heart, did not hesitate to order the arrest and incarceration of Dunmore's agent. In retaliation, the Virginia Governor demanded that Lt. Gov. Penn dismiss Arthur immediately.[23] In his response, Penn stated that "Mr. St. Clair is a gentleman, who for a long time had the honor of serving his majesty in the regulars with reputation, and in every station of life has preserved the character of a very honest, worthy man...you must excuse my not complying with your Lordship's requisition of stripping him, on this occasion, of his offices and livelihood, which you will allow me to think not only unreasonable, but somewhat dictatorial."[24] The dispute ended, however, when Lord Dunmore was soon forced to seek refuge on a British warship rather than a frontier fort.[25]

While establishing his new homestead and devoting endless hours to his diverse public duties, the larger struggles--over the Stamp Act and the Townshend Acts as well as the Boston Massacre and the debate over taxation--must have seemed like distant distractions to this former British Officer who was living on the edge of the known world. Despite his pride in having served his King and Country during the late war, this honest, hardworking Scotsman had gradually evolved into a proud, patriotic American.

In May 1775, only a month after the Battles of Lexington and Concord, the citizens of Westmoreland County met to debate British aggression. In addition to being appointed one of the members of the new Committee of Safety,[26] Arthur was also the primary author of the Resolutions that were adopted, including the preamble which stated that: "we declare to the world, that we do not mean by this Association to deviate from the loyalty which we hold it our bounden duty to observe; but, animated with the love of liberty, it is no less our duty to maintain and defend our just rights which, with sorrow, we have seen of late wantonly violated in many instances by wicked ministry and a corrupted Parliament..."[27] As colonial government collapsed, Arthur reported to Lt. Gov. Penn that "...every thing seems to be running into the wildest confusion. If some conciliating plan is not adopted by the Congress, America has seen her golden days, they may return, but will be preceeded by scenes of horror."[28]

Arthur described the next step many years later: "My first connection with the United States began in the year 1775. Congress had appointed commissioners to repair to Fort Pitt to treat with the Indians, and induce them to a neutrality during our contest with Great Britain...On their way to the rendezvous they called upon me, and requested that I would accompany them and act as their secretary during the negotiations, to which I consented."[29] During their time together, Arthur urged the commissioners to obtain permission for him to lead a volunteer expedition against Detroit. Commissioner James Wilson of Pennsylvania--also a native of Scotland who became Arthur's lifelong friend--did, indeed, recommend this plan to Congress while Arthur eagerly enlisted over 400 recruits.[30] The proposal, however, was rejected.

Instead, on January 3, 1776, at the recommendation of Pennsylvania's Committee for Safety, Arthur was elected by the Continental Congress to serve as Colonel of Pennsylvania's 2nd Battalion in the new Continental Army.[31] President John Hancock immediately summoned him to Philadelphia. The scene was later described by another of Arthur's closest friends, James Wilkinson: "In this situation the American Revolution found him, surrounded by a rising family in the enjoyment of ease and independence, with the fairest prospects of affluent fortune, the foundation of which had been already established by his intelligence, industry and enterprise. From this peaceful abode..." Wilkinson reported, "he [St. Clair] was drawn by the claims of a troubled country....therefore, without application or expectation on his part, he received the commission of a Colonel...He obeyed the summons, and took leave not only of his wife and children, but in effect, of his fortune, to embark in the cause of liberty and the United Colonies."[32] For the next seven years, from Fort Ticonderoga to Yorktown, Arthur St. Clair repeatedly served on the front line of America's war for Independence.

When he reached Philadelphia, Arthur's first assignment was to work with America's most distinguished citizen, Benjamin Franklin. Their task was to evaluate the military qualifications of a French Artillery Officer who was seeking employment in the Army.[33] In March 1776, after approving the applicant and having completed recruitment for his new Battalion, Arthur was ordered to lead his men North in support of the American invasion of Canada. By way of introduction, President Hancock wrote to his Massachusetts colleague Thomas Cushing that "This St. Clair was a Regular Officer, he married Mr. Bayard's Daughter of Boston, and a fine fellow he is."[34] To Gen. Philip Schuyler, the President stated that Col. St. Clair was "a Gentleman of Reputation, & a Good Officer, he served many Years a Captain in the Regular Army..."[35]

Robert Morris, the great Philadelphia financier, expressed even stronger sentiments in a letter to Gen. Charles Lee: "Col. St. Clair of the 2nd Battalion has seen much service; was in the King's army a Lieutenant, is a sensible, worthy man, much esteemed in Bedford County, where he is ------- and has acquired considerable property; he is also much esteemed and respected here."[36]

Since the Army had already been repulsed at Quebec the previous New Year's Eve, the invasion was doomed by the time Arthur and his troops met the retreating American forces at Sorel on May 16. Nevertheless, as described in *A Battlefield Atlas of the American Revolution*, Gen. Sullivan "remained determined to...defend upper Canada to the last extremity."[37] In pursuit of that objective, Gen. Thompson was captured while leading his troops back along the St. Lawrence River. Arthur, as next in command, was just barely able to save "his small, broken detachment from capture and defeat."[38] In the end, after a disastrous eight month campaign and the loss of five thousand Americans to death, desertion or disease, the American Army arrived at Fort Ticonderoga.[39] It was there, on Sunday, July 28, 1776, that Col. Arthur St. Clair had the honor of reading the Declaration of Independence to the assembled troops.[40]

The previous month, after returning from an inspection of Canada, Congressman Samuel Chase of Maryland had recommended to Gen. Horatio Gates that "Colonel Sinclair [St. Clair] will be of great Service. He has prudence, bravery and a Knowledge of the Country. If he would accept I believe he is the most proper person in Canada to be your adjutant General."[41] The rest of Congress concurred in Chase's evaluation. On August 9, 1776, when it created six new brigadier generals, Arthur was tied for the second highest number of votes.[42] Later that month, Arthur's close friend, Judge Thomas Smith, sent him congratulations from Philadelphia: "I can assure you, from undoubted authority, that your military character stands as high with Congress as that of any general on the continent, and I flatter myself that you have as good a chance for even a more elevated rank than that to which you are lately raised."[43]

Arthur was pleased, but unimpressed. "I have come to that time of life" he wrote less than a month after his promotion "...that puts me out of danger of that flutter and emotion that sudden and unexpected elevation gives some people. I assure you I would rather experience the heartfelt satisfaction of discharging one social duty, one debt of gratitude, than have as many 'Honours' and 'Excellencys' affixed to my name as would fill a quire of paper." And then he added, in an offhanded remark that would prove painfully prophetic, "You know I am a bad politician."[44]

On November 23, 1776, in response to Gen. Howe's anticipated march on Philadelphia, Congress directed Gen. Washington to order a large number of troops from the Northern Department to join him in defense of the Capital.[45] In response, Arthur headed south with approximately 1,200 men,[46] most of whom were nearing the completion of their service. Many, however, promised to reenlist if they were furloughed long enough to return home for a brief visit. Arthur not only agreed, but, "out of his own private funds supplied some of the money necessary to pay expenses of reenlistment."[47]

By late December, Arthur had joined Washington in time for the historic crossing of the Delaware River on Christmas night 1776. He led Gen. Sullivan's column as it advanced into Trenton in "the most audacious" victory of the war.[48] On learning of the defeat, Gen. Howe ordered Gen. Cornwallis to march to Trenton with 8,000 British troops to put an end to the rebels. When the British Army arrived in late afternoon on New Year's Day 1777, Cornwallis felt certain that Washington's troops could not escape in time to avoid defeat.[49] Arthur, however, as Wilkinson later reported, had carefully observed the terrain and proposed an exit strategy which Washington immediately adopted. By the following morning, when Cornwallis discovered that the Americans were gone, Washington's troops were only two miles from Princeton. There, Arthur led the final assault which forced the remaining British to flee. To avoid Cornwallis' advancing Army, Washington reluctantly decided to cap his double victory by establishing winter quarters at Morristown, New Jersey.[50]

On February 19, 1777, the Continental Congress promoted five Officers to the rank of Major General, two of whom--Thomas Mifflin and Arthur St. Clair--would ultimately become Presidents of Congress.[51] In his letter of congratulations, James Wilson, now a Pennsylvania congressman, added that "I have good Reason to believe...that the important Command of Ticonderoga is destined for you[r] next Campaign." And then, in a painful twist of fate, he added: "I presage it a Theatre of Glory."[52] Arthur, however, preferred to remain with his Commander-in-Chief in the Southern Department but, on April 1, he was ordered to head north to take charge of Fort Ticonderoga.[53] On April 18, Gen. Washington thanked Arthur "for the desire you express for serving in this department," but "I applaud your resolution of submitting cheerfully to whatever post is assigned you."[54]

Arthur assumed command at Fort Ticonderoga on June 12, 1777. He immediately informed Gen. Schuyler, the new head of the Northern Department, of the bleak conditions he found: "If the enemy intend to attack us, I assure you, sire, we are very illprepared to receive them. The whole amount of Continental troops, fit for duty, is fifteen hundred and seventy-six...Besides these, there are three regiments of Hampshire militia, engaged for no particular term, and who go off whenever they please."[55] Five days later, in a letter to Wilson, Arthur presented an even more candid description: "I am much disappointed in the strength of the garrison and the state of the fortifications at this place. Instead of their having been improved during the winter, which was expected, they are much worse than when I left them [in 1776]...our numbers are greatly unequal to the vast extent of ground we must occupy... Our works would demand ten thousand men, and I hav not more than twenty-two hundred...Men, however, might be got here had we provisions, but we are so short in that article that I dare not call in the militia, as in a couple of weeks, they would eat up our whole stock of meat." In closing, Arthur added a most uncharacteristic note of alarm: "My dear friend, if you should not hear from me again, which may probably be the case, remember that I have given you this account of our situation, and do not suffer my reputation to be murdered after having been sacrificed myself."[56]

That same day, on the floor of Congress, Gen. Gates argued that "Tyconderoga is the proper and only Post for the Commander in Chief of the Northern Army [Gen. Schuyler], from the Middle of June, to the Middle of November; and if he is not there in that Term Tyconderoga is in

Danger of being lost." Gates went on to state that "I have the best Opinion of the Major General now in Command there [Gen. St. Clair]. He is a tried, and an approved good Soldier. But if he has it in his Power to play only half the Game, it is Odds but the Game is lost."[57] Playing "only half the Game," however, would have been better than the conditions Arthur actually faced. And, contrary to Gen. Gates' advice, Gen. Schuyler was home in Albany as the enemy drew nearer.

On June 26, Arthur reported to Gen. Schuyler that "The scene thickens fast, and Sunday next, it seems, is fixed for the attack on this place. We must make the best of it we can, and I hope at least to cripple them so as they may not be able to pursue their fortune, should it declare in their favor...I have some thoughts, if they are not numerous, of attacking them." Two days latter, Arthur added that the "scout on which I depended much for intelligence, is not yet returned, nor, I fear, ever will now."[58] How large a force he would face remained a mystery. Nevertheless, on June 30, Arthur sent a remarkably optimistic letter to Congress that had a devastating impact on his military career. In it he stated that "My people are in the best Disposition possible and I have no Doubt about giving a good Account of the Enemy should they think proper to attack us."[59] But then, a new threat materialized.

In the opinion of historian Benson Bobrick, "the remnant at Ticonderoga had prepared as best they could for the impending siege," but they were no match for Gen. Burgoyne's engineer who accomplished the nearly impossible task of hauling heavy artillery to the summit of Sugar Loaf Hill within striking distance of the Fort. On the morning of July 5, when Arthur's spyglass caught the first sight of the British guns, he realized that the Fort known as the "northern Gibraltar" was no longer defensible.[60] That same day, at a Council of General Officers which included Arthur and his three Brigadiers General, it was unanimously decided "that it is impossible, with our force, to defend Ticonderoga and Mount Independence, and that...a retreat ought to be undertaken as soon as possible, and that we shall be very fortunate to effect it."[61]

Over the next 6 harrowing days, Arthur and his Army did manage to escape, finally arriving at Fort Edward on July 12.[62] The night before he left Ticonderoga, Arthur had sent a message to Gen. Schuyler, providing basic details. On July 8, he wrote again: "I account myself very happy in effecting this retreat, as the loss of the army, small as it is, would have been a blow that this part of the country would have felt severely, and that must inevitably have happened in a very few days."[63] Arthur had no doubt that by surrendering the Fort in order to save his Army, his troops would live to fight again once they were united with the rest of Schuyler's forces.

In Philadelphia, however, the fall of Ticonderoga hit Congress like a thunderbolt. The fact that it was difficult for Arthur to prepare a full report while in flight and that the messages he did send were slow to reach Gen. Schuyler made a bad situation even worse. On July 18, President Hancock wrote to Gen. Schuyler that "The Loss of Ticonderoga still remains a very mysterious Affair for Want of proper Information nor have we as yet received any Account of the Fate of the Garrison under the Command of General St. Clair, only from Report, which is of such a Nature as to increase our apprehensions without removing our Suspence." The President later added a postscript: "Since writing the foregoing, Congress have received a Letter from General St. Clair of the 14th Instant inclosing a Copy of the proceedings of a Council of War."[64]

According to the ever caustic Sam Adams, "Schuylers Letters are rueful indeed! ...with such a Mixture as would excite one to laugh in the Midst of Calamity. He seems to contemplate his own Happiness in not having had much or inded any Hand in the unhappy Disaster. He throws Blame on St. Clare [sic] in his Letter of July 9th." In early August, describing the fall of Ticonderoga to another friend, Adams added that "I cannot at present acount for it...There seems to me to be the evident Marks of Design."[65] James Lovell, another Massachusetts delegate, wrote that "Here the general Cry is treachery and some go so far as to name the sum given, however these reflections are always to be expected on such occasions."[66] Thomas Burke's thoughts were less conspiratorial. The North Carolina congressman wrote that "Many of us have long expected that Ticonderoga would be evacuated at the Approach of an Enemy because we had no hopes of having a force there competent to its defense...We have relied too much on Fortifications without sufficient force or discipline to defend them."[67]

On July 29, Congress Resolved "That an enquiry be made into the reasons of the evacuation of Ticonderoga and Mount Independence, and into the conduct of the general officers who were in the northern department at the time of the evacuation." The following day, Congress ordered that "Major General St. Clair...is hereby directed forthwith to repair to head quarters."[68] Gen. Schuyler was also summoned.[69] The fact that the New England States had "no confidence" in Gen. Schuyler, a New Yorker, further complicated an already tense situation. New England delegates insisted that both Schuyler and St. Clair should be recalled and that their region's favorite, Gen Gates, should assume the command.[70] On August 4, the switch became official.[71]

During the months that followed, Arthur tried repeatedly to explain what the situation had been on the ground when the Fort fell. As early as July 17, 1777, he wrote a long letter to Gen. Washington in which he described each detail and the rationale for his decisions. Arthur informed his Commander-in-Chief that "I had no alternative but the evacuation of my posts, or the loss of the army...I was actuated by no motives but what sprang from a sincere regard for the public welfare."[72]

Gen. Washington demonstrated his confidence in Arthur throughout these difficult months. Repeatedly, the Commander-in-Chief urged Congress to resolve the situation as quickly as possible: "It would be well, [if] the intended inquiry into the Conduct of Genl Sinclair [sic] could be brought to a speedy issue, and if he is acquitted, to the satisfaction of Congress, as his general character as an officer is good, that he may be again restored to the service."[73] Even before the charges were resolved, Washington included Arthur in War Councils.[74]

Arthur also played an active part in the Battle of Brandywine where his horse was shot from under him. But, because of his pending Court Martial, he was not permitted to lead his own forces. A few days later, having received word that his wife was ill, Arthur was granted a brief leave, but, by November 1777, after the fall of Philadelphia, he returned to headquarters where he, too, endured the brutal winter of 1777-78, at Valley Forge.[75] Arthur was again at Washington's side in June 1778, for the battle at Monmouth Court House in New Jersey.[76]

Arthur argued his case to New York Delegate John Jay: "That as to myself, I was perfectly easy; I was conscious of the uprightness and propriety of my conduct, and despised the vague censure of an uninformed populace." Furthermore, despite the fact that Gen. Schuyler had tried to shift the blame to his deputy, Arthur came to his commander's defense by stating clearly that because Schuyler was not there, "he was totally unacquainted with the matter." Arthur pointed out that "had our army been made prisoners, which it certainly would have been, the State of New York [which Jay represented], would have been much more exposed at present."[77]

In mid-September 1777, Arthur's close friend Col. Wilkinson, who was still assigned to the Northern Department, informed Arthur that "Gen. Gates...tells me, confidentially, that nothing could give him so much satisfaction as your presence here, though I find his supporters are, unfortunately, your enemies; hence his silence."[78] One month later, in celebration of the British Army's surrender at Saratoga, Col. Baldwin, who was also with Gen. Gates, sent congratulations to Arthur "on the important conquest over General Burgoyne..." Baldwin added that "by this time, the people in general have altered their sentiments with respect to the evacuation of Ticonderoga. The officers, and all who I now hear speak about it, say that a better plan could not have been adopted, and nothing but your leaving that place could have given us the success."[79]

The inquiry Congress had ordered dragged on for months as its characteristic inefficiency and the absence of key delegates necessitated one delay after another. Finally, on February 5, 1778, "a variety of evidence" was forwarded to Gen. Washington with instructions "to appoint a court martial." Washington responded at the end of that month that he was unable to pursue such a course since Congress had failed to issue any specific charges.[80] In early June, in a letter to Washington, President Henry Laurens expressed his own outrage at the delay: "I am quite in opinion with those Gentlemen who say 'the not proceeding in this matter is cruel & oppressive'--although I am as well convinced, the delay has not been calculated or intended to distress the parties affected--it has arisen from a vapid desultory habit, which if I am not mistaken, I have seen, squander Millions & endanger States." In his usual blunt style, Laurens then added: "I speak with warmth & I believe with equal truth."[81] It took until June 20 before Congress did approve charges against Gen. St. Clair and Gen. Schuyler.

By the time Arthur's Court Martial finally began on August 23, 1778, Gen. Gates was prepared to speak out publicly in defense of his friend. Under oath, Gates testified that "From my long acquaintance with you as an officer, and particularly your usefulness to me as a brigadier-general in the campaign of 1776, it excites my astonishment that there should be such charges as cowardice, treachery, or incapacity exhibited against you. From my knowledge of you, both as an officer and a gentleman, I have the highest opinion of your courage, honor, capacity, and fidelity."[82]

Gen. St. Clair and Gen. Schuyler were court martialled, fifteen months after Fort Ticonderoga fell. Both were acquitted "with the highest honour" of all charges against them.[83] In December 1778, Congress confirmed the verdicts.[84]

Shortly after Congress approved Arthur's acquittal, he received a warm note of congratulations from his friend, the Marquis de Lafayette: " ...I sincerely give joy to your country, that, NOTWITHSTANDING ALL CABALS, due justice is at last paid to such a citizen and soldier as you are..."[85] Once his reinstatement was final, Arthur was assigned command of a division composed of the Pennsylvania line[86] just as a heated dispute over their terms of enlistment threatened to break out into full scale mutiny. On March 6, 1779, Arthur wrote to Joseph Reed, the President of Pennsylvania, that "...a very disagreeable circumstance has occurred in our line...The officers, it seems, have formed a committee to state their grievances to the field officers...if they do not receive entire satisfaction on these points, on or before the 15th of April, every officer of the line will then resign their commissions..." Arthur added that "it is my duty to inform you explicitly that their complaints are but too well founded; that I believe necessity has, in a great measure, compelled them to the steps they have taken..."[87] At Arthur's urging, his close friend Thomas Smith introduced legislation in the Pennsylvania Assembly which diffused the crisis.[88]

In mid-August 1780, Gen. Gates suffered the greatest humiliation of the war when his newly rebuilt Southern Army was "virtually destroyed" by Gen. Cornwallis at Camden, North Carolina. To make matters even worse, Gates fled from the battle, covering 180 miles in only three and a half days.[89] At least one member of Congress--John Hanson of Maryland, the future President--suggested that Arthur would be an excellent candidate to succeed Gates.[90]

Another startling development, however, sent Arthur north rather than south. On October 1, he was ordered to take immediate command of West Point after Gen. Benedict Arnold's treason had been discovered. Even though he was recovering from an illness, Arthur responded immediately since a British attack seemed likely. On the way, he wrote a hurried personal letter to his wife, expressing his pleasure in a letter he had recently received from his second son, John Murray: "...the writing... was better than I expected," he told her. And then, after five agonizing years at war, Arthur expressed every soldier's most heartfelt desire: "I long much to see you all."[91]

On New Year's Day 1781, the Pennsylvania troops quartered at Morristown ushered in the new year "in a manner that shook the American cause to its foundations." Angered once again over their terms of enlistment, after a ration of rum was passed around they refused to obey their officers. Two captains and a lieutenant who tried to impose order were killed and other officers were injured. As the mutiny spread, the authorities became so desperate that, in the words of historian John C. Miller, "the mutinous troops virtually wrote their own terms for laying down their arms."[92] Since the revolt nearly destroyed Arthur's division, Washington ordered him to begin immediately to rebuild his forces and informed him that when the task was completed he should join Gen. Greene's Southern Army. On July 22, 1781, Arthur cautioned the Commander-in-Chief that the recruitment process was far from completed since "there will be much difficulty and delay in equipping the troops after they are raised, as the State of Pennsylvania has no money and little credit..."[93]

Plans changed again in early September. When Gen. Washington received word that the French fleet was headed toward the Virginia coast, he and the Comte de Rochambeau left Philadelphia on September 5,

1781, to confront the British forces under Gen. Cornwallis at Yorktown.[94] As they marched, Washington issued an appeal for all available troops to join him. On September 29, Arthur sent word to his commander that his troops had been delayed because "Congress had ordered me to draw all the levies of this State to Philadelphia, from an apprehension that strongly prevailed...that Sir Henry Clinton, with a body of about five thousand men, intended, by way of diversion to visit this city and either plunder or destroy it." He then added, in obvious relief, that "Your Excellency's letter was immediately communicated to Congress, and this day they have repealed the order and left me at liberty to join the army, which I shall do with as much expedition as possible..."[95]

On October 15, Arthur and his troops reached Washington's Headquarters on the outskirts of Yorktown. The following day he wrote a brief letter to his wife informing her that "I arrived here last night after a journey of nine days...Lord Cornwallis has not yet given up the ghost, but he will be now constrained to surrender, and I think myself very fortunate to have got up before it took place..."[96]

Cornwallis' surrender at Yorktown on October 19, 1781, clearly marked the beginning of the end of the Revolutionary War.[97] It would be more than a year, however, before the British abandoned Charleston and even longer before they withdrew from New York. Meanwhile, in mid-November 1781, Arthur informed Gen. Greene, the Commander of the Southern Department, that "I am now on my march, with the Pennsylvania and Maryland troops, to join your army..."[98] After encountering great difficulties along the way, Arthur finally reached Greene on December 27, at Jacksonburgh.[99] In response to a letter from Arthur at that time, Washington reminded him that "there is no accounting for the events of war." But, he reassured Arthur, "If your attempt should fail, whatever may be the censures of the people at the moment of the event, yet, I doubt not that your character will eventually obtain that justice which I flatter myself your conduct will ever merit, an instance of which you have already had in the course of this war."[100]

After reaching South Carolina, Arthur and his troops played a critical role in the siege of Charleston, waiting patiently for the British to evacuate without further bloodshed or destruction. For a soldier, it was a dreary business, especially when family concerns had gone unattended for so long. In early 1782, Arthur wrote to Gen. Washington again, notifying him that "The situation of my private affairs requires my attention to them this summer, which, if I do not give, they must go to absolute ruin."[101]

Even before he left South Carolina, Arthur wrote to the President of Congress, urgently requesting that the funds he had advanced to cover the expenses of his troops be reimbursed as quickly as possible. When he returned to Philadelphia in May 1782, he immediately held a series of meetings with his friend Robert Morris, the Superintendent of Finance, who was sympathetic but unable to offer much help. Arthur later shared the private nature of those conversations with Washington: "I let him very explicitly into my present circumstances, which is, in short, Sir--I am not master of one single shilling, nor will any thing that I am possessed of command it; I am in debt, and my credit exhausted, and were it not for the rations I receive, my family would actually starve..." Despite his pride, Arthur added that "This is rather hard, after sacrificing, as I have done, ease and independence, and the best part of my life..."[102] Arthur then took an extended leave of absence, with Washington's permission, to deal with his mounting personal affairs.

Throughout his own financial crisis, Arthur never lost sight of the similar plight of his fellow officers. In January 1783, he wrote to Pennsylvania Delegate Thomas FitSimmons: "The situation of these men is truly deplorable...As these gentelmen look up to me, for advice at least (other assistance I can not afford them, as I find myself in the same situation), I hope I may stand excused for taking the liberty to address you on this subject...An advance of money is of the utmost consequence even to their existence, and, should it be denied, they must be driven to desperation."[103]

On February 19, 1783, Gen. Washington informed Arthur "...in this private and friendly manner...that, in case you wish to retain a command in this army, it will be essential for you to come on immediately..."[104] Arthur responded at once while both the army and the nation anxiously waited for the arrival of the definitive peace treaty. Despite the uncertainty, on June 11, Congress directed the Secretary at War to complete the furlough of Delaware, Maryland, Pennsylvania and Virginia troops.[105] Two days later, the sergeants from one of the regiments already in Philadelphia, sent to Congress what James Madison termed "a very mutinous remonstrance..." To Madison's relief, "The prudent & soothing measures taken by the Secy. at war & Gl. Sinclair [St. Clair] have I believe obviated the embarrassment."[106] Arthur informed Gen. Wayne of these developments but warned that "The entire derangement of our finances put it out of the power of the public to make the provision they wished, and that ought to have been made before a dissolution of the army took place."[107] Stated simply, thousands of soldiers were being dismissed without any hope of immediate compensation for their service.

In less than a week, this combustible situation exploded. On June 19, Arthur received word from the War Office that "The Troops at Lancaster have mutinied, and are now on their march to this city."[108] By order of Congress, Arthur was directed to return to Philadelphia "without delay."[109] As they reached the capital, the Lancaster rebels were joined by other angry veterans who supported their protest. By midday on Saturday, June 21, over 400 rogue soldiers, some with fixed bayonets, surrounded the Pennsylvania State House where both Congress and the State Legislature met.[110] While a committee of Congress failed in its desperate attempt to convince State Officials to call out the militia, Arthur negotiated directly with the rebels. President Boudinot informed Gen. Washington that "matters continued thus till half past 3 O'Clock this afternoon..."[111] Two days later, in a letter to Gov. Livingston of New Jersey, the President added that "Congress... were suffered by the Rioters to pass unmolested, Genl. St. Clair having persuaded them to return to their Barracks."[112]

Madison sketched a slightly more dramatic scene: "...the Soldiers remained in their position, without offering any violence, individuals only occasionally uttering offensive words and wantonly pointing their muskets to the Windows of the Hall of Congress...But it was observed that spirituous drink from the tipling houses adjoining began to be liberally served out to the Soldiers, & might lead to hasty excesses."[113] Arthur later informed Washington that he finally "got them sent to their quarters, and, indeed, without vanity, I believe it was fortunate that I was able to come to town, as my presence had some effect in restraining them from greater enormities..."[114] Within days, the ringleaders were arrested, the remainder of the rebels returned to their duties and eventually Congress granted the participants pardons.[115]

But, by Tuesday afternoon, June 24, Congress had had enough of military mutineers and cowardly state officials. President Boudinot, a New Jersey native, made arrangements for Congress to reconvene at Princeton early in July.[116] For the duration of the First American Republic, the capital of the United States shifted between New Jersey and Maryland and ultimately to New York. It was only after Washington's inauguration that Philadelphia briefly reclaimed the title before the seat of government found a permanent home in the District of Columbia in 1800.[117]

Arthur's patience with Congress had also been exhausted by the summer of 1783. When he perceived an insult by not being selected to conduct the investigation of the Pennsylvania mutiny, he wrote an intemperate letter to Congress which President Boudinot was kind enough to hold back in the hope that Arthur would reconsider. The President assured him that no insult had been intended but that "If on the second reading you choose your letter should be read in Congress, it shall be done without delay."[118] The letter went unread.

As Arthur transitioned back into civilian life in the Fall of 1783, "he found himself ruined financially." His 19th Century biographer, William Henry Smith, states that "The comfortable fortune, and the valuable offices, which were all his in 1775...were all gone--all given freely, and without a regret, for freedom and a republic."[119] In that spirit, Arthur proudly concluded his Revolutionary War service on December 8, 1783. Along with Pennsylvania President John Dickinson and financier Robert Morris, Major Gen. Arthur St. Clair officially welcomed Gen. George Washington back to Philadelphia on the Commander-in-Chief's farewell visit.[120] Two weeks later, in Annapolis, Washington surrendered his commission to Congress and retired to Mount Vernon.

That same month, Arthur was elected as the President of the Society of the Cincinnati for the State of Pennsylvania. It was a new fraternal organization consisting of former Revolutionary War officers. At its first general meeting in Philadelphia in May 1784, George Washington, now retired, was unanimously elected President of the national Society. Surprisingly, Horatio Gates, once Washington's bitter rival, was elected Vice President. Arthur St. Clair, Elias Boudinot and Thomas Mifflin were the only Presidents of Congress who qualified for membership.[121]

During his years of military service, Arthur had privately opposed the Pennsylvania State Constitution of 1776, a peculiar blend of a plural executive and a unicameral legislature. Now, as a civilian, he was determined to correct the situation. In October 1783, Arthur was elected from the county of Philadelphia to serve on the Council of Censors, a bizarre body that was responsible for inquiring "whether the State Constitution had been preserved inviolate." He was then selected for the Council's five member committee which reported "those articles of the Constitution which are materially defective and absolutely require alteration and amendment." Their report did receive majority support from the Council, but lacked the two-thirds vote required for calling a new State Constitutional Convention. Arthur was also elected to the office of Vendue Master of Philadelphia, "an honorable, and very lucrative position, through which the public revenues were received at that time."[122] Arthur's financial plight finally began to brighten, at least for the moment.

When the Pennsylvania Assembly met on November 11, 1785, fifty-five percent of the deeply divided legislature elected Arthur as its newest Delegate to the Continental Congress. His close friend and confidant, James Wilson, was also reelected. Arthur took his seat the following February.[123] His congressional career in New York began slowly. On March 2, he reported to Wilson that "Since my arrival here nothing of any Moment has been upon the Carpet and if there had been it could not have been proceeded in as we have not at any time had more than seven States..."[124]

During the long gaps in congressional activity, Arthur even found time to pursue personal correspondence. In late March he wrote to his married daughter Elizabeth Lawrence, whom he greeted as "My Dear Betsy." Since she had apparently scolded him for not writing when, in truth, his original letter had simply been delivered late, Arthur playfully commented that her attack had "convinced me of two things...That Women are not always the most reasonable Creatures in the World...and that the most gentle of them, can now and then scold at good round rate." He added that he once thought that she might be the exception, but that she "kindly determined to undeceive me..."[125] Arthur also exchanged correspondence with his oldest son, Daniel, who had been a Lieutenant in the 3rd Pennsylvania Regiment from 1777-81. He urged Daniel to pursue a law career, even though he acknowledged that "The prejudice against Lawyers is one of those Opinions which rages in America..." Daniel, however, believed that the military was a more honorable profession.[126] Arthur won the argument.

It wasn't until August 3 that heated debate brought renewed life to the floor of Congress. On that day, former President John Jay, who now served as Secretary for Foreign Affairs after a distinguished diplomatic career (which included negotiating the Paris Peace Treaty), introduced a detailed proposal for a commercial treaty with Spain. Jay pointed out that not only was Spain "by far the greatest Consumer of all the European Kingdoms..." but that the Spanish "paid...in Gold and Silver," for American exports "whereas all other Nations pay with Manufactures..." Based upon the insistence of the Spanish minister that access to the Mississippi River would not be permitted in Spanish territory, Jay recommended that the treaty "should be limited to twenty five or thirty years, and that one of the Articles should stipulate that the United States would forbear to use the Navigatin of that River below their territories to the Ocean." Jay argued that "As that Navigation is not *at present* important, nor will probably become much so in less than twenty five or thirty years, a forbearance to use it while we do not *want it,* is no great sacrifice."[127]

Arthur was absent when the debate began, but on August 18, two days after returning to Congress, he delivered a detailed critique of Jay's proposal. He endorsed the commercial aspects of the treaty which, he said, as "the poet has beautifully expressed...binds the round of Nations in a golden Chain." Arthur pointed out, however, that "It will have and must have political Consequences." On the critical issue of access to the Mississippi, he clearly sided with Jay: "There appears to me to be more dignity, more policy certainly in waving the Exercise of a Right we cannot maintain, & obtaining something for the Waiver, than by pertinaciously insisting upon it, lose the Advantage and endanger the Right itself."[128]

Arthur's speech also included a fascinating insight into his views on western migration just sixteen months before the vast Northwest Territory was entrusted to his care. In response to those who argued that free navigation of the Mississippi was essential to opening up the west, Arthur cautioned restraint: "I am well acquainted with the Manners of our Frontier People and it was the employment of a great part of my Life to improve and civilize them." Because of the hardships they face and their distance from "the Center of Power...they acquire a turbulence and ferocity of Disposition that renders them but indifferent Citizens at the best..." He warned that "Care then Sir should be taken to check this Spirit and if it cannot be checked Government should go hand in hand with it..."[129]

Four days later, Arthur recorded a remarkable observation in his private notes: "Shutting the Missippi [sic] will prevent emigration--a most desirable End. If Countries are too full of People for Agriculturists they will turn themselves to Manufactures--the very thing America wants."[130] As the debate over navigation dragged on, the Southern States made increasingly clear that they would never ratify Jay's compromise. The Spanish eventually lost interest in the negotiations and the entire issue was ultimately postponed until the Second Republic began.[131]

In mid-September 1786, Arthur turned his attention to the plight of America's Indian Tribes. He introduced a Motion "That the Secretary of Congress take order for preparing a Proclamation...strickly charging and commanding all and every of the said States and all and every of their Citizens to behave towards the said Indian Nations and every individual of them in such manner as civilized Nations do...towards Nations and individuals of Nations with which they are at Peace, that the national Character may not be injured and the good of the Union maintained."[132] Arthur's specific target was the State of Virginia which he had learned was in the process of waging war against some of the friendly Tribes. Arthur was appointed to chair a five member committee to look into such charges. Virginia claimed self-defense while others blamed the illegal British forts along the frontier for inciting the Indians. In the end, the committee's report was simply ignored.[133]

Arthur left Congress in mid-October. A few weeks later, however, he was again selected by the Pennsylvania Assembly for another congressional term. By the time he returned to New York on January 25, 1787, Congress had not yet elected a new President.[134] In Arthur's absence, Rufus King of Massachusetts had speculated that either "Mr. Nash of No. Carolina, or Mr. Jno [John] Langdon of N Hampshire" would probably be chosen.

William Pierce of Georgia speculated that his colleague, George Walton, would be selected. Since none of those three States had yet had the honor of providing a President, the odds seemed in their favor. Nash, however, died in December 1786; Langdon did not arrive until September 1787; and, Walton was no longer a delegate.[135] Another North Carolina candidate, William Blount, had, according to congressional historian Edmund Cody Burnett, "fixed his eye upon the presidency," but the first round of balloting on January 17, indicated no clear favorite among several candidates. When Congress next obtained a quorum, on February 2, 1787, Arthur St. Clair of Pennsylvania became the only professional soldier ever elected President of Congress.[136] According to Madison, the selection had been decided after "some contest between the friends of Mr. Blount & Genl. Sinclair [St. Clair]..."[137]

While adjusting to his new national responsibilities, Arthur came under intense pressure from his home State to settle his accounts in Philadelphia where he had served as Vendue Master since 1783. John Nicholson, the Comptroller General of Pennsylvania, had initiated legal proceedings to resolve the matter. On February 12, Arthur responded to Nicholson's accusations: "It is most certain I did not know that old Ballance had not been paid off. Tho I acknowledge now, as I did then, that is not Justification--but if you had been pleased to have been more explicit, it would have led me to enquire more particularly, and I certainly had not left the City until provision had been made for the payment, tho' it had been attended with giving you the trouble to cut up more of my Certificates. It is true Sir many of them have been for Sale, and for purposes I am not ashamed of--for discharging Debts contracted during the progress of the Revolution--which cost me a great part of my Property when many others were making their Fortunes."[138]

Arthur also received letters of support from old friends and military colleagues. When, as President, he had the pleasure of sending a congressional gold medal to his old friend, Gen. Horatio Gates, Gates replied that "Nothing could add to this distinguished mark of the favor and approbation of Congress but my receiving it in so polite a manner from the hands of your Excellency; from you, sir, whom, in the course of thirty years, I have so often had the honor to accompany on a vast variety of military service. Permit me, likewise, to declare the satisfaction I feel in seeing your Excellency's merits crowned by the high station you now fill with such acknowledged ability."[139]

At the same time, Madison outlined pending national business in a letter to Washington. At the top of his list was the ongoing failure of both Britain and the States to comply with all provisions of the peace treaty. As a justification for not surrendering their forts along the frontier, the British repeatedly pointed to the refusal of the States to compel the payment of debts owed to loyalists.[140] In a fascinating offhanded comment, he told Washington that "Those who may lean towards a monarchical Govt. and who I suspect are swayed by very indigested ideas, will of course abandon an unattainable object whenever a prospect opens of rendering the Republican form competent to its purpose."[141]

The most pressing issue was Virginia's call for a Convention to consider amendments to the Articles of Confederation. As historian Richard B. Morris has stated: "Congress...understandably showed no great warmth to a proposal that set up a mechanism to bypass that body."[142] But the Delegates knew better than anyone that some adjustments were desperately needed. Therefore, on February 21, 1787, they approved the following resolution: "Congress having had under consideration the letter of John Dickinson esqr chairman of the Commissioners who assembled at Annapolis during the last year...and entirely coinciding with them as to the inefficiency of the federal government and the necessity of devising such farther provisions as shall render the same adequate to the exigencies of the Union do strongly recommend to the different legislatures to send forward delegates to meet the proposed convention on the second Monday in May next at the city of Philadelphia ...for the purpose of revising the Articles of Confederation and perpetual Union..."[143]

The opening of the Convention in May 1787 further exasperated the eternal struggle to establish a congressional quorum since ten members of Congress--including such pivotal players as James Madison, Rufus King and former President Nathaniel Gorham--were preoccupied throughout the summer with their duties in Philadelphia rather than New York.[144] Another former President, Richard Henry Lee, had also been elected to serve in both bodies, but believed it was his responsibility to remain in Congress, especially since he presumed that Congress would ultimately review the work of the Convention. Many of his congressional colleagues disagreed.

Since Congress was not able to muster a quorum after May 11 because so many members had migrated to Philadelphia for the Convention, Arthur informed Secretary Charles Thomson on May 18 that "Having some pressing Business in a distant part of Pennsylvania that cannot well be done without my being personally present, I avail myself of the Situation of Congress at this time to attend to it"[145] Even the Secretary himself took the opportunity to travel home to Philadelphia that month.[146] Several weeks later, when Thomson returned to New York, he discovered that Arthur was still away. "I cannot account for the absence of the president."

Thomson wrote to a friend, "it has I assure you given a good deal of offence. If I knew where to direct a letter to him I would take the liberty to write and urge him to come on as speedily as possible."[147] When a quorum was finally reestablished on Wednesday, July 4, 1787, the President had not yet returned. William Grayson of Virginia was selected to temporarily preside as Chairman.[148] Arthur finally resumed his duties on July 17, referring to his two-month leave as "A Recess..."[149]

In Arthur's absence, Congress acted with remarkable speed in early July to tackle its most important piece of postwar legislation: The Northwest Ordinance of 1787. Authorship of this seminal document has been assigned to at least four candidates, but Dr. Manasseh Cutler, a representative of the newly formed Ohio Company of Associates, appears to be the most credible candidate to claim the title.[150] On the morning of July 5, 1787, Cutler arrived at Congress where he subsequently presented his group's detailed proposal for governing the frontier. On July 13, according to Cutler's description, "the ordinance establishing a government in the western Federal Territory" was enacted by Congress. "The amendments I proposed," he wrote, "have all been made except one..."[151]

As historian Richard B. Morris described The Ordinance, it "combined a structure of territorial government and a schedule of admission to statehood with a set of provisions regarding property, contracts, and basic civil rights."[152] At first, the entire Northwest Territory (which was eventually divided into the States of Ohio, Michigan, Indiana, Illinois, Wisconsin and eastern Minnesota) was to be headed by a governor, secretary and three judges, all to be appointed by Congress. The second stage would be triggered when a part of that territory reached five thousand free adult male inhabitants. At that point, the settlers would be entitled to elect their own bicameral legislature which would serve alongside the appointed governor. Finally, when that territory attained sixty thousand free residents, it would become eligible for admission into the Union "on an equal footing" with the original thirteen States. Article Six of the Ordinance clearly stated that "There shall be neither slavery nor involuntary servitude in the said territory..."[153]

Speculation began immediately concerning who would be selected to govern this vast territory. In early August, Massachusetts Congressman Samuel Holten reported to former President Nathaniel Gorham that "My present thought is that I should favor G. Sinclair [St. Clair] to be Govr..."[154] Not surprisingly, the Ohio Company preferred one of their own directors, former Brigadier-General Samuel Holden Parsons of Connecticut. Cutler later insinuated that President St. Clair was withholding his influence because of his own interest in the office. Cutler's allegation, however, has never been substantiated.[155]

Despite the long-term implications pertaining to the Ordinance, Congress still could not retain a quorum. On August 13, while suffering from sever gout in his right hand,[156] Arthur, as President, pleaded with the governors of Georgia, Maryland, Connecticut, Rhode Island and New Hampshire to hasten the arrival of their delegations. "The want of a due Representation in Congress...has very greatly embarrassed the Affairs of the Union...What, Sir, must the Nations of the World Think of Us when they shall be informed that we have appointed an Assembly and... during the Course of almost a whole Year, it has not been capable, except for a few Days, for want of a sufficient number of Members, to attend to these matters." He added that "...the national Convention...will soon rise, and it appears to be of great Consequence that, when their Report comes under the consideration of Congress, it should be a full Congress and the important Business which will be laid before them meet with no unnecessary Delay."[157]

Throughout all of 1787, there were only "112 days on which the Congress assembled and transacted business...there were only 2 days on which there was a delegate present for each of the 13 States." But, as the editor of the Journals of the Continental Congress stated in Volume XXXII, " Despite the handicap of poor attendance a grat amount of business was done by the Congress during the year..."[158]

The Constitutional Convention did complete its work on September 17. Over the next several days, those delegates who were also members of Congress traveled back to New York with the final document. On September 20, the proposed Constitution was officially presented to Congress. One week later, Arthur presided over two days of intense debate concerning how Congress should proceed. On Friday, September 28, over the heated objections of former President Richard Henry Lee, who insisted that Congress should exercise its authority by amending and voting on the document,[159] Congress decided to adhere to the Convention's plan by simply transmitting copies of the proposal "to a convention of Delegates chosen in each state by the people thereof in conformity to the resolves of the Convention..."[160] Accordingly, the proposed State Ratification Conventions proceeded without Congress taking any official position.

As soon as the new Constitution had been safely dispatched to the States, congressional focus shifted back to the selection of officials to lead the Northwest Territory. On October 5, "Congress proceeded to the election of a governor for the western territory pursuant to the Ordinance of the 13th of July last and the ballots being taken The Hon Arthur St.

Clair was elected." Former Major Winthrop Sargent, a founder of the Ohio Company, was then chosen to serve as Secretary.[161] Eleven days later, Parsons, the Company's original candidate for Governor, and two other men were elected as Judges for the territory.[162] Together with the Governor, they would also serve as the first legislature.

On Tuesday, October 23, Congress adopted the following Resolution: "We reposing special trust and confidence in your integrity prudence and ability have constituted and appointed and by these presents do constitute and appoint you the said A. S. [Arthur St. Clair] Governor in and over the territory of the United States of America north west of the river Ohio and commander in chief of the militia therein, to order rule and govern the same conformably to the Ordinance of the 13 July 1787... And we do... give and grant to you the said A S all the powers authorities and prerogatives assigned to the governor of the said territory in and by the said Ordinance." Arthur's commission was "to take effect from the first day of february 1788..."[163]

Thus began the next chapter in the history of the United States. Many Revolutionary soldiers would finally receive the compensation in land which the inflated continental currency could never match.[164] For average Americans, dreams of homesteads now seemed within reach. And, as some brave souls had predicted during the darkest days of the Revolutionary War, the sale of western lands did indeed help to cover the nation's war debt. Historian Merrill Jensen estimated that by the 1830s, the United States had sold "more than forty-four million dollars worth of land..."[165] It is not surprising that Daniel Webster later stated: "I doubt whether one single law of any law-giver, ancient or modern, has produced effects of more distinct, marked, and lasting character than the Ordinance of 1787."

Arthur took leave of Congress on October 29.[166] As he prepared for the demands of his new office and the relocation of his family back to Ligonier, Pennsylvania,[167] most of the States were preoccupied with their own Ratification Conventions. All but forgotten, the Continental Congress did not attain a quorum again until January 21, 1788. The following day, Cyrus Griffin of Virginia was elected as the fourteenth and last "President of the United States in Congress Assembled."[168]

On Wednesday, July 9, 1788, Governor Arthur St. Clair's barge landed at the foot of Fort Harmar near the confluence of the Muskingum and Ohio Rivers. Government had come to the wilderness. Sergeant Joseph Buell captured the historic moment in his journal: "On landing he [Gov. St. Clair] was saluted with thirteen rounds from the field piece. On entering the garrison the music played a salute; the troops paraded and presented their arms."[169] The following Tuesday, Arthur and his party were officially welcomed to the nearby settlement of Marietta.[170] There, as Governor, he delivered his first formal address to the inhabitants of the Territory. He pledged that "it is very much my desire, to do every thing within the compass of my power for the peace, good order, and perfect establishment of the settlement..."[171]

Arthur began at once to enact territorial laws and establish the government. He was also responsible for pursuing peace with the Indians within his domain. Despite repeated threats from some, and the incitement emanating from the British frontier forts that still stood in violation of the 1783 Peace Treaty, Arthur did manager to open a major tribal council in mid-December. By January 9, 1789, he he was able to finalize two separate treaties with most of the tribes. The Mohawks, Miamis and Shawnese, however, remained hostile. As a result, Arthur realized that force would be required before settlers felt safe enough to migrate throughout the region. He traveled back to New York that spring in order to consult directly with Secretary of War Henry Knox.[172]

As Governor of the Northwest Territory, Arthur was also an honored guest at Federal Hall in New York City on April 30, 1789, as his friend George Washington was sworn into office as the first President of the United States under the Second Republic.[173] One month later, the President and Mrs. Washington invited Arthur to join them for a small dinner party at their official residence, which Arthur himself had occupied less than two years earlier during his own presidency.[174]

That July, while still in New York, he received news from his old confident, former congressman James Wilson of Philadelphia, who informed Arthur that "it is in the serious contemplation of some here to have you placed in the chair of the President of Pennsylvania [i.e., Governor]."[175] Arthur was seriously tempted since his current annual salary of $1,500 was simply inadequate to meet the needs of his family.[176] He finally permitted his name to be entered in the contest the following year after the State's new Constitution was adopted in September 1790. Arthur received support from Robert Morris and Benjamin Rush as well as Wilson, but, in the end, the election wasn't even close. The incumbent, Thomas Mifflin (who had also served as President of Congress from 1783-84), was a natural politician. Mifflin carried every county in the State and won the city of Philadelphia by a vote of 1,761 to 96.[177]

A far more serious defeat awaited Arthur back on the frontier. In October 1791, with only 2,000 troops (1,000 fewer than had been promised by Secretary Knox) and inadequate supplies, Arthur was notified by the War Department that "The President still continues anxious that you should, at the earliest moment, commence your operations."[178] Ever the good soldier,

Arthur did as ordered. As a result, a surprise attack by the Indians along the eastern fork of the Wabash River decimated his ranks.[179]

On March 27, 1792, after an exhaustive review, a congressional inquiry exonerated Arthur of any blame for the defeat: "The committee conceive it but justice to the commander-in-chief, to say that, in their opinion, the failure of the late expedition can, in no respect, be imputed to his conduct, either at any time before or during the action; but that, as his conduct, in all the preparatory arrangements, was marked with peculiar ability and zeal, so his conduct, during the action, furnished strong testimonies of his coolness and intrepidity."[180] Even though he was fully exonerated, Arthur's military reputation had been seriously tarnished. (Over two years later, with a far larger army and adequate supplies, Major General Anthony Wayne was able to defeat the warring tribes at the Battle of Fallen Timbers in August 1794.[181])

Despite Arthur's humiliation, President Washington continued to extend his confidence and friendship.[182] The day after the congressional vote, Washington even wrote to Arthur, expressing the hope that "you may enjoy uninterrupted happiness."[183] Arthur did indeed retain his civilian office as Governor throughout the Washington and Adams Administrations. At times, however, he felt like "a poor devil banished to another planet," as he confided to Alexander Hamilton in 1793.[184] Fortunately, in 1796, Arthur was able to pursuade his son, Arthur, Jr., a successful Pittsburgh attorney, to become the territory's Attorney General.[185]

During his tenure as Governor, Arthur also managed to inspect much of the region under his jurisdiction, including French settlements at Kaskaskia and Cahokia along the Mississippi River. St. Clair County, Illinois, just East of St. Louis, stands today as a living memorial to that historic 1790 visit.[186]

A decade later, nearing the end of his long public life, Arthur spoke from his heart concerning Native Americans in an address to the Ohio Territorial Legislature: "It has long been a disgrace to the people of all the States bordering upon the Indians, both as men and as Christians, that, while they loudely complained of every injury or wrong received from them...they were daily offering to them injustice and wrongs of the most provoking character, for which I have never heard that any person was ever brought to due justice and punishment, and all proceeding from the false principle that, because they had not received the light of the gospel they might be abused, cheated, robbed, plundered, and murdered at pleasure, and the perpetrators, because professed Christians, ougth not to suffere for it. What kind of Christianity is this, or where is it to be found? Surely, not in the gospel of Jesus Christ."[187]

Considered wise by some and autocratic by others,[188] Arthur continued to nurture the Ohio region even after the Indiana Territory to the West was split off in 1800.[189] Local leaders, however, eager to take the reigns of power, grew impatient to complete the Statehood process and became increasingly vicious in their attacks on the Governor.[190] Nevertheless, Arthur persisted in his belief that statehood was premature, and he challenged "all the World to produce one instance, in the whole of my Administration, where...an Act to which the interest and welfare of the people was not the leading...motive.[191] The new Jefferson Administration, anticipating another loyal Republican State, eventually sided with Arthur's enemies.[192] On December 14, 1802, the Governor was notified by Secretary of State Madison that the President had relieved him of the office he had held for nearly fifteen years. Arthur asked the Secretary "to present my humble thanks to the President for that favor, as he has thereby discharged me from an office I was heartily tired of, about six weeks sooner than I had determined to rid myself of it..."[193] The following year, the State of Ohio was admitted to the Union.[194]

Arthur, now a private citizen, returned to western Pennsylvania and his home, two miles north of Ligonier. At long last he was permanently reunited with his wife, Phoebe, who, according to one biographer, suffered from great anxiety and mental strain.[195] Still a staunch Federalist, Arthur unsuccessfully petitioned the Republican Congress for the sizable reimbursement his country still owed to him. (It was not until 1857, thirty-nine years after his death, that Congress finally appropriated "a considerable sum for the benefit of his surviving heirs.") In 1810, unable to meet his financial obligations,[196] Arthur lost almost all of his possessions except for "a few books of my classical library."[197] He and his wife were even forced to abandon their home.

Nearly penniless, Arthur and Phoebe along with several grandchildren retreated a few miles to a double log cabin on Chestnut Ridge on land owned by their eldest son, Daniel.[198] There, assisted by their daughter Louisa,[199] they lived out their final years running a tavern where they served plain meals and "selling supplies to the wagoners who traveled the road" to Pittsburgh. The State of Pennsylvania eventually did grant him a small annuity, but they struggled every day to survive.[200] Through it all, Arthur maintained his dignity. In 1815, Elisha Whittlesey, a future congressman, visited the old patriot. Years later, Whittlesey recalled that "I never was in the presence of a man that caused me to feel the same degree of esteem and veneration...Poverty did not cause him to lose his self respect..."[201]

Following a freak accident in which he was thrown from his wagon, Arthur died on August 31, 1818, at the age of 82. His wife Phoebe, after

58 years of married life, survived her husband by only eighteen days.[202] Having been separated so often in life, they now rest side by side at St. Clair Cemetery in Greensburg, Pennsylvania.[203]

Years earlier, in a letter to his intimate friend and confidant James Wilson, Arthur articulated his core philosophy which never wavered throughout his long and tumultuous life: "I hold that no man has a right to withhold his services when his country needs them," he wrote. "Be the sacrifice ever so great, it must be yielded upon the altar of patriotism."[204]

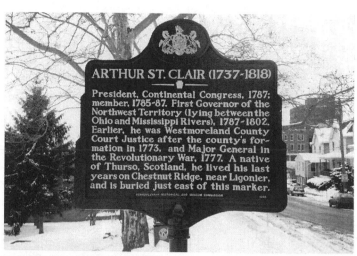

ARTHUR ST. CLAIR (1737-1818)

President, Continental Congress, 1787;
member, 1785-87. First Governor of the
Northwest Territory (lying between the
Ohio and Mississippi Rivers), 1787-1802.
Earlier, he was Westmoreland County
Court Justice after the county's formation in 1773, and Major General in
the Revolutionary War, 1777. A native
of Thurso, Scotland, he lived his last
years on Chestnut Ridge, near Ligonier,
and is buried just east of this marker.

President Arthur St. Clair
and his wife Phoebe
are buried sided by side
at St. Clair Cemetery in
Greensburg, Pennsylvania.
After 58 years of marriage
and seven children
they died only 18 days apart.

The birth year printed on
the highway marker (above)
is inaccurate.
According to the latest research
by the Library of Congress
Arthur St. Clair was born
in 1736.

WHILE ARTHUR ST. CLAIR
WAS PRESIDENT

February 1787 - November 1787

Two days after Arthur St. Clair was elected President, Shays Rebellion in Massachusetts was finally crushed when Gen. Benjamin Lincoln captured 150 of the remaining rebels. Their leader, Daniel Shays, escaped to Vermont.[205] The Rebellion sparked a wave of backcountry resistance across the nation. Resentment toward heavy-handed debt collection and suffocating new taxes spread from debtors who forcefully prevented the sale of cattle seized for taxes in York, Pennsylvania to the angry mob that burned down the Court House in King William County, Virginia. As historian Richard B. Morris observed, "the spread of the Shays' contagion conveyed a sense of urgency to the nationalists, who now recognized that... there was a need for a central government that could maintain civil order in the states."[206]

This message was certainly not lost on the delegates to the Constitutional Convention who met in Philadelphia from May through September 1787. In his opening remarks on May 29, Gov. Edmund Randolph of Virginia specifically cited the recent rebellion in Massachusetts as a dramatic example of the failure of the existing confederacy.[207] Even though the Convention's deliberations were held in strictest secrecy, the mere existence of that historic conclave totally eclipsed the Continental Congress which still struggled on in New York.

What is truly amazing is the fact that Congress accomplished as much as it did during 1787. In mid-February, it passed the Post Office ordinance and authorized the Postmaster General to contract for mail delivery. In April, Congress debated the politically charged issue of where to locate the nation's permanent capital.

In the diplomatic realm, Congress took another important step forward in early May, when it officially received the first British Consul to the United States, Phinease Bond. Five months later circumstances were reversed when it voted to accept John Adams' request that he be permitted to return to America when his commission as the first United States Minister to Great Britain expired. In October, Congress voted to extend

Thomas Jefferson's commission as Minister to France. During this period, it also ratified a commercial treaty with Morocco.[208] By far, however, the adoption of the Northwest Ordinance of 1787 and Arthur's subsequent election as the first Governor of that vast territory were the crowning accomplishment of Congress during Arthur St. Clair's presidency.

While the United States struggled through its adolescent growth, the ancient Kingdom of France faced far greater crises which stemmed, in part, from that Kingdom's extensive financial support of the American Revolution which had been orchestrated by the Comte de Vergennes, the French Foreign Minister. His death in early 1787 cost the United States its most valuable contact in Europe.

The price of Vergennes' policies, however, fell much harder on his Sovereign, Louis XVI. To deal with France's financial crisis, the King called the Assembly of Notables to meet in February 1787. But, led by opposition from the clergy, it rejected the "radical" reform program that had been proposed by the King's Finance Minister, Charles Alexandre de Calonne. The minister's removal two months later simply exacerbate the financial crisis which eventually led to riots and revolution.[209]

One of the clearest indications that the Revolutionary War was truly over was the career of Lord Charles Cornwallis. After his ignominious surrender of the British Army at Yorktown in October 1781,[210] Cornwallis eventually returned to England. A few years later, his star rose again in 1787 when he was appointed by Pitt the Younger to serve as Governor General of India under the 1784 India Act which extricated royal government from the clutches of the East India Company. Cornwallis, who demanded extensive powers to purge the local administration, arrogantly viewed all things Indian as corrupt, thus triggering a dangerous racial division for decades to come.[211] Displeased with the support he received from London, Cornwallis finally resigned his office in 1793. Even then, his biography was incomplete. In 1798, two years after President Washington had retired to Mount Vernon for the last time, Lord Cornwallis embarked on his most challenging assignment: Viceroy of Ireland.[212]

Chapter 13

President
ARTHUR ST. CLAIR
of
PENNSYLVANIA

Notes

Abbreviation Key

JCC   Journals of the Continental Congress
LDC   Letters of Delegates to Congress
PHL   The Papers of Henry Laurens

[1] Under Article II, Section 1 of the United States Constitution: "No Person except a natural born Citizen...shall be eligible to the Office of President."

[2] The Old Northwest Territory included what are now the states of Ohio, Indiana, Michigan, Illinois and Wisconsin as well as part of Minnesota.

[3] Frazer Ells Wilson, Arthur St. Clair: Rugged Ruler of the Old Northwest (Garrett & Massie, Richmond, Virginia, 1944), pp. 57-58. The first county established in the present-day state of Illinois, just east of St. Louis, was St. Clair County. Belleville, the county seat, is still home to the "St. Clair Mansion" on Church Street, which was built by William St. Clair, a relative, in the early 1800s. When William died in 1799, he left his estate to Gov. St. Clair's son, Arthur St. Clair, Jr., who was then Attorney General of the Northwest Territory.

[4] Merriam-Webster's Geographical Dictionary, 3rd Edition (Merriam-Webster, Inc., Springfield, Massachusetts, 1998), p. 1181.

[5] Biographical Directory of the American Congress: 1774-1961 (Government Printing Office, Washington, DC, 1961), pp. 1556-155. See also: William Henry Smith, The St. Clair Papers: The Life and Public Services of Arthur St. Clair (Robert Clarke & Co., Cincinnati, 1882), Vol. 1, p. 2; and, Wilson, op. cit., p. 3.

[6] Paul H. Smith, Editor, LDC: 1774-1789 (Library of Congress, Washington, DC, 1996), Vol. 24, pp. xxix-xxx. See also: Dumas Malone, Dictionary of American Biography (Charles Scribner's Sons, New York, 1943), Vol. XVI, pp. 293-295.

[7] Converted to the "new style" of dating, the date of Arthur St. Clair's birth would be April 3.

[8] As cited in Wilson, op. cit., p. 2.

[9] Malone, op. cit., Vol. 16, p. 293.

[10] Wilson, op. cit., p. 4.

[11] "The Royal American regiment...consisted of four battalions of 1,000 men each." Smith, op. cit., Vol. 1, p. 3 footnote.

[12] Smith, op. cit., Vol. 1, p. 4.

[13] See Introduction.

[14] In the official narrative of Arthur St. Clair's Indian Campaign, as cited in Wilson, op. cit., pp. 5-6.

[15] Smith, op. cit., Vol. 1, p. 6.

[16] Smith, op. cit., Vol. 1, p. 6

[17] Wilson, op. cit., pp. 8-9.

[18] Smith, op. cit., Vol. 1, pp. 6, footnotes 1; and pp. 7-8, footnote 3.

[19] Wilson, op. cit., p. 9.

[20] Malone, op. cit., Vol. 16, p. 294.

[21] Wilson, op. cit., p. 11.

[22] David Hawke, In The Midst Of A Revolution (University of Pennsylvania Press, Philadelphia, 1961), p. 79.

[23] Smith, op. cit., Vol. 1, p. 10.

[24] Smith, op. cit., Vol. 1, p. 291; Governor Penn to Lord Dunmore, March 31, 1774.

[25] John C. Miller, Triumph of Freedom (Little, Brown & Company, Boston, 1948), p. 40.

[26] Malone, op. cit., Vol. 16, p. 294.

[27] Smith, op. cit., Vol. 1, p. 364; Resolutions Adopted at Hannastown, Westmoreland County, Pennsylvania, May 1775.

[28] Smith, op. cit., Vol. 1, p. 355; Arthur St. Clair to Governor Penn, May 25, 1775.

[29] As quoted in Smith, op. cit., p. 14.

[30] LDC, op. cit., Vol. 2, p. 10; Richard Smith's Diary, September 13, 1775. Smith, op. cit., p. 15.

[31] Worthington Chauncey Ford, Chief, Division of Manuscripts, JCC: 1774-1789 (Government Printing Office, Washington, DC, 1906), Vol. IV, pp. 23-24.

[32] As quoted in Wilson, op. cit., pp. 23-24.

³³ LDC, op. cit., Vol. 3, p. 109; Richard Smith's Diary, January 17, 1776. According to a February 5, 1776, entry in Smith's Diary, the Foreign Officer was Dohickey Arundel. Franklin and St. Clair did give find him qualified, but others raised objections because he was a "Papist." p. 204.

³⁴ LDC, op. cit., Vol. 3, p. 183; John Hancock to Thomas Cushing, February 1, 1776.

³⁵ LDC, op. cit., Vol. 3, p. 494; John Hancock to Philip Schuyler, April 6, 1776.

³⁶ LDC, op. cit., Vol. 3, p. 269; Robert Morris to Charles Lee, February 17, 1776.

³⁷ Craig L. Symonds, <u>A Battlefield Atlas of the American Revolution</u> (The Nautical & Aviation Publishing Company of America, Inc., 1986), pp. 23-25.

³⁸ Wilson, op. cit., p. 25.

³⁹ Smith, op. cit., Vol. 1, p. 23.

⁴⁰ Wilson, op. cit., p. 27.

⁴¹ LDC, op. cit., Vol. 4, p. 202; Samuel Chase to Horatio Gates, June 13, 1776.

⁴² JCC, op. cit., Vol. V, p. 641. See also: LDC, op. cit., Vol. 4, p. 651; William Williams to Joseph Trumbull, August 10, 1776.

⁴³ Smith, op. cit., Vol. 1, p. 373; Thomas Smith to General St. Clair, August 22, 1776.

⁴⁴ Smith, op. cit., Vol. 1, p. 376; General St. Clair to Lieutenant-Colonel Allen; September 1, 1776.

⁴⁵ JCC, op. cit., Vol. VI, p. 977.

⁴⁶ LDC, op. cit., Vol. 5, p. 586; William Paca to the Maryland Council of Safety, December 7, 1776.

⁴⁷ Smith, op. cit., Vol. 1, pp. 378-379, footnote 1.

⁴⁸ Smith, op. cit., Vol. 1, pp. 31-32; see also, Symonds, op. cit., p. 31.

⁴⁹ Symonds, op. cit., p. 33.

⁵⁰ Smith, op. cit., pp. 35-36 & 41-42.

⁵¹ JCC, op. cit., Vol. VII, p. 133. Gen. Stirling, Gen. Stephen and Gen. Lincoln were also elected Majors General at the same time.

⁵² LDC, op. cit., Vol. 6, p. 333; James Wilson to Arthur St. Clair, February 20, 1777.

⁵³ JCC, op. cit., Vol. VII, p. 217.

⁵⁴ Smith, op. cit., Vol. 1, p.393; General Washington to General St. Clair, April 18, 1777.

⁵⁵ Smith, op. cit., Vol. 1, p. 399; General St. Clair to General Schuyler, June 13, 1777.

[56] Smith, op. cit., Vol. 1, pp. 402-404; General St. Clair to James Wilson, June 18, 1777.

[57] LDC, op. cit., Vol. 7, pp. 215-216; Horatio Gates' Notes for a Speech to Congress, June 18, 1777. Gen. Gates requested to address Congress directly after being informed that Gen. Schuyler, not Gates, had been appointed as the Commander of the Northern Department. The imprecise wording of President Hancock's letter to Gen. Gates on March 25, 1777, was the source of the confusion.

[58] Smith, op. cit., Vol. 1, pp. 410-411; General St. Clair to General Schuyler, June 26, 1777 and June 28, 1777.

[59] LDC, op. cit., Vol. 7, p. 360; Samuel Adams to Richard Henry Lee, July 22, 1777.

[60] Benson Bobrick, Angel in the Whirlwind (Simon & Schuster, New York, 1997), pp. 250-253.

[61] Smith, op. cit., Vol. 1, pp. 420-421; The Evacuation of Ticonderoga and Mount Independence.

[62] Smith, op. cit., Vol. 1, p. 69.

[63] Smith, op. cit., Vol. 1, p. 424; General St. Clair to General Schuyler, July 8, 1777.

[64] LDC, op. cit., Vol. 7, p. 352; John Hancock to Philip Schuyler, July 18, 1777.

[65] LDC, op. cit., Vol. 7, pp. 359 & 435; Samuel Adams to Richard Henry Lee, July 22, 1777; and, to John Langdon, August 7, 1777.

[66] LDC, op. cit., Vol. 7, pp. 426-427; James Lovell to William Whipple, August 5, 1777.

[67] LDC, op. cit., Vol. 7, p. 362; Thomas Burke to Richard Caswell, July 22, 1777.

[68] JCC, op. cit., Vol. VIII, pp. 585 & 590.

[69] JCC, op. cit., Vol. VIII, p. 596.

[70] LDC, op. cit., Vol. 7, p. 393; New York Delegates to the New York Council of Safety, July 29, 1777; see also, p. 401, footnote 1; Samuel Adams to James Warren, August 1, 1777.

[71] JCC, op. cit., Vol. VIII, p. 604.

[72] Smith, op. cit., Vol. 1, pp. 431-433; General St. Clair to General Washington, July 17, 1777.

[73] Fitzpatrick, op. cit., Vol. 9, p. 322: General Washington to the President of Congress, October 7, 1777.

[74] Fitzpatrick, op. cit., Vol. 9, p. 263, footnote 74; and, Vol. 10, pp. 77-78, 85 & 245.

[75] Wilson, op. cit., pp. 31-32.

[76] Smith, op. cit., Vol. 1, pp. 99-101.

[77] Smith, op. cit., Vol. 1, p. 433; General St. Clair to John Jay.

[78] Smith, op. cit., Vol. 1, p. 443; Colonel Wilkinson to General St. Clair, September 21, 1777.

[79] Smith, op. cit., Vol. 1, pp. 444-445; Colonel Baldwin to General St. Clair, October 17, 1777.

[80] John C. Fitzpatrick, Editor, The Writings of Washington (Government Printing Office, Washington, DC, 1933), Vol. 10, p. 518; General Washington to the President of Congress, February 27, 1778.

[81] LDC, op. cit., Vol. 10; p. 46; Henry Laurens to George Washington, June 8, 1778.

[82] Smith, op. cit., Vol. 1, p. 448; The Court-Martial of Gen. Arthur St. Clair, Major General Benjamin Lincoln, President & John Laurence, Judge Advocate, August 1778.

[83] LDC, op. cit., Vol. 7, p. 417, footnote 1; John Hancock to Philip Schuyler and Arthur St. Clair, August 5, 1777.

[84] JCC, op. cit., Vol. XII, pp. 1225-1226. The vote on Gen. St. Clair took place on December 16, 1778. A similar vote had been taken concerning Gen. Schuyler on December 3, 1778, p. 1186.

[85] Smith, op. cit., Vol. 1, p. 458; Marquis de Lafayette to General St. Clair, January 1779. Some speculate that Arthur's Court Martial was only part of the much larger effort by Washington's enemies to have him replaced as Commander-in-Chief by Gen. Gates, a conspiracy popularly known as the Conway Cabal. See Chapter 10, p. 307-309, for further details.

[86] Smith, op. cit., Vol. 1, p. 101.

[87] Smith, op. cit., Vol. 1, p. 462-467; General St. Clair to President Reed, March 6, 1779.

[88] Burton Alva Konkle, The Life and Times of Thomas Smith, 1745-1809 (Campion & Company, Philadelphia, 1904), 109.

[89] Symonds, op. cti., p. 87. Gen. Gates described his defeat as "unfortunate" as he tried to salvage his reputation. Bobrick, op. cit., pp. 402-403.

[90] LDC, op. cit., Vol. 16, p. 51; John Hanson to Thomas Sim Lee, September 11, 1780.

[91] Smith, op. cit., Vol. 1, p. 529, footnote 1; Arthur St. Clair to Phoebe St. Clair, October 1780.

[92] Miller, op. cit., pp. 542-544.

[93] Smith, op. cit., Vol. 1, p. 553; General St. Clair to General Washington, July 22, 1781.

[94] Smith, op. cit., Vol. 1, p. 556; General St. Clair to General Irvine, September 6, 1781.

[95] Smith, op. cit., Vol. 1, p. 559; General St. Clair to General Washington, September 29, 1781.

[96] Smith, op. cit., Vol. 1, p. 560; General St. Clair to Mrs. St. Clair, October 16, 1781.

[97] Bobrick, op. cit., pp. 463-464. The end came not a moment too soon. Even as the surrender ceremonies were taking place, Gen. Clinton was sailing toward Yorktown with 25 ships and 7,000 troops to relieve Cornwallis, only to discover that he was too late.

[98] Smith, op. cit., Vol. 1, p. 564; General St. Clair to General Greene, November 14, 1781.

[99] Smith, op. cit., Vol. 1, p. 113.

[100] Smith, op. cit., Vol. 1, p. 567; General Washington to General St. Clair, November 30, 1781.

[101] Smith, op. cit., Vol. 1, p. 569; General St. Clair to General Washington, February 4, 1782.

[102] Smith, op. cit., Vol. 1, p. 572; General St. Clair to General Washington, November 26, 1782.

[103] Smith, op. cit., Vol. 1, p. 579; General St. Clair to Hon. Thomas Fitzsimmons, January 21, 1783.

[104] Smith, op. cit., Vol. 1, p. 577; General Washington to General St. Clair, February 19, 1783.

[105] JCC, op. cit., Vol. XXIV, p. 390; June 11, 1783.

[106] LDC, op. cit., Vol. 20, p. 336; James Madison to Edmund Randolph, June 17, 1783.

[107] Smith, op. cit., Vol. 1, p. 586; General St. Clair to General Wayne; June 15, 1783.

[108] Smith, op. cit., Vol. 1, p. 587; Major Jackson to General St. Clair, June 19, 1783.

[109] LDC, op. cit., Vol. 20, pp. 343-344; Elias Boudinot to William Jackson, June 19, 1783.

[110] Eugene R. Sheridan and John M. Murrin, Editors, Congress at Princeton (Princeton University Library, Princeton, 1985), p. xl.

[111] LDC, op. cit., Vol. 20, pp. 349-350; Elias Boudinot to George Washington, June 21, 1783, 4 O'Clock P.M.

[112] LDC, op. cit., Vol. 20, pp. 357-358; Elias Boudinot to William Livingston, June 23, 1783.

[113] LDC, op. cit., Vol. 20, pp. 351-352; James Madison's Notes of Debates, June 21, 1783.

[114] Smith, op. cit., Vol. 1, p. 589; General St. Clair to General Washington, July 2, 1783.

[115] Smith, op. cit., Vol. 1, p. 115. Four years later, the impact of this incident convinced many delegates to the Constitutional Convention that Congress should never again be at the mercy of any state government and thus came into existence the formation of the District of Columbia as the permanent seat of national government.

[116] LDC, op. cit., Vol. 20, p. 368; Elias Boudinot's Draft Statement on the mutiny, June 26, 1783.

[117] The American Story in Art (National Society of the Daughters of the American Revolution, 1986), pp. 13 & 18.

[118] LDC, op. cit., Vol. 20, p. 411; Elias Boudinot to Arthur St. Clair, July 9, 1783.

[119] Smith, op. cit., Vol. 1, p. 116.

[120] Douglas Southall Freeman, Washington (Charles Scribner's Sons, New York, 1968), abridged edition, p. 508.

[121] Smith, op. cit., Vol. 1, pp. 590-593.

[122] Smith, op. cit., Vol. 1, pp. 116-117 & 593-598.

[123] LDC, op. cit., Vol. 23, pp. xxiv & 109; Charles Pettit to Nathanael Greene, January 20, 1786.

[124] LDC, op. cit., Vol. 23, p. 173; Arthur St. Clair to James Wilson, March 2, 1786.

[125] LDC, op. cit., Vol. 23, p. 206; Arthur St. Clair to Elizabeth Lawrence, March 22, 1786.

[126] LDC, op. cit., Vol. 23, pp. 576-577, and, footnotes 1 & 2; Arthur St. Clair to Daniel St. Clair, September 1786.

[127] JCC, op. cit., Vol. XXXI, pp. 467-484.

[128] LDC, op. cit., Vol. 23, pp. 491-495; Arthur St. Clair's Speech, August 18, 1786.

[129] LDC, op. cit., Vol. 23, p. 494.

[130] LDC, op. cit., Vol. 23, p. 518; Arthur St. Clair's Notes, August 22?, 1786.

[131] Frank Monaghan, John Jay (The Bobbs-Merrill Company, New York, 1935), pp. 260-261.

[132] JCC, op. cit., Vol. XXXI, pp. 656-658.

[133] LDC, op. cit., Vol. 23, p. 574, footnote 4; Timothy Bloodworth to Richard Caswell, September 29, 1786.

[134] LDC, op. cit., Vol. 23, p. xxiv; and, Vol. 24, p. xxv.

[135] LDC, op. cit., Vol. 24, p. 30 and footnote 2; Rufus King to Daniel Kilham, November 19, 1786.

[136] Burnett, op. cit., pp. 673-674.

[137] LDC, op. cit., Vol. 24, p. 95; James Madison to James Monroe, February 11, 1787.

[138] LDC, op. cit., Vol. 24, pp. 79-80 & 96-97; Arthur St. Clair to John Nicholson, January 30, 1787 & February 13, 1787.

[139] Smith, op. cit., Vol. 1, p. 605; General Gates to President St. Clair, August 31,1787.

[140] LDC, op. cit., Vol. 24, p. 220, footnote 1.

[141] LDC, op. cit., Vol. 24, pp. 110-111; James Madison to George Washington, February 21, 1787. See also Chapter 12, pp. 372-373, for a further discussion of the issue of monarchy at this phase of the Continental Congress.

[142] Richard B. Morris, The Forging of the Union (Harper & Row, Publishers, New York, 1987), p. 257.

[143] JCC, op. cit., Vol. XXXII, pp. 71-72. See also: Irving Brant, The Fourth President: A Life of James Madison (The Bobbs-Merrill Company, Indianapolis, 1970), pp. 135-136. Since only five States attended the Annapolis Meeting in September 1786, its one Resolution was to call for a Convention to revise the Articles of Confederation to be held in Philadelphia the following May.

[144] LDC, op. cit., Vol. 24, pp. xviii-xxvii. See also: LDC, op. cit., Vol. 24, pp. 275-276, footnote 1. The ten congressional delegates who also served as Members of the Constitutional Convention in the summer of 1787 were: Gorham and King (MA); Madison (VA); Blount (NC); Butler (SC); Few & Pierce (GA); Gilman & Langdon (NH); and, Johnson (CT).

[145] LDC, op. cit., Vol. 24, p. 281; Arthur St. Clair to Charles Thomson, May 18, 1787.

[146] LDC, op. cit., Vol. 24, p. 279, footnote 1. Thomson's deputy, Roger Alden, managed the Secretary's Office until Thomson returned to New York on June 24, 1787.

[147] LDC, op. cit., Vol. 24, p. 350; Charles Thomson to William Bingham, July 8, 1787.

[148] JCC, op. cit., Vol. XXXII, p. 297.

[149] LDC, op. cit., Vol. 24, p. 372; Arthur St. Clair to John Wendell, July 24, 1787.

[150] Harlow Lindley, Chairman, History of the Ordinance of 1787 and the Old Northwest Territory (Northwest Territory Celebration Commission, Marietta, Ohio, 1937), pp. 16-25. Some attributed authorship to Jefferson who chaired a congressional committee in 1784 when an earlier proposal was issued. The 1787 act, however, shows little similarity to that earlier measure and Jefferson had been out of the country for years when the final law was adopted. Others, including Daniel Webster, believed that Nathan Dane of Massachusetts was the author while Rufus King's son claimed the honor for his distinguished father. Scholarly research during the 1876 Centennial, however, pointed to Cutler.

[151] As cited in Lindley, op. cit., p. 25.

[152] Morris, op. cit., p. 231.

[153] Henry Steele Commager, Editor, <u>Documents of American History</u> (Appleton-Century-Crofts, New York, 1963), The Northwest Ordinance, p. 132.

[154] LDC, op. cit., Vol. 24, p. 397; Samuel Holten to Nathaniel Gorham, August 8, 1787.

[155] As cited in Lindley, op. cit., p. 26.

[156] LDC, op. cit., Vol. 24, p. 434; Arthur St. Clair to Thomas FitzSimons, September 20, 1787.

[157] LDC, op. cit., Vol. 24, pp. 403-404; Arthur St. Clair to Certain States, August 13, 1787. At the same time, Secretary Thomson wrote to the States informing them that "since the first Monday in November last the United States have not been represented more than three days by 10 States, thirty days by 9 states And forty days by 7 & 8 states." Vol. 24, p. 399; Charles Thomson to the States, August 10, 1787.

[158] JCC, op. cit., Vol. XXXII, pp. vii-viii; Prefatory Note.

[159] Chapter 11. Above all, the Continental Congress wanted to avoid activating the amending process of the Articles of Confederation which required unanimous consent. Since the State of Rhode Island did not even send delegates to the Constitutional Convention it was widely assumed that Rhode Island would, in effect, exercise a veto over the document if given the opportunity.

[160] JCC, op. cit., Vol. XXXIII, p. 549.

[161] JCC, op. cit., Vol. XXXIII, p. 610. See also Lindley, op. cit., p. 22.

[162] JCC, op. cit., Vol. XXXIII, p. 686.

[163] JCC, op. cit., Vol. XXXIII, p. 699.

[164] Wilson, op. cit., p. 45.

[165] Merrill Jensen, <u>The New Nation: A History of the United States During the Confederation 1781-1789</u> (Alfred A. Knopf Publishers, New York, 1950, p. 359.

[166] LDC, op. cit., Vol. 24, p. xxv.

[167] Wilson, op. cit., p. 42. Even though several of Arthur's children did eventually join him in Ohio, his wife, totally unsuited to frontier life, remained in slightly-more-civilized Ligonier, Pennsylvania throughout his governorship.

[168] LDC, op. cit., Vol. 24, p. xvii.

[169] As cited in Lindley, op. cit., p. 45.

[170] Wilson, op. cit., p. 46. The Ohio Company presented Gov. St. Clair with "fifteen acres of ground in the town [Marietta] for his family and personal use." While such "considerations" were both common and legal at the time, Arthur did not engage in wild land speculation like so many of his era.

[171] Smith, op. cit., Vol. II, pp. 53-56; Governor St. Clair's Address at Marietta, July 15, 1788.

[172] Smith, op. cit., Vol. I, pp. 156-158.

[173] Smith, op. cit., Vol. I, p. 158, footnote 2.

[174] Smith, op. cit., Vol. II, pp. 120-121, footnote 1; The other guests included Vice President John Adams, former President John Jay, New York Gov. George Clinton, Speaker Frederick Muhlenburg and the Ambassadors from France and Spain. For additional information on the President's House at No. 3 Cherry Street in New York City, see Chapter 11, p. 347.

[175] Smith, op. cit., Vol. II, pp. 119-120; James Wilson to Arthur St. Clair, July 13, 1789.

[176] Wilson, op. cit., p. 215. Arthur maintained that, as Governor of the Northwest Territory, "...the general government never contributed one cent, except the salary, which was not equal to my travelling expenses for a good many years." See also, Wilson, op. cit., p. 41.

[177] Kenneth R. Rossman, <u>Thomas Mifflin and the Politics of the American Revolution</u> (The University of North Carolina Press, Chapel Hill, 1952), pp. 192-196.

[178] As cited in Smith, op. cit., Vol. I, p. 173.

[179] Smith, op. cit., Vol. II, p. 265; General St. Clair to the Secretary of War, November 9, 1791. In his report, Gen. St. Clair stated that: "I have nothing, sir, to lay to the charge of the troops but their want of discipline, which, from the short time they had been in service, it was impossible they should have acquired, and which rendered it very difficult, when they were thrown into confusion, to reduce them again to order, which is one reason why the loss has fallen so heavy upon the officers, who did every thing in their power to effect it. Neither were my own exertions wanting; but, worn down with illness, and suffering under a painful disease, unable either to mount or dismount a horse without assistance, they were not so great as they otherwise would, and, perhaps, ought to have been. We were overpowered by numbers.."

[180] Smith, op. cit., Vol. II, pp. 286-299; Report of a Special Committee of the House of Representatives on the Failure of the Expedition Against the Indians, March 27, 1792.

[181] Lindley, op. cit., pp. 57-58. Gen. Wayne's victory over the Northwest Indians led to the Treaty of Greenville on August 5, 1795.

[182] Washington Irving, <u>Life of George Washington</u> (G. P. Putnam, New York, 1859), Vol. 5, p. 119.

[183] Smith, op. cit., Vol. II, p. 284; President Washington to General St. Clair, March 28, 1792.

[184] Smith, op. cit., Vol. II, p. 317; Governor St. Clair to Alexander Hamilton, August 9, 1793.

[185] Smith, op. cit., Vol. I, pp. 196 & 214. In 1799, when the Territory elected its first Delegate to Congress, Arthur, Jr. lost to territorial Secretary William Henry Harrison, the future President, by one vote in the new General Assembly.

186 Smith, op. cit., Vol. I, pp. 164-166; see also Wilson, op. cit., pp. 57-58 & 62. According to Wilson, Secretary Sargent insisted on naming it in Gov. St. Clair's honor.

187 Smith, op. cit., Vol. II, p. 503; Address of Governor St. Clair to the Territorial Legislature, at the Opening of the Second Session, at Chillicothe, November 5, 1800.

188 Wilson, op. cit., p. 135.

189 Lindley, op. cit., p. 49. Ohio and Eastern Michigan retained the title of Northwest Territory in 1800 when the rest of the area became known as the Indiana Territory under the governorship of William Henry Harrison (who briefly served as the 9th President of the United States in 1841). By 1809, the land west of Indiana was known as the Illinois Territory. By 1818, the year Arthur St. Clair died, the States of Ohio, Indiana and Illinois had been established and the rest of the area was known as the Michigan Territory. Finally, by 1848, Michigan and Wisconsin had also been declared States and the Northwest portion of the original territory became eastern Minnesota.

190 Wilson, op. cit., p. 189.

191 Smith, op. cit., Vol. II, p. 482; Governor St. Clair to James Ross, December 1799: "A multitude of indigent and ignorant people are but iill qualified to form a constitution and government for themselves; but that is not the greatest evil to be feared from it. They are too far removed from the seat of government to be much impressed with the power of the United States...though at present they seem attached to the General Government, it is in fact but a passing sentiment, easily changed or even removed, and certainly not strong enough to be counted upon as a principle of action..." See also, p. 573; Governor St. Clair to Thomas Jefferson, President, February 13, 1802.

192 Wilson, op. cit., pp. 201 & 204; see also Smith, op. cit., Vol. I, p. 245. President Jefferson's specific rationale for dismissing Governor St. Clair included what Jefferson refered to as "an intemperance and indecorum of language toward the Legislature of the United States..." Wilson, op. cit., p

193 Smith, op. cit., Vol. I, pp. 599-600; Arthur St. Clair to James Madison, December 21, 1802.

194 Wilson, op. cit., p. 202. "...the first seven governors of Ohio belonged to the Jeffersonian party and the seven presidents, elected in later years, were all of the opposite party."

195 Wilson, op. cit., p. 231.

196 Malone, op. cit., Vol. XVI, p. 295.

197 Smith, op. cit., Vol. I, pp. 250-252.

198 Wilson, op. cit., pp. 220 & 222.

199 Wilson, op. cit., p. 235. See also pp. 238-245, for the legend of "Louisa and the Chief's Son" which describes the unverified tale of how the 16 year old daughter of the Northwest Governor fell in love with the warrior son of Chief Joseph Bramt of the Mohawks.

200 Smith, op. cit., Vol. I, pp. 252-253. See also, Wilson, op. cit., p. 222.

[201] As cited in Smith, op. cit., Vol. I, p. 253.

[202] St. Clair tomb, St. Clair Cemetery, Greensburg, Pennsylvania.

[203] Smith, op. cit., Vol. I, p. 254.

[204] As quoted in Smith, op. cit., Vol. 1, p. 14.

WHILE ARTHUR ST. CLAIR WAS PRESIDENT

Notes

Abbreviation Key

JCC   Journals of the Continental Congress
LDC   Letters of Delegates to Congress
PHL   The Papers of Henry Laurens

[205] For the details of Shays Rebellion, see Chapter 12. See also, Richard B. Morris, Editor, Encyclopedia of American History (Harper & Row, New York, 1961), pp. 115-116.

[206] Richard B. Morris, The Forging of the Union: 1781-1789 (Harper & Row, New York, 1987), p. 265.

[207] E. H. Scott, Editor, Journal of the Federal Convention Kept by James Madison (Scott, Foresman and Co., Chicago, 1898), pp. 59-60.

[208] Paul H. Smith, Editor, LDC: 1774-1789 (Library of Congress, Washington, DC, 1996), Vol. 24, pp. xii-xvi; Chronology of Congress.

[209] Encyclopaedia Britannica, Inc., (William Benton, Publisher, Chicago, 1966), Vol. 9, pp. 724-726.

[210] Chapter 7.

[211] J. Steven Watson, The Reign of George III (Clarendon Press, Oxford, 1960), pp. 306 & 322.

[212] Donald Grove Barnes, George III and William Pitt, 1783-1806 (Octagon Books, Inc., New York, 1965), pp. 354-356.

Chapter 14

President
CYRUS GRIFFIN
of
VIRGINIA

The Most Forgotten Father

Colonial Williamsburg, that great guardian of America's Revolutionary heritage, has done the unthinkable. It has misplaced the fourteenth and final President of the Continental Congress.

The first President, Peyton Randolph, rests in peace in the crypt of the Wren Chapel at the College of William and Mary.[1] Many other giants of that age, including Lord Botetourt, the popular colonial governor (1770-71), and Benjamin Harrison, the patriot, are also accorded recognition and honor throughout the city. And yet, the last President of America's First Republic, Cyrus Griffin, remains unmourned and unacknowledged in Bruton Parish Churchyard beside the Table Tomb he so lovingly commissioned for his dear wife, Lady Christina Stuart Griffin. There, in an unmarked grave, buried "at the smallest expence possible in every respect," according to the dictate of his Will,[2] Cyrus Griffin's remains have been interred in obscurity for two centuries. Of all the Founding Fathers, he is surely the most forgotten.[3]

Equally overlooked in the annals of American History is the critical role that the descendants of French Huguenots, including Cyrus Griffin, played in the founding of the United States. Cyrus was the fourth of the fourteen Presidents of the Continental Congress who could trace his ancestors to those brave souls who fled the Protestant persecution which culminated in King Louis XIV's revocation of the Edict of Nantes in 1685. As the author of *The Huguenots in America* states, "they were the first major Continental European refugee group to settle in the British colonies of North America since the arrival of the Puritans half a century earlier."[4] That author conservatively estimates that the total Huguenot migration to British North America did not exceed 2,000 by 1700.[5] And yet, those courageous men and women who fled their homes for religious liberty during the 17th Century set a powerful example of courage and tenacity for their descendants a century later.

The fact that twenty-eight percent of the Heads of State of the First American Republic--Laurens, Jay, Boudinot and Griffin--came from families who had emigrated from France as a result of the Huguenot Diaspora is truly amazing. Not only were these new pilgrims exceptionally brave, they were also remarkably adaptable. Many Anglicized their names and even joined other Protestant denominations in order to integrate into their new home across the Atlantic. These skills also served their grandchildren well in helping to found a new nation.[6]

Cyrus was directly linked to these Hugunot immigrants through his mother, Mary Ann Bertrand. Her father, John, had been a Protestant minister in France before he and his brother Paul sought exile in London. There, on September 29, 1686, John Bertrand married Charlotte Jolie, a French nobleman's daughter. They soon emigrated to America where they gave birth to Mary Ann and a son named William (who died in 1760).[7] The family settled in Lancaster County, Virginia."[8]

On his father's side, some historians speculate that Cyrus was descended from Llewllyn Griffin, the last King of Wales, who died in battle in 1282. More reliable, however, is the fact that two Welshmen, Thomas Griffin and his brother Samuel, arrived in America by 1651, when Thomas Griffin procured land on the Rappahannock River in Virginia. Samuel apparently returned to Wales, but Thomas Griffin made his home in America. He eventually married a woman named Sarah. Their first child, Leroy Griffin, served as a Justice of the Peace of Rappahannock County from 1680-1695. Leroy Griffin married Winifred Corbin, the daughter of Col. Gawin Corbin. They named their oldest son Thomas, in honor of his grandfather.

Thomas Griffin, the grandson of the founder, represented Richmond County in the Virginia House of Burgesses from 1718-1723. While his wife is unknown, they named their oldest son Leroy in honor of Thomas' father. Young Leroy Griffin, like his father and grandfather, took an active role in public affairs. He became the High Sheriff of Richmond County. He also owned a successful tobacco plantation. On October 5, 1734, Leroy Griffin married Mary Ann Bertrand. They raised eight children, four of whom actively participated in the founding of their new nation. Their eldest, Dr. Corbin Griffin, was a member of the York County Committee of Safety from 1775-76, and worked as a surgeon in the Virginia line during the American Revolution. He eventually settled in Yorktown, Virginia where his home, "Griffin House," still stands.[9]

William Griffin, their second son, was a colonel of the militia and served as Sheriff of King and Queen County, Virginia in 1782. Their third son, Samuel, was a lawyer and legislator who also served in uniform as a colonel in the Revolution and was wounded at the Battle of Harlem Heights in October 1776. He was later appointed to the Virginia Board of War. In 1778, Samuel married Betsy Braxton, the daughter of Carter Braxton, one of the Signers of the Declaration of Independence. Samuel was elected as a member of the Virginia House of Delegates in 1786. At the start of the Second American Republic, Samuel served three terms as a member of the new United States House of Representatives from Virginia (1789-1795).[10]

Leroy and Mary Ann Griffin had five other children including Leroy, Jr., Thomas Bertrand and John Tayloe. Their only daughter, Elizabeth, married Col. Richard Adams, a wealthy Richmond landowner.[11] Their sixth son, Cyrus, the future President, was born in Faarnham Parish in Richmond County, Virginia on July 16, 1748, only two years before his father died.[12]

At the age of 18, like many young men from prosperous 18th Century Virginia families, Cyrus traveled overseas in 1766 to study at Edinburgh University. There he formed a close friendship with one of his fellow students, Charles Stuart, Lord Linton, the son and heir of the Sixth Earl of Traquair. During the reign of Charles I, Lord Linton's ancestor had been one of the most powerful men in Scotland. During the 1630s, while serving as Scottish Treasurer, the First Earl had guaranteed that taxes flowed south to the king.[13] Over a hundred years later, the family remained fiercely loyal to the Catholic faith. As a minority in a Protestant realm, the castle at Traquair, approximately 25 miles south of Edinburgh, still housed a chapel where services were held regularly.[14]

At some point, Lord Linton invited Cyrus to join him at his family's estate over a school holiday. What unfolded is described in an amusing 1923 book entitled "Love Stories of Famous Virginians" by Sally Nelson Robins. Upon arrival, Cyrus was introduced to Linton's three sisters: Lady Christina, Lady Mary and Lady Louisa. According to John Adams' description years later, Lady Christina spoke French "like a Paris lady."[15] Robins describes her as "so beautiful and so fascinating" that Cyrus could not resist her charms. She, in turn, was obviously struck by the "tall and handsome" American with the piercing blue eyes.[16]

All sources agree that the old Earl was vehemently opposed to the notion of his daughter marrying a Protestant commoner from America. The next step, however, remains shrouded in lore. While an old scrap book kept by Cyrus' grandson claimed that the Earl reluctantly consented and even permitted the couple to be married by a priest in Traguair chapel,[17] most assert that the eager young lovers eloped to avoid her father's rage. Robins maintains that during their escape Lady Christina fell and broke her ankle "which rendered her lame all the rest of her life..."[18]

According to a 1965 research article by another writer, their marriage was entered in the "Register of Marriages Within the City of Edinburgh" on April 29, 1770. That article maintains that Lady Christina's father was listed as "Deceast" in order to avoid the requirement of giving prior notice before they could marry, which would have delayed the ceremony. If true, this document would clearly contradict the grandson's conjecture.[19] Over a century later, the story of these defiant young lovers served as the basis for "The Griffins," a romantic novel published in 1904 by Mary Stuart Young.[20]

It is also unclear whether Christina and her husband were ever permitted to return to the Castle. Robins claims that their first son, John, was even born at Traquair on April 20, 1771.[21] Whatever happened, Cyrus and his young family moved to London in late May 1771, to continue his study of law at Middle Temple, one of London's four Inns of Court.[22] There, in the greatest city of the Empire, they struggled to survive for the next three years. Cyrus' new brother-in-law, Richard Adams, very generously came to their aid. Adams notified his London merchant that since Cyrus "has lately been privately married to the oldest daughter of the Earl of Traquair ...we are apprehensive that Mr. Griffin...may have occasion for more money than he can readily command..." Therefore, Adams wrote, "I shall...esteem it a great favor if you will present him the enclosed and give him any assistance in this way in your power. You will find him a solid, sensible young man well worthy your notice and friendship."[23]

Finally, in 1774, after living abroad for eight years, Cyrus returned to America with his beautiful wife and young son. Christina gave birth to their first daughter, Mary, that same year. Two more children--Louisa and Samuel--were born in America. From the moment they settled in Virginia, everyone referred to Mrs. Griffin as Lady Christina. After only a year, however, Cyrus returned to London alone in the hope of securing his wife's share of her family's fortune. Citing Scottish law and the fact that Christina's brother's marriage had not yet produced an heir, Cyrus unsuccessfully petitioned Lord Germain, a member of the government, for assistance in his quest.[24]

While in England, Cyrus became increasingly alarmed over the rapid deterioration in relations between America and the Mother Country. In a remarkably bold move, he prepared "A Plan of Reconciliation with the American Colonies" in which he outlined what he perceived to be a constructive path toward peace. It called for the appointment of a commission which would meet with members of the Continental Congress as individual citizens in an attempt to review all American grievances since the end of the French & Indian War in 1763. Specific disagreements that could not be resolved through that process would then be referred to the next Parliament with the right of the American Colonies to be represented by counsel. If these efforts failed, each party would "remain in possession of their prisoners, captives and conquests till the final termination of this unhappy dispute."[25]

On Saturday, December 30, 1775, armed with a letter of introduction from their mutual friend, the Reverend Isaac William Gibberne, Cyrus anxiously carried his Plan to the home of Lord Dartmouth, the new Privy Seal, who, only five weeks earlier, had relinquished his position as Secretary of State for the American Department.[26] Cyrus had hoped to present his Plan in person but was disappointed to learn that his lordship was not receiving visitors. Instead, Cyrus scribbled a brief note which he left with the Plan. In it, he acknowledged that his "intrusion would be highly impertinent if we were not told from history that the efforts of the most inconsiderable person may some-times be of the greatest service to the Community." Even though nothing ever came of Cyrus' proposal, Dartmouth did retain it in his files where it still remains in the possession of the Earl's descendants.[27]

Having failed in his efforts at personal and political diplomacy, Cyrus was eager to return home to his family and his country. Lord Germain, the new Secretary of State for the American Department, granted him a passport in March 1776. Cyrus anxiously set sail for America and whatever his fate might be in the struggle ahead.[28]

Shortly after he was reunited with his family, and just as he was starting to build his law practice, American Independence was officially proclaimed. Following in his grandfather's footsteps, Cyrus responded to the challenge by successfully seeking election to the Virginia legislature from Lancaster County. On May 5, 1777, Cyrus first took his seat in the Virginia House of Delegates. As one of the best trained lawyers in the state, it is hardly surprising that he was immediately appointed to the Committee for Courts of Justice. It was one of four committees during that session where he served with Patrick Henry and Thomas Jefferson.[29]

After only a one year apprenticeship in the State House, Cyrus was elected by his Virginia colleagues on May 29, 1778, as a delegate to the Continental Congress.[30] Just over a month later, Congress itself returned to Philadelphia after the British evacuation of the American capital. It was there that Cyrus presented his credentials on August 19, 1778, just as the dispute between Arthur Lee and Silas Deane began to divide that assembly.[31] For the next two months Cyrus served alongside his Virginia colleague, Richard Henry Lee, Arthur Lee's older brother.[32] At first, Cyrus even voted with his fellow Virginians;[33] but soon, Cyrus and the Lee clan became bitter rivals.

Like President Henry Laurens, Cyrus also became increasingly disillusioned with Congress itself. On October 6, 1778, he wrote a remarkable letter to Thomas Jefferson who was again serving in the Virginia House. Cyrus stated in the opening lines that "There are but few Men indeed with whom I could wish to be thus candid." He then poured out his frustration with the national government: "Congress exhibit not more than two or three Members actuated by Patriotism. Great questions are carried every day in favor of the Eastward, and to the prejudice of the Southern States...I will not sit in a house whose proceedings I cannot assent to with honor, nor is it in my abilities to oppose them with success." He told Jefferson that "It would astonish you to think how all affairs proceed upon the interested Principle: Members prostituting their votes in expectation of mutual assistance upon favorite Points. I am apprehensive that in getting free from oppression in one quarter, we are likely to establish it in another..."

In discussing the Lee-Deane affair, it became obvious that Cyrus had broken with the Lees. "We are plagued to death with quarrels and recriminations relative to our Commissioners abroad;" he said. "These men will involve the Continent in perdition. It is absolutely necessary that Dean [sic] should be sent over to Europe for the most valuable purpose in the world, but some gentlemen are determined to ruin an innocent Character, notwithstanding he alone has the great merit of concluding that valuable Treaty with the Minister of France."[34]

Cyrus left Philadelphia two weeks later but, despite his intense frustration, he returned just before Christmas 1778, and continued his work as a member of Congress without interruption for another eighteen months.[35] On March 1, 1779, he took on even more responsibility when he became a member of the powerful Committee on the Treasury.[36] Later that year, when the committee authorized a $10,000 reimbursement to Silas Deane to cover his expenses since the previous June, Henry Laurens, long a Deane opponent, poured out his anger to his friend and colleague, Richard Henry Lee: "I opposed the Payment of that or any Sum to Mr. Deane until he should account for the large Sums of Public Money which have been in his hands..." Laurens, one of the most successful businessmen of the South, added that "this deficiency of firmness & perseverance is the source of much irregularity & much evil in public business."[37]

Cyrus' continued service in Congress and on the Treasury Committee made him an obvious target for his enemies. By mid-1779, the powerful Lee Family and its allies had expanded their attack on Silas Deane by challenging the private ethics and public policy of several of Deane's key supporters including Samuel Chase of Maryland, Robert Morris of Pennsylvania and Meriwether Smith and Cyrus Griffin of Virginia. In June of that year, the Virginia House passed legislation which required all of its congressional delegates to take an oath that they would "not directly or indirectly engage in any merchandize, either foreign or domestick." The legislature then pro-ceeded to reelect both Cyrus and Meriwether Smith for the next congressional term.[38]

Smith expressed his outrage to Jefferson, now the Governor of Virginia, complaining that the new conditions attached to congressional service "are very injurious to my personal Interest and Honour..." He added that "my Enemies, not content with attempting to displace me by a direct Vote, have availed themselves of a circumstance to procure a Law which either removes me from Office or deprives me of a considerable Means of Subsistance."[39]

Cyrus was equally irate. While recovering from an illness which confined him "to the Bed and house" for fifteen days, he wrote to an old friend on August 10, 1779, that "the Lee party in the Virginia assembly were strenuous of opposition to Smith and myself, and almost carried the point of exclusion." He shared with his friend that "truly I find it impossible to remain in Congress a long time; I am already some Thousand Dollars out of pocket; my constitution will not support excessive confinement; I only wish to see our brave army placed upon such a respectable footing as their... Patriotism deserve...and the curency of the united states in a fair way of appreciating: and then farewell to public Business eternally."[40] Cyrus had no way of knowing that he would actually continue in public service for the remaining thirty-one years of his life.

By mid-September 1779, a ray of optimism briefly broke through in a letter Cyrus sent to his close friend, Lt. Col. Burgess Ball.[41] In speculating on the latest British activity and the potential impact of the French fleet, Cyrus stated that "I am *almost* as sanguine as yourself that the present Campaign will finish the Contest; the opposition to Great Britain is very formidable indeed..." But then, as if jolted back to reality, he added "and yet when so conspicuous a nation begins to fall, perhaps she may go on to the brink of destruction, and of consequence the war may be lengthened a considerable time to come."[42] Unhappily for Ball, Cyrus' fears were realized. Ball was captured by the British when Charleston fell eight months later.[43]

On October 14, 1779, Cyrus' congressional focus expanded to include judicial affairs when he was appointed to fill a vacancy on the Committee on Appeals.[44] The committee's formation could be traced to 1775 when Gen. Washington had urged Congress to establish a procedure for adjudicating disputes over vessels and cargoes that were periodically captured by the infant American navy as well as privateers. By sheer coincidence, the first such appeal was requested by Pennsylvania on July 4, 1776. By 1779, the process had evolved into individual Admiralty Courts (also known as prize courts) at the State level with appeals directed to this specific congressional committee.[45]

This new assignment placed even greater demands on Cyrus' already hectic schedule. In addition to the Committee on Appeals, he also served on several other important bodies including the Committee of Commerce which "met almost daily in 1779."[46] What made matters even worse was that from November 1, until James Madison finally presented his credentials in March 1780, Cyrus was also the only Virginia Delegate to attend Congress. Patrick Henry, among others, had been elected, but never appeared.[47] As a result, Cyrus could participate in committee work but, according to Virginia law, at least two delegates had to be present in order for the State to cast its vote in the full body.

In a letter to the Virginia House of Delegates on November 9, 1779, Cyrus pleaded for help: "I am at present alone in this important delegation; perhaps abundantly more important than my Constituents suppose. A majority of states in Congress shew a manifest inclination to lessen the weight of Virginia in the general scale of the union; and the Continental Credit is already upon the very brink of ruin. At such a period the assembly are satisfied that my abilities and Influence are greatly inadequate to represent so vast a Country as Virginia, even upon the supposition I had the power of voting in Congress. I feel exceedingly for the rights of my Country, and the Welfare of America, and I hope to be excused when I express some degree of astonishment that at least three members are not sent forward to Philadelphia, and members too of the first abilities and character."[48] In response to Cyrus' plea, the Virginia Assembly solved at least part of the problem when it passed a law late that Fall authorizing Cyrus to cast the State's vote by himself.[49]

By the beginning of 1780, after Pennsylvania had refused to accept the Com- mittee on Appeals' reversal of its State court in the trial of the sloop *Active*, it had become obvious to Cyrus and his congressional colleagues that the Committee had to shed its legislative ties in order to strengthen its judicial authority.[50] Accordingly, on Saturday, January 15, 1780, the Continental Congress created the Court of Appeals in Cases of Capture to hear "all appeals from the Courts of Admiralty in the several States."[51] It would consist of three judges, none of whom could be members of Congress. Any two judges would constitute a quorum. As Professor Henry J. Bourguignon states in his book *The First Federal Court,* "Though not explicitly provided, the new court apparently could review questions of fact as well as law." The Court's inability to enforce its decrees was clearly its Achilles' heel. As was true on so many important issues, Congress simply left it up to the States to ensure that the Court's rulings were implemented.[52]

One week after establishing the Court, Congress elected its first three judges: George Wythe of Virginia, Titus Hosmer of Connecticut and William Paca of Maryland. Wythe, perhaps the most respected legal mind in Virginia, declined.[53] Three months later, on April 28, 1780, Cyrus was elected to fill the "Virginia seat" on the Court.[54] In order to do so, however, he first had to resign his membership in Congress.

Until he did so, Cyrus remained active, as always, during his final months as a delegate. In mid-March he shared his thoughts on the upcoming Court Martial of Dr William Shippen in an exchange of letters with John Morgan who was then gathering evidence to prosecute Shippen, the Director General of the Medical Department of the Army.[55] As in the Lee-Deane affair, these outside events again brought Cyrus into conflict with the powerful Lee Family. Dr. Shippen was married to Lee's sister, Alice. Richard Henry Lee even stayed with the Shippens whenever he was in Philadelphia attending Congress.[56]

As before, Cyrus paid a heavy price for dueling with the "Sons of Stratford." That October, when the Virginia Congressional Delegates who had served over the past year presented their expense accounts to the state legislature, most were approved as "fairly stated and fully reasonable." Cyrus Griffin and Meriwether Smith, however, were not as fortunate. Their reports were rejected and they were required to justify specific items. The issue dragged on for months without a satisfactory resolution.[57]

Despite such personal attacks in the Virginia legislature, Cyrus did maintain the support of his congressional colleagues. President Samuel Huntington sent him official notification on May 1, 1780, that he had been appointed to the Court of Appeals.[58] Three days later, Cyrus thanked Congress "for the confidence they repose in my Integrity and abilities..."[59] He wrote to Governor Jefferson on June 9, concerning his new appointment. Without any explanation, he told Jefferson that "It is probable I shall not act in that Commission long."[60] One week later, he wrote to Jefferson again. "As this will be the last letter I shall have the honor of writing your excellency in my official capacity [as a delegate] –" Cyrus said, "I hope to obtain the governor's approbation that whilst alone and at the head of the Delegation to Congress I have done my part in making those representations and giving that Intelligence from time to time, which the executive ought constantly to be informed of."

With a sense of pride, Cyrus went on to say that "I do not recollect any one matter of importance that was omitted in my communications to your excellency..." And then, switching to a more intimate tone, he added that "I confess as an Individual that I felt a pride and pleasure in corresponding with a great character, exclusive of that sacred duty which my honorable appointment demanded of me."[61] That same day, Cyrus cast his last vote as a member of Congress during that session and embarked on his new career on America's first Federal Court.[62]

Cyrus was scheduled to join Judges Hosmer and Paca on the bench as soon as possible, but Hosmer, who was ill when he accepted the appointment, died the following August without ever hearing a case. Paca, who, like Cyrus, had also studied in London, did play an active role on the Court for its first two years. Even though Cyrus had indicated to Jefferson that his judicial duties might be fairly brief, Cyrus ultimately served on the Court of Appeals for its entire duration, leaving in 1787, after having heard approximately fifty cases.[63]

It appears from the record that Cyrus and Judge Paca took their Oath of Office from President Huntington on June 14, 1780, the day after Cyrus had resigned his congressional seat.[64] The Court decided its first case only nine days later.[65] In mid-July, Cyrus acknowledged a letter of congratulations he had received from Gov. Jefferson which "has given me the greatest pleasure I have felt since my entrance into public life." He added that "if I can preserve the friendship of a Jefferson and a very few others, I shall think myself perfectly happy and safe."[66] Unfortunately, Cyrus eventually learned how fickle that friendship could be.

In February 1781, Cyrus wrote to President Huntington, urging Congress to fill the vacancy created by Hosmer's death the preceding summer. In typical fashion, not only did Congress take no official action, but one member even suggested that the number of judges be reduced to one in order to cut costs. That proposal was rejected.

The following year, Cyrus agreed to take on an additional assignment when he was selected to serve on the commission to settle the long-standing boundary dispute between Pennsylvania and Connecticut.[67] The process was authorized under Article IX of the Articles of Confederation.[68] In the official letter that the new President, John Hanson, sent to prospective members of the Commission, he stated that: "As the peace of two States and consequently of the whole Union depends upon an amicable settlement of this dispute, I trust you will view your appointment in so important a light, that it will be unnecessary, to use arguments to induce you to undertake the business and to meet punctually at the time & place appointed."[69]

Seven men were initially selected to serve on this commission. In critiquing each nominee in a letter to the Governor of Connecticut, one member of that State's Congressional Delegation commented that "Judge Griffin as he now lives in this City [Philadelphia] will doubtless attend as he has not refused; he belongs to Virginia, is a Gentn of good understanding, of great Integrity & Candor..."[70] When the trial opened in Trenton on November 12, 1782, only five of the original seven, including Cyrus, were serving on the bench.[71] The State of Pennsylvania was represented by four attorneys, including James Wilson, a future Supreme Court Justice during the Second Republic. Connecticut's legal team included Eliphalet Dyer, a member of Congress who was also a distinguished State Judge.[72] Despite Connecticut's attempt to adjourn the proceedings, the case was heard and the Commission ruled unanimously "that the State of Connecticut has no right to the lands in controversy." The Commission's final report was presented to Congress on January 3, 1783."[73] This case clearly demonstrated that the Articles of Confederation could work if the States lived up to their commitments as well.

While Cyrus was away helping to adjudicate the boundary dispute, Judge Paca resigned from the Court of Appeals in late 1782, to become Governor of Maryland.[74] His departure finally forced Congress to appointment two additional members to the Court--George Read of Delaware and John Lowell of Massachusetts--who were elected on December 5, 1782.[75] George Read, who had briefly served as President of Delaware during the British occupation in 1777-78, was also the man who had nearly derailed Delaware's vote for Independence in July 1776, but later added his signature to the Declaration.[76] John Lowell, a member of the Continental Congress at the time of his appointment, was the patriarch of a notable New England family which ultimately included the great American poet, James Russell Lowell, his grandson.[77]

The Court usually held two terms throughout the year, from May to June and again from September to October. Its workload varied widely. The Spring of 1783, for example, was an especially busy period with a large number of cases pending. The two newly appointed judges, however, kept postponing their arrivals because of previous commitments back home. Cyrus grew increasingly frustrated. That April, one member of Congress reported that "Judge Griffin who has allway [sic] been ready to attend & has been so much perplexd with the continued dissappointments from the other Judges & wearied out by delays moved Congress for Liberty to resign his office..."[78] Friends convinced Cyrus to withdraw his resignation and eventually his new colleagues did arrive.

In 1784, after deciding a dozen cases in May, no new business came before the Court for the next year and a half. As a result, in 1785, Congress, threatened to replace their judicial salary with a per diem when cases arose. As the Presiding Judge, Cyrus sent a letter of protest to Congress concerning the situation.[79] In response, the Continental Congress passed the following Resolution on February 9, 1786: "Resolved, That Congress are fully impresed with a sense of the ability, fidelity and attention of the judges of the court of Appeals, in the discharge of the duties of their Office; but that as the war was at an end, and the business of that court in a great measure done away, an attention to the interests of their constituents made it necessary that the salaries of the said judges should cease."[80]

In May 1787, the Court met one last time in New York to resolve the final five cases on its docket just as the Constitutional Convention was opening in Philadelphia that same month.[81] The entire government was about to enter a critical transformation which would ultimately enshrine the concept of separation of powers which Cyrus and his colleagues on the Court of Appeals had helped to establish.

Since the Court had been based in Philadelphia for most of its existence, Cyrus had even moved his family there for much of that decade.[82] As a result, his political fortunes back in Virginia met with mixed results because of his long absences. In 1784 and again in 1786, for example, Cyrus failed to win election to the State's Executive Council; but the voters of Lancaster County did return him to his old seat in the Virginia House of Delegates where he became friends with fellow Delegate John Marshall.[83]

On October 23, 1787, five weeks after the Constitutional Convention had completed its work, Cyrus was elected by the Virginia House of Delegates to resume his seat in Congress. While representation from some States tended to diminish in character during the final years of the Continental Congress, Virginia's remained exceptionally impressive even though regular attendance was often a problem. Cyrus Griffin and Richard Henry Lee, both Presidents of the First American Republic, served during those final years alongside James Madison and James Monroe, two of the early Presidents of the Second Republic. No other State could boast of such a distinguished delegation.[84]

Cyrus returned to New York where he moved into "the best Boarding house" in the city along with Madison and several other delegates."[85] He took his seat in Congress on Tuesday, November 20, 1787. That Thursday, James Madison arrived.[86]There was still no quorum, however, since the nation's attention had been diverted to the Ratification Conventions which were already starting in the individual States. Two months earlier, all eyes had been focused on Congress as Richard Henry Lee had argued in vain that Congress must amend and vote on the proposed Constitution before it could be submitted to the States. That debate ended on September 28, when a clear majority agreed with the framers that Congress should simply transmit the document without comment. To have done otherwise, most delegates argued, would have triggered the amending process of the Articles of Confederation which required a unanimous vote.[87]

Madison, widely acknowledged as the Father of the Constitution, was certainly not optimistic concerning what he hoped would be the final months of the Continental Congress. In a letter to Gen. Horatio Gates in mid-December 1787, he complained that "No authority equal to the business exists in the recess of Congress; and the Authority of Congress has been out of existence for some time, and if we are to judge from the present aspect of things, will continue so for some time longer."[88] Madison's pessimism did not take into account the fact that only a few months earlier, while he was attending the Convention in Philadelphia, Congress had actually adopted one of its most important pieces of legislation: The Northwest Ordinance.[89]

At the same time, Cyrus wrote to his close friend, former Congressman Thomas FitzSimons, who, like Cyrus' wife, was living in Philadelphia: "For some days past I have been confined with a violent cold and disagreeable affection of the head--but as nothing very alarming is to be feared I wish my poor little woman to know but little of it." Later in the letter, in an apparent reference to a request he received from a New York church, Cyrus commented that "having but little property of my own and scarcely any thing by my wife, I should not be justifiable in spending that little at a distance from my own country even for the purposes of *Religion*..." At the end he lamented that "There are but four states rep[r]esented in Congress and I see no probability of a majority for weeks to come." In contrast, he pointed out that "Our foreign correspondence contain the strongest reasons why a fixed and efficient government should be organised with all expedition."[90]

Another Virginia Delegate who traveled to New York with Cyrus concurred with his colleagues on the mood in Congress. He wrote that "The new Constitution is the only subject of Conversation in every Company in this place; I am inclined to think a Majority of the States will adopt it through choice & that the Minority will be reduced to accede by necessity. Our present political System is in utter Confusion. A change must & will soon take place. God grant it may be for the better."[91]

By mid-January 1788, Cyrus reported to FitzSimons that four States had already ratified the Constitution but that "If Mass. should be so unwise and dishonest to reject the system, N. York and Virginia will not hesitate one moment to follow the example--and then farewell to a federal Government of the whole; the baneful, the fatal consequences not one of us can forsee in their extent." On a personal note, Cyrus displayed his wry sense of humor when he wrote that "I intended to Philadelphia for a little--but as my cold is bad, and what is still worse my pay would cease when absent from the Seat of Congress. I believe dear Madam had better spend the long nights without a partner, than the short days without Soup."[92]

On Monday, January 21, 1788, Congress finally established a quorum for the first time in over two months. The next day, Judge Cyrus Griffin of Virginia was elected by his colleagues as the fourteenth and last President of the Continental Congress.[93] He was the third Virginian so honored. Along with Peyton Randolph and Richard Henry Lee, Cyrus' election clearly established Virginia as the birthplace of Presidents, a title it held for over a half century. Madison informed Gov. Randolph of Virginia that "our friend C. Griffin" was elected and that "There was no competition in the case which you will wonder at as Virginia has so lately supplied a president [Richard Henry Lee]. N. Jersey did not like it I believe very well, but acquiesed."[94]

One of the delegates fell ill the day after the election and just as suddenly, the quorum was lost. Massachusetts Congressman Samuel Otis described the dismal scene in early February 1788: "I need not enlarge upon the weak state of the Foederal Government; Many circumstances contribute to debase its dignity. The Tre[a]sury of the USA being without supplies, Their troops stationed to secure the frontiers, and the Civil list of Congress destitute of provision; And even the small pittance necessary for the subsistence of the Presidents household, even in the most eligible stile, of republican neatness & simplicity, only attainable from other inadequate appropriations; Are facts which evince the most degrading poverty in the foederal Government...In this situation...can it be wondered at that a Government, not destitute indeed of resources, but so supine in her application of them, should be viewed in a ridiculous light by her own Citizens, & a contemptible one by other Nations...Under these circumstances however Congress thot it their duty at least to preserve the forms, & proceeded to the election of Cyrus Griffin Esq their President..."[95]

Cyrus expressed similar sentiments in a letter to his dear friend FitzSimons: "I feel no addition of real satisfaction in being thus elevated, but truly and with sincerity I expereince the reverse. My family are the great object I have in contemplation, and if this promotion in its consequences shall redound to the advantage of my children my utmost wishes will be accomplished, so far as private considerations are permitted to operate--at all times and upon all occasions I would sacrifice my ease to their emolument." Cyrus was well aware that his role was most likely to preside over the final days of the Continental Congress, "And as to the public," he wrote, "it is not in my power to do any essential services, but I will discharge my duty with honesty and to the best of my abilities."

Switching to the loneliness of his office since his wife and family were still living in Philadelphia,[96] Cyrus confided to FitzSimons that "I am almost tired to death with this kind of life, in a croud thro' the day and solitary at night--the family must certainly be set in motion in April or May unless something material should intervene to prevent a Journey to N. York and if then yourself and Mrs. FitzSimons can make it convenient to spend some time with us how extremely rejoiced I should be..."[97]

Meanwhile, all eyes had been fixed on the Massachusetts Ratification Conven-tion. As James Madison wrote earlier to Rufus King in Boston, "It is impossible to express how much depends on the result of the deliberations of your Body."[98] The Massachusetts vote had been very much in doubt until January 31, when Gov. John Hancock, the former President, publicly came out in support of the proposed Constitu-tion, urging amendments after its adoption. Six days later, the Massachusetts Delegates voted to ratify.[99] Even though the outcome in Virginia and New York still remained uncertain, there was reason to hope that the required nine States would join, thereby helping to turn the tide where anti-Federalist sentiments ran deep.

While the nation's future hung in the balance, Congress still had work to do. On Tuesday, February 26, 1788, it met in formal session to welcome the new French Minister Plenipotentiary, the Comte de Moustier.[100] In his remarks, the Minister assured Congress that "The relations of friendship and Affection which subsist between the King my Master and the United States, have been established on a basis which cannot but daily acquire a new degree of solidity." As President, Cyrus then rose to welcome the new Minister: "Sir: It will always give us pleasure to acknowledge the friendship and important good offices which we have experienced from his Most Christian Majesty and Your generous Nation; and we flatter ourselves that the same principles of magnanimity...will continue to operate, and to render them still more extensive in their benefits to the two Countries."[101]

A few days later, Cyrus wrote to FitzSimons that "we are told that the King has consented to the Protestant Edict in France, which not only *tolerates* all *non-Catholics*, but gives them admission into Government &c..." Cyrus, as a descendent of French Huguenots, was delighted by the news. He predicted that "France is hastening by this and other great affairs already in agitation to adopt the real principles of freedom & human

Nature, and will in all probability be exhibited as one of the most illustrious nations the world has ever seen." Only sixteen months later, with the fall of the Bastille, French politics would encounter a profound upheaval.

Cyrus also proved a poor prophet when reporting to FitzSimons on the latest developments concerning ratification. While expressing the hope that "perhaps Rhode Island may take up the discussion and accord with the plan," he also noted that "we are parting with our valuable friend Madison to Virginia from Congress, but still I am doubtful that all his virtues and abilities will avail nothing."[102]

As always, Cyrus' letter to FitzSimons was of special interest because of its insight into his personal life. He opened by stating that "My little woman has forgotten to write to me about a change of lodgings...I shall be very happy that you advise lady C. what is the better plan to be adopted; I do not like my family to be in a house with boarders...if the family come to N. York it may not be convenient until the last of April, perhaps not at all." And, in closing, he told FitzSimons that "the weather fret's my constitution to atoms almost--it is too cold for a southern fabrick."[103]

On March 24, Cyrus reported to Madison that "We are still going forward in the same tract of Seven states, of course not a great deal can be done, and indeed not a great deal to do. A prospect of the new Constitution seems to deaden the activity of the human mind as to all other matters; and yet I greatly fear that constitution may never take place; a melancholy judgment most certainly--and would to heaven that nothing under the Sun shall be more erroneous!" And then, in a clear rebuttal to some who would later claim that Cyrus was an anti-Federalist,[104] he added that "The constitution is beautiful in Theory--I wish the experiment to be made--in my opinion it would be found a government of sufficient energy *only*."[105] To another correspondent, Cyrus stated that "I hope the United States at home will adopt a Constitution beautiful in theory and which will be found a Government of Safety, and of Energy."[106]

Cyrus wrote to Madison again on April 7, lamenting the fact that attendance was now down to only six States and that even the New York Delegation was not present despite the fact that Congress was meeting in New York. Clearly discouraged, he told Madison that "it seems to me the period is fully arrived to close the Confederation."[107]

As a realist, however, Cyrus had to deal with the situation as it existed He wrote to FitzSimons that "At present I discover no probability that Congress will adjourn to Philadel--the southern states not being fully represented--and as my family, when seperate from me are very expensive, money difficult to be gotten, and their situation in a boarding house not the most agreeable, I think they had better conclude and come to this place, to set out about the last day of April in order to reach N. York, on the first Friday or Saturday in May." Cyrus also confided in FitzSimons concerning his personal finances: "But, my dear sir, how does the money hold forth-- and if not, can you negotiate a Bill upon me."[108]

That same day, Cyrus wrote again to Madison, reporting that Jefferson had sent a package for him from France and that John Adams, who was preparing to leave England, "approves highly the proposed Constitution." In anticipation of Virginia's Ratification Convention, Cyrus said that "We all rejoice greatly at your election..." and he stated that "In point of virtues and real abilities the federal members are much superior. Henry is weight and powerful," he wrote, "but too interested--Mason too passionate--the Governor [Randolph] by nature timid and undecided..."[109] Two weeks later, in response to Madison's most recent letter, Cyrus' mood had shifted : "I am very sorry to hear that your calculations render the adoption of the constitution so uncertain--I did once think that my conclusion upon the matter was erroneous--but alas! my dear sir, without a change of opinion when the members assemble I fear the system will be lost..."[110]

At the same time, Cyrus finalized plans for his family's journey to New York. He told FitzSimons that "I now send a Boy under your freindly [sic] direction...to drive my family to this place...The President's Coach was demolished before I came to the house or I would send it...all expences I will pay most gladly." He added that "I beg leave to thank you, my dear sir, and your very kind lady for so much goodness to a very helpless family--we seem to have been united to give trouble to others--and when it will finish heaven only knows. I hope you intend to pay us a visit this summer..."[111]

On May 5, Cyrus told Madison that "Maryland has acceded to the proposed Constitution by a great majority" even though the Governor, his former colleague, Judge Paca, vigorously opposed it. He added that "South Carolina will adopt the system very soon." Despite serious doubts concerning Virginia and New York, Cyrus stated that "from the present appearance of things I rather incline to believe that in the course of 12 months we shall have the Government in operation--yet I am not so sanguine as Hamilton or Gen. Knox." This time, Cyrus' prediction proved accurate. As for the existing government, Cyrus informed Madison that "Once more we are going on with the business of Congress--but have finished nothing of consequence."[112] Three days later he sent a circular letter to the five States not in attendance--New York, North Carolina, Rhode Island, Connecticut & Georgia--requesting "that the Gentlemen from your State would attend upon the national business, and particularly at this interesting period."[113]

In his next letter to Madison, Cyrus reported that John Adams had been told by George III "that he wished always to cultivate a good understanding with the united states, and would amply comply with the Treaty whenever America manifested the same disposition." But at Court, Adams reported that "the Courtiers jest very much upon our debelitated situation, but all seem to think that the new Constitution if adopted will place this Country upon a respectable foundation--and until that period arrives they can have no permanent Intercourse with us."[114]

In mid-June, Cyrus was again optimistic. He wrote to FitzSimons that "I am not a little happy that the important business of the proposed Constitution is going on so well in Virginia...New Hampshire will certainly adopt the system...From the appearance of things taken altogether we have good reason to conclude that the union will be complete."[115] But then he received word that Madison was ill. "We are all extremely uneasy at your Indisposition," he told his Virginia friend, "how much to be regretted indeed! And particularly when such important matters are under deliberation--but I hope that kind Heaven has restored you before this day, to be a farther blessing and honor to your Country!" Cyrus then closed with a personal note: "Above all things take charge of your health. Most affly."[116]

Exactly one week later, on June 25, Cyrus notified Madison by express rider that New Hampshire had become the ninth State to ratify the Constitution.[117] The new government was finally an established fact. That same day, even before the President's note had arrived, the Virginia Convention itself ratified the document by a vote of 89 to 79.[118] Samson had once again triumphed over Goliath as soft-spoken James Madison won the debate over the Anti-Federalists' most formidable opponent, Patrick Henry. The fear of being left out of the new union even convinced the New York Delegates to narrowly approve the Constitution by a vote of 30 to 27 when their Convention finally met that July. Only North Carolina and Rhode Island stood apart.[119]

Now that it was a *fait accompli*, the Continental Congress eagerly began to plan for the transition to the new government. A delegate from New Hampshire reported to a friend on July 29, that: "I expected this day to have been able to inform you of the place in which the new Congress will meet. But the President was so unwell that he could not attend & the business was postponed. Congress have agreed that the Electors of President shall be appointed on that first Wednesday of Janr., the President be chosen the first Wednesday of Feb. & Congress assemble the first Wednesday of March next...I believe notwithstanding the meeting of the new Congress is so late there will not be necessity of another Congress under the present Confederation after Novr. next."[120]

Contrary to that prediction, the Continental Congress struggled on for another seven months. Cyrus and his wife also continued to host elegant dinners at the President's House. In August 1788, their guests included Jacques Pierre Brissot de Warville, a 34 year old Frenchman who was a member of the lower bourgeoisie. De Warville was on a six month tour of America when he was invited to dine at the President's table. He later described Cyrus as "a handsome, well-built Virginian, witty, soft-spoken, affable, and polite." Surprisingly, he was not as favorably impressed by the women. "I met seven or eight ladies, all wearing large hats, feathers, etc... Two of them wore dresses which exposed much of their bosoms. I was scandalized by such indecency in republican women."

De Warville's description of the final days of America's First Republic are especially noteworthy: "A President of Congress is far from being surrounded by the ceremony enjoyed by European monarchs--and so much the better. His position is not permanent--and again, so much the better. He never forgets that he has been a simple citizen, and that he will become one again. He does not give sumptuous dinners--once more, so much the better, for this means that he is surrounded by fewer parasites and has less opportunity to corrupt others."

De Warville also recorded that "at this dinner many customs observed else-where were not followed: no tiresome introductions, none of those toasts that become so wearisome in a large company. After the ladies withdrew, little wine was drunk. These details are sufficient to give you an idea of the temperance practiced in this country. Temperance is the supreme virtue of republicans." De Warville later attempted to impose those republican principles on his own country when he became a leader of the French Revolution; but, like so many French idealists, he fell victim to the guillotine in November 1793.[121]

A less complimentary view of the First Republic was penned by John Adams' daughter, Nabby. While living in New York City during the summer of 1788, she wrote to her mother on May 20 that "Congress are sitting; but one hears little more of them if they were inhabitants of the new-discovered planet. The President is said to be a worthy man; his wife is a Scotch woman, with the title of Lady Christiana Griffin; she is out of health, but appears to be a friendly-disposed woman; we are engaged to dine there next Tuesday."[122]

Later that summer Nabby reported to her mother that "We have dined to-day at President Griffin's, with a company of twenty-two persons, including many members of Congress, &c. Had you been present you would have trembled for your country, to have seen, heard and observed the men who are its rulers. Very different they were, I believe, in times past...there were very few whose behavior bore many marks of wisdom...The

President of Congress gives a dinner one or two or more days every week, to twenty persons--gentlemen and ladies...on Fridays, Lady Christiana, the Presidentess" sees company.[123]

That Fall, the Virginia House reelected Cyrus and James Madison as two of their delegates to Congress.[124] The new Federal Year officially began on Monday, November 3, 1788, with only two members present along with the ever-vigilant Secretary, Charles Thomson. Cyrus presented his credentials on November 15, and remained in New York for the rest of the session.[125] He also took the time to recommend his secretary, John Livingston, for the office of Clerk in the new Senate.[126] Over the next three and a half months, delegates from a total of ten States--including North Carolina and Rhode Island, which had not yet ratified--submitted their certificates of election. Only Connecticut, Delaware and Georgia did not attend. During these final few months, as Thomson completed his official Journal, the Continental Congress "never transacted any business."[127]

As the transition progressed, Alexander Hamilton offered an interesting observation on New York politics: "I am well informed, that his Excellency [New York Gov. George Clinton] never made a visit to, or had any intercourse of civilities with either of the two last Presidents of Congress...As that body sat in the state, it was unquestionably the duty of the Governor to pay the first attentions to the President after his election. This rule has been understood throughout America, and its propriety is felt evident. The omitting to pay those attentions was a mark of disregard to the government of the Union, for which there can be no excuse..."[128]

Finally, on Monday, March 2, 1789, the First American Republic completed its historic mission.[129] The next evening, thirteen shots were fired from the fort opposite Bowling Green in New York in honor of the Confederation. At dawn the following morning, Wednesday, March 4, an eleven gun salute (in recognition of the eleven States that had already joined the Union) greeted the new era.[130]

Some things did not change, however. As always, it was difficult to obtain a quorum. Even though the new Congress was scheduled to meet on March 4, Cyrus lamented to a friend five days later that "There are only eight Senators and 18 Representatives assembled--a very unfortunate thing."[131] By April, the new Congress was finally in place and the Electoral Votes were counted. Cyrus was there at Federal Hall in New York City on April 30, 1789, when his successor, George Washington, was sworn in as the first President of the United States under the Second Republic.[132] At the end of that momentous day, President Washington retired to the same house at 3 Cherry Street that had been occupied by his four presidential predecessors.[133]

Since Mrs. Washington had not yet arrived in New York, plans for an Inaugural Gala had been canceled. On Thursday, May 7, however, Cyrus and Lady Christina did join the new President at "a very splendid ball" that was given "at the Assembly Room...on the east side of Broadway, a little above Wall Street..." One week later, the French Minister hosted an even more elegant evening. On May 28, the morning after Mrs. Washington's arrival, "The principal women of the metropolis" including Lady Christina, "hastened to pay their compliments to the wife of the President."[134]

As the new administration was being formed, Cyrus wrote to President Washington in mid-July "to offer his farther Services to the union, either in the diplomatic line or as one of the Judges of the Supreme Court.[135] Washington responded on August 18: "I have invariably avoided giving any sentiment or opinion; for the purpose of reserving myself unembarrassed with promises until all the Candidates are known and the occasion, when decision shall become necessary on my part."[136] Not long after, however, Washington did ask Cyrus to return to national service by appointing him to join David Humphreys and Benjamin Lincoln as temporary Commissioners to the Creek Indians of Georgia. The new Commissioners sailed from New York for Savannah on September 1.[137]

During his absence, Cyrus was elected by the Virginia House of Delegates as a member of the State's Privy Council, a lucrative position which the State legislature later rescinded because Cyrus' presidential appointment appeared to conflict with State law.[138] Meanwhile, the negotiations with the Indian Tribe broke down when the lower Creeks appeared willing to enter a treaty but the upper Creeks refused.[139] After years of public service, Cyrus was suddenly left without an office or an income.

President Washington took note of these developments. In late November, he shared his thoughts with his new Attorney General, Edmund Randolph. The fact that Edmund Pendleton had declined to accept the position as Federal District Judge for Virginia after being nominated "has embarrassed me" the President said. He next considered appointing George Wythe, but was informed that Wythe would also decline. "Under these circumstances," Washington reported, "I have, by the powers of the Constitution, appointed Mr. Cyrus Griffin during the recess of the Senate. My reasons for this appointment in preference to any other except Mr. Wythe are, because he has (as I am informed) been regularly bred to the Law; has been in the Court of appeals; Has been discontinued of the Council in Virginia (contrary to the expectation of his friends here at the time, who thought that his temporary appointment as a negotiator with the southern Indians would not bring him under the disqualifying law of

Virginia) and thereby thrown entirely out of employment, and because I had it in my power to ascertain with precision his acceptance."

Washington added that "I shall say nothing of his being a Man of amiable character and of competent abilities, because in these respects some of the present Judges in that State may be his equals; but to what I have said, may be added, he has no employment now, and needs the emolument of one as much as any of them."[140] In fact, Washington ultimately selected three of the four Judges who had served on the Federal Court of Appeals during the First Republic--Griffin (VA), Paca (MD) and Lowell (MA)--for appointment to the new Federal District Courts in their respective States.[141]

As grateful as Cyrus was, he clearly preferred a diplomatic assignment. On December 11, 1789, he wrote to Jefferson, who had been nominated by Washington to be Secretary of State. "In case you do not return to France; but shall judge it better to accept the ardent wishes of the President," Cyrus said, "let me solicit my kind friend to mention me for that foreign employment, if there shall be no particular objection." For reasons unknown, he then stated that "The appointment I understand would be acceptable to the French, and generally expected throughout the united states, honorable and advantageous to me, and" he argued, despite his distinguished judicial career, "more consonant to my turn of mind than a legal character." Cyrus added that "I should hope also that the elevated stations I have filled in the Republic would add some consequence to the Individual."[142]

In his response, Jefferson told Cyrus that "If he [Washington] chuses to make use of me here, I shall at all times and places be ready to render you any service in my power. This however could only be on my arrival at New York, as I do not feel myself on such a footing with the President as to suggest any person to him but in the course of a conversation when a fit occasion could be made."[143] Cyrus' interest in the appointment was hardly a secret. In late November, Jefferson's former deputy, William Short, who was also eager for the position, had written to Jefferson from Paris warning him that "several people are trying already to succeed you I cannot help mentioning it. They speak of Cyrus Griffin and say also that it is expected G. Morris will make great exertions."[144] Short was ultimately named *chargé d'affairess*.[145]

In the end, Cyrus did accept the appointment as the Federal District Judge for Virginia. When he first called his Court to order in Richmond on December 17, 1789, the only business to be transacted was the swearing in of four local attorneys, including his friend, thirty-four year old John Marshall.[146] Of the hundreds of cases that Cyrus subsequently heard over the next twenty-one years, at least three remain permanently etched in American history.

The first of the three became a test case which dealt with the collection of debts owed to British merchants prior to the Revolution. Article Four of the peace treaty between Great Britain and the United States stipulated "that creditors on either side shall meet with no lawful impediment to the recovery of the full value in sterling money, of all *bona fide* debts heretofore contracted."[147] After the war, however, the repayment of American debts became an intense political debate. This was especially true in Virginia where such debts were estimated at £2,000,000 sterling.[148]

For their part, Virginians were still furious that the British had carried off a large number of their slaves during the war and that Britain was failing to live up to its obligations by refusing to vacate their frontier forts. The State legislature had adopted several laws to protect Virginians from British creditors even though the new Constitution mandated that treaties trumped State action. In this deeply contentious atmosphere, over two hundred cases concerning the repayment of prewar British debts were brought before Cyrus' Court during its early years. The most famous was *Jones v. Walker* which was later renamed *Ware v. Hylton* when the original defendant died. It opened in Richmond in November 1791.[149] Cyrus was joined on the bench by two Supreme Court Justices who rode circuit twice a year, as mandated in the Judiciary Act of 1789.[150] The defendant was initially represented by four distinguished attorneys, including John Marshall and Patrick Henry.[151]

This case, which dragged on for two years in the Circuit Court, raised a number of critical issues concerning the formation of the new national government such as the concept of federalism, separation of powers, and the meaning of the supremacy clause of the US Constitution.[152] When the case was finally decided on June 7, 1793, Cyrus was sitting with Chief Justice John Jay and Associate Justice James Iredell. All three agreed to strike down three of the defendant's special pleas, thereby strength-ening the national government, but Cyrus and Justice Iredell, who were known to be sympathetic to the creditors, overruled Jay on a fourth. The Chief Justice, however, had the final word. When the case came before the US Supreme Court on appeal in March 1796, Jay's position--that treaties were supreme and the debts must be paid--prevailed. By then, Jay, as President Washington's special representative two years earlier, had negotiated a new treaty with Britain which called for the creation of "arbitration commissions" to help to resolve the remaining disputes.[153]

On May 23, 1796, again seeking a Supreme Court appointment, Cyrus sent Washington a truly remarkable letter in which he poured out his soul in an effort to win the President's support. Concerned that some of his enemies--Edmund Randolph or the Lees, in particular--might be speaking ill of him, Cyrus made clear that "I do not game. I have not speculated in the amount of one shilling in my life; and I am temperate & retired, confining myself to Books, my Family, and the duties of my station." He added that "there lives not a Judge upon Earth of more discretion in his office, my opinion upon any question was never known until given Judicially." In conclusion, he admitted "That I have faults, that I have follies and deficiencies I do not deny__but...I have never said one syllable derogatory to your personal or political character..."[154] Washington replied that "I am sorry, that, without being accused, you should think it necessary to go into a lengthy justification of your conduct and principles.__What the entire design of your letter of the 23d Ult. my be, I am at a loss, to conceive..." Part of Cyrus' objective was perfectly clear. He wanted a raise. His salary of $1,800 per year was approximately half of what Associate Justices of the Supreme Court earned.[155] His plea, however, fell on deaf ears.

Two years later, Cyrus renewed his quest in a letter to President Adams: "I could wish most fervently to change my Situation upon the Bench, and would willingly take some other respectable employment.__ Indeed, Sir, I am the very oldest civil Officer under the general Government; that is, I have served more years than any other man, from early in the year 1778 to the present period, and sometimes in very high Stations, at the expence of all the property I possessed; and now with a large family & nothing but a small Salary to maintain them..." He added that "the Supreme Judges tell me, that the business of the Circuit Court for Virginia is considerably more than all the Union together."[156] Once again, Cyrus' request went unfulfilled.

Continuing his judicial career, the next historic trial that Cyrus heard resulted from the 1798 Alien and Sedition Acts that marked the low point of the Adams Administration. Section 2 of the Sedition Act declared "That if any person shall write, print, utter, or publish...any false, scandalous and malicious writing or writings against ...the President of the United States,with intent to defame...the said President, or to bring them...into contempt or disrepute...shall be punished by a fine not exceeding two thousand dollars, and by imprisonment not exceeding two years."[157] In defiance of the Act, the *Aurora*, the mouthpiece of Jefferson's emerging Republican Party, viciously attacked Adams, the Federalist President, at every opportunity. It declared that he was "unhinged" by the "delirium of vanity."[158] Political pamphleteer James T. Callender, who wrote for the

Aurora, was, in the opinion of Jefferson's biographer Merrill D. Peterson, "The most scurrilous of Republican scribes…"[159]

In his diatribe, *The Prospect Before Us*, Callender charged that "Mr. Adams has only completed the scene of ignominy which Mr. Washington began."[160] Jefferson, who "saw some of this in page proof," sent $100 to Callender even though he later claimed that it was simply a charitable contribution.[161] Callender was arrested. His trial before the Federal Court in Richmond began in early June 1800. Since it was "the first case brought in staunchly Republican Virginia under the Sedition Act" it generated tremendous interest. Supreme Court Associate Justice Samuel Chase, who joined Cyrus on the bench, was already well known for his outspoken support of the new law.[162] In contrast, Cyrus "was restrained in manner and gave an impression of timidity," but, according to Chase's biographer, Cyrus "could be resolute in action and was an excellent administrator."[163]

Chase repeatedly ruled out of order any challenge by Callender to the constitutionality of the Act. With Secretary of State John Marshall present in the courtroom, Chase stated that it was exclusively the prerogative of the Court, not the jury, to determine questions of law. Chase's biographer contends that this was the spark that ignited Marshall's doctrine of judicial review when he later became Chief Justice. Even though the defense attorneys refused to proceed under Chase's iron rule, the jury took only two hours to find the defendant guilty. Callender was fined $200, sentenced to nine months in jail and required to post a $1,200 bond.[164]

When Jefferson's Republican Party came to power in 1801, leaders in the House of Representatives called for Chase's impeachment based upon his conduct in several trials concerning the Sedition Act, including Callender's. As part of his defense, Chase argued that if he was guilty then certainly the District Judges who had served with him, including Cyrus, must also be indicted. By the time Chase was impeached in 1804, however, Cyrus had adapted to the political winds and had made clear his loyalty to his old friend Jefferson. In addition, Cyrus' son-in-law, Mary's husband, was also a Member of Congress at that time.[165] Cyrus and Chase both survived. On March 1, 1805, with Vice President Aaron Burr presiding over the trial, Justice Samuel Chase was found not guilty on all eight counts.[166]

The third and most prominent case that Cyrus participated in during his years on the Federal Bench involved several of the key players related to the Callender case, but under radically different circumstances. Aaron Burr, no longer Vice President, was charged with treason for conspiring to carve out a new nation in the western United States with himself at its head.[167] His trial, which was largely orchestrated by President Jefferson from the Executive Mansion, opened in Richmond on Friday, May 22, 1807.[168] John Marshall, Jefferson's bitter political opponent, now the Chief Justice, presided over the trial. "The upright and learned Cyrus Griffin,"[169] still District Judge for Virginia, sat at Marshall's side. Former Virginia Gov. Edmund Randolph--the favorite nephew of America's first President, Peyton Randolph--was lead attorney for Burr. The room itself was packed with historic personalities including Winfield Scott, then a young attorney, who later served as General of the Army; and, Gen. Andrew Jackson, who was elected President two decades later.[170]

Increasingly angered over Marshall's management of the trial, the President expressed his frustration with Cyrus, as well, when he wrote to the lead prosecutor: "Will not the associate judge assume to divide his court and procure a truce at least in so critical conjecture?"[171] In public, at least, Cyrus deferred to the Chief Justice. On August 31, Jefferson's worst fear came true when Marshall, in effect, derailed Jefferson's carefully crafted case against Burr by tightening the Court's definition of "treason," thereby dismissing 140 prosecution witnesses. The following day, the jury demonstrated its disgust at not being permitted to hear the evidence when it handed down a verdict of "not proved to be guilty under this indictment by any evidence submitted to us." Burr objected to the wording of the verdict. In response, Marshall ordered that it be officially recorded as "not guilty."[172]

Despite his quiet demeanor in public, Cyrus did not hesitate to exercise independent judgment, even if it conflicted with his Supreme Court colleagues. John Jay, James Wilson and James Iredell were among those who could attest to that fact.[173] President Jefferson, however, never forgave Cyrus for allowing Marshall free reign in Burr's Trial. On May 25, 1810, as Cyrus' health failed, Jefferson wrote to the new President, James Madison, urging him to appoint John Tyler, Jr. to the District Court in Virginia as soon as "so wretched a fool as Griffin" died.[174] In a letter to Tyler, Jefferson stated that "We have long enough suffered under the base prostitution of law to party passions in one Judge [Marshall], and the imbecility of another [Griffin]."[175] As Adams knew all too well, Jefferson could strike out at former friends with a vengeance.

Around 1790, his first full year on the Federal Bench, Cyrus and his wife moved from Yorktown to Williamsburg where they rented a house on Duke of Glouster Street in the center of the city. In 1806, they moved again to his brother Samuel's home on Francis Street near the college.[176] Lady Christina died there on October 8, 1807, and was buried at Bruton Parish Churchyard a few blocks away.[177] After losing his wife, Cyrus' health steadily declined. Three years later, his older brother, Samuel, also passed away.[178] Only 17 days later, Cyrus died in Yorktown on December 10,1810.[179]

Today, that impetuous young lover who once won the heart of a Scottish noblewoman and later took the helm of his new nation, rests beside his "dearly beloved Christina" in an unmarked grave.[180]

BRUTON PARISH CHURCH
Colonial Williamsburg

In his Will, Cyrus Griffin, the 14th
and final President of the United
States under the First American
Republic, directed that: "My body
to be deposited in the Church
Yard of Williamsburg near that of
my dearly beloved Christina at
the smallest expence possible
in every respect."

Two centuries later, he rests in
an unmarked grave to the left of
his wife's table tomb (pictured
below).

WHILE CYRUS GRIFFIN
WAS PRESIDENT

January 1788 - March 1789

The new Constitution dominated debate during the final year of the Continental Congress. By the time Cyrus Griffin became President on January 22, 1788, the States of Delaware, New Jersey and Georgia had already unanimously ratified the new charter.[181] Two other States had done so with overwhelming majorities: Pennsylvania (46-23) and Connecticut (128-40).[182] Two weeks after Cyrus' election, the critical State of Massachusetts gave its assent by a vote of 187-168, when popular Gov. John Hancock, the former President, finally spoke out in favor of ratification.[183] In March, when Rhode Island held a plebiscite rather than a convention, the proposed Constitution lost overwhelmingly at the polls: 2,711 to 239.[184] Fortunately, momentum was regained the following month when Maryland approved the document, 63-11.[185]

In May 1788, with the proposed Constitution indelibly stained by South Carolina's demands concerning slavery, that State did vote to ratify, 149-73. Like several States, it also proposed specific amendments to be added if and when the new government was formed. Later that month, under the political muscle of Gov. George Clinton, the prospects for adoption in New York appeared extremely dim when 46 Antifederalists were elected as delegates to that State's Ratification Convention compared to only 19 who supported the Constitution, all of whom represented the City of New York. There was even talk of the City seceding from the State if the Convention failed to ratify.[186]

June was the decisive month. The Virginia Ratification Convention opened in Richmond on June 2, 1788. Two days later, Patrick Henry and George Mason led the opposition, which included James Monroe and others who demanded amendments prior to a final vote. James Madison, the document's primary author, fought for its unconditional adoption with support from George Wythe, John Marshall and fellow Federalists. As the debate intensified in Virginia, the New York delegates met at Poughkeepsie on June 17, and elected Gov. Clinton to preside over their deliberations.[187] Despite the series of letters published by Madison, Hamilton and Jay prior to the New York Convention--now known as the Federalist Papers--the State still seemed hopeless.

While the fate of the Republic appeared to hang in the balance elsewhere, the New Hampshire Convention reconvened in mid-June. There, on June 21, 1788, the Granite State voted to ratify 57-46.[188] As the required ninth State, the deed had been done. The Constitution had been adopted! The Continental Congress received formal notification from New Hampshire on July 2, the twelfth anniversary of the vote for Independence.[189]

The United States of America now had a new lease on life. On June 25, even before receiving word from the North, Virginia also ratified by a vote of 89-79.[190] Anti- federalists in New York, however, did not give up without a fight. Binding amendments were introduced, a proposal permitting the State to secede was debated and Hamilton very reluctantly suggested a second national convention to review amendments. Finally, on July 25, 1788, through the efforts of former President John Jay and others, New York voted 30-27 to join the Second American Republic.[191]

Unlike New York, North Carolina refused to be intimidated. At the conclusion of its Convention on August 2, the State's Antifederalists voted to withhold ratification until the laundry list of amendments it proposed could be addressed. Over a year later--November 21, 1789--North Carolina did ratify by a vote of 194-77.[192] Rhode Island was the last of the original thirteen. On May 29, 1790, Rhode Island finally adopted the Constitution in Convention by a vote of 34-32.[193]

As soon as Congress received official notification from New Hampshire that the mandatory ninth State had ratified, it immediately established a committee on July 2, 1788, to "report an Act to Congress for putting the said constitution into operation in pursuance of the resolutions of the late federal Convention."[194] At the conclusion of its fifteen year history, the work of that committee was, in effect, the last major contribution of the Continental Congress toward the formation of the United States.

Contrary to popular belief, two of the giants of the Revolution played no direct part in either drafting nor adopting the new Constitution. John Adams, the first United States Minister to Great Britain, did not return to American until Tuesday, June 17, 1788, months after Massachusetts had ratified the Constitution.[195] Thomas Jefferson, the American Minister to France, remained in Europe a year and a half longer, landing at Norfolk on November 23, 1789.[196] During their assignments overseas, both men had intensely observed the momentous developments throughout that continent.

In Britain, the year 1788 devolved into a "Regency Crisis" because of the King's deteriorating health and the political void it created.[197] On June 11, His Majesty suffered severe abdominal 'spasms' which lasted throughout the day. Over the next nine months, as his condition became increasingly precarious, his conduct became extremely erratic.[198] By November 1788, the King was seriously ill with what is now believed to have been porphyria, but was best described at the time as bouts of madness.[199] One member of the Court wrote that "as the poor King grew worse, general hope seemed universally to abate...the Prince of Wales took the government of the House into his own hands...The Queen...spent the whole day in patient sorrow and retirement with her daughters."[200] On December 5, the King was placed in the care of the Rev. Francis Willis who ran a private insane asylum. For the next five weeks, the Monarch's life was a living hell. And then, in February, George III slowly regained his composure and his crown.[201]

In celebration of King George III's recovery, a special Thanksgiving Service was held at St. Paul's Cathedral on April 23, 1789, exactly one week before his former subject-turned-traitor, George Washington, was sworn in as President of the United States of America.[202]

In France, an even more insidious crisis soon shatter King Louis XVI's reign. On July 5, 1788, under mounting pressure from provincial parliaments across France, the King reluctantly agreed to call a meeting of the Estates-General, the national legislative assembly which consisted of equal representation from nobles, clergy and commoners. It would mark the first gathering of that body in 175 years. By that winter, the demand arose that the number of commoners should be double either of the other two classes. When the French government capitulated on that critical point in December, the stage was set for "the political triumph of the progressive middle class over the forces of reaction."[203]

Thus, in a desperate attempt to stem the financial crisis which was undermining his reign, King Louis XVI permitted the opening of the 1,200 member Estates-General at Versailles on May 5, 1789, only days after Washington's inauguration and the beginning of the Second American Republic.[204]

Chapter 14

President
CYRUS GRIFFIN
of
VIRGINIA

Notes

Abbreviation Key

JCC   Journals of the Continental Congress
LDC   Letters of Delegates to Congress
PHL   The Papers of Henry Laurens

[1] Chapter 1.

[2] Cyrus Griffin's Will, York County Records, Wills & Inventories (1783-1811), Book 23, p. 810. (As cited in the archives of The Colonial Williamsburg Foundation).

[3] In a letter dated April 21, 1994, in response to this author's inquiry, John E. Ingram, Curator of Special Collections at The Colonial Williamsburg Foundation wrote the following: "Unfortunately, the registers for Bruton Parish for the years 1810-1811 no longer exist. I also searched our research query file, and the latest information there agrees with you, that is, Cyrus Griffin is reputed to lie in the Bruton graveyard, (as he wished), but there is no marker and no evidence that such is the case."

[4] Jon Butler, The Huguenots in America (Harvard University Press, Cambridge, 1983), pp. 1 & 14. The Edict of Nantes had been issued by King Henry IV in 1598. Henry, who gave up the Protestant faith in order to claim the throne (according to legend he remarked that "Paris is worth a Mass"), granted French Protestants freedom of worship under very strict guidelines which became even less favorable after Henry's death and the rise of Cardinal Richelieu. Louis XIV revoked the Edict in 1685, but Louis XVI restored most of its provisions not long before the French Revolution.

[5] Butler, op. cit., p. 49.

[6] Today, the only remaining French Huguenot Church in the United States that is not affiliated with another denomination is located in the heart of historic Charleston, South Carolina. Services there are still conducted in French once a year.

[7] Sally Nelson Robins, Some Colonial Families, The American Historical Register, 1895, p. 1234.

[8] Robins, Colonial Families, op. cit., p. 1233.

[9] Robins, Colonial Families, op. cit., p. 1233.

[10] Biographical Directory of the American Congress: 1774-1761 (Government Printing Office, Washington, DC., 1961), pp. 975-976. See also: Margaret C. S. Christman, Research Historian, Unraveling a Mistaken Identity (National Portrait Gallery, Washington, DC), online article.

[11] Sally Nelson Robins, Love Stories of Famous Virginians (The Dietz Printing Co., Richmond, 1923), pp. 134-135.

[12] Henry S. Rorer, Cyrus Griffin; Virginia's First Federal Judge, *Northern Neck of Virginia Historical Magazine,* Vol. 15, 1965, p. 1347. As happens so often during this historic period, Cyrus Griffin's year of birth is listed as 1748 by some sources and 1749 by others. Both the Biographical Directory of the American Congress and the LDC (Library of Congress, Washington, DC, 1998) agree on the year 1748.

[13] Mark Kishlansky, A Monarchy Transformed (The Penguin Press, London, 1966), p. 139.

[14] Rorer, Cyrus Griffin, op. cit., p. 1348.

[15] Charles T. Cullen, The Papers of John Marshall (The University of North Carolina Press, Chapel Hill), Vol. II, p. 258; John Adams to John Marshall, September 5, 1800.

[16] Robins, Love Stories, op. cit., pp. 134-135. The fact that Cyrus Griffin had blue eyes was established by Margaret C. S. Christman, Research Historian, op. cit., p. 1.

[17] Robins, Colonial Families, op. cit., p. 1236. She states that "In an old scrap-book of James Lewis Corbin Griffin, a grandson of Cyrus Griffin, we find they were married at Traquair by a Romish priest; but there is also a tradition in the Griffin family that they fled from Traquair at night, and that the grand lady, unused to sudden journeys across a rough country, fell and hurt her slender ankle."

[18] Robins, Love Stories, op. cit., pp. 136-137.

[19] Rorer, Cyrus Griffin, op. cit., p. 1348.

[20] Allen Johnson & Dumas Malone, Editors, Dictionary of American Biography (Charles Scribner's Sons, New York, 1943), p. 619, footnote.

[21] Robins, Colonial Families, op. cit., p. 1236. See also: Cullen, op. cit., Vol. III, p. 244. In 1800, Cyrus' oldest son, John, was appointed one of three Judges of the Indiana Territory by President John Adams.

[22] Rorer, Cyrus Griffin, op. cit., p. 1348.

[23] As cited in Robins, Love Stories, op. cit., p. 135.

[24] Rorer, Cyrus Griffin, op. cit., p. 1349. Cyrus Griffin's father-in-law, the 6th Earl, did not die until 1779 at which time Lord Linton assumed the title. While Robins contends that the new Earl died without leaving a male heir, Rorer states that Lord Linton, now the 7th Earl, and his wife Mary did give birth to a son in 1781.

[25] Henry S. Rorer, Cyrus Griffin's Plan of Reconciliation with the American Colonies, *The Journal of Southern History*, Vol. 5, No. 1 (February 1939), pp. 99-100.

[26] Rorer, Cyrus Griffin's Plan, op. cit.,, p. 98. See also: B. D. Bargar, <u>Lord Dartmouth and the American Revolution</u> (The University of South Carolina Press, Columbia, 1965), pp. 180-181. After intense discussions, Lord Dartmouth (who was surprisingly friendly toward the American Colonies) was promoted to the Office of Privy Seal by his stepbrother, Lord North on November 10, 1775, despite the fact that George III felt that Dartmouth was "carrying obstinacy greatly too far..."

[27] Rorer, Cyrus Griffin's Plan, op. cti., p. 99. Rorer states in his 1939 article that "the present Earl of Dartmouth...has very graciously furnished the writer with" a copy of the Plan. According to Rorer, Cyrus Griffin's cover letter was discovered in 1895 and is now included in the Historical Manuscripts Commissions official files.

[28] Rorer, Cyrus Griffin's Plan, op. cti., p. 101. See also: Rorer, Cyrus Griffin, op. cit., p. 1350.

[29] Rorer, Cyrus Griffin; op. cit., p. 1350. See also: Paul H. Smith, Editor, <u>LDC: 1774-1789</u> (Library of Congress, Washington, DC, 1981), Vol. 7, p. xx. Even though Jefferson was reelected to the Continental Congress on June 20, 1776, he "did not attend in 1777."

[30] <u>LDC</u>, op. cit., Vol. 10, p. xxii.

[31] Worthington Chauncey Ford, Chief, Division of Manuscripts, <u>JCC: 1774-1789</u> (Government Printing Office, Washington, DC, 1908), Vol. XI, p. 811.

[32] <u>LDC</u>, op. cit., Vol. 10, p. xxii.

[33] <u>LDC</u>, op. cit., Vol. 10, p. 708.

[34] <u>LDC</u>, op. cit., Vol. 11, pp. 32-33; Cyrus Griffin to Thomas Jefferson, October 6, 1778.

[35] <u>LDC</u>, op. cit., Vol. 11, p. xxiv. See also: Vol. 12, p. xxiv; Vol. 13, p. xxii; Vol. 14, p. xxiii; Vol. 15, p. xxiii.

[36] <u>JCC</u>, op. cit., Vol. XIII, p. 263.

[37] <u>LDC</u>, op. cit., Vol. 13, pp. 433-435; Henry Laurens to Richard Henry Lee, August 31, 1779.

[38] <u>LDC</u>, op. cit., Vol. 12, p.340, footnote 1. See also: Vol. 13, p. 156, footnote 2.

[39] <u>LDC</u>, op. cit., Vol. 13, pp. 155-156; Meriwether Smith to Thomas Jefferson, July 6, 1779.

[40] <u>LDC</u>, op. cit., Vol. 13, p.345; Cyrus Griffin to Burgess Ball, August 10, 1779.

[41] <u>LDC</u>, op. cit., Vol. 13, p. 519; Cyrus Griffin to Burgess Ball, September 21, 1779. In this letter, Cyrus' affection for Ball is clearly reflected in the sentence: "No person upon Earth can be more welcome to what little satisfaction I am able to give him in the way of writing now and then."

[42] LDC, op. cit., Vol. 13, pp. 519-520; Cyrus Griffin to Burgess Ball, September 21, 1779.

[43] LDC, op. cit., Vol. 13, p. 346, footnote 1. Lt. Col. Burgess Ball (1749-1800) had been transferred to the 1st Virginia Regiment of Foot in September 1778. He was captured when Charleston surrendered in May 1780. Cyrus also corresponded with Benjamin Franklin that September. Lady Christina's father had died in Paris on March 28, 1779. Franklin was obviously serving as an intermediary between Cyrus and his late father-in-law's family. "We thank you," Cyrus told Franklin, "for the trouble of attaching a Bond executed by the late Earl of Traquair." The details concerning this bond are not clear. LDC, op. cit., Vol. 13, pp. 605-606; Cyrus Griffin to Benjamin Franklin, September 1779.

[44] JCC, op. cit., Vol. XV, p. 1171.

[45] Henry J. Bourguignon, The First Federal Court: The Federal Appellate Prize Court of the American Revolution, 1775-1787 (The American Philosophical Society, Philadelphia, 1977), pp. 39 & 78.

[46] LDC, op. cit., Vol. 14, p. 264. See also: Vol. 14, p. 443, footnote 3.

[47] LDC, op. cit., Vol. 14, pp. xxiii-xxiv. See also: Vol. 15, pp. xxii-xxiii. See also: Vol. 15, p. 108, footnote 2. During this period Cyrus and eventually Madison were living at the Philadelphia home of Mrs. Mary House at Fifth and Market Streets.

[48] LDC, op. cit., Vol. 14, p. 166; Cyrus Griffin to the Virginia House of Delegates, November 9, 1779.

[49] LDC, op. cit., Vol. 14, p. 9, footnote 2.

[50] Bourguignon, op. cit., p. 40.

[51] JCC, op. cit., Vol. XVI, pp. 61-64. See also: LDC, op. cit., Vol. 14, p. 386; Samuel Huntington to Titus Hosmer, William Paca, and George Wythe, February 2, 1780.

[52] Bourguignon, op. cit., p. 115.

[53] Bourguignon, op. cit., pp. 116-118. Thomas Jefferson, among other prominent Virginians, had studied law under George Wythe.

[54] JCC, op. cit., Vol. XVI, p. 397.

[55] LDC, op. cit., Vol. 14, p. 505; Cyrus Griffin to John Morgan, March 15, 1780.

[56] Chapter 11, endnote 19.

[57] LDC, op. cit., Vol. 15, p. 310, footnote 3.

[58] LDC, op. cit., Vol. 15, p. 70; Samuel Huntington to Cyrus Griffin, May 1, 1780.

[59] LDC, op. cit., Vol. 15, p. 78; Cyrus Griffin to Samuel Huntington, May 4, 1780.

[60] LDC, op. cit., Vol. 15, p. 278, Cyrus Griffin to Thomas Jefferson, June 9, 1780.

[61] LDC, op. cit., Vol. 15, pp. 309-310; Cyrus Griffin to Thomas Jefferson; June 13, 1780.

[62] JCC, op. cit., Vol. XVII, p. 507.

[63] Bourguignon, op. cit., p. 118.

[64] Bourguignon, op. cit., p. 119. At that time, 1780, the salary for the Judges of the new Court of Appeals was $2,250 each per year compared with Secretary Thomson's salary of $3,000; and, $4,000 for the Secretary for Foreign Affairs. Robert Morris, the Superintendent of Finance, was paid $6,000.

[65] Bourguignon, op. cit., p. 118.

[66] Charles T. Cullen, Editor, The Papers of Thomas Jefferson (Princeton University Press, Princeton, 1983), Vol. 3, p. 483; Cyrus Griffin to Thomas Jefferson, July 11, 1780.

[67] LDC, op. cit., Vol. 19, p. 51; Connecticut Delegates to Jonathan Trumbull, Sr., August 10, 1782.

[68] JCC, op. cit., Vol. XXIV, p. 7.

[69] LDC, op. cit., Vol. 19, p. 103; John Hanson to William Whipple and Others, August 28, 1782.

[70] LDC, op. cit., Vol. 19, p. 207; Eliphalet Dyer to Jonathan Trumbull, Sr., September 25, 1782.

[71] JCC, op. cit., Vol. XXIV, p. 7.

[72] LDC, op. cit., Vol. 19, p. 399; James Madison to Edmund Randolph, November 19, 1782. See Also: James Grant Wilson & John Fiske, Editors, Appletons' Cyclopaedia of American Biography (D. Appleton and Company, New York, 1887), Vol. II, p. 286.

[73] JCC, op. cit., Vol. XXIV, pp. 6-32..

[74] Bourguignon, op. cit., p. 117.

[75] Bourguignon, op. cit., pp. 118-120. Se also, Cyrus Griffin to Samuel Huntington, February 22, 1780.

[76] G. S. Rowe, Thomas McKean (Colorado Associated University Press, Boulder, 1978), p. 81. On July 1, 1776, when Congress took its first informal poll on the issue of Independence in the Committee of the Whole, the Delaware Delegation split with Thomas McKean voting aye and George Read voting no. McKean then sent for the ailing Caesar Rodney, the absent third delegate. Rodney, despite his illness, rode all night through a thunderstorm in order to cast his vote with McKean and thereby put Delaware in the affirmative column the next day when the final vote came up on the floor of Congress. Rodney's historic ride is depicted on Delaware's commemorative quarter. On August 2, 1776, Delegate George Read cast his fate with his colleagues when he decided to sign the Declaration of Independence.

[77] Dumas Malone, Dictionary of American Biography (Charles Scribner's Sons, New York, 1943), pp. 464-465.

[78] LDC, op. cit., Vol. 20, p. 134; Eliphalet Dyer to Thomas Shaw, April 2, 1783.

[79] Maeva Marcus, Editor, The Documentary History of the Supreme Court of the United States, 1789-1800 (Columbia University Press, New York, 1985), Vol. 1, Part 2, p. 630; Cyrus Griffin to George Washington, July 10, 1789. See also: Bourguignon, op. cit., p. 124.

[80] JCC, op. cit., Vol. XXX, pp. 60-61..

[81] Bourguignon, op. cit., pp. 124-125.

[82] Gaspare J. Saladino, American National Biography Online (www.anb.org.nuncio.cofc. edu/articles)

[83] Saladino, op. cit.

[84] LDC, op. cit., Vol. 24, p. xxvii.

[85] LDC, op. cit., Vol. 24, p. 588, John Brown to James Breckinridge, December 16, 1787. Brown, another member of the Virginia Delegation in 1787, lived in that same boarding house with Cyrus Griffin and James Madison.

[86] JCC, op. cit., Vol. XXXIII, p. 716.

[87] Chapter 11. Since Rhode Island had even refused to attend the Constitutional Convention, the congressional delegates knew that requiring unanimous consent for the new Constitution would have doomed it to defeat.

[88] LDC, op. cit., Vol. 24, p. 579; James Madison to Horatio Gates, December 11, 1787.

[89] Chapter 13.

[90] LDC, op. cit., Vol. 24, p. 584; Cyrus Griffin to Thomas FitzSimons, December 16, 1787.

[91] LDC, op. cit., Vol. 24, p.588; John Brown to James Breckinridge, December 16, 1787.

[92] LDC, op. cit., Vol. 24, p. 611; Cyrus Griffin to Thomas FitzSimons, January 13, 1788.

[93] JCC, op. cit., Vol. XXXIV, pp. 1 & 9.

[94] LDC, op. cit., Vol. 24, p. 628; James Madison to Edmund Randolph, January 27, 1788.

[95] LDC, op. cit., Vol. 24, pp. 637-638; Samuel A. Otis to James Warren, February 6, 1788.

[96] LDC, op. cit., Vol. 25, p. 51; Samuel Otis to George Thatcher, April 13, 1788. Otis told Thatcher that Mrs. Griffin was still in Philadelphia "and I suspect she is averse from any farther advances East." He was wrong.

[97] LDC, op. cit., Vol. 24, p. 650; Cyrus Griffin to Thomas FitzSimons, February 18, 1788.

[98] LDC, op. cit., Vol. 24, p. 617; James Madison to Rufus King, January 23, 1788.

[99] Chapter 3.

[100] LDC, op. cit., Vol. 25, p. 516, footnote 2. See also: Rufus Wilmot Griswold, The Republican Court (D. Appleton & Co., New York, 1867), p. 83. Moustier entertained frequently and ostentatiously. He boasted that he had once told President Griffin that "he was but a tavern-keeper." Moustier, who remained loyal to the Bourbons, died a refugee in England in 1817.

[101] JCC, op. cit., Vol. XXXIV, pp. 62-65.

[102] LDC, op. cit., Vol. 25, p 6; Cyrus Griffin to Thomas FitzSimons, March 3, 1788.

[103] LDC, op. cit., Vol. 25, p 6; Cyrus Griffin to Thomas FitzSimons, March 3, 1788.

[104] LDC, op. cit., Vol. 25, p. 201; Jonathan Hazard to John Collins, July 2, 1788. Hazard told his friend that "I have Indevered Ever since I have been hear [sic], to find his [Griffin's] mind in Regard to the constitution, but it hath been out of power, but I am Led to believe he would have been as well pleased, had the constitution been Rejected as he now is."

[105] LDC, op. cit., Vol. 25, p. 26; Cyrus Griffin to James Madison, March 24, 1788.

[106] LDC, op. cit., Vol. 25, p. 52; Cyrus Griffin to Samuel Johnston, April 14, 1788.

[107] LDC, op. cit., Vol. 25, p. 43; Cyrus Griffin to James Madison, April 7, 1788.

[108] LDC, op. cit., Vol. 25, pp. 51-52; Cyrus Griffin to Thomas FitzSimons, April 14, 1788.

[109] LDC, op. cit., Vol. 25, p. 53; Cyrus Griffin to James Madison, April 14, 1788.

[110] LDC, op. cit., Vol. 25, p. 83; Cyrus Griffin to James Madison, April 28, 1788.

[111] LDC, op. cit., Vol. 25, p. 82; Cyrus Griffin to Thomas FitzSimons, April 27, 1788.

[112] LDC, op. cit., Vol. 25, p. 88; Cyrus Griffin to James Madison, May 5, 1788.

[113] LDC, op. cit., Vol. 25, p. 90; Cyrus Griffin to Certain States, May 8, 1788.

[114] LDC, op. cit., Vol. 25, p. 105; Cyrus Griffin to James Madison, May 19, 1788.

[115] LDC, op. cit., Vol. 25, p. 174; Cyrus Griffin to Thomas FitzSimons, June 16, 1788.

[116] LDC, op. cit., Vol. 25, p. 177; Cyrus Griffin to James Madison, June 18, 1788.

[117] LDC, op. cit., Vol. 25, p. 191; Virginia Delegates to James Madison, June 25, 1788.

[118] Irving Brant, James Madison: Father of the Constitution (The Bobbs-Merrill Company, Inc., Indianapolis, 1950), pp. 226-227.

[119] Jack N. Rakove, Original Meanings (Alfred A. Knopf, New York, 1996), pp. 114-128.

North Carolina ratified the Constitution in November 1789; and, in May 1790, Rhode Island finally did so by a margin of only two votes!

[120] LDC, op. cit., Vol. 25, p. 261; Paine Wingate to Samuel Lane, July 29, 1788.

[121] J. P. Brissot de Warville, New Travels in the United States of America 1788 (The Belknap Press, Cambridge, 1964), p. 150.

[122] Griswold, op. cit., pp. 91-92; Abigail Adams Smith to Abigail Adams, May 20, 1788. The planet John Adams' daughter made reference to was Uranus which was discovered by William Herschel in 1781.

[123] Griswold, op. cit., pp. 96-97. Abigail Adams Smith to Abigail Adams, Summer 1788.

[124] LDC, op. cit., Vol. 25, p. 459. Also elected that day by the Virginia House were John Brown, John Dawson and Mann Page.

[125] LDC, op. cit., Vol. 25, p. 510, footnote 7. "In the expense accounts that he submitted to the Virginia treasurer, Griffin claimed continuous delegate service from November 1, 1787, to March 4, 1789..."

[126] LDC, op. cit., Vol. 25, p. 467; Cyrus Griffin to George Read, December 1788. John Livingston had served as secretary for Presidents Gorham, St. Clair and Griffin. He did not get the position, nor was any member of the Livingston family appointed to the new government by President Washington.

[127] JCC, op. cit., Vol. XXXIV, pp. 604-605. The last entry in the Journals is that on that final day, Monday, March 2, 1789, Mr. Philip Pell of New York presented his credentials.

[128] Harold C. Syrett, Editor, The Papers of Alexander Hamilton (Columbia University Press, New York, 1962), Vol. V, pp. 262 & 286-287; H. G. Letter IX, March 3, 1789. The 16 H. G. Letters are now known to have been written by Alexander Hamilton to a ficticious correspondent. Published in the *Daily Advertiser,* the letters were a sustained attack on New York Governor George Clinton.

[129] LDC, op. cit., Vol. 25, p. 508; Hugh Williamson to Samuel Johnston, March 2, 1789. North Carolina Delegate Hugh Williamson even wrote in his letter on March 2 that "I think it probable that my Privilege of franking Letters after to day may be disputed at the Post Office."

[130] George Adams Boyd, Elias Boudinot: Patriot and Statesman, (Princeton University Press, Princeton, 1952), p. 154.

[131] LDC, op. cit., Vol. 25, p. 509; Cyrus Griffin to Beverley Randolph, March 9, 1789.

[132] Boyd Stanley Schlenther, Charles Thomson (Associaed University Presses, London, 1990), p. 190.

[133] Douglas Southall Freeman, Washington (An Abridgment by Richard Harwell),

(Charles Scribner's Sons, New York, 1968), p. 563. See also: Chapter 11, p. 161; and, Griswold, op. cit., pp. 166-168.

[134] Griswold, op. cit., pp.154 -165.

[135] Marcus, op. cit., Vol. 1, Part 2, p. 630; Cyrus Griffin to George Washington, July 10, 1789. One month later, August 14, 1789, concerned that his first letter had been too boastful, Cyrus again wrote to Washington, informing him that if his earlier letter was inappropriate it was due to "misinformation concerning the manner, and from an ardent desire to continue in the employment of the union..." Vol. 1, Part 2, pp. 649-650.

[136] John C. Fitzpatrick, Editor, The Writings of George Washington (Government Printing Office, Washington, DC, 1940), Vol. 30, p. 383; George Washington to Cyrus Griffin, August 18, 1789.

[137] Fitzpatrick, op. cit., Vol. 30, p. 404; George Washington to Arthur Campbell, September 15, 1789.

[138] Rorer, Cyrus Griffin, op. cit., p. 1353.

[139] Syrett, op. cit., Vol. 5, p. 456; Alexander Hamilton to George Washington, October 20, 1789.

[140] Fitzpatrick, op. cit., Vol. 30, pp. 472-473; George Washington to Edmund Randolph, November 30, 1789. John Marshall, the future Chief Justice, also turned down President Washington's offer to be appointed Attorney for the District of Virginia; Vol. 38, p. 463; George Washington to John Marshall, November 23, 1789.

[141] Biographical Directory of the American Congress, op. cit., pp. 1239 & 1418.

[142] Cullen, op. cit., Vol. 16, pp. 14-15; Cyrus Griffin to Thomas Jefferson, December 11, 1789.

[143] Cullen, op. cit., Vol. 16, pp. 15-16; Thomas Jefferson to Cyrus Griffin, December 11, 1789.

[144] Cullen, op. cit., Vol. 15, p. 564; William Short to Thomas Jefferson, November 30, 1789.

[145] Wilson, op. cit., Vol. V, p. 516.

[146] Rorer, Cyrus Griffin, op. cit., p. 1354.

[147] Henry Steele Commager, Editor, Documents of American History (Appleton-Century-Crofts, New York, 1963), p. 118; Treaty of Peace with Great Britain, September 3, 1783.

[148] Charles F. Hobson, The Recovery of British Debts in the Federal Circuit Court of Virginia, 1790-1797, *The Virginia Magazine of History and Biography*, Vol. 92 (April 1984), p. 179.

[149] Marcus, op. cit., Vol. 2, pp. 123-124.

[150] Commager, op. cit., pp. 153-154. Under the provisions of the Judiciary Act of 1789, the United States was divided into three judicial Circuits. Each year, two Justices of the US Supreme Court had to ride circuit in their assigned area and hear cases in conjunction with the Federal District Judge for that State. Two of the three judges would constitute a quorum.

[151] Hobson, op. cit., p. 187.

[152] Marcus, op. cit., Vol. 2, p. 339

[153] Hobson, op. cit., pp. 189-194. Jay had resigned as Chief Justice before the Supreme Court heard the case in 1796. Despite the victory of British creditors in *Ware v. Hylton,* American juries continued to frustrate British plaintiffs by subtracting interest on those debts during the Revolutionary War years. Secretary of State Thomas Jefferson, despite his reputation for articulating the rights of man, described his position on the payment of interest on British debts as: "No slaves, no interest." See also: Marcus, op. cit., Vol. 2, p. 339, footnote 4.

[154] Marcus, op. cit., Vol. 1, Part 2, pp. 848-851; Cyrus Griffin to George Washington, May 23, 1796.

[155] Syrett, op. cit., Vol. XVII, pp. 499 & 502. In 1794, Cyrus Griffin earned $1,800 per year as a Federal District Judge compared with Associate Justice James Wilson's $3,500 and Chief Justice John Jay's $4,000.

[156] Marcus, op. cit., Vol. 1, Part 2, pp. 869-870; Cyrus Griffin to John Adams, November 10, 1798.

[157] Commager, op. cit., pp. 177-178.

[158] As cited in David McCullough, John Adams (Simon & Schuster, New York, 2001), p. 498.

[159] Merrill D. Peterson, Thomas Jefferson & the new nation (Oxford University Press, New York, 1970), 569. It was Callender who also exposed Alexander Hamilton's scandal in the Reynolds affair.

[160] As cited in Rorer, Cyrus Griffin, op. cit., p. 1354.

[161] Peterson, op. cit., pp. 635-636.

[162] Marcus, op. cit., Vol. 3, pp. 435-436.

[163] Jane Shaffer Elsmere, Justice Samuel Chase (Janevar Publishing Company, Muncie, IN, 1980), p. 119.

[164] Elsmere, op. cit., pp. 63 & 121-122.

[165] Biographical Directory of the American Congress, op. cit., p. 976. Mary, Cyrus Griffin's oldest daughter married her cousin, Thomas Griffin. He served in Congress from 1803-1805. He also served as Chief Justice of the Virginia State Court of Quarter Sessions in Yorktown from 1805-1810, while Cyrus was still Federal District Court Judge.

[166] Elsmere, op. cit., pp. 174 & 295. James T. Callender eventually concluded that Thomas Jefferson had not adequately come to his defense and turned his poison pen on the new President, as well.

[167] John Dos Passos, The Conspiracy and Trial of Aaron Burr, *American Heritage Magazine,* Vol. XVII, No. 2, (February 1966); p. 70.

[168] Peter Charles Hoffer, The Treason Trials of Aaron Burr (University Press of Kansas, Lawrence, KS, 2008), pp. 8-9.

[169] William Wirt Henry, The Trial of Aaron Burr, *The Virginia Law Register,* Vol. 3, No. 7, (November 1897), p. 500.

[170] Joseph P. Brady, The Trial of Aaron Burr (The Neale Publishing Company, New York, 1916), p. 14.

[171] Albert J. Beveridge, Life of John Marshall (Houghton, Mifflin, Boston, 1916), Vol. 3, p. 520.

[172] Brady, op. cit., p. 171. Burr was then charged with violating the Neutrality Act, but the prosecution decided to drop the case.

[173] Marcus, op. cit., Vol. 3, pp. 133-134.

[174] As cited in Rorer, *Cyrus Griffin,* op. cit., p. 1355; Thomas Jefferson to James Madison, May 25, 1810.

[175] Merrill D. Peterson, Editor, Thomas Jefferson Writings (The Library of America, New York, 1984), pp. 1225-1226; Thomas Jefferson to John Tyler, Jr, May 26, 1810. Tyler was the father of John Tyler (1790-1862) who became the 10th President of the United States under the Second Republic. Jefferson, who viscously attacked several of his former colleagues, most notably John Adams, was especially interested in the Virginia Judgeship because he himself became a defendant in a case held in Richmond on December 5, 1811, a year after Cyrus Griffin's death. In that case, Marshall and Tyler ruled that the Court had no jurisdiction and therefore found in favor of Jefferson, the defendant. See also: Rorer, *Cyrus Griffin,* op. cit., p. 1355. In his article, Rorer makes clear that Cyrus Griffin was the intended target of the "imbecility" remark.

[176] Colonial Williamsburg Foundation Archives, Letter of Cyrus Griffin to Unknown, October 7, 1806.

[177] William A. R. Goodwin, Bruton Parish Church Restored and Its Historic Environment (Bruton Parish Publication, Williamsburg, 1907), p. 81. See also: *Virginia Magazine of History,* Vol. 17, p. 435.

[178] Rorer, Cyrus Griffin, op. cit., p. 1356. See also: *William and Mary Quarterly,* Vol. 7, 1898-1899, pp. 60-61. Samuel Griffin died on November 23, 1810.

[179] York County Records, Wills & Inventories, Book 23, p. 810. Other sources set December 14, 1810, as the date of Cyrus' death, but this source appears more credible. See also: *Richmond Enquirer,* December 10, 1810, p. 3.

[180] Cyrus Griffin's Will, op. cit. Like President Nathaniel Gorham, there has never been a biography of President Cyrus Griffin nor even a doctoral dissertation. Prior to this chapter, the longest piece ever written about his life was the eleven page article by Henry S. Rorer which appeared in the *Northern Neck of Virginia Historical Magazine* in 1965.

WHILE CYRUS GRIFFIN
WAS PRESIDENT

Notes

Abbreviation Key

JCC   Journals of the Continental Congress
LDC   Letters of Delegates to Congress
PHL   The Papers of Henry Laurens

[181] Bernard Bailyn, Editor, The Debate on the Constitution (The Library of America, New York, 1993), Vol. 2, pp. 1064-1065.

[182] Leonard W. Levy, Editor-in-Chief, Encyclopedia of the American Constitution (Macmillan Publishing Company, New York, 1986), Vol. 3, p. 1513.

[183] Chapter 3.

[184] Bailyn, op. cit., Vol. 2, pp. 1066 & 1074.

[185] Levy, op. cit., Vol. 3, p. 1513.

[186] Bailyn, op. cit., Vol. 2, pp. 1066-1067.

[187] Bailyn, op. cit., Vol. 2, p. 1067.

[188] Levy, op. cit., Vol. 3, p. 1513.

[189] Bailyn, op. cit., Vol. 2, p. 1068. While July 4, 1776, is mistakenly celebrated as the birthday of the United States, that was the day the Declaration was adopted. The actual vote for Independence took place two days earlier on July 2, 1776. As John Adams confided in a letter to his dear wife: "The Second Day of July 1776, will be the most memorable Epocha, in the History of America...It ought to be commerated, as the Day of Deliverance..." L. H. Butterfield, Editor, The Book of Abigail and John: Selected Letters of the Adams Family, 1762-1784 (Harvard University Press, Cambridge, 1975), p. 142; John Adams to Abigail Adams, July 3, 1776.

[190] Levy, op. cit., Vol. 3, p. 1513.

[191] Jack N. Rakove, Original Meanings (Alfred A. Knopf, New York, 1996), pp. 125-127.

[192] Bailyn, op. cit., Vol. 2, pp. 1069 & 1072.

[193] Sol Bloom, Director General, <u>History of the Formation of the Union Under the Constitution</u> (Government Printing Office, Washington, DC, 1943), p. 60.

[194] Roscoe R. Hill, Editor, <u>JCC: 1774-1789</u> (Government Printing Office, Washington, DC, 1937), Vol. XXXIV, p. 281.

[195] David McCullough, <u>John Adams</u> (Simon & Schuster, New York, 2001), p. 389.

[196] Merrill D. Peterson, <u>Thomas Jefferson and the New Nation</u> (Oxford University Press, New York, 1970), p. 390.

[197] J. Steven Watson, <u>The Reign of George III: 1760-1815</u> (Clarendon Press, Oxford, 1960), pp. 304-305.

[198] Stanley Ayling, <u>George The Third</u> (Alfred A. Knopf, New York, 1972), pp. 329-335.

[199] John Brooke, <u>King George III</u> (McGraw-Hill Book Company, London, 1972), pp. 337-339. Porphyria, believed to be an hereditary disease, was unknown in the 18th Century. In 1966, a careful review of the King's medical records by two British psychiatrists and historians of medicine led to this diagnosis. Further study indicated that George III suffered from at least four bouts of this disease: 1788-89, 1801, 1804 and "the King's permanent disablement in 1811" (four years before his death). A study of his family's history also uncovered that four of his sons and at least one grand-daughter suffered from similar symptoms.

[200] Ayling, op. cit., p. 332.

[201] Brooke, op. cit., pp. 331-336.

[202] Donald Grove Barnes, <u>George III and William Pitt, 1783-1806</u> (Octagon Books, Inc., New York, 1985), p. 200.

[203] William Benton, Publisher, <u>Encyclopedia Britannica</u> (William Benton, Publisher, Chicago, 1966), Vol. 9, p. 726.

[204] William L. Langer, Editor, <u>An Encyclopedia of World History</u> (Houghton Mifflin Company, Boston, 1972), p. 628.

Chapter 15

Secretary
CHARLES THOMSON
of
PENNSYLVANIA

Beyond The Call Of Duty

During the First American Republic, the greatest patriot of all never occupied the President's chair, nor was he provided a mansion and carriage at public expense. But, as Secretary of Congress for its entire fifteen-year history, Charles Thomson was the driving force behind the gavel and the living institutional history of the nation's first government. Without his prodding and pleading, Congress would never have survived. Without his faithful service, the record of the First American Republic would be lost to history.

Charles Thomson's life was itself the perfect embodiment of the American Dream. He arrived on these shores as a penniless orphan at the age of ten and now, over two centuries later, he and his wife rest beneath a magnificent obelisk in historic Laurel Hill Cemetery in the heart of Philadelphia. Throughout his long and immensely productive career he left a unique and indelible mark on state and national government, natural science and biblical scholarship. His friends and correspondents for decades included Franklin and Jefferson.[1] It was also Charles Thomson, the Secretary of Congress, who officially notified Washington of his election as the first President of the Second American Republic and accompanied him from Mount Vernon to the inaugural ceremonies in New York.

After American independence had been won, several prominent colleagues, including John Jay, urged Charles to write the definitive history of the Revolution since "no other person in the world is so perfectly acquainted with the rise, conduct and conclusion of the American Revolution as yourself..."[2] It even appears that Charles began work on such a manuscript but in later years he destroyed most of his personal papers.[3] As he wrote to a friend, Charles refused to "undeceive future generations" concerning the "supposed wisdom and valor of our great men."[4] Despite that enormous loss to our nation's narrative, other dedicated individuals and institutions have struggle to fill in the gaps. Many of those myths can finally be reexamined as 21st Century America reflects anew on its birth.

Charles Thomson's personal story began on November 29, 1729, in the town of Gorteade, County Derry, in what is today Northern Ireland. His ancestors had emigrated to Ireland in the 17th Century.[5] John Thomson and his wife (who's name is unknown) gave birth to five sons and one daughter. Charles was the third oldest. In 1739, only months after the death of his wife, John Thomson and three of his sons set sail for America as part of a Scotch-Irish wave of immigration across the Atlantic that totaled nearly 40,000 by 1750. Tragically, as the American coast came into view, the father died on board ship and was buried at sea. Even though Charles was only ten, he later recalled that "I stood by the bedside of my expiring and much loved father, closed his eyes and performed the last filial duties to him."[6]

When the ship landed at New Castle, Delaware, the captain confiscated their father's savings before putting the boys ashore. Charles was eventually given shelter by a blacksmith's family that was eager to engage him as an indentured apprentice. Even at that young age, however, Charles was determined to carve out a better life for himself. As he fled New Castle by foot, setting out along the main road toward Wilmington, he met a lady who asked about his journey. Charles shared his story and added "that he saw men of education useful to themselves and others, and he thought if he had the chance he could be successful in that way."[7] Through this stranger's kindness and financial assistance from his brother, Alexander, Charles was placed in a private school two miles from New London, Pennsylvania which had just been established by the Rev. Francis Alison, a prominent Presbyterian minister.[8]

The Rev. Alison, one of the finest classical scholars in America, had an illustrious career during which he helped to educate and inspire a whole generation of American patriots including Thomas McKean, the future President, and three other signers of the Declaration of Independence.[9] Over the next five or six years, under Alison's guidance, Charles excelled in a wide range of subjects, especially Greek and Latin. It was also through Alison that the eager young student met Benjamin Franklin, who shortly thereafter founded the Academy of Philadelphia (now the University of Pennsylvania). In December 1750, Charles accepted a position as Latin and Greek Tutor at Franklin's academy. One year later, he was reunited with the Rev. Alison when his mentor became the Academy's new Rector.

In 1755, their idyllic environment was shattered when the Academy was chartered as a college and the new Anglican provost made life uncomfortable for Presbyterian members of the faculty. Charles resigned his position that July, but continued his teaching career as head of the Latin program at the prestigious Friends Public School which had been founded by the Quakers in 1689.[10] Charles recorded his educational philosophy in his memorandum book: "The end of learning should be to remove prejudices, govern the passions & make men good, honest & virtuous, good Children, good parents, good friends & good citizens." One of his students at the school described Charles as "...master of every art and of every science."[11]

Through his daily interaction with the Quakers, Charles also developed valuable insights into Pennsylvania politics, which was still dominated by that pacifist sect. At that time, the "Broadbrims" (as John Adams often referred to members of that religion because of their style of dress)[12] not only controlled the Assembly but they were also attempting to undermine the authority of the proprietary government in order to consolidate power in their own hands.

Through the Quakers, Charles was also exposed to the intricacies of Indian affairs. In November 1756, during the French & Indian War, Charles was included in a Quaker delegation which attended a conference with ten Indian tribes, including the Delawares (who had killed or captured nearly 400 Pennsylvania settlers the previous spring). Initially, Charles served as secretary to the delegation. By the following summer, Quaker leaders also had arranged for Charles to serve as clerk to the the self-proclaimed "King" of the Delawares, a quirky yet charismatic chief by the name of Teedyuscung. As Charles later recorded: "I was obliged to enter deep into their politics and investigate their claims."[13]

Charles' intense two-year involvement in Indian Affairs climaxed at the Conference in Easton, Pennsylvania in October 1758. As a result of those negotiations, hostilities abated along the Pennsylvania frontier. At that conference Charles was also adopted into the Delaware tribe and given the Indian name "Wegh-wu-law-mo-end" which translates as "The Man who speaks the Truth." Years later, when asked how his name had come to be associated with speaking the truth, Charles replied that "I had resolved in spite of consequences, never to put my official signature to any account, for the accuracy of which I could not vouch as a man of honor."[14]

In 1759, Charles summarized the lessons he had learned in "An Enquiry into the Causes of the Alienation of the Delaware and Shawenese Indians from the British Interest." Even former Virginia Militiaman George Washington came under fire for treating the Indians more as slaves than allies during the early days of the war.[15] Charles concluded that Indians "are capable of being our most useful Friends or most dangerous Enemies.

And whether for the future, they are to be the one or the other, seems now to be in our own Power."[16] He sent the manuscript to Franklin who was by then serving as a colonial agent in London. Franklin distributed copies throughout the British Government in the hope of replacing Pennsylvania's proprietary government with a Royal Charter.

In the midst of his teaching and frontier duties, Charles fell in love with Ruth Mather of Chester, Pennsylvania. After their marriage in 1758, they rented a house on Market Street near the Franklin home.[17] Little is known of their married life but, in 1769, Ruth gave birth to twins who died in infancy. A contemporary of the Thomsons recorded that around that time Ruth lost her sense of reason "from an hereditary infirmity" likely triggered by the death of her children.[18] That December, Deborah Franklin reported to her husband, who was still living in England, that "Nabor Thomson has bin gon ever senes the begining of the summer and my worthey mrs. Thomson has labered under a verey maloncoley disorder..."[19] Some have speculated that Ruth's death early the next year might have been suicide, but no definitive record exists. Charles, who remarried four years later into a prominent Philadelphia family, never again fathered children.

During the decade leading up to his first marriage, Charles also helped to organize a small discussion group dedicated to self-improvement which was clearly patterned on the "Junto" made famous by Benjamin Franklin in the 1740s. Franklin's illegitimate son, William (the future Royal Governor of New Jersey), joined Charles in launching the "Young Junto." In December 1766, the members officially named it "The American Society for promoting and propagating useful knowledge." Its mission statement proclaimed that "Knowledge is of little use when confined to mere Speculation; but when speculative Truths are reduced to Practice, when Theories, grounded upon Experiments, are applied to common Purposes of Life, and when, by these, Agriculture is improved, Trade enlarged, and the Arts of Living made more easy and comfortable...Knowledge then becomes really useful..."[20]

One year later a rival group, The Philosophical Society, was organized which featured a more conservative cast of characters By December 1768, however, personal animosities were set aside in the cause of science when the two groups formally merged into the The American Philosophical Society. Benjamin Franklin, though still in London, was elected to head the new club and Charles was elected as one of the organization's three secretaries. The Society quickly became the center of scientific and practical knowledge throughout North America. It also reflected Charles' lifelong passion for exploring and understanding the natural world, a characteristic he shared with Franklin, Jefferson and so many of the Founding Fathers. They were, in every sense, men of The Enlightenment.

Charles Thomson, however, was also a man of faith. For him, the exploration of God's Universe was simply an holistic approach to creation. By ancestry and tradition, he strongly identified with Presbyterianism during these years and served as an elder in the First Presbyterian Church in Philadelphia. Since colonial Americans viewed members of his denomination as the opposition to the established Church of England, his religious identification also had profound political implications in the decade leading up to the American Revolution. By 1765, a Synod composed of delegates from Presbyterian congregations across the East Coast was held at Philadelphia. The Synod also established committees of correspondence with Congregational Churches in New England.[21]

Thus, through his friendship with Franklin, his working relationship with the Quakers, his involvement in Indian affairs, his leadership of the American Philosophical Society and his deep ties to the Presbyterian Church, Charles became intimately familiar with Pennsylvania politics and its competing factions. What ultimately transformed Charles into a leader of resistance to British policy, however, was his immersion into the world of business. In 1760, two years after his marriage to Ruth, Charles left academia to open his own dry goods store on Market Street, nearly opposite the King of Prussia tavern. His initial inventory included a wide range of items from blankets and pewter plates to pipes and gun powder.[22] Through his characteristic diligence and determination, Charles became a recognized Philadelphia merchant who actively engaged in maritime trade. Not surprisingly, as Britain began to impose new taxes to offset the enormous cost of its victory in the French & Indian War, American merchants such as John Hancock, Henry Laurens and Charles Thomson were among the first to feel the impact. Repeatedly, short-sighted colonial policies drove America's best and brightest into open revolt.

By 1764, as rumors concerning yet another new tax began to circulate, Charles began to form an alliance with John Dickinson, a wealthy young man from a prominent family, three years his junior, who had also studied under the Rev. Alison. Their intense opposition to the threat of a Stamp Tax cemented their close friendship which lasted for the rest of their lives. Both men viewed the tax as a dangerous departure from established colonial policy. For the first time, Parliament was attempting to raise revenue from Americans rather than merely regulating trade.

Initially, Franklin was caught on the wrong side of the issue. Since Franklin's primary objective at that time was to replace the Penn Family's proprietary government with a Royal Charter, he was extremely hesitant to criticize the British Government even on such an important issue. In July 1765, in response to two letters from Charles updating him on

America's resistance to the impending Stamp Act, Franklin assured "my good neighbour, I took every step in my power to prevent the passing of the stamp act no body could be more concerned in interest than myself to oppose it sincerely & heartily." Unfortunately, as Franklin explained, Parliament "was provoked by American Claims of Independence & all Parties joined in resolving by this act to settle the point. We might as well have hindered the sun's setting." From London, the only course of action that Franklin could offer, given his delicate balancing act, was to "let us make as good a night of it as we can. We may still light candles."[23]

In America, the threat seemed far more ominous. On October 5, 1765, as John Dickinson prepared for the opening of the Stamp Act Congress in New York City,[24] over a thousand citizens gathered outside the State House in Philadelphia to organize resistance to the new tax. After Charles and several others delivered impassioned speeches to the crowd, a prominent five-member delegation, including Charles and wealthy financier Robert Morris, was selected to demand the resignation of John Hughes, the newly appointed stamp agent. Hughes fiercely refused to step down; but, under intense pressure, he ultimately agreed not to attempt to enforce the Act. Following another meeting on November 7, one week after the tax went into effect, approximately 400 Philadelphia merchants joined with their colleagues throughout the colonies by agreeing to boycott British goods until the Stamp Act was repealed.[25]

Charles shared his fears and anger in a letter to business associates in London that same day: "Where this will end God knows," he told them, "but if relief does not come, and that speedily we who have imported Goods from Great Britain are ruined..." In words that would ring true throughout the colonies, he then stated that "Since I have concerned in trade I have very little attended to Politics; but such is the present Crisis that none who have the least regard for public or private Interest can be silent." He warned his associates that "The affections of more than two millions of as loyal subjects as ever existed are in a fair way to be alienated from G. B." and that the current policy had awakened a "spirit of liberty... that will hazard much before it will submit to Slavery."[26]

As events unfolded, Franklin--who had initially nominated Hughes, to serve as stamp agent for Pennsylvania--gradually recalibrated his own position concerning the tax. He even incorporated part of Charles' correspondence into articles he arranged to have printed in London newspapers.[27] In May 1766, after the tax had been repealed, Charles wrote to "My Worthy and much Esteemed Friend," thanking Franklin "for the pains you have taken to bring that happy event." Charles stressed that "Our hearts are still towards Britain, our love and allegiance to our King is entire and unshaken, and I am sure never did a dutiful and Affectionate Son feel more sincere pleasure from a Reconciliation with a much loved parent unjustly offended at him, than the Americans feel at the prospect of reestablishment of harmony, peace and Concord between Great Britain and them." Charles ended the letter by rejoicing "that an affair which might have had such terrible Consequences is thus hapily accommodated. May there never arise a like occasion!"[28]

Charles, through his oratory and organizational skills, and Dickinson, through his writing and reputation, had emerged as two of the key leaders of the local resistance movement. The critical lessons they learned through the Stamp Act crisis served them well in the political battles ahead. No longer was the debate over proprietary government. The new challenge concerned the fundamental rights of the people. Were colonial Americans entitled to full British citizenship or were they merely cogs in Britain's mercantilistic empire? The repeal of the Stamp Act in early 1766 provided only a brief respite in that ongoing debate.

The very next year Parliament demonstrated once again what historian Barbara Tuchman later referred to as "the march of folly" when it imposed a new tax on a wide variety of items such as tea, paper and glass.[29] These Townshend duties reignited colonial anger as Charles later made clear in a letter to Franklin: "The colonies see plainly that the Ministry have adopted a settled plan to subjugate America to arbitrary power and that all the late acts respecting them lead to this purpose." Charles conceded that "the impositions already laid are not very grievous; but if the principle is established...there is no security for what remains. The very nature of freedom supposes that no tax can be levied on a people without their consent given personally or by their representatives." He proudly stated that since "almost every farmer is a freeholder, the spirit of Liberty will be kept awake and the love of freedom deeply rooted; and when strength and liberty combine it is easy to foresee that a people will not long submit to arbitrary sway."[30]

Starting on November 5, 1767, a series of 14 "Letters from a Pennsylvania Farmer," which denounced the Townshend Acts, began to appear anonymously in the *Pennsylvania Chronicle*.[31] Assembly Speaker Joseph Galloway, Franklin's ally in the campaign against proprietary government, denounced the articles as "damned ridiculous...Only a compilation by Dickinson and Thomson!"[32] The "Letters" were widely reprinted throughout the colonies as Dickinson's authorship became known.

Charles' goal in this new struggle was to motivate his fellow Philadelphia merchants to join their cohorts in Boston and New York in yet another boycott of British goods. To his great disappointment, meetings of merchants in the spring of 1768, failed to reach any consensus. Undaunted, Charles submitted several letters which were published in the *Pennsylvania Gazette* in 1768. Signed "A Freeborn American," Charles challenged his readers: "Where are those *heroic resolves,* that zeal for the preservation of government and liberty, that shone so brightly in the time of the detestable *Stamp Act?*" He urged them to "Revere the mother-country; but never, never let that veneration degenerate into a weak, pitiful submission to tyrannical measures... Let the spirit of liberty and loyalty invigorate every breast, and, in the use of proper means, with the blessing of heaven, we may justly hope for success."[33]

While the battle continued to rage in the Philadelphia press, the boycott went into effect in Boston and New York on January 1, 1769. That February, Charles was able to persuade 48 of the more radical merchants to join with him in pledging not to submit any orders to Britain until the Townshend duties were repealed. Finally, one month later, a larger meeting was held and the Philadelphia merchants adopted the boycott. Through this torturous process, Charles realized that effective resistance would require expanding his base by including large segments of the population that traditionally had been left out of Pennsylvania politics such as the working class, farmers and western settlers.

June 5, 1770, marked a milepost in Pennsylvania politics. Realizing that disgruntled conservative merchants would attempt to rescind the boycott at a meeting scheduled that day, Charles packed the event with the newly politicized workers who were loyal to his cause. While the ploy only delayed the inevitable, it opened Pandora's Box in ways that even Charles would eventually find disturbing. For the moment, however, Charles, Dickinson and Thomas Mifflin (a future president and governor) were the leaders of the most energized force in Philadelphia politics. When word arrived that Parliament had again succumbed to pressure and withdrawn all the new taxes, except that on tea, these resistance leaders were ultimately forced to admit defeat, but their new coalition remained poised to meet the next challenge to their liberties.

Pennsylvania Speaker Joseph Galloway unsuccessfully tried to warn his friend Franklin to avoid Charles: "Pray be cautious in future what you write to that Man, who is void of Principle or Virtue. I have found him so on more Occasion than one, and I am confident you will also shd you continue your free Correspondence."[34] By then, however, Franklin realized that the political sands were shifting.

During the relative political calm of the early 1770s, Charles switched his focus exclusively to business. In the fall of 1770, having recently lost his first wife and infant children, Charles decided to terminate his commercial activities in the city and moved forty miles southeast of Philadelphia to Batsto, New Jersey. There, along the banks of the Mullica River, he became an active partner with another political colleague, John Cox, Jr. Since they had both invested in a bog iron furnace at that location several years earlier, they were determined to redirect their energies to their new business. At the same time, their mutual friend, Dickinson, was taking a new wife and temporarily withdrew from colonial politics and the Pennsylvania Assembly.[35]

Despite these new endeavors, all three men continued to keep a close eye on Pennsylvania politics. In August 1772, a collection of Philadelphia tradesmen and mechanics known as "The Patriotic Society" urged them to run for the colonial Assembly.[36] Knowing that they would still be in the minority, they declined. By the following year, however, all three patriots stood ready to respond as the ships loaded with East India Tea headed toward Philadelphia. On October 16, 1773, Charles and other resistance leaders addressed a mass meeting which denounced anyone who might aid in the importation or sale of the tea. At the end of the meeting, a twelve-member committee was elected to demand the resignation of the designated tea agents. Most agreed. Those that hesitated were intimidated into compliance.[37]

Charles was added to the committee at the next mass meeting in early December and, as usual, served as its secretary. When the ship carrying the tea came into sight on Christmas night, Charles was among the members of the committee who convinced Captain Ayres to anchor clear of the harbor while they escorted him into the city. There, on the morning of December 27, 1773--eleven days after the Boston Tea Party--a crowd of 8,000 angry Philadelphians convinced the Captain to immediately head back to England without unloading his cargo. Charles conveyed this information to Sam Adams, the leader of Boston's Sons of Liberty.

The colonies braced themselves for Britain's reaction. On May 19, 1774, Paul Revere galloped into Philadelphia bearing news of the Intolerable Acts which would soon close Boston Harbor and suspend Massachusetts Government. The citizens of Boston were pleading with their Pennsylvania brethren to join in an immediate boycott and to unite in opposition. A mass meeting was called for the evening of May 20 in order to formulate a response. As Charles later described the scene, he and his patriotic allies, Thomas Mifflin and Joseph Reed, both future Governors of Pennsylvania, devised a plan to persuade their popular yet reluctant colleague John Dickinson to take the lead in urging solidarity with Boston. At the meeting at City Tavern that night, Charles "pressed for an immediate declaration in favour of Boston," even fainting in the midst of his oration (either because of the heat or the theatrical demands of the moment). By prearrangement, Dickinson then rose and successfully urged more moderate measures over the objections of those who opposed any link to the Massachusetts radicals. The ruse worked perfectly. A nineteen-member committee of correspondence was elected which informed Boston that Philadelphia supported creation of a continent-wide congress.[38] In a private letter to Sam Adams, Charles also pledged that he and his colleagues would continue to encourage stronger measures. Adams thanked Charles for his "Zeal in the Common Cause of America..."[39]

Just as Charles had struggled to enlarge the base during earlier crises, his new goal was to link the various political factions into a united response throughout Pennsylvania. Some of his working class allies failed to appreciate the need for unity and grew increasingly disgruntled with his more measured approach.[40] Nevertheless, Charles, Dickinson and Reed dominated another mass meeting held outside the State House on June 18, 1774. An organizing committee was elected that evening to begin preparations for the opening of the congress early that fall. In characteristic fashion, Charles was selected secretary of that group which met every Monday afternoon at Carpenters' Hall, the newly constructed home of one of the colonial guilds.[41]

In order to merge the German immigrants along the Pennsylvania frontier into the movement, Charles traveled to Lancaster, Bethlehem and other locations with Dickinson, Mifflin and their wives and Mrs. Dickinson's first cousin, Hannah Harrison, who later that summer became Charles' second wife. The group returned on July 3, two months before congress was scheduled to open.

Charles and his colleagues were ultimately successful in persuading the Quakers and conservative Assembly members to endorse the calling of a congress. Charles even orchestrated most of the logistics for that event. Nevertheless, his old enemy, Speaker Galloway, still controlled the Assembly and had every intention of dominating Pennsylvania's delegation. Since Charles, Dickinson and Reed were not current members of the legislature, Galloway shrewdly limited the selection of congressional representatives to Assemblymen. As a result, Mifflin was the only patriot leader included in Pennsylvania's delegation when the First Continental Congress opened that fall. That fact did not prevent Charles from greeting his distinguished guests as they arrived from across the continent. On Tuesday morning, August 30, 1774, he first met John Adams. Later that day, Adams recorded in his diary that "This Charles Thompson [sic] is the Sam Adams of Phyladelphia--the Life of the Cause of Liberty, they say."[42]

Surprisingly, Charles chose that precise moment to marry Hannah Harrison, the wealthy spinster, two years his junior, who had been his traveling companion earlier that summer. Since their marriage took place on September 1, 1774, only weeks after the death of her mother, biographers speculate that issues related to her inheritance most likely delayed an earlier ceremony.[43] When Charles came into the city on the following Monday, September 5, 1774--the day Congress opened--he was informed that the delegates requested his immediate attendance.[44] Earlier that day, Thomas Lynch, Sr. of South Carolina had nominated Charles, "a Gentleman of Family, Fortune, and Character," to be Secretary of Congress.[45]

As Charles entered Carpenters' Hall, where he had devoted so many hours to preparing for that gathering, President Peyton Randolph informed him that "Congress desire the favor of you, sir, to take their minutes." Charles "bowed in acquiescence," and took his seat at the desk."[46] Whether his selection came as a surprise or was carefully scripted "out of doors" (as so many important moments in Congress were), Galloway's "Sworn opposite" had gained admittance, despite the Pennsylvania Speaker's determination to keep him out.[47] Sensing the mood of the body, however, Galloway "did not think it prudent to oppose it."[48] It is ironic that one of the few delegates who did initially object to a non-member serving in that position was John Jay of New York, a future President, who, over the years, would became one of Charles' closest friends and colleagues.[49]

At 9:00 am on Saturday, September 10, 1774, having settled his personal affairs, Charles resumed his official duties as Secretary, which ultimately stretched across the entire fifteen-year history of the Continental Congress.[50] His previous public service had prepared him exceptionally well for that unique and monumental task. The Journal he so faithfully penned year after year eventually grew into 34 printed volumes.[51] In it, Charles recorded almost every official congressional action leading up to, and including, the entire Revolutionary War. In its pages he also captured those critical post-war years when defeat was nearly snatched from the jaws of victory. Since each Journal was eventually published and sent to the States, Charles also maintained two "Secret Journals," (one for foreign affairs, one covering sensitive domestic issues) which only the delegates and top generals were privy to.[52] As he later described his initial method: "... what congress adopted, I committed to writing; with what they rejected, I had nothing farther to do..."[53] His responsibilities, however, extended far beyond pen and parchment. As Secretary, he officially attested to the authenticity of every document and carefully maintained the archives of the new nation.[54] He also oversaw the printing and distribution of congressional documents and assisted the President in maintaining correspondence with state leaders and military officers. As the years passed, his responsibilities steadily grew as new delegates increasingly turned to him as the only source of institutional history.[55]

As a political leader and senior congressional official, Charles continued to interact socially with the delegates throughout his long career. After Congress adjourned for the day on September 12, for example, Charles joined Adams, Mifflin and others for dinner at Dickinson's Fair Hill estate on the outskirts of the city.[56] Twelve days later, Charles and his new wife hosted Adams, Dickinson and others at their home.[57] In the early days, Charles also remained active in Pennsylvania politics. On October 3, John Adams delighted that Charles, Dickinson and Mifflin had all been elected to the Pennsylvania Assembly. He felt certain that it "will make a great Weight in favour of the American Cause."[58] Two immediate results were the replacement of Galloway as Speaker and Dickinson's appointment to Pennsylvania's congressional delegation.[59] What is truly surprising is that unlike all of his congressional colleagues, it was the only time throughout Charles Thomson's long life that he was actually an elected member of a legislative body.

On October 22, Charles recorded the election of Henry Middleton as the second President when Peyton Randolph was called back to Virginia.[60] Four days later, after the Petition to the King had been adopted and signed, the First Continental Congress concluded its work with one final dinner at City Tavern. In appreciation to Charles for his voluntary service, the delegates presented him with a piece of silver plate worth £50 sterling.[61] After the members left Philadelphia, Charles and Dickinson oversaw the publication of the *Journal of the Proceedings of the Congress*.[62] Rhode Island Delegate Samuel Ward later expressed his thanks to Charles for "a Journal extraordinary."[63] Not surprisingly, Galloway was irate. Over the winter he engaged in a journalistic battle with "the Pennsylvania Farmer and his old Assistant Charles Thompson [sic]."[64]

By the time the Second Continental Congress opened on Wednesday, May 10, 1775, American blood had already been shed on Lexington Green and Concord Bridge. Peyton Randolph and Charles Thomson were reelected to their respective offices, but the meetings were henceforth held in the Pennsylvania State House.[65] Congressional membership also saw several significant changes. Galloway had resigned from Congress in disgust and eventually joined the loyalist forces.[66] Benjamin Franklin had just returned to America in time to take his seat. The Massachusetts Delegation also added a powerful and prominent new member, John Hancock, who was elected as the Third President on May 24, when Randolph was again called back to Williamsburg. Replacing him in the

Virginia Delegation was Thomas Jefferson.[67] By mid-June, Washington was selected as Commander-in-Chief of the new Continental Army and Thomas Mifflin traded his legislative duties for a military commission as he rode with Washington to the battlefield in Boston.[68]

When the final debate over Independence began one year later, Charles and his friend, Dickinson, found themselves on opposite sides of that fundamental issue. Dickinson persisted in hoping for reconciliation with the Mother Country and argued that even if a break should become inevitable, Congress was not yet prepared to take on the burden of nationhood.[69] Charles, on the other hand, had long believed that separation was essential for salvation.[70] As Secretary, he had no vote, but when the Declaration of Independence was published in *The Pennsylvania Gazette* on July 10, 1776, the only names that appeared were President John Hancock and Secretary Charles Thomson. The final engrossed parchment (which now resides behind bombproof glass in the National Archives) was not available for the delegates to sign until August 2, 1776.[71]

Despite their political disagreements, the relationship between Charles and his friend Dickinson held strong. Only a few weeks after the vote on Independence, Charles confided to him his personal disgust over military egos when he reported on Gen. John Sullivan's threat to resign "thinking his honour hurt by the promotion of Gates..." "What shall we say of this phantom *honour*, the soldier's deity & object of worship," Charles sarcastically asked. "I would not have a soldier devoid of it; But I think it a plant better suited for the gardens of monarchy; than those of a republic."[72] Unlike so many members of Congress, Charles was never dazzled by a uniform nor did he lust after military glory.[73]

Throughout his long tenure as Secretary, Charles was always conscious of his unique role in the founding of the new nation. His duties continued to increase as Congress struggled with military affairs, fiscal crises and the debate over confederation.[74] During the First American Republic's fifteen-year history, in addition to keeping the official Journal, which he distributed to the States, Charles maintained separate secret journals on both foreign and domestic affairs.[75] He also carefully endorsed and filed committee reports, all official documents and most correspondence. Approximately 50,000 of those papers, which are permanently preserved at the National Archives, are now inventoried in the five-volume *Papers of the Continental Congress*.[76] Charles also monitored legislative developments in the States and even prepared special reports for the delegates, upon request.[77] Despite his herculean task, Charles was nevertheless criticized by some delegates who disagreed with his methods or detected what they perceived to be bias in the performance of his duties, a charge he absolutely denied.

Even though Charles had made clear from the start that he would only record motions that had been adopted in the official Journal, John Adams bitterly complained in his Autobiography that all important debates should also have been recorded, similar to the *Congressional Record* today. In reference to a debate in March 1776, for example, Adams wrote: "Here is an Instance, in addition to many others, of an extraordinary Liberty taken by the Secretary, I suppose at the Instigation of the Party against Independence, to suppress, by omitting on the Journals the many Motions that were made disagreable to that sett. These motions ought to have been inserted verbatim on the Journals, with the names of those who made them."[78] Despite such disagreements, Charles and John Adams did retain their casual relationship. For example, while Congress was briefly billeted in Baltimore, Adams reported to his wife that "Yesterday, I took a long Walk with our Secretary Mr. Thompson..."[79]

On August 2, 1777, Congress reached a compromise when it resolved: "That all proceedings of Congress, and all questions agitated and determined by Congress, be entered on the journal, and that the yeas or nays of each member, if required by any State, be taken on every question as stated and determined by the house."[80] But the work of its various committees--the lifeblood of Congress then, as now--was only included in the Journal when a committee report was actually debated on the floor of Congress and a vote was taken, regardless of the outcome. Sometimes there were exceptions to the rule, and, on occasions, the press of business caused Charles to overlook a specific vote or even record an item incorrectly.[81] A far more frustrating problem for the Secretary, however, was the retrieval of documents that were temporarily loaned to individual members or committees.[82] One task that demanded a tremendous amount of time and energy within the Secretary's office was the process of making multiple copies of documents for the chief executives of each state, military commanders and American foreign diplomats.

What is truly amazing was the overall efficiency of the Secretary's office despite the challenges facing a new nation in the midst of war. Not only did Charles have to create the entire process from scratch, he was also forced to transport his operation on short notice as the British threatened to occupy Philadelphia. The first scare came on December 12, 1776, when Congress relocated to Maryland for over two months. Despite the logistical nightmare, Charles was there at President Hancock's side when the delegates resumed their work in Baltimore on Friday, December 20.[83] After Congress returned to Philadelphia on March 12, 1777, the fear of invasion remained ever constant.[84] Six months later, on the evening of September 18, Congress fled once again as the British Army approached the capital. The delegates first stopped at Lancaster, where they met for only one day--Saturday, September 27, 1777--before seeking safety across the Susquehanna River in York, Pennsylvania. There, on September 30, the Continental Congress settled in for the next nine months as it resumed debate on the proposed Articles of Confederation.[85]

While Congress was in exile, Gen. Howe, the British Commander, gave the order that fall to destroy the country estates of seventeen known patriots. In addition to John Dickinson's mansion, Fair Hill, Charles and Hannah's home, Somerville, was burnt to the ground.[86]

On October 29, after two-and-a-half years as President, Hancock announced to his fellow delegates that he was taking a leave of absence to regain his health. That afternoon, Congress resolved "That the secretary officiate as president until a new choice is made." Over the years, in additional to his other responsibilities, Charles occasionally served in that capacity during brief presidential absences. Three days later, on November 1, 1777, Henry Laurens of South Carolina was elected as the fourth President of Congress.[87]

Randolph and Middleton, the first two Presidents, had been elder statesmen nearing the end of their long and distinguished careers. Hancock, who was eight years younger than Charles, had been well respected for his sober work ethic and widely admired for his gregarious personality. As Secretary, Charles had enjoyed a close working relationship with all three men. Henry Laurens, however, perhaps the hardest working of all fourteen Presidents, was never known for his social graces. He had spent his entire life as a successful, hard-headed businessman who, unlike Hancock, had not inherited his fortune. To President Laurens, five years older than Charles, the Secretary of Congress was not his colleague but his clerk.

During the winter of 1777-78, as the Continental Army struggled through the bitter cold at Valley Forge, the relationship between President Laurens and Secretary Thomson gradually imploded. In early January, Laurens complained to a correspondent that "I have waited much too long" for copies of congressional documents that he had requested from the Secretary's Office.[88] In March, when the Pay Master of the Northern Department complained to the President that he had been addressed incorrectly in a recent letter, the President placed the blame on the Secretary. When Charles responded, Laurens "received a reply so rugged, as had nearly carried me beyond the limits within which every Gentleman will confine himself in a Public Assembly." The President "treated the asperity of Mr. Secretary with silent contempt, & appealed by reading Your [the complainant's] Letter, to Congress." Charles ended the debate when he cited related Resolutions to prove the accuracy of his original advice.[89]

On April 21, 1778, President Laurens again cited a specific example where, in his opinion, "The Secretary persists in keeping the Journal thus unfairly misrepresenting the proceedings of the House."[90] Back in Philadelphia on September 27, after the British had withdrawn, Laurens confided to New York Gov. George Clinton that "All our Public Offices, which have hitherto been conducted as well, I presume, as circumstances in an infant State would admit of, now call for inspection and improvement, and none more than the Secretary's Office..."[91] On December 9, 1778, Laurens turned his anger on Congress itself during the investigation of Arthur Lee's accusations concerning Silas Deane's management of public funds overseas.[92] In a fiery speech to the delegates, President Laurens tendered his resignation. John Jay of New York, who supported Deane in the bitter Lee-Deane Affair, was elected as the fifth President the following day.[93]

The Lee-Deane Affair bitterly divided Congress for years. At one point, Richard Henry Lee of Virginia, another future President and the elder brother of Arthur Lee, drug Charles into the argument by accusing him of withholding evidence that Deane had given the British a copy of the preliminary treaty of alliance with the French.[94] Lee thus sided with Laurens in his criticism of the Secretary. In May 1779, in a private letter to Laurens, Richard Henry Lee scathingly denounced Charles "as unfit to be the Secretary of Congress as any other W-h-e in Philadelphia." Analyzing that statement, researchers at the Library of Congress concluded that "Despite the confusion of how Lee placed his dashes, he was doubtless suggesting that Charles Thomson was no more to be trusted than a common whore."[95] Their feud lasted for years.

The dispute with Laurens exploded on September 1, 1779, when the former President brought charges against Charles before a congressional committee. "My complaint against the Secretary of Congress for disrespectful behavior to a Member of that Assembly probably would not have been made on the circumstances of Yesterday," Henry stated, "had not his behavior upon that occasion been an unprovoked repetition of insults which the Secretary had at divers preceding times offered to Delegates of Congress and to myself in particular." Laurens then recited several perceived slights over the previous two years before detailing the latest incident: "The particular complaint made Yesterday, is of Mr. Thomson's affrontive answers when I requested him to let me have only two Copies of the Journal for my State...His first answer was--I won't. I replied, you won't Mr. Thomson, what language is this? I tell you I want them for my State--to which he again answered, I won't, but added, till I have given every Member present one; Mr. Thomson then descended from the Platform;

I reached out my hand to take another Copy, he snatched from me and said, you shan't have it--this repeated insult brought instantly to my mind his former conduct & provoked me to say, he was a most impudent fellow, that I had a good mind to kick him; he turned about, doubled his fist and said you dare not, I recollected the time and place and let him pass on. When he had humoured himself he returned with many spare Journals in his hands and gave me one, I barely asked him if he might not as well have done this at first."[96]

In his defense five days later, Charles told the Committee that "Of the five presidents under whom...I have had the honor to serve Congress, I flatter myself I enjoyed the confidence, esteem & friendship of four; and I deem it unfortunate that I cannot boast the same of the one who is the present complainant." Charles argued that his initial efforts to establish a rapport with President Laurens had been consistently rebuffed and "I confess freely that I was too proud a spirit to brook indignities and that I scorned to court any man however high in office, by fawning, cringing or servility." Charles stated that even though Laurens had "continued by a thousand undescribable ways to tease, irritate and provoke me...I wished to forget them, that I might preserve some respect for a man so highly honoured by his country." Now that charges had been filed against him, however, Charles responded in detail to each of the six specific complaints, concluding with his view of the recent confrontation over the Journals. In conclusion, he told the committee that "I have now lived fifty years and never before received such an insult."[97]

To the relief of the committee members, on September 8 John Dickinson managed to reach an understanding with both litigants whereby Charles made clear that "it was not my Intention to give him [Laurens] any Offence...and that it...is my wish on all Occasions to treat him with Respect." In response, Laurens agreed that "I shall at all Times treat Mr [Thomson] with Respect--and...I am willing, that the Committee should obtain Leave of Congress to be discharged from making a Report."[98] Even though this ended the formal proceedings, Charles later added a stinging notation on the file copy of the proceedings: "This outrageous language & insolent behaviour may be attributed to his [Laurens] want of education and to his having been bred among negro slaves over whom he had been accustomed to tyrannize & against whom he could vent his ill hummours & turbulent passions not only with impunity but to effect."[99]

At the end of that month, John Jay relinquished the chair in order to accept his latest assignment as Minister to Spain. The following day, September 28, 1779, Samuel Huntington of Connecticut was elected America's sixth President.[100] Five week's later, when the Connecticut

Delegates' credentials temporarily expired, Charles again presided over Congress--from November 4-9--until President Huntington was able to resume his duties.[101] Despite the press of daily business, Charles was also eager "to facilitate the transmitting to posterity the rise & progress of these infant States..."[102] He hoped "to have as complete a collection of the public papers of every state as I can deposited here..."[103] In return, he pledged to send congressional Journals to the States on a more frequent basis.

In early January 1780, Charles' refusal to suffer fools gladly apparently led to a brief physical altercation with a little-known Pennsylvania delegate, James Searle. The only mention of the event is found in Samuel Holten's diary: "Mr. Searle cained the secy. of Congress, & the secy returned the same salute."[104] On March 20, 1780, Virginia's newest delegate--James Madison--began his long congressional career. Unlike Searle, Madison never resorted to physical violence but he occasionally did criticize the accuracy of Charles' Journal and even kept his own notes at one point.[105]

At the end of 1780--Christmas Day, to be exact--Charles sent a long and surprisingly optimistic letter to Dickinson despite the fact that Charleston was then occupied and the Treasury was empty. "After many fruitless attempts and a war of six years," Charles wrote, "our enemies must be convinced that it is not in their power to subdue us by force... their hopes of subjugating us, if they still retain any, must rest wholly on the derangement of our finances." In confronting that fiscal crisis, Charles believed that "The people of America are in general sensible and intelligent; Convince them that taxes are necessary and they will cheerfully pay them. It appears to me that during the present controversy, the people have been always readier to pay than the legislatures to lay or call for taxes."

"The United States are just entering upon the stage of political existence," Charles stated. "The novelty of their appearance will naturally attract the attention of other nations and from our conduct at our first outset they will form their opinions with regard to our character and the rank we are to sustain among them...If we exert ourselves with zeal and vigor in defending our rights and maintaining our fredom, we shall be honored and respected and will meet with countenance and support." He reminded Dickinson that "When we first engaged in this contest we declared that rather than submit to the domination of Britain we would sacrifice not only our fortunes but our lives. This is now the time," Charles argued, "to demonstrate the sincerity of those declarations."[106]

Charles' optimism seemed partially fulfilled when the Articles of Confederation, which had finally been ratified, went into effect on March 1, 1781.[107] Even though President Huntington and Secretary Thomson retained their positions without any interruption, the day to day operation of government began to shift from countless committee to established departments. On May 14, Congress received Robert Morris' letter of acceptance to serve as Superintendent of Finance. On August 10, Robert R. Livingston of New York was elected as Secretary for Foreign Affairs.[108] As part of that transformation, Charles reported to Dickinson that "Congress have ordered my accounts to be settled up to the first of March last and have acknowledged the public endebted to me to that day in the sum of five thusand some hundred dollars specie value. But," he added, "when they will be enabled to pay me I know not."[109]

On July 6, 1781, having served 21 months as President, Samuel Huntington submitted his resignation to Congress because of "his ill state of health..." Three days later, Samuel Johnston of North Carolina was elected to succeed him, but he declined because he was determined to return home.[110] On July 10, Thomas McKean, a delegate from Delaware and the Chief Justice of Pennsylvania, agreed to accept the position, but only until his Court reopened in the fall.[111] McKean thus became the seventh President of Congress and the first elected under the Articles of Confederation. When the news that Cornwallis had surrendered at Yorktown reached Congress on October 24, McKean agreed to postpone his own departure at such a critical moment. Edmund Randolph of Virginia, the favorite nephew of the late Peyton Randolph, the first President, at once offered a motion that a service of thanksgiving be held that same afternoon.[112] One week later, as the victorious troops marched through Philadelphia, President McKean received the captured flags.[113]

On the first Monday of November (the date prescribed in the Articles for the annual opening of Congress), John Hanson of Maryland was elected, for a set term of one year, as the eighth President.[114] Charles also used this transitional moment to revise several procedures within his Office. Henceforth, all information pertaining to committees and committee appointments would be recorded in a new Committee Book rather than the official Journal. In similar fashion, letters sent and received would only be listed in his Dispatch Book.[115] On January 28, 1782, Congress decided to transfer primary responsibility for most official correspondence from the elderly President to the heads of the executive departments, especially the Secretary.[116] Charles, however, was not an empire builder. When he felt that an issue fell under the purview of another department, he did not hesitate to forward the pertinent documents to one of his colleagues.[117]

By May 1782, even though New York City and Charleston were still occupied by British troops, Congress had adopted some of the trappings of a European Court. When French Minister La Luzerne was "granted an audience" to announce the birth of the Dauphin (the royal heir), the

President sat "in a chair on a platform raised two steps from the floor with a large table before him. The members of Congress in chairs on the floor to his right and left...The Secretary of the United States in Congress assembled stood on the right of the president on the first step of the platform."[118] In a later debate, Arthur Lee (by then a member of Congress) argued that "Gentlemen might despise etiquette...but... Every civilized nation had found it necessary to settle it. We should not affect to be wiser than all the world."[119]

Charles was also instrumental in designing the Great Seal of the United States. Three previous committees--one of which included Franklin, Jefferson and John Adams--had failed to win congressional approval. Working with William Barton, "a young Philadelphia lawyer with a knowledge of heraldry," Charles sketched out the design of the American Eagle with an olive branch in one talon and arrows in the other. He also kept the *E Pluribus Unum* (From Many One) motto proposed earlier. Charles, the former Latin scholar, then inserted the phrases *Annuit Coeptis* (He Has Favored Our Undertaking) and *Novus Ordo Seclorum* (A New Order of the Ages) on the opposite side.[120] The Great Seal was finally adopted by Congress on June 20, 1782.[121] For the rest of his term as Secretary, Charles took enormous pride in being the keeper of the Great Seal which he affixed to all official papers.[122]

As mandated by the Articles of Confederation, the new Congress opened its annual session on Monday, November 4, 1782. John Hanson, who died one year later, was more than eager to turn over his Office to New Jersey Delegate Elias Boudinot who was elected the ninth President that same day.[123] Three days later, Charles' old friend, John Dickinson, was elected President of the State of Pennsylvania (in effect, Governor).[124]

On November 11, Charles' focus switched to his dedicated staff when he informed Superintendent Robert Morris that "one of the clerks in My Office died yesterday and has left a widow advanced in years & very infirm, in low circumstances." Charles urged assistance for the woman since his clerk's last illness "has involved expence above his circumstances & his past services merit some reward above his pay."[125] In similar fashion, when his deputy, George Bond, retired the following year, Charles arranged for him to received a $500 bonus in appreciation for his service.[126]

On January 15, 1783, Congress was informed by Gen. Greene that Charleston had finally been evacuated by the British in mid-December. Charles immediately notified several Philadelphia newspapers.[127] Throughout these years, his role as Secretary continued to grow. In late February, when a debate arose over which types of motions required nine votes rather than seven, Madison recorded that "Some were of opinion that the Secretary ought to make an entry according to his own judgment and that that entry sd. stand unless altered by a positive instruciton from Congs." Some objected, saying that "it wd. make the Secy. the Sovereign in many cases, since a reversal of his entry wd. be impossible." The issue was never resolved.[128] The next major development concerning the Secretary's position occurred in early June when Robert R. Livingston, the Secretary for Foreign Affairs, submitted his resignation. Charles was directed "to receive into my care the papers of your Office till a successor can be appointed." Charles informed Livingston that "I am determined to have nothing to do with the business of the Office..."[129] That commitment proved to be very difficult at times since the position went unfilled for over a year.

Saturday, June 21, 1783, marked a pivotal moment in the history of the Continental Congress. As 500 disgruntled soldiers demanding back pay surrounded the State House, where both Congress and the Pennsylvania Assembly were in session, the delegates voted to withdraw from the city if their safety could not be guaranteed. Throughout the weekend, Alexander Hamilton negotiated in vain with State officials while Major Gen. Arthur St. Clair, a future President, attempted to disperse the troops. When Pennsylvania authorities refused to take action, President Boudinot sent word that the delegates would reconvene in New Jersey, his home State.[130]

When Congress met in Princeton, New Jersey, at the end of June,[131] most members assumed that it would be only a brief interlude until the crisis passed. But, as events unfolded, the Continental Congress would never again return to Philadelphia. That fact not only worked a tremendous hardship on many, like Charles, who called Philadelphia home, but it clearly helped to hasten the end of the First American Republic as Congress repeatedly switched from one location to another, thereby making a quorum increasingly difficult to attain.

Not only did Charles have to pack and relocate the Secretary's Office, by now a sizable undertaking, but the relocation to Princeton (June 30-November 4, 1783)[132] also marked the longest separation that he and his devoted wife would ever endure. The one benefit that derived from their painful separation was a treasure trove of letters that provide a remarkable insight into that period. On the first day, Charles "found the members extremely out of humour and dissatisfied with their situation." Despite that fact, as Charles reported to his wife, some members "could never think of returning unless the citizens of Philadelphia would make reparation for the wounded honor of Congress." Charles, however, was eager to go home and "wished them to consult their reason and not their passions..." Charles was especially angry at his old friend John Dickinson, then the President of Pennsylvania, for his failure to apologize to Congress. "I fear that his cursed pride will undo his country. He has his virtues but they are suited to other times." Even President Boudinot told Charles that same evening that "this place would not do...that Congress must either go back to Philada. or remove to some other place."[133]

In his next letter in early July, Charles told Hannah that "I see folly, weakness and passion marking the characters of those who ought to be distinguished by their wisdom and prudence." Furthermore, since only seven States had arrived, no major business could yet be transacted. [134] On July 4, President Boudinot hosted a dinner to celebrate the anniversary of Independence but the celebration fell flat because the fireworks failed to arrive in time. "I confess," Charles wrote, "I was very little entertained, and wished myself, a thousand times in Philadelphia with my dear Hannah."[135] Two days later, on a more serious note, Charles confided to Hannah that "when I look forward I see a dark cloud and gloomy prospects for America.... Those jarring principles which were kept down by common danger [i.e., the war] begin to operate. And pride & passion seem to occupy the seat of reason."[136]

On July 23, Congress received a petition which had been drafted by Thomas Paine and signed by 873 citizens of Philadelphia, urging the government to return. But, when Dickinson and the State failed to endorse the petition, the delegates dismissed it.[137] Two days later, Charles lamented that "private and not public views too frequently influence the conduct of men at the helm of government...I confess I have my fears, that the predictions of our enemies will be found true, that on the removal of common danger our Confederacy & Union will be a rope of sand." "Were I to hazard a conjecture," he wrote, "it would be that the four eastern states will form one confederacy...New Y will be compelled to join this confederacy either voluntarily or by force...New Jersey, Pennsylvania, Delaware and Maryland will form another Union." As for the oldest and largest State: "The haughtiness of Virginia...will induce it to set up for itself. And if ever royal government is set up in N. America, here it will first erect its throne." For the remaining three Southern States, Charles feared that they "may league together but without any close confederacy. For such is the fiery pride of South Carolina..." he predicted with uncanny accuracy, "she will not cordially join in any Union till she is taught wisdom by sore suffering."[138]

At the end of July, Charles wrote that "every day's experience evinces that this is not a proper place." Nevertheless, he told Hannah: "For my own part I am determined to continue. I have contributed as much as in my power to erect the building & it shall tumble about my ears before I quit it."[139] His mood continued to darken over the next week. "I am in such a dull, stupid humour," he told her, "that I may be said to exist not to live...I long to see you and to be roused from this apathy."[140] Fortunately, Charles was able to journey home to Philadelphia to see his wife for several days in mid-August.[141] A few weeks after he returned to Princeton, Charles had regained some of his optimism when he stated that "I entertain a fond hope that the same kind providence which has conducted us so far in our journey will open a way for the future happiness and prosperity of the United States."[142] In late August, Gen. Washington also arrived in Princeton at the invitation of Congress. For nearly two months he leisurely consulted with the delegates on post-war policies as the entire government waited anxiously for news concerning the final peace treaty.[143]

Occasionally, Charles would apologize to Hannah for his long political tirades. "You see, my dear, what it is to have a politician for a husband. Instead of love letters you are only to be entertained with business or politics." He confessed that "my mind has been lately much agitated and I have deliberated very seriously on my future plan of life." Of one thing he was certain, "My comfort and happiness greatly depends upon being with you." Looking toward the future, Charles wrote "that I thought I might upon the return of peace and the attainment of those blessings for which we contended, continue to enjoy the profits arising from my Office, especially as the office is necessary and I flatter myself I should not be unservicable to my country in the exercise of it...But I must premise that when I retire it will not be to ease and affluence. I must attend to some business for our support. However as our wants are not many and our expenses not very great, I think by attention to our farms we may live decently without much trouble or uneasiness of mind."[144]

On September 8, 1783, Congress elected John Rutledge of South Carolina to serve as Chairman in the absence of the President. The next day, since both President Boudinot and Chairman Rutledge were not in attendance, Congress elected Daniel Carroll of Maryland to fill the Chair.[145] Charles described this process as "carrying republicanism beyond even the Dutch. They have their president of the week, Congress their chairman of the day." He sadly confided to Hannah that "experience [shows?] that though a seat in Congress may give great self importance it does not in an equal degree confer wisdom and prudence."[146]

That fall, Charles initiated a monthly "Memorandum Book" in which his clerks recorded the work the Secretary's Office performed for the delegates.[147] During that same period, debate intensified concerning the selection of a permanent home for Congress. Charles favored "a delightful

Spot" in Pennsylvania along the Delaware River, just opposite Trenton, New Jersey. He hoped it would "hereafter be distinguished by the name of *Statesburg*."[148] For political reasons, the delegates considered building two capitals, one in the Eastern or Middle States and one in the South. "But in the present state of affairs," Charles wrote, "to talk of building cities, when they can scarcely furnish money to buy paper on which to draw a plan of them...appears to me something different from wisdom, prudence or policy."[149] Setting reality aside, Charles reported on October 21, that "The dye is cast."[150] Congress did agree to construct two capitals, one along the banks of the Delaware River and another along the Potomac. During the interim, Congress would meet "alternately at equal periods...in Trenton and Annapolis."[151]

On October 31, news finally reached Congress that the definitive peace treaty had been signed in Paris. The delegates heaved a huge sigh of relief. The following Monday, November 3, 1783, marked the opening of the new Congress. Former Major Gen. Thomas Mifflin of Pennsylvania, who was not in attendance, was unanimously elected as the tenth President. In his absence, Maryland Delegate Daniel Carroll was asked to serve as Chairman until Congress completed its work in Princeton the following day.[152]

When Congress attempted to reconvene at the Maryland State House in Annapolis on November 26, 1783, poor attendance forced the delegates to adjourn from day to day until Saturday, December 13, when seven States finally constituted a quorum.[153] Unfortunately, nine States were required to ratify the final peace treaty, copies of which had to be exchanged by Great Britain and the United States in Paris no later than March 3, 1784. Tension steadily increased as the deadline grew closer. For Charles, the move, as always, produced a special hardship. In response to a request for information from one correspondent, he was forced to reply that "The papers in my Office are so deranged by the removal that I cannot send you any thing except a copy of the journals as far as they are printed..."[154]

Despite the challenges facing Congress, Tuesday, December 23, 1783, marked the crowning moment of the American Revolution. That morning, as directed, Gen. Washington and his closest military aides entered the State House in full uniform, where they were greeted by President Mifflin, Secretary Thomson, other department heads and the members of Congress. After brief remarks, the Commander-in-Chief surrendered his commission to the President of Congress and withdrew.[155] Unlike most great military victories throughout history, civilian rule had triumphed. The new Republic had survived!

A quorum of nine States was finally established on Wednesday, January

14, 1784. The peace treaty was immediately brought before the body and unanimously ratified. The delegates promised "that we will sincerely and faithfully perform and observe" its provisions and "never suffer them to be violated by any one or transgressed in any manner as far as lies in our power." The votes of New Hampshire and New Jersey were not counted since only one delegate was present from each (two were required under the Articles of Confederation). New York and Georgia were absent.[156]

Charles immediately wrote to congratulate both Franklin and Jay. He assured Franklin that "I have a great confidence in the good sense of my country men in general..." Then, looking toward the future, Charles added: "Though you and I have lived to see a great work accomplished, yet much still remains to be done to secure the happiness of this Country." To Jay, Charles confided that "There has been a scene for six months past over which I would wish to draw a veil...However the prospect begins to brighten and as I love to indulge a hope which corresponds with my fond wishes I flatter myself that prudence and good sense will prevail."[157]

The struggle, however, was still not officially over. If ratified copies of the Treaty were not exchanged in Paris by the deadline, either side was free to reopen negotiations. The formal end of hostilities was now hostage to the calendar as three copies were entrusted to three different couriers to avoid any mishap. Shipping schedules and rough seas, however, conspired against them. It was almost five weeks after Congress had ratified the document before any of the three copies successfully set sail.[158] Fortunately, when Henry Laurens (who was in Bath, England attempting to regain his health) requested that the deadline be extended, he was assured by David Hartley, the British negotiator, that an extension of the deadline would not be necessary "as the delay in America appears to have arisen merely in consequence of the inclemency of the season."[159]

Charles was relieved when Congress received the news from Laurens, but he could not forget the painful experiences of recent months. He candidly shared his feelings in a letter to Pennsylvania Delegate Richard Peters who had recently resigned: "Considering what a deep share I have taken in this controversy and how anxious I have ever been not only for the success of our cause but for the honor and dignity of the United States...a recollection of the events which have taken place these six months past must give me the most pungent pain...But now that the war is closed with honor and success and the Eyes of all Europe are turned upon that council which it was supposed directed the measures of this Continent in high expectation of seeing traits of wisdom, dignity and prudence, and what a scene they have exhibited? Oh that it could be oblitereated from the annals of America & utterly effaced from my memory!"[160]

Because Hannah had also moved to Annapolis, even Charles' mood could not prevent him from enjoying the Maryland capital's charms. "Coming to the gay city of Annapolis where pleasure holds her court, is it to be conceived that I, old & experienced as I am, could be so bad a courtier as not to conform to her customs...I have attended Balls, plays & assemblies and...Mrs. T. has had her tea parties dignified with the title of *Conversations*."[161] Congress, however, was still only a dim reflection of its former self.

Jefferson shared his true feelings that spring with Count van Hogendorp, one of several European travelers who could not resist publishing their observations. "The members of Congress are no longer, generally speaking, men of worth or of distinction," Jefferson told the Count. "For Congress is not, as formerly, held in respect...Moreover the government of the States and the foreign missions absorb the men of first rank in the Union." Jefferson described Congress as "composed of rich and frivolous young men; old men from the country who ignore what goes on in the world; officers, who, having no longer military status enter into this national assembly out of vanity, perhaps lawyers who appear only when the State who elects them needs their help...and, in short, of few men who, gifted with high principles and the necessary attainments, have enough patriotism to sacrifice their private purposes to the public interest."[162] Charles wholeheartedly agreed: "I wish the states would send forward men of enlarged Minds & conciliating tempers."[163]

Through it all, Charles was the pragmatist who kept the wheels of government turning through good times and bad. In May 1784, when Congress switched its attention to securing commercial treaties with other nations, it was Charles who personally oversaw the twenty separate commissions that were issued "for treating with the Courts" of Russia, Germany, Prussia, Denmark, Saxony, Hamburg, England, Spain, Portugal, Naples, Sardinia, Venice, Genoa, Tuscany, The Porte, Morocco, Algiers, Tunis, Tripoli and, despite Congress' anti-Catholic bias, even The Pope (then temporal ruler of the Papal States). In addition to the commissions, Charles also prepared duplicate copies of the "Instructions for Negotitating Treaties of Amity and Commerce" which earlier had been approved by Congress.[164] That same month, Congress elected former President Jay as the new Secretary for Foreign Affairs.[165] When Charles informed Jay of the election, he stressed that "it is not only time but highly necessary for us to think and act like a sovereign as well as a free people."[166]

On Thursday, June 3, 1784, Congress voted to adjourn for nearly five months, scheduling its next session for Trenton, New Jersey in the fall. To fill the interim, the delegates established a Committee of the States (one member from each State) as authorized in the Articles of Confederation.[167] This new body initially met in Annapolis the following day and elected Delegate Samuel Hardy of Virginia as its Chairman. Charles attended the Committee's first meeting and helped to staff the new group.[168] He then turned over those tasks to his new deputy, Benjamin Bankson, and returned to Philadelphia in order to organize his files and enjoy a much needed rest after a decade of congressional service.[169] Twenty times that summer the Committee was able to muster a quorum, but little was actually accomplished.[170]

Writing from his home in Philadelphia on July 28, Charles informed the Committee of the States that he had just received a letter from Franklin in Paris confirming that the ratified treaties had been exchanged on the evening of May 12, 1784. "Thus," Franklin wrote, "the great and hazardous interprize we have been engaged in, is, God be praised, happily compleated...an event I hardly expected I should live to see." Franklin also cautioned his countrymen that "our future safety will depend on our Union and our virtue. Britain will be long watching for advantages to recover what she has lost."[171] In his reply, Charles told Franklin that "From the first appeal to arms, through the whole contest, I never had a doubt of the issue; but I was afraid it would come upon us before we had acquired national principles, habits and sentiments, which would enable us to improve it to advantage and to act becoming our station and dignity."[172]

When the delegates from New Hampshire, Massachusetts and New Jersey left Annapolis on August 11, the remaining six members acknowledged that the experiment had failed.[173] Jacob Read, the South Carolina member of the Committee, told Charles that "we are rendered Useless & impotent."[174] Charles immediately wrote to the Chairman: "Can it be possible that gentlemen will take such a rash step as to dissolve the Commee. and leave the United States without any head or visible authority?"[175] Chairman Hardy responded that "Its tendency to lessen the dignity of the foederal Government in the Eyes of our own Citizens as well as those of foreigners cannot be denied." But, in the Committee's defense, Hardy pointed out that they had been left "without a Competent Number to proceed to business."[176] On August 19, the remaining members asked Charles to take possession of its records and urged that a new Committee be appointed to meet in either Philadelphia or Trenton.[177]

Once again, the Secretary of Congress had to do his best to fill the congressional void. Over the next two and a half months Charles served as the only visible symbol of the newest nation on Earth. In the opinion of at least one author, the Secretary's ever-expanding role made Charles the de facto Prime Minister.[178] It was an awesome responsibility. On September

18, he wrote to Jay, who was back in New York: "I wish exceedingly to see and converse with you not only on the subject of your acceptance but on the general State of our Affairs." Charles pointed out that not only had the Committee of the States disbanded but that their mutual friend, Robert Morris, was "winding up his Affairs so as to quit his Office" and that their "Ministers abroad are left wholly to themselves without the least information of what is passing here."[179]

In late September 1784, five States--Georgia, South Carolina, Virginia, Delaware and Pennsylvania--did send representatives to Philadelphia in the hope of establishing a new Committee of the States, but they never attained a quorum.[180] Charles shared his frustration with his friend Jefferson who was by then serving in Paris: "Though this invisibility of a foederal head will have little effect on our affairs here, or on the minds of the citizens of the United States who can easily reconcile themselves to it...yet I am apprehensive it will have an ill aspect in the eyes of European Nations & give them unfavourable impressions, which will require all your address & abilities to remove."[181]

On Monday, November 1, 1784, only six delegates from five States had assembled at the French Arms Tavern in Trenton, the unlikely seat of the new government.[182] While waiting for additional delegates, Charles made arrangements to bring the President's furniture, household items and coach to Trenton.[183] When Congress finally reached a quorum on November 30, Richard Henry Lee of Virginia, "a leading member of the anti-Thomson faction," was elected as the eleventh President.[184] Three weeks later, Charles confided to Dickinson that "I fear much that public calamity and a sad experience of the evils that will result from disunion will alone convince us of the advantages resulting from a foederal government and the necessity of preserving it."[185]

In late December, two important developments took place in Trenton which gave Charles renewed hope. On December 20, Congress reversed its vote of the previous year to establish two permanent capitals.[186] The next day, John Jay was sworn in as the new Secretary for Foreign Affairs.[187] Together, Charles and his friend Jay would attempt to stabilize the ship of state during its final years.

On Christmas Eve 1784, prior to adjournment, Congress voted to reconvene in New York City early the next year.[188] When Charles left for New York in January, Hannah accompanied him for a brief visit before returning to Philadelphia. She found the city "more agreeable than I expected."[189] Surprisingly, unlike the lengthy delays of the past, a quorum was established by Thursday, January 13.[190] As President Lee selected an elegant mansion at 3 Cherry Street that would serve as the official presidential residence for the remainder of the First Republic (as well as President Washington's first home after his inauguration), Congress settled into its eighth capitol at City Hall.[191]

In early March, Charles notified Gen. Henry Knox that Congress had elected him to serve as Secretary of War.[192] Charles also found time to catch up on some of his personal correspondence. In an exchange of letters with Jefferson, they, as always, not only wrote about politics, but traded information on new scientific instruments and shared observations on agriculture, climate and even the heavens. Charles confessed, however, that "My time and attention are so engrossed with the duties and business of my office that I have no leisure for those philosophical researches I once was so fond of. And from what I can observe," he wrote, "Congress seemed disposed rather to increase than to lessen those duties."[193] Since Hannah was back in Philadelphia, Charles had resumed their intimate correspondence. He described his "dark and gloomy" room which didn't even look out onto the street.[194]

Charles also informed Hannah that he had attended a recent conference concerning a bill in the New York legislature which called for the gradual abolition of slavery. He mentioned that "our old acquaintance [Thomas] Paine" was one of the key participants. (In a footnote to this letter, the researchers at the Library of Congress noted that "The paucity of commentary on the subject of antislavery in the surviving congressional correspondence is striking." The researchers pointed out that the preceding year, Congress had "voted on and rejected a report recommending that a Quaker appeal for ending the slave trade be referred to the states."[195] In contrast, Indian Affairs received a great deal of attention from Congress over the years. Various wars and negotiations were conducted with a wide range of Indian Tribes.[196] The Indians, however, were seldom the beneficiaries as they were steadily pushed further from the Atlantic coast as white settlers continued to move westward.[197])

On April 3, 1785, Charles updated Hannah on the most recent efforts of his congressional enemies, led by Elbridge Gerry, to drive him from Office. Their plan had been to enhance the powers of the Secretary of Congress, especially in relation to the States, but require that annual elections be held to fill the Office, thereby removing Charles from that position.[198] "I had strong suspicions that the moving this matter originated in the ambition of one and the malice and resentment of another..." he told her.[199] By now Charles was even convinced that Arthur Lee had tried twice to poison him, once in Princeton an again in Annapolis.[200] Charles assured her that his enemies had acted "with so little skill in political manoeuvres" that it became obvious that they were motivated by "an object of ambition rather than of public utility..." When the vote was taken on March 31, his career was secure and his powers enhanced.[201]

Once his immediate future was resolved, Charles returned to Philadelphia the weekend of April 16 to complete arrangements for moving Hannah and their large household, including a cow, to New York (in his absence, his deputy kept the Journal from April 18 through May 6).[202] While home, Charles took the time to write to Washington (now a private citizen) concerning the preservation of the General's papers.[203] Back in New York, Charles had selected an elegant house for their residence; but first, as Hannah reported to a friend, "Our landlord is a cleansing the house...with paper & paint from top to bottom, which prevents us from unpacking, 'til that is done. It also excuses me from accepting of Invitations out as my cloaths are not unpacked."[204] For the first time in almost two years, the United States finally had a real capital. Most government departments had been ordered to move to New York by the beginning of May.[205]

On Friday, May 20, 1785, Congress adopted "An Ordinance for ascertaining the mode of disposing of Lands in the Western Territory," the first important step toward settling that vast frontier. One week later, after the documents had been copied by his staff, Charles forward the Ordinance to the Governors of each State.[206] Charles wrote to the Governors again on June 9, notifying them that Congress had passed a Resolution "That... recommended to the several States, to make provision for Officers, soldiers or seamen, who have been disabled in the service of the United States..." He stressed that "the condition of many of these unfortunate Men, who have a claim not merely on the humanity but on the gratitude & Justice of their Country, demands immediate attention."[207]

In mid-July, in a letter to Dickinson--still the chief executive of Pennsylvania--Charles articulated his plan for leading Congress out of its current morass. "It must be allowed that the federal government is weak and inefficient," he wrote. "But the question is to what cause is this owing? To an imperfection in the Confederation or to a deficit in the constitutions of the several States?" Borrowing from Shakespeare, he told Dickinson that "There is a tide in the opinions as well as affairs of a people which if carefully watched and improved facilitate great events." Charles believed that the first step required was to vest Congress "with the power of regulating trade & raising a revenue by duties on importations." He argued that once that was done and "the benefits arising from it being sensibly felt, the minds of the people will be better disposed for granting other necessary powers and the federal government will without any convulsion be gradually improved."[208]

By the summer of 1785, Charles was sending out detailed attendance lists to shame absent States into dispatching their delegates and ordering the Treasurer of the United States "to remove to this place by the first of October..."[209] The fact that President Lee was absent from mid-August through the end of September because of his health further increased the Secretary's responsibilities even though Samuel Holton of Massachusetts served as interim Chairman.[210] On August 17, Congress directed Charles to transmit monthly attendance lists to each State; and, on August 29, the body transferred "additional duties to the Secretary when it relieved the delegates "of the housekeeping chores previously performed by the committees of the week;.[211] The Secretary's role had morphed into an unacknowledged Home Office.

On September 21, 1785, Charles wrote a brief letter to Franklin, welcoming him back to America: "Being deprived of the pleasure of waiting on you in person, I embrace the earliest opportunity, with all the warmth and all the sincerity of friendship to congratulate you on your safe arrival and heartily welcome you to your native country."[212] His tone was decidedly different when he wrote Samuel Elbert, the Governor of Georgia, in early October: "Not having received an answer to my letters of 28th & 31st May, 2d & 9th June, 28th July, 24th & 29th August, I take the liberty of referring to them, not doubting but the resolutions of Congress therewith transmitted will in due time be attended to."[213]

In his next letter to Jefferson, in early November, Charles described slavery as "a cancer that we must get rid of. It is a blot in our character," he said, "that must be wiped out. If it cannot be done by religion, reason & philosophy," he accurately predicted,"confident I am that it will one day be by blood." Charles confessed that "I am more afraid of this than of Algerine piracies or the jealousy entertained of us by European powers." He concluded by again pointing out to Jefferson that "the duties of my office are much enlarged."[214]

The new congressional year began on November 4, 1785, but a quorum did not assemble until Wednesday, November 23, at which time former President John Hancock was elected to return to the seat he previously occupied. In his absence, Delegate David Ramsay of South Carolina was selected to serve as Chairman.[215] Hancock, who had recently relinquished the Governorship of Massachusetts, repeatedly promised to journey to New York as soon as his health would permit. The long wait did not improve Congress' reputation despite Ramsay's dedication and the Secretary's best efforts. Fortunately, unlike Princeton or Trenton, New York did provide plenty of distractions. Hannah reported that "This City is grown very gay Plays 3 times a week an Assembly and Concert every other Thursday."[216] Above all, Hannah was there at his side.

On February 1, 1786, Charles sent a circular letter to all of the States informing them that "So few States have attended that for these three months past little has been done besides adjourning from day to day."[217] He sent another plea to the Governors of Rhode Island, Delaware and North Carolina toward the end of February: "...since the first Monday in Novr there have seldom been even seven states represented and never above eight so that it was impossible to take up the great business of the Confederacy. What the result may be of this inattention of the states to the Concerns of the Union, is uncertain; but I hope your Excellency will use your Endeavours to urge the Attendance of your Delegates as speedily as possible..."[218]

Despite the legislative imbroglio, the young government did address Indian affairs. Between November 1785 and late January 1786, it signed treaties with the Cherokees, Choctaws, Chickasaws and the Shawnees.[219] That April, Charles notified the Governors concerning these developments: "Considering how much the security, comfort and happiness of the frontier settlements depend on being at peace with the neighbouring Indians, and how important it is to the whole Confederacy that the Savages on our borders be impressed with a sacred regard for treaties and with a firm, unshaken confidence in our justice, honor and national faith solemnly pledged, I have no doubt but your Exy will exert the means in your power to enforce a due observance of the several articles of these treaties so far as they concern your state."[220]

Charles' optimism broke through in a letter to Jefferson that same month. "I will venture to assert," he wrote, "there is not upon the face of the earth a body of people more happy or rising into consequence with more rapid strides than the inhabitants of the United States of America... and what is more, the people are well clad, well fed, and well housed." In his response later that month, Jefferson touched on their mutual interest in science when he described "the application of steam as an agent for working grist mills." Jefferson accurately predicted that it is "likely to have extensive consequences."[221]

Since Hancock had not yet arrived, David Ramsay continued to serve as Chairman until May 12, when his term as a South Carolina delegate expired. On May 15, Nathaniel Gorham of Massachusetts was selected to fill the Chair.[222] Finally, on June 5, 1786, Congress was notified that, because of poor health, John Hancock had reluctantly submitted his resignation. The following day, Congress elected Chairman Gorham as the twelfth President to complete Hancock's unexpired term.[223] On July 4, President Gorham had the honor of hosting a public levee at the President's House to celebrate the first decade of Independence.[224]

Charles' role as national archivist was clearly a labor of love. When Gen. Nathanael Greene died that summer, Charles made certain that his papers were retrieved. "The regard I have for the memory of a Man who has performed such essential services to his country," Charles wrote, "makes me most earnestly wish to preserve those documents which alone will enable some future historian to do justice to his merit, and transmit his fame to posterity."[225]

That September, delegates from Virginia, Delaware, Pennsylvania, New Jersey and New York met in Annapolis to propose amendments to the Articles of Confederation. Given the poor attendance, they decided to send a letter to Congress and each of the States, urging that a convention be held in the spring.[226]

In October, Congress demonstrated a sudden burst of energy. For more than a year, the delegates had debated a proposal for establishing a Board to liquidate and settle all accounts between the United States and individual States. That ordinance was finally adopted on Friday, October 13, by a vote of 7 to 2 with Maryland's delegation divided.[227] Three days later, Charles transmitted a copy to the States, urging their legislatures to pass laws to assist in its implementation.[228] On October 21, Charles sent two additional notices to the States. The first informed them that Congress had established a national Mint "for regulating the value and alloy of Coin."[229] The second called for increasing America's standing Army to a total of 2,040 non-commissioned Officers and privates. The motivation for the bill was the outbreak of Shay's Rebellion in Western Massachusetts.[230]

The new Congress was scheduled to convene on Monday, November 6, 1786, but Charles and a handful of delegates waited impatiently for over two months before a quorum arrived on January 17, 1787.[231] Unfortunately, several members left the next day before a new President could be chosen. Finally, on February 2, 1787, retired Major Gen. Arthur St. Clair was elected as the thirteenth President of the United States.[232] Later that month, in response to the request of the Annapolis conference the preceding fall, Congress adopted the following motion: "Resolved that in the opinion of Congress it is expedient that on the second Monday of May next a Convention of delegates who shall have been appointed by the several States be held at Philadelphia for the sole and express purpose of revising the Articles of Confederation..."[233] As Charles explained to the Governor of New Hampshire, any amendments to the Articles which might be proposed by the Convention would then have to be "agreed to in Congress" before being confirmed by the States.[234]

As plans proceeded for the Philadelphia meeting, Delegate Lambert Cadwalader of New Jersey reported to a friend that "A Spirit of Economy prevails at present in Congress to so great a Degree that we have...limited the Presidents Expences to 8,000 Dllrs per Annm., lowerd Jay to 3,500 from 4000; Thompson to 2,600 & reduced the Commissrs of the Treasury to 2000 each besides cutting down those of the other Departments (except the Secretary of War)..."[235]

The Philadelphia Convention was scheduled to open on May 14, 1787; but, as usual, a quorum could not be reached until Friday, May 25. George Washington was elected to serve as President and, on May 30, Nathaniel Gorham, the immediate past President of Congress, was elected to Chair the Committee of the Whole (where much of the debate took place).[236] While fifteen delegates to Congress had been elected as members of the Convention, only ten--including Gorham and Madison--actually attended. Abraham Clark of New Jersey and former President Richard Henry Lee of Virginia believed that their congressional responsibilities took priority. They remained in New York. Three other men had also been elected to both, but attended neither.[237]

Because of the Convention, Congress was unable to transact business from May 12 through July 3.[238] Both President St. Clair and Secretary Thomson used the recess to return to their respective homes to attend to personal business.[239] Whether Charles met with Convention delegates while home in Philadelphia is unclear. It is also possible that during that period he penned his 38-page pamphlet: *Notes on Farming*. Later that summer, when he sent copies to a friend, he stated that "Farming is a branch of natural philosophy and it is only by experiments that we can hope for success in improving it. A few successful experiments clearly pointed out are better than a whole volume of theory."[240]

When Charles returned to New York on June 22, he was convinced that "the peace of the Union & the happy termination of the measures of the Convention depend on the meeting & continuance of Congress & keeping up the form of government until the New plan is ready for Adoption."[241] His wish was fulfilled on July 4, the Declaration's eleventh anniversary, when seven States assembled. Since President St. Clair had not yet returned, Delegate William Grayson of Virginia was chosen as Chairman.[242] As Charles wrote to a friend four days later, "I cannot account for the absence of the president. It has I assure you given a good deal of offence."[243]

Despite all the obstacles, Congress then proceeded to act on one of the most important pieces of legislation it its fifteen year history. On Friday, July 13, 1787, the delegates adopted "An Ordinance for the government of the territory of the United States North West of the river Ohio."[244] From that vote sprang five future States--Ohio, Indiana, Michigan, Illinois and Wisconsin--and the model for further expansion across the entire continent. Charles was especially pleased that Article 6 of the Northwest Ordinance prohibited slavery throughout that territory. "I am so much a friend to that article," he wrote, "that let the consequences be what they may I would not wish it altered." (Researchers at the Library of Congress, however, have concluded that "article 2 of the ordinance was long used to protect the property rights of slave-owning French settlers in the Illinois country."[245])

President St. Clair returned to Congress on July 17.[246] One week later, the delegates took an important step toward settling all outstanding Revolutionary War claims against the national government. Individuals would have between eight months and a year to file such claims.[247]

On Monday, September 17, 1787, the Philadelphia Convention completed its work and adjourned.[248] By that Thursday, many of the delegates had returned to New York, bringing with them the proposed Constitution. Since amendments to the Articles of Confederation required the unanimous ratification of the States, the fact that Rhode Island had refused to attend the Convention made adoption through that route highly unlikely. Instead, Article VII of the new document stipulated that "The Ratification of the Conventions of nine States, shall be sufficient for the Establishment of this Constitution between the States so ratifying the Same."[249] Former President Richard Henry Lee argued strenuously that Congress had already decided earlier in the year that it must vote on the document before sending it to the States. The pragmatic majority easily defeated Lee's motion.[250] Instead, as mandated by Congress on September 28, Charles sent copies of the new Constitution to the States, directing them to submit it "to a Convention of Delegates chosen in Your State by the people."[251]

On October 5, Congress proceeded to elect President Arthur St. Clair as the first Governor of the new Northwest Territory.[252] He continued to preside over Congress until October 29, when he took leave of the delegates and departed for the frontier.[253] Charles later wrote to the new Governor: "I heartily wish you success...& happiness in the administration of your government."[254] When the new congressional year began on Monday, November 5, 1787, South Carolina and Georgia were the only States fully represented.[255] Instead, the nation's attention was fixed on the Ratification Conventions being held that fall in Delaware, Pennsylvania and New Jersey. In early January 1788, Georgia and Connecticut were added to the list of States favoring the new union.[256]

During that winter, Hannah reported to a friend that "I caught a violent cold which confined me better than six weeks. As soon as I got better C. T. was confined for some time..." Through it all, Hannah was remarkably resilient. As she had earlier confided to a friend: "I consider myself a Sojourner or a traveller that holds himself ready to start when the Stageman calls."[257]

At long last, on January 21, 1788, Congress again reached a quorum of seven States. The next day the delegates elected Cyrus Griffin of Virginia as the fourteenth and final President of the United States during the First American Republic.[258] At the same time, the critical Massachusetts Ratification Convention was already underway, with the outcome still in serious doubt. Former President Hancock had by then been reelected as Governor. Once he threw his support behind the Constitution, his State voted to ratify on February 6.[259] On February 26, the attention of Congress turned to international relations when President Griffin and the members officially received the new French Minister, the Comte de Moustier.[260]

By mid-April, the focus shifted back to ratification. As the Maryland Convention debated the Constitution, Charles told a former delegate that "unless that [ratification] takes place I confess to you my fears for the safety, tranquility and happiness of my country are greater than at any period of the late war." And then, as the undisputed authority on the Continental Congress, Charles added a dire warning: "The present federal government is at the point of expiring. It cannot I think survive the present year and if it could experience must have convinced every man of reflection that it is altogether inadequate to the end designed."[261] To his relief, Maryland overwhelmingly said yes at the end of that month.

In late May, only days after South Carolina had become the eighth State to ratify the Constitution, Charles shared his reflections on the American Revolution with his friend William Ellery, a former Rhode Island delegate who had signed the Declaration of Independence.[262] "Sensible of our inexperience in the art of government and of the self sufficiency of those who would probably take the reins I dreaded the mischief that might flow from the wanton abuse of power and liberty too easily acquired," he wrote. "I confess we have escaped better than I expected. I am therefore encouraged to hope for a favorable issue..." Charles, the scholar, concluded with a line from Virgil's Aeneid: "Perhaps it may one day be a pleasure to remember these sufferings."[263]

June proved to be the pivotal month when both New Hampshire and Virginia held their Conventions. On June 30, Charles had the pleasure of informing Dickinson "that authentic accounts have been recd. of New Hampshire having ratified the New Constitution, So that now nine states have adopted it." Already looking toward the future, Charles expressed his hope "that all the States which adopt the Constitution should be present when Congress proceed on the measures necessary for putting it in Operation."[264] What Charles did not know at the time was that four days earlier Virginia had also voted 89-79 to ratify after Patrick Henry's determined opposition failed to trump James Madison's articulate advocacy.[265]

The toughest battle of all came in July when the New York Convention opened in Poughkeepsie with Gov. George Clinton leading the anti-federalist forces. If the State voted no, New York City's dream of becoming the permanent capital would have been crushed. Even though the pro-federalist newspaper articles written by Hamilton, Madison and Jay would later attain sacred status as the *Federalist Papers,* they were no match for Gov. Clinton's political machine. It was the news of New Hampshire's ratification and the fact that the new Republic was thereby a *fait accompli* that added New York to the plus column by a vote of 30-27. (It was truly anti-climactic when North Carolina finally ratified 17 months later; and, reluctant Rhode Island begrudgingly approved six months after that by a vote of 34-32.)[266]

Once the birth of the Second Republic was assured, a wide range of issues, including Kentucky's push for statehood, were eagerly deferred to the new government. Charles informed Samuel McDowell, one of the leaders of that movement, that "though Congress think it expedient that the district be made a separate State...the present State of the government of the Confederacy renders it highly improper for them to proceed further than to express their opinion that the district ought to be an Independent member of the Union, as soon as circumstances will permit measures to be taken for that purpose."[267]

Social events, however, were very much in vogue. Hannah reported in August that "Our President keeps an open house, Lady Christina has very large tea parties, there were seventy Gentlemen & Ladies counted at one of her Levee's and on one of the hottest days we have had."[268]

Congress devoted part of the summer and early fall of 1788 to developing plans for implementing the Constitution. On September 13, it created a three-step process starting on the first Wednesday of January with the appointment of Presidential Electors in each of the States that had by then ratified the Constitution. On the first Wednesday of February, those Electors would then be required to meet in their respective States to cast their votes for President. Finally, the new Congress would convene on the first Wednesday in March in New York City where it would count the electoral votes and launch the Second American Republic.[269] Charles sent copies of that Resolution to the States later that same day.[270]

On October 6, as the delegates tried to attend to pending business prior to the start of the new Congress, they were forced to relocate to the office of the Secretary for Foreign Affairs while City Hall was being renovated to accommodate the new bicameral legislature.[271] The last official session of the Continental Congress was held in the Foreign Affairs office on Friday, October 10, 1788.[272] Charles faithfully recorded attendance after that date, but he and Secretary Jay--both of whom had been there the day Congress began over fourteen years earlier--were often the only link to the national government during its final months.

Charles was not idle, however. In preparation for the new government, he wrote to the States on October 22: "As the Government which is soon to commence under the new Constitution is vested with the power of regulating commerce with foreign Nations, and of laying and collecting duties & imports, it will be of importance to them to be informed of the actual state of the commerce & the laws of each State imposing duties or regulating trade; I shall therefore take it as a favor if Your Excellency will cause copies of such laws of Your State as relate to this subject to be forwarded to this Office as soon as possible."[273]

On Monday, March 2, 1789, Charles recorded his last entry in the official Journal.[274] The First American Republic had completed it course. Peyton Randolph and Henry Middleton, the first two Presidents, did not live long enough to celebrate that day, nor did their colleague, John Hanson. Four former Presidents--John Hancock, Samuel Huntington, Thomas Mifflin and Arthur St. Clair--were then serving as Governors. Henry Laurens had retired from public life and Nathaniel Gorham, who almost ran for the new Congress, had returned to business instead. Thomas McKean was still Chief Justice of his State and would later be elected Governor. Cyrus Griffin, the outgoing President, would soon become a Federal Judge. At Washington's request, John Jay continued as America's top diplomat for several months and was also appointed as the nation's first Chief Justice and later elected Governor. Only two of the first fourteen Presidents chose to remain as legislators. Elias Boudinot was elected as a member of the first House of Representatives while Richard Henry Lee was selected by his State legislature as an original member of the United States Senate.

The Second American Republic was scheduled to start on Wednesday, March 4, as outlined in the Resolution adopted the previous September. On March 7, however, Charles reported that the new delegates "have not assembled in sufficient number to form a house..."[275] Two weeks later, his disappointment turned to anger as he wrote to George Read, the newly elected Senator from Delaware, that "I am extremely mortified that you did not come...Those who feel for the honor and are solicitous for the happiness of this country are pained to the heart at the dilatory attendance of the members appointed to form the two houses." He pointed out that "It is now almost three weeks since the day appointed for the meeting of the two houses and...there are not enough arrived to form either house and to count the ballots, to see who is elected President or Vice-President." Charles plaintively asked: "What must the world think of us?"[276]

The House of Representatives finally reached a quorum on April 1, 1789. Five days later, when the Senate convened, the two bodies proceeded immediately to count the Electoral votes in the Senate chamber.[277] To no one's surprise, George Washington was unanimously elected as the first President of the Second Republic while John Adams was elected as America's first Vice President. Charles' future was less certain. The day after Washington's election, Charles confided his feelings to Robert Morris: "I cannot express the anxiety I feel on the determination I had taken to retire to private life, while so many of my friends whom I love and esteem express such an earnest desire that I should continue in a public line." Charles then sketched out the details under which he said he would be willing to continue: "That the keeping of the Great Seal, with the duties thereto annexed...& the custody and care of the papers, which belonged to the late Congress, be committed to me, this office to be made the depository of the Acts, Laws and Archives of Congress; that the same salary be continued to me...& my stile be Secretary of the Senate and of the United States or Congress..." Charles would also require a deputy "to do the ordinary busines of the House, so that I may not be under the necessity of attending except on special occasions..." Charles stated that if these conditions were met "I am ready to serve them to the utmost of my power..."[278]

Benjamin Franklin had offered Charles some sage advice a few months earlier: "My good friend...if the reproach thrown on Republicks, that they are apt to be ungrateful, should ever unfortunately be verified with respect to your services, remember you have a right to unbosom yourself in communicating your griefs to Your affectionate ancient friend & most obed. humble servant. B. Franklin."[279] Franklin's words rang all too true when, on April 8, Charles' enemies, especially the old Lee-Adams alliance, orchestrated his defeat for the Secretary of the Senate position while Charles was away on Senate business. Samuel Alleyne Otis, the former Speaker of Massachusetts and younger brother of the godfather of the American Revolution, James Otis, was elected instead.[280]

Charles had left the city on April 7. The Senate had selected him to officially notify George Washington concerning his election and to accompany the President-elect back to New York. Whether Charles' selection was a mark of distinction by his friends or a clever ploy by his enemies remains open to debate. In either case, Charles arrived at Mount Vernon on Tuesday the 14th. After the formal notification, Washington told Charles that "it was a peculiar gratification to have received the communication from you." After two nights as the General's guest, they set out on the morning of April 16, bidding farewell to Mrs. Washington, who would join her husband a month later. For the next week, Charles and Washington's aide, Col. Humphreys, were at the President-elect's side as they journeyed north, attending receptions and banquets at every stop.[281] In Elizabeth, New Jersey they were greeted by a five member congressional delegation, including former President Boudinot. On April 23, they completed their journey when, to the cheers of thousands of citizens, they arrived by boat at the foot of Manhattan.[282]

The Inauguration was held at Federal Hall exactly one week later. There, on the morning of Thursday, April 30, 1789, the dignitaries-- including five former Presidents--gathered on the balcony overlooking the throngs who had come to witness that historic moment. Former President Boudinot was there, of course, as were many military leaders from the Revolutionary War, including Maj. Gen. Arthur St. Clair, the former President of Congress who now served as Governor of the Northwest Territory. Cyrus Griffin, the last President of Congress, was also present as was former President John Jay, now acting Secretary of State. The one man missing was Secretary Charles Thomson. In an act of extreme political spite, former President Richard Henry Lee, Chairman of the Senate Inaugural Committee, settled a decade-long feud by refusing to provide a reserved seat for the Secretary on the pretense that he was no longer a government official. Charles' friends in Congress did not have time to reverse the snub.[283] As a result, despite his years of dedicated service, Charles was forced to watch from the street below.

That same day, Charles drafted a letter of resignation to Congress which he never sent. In it, he stated that "I was struck with surprize at being passed by unnoticed in the arrangement made by the comee. who I understand were appointed to take order respecting the ceremonial for his inauguration, while some other officers under the late government were invited to attend that solemn occasion. To what cause this has been owing I am altogether a stranger."[284] Instead of lamenting his fate, Charles devoted his energy to other endeavors. In May he had a special set of the Journals of the Continental Congress bound for the President."[285] He was also supporting the creation of a new "Home Department" which would cover a wide range of domestic duties, including many which he had previously handled. Otis, now Secretary of the Senate, was obviously concerned.

"How Charle will succeed in the home department," he wrote, "[I] am not able to say. He is artful, industrious and ambitious and will leave no Stone unturned."[286]

In May, the House began work on the creation of executive departments. Two months later, while Charles was doing battle with the outgoing Treasury Board concerning his salary,[287] the House approved legislation pertaining to the Departments of Treasury, War and Foreign Affairs, but was still debating the proposal for a new Home Department. Elbridge Gerry, perhaps Charles' most bitter enemy, led the fight against it. "The people...will be apt to think we are providing sinecures for men whom we favor..." he argued. "They will suppose that we contemplate the establishment of a monarchy, by raising round the Executive a phalanx of such men as must be inclined to favor those of whom they hold their places." The proposal was defeated on July 23, and the duties scattered among other offices.[288]

Once the bill to establish a Home Department was defeated, Charles knew that his congressional career had come to an end. That same day he sent his letter of resignation, not to Congress, but to his friend and colleague, President Washington. "I present myself before you to surrender up the charge of the books, records and papers of the late Congress which are in my custody &...to deliver into your hands the Great Seal of the federal Union." In characteristic style, Charles also took the opportunity to recommend two of his dedicated assistants for positions in the new government. Charles then closed that momentous chapter of his life: "And now with most sincere and ardent wishes for the prosperity of our country and a fervent prayer for your health and hapiness I bid you an affectionate Farewell."[289]

President Washington replied the next day: "The present age does so much justice to the unsullied reputation with which you have always conducted yourself in the execution of the duties of your office, and posterity will find your name so honourably connected with the verification of such a multitude of astonishing facts, that my single suffrage would add little to the illustration of your merits." Washington then added: "Accept, then, this serious declaration, that your services have been important as your patriotism was distinguished; and enjoy that best of all rewards, the consciousness of having done your duty well."[290]

Some historians have speculated on why Washington did not offer Charles a position in the new Administration as he did to Hamilton, Jefferson and Jay. In response to such an inquiry at that time, the President simply stated that it was the Secretary's "earnest wish to retire from the bustle of public life, and enjoy the evening of his days in domestic tranquility."[291] From a political perspective, however, Charles might simply have been too closely identified with the Continental Congress. Despite its awesome accomplishments, especially during its first decade, the final years of Congress were widely viewed as a failure. Like Banquo's ghost, Charles could have become a constant reminder of a past that Washington was remarkably successful in exorcising from American history.[292]

Charles and Hannah returned to Harriton, their estate on the outskirts of Philadelphia near Bryn Mawr. In July 1790, Hannah reported to a friend that Charles was happy in retirement: "He can leave posts and places to be scrambled for by those who will."[293] In sharp contrast, his friend, Pennsylvania Senator William Maclay, believed that Charles actually "wishes to die in an eminent office."[294] In fact, Charles and his supporters were actively exploring various routes back to public life. His name was prominently mentioned as a candidate for either the United States House or Senate in 1790, and he foolishly permitted supporters to place his name on the ballot for Governor of Pennsylvania that year. The results were dismal.

In July 1792, Charles wrote to his brother that he was enjoying "a great share of health since I quit public Business and what is still more a great deal of tranquility & peace of mind."[295] That same fall, however, Charles again sought election to the House, but this time he discarded his Federalist identity by running on the Republican ticket. For some reason, he withdrew his name at the last minute, leaving many of his supporters angry and dispirited. He never sought elective or appointive office again.[296] In 1793, Charles even declined President Washington's request that he come out of retirement long enough to help to negotiate a treaty with Western Indian Tribes.[297]

Despite his continued interest in national affairs, Charles had already begun an entirely new journey during his final months in New York which he later described as an "agreeable & useful employment to my mind."[298] As a spiritual man who was both a scholar and a skeptic, Charles instinctively distrusted religious dogmas based on conjecture rather than research. Fragments of a manuscript preserved by the Historical Society of Pennsylvania provide a clear explanation in Charles' own words for why he undertook his next monumental project, the translation of the Old Testament from the earliest Greek version, the Septuagint Bible. Charles wrote that "the quotations which the writers of the New Testament make from the Old, either to show that the predictions of the prophets are fulfilled in J[esus] C[hrist] or to confirm and enforce the doctrines they delivered...are chiefly taken from the Sept[uagint]; and ...upon inquiry, I could not find that there was any translation of this into English..."[299] And thus, Charles devoted his considerable intellect and energy over the next twenty years to filling that scriptural void.

The Septuagint had been drawn directly from the ancient Hebrew and Aramaic scrolls in Alexandria, Egypt. It is "the only version of the Old Testament dating from the third century before the Christian Era," started during the reign of Ptolemy II, the founder of the Great Library.[300] It is the text that was common during the time of Christ and referenced by him and his disciples.[301] What is most amazing is that Charles was the first person in history ever to translate the Septuagint into English.

By August 1793, Charles had completed the first draft of both the Old and the New Testament. Seven years later, he was still working on the fourth revision. On January 11, 1808, President Jefferson wrote to "My Dear and Antient Friend" that "I see by the newspapers your translation of the Septuagist is now to be printed, and I write this to pray to be admitted as a subscriber." The President added that "I have learnt from time to time with great satisfaction that you retain your health, spirits and activity of mind and body." Unlike Jefferson's complicated relationship with some of his other old friends such as John Adams and Cyrus Griffin, Jefferson never turned his wrath on Charles.[302] Their close bond was always more intellectual than political.

Years later, Charles explained the methodology he used in his translation: "Attached to no system nor peculiar tenets of any sect or party, I have sought for truth with the utmost ingenuity, and endeavored to give a just and true representation of the sense and meaning of the Sacred Scriptures; and in doing this, I have further endeavored to convey into the translation, as far as I could, the spirit and manner of the authors, and thereby give it the quality of an original."[303] Decades later, Charles' published edition still received high praise from other biblical scholars. Dr. Francis Bowen, a 19th Century Harvard professor, stated that "This solitary and unaided scholar... having at his disposal none of the rich means and appliances of scholarship which were collected in the Jerusalem chamber of Westminster Abbey...has yet produced a work which may well challenge comparison with the best results of the united labors...of two companies containing thirty or forty of the best scholars in England and America."[304]

The four volumes, which also included Charles' original translation of the New Testament, were published by April 1809. One thousand copies were priced at ten dollars each. Against his editor's advice, Charles had refused to provide a preface or to include "any published commendations from others..."[305] As a result, sales were disappointing and the first English translation of the Septuagint Bible never received the recognition it deserved outside of scholarly circles. In March 1825, Charles' nephew, John Thomson, presented his uncle's desk copy of the Septuagint (which included post-publication corrections Charles had made in longhand) to the Library Company of Philadelphia, the oldest public library in America, which had been founded in 1731 by Benjamin Franklin.[306] The latest edition of Charles' Septuagint Bible was published in 1954.[307]

Throughout his retirement, Charles thought of himself as a country gentleman who pursued scholarly interests while supervising his farm. The black farmhands who worked the fields were all free men and women. When one servant, Old Gregory, became crippled and could no longer look after himself, Charles and Hannah brought him to Harriton where he was cared for until he died four years later. Unlike many of his revolutionary colleagues, Charles and Hannah remained financially stable for the rest of their lives thanks to a variety of investments, including agriculture and real estate.[308] They lived fairly simple yet comfortable lives, continuing to take delight in each other's company. Hannah's two nieces--Amelia and Mary--lived with them for several years and, after Charles retired, Amelia's eldest son, Charles McClenachan, lived at Harriton full time as the child they never had.[309]

Starting with the death of his brother, Alexander, in April 1807, Charles' world was devastated by the suffering and death of those closest to him over the next ten months. That same spring, Hannah suffered a severe stroke. Early that fall, five days after their thirty-third wedding anniversary, Charles recorded in his daybook that "My dear Hannah expired 20 mins. after 5.p.m...after a long & gradual decline..."[310] The following February, his closest friend, John Dickinson, also passed away. In a letter to Jefferson, Charles confessed that he felt like "an old tree stript of its foliage."[311] Fortunately, Charles' only sister, Mary, came to live with him shortly after Hannah died.

In 1804, and again in 1808, Charles performed his final public role when he served as a presidential elector; first for Jefferson and then Madison. But, in 1812, when Madison failed to check the congressional call for war, Charles opposed the conflict and urged an end to the Virginia presidential dynasty.[312] During those years following Hannah's death, his real solace was a return to scriptural studies. Utilizing his own translation of the New Testament, Charles wrote another scholarly study to disprove the notion that the four Gospels were somehow contradictory. By arranging the facts presented by the Evangelists in parallel columns, Charles demonstrated to his own satisfaction that there were no contradictions in the stories they told. *A Synopsis of the Four Evangelists*, which was published in 1815, did include a preface.

Jefferson wrote from Monticello in early 1816, pointing out that after 52 years of friendship they were "monuments of another age." He told Charles that he had purchased a copy of the Synopsis "as soon as I saw it advertised." In that same letter, Jefferson uncharacteristically shared a little of his own religious philosophy with his old friend, something he seldom did with anyone. When word of it later leaked out, Jefferson wrote early the following year, telling Charles to "Say nothing of my Religion; it is known to my God and myself alone." "It is a singular anxiety," Jefferson added, "which some people have that we should all think alike...What a world of physical and moral monotony would it be!"[313]

Charles suffered a "paralytic stroke" in 1816, and later a second attack by which he was "struck dumb." Sometime after that, however, "I woke as from a trance and found a wonderful change in my whole system.."[314] In May 1816, he told Jefferson that "I write and read without spectacles" but "My hearing is so dull that I can take no share in common conversation." "My memory is like a riddle." he wrote. "But...How few at my age enjoy greater comforts!"[315]

A few years earlier, in 1811, another personal tragedy had struck when Charles McClenachan, who grew up at Harriton, suddenly died.[316] After that, McClenachan's family and several of Hannah's other relatives eagerly awaited the day when they would inherit the estate which had originally belonged to Hannah's father. Charles and his sister Mary, however, were joined at Harriton by their nephew, John Thomson, and his children. Alarmed, Hannah's family eventually initiated legal proceedings to have Charles and his relatives evicted. The Court date was set for Monday, August 16, 1824. Instead, at 2 o'clock that morning, Charles died at the age of 94, fifty years after the opening of the Continental Congress, the real birthday of the United States.[317]

As clearly stipulated in his Will, Charles was buried two days later next to Hannah in her family's plot at Harriton. John Thomson took charge of his uncle's papers before being forced to leave the estate. Fourteen years later, when a new cemetery was developed just outside of Philadelphia, John Thomson sought permission to move his uncle's remains. When his request was rebuffed, he took direct action by digging up the graves of Charles, Hannah and his own son in the middle of the night of August 13, 1838. Today, they rest beneath a beautiful 21 foot granite obelisk along the banks of the Schuylkill River in historic Laurel Hill Cemetery.[318]

Nine days after his death, the *Norristown Herald* ran the following obituary for Charles Thomas, formerly Secretary of Congress:

> Farewell thou hoary headed patriot and sage!
> A great nation will truly feel thy loss.
> A few years more and all your contemporaries will be mingled with the dust.
> But their memories should be the theme of gratitude for ages yet unborn.[319]

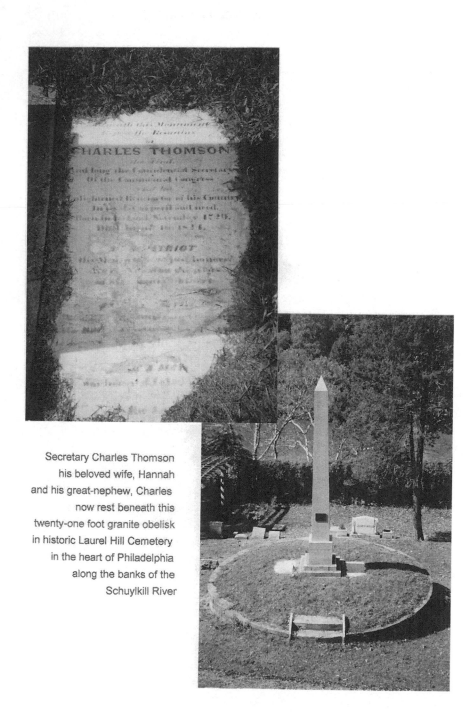

Secretary Charles Thomson
his beloved wife, Hannah
and his great-nephew, Charles
now rest beneath this
twenty-one foot granite obelisk
in historic Laurel Hill Cemetery
in the heart of Philadelphia
along the banks of the
Schuylkill River

Chapter 15

Secretary
CHARLES THOMSON
of
PENNSYLVANIA

Notes

Abbreviation Key

JCC   Journals of the Continental Congress
LDC   Letters of Delegates to Congress
PHL   The Papers of Henry Laurens

[1] Collections of the New-York Historical Society for the Year 1878 (New York Historical Society, New York, 1879), p. 262; Thomas Jefferson to Charles Thomson, January 9, 1816. Jefferson referred to Thomson as "My Dear & Ancient Friend" and stated in the opening sentence of his letter that their acquaintance was in its 52nd year. Thomson had known Franklin from 1750 until Franklin's death in 1790.

[2] Collections of the New-York Historical Society for the Year 1878, op. cit., pp. 175-175; John Jay to Charles Thomson, July 19, 1783.

[3] Boyd Stanley Schlenther, Charles Thomson: A Patriot's Pursuit (University of Delaware Press, London, 1990), pp. 204-205.

[4] As cited in Kenneth R. Bowling, "Good-by 'Charle': The Lee-Adams Interest and the Political Demise of Charles Thomson, Secretary of Congress, 1774-1789, The Pennsylvania Magazine of History and Biography, Vol. 100, No. 3 (July 1976), pp. 314-315.

[5] Henry Bartholomew Cox, The Mind of Charles Thomson (The Scotch-Irish Foundation, Philadelphia, 1973); A Paper read at the Annual Meeting of the Harriton Association, March 20, 1973. [Harriton is the name of Charles & Hannah Thomson's estate outside of Philadelphia where they lived during the final decades of their lives.]

[6] As cited in Lewis R. Harley, The Life of Charles Thomson (George W. Jacobs & Co., Philadelphia, 1900), p. 18.

[7] As cited in Schlenther, op. cit, p. 19; John Watson, Biographical Notes.

[8] J. Edwin Hendricks, Charles Thomson and the Making of a New Nation, 1729-1824 (Associated University Presses, Cranbury, NJ, 1979), p. 25.

[9] Harley, op. cit, p. 29.

[10] Schlenther, op. cit., p. 25.

[11] As cited in Schlenther, op. cit., p. 26.

[12] Paul H. Smith, Editor, <u>LDC: 1774-1789</u> (Library of Congress, Washington, DC, 1976), 26 Volumes; Vol. 1, p. 155; John Adams to Abigail Adams, October 7, 1774.

[13] As cited in Schlenther, op. cit., p. 33.

[14] As cited in Harley, op. cit, p. 50.

[15] Schlenther, op. cit., p. 36.

[16] Charles Thomson, *An Enquiry into the Causes of the Alienation of the Delaware and Shawanese Indians from the British Interest*, as cited in Hendricks, op. cit., p. 22.

[17] Hendricks, op. cit., p. 20.

[18] As cited in Schlenther, op. cit., p. 255. Deborah Logan, Charles Thomson's contemporary, recorded numerous events concerning Thomson's life in her diary which is preserved as the Logan Papers in the Historical Society of Pennsylvania in Philadelphia.

[19] William B. Willcox, Editor, <u>The Papers of Benjamin Franklin</u> (Yale University Press, New Haven, 1972), Vol. 16, p. 262; Deborah Franklin to Benjamin Franklin, December 13, 1769.

[20] As cited in Schlenther, op. cit., pp. 75-76.

[21] Harley, op. cit., pp. 62-63.

[22] As cited in Schlenther, op. cit., p. 48. According to Schlenther, identical ads for Charles Thomson's new shop--which included a reference to specific items--ran in the *Pennsylvania Gazette* on October 2, 1760 and November 27, 1760.

[23] <u>Collections of the New-York Historical Society for the Year 1878</u>, op. cit., pp. 4-5; Benjamin Franklin to Charles Thomson, July 11, 1765.

[24] C. A. Weslager, <u>The Stamp Act Congress</u> (Associated University Presses, Newark, 1976), pp. 107-108.

[25] Schlenther, op. cit., pp. 64-65.

[26] <u>Collections of the New-York Historical Society for the Year 1878</u>, op. cit., pp. 7-12; Charles Thomson to Messrs Cook, Lawrence & Co., November 9, 1765.

[27] <u>Collections of the New-York Historical Society for the Year 1878</u>, op. cit., p. 13; Benjamin Franklin to Charles Thomson, February 27, 1766.

[28] <u>Collections of the New-York Historical Society for the Year 1878</u>, op. cit., pp. 15-16; Charles Thomson to Benjamin Franklin, May 20, 1766.

[29] Barbara W. Tuchman, <u>The March of Folly</u> (Alfred A. Knopf, New York, 1984). Chapter

Four of her book is devoted to "The British Lose America." For a discussion of the Townshend Taxes, see Introduction.

[30] Collections of the New-York Historical Society for the Year 1878, op. cit., pp. 21-25; Charles Thomson to Benjamin Franklin, November 26, 1769.

[31] Mark M. Boatner III, Encyclopedia of the American Revolution (David McKay Company, Inc., New York, 1974), pp. 362-363.

[32] As cited in Schlenther, op. cit., p. 78.

[33] *Pennsylvania Gazette*, May 12, 1768.

[34] Willcox, op. cit., Vol. 17, p. 229; Joseph Galloway to Benjamin Franklin, September 27, 1770.

[35] Schlenther, op. cit., pp. 95-98.

[36] John J. Zimmerman, "Charles Thomson, 'The Sam Adams of Philadelphia,'" *The Mississippi Valley Historical Review*, Vol. 45, No. 3 (December 1958), p. 480.

[37] Hendricks, op. cit., p. 93.

[38] Charles Thomson, "Early Days of the Revolution in Philadelphia," *The Pennsylvania Magazine of History and Biography*, Vol. 2, No. 4 (1878), pp. 413-415; Charles Thomson to William Henry Drayton, c. 1778-1779.

[39] As cited in Schlenther, op. cit., p. 107; Sam Adams to Charles Thomson, May 30, 1774.

[40] Boyd Stanley Schlenther comments in his excellent biography of Charles Thomson that some of the new working-class recruits demonstrated a "growing anti-intellectualism" that increasing disturbed Charles; op. cit., p. 113. The situation sounds erily familiar to the Tea Party politics of the early Obama Administration and many similar protest movements throughout United States history.

[41] Schlenther, op. cit., p. 113.

[42] L. H. Butterfield, Editor, The Diary and Autobiography of John Adams (The Belknap Press, Cambridge, 1961), Vol. 2, p. 115.

[43] Schlenther, op. cit., p. 117. See also Butterfield, op. cit., Vol. 2, p. 118. Surprisingly, on September 1, 1774, (the morning of Charles Thomson's marriage) John Adams recorded that Charles joined him at Thomas Mifflin's home for breakfast.

[44] *American Quarterly Review* (March 1827), as cited in Paul H. Smith, Editor, LDC: 1774-1789 (Library of Congress, Washington, DC, 1976), Vol. 1, p. 12, footnote 8.

[45] Butterfield, op. cit., Vol. 2, p. 123.

[46] As cited in Harley, op. cit, p. 87. See also: Worthington Chauncey Ford, Chief, Division of Manuscripts, JCC: 1774-1789 (Government Printing Office, Washington, DC, 1904), Vol. I, p. 14.

[47] LDC, op. cit., Vol. 1, pp. 20-23; Silas Deane to Elizabeth Deane, September 5, 1774. Silas Deans added that "I doubted in my own mind the propriety [of selecting a non-delegate], but did not oppose it, as by opposing I most probably should have had the Task myself which is Too Burthensome to one who wants all spare hours for relaxation." If Deane had become Secretary, he probably would not have been sent to Paris, thereby avoiding the greatest internal division that Congress confronted during its entire history: The Lee-Deane Affair.

[48] LDC, op. cit., Vol. 1, p. 27; Joseph Galloway to William Franklin, September 5, 1774.

[49] LDC, op. cit., Vol. 1, pp. 25-26; James Duane's Notes of Debates, September 5, 1774. Jay argued that an elected Member of Congress should have preference, but most felt that the secretary's duties would prevent that delegate from participating in the deliberations, thereby denying his colony full representation.

[50] JCC, op. cit., Vol. 1, p. 29.

[51] LDC, op. cit., Vol. 18, p. 312, footnote 1. Researchers at the Library of Congress point out that "the entries found in the printed journals [1904 edition] are often a composite of sources, drawn from Thomson's secret journals of Congress (both foreign and domestic), as well as his regular rough journals, and various draft motions, resolutions, and committee reports, not all of which are even located in the PCC [Papers of the Continental Congress]." See also Vol. 20, p. 17, footnote 1. The researchers point out that an entry in James Madison's Notes of Debates "provides an instructive reminder of the striking gaps found in Secretary Charles Thomson's journal of Congress, which contains no entries for the dates March 11 through 17 [1783], although the editor of the modern edition of the journals created a number of entries for these days drawn from various other documents..."

[52] LDC, op. cit., Vol. 11, pp. xxvii-xxviii.

[53] LDC, op. cit., Vol. 1, p. 12, footnote 8.

[54] LDC, op. cit., Vol. 20, p. 541; Charles Thomson to Elias Boudinot, August 11, 1783. As Secretary Thomson told President Boudinot: "It has been my Study not only to preserve the papers entrusted to my care but to have them so arranged as to be ready to be produced whenever called for."

[55] LDC, op. cit., Vol. 11, p. 407; John Jay to Benjamin Franklin, January 3, 1779.

[56] Butterfield, op. cit., Vol. 2, pp. 132-133.

[57] LDC, op. cit., Vol. 1, p. 93.

[58] Butterfield, op. cit., Vol. 2, p. 147.

[59] LDC, op. cit., Vol. 1, p. 156, footnote 4 & p. 194. John Dickinson took his seat as a congressional delegate on October 17, 1774.

[60] LDC, op. cit., Vol. 1, p. 233.

[61] LDC, op. cit., Vol. 1, pp. 246 & 249.

[62] LDC, op. cit., Vol. 1, pp. 266-267, footnote 1.

[63] LDC, op. cit., Vol. 1, p. 270; Samuel Ward to John Dickinson, December 4, 1774.

[64] LDC, op. cit., Vol. 1, p. 325; Joseph Galloway to Samuel Verplanck, April 1, 1775.

[65] JCC, op. cit., Vol. II, p. 12.

[66] LDC, op. cit., Vol. 1, p. 342; Joseph Hewes to Samuel Johnston, May 11, 1775. Hewes reported that "Galloway has turned apostate." He told Johnston that "A few days ago a Box was left at his Lodgings in this City directed for Jos. Galloway Esqr. He [Galloway] opened it...and was much surprised to find it contained a Halter with a note in these words 'all the Satisfaction you can now give your injured Country is to make a proper use of this and rid the World of a Damned Scoundrell.'"

[67] JCC, op. cit., Vol. II, pp. 12, 58-59, 101.

[68] LDC, op. cit., Vol. 1, p. 531; Samuel Adams to Joseph Warren, June 22, 1775.

[69] LDC, op. cit., Vol. 4, p. 251, 1.

[70] LDC, op. cit., Vol. 21, p. 772; Charles Thomson to Benjamin Franklin, August 13, 1784.

[71] Robert G. Ferris, Editor, Signers of the Declaration (US Government Printing Office, Washington, DC, 1975), pp. 21-23.

[72] LDC, op. cit., Vol. 4, p. 562; Charles Thomson to John Dickinson, July 29, 1776.

[73] LDC, op. cit., Vol. 7, p. 359; Charles Thomson to George Washington, July 21, 1777. Charles Thomson also respected the demarcation between political and military authority. After offering unsolicited military advice to the Commander-in-Chief, the Secretary added: "But I am transgressing my line and I fear trespassing on your time."

[74] LDC, op. cit., Vol. 8, p. 364; John Penn to Theodorick Bland, December 1, 1777. One of the many tedious aspects of the Secretary's job was adjudicating disagreements pertaining to the official record. In late 1777, for example, the Secretary had to write out all of the Journal Resolutions pertaining to the appointment of colonels in the Continental Army in order to settle a dispute concerning rank between two Army officers.

[75] LDC, op. cit., Vol. 14, p. 87, footnote 1. The official 34 volume JCC which was published by the Library of Congress starting in 1904 are actually a composite of several of the Secretary's Journals and occasionally other documents.

[76] John P. Butler, Compiller, Index: The Papers of the Continental Congress, 1774-1775 (US Government Printing Office, Washington, DC, 1978), Vol. 1, p. v. At the start of the Second American Republic in 1789, most of these Papers were housed in the State Department. In 1903, responsibility was transferred to the Library of Congress until 1952, when the Papers found a permanent home in the National Archives. The 50,000 documents total approximately 170,000 manuscript pages.

[77] LDC, op. cit., Vol. 13, pp. 536-538; Charles Thomson to Thomas Mifflin, September

22, 1779. At Mifflin's request, the Secretary compiled a fascinating Report on the status of State Governments in 1779.

[78] Butterfield, op. cit., Vol. 3, p. 375.

[79] LDC, op. cit., Vol. 5, p. 250; John Adams to Abigail Adams, February 10, 1777. See also Vol. 8, p. 646, footnote 1. In 1778, Secretary Thomson even hired one of John Adams' former law clerks, John Thaxter, Jr.

[80] JCC, op. cit., Vol. VIII, p. 599.

[81] LDC, op. cit., Vol. 3, p. 457, footnote 1 & p. 568, footnote 1, provide specific examples of omissions that are occasionally annotated in the 26 volumes. An example of entering incorrect information can be found in Vol. 9, p. 680, footnote 1. See also: Vol. 7, p. 375; Starting on July 25, 1777, "Thomson resorted to a form of personal shorthand..."; and, Vol. 17, p. 556.

[82] LDC, op. cit., Vol. 21, pp. 350-351; Charles Thomson to Thomas FitzSimons, February 12, 1784.

[83] JCC, op. cit., Vol. VI, pp. 1027-1028.

[84] JCC, op. cit., Vol. VII, p. 169. See also LDC, op. cit., Vol. 6, p. 433, footnote 1: "Thomson did not return to Philadelphia and resume keeping the journals until March 24, the entries for March 14-23 were kept by President Hancock and his secretary, Jacob Rush."

[85] JCC, op. cit., Vol. VIII, pp. 754-756.

[86] Schlenther, op. cit., p. 152. After the British eventually evacuated Philadelphia, Charles and Hannah Thomson used his city house at the corner of Spruce and Fourth Streets as their primary residence for the duration of the First American Republic. In 1789, they retired to Hannah's estate, Harriton, outside of Bryn Mawr.

[87] JCC, op. cit., Vol. IX, pp. 846 & 854.

[88] LDC, op. cit., Vol. 8, pl. 691; Henry Laurens to George Read, January 1778.

[89] LDC, op. cit., Vol. 9, pp. 278-279; Henry Laurens to Jonathan Trumbull, Jr., March 12, 1778.

[90] LDC, op. cit., Vol. 9, p. 427; Henry Laurens' Notes on Half Pay, April 21, 1778.

[91] LDC, op. cit., Vol. 10, p. 702; Henry Laurens to George Clinton, September 27, 1778.

[92] For the details of Henry Laurens resignation as President, see Chapter 4. LDC, op. cit., Vol. 11, p. 441, footnote 3; One month after his resignation, Henry Laurens engaged in a duel with Pennsylvania Delegate John Penn over a perceived insult. Neither man was wounded. The French Minister, Gerard, reported that it was one of eight or nine duels he had heard about "in recent weeks." For an overview of the Lee-Deane Affair, see Chapter 11. See also Vol. 18, pp. 195-196 & 558. Deane returned to Europe supposedly to retrieve

his papers for use in his defense, but instead, in early 1781, he offered his services to the British Government in the hope of promoting negotiations to end the war by persuading one of the American colonies "to return to its former allegiance." In the summer of 1782, once his treachery became known, even an American vessel of war named after him was changed to "The Hague," in honor or the new Dutch allies.

93 JCC, op. cit., Vol. XII, pp. 1202-1206.

94 Fred S. Rolater, "Charles Thomson, 'Prime Minister' of the United States," *The Pennsylvania Magazine of History and Biography*, Vol. 101, No. 3 (July 1977), p. 332.

95 LDC, op. cit., Vol. 12, p. 550 & footnote 5; Richard Henry Lee to Henry Laurens, May 27, 1779.

96 LDC, op. cit., Vol. 13, pp. 442-444; Henry Laurens to a Committee of Congress, September 1, 1779. See also Vol. 14, p. 8, footnote 7. One of the charges Laurens alleged against the Secretary was the inadequacy of the commission Charles had prepared for John Adams when he was assigned to the French Court. Adams himself, however, later stated that "I think [my commission]...a very decent, respectable and honorable commission...I see no reason to object to it."

97 LDC, op. cit., Vol. 13, pp. 458-465; Charles Thomson to a Committee of Congress, September 6, 1779.

98 LDC, op. cit., Vol. 13, p. 445, footnote 1.

99 LDC, op. cit., Vol. 13, p. 466, footnote 14.

100 JCC, op. cit., Vol. XV, pp. 1113-1114.

101 LDC, op. cit., Vol. 14, p. 142, footnote 1.

102 LDC, op. cit., Vol. 14, pp. 216-217.

103 LDC, op. cit., Vol. 14, p. 540; Charles Thomson to Jonathan Trumbull, Sr.; March 23, 1780.

104 LDC, op. cit., Vol. 14, p. 348; Samuel Holton's Diary, January 18-19, 1780.

105 LDC, op. cit., Vol. 26, p. xlvi. See also: Vol. 19, p. 341, footnote 1. From November 4, 1782-June 21, 1783, James Madison kept his own detailed Notes of Debates in the Continental Congress.

106 LDC, op. cit., Vol. 16, pp. 485-498; Charles Thomson to John Dickinson, December 25, 1780.

107 JCC, op. cit., Vol. XIX, pp. 213-214. The Articles of Confederation, which were approved by Congress in late 1778, were finally ratified when Maryland agreed to sign following Virginia's concession of its western lands.

108 JCC, op. cit., Vol. XX, p. 499 & Vol. XXI, pp. 851-852.

109 LDC, op. cit., Vol. 17, pp. 206-207; Charles Thomson to John Dickinson, May 1, 1781.

Wisely, the financially strapped Congress made immediate provisions for covering the balances of the under-secretaries and clerks first.

[110] JCC, op. cit., Vol. XX, p. 724.

[111] Chapter 7.

[112] JCC, op. cit., Vol. XXI, p. 1071.

[113] G. S. Rowe, Thomas McKean: The Shaping of an American Republicanism (Colorado Associated University Press, Boulder, 1978), p. 163.

[114] JCC, op. cit., Vol. XXI, p. 1100.

[115] LDC, op. cit., Vol. 18, p. 179, footnote 1. See also: p. 654. Starting on July 22, 1782, "Charles Thomson's Notes of Debates" are frequently cited in the LDC.

[116] JCC, op. cit., Vol. XXII, pp. 55-57.

[117] LDC, op. cit., Vol. 18, p. 209; Charles Thomson to Robert Morris, November 21, 1781. In this specific instance, prior to the 1782 reorganization mandated by Congress, Secretary Thomson forwarded a letter to Superintendent Morris with the comment that "As the letter is to go from your Office it may be proper that the papers on which the letter is grounded should be lodged there."

[118] LDC, op. cit., Vol. 18, pp. 504, footnote 2; and, 506-507; Charles Thomson's Report on the Audience with La Luzerne, May 13, 1782. Even the color of the green table cloths had been specified in planning the event.

[119] LDC, op. cit., Vol. 19, p. 106. Charles Thomson's Notes of Debates, August 28, 1782.

[120] Edward W. Richardson, Standards and Colors of the American Revolution (University of Pennsylvania Press, 1982), pp. 10-12.

[121] JCC, op. cit., Vol. XXII, pp. 338-339. Uncharacter-istically, the Journal provides remarkable detail concerning the meaning of each symbol.

[122] Schlenther, op. cit., p. 193. The slightly modified version of Charles Thomson's design for the Great Seal is found today on the back of a one dollar bill.

[123] JCC, op. cit., Vol. XXIII, p. 708. See also Chapter 8, p. 258. John Hanson died on November 15, 1783, at Oxon Hill, Maryland.

[124] LDC, op. cit., Vol. 19, p. 431, footnote 1.

[125] LDC, op. cit., Vol. 19, pp. 370-371; Charles Thomson to Robert Morris, November 11, 1782. Congress authorized the payment.

[126] Eugene R. Sheridan and John M. Murrin, Editors, Congress at Princeton (Princeton University Press, Princeton, 1985), p. 37, footnote 4. See also: LDC, op. cit., Vol. 19, p. 525; December 1782. When Charles submitted the 1783 budget for the his Office it totaled $8,300, including his salary as well as the wages for his deputy and three clerks.

[127] LDC, op. cit., Vol. 19, p. 585; James Madison's Notes of Debates, January 15, 1783.

[128] LDC, op. cit., Vol. 19, p. 751; James Madison's Notes of Debates, February 28, 1783.

[129] LDC, op. cit., Vol. 19, pp. 306-307; Charles Thomson to Robert R. Livingston, June 4, 1783.

[130] See Chapters 9 & 13 for details pertaining to the mutiny and Congress' departure.

[131] JCC, op. cit., Vol. XIV, p. 411.

[132] LDC, op. cit., Vol. 20, p. xxvi. The Continental Congress met at Nassau Hall on the campus of the College of New Jersey, now Princeton University. Delegate James Madison of Virginia was one of its graduates.

[133] Sheridan, op. cit., pp. 3-13; Charles Thomson to Hannah Thomson, June 30, 1783.

[134] Sheridan, op. cit., pp.16-18; Charles Thomson to Hannah Thomson, July 4, 1783.

[135] LDC, op. cit., Vol. 25, pp. 748-750; Charles Thomson to Hannah Thomson, July 5, 1783.

[136] Sheridan, op. cit., pp. 19-20; Charles Thomson to Hannah Thomson, July 6, 1783.

[137] Sheridan, op. cit., pp. 27; Charles Thomson to Hannah Thomson, July 24, 1783.

[138] Sheridan, op. cit., pp. 28-31; Charles Thomson to Hannah Thomson, July 25, 1783.

[139] Sheridan, op. cit., p. 37; Charles Thomson to Hannah Thomson, July 30, 1783.

[140] LDC, op. cit., Vol. 25, p. 755; Charles Thomson to Hannah Thomson, August 6, 1783. Washington was first received by Congress on August 26, 1783.

[141] Sheridan, op. cit., p. 42; Charles Thomson to Hannah Thomson, August 19, 1783.

[142] Sheridan, op. cit., p. 61; Charles Thomson to Hannah Thomson, September 18, 1783.

[143] James Thomas Flexner, George Washington in the American Revolution (1775-1783) (Little, Brown and Company, Boston, 1968), Vol. 2, pp. 518-519.

[144] Sheridan, op. cit., p. 76; Charles Thomson to Hannah Thomson, October 19, 1783.

[145] JCC, op. cit., Vol. XXV, pp. 538-539.

[146] LDC, op. cit., Vol. 25, p. 759; Charles Thomson to Hannah Thomson, September 10, 1783.

[147] LDC, op. cit., Vol. 21, pp. 7-9; Charles Thomson Memorandum Book, October 1 -November 1, 1783. With occasional gaps, the Mem- orandum Book was kept until September 15, 1788.

[148] Sheridan, op. cit., p. 65; Charles Thomson to Hannah Thomson, October 13, 1783.

[149] Sheridan, op. cit., pp. 72-73; Charles Thomson to Hannah Thomson, October 17, 1783.

[150] Sheridan, op. cit., p. 81; Charles Thomson to Hannah Thomson, October 21, 1783.

[151] JCC, op. cit., Vol. XXV, pp. 711-712,

[152] JCC, op. cit., Vol. XXV, pp. 799 & 807. See also: LDC, op. cit., Vol. 21, p. 120; Elias Boudinot to the Ministers Plenipotentiary, November 3, 1783.

[153] JCC, op. cit., Vol. XXV, pp. 809-810. December 13, 1783, also marked the beginning of future President James Monroe's membership in the Continental Congress.

[154] LDC, op. cit., Vol. 21, p. 204; Charles Thomson to John Debrett, December 16, 1783.

[155] JCC, op. cit., Vol. XXV, p. 837.

[156] JCC, op. cit., Vol. XXVI, pp. 23-29. The State of New York also failed to vote on the Declaration of Independence on July 4, 1776, because its lone delegate, Alexander Hamilton, had no instructions form the New York Assembly on that date. New York did add its vote and name later, in time for New York delegates to sign the document on August 2, 1776.

[157] LDC, op. cit., Vol. 21, pp. 280-286; Charles Thomson to John Jay, January 14 & 15, 1784; and, Charles Thomson to Benjamin Franklin, January 15, 1784.

[158] Edmund Cody Burnett, The Continental Congress (The Macmillan Company, New York, 1941), pp. 593-594.

[159] David R. Chesnutt and James Taylor, Editors, PHL (University of South Carolina Press, Columbia, 2003), Vol. 16, p. 422; Henry Laurens to Charles Thomson, March 28,1784.

[160] LDC, op. cit., Vol. 21, pp. 293-294; Charles Thomson to Richard Peters, January 19, 1784. Richard Peters, like Secretary Thomson, had suffered through the previous year. He was reelected on November 13, 1783, but resigned three days later.

[161] LDC, op. cit., Vol. 21, p. 488; Charles Thomson to George Clymer, April 3, 1784.

[162] LDC, op. cit., Vol. 21, p. 494, footnote 3. Count von Hogendorp "traveled in America from Boston to Mount Vernon between November 1783 and June 1784..." The fact that Jefferson was so sanctimonious is amusing given the fact that he declined his first appointment to France and proved to be a disastrous war time Governor of Virginia, almost loosing the State to British invaders and barely avoiding censure by his own legislature.

[163] LDC, op. cit., Vol. 21, p. 630; Charles Thomson to Thomas Jefferson, May 19, 1784.

[164] LDC, op. cit., Vol. 21, pp. 620-621; Charles Thomson to Thomas Jefferson, May 16, 1784. In typical fashion, Elbridge Gerry then criticized the titles Secretary Thomson had inserted for each sovereign.

165 JCC, op. cit., Vol. XXVI, p. 355.

166 LDC, op. cit., Vol. 21, p. 694; Charles Thomson to John Jay, June 18, 1784.

167 JCC, op. cit., Vol. XXVII, p. 555.

168 JCC, op. cit., Vol. XXVII, p. 561.

169 LDC, op. cit., Vol. 21, p. 696; Charles Thomson to Samuel Hardy, June 20, 1784.

170 JCC, op. cit., Vol. XXVII, pp. 561-638.

171 LDC, op. cit., Vol. 21, p. 745; Charles Thomson to Samuel Hardy, July 28, 1784.

172 LDC, op. cit., Vol. 21, p. 772; Charles Thomson to Benjamin Franklin, August 13, 1784.

173 LDC, op. cit., Vol. 21, p. 781, footnote 1. In addition to the sudden departure of New Hampshire, Massachusetts and New Jersey; Rhode Island, New York, Delaware and Connecticut had had already been absent. Only six States remained in Annapolis on August 19, 1784, when the Committee was dissolved.

174 LDC, op. cit., Vol. 21, p. 765; Jacob Read to Charles Thomson, August 13, 1784.

175 LDC, op. cit., Vol. 21, p. 776; Charles Thomson to Samuel Hardy, August 13, 1784.

176 LDC, op. cit., Vol. 21, p. 777; Samuel Hardy to Charles Thomson, August 16, 1784.

177 JCC, op. cit., Vol. XXVII, pp. 636-638.

178 Rolater, op. cit., p. 322-348.

179 LDC, op. cit., Vol. 21, p. 792; Charles Thomson to John Jay, September 18, 1784.

180 LDC, op. cit., Vol. 21, p. 794; Charles Thomson to Certain States, September 27, 1784.

181 LDC, op. cit., Vol. 21, p. 807; Charles Thomson to Thomas Jefferson, October 1, 1784.

182 JCC, op. cit., Vol. XXVII, p. 6, footnote 1. The French Arms Tavern was located "on the Southwest corner of King and Second Streets (modern State and Warren Streets)."

183 LDC, op. cit., Vol. 22, p. 15; Charles Thomson to Richard Phillips, November 11, 1784.

184 JCC, op. cit., Vol. XXVII, p. 649. See also: LDC, op. cit., Vol. 22, p. 307, footnote 2.

185 LDC, op. cit., Vol. 22, p. 81; Charles Thomson to John Dickinson, December 22, 1784.

186 JCC, op. cit., Vol. XXVII, p. 696.

187 LDC, op. cit., Vol. 22, p. 82, footnote 4.

[188] JCC, op. cit., Vol. XXVII, p. 710.

[189] Hannah Thomson, "Letters of Hannah Thomson," *The Pennsylvania Magazine of History and Biography*, Vol. 14, No. 1 (April 1890), p. 29; Hannah Thomson to John Mifflin, January 15, 1785.

[190] JCC, op. cit., Vol. XXVIII, p. 3.

[191] Chapter 11. See also: LDC, op. cit., Vol. 22, p. 391, footnote 3.

[192] LDC, op. cit., Vol. 22, p. 260; Charles Thomson to Henry Knox, March 9, 1785. Henry Knox, a bookseller by profession, launched a brilliant military career when he transported the cannons captured at Fort Ticonderoga in New York to the cliffs above Boston Harbor, thereby making it possible for Gen. Washington to drive the British out of Boston in March 1776.

[193] Collections of the New-York Historical Society for the Year 1878, op. cit., pp. 199-200; Charles Thomson to Thomas Jefferson, March 6, 1785.

[194] LDC, op. cit., Vol. 22, p. 282; Charles Thomson to Hannah Thomson, March 22, 1785.

[195] LDC, op. cit., Vol. 22, p. 284, footnote 2.; Charles Thomson to Hannah Thomson, March 22, 1785. See also: Vol. 21, p. 266, footnote 3.

[196] LDC, op. cit., Vol. 22, pp. 286-287; Charles Thomson to Certain States and Charles Thomson to the Indian Commissioners, March 24, 1785. These represent only two of scores of letters among the delegates pertaining to Indian Affairs.

[197] LDC, op. cit., Vol. 22, p. 469; Charles Thomson to the Indian Affairs Commissioners, June 21, 1785. In 1779, Thomas Killbuck and John Killbuck, two Indian youth from the Delaware Tribe, had been placed in the care of Congress and subsequently educated at the College of New Jersey (i.e., Princeton University). In 1785, both men expressed their desire to return to their Native Country.

[198] LDC, op. cit., Vol. 22, p. 330; Charles Thomson to Certain States, April 12, 1785. See also: JCC, op. cit., Vol. XXVIII, p. 212.

[199] LDC, op. cit., Vol. 22, p. 305; Charles Thomson to Hannah Thomson, April 3, 1785.

[200] Schlenther, op. cit., p. 178.

[201] LDC, op. cit., Vol. 22, pp. 305-306; Charles Thomson to Hannah Thomson, April 3, 1785. See also: JCC, op. cit., Vol. XXVIII, p. 212.

[202] LDC, op. cit., Vol. 22, p. 307, footnote 1. See also: pp. 388-389; Charles Thomson's Shipping List, May 9?, 1785.

[203] LDC, op. cit., Vol. 22, pp. 352-353; Charles Thomson to George Washington, April 22, 1785.

[204] Thomson, Hannah, op. cit., p. 29.

[205] LDC, op. cit., Vol. 22, p. 314, footnotes 1 & 2.

[206] LDC, op. cit., Vol. 22, p. 412; Charles Thomson to Richard Caswell, May 28, 1785.

[207] JCC, op. cit., Vol. XXVIII, pp. 435-437. See also: LDC, op. cit., Vol. 22, pp. 447-448; Charles Thomson to the States, June 9, 1785.

[208] LDC, op. cit., Vol. 22, pp. 519-522; Charles Thomson to John Dickinson, July 19, 1785.

[209] LDC, op. cit., Vol. 22, pp. 547; Charles Thomson to Certain States, August 3, 1785; and, p. 549; Charles Thomson to Michael Hillegas, August 5, 1785.

[210] LDC, op. cit., Vol. 22, p. 573, footnote 2. See also: JCC, op. cit., Vol. XXVIII, p. 631.

[211] JCC, op. cit., Vol. XXIX, pp. 632 & 664. See also: LDC, op. cit., Vol. 22, p. 623; and, pp. 627-628, footnote 3.

[212] LDC, op. cit., Vol. 22, p. 644, footnote 2; Charles Thomson to Benjamin Franklin, September 21, 1785.

[213] LDC, op. cit., Vol. 22, p. 662; Charles Thomson to Samuel Elbert, October 5, 1785.

[214] LDC, op. cit., Vol. 22, pp. 716-717; Charles Thomson to Thomas Jefferson, November 2, 1785.

[215] JCC, op. cit., Vol. XXIX, p. 883. David Ramsay of Charleston, South Carolina was a doctor, politician and an historian who wrote the History of the Revolution of South Carolina. His third wife was Martha Laurens, the eldest daughter of former President Henry Laurens. Their home still stands at No. 92 Broad Street in historic Charleston.

[216] Thomson, Hannah, op. cit., p. 31; Hannah Thomson to John Mifflin, December 8, 1785.

[217] LDC, op. cit., Vol. 23, p. 131; Charles Thomson to the States, February 1, 1786.

[218] LDC, op. cit., Vol. 23, pp. 162-163; Charles Thomson to Certain States, February 24, 1786.

[219] LDC, op. cit., Vol. 23, p. 242, footnote 2.

[220] LDC, op. cit., Vol. 23, p. 250; Charles Thomson to the States, April 22, 1786.

[221] Collections of the New-York Historical Society for the Year 1878, op. cit., pp. 205-206; Charles Thomson to Thomas Jefferson, April 6, 1786: and, p. 207; Thomas Jefferson to Charles Thomson, April 22, 1786.

[222] JCC, op. cit., Vol. XXX, p. 264.

[223] JCC, op. cit., Vol. XXX, pp. 328 & 330.

[224] LDC, op. cit., Vol. 23, p. 375; Charles Thomson to John Jay, June 29, 1786.

[225] LDC, op. cit., Vol. 23, p. 569; Charles Thomson to Jeremiah Wadsworth, September 26, 1786.

[226] JCC, op. cit., Vol. XXXI, pp. 677-680. The letter from the Annapolis Conference was signed on September 14, 1786, by John Dickinson of Pennsylvania who served as Chairman of the gathering.

[227] JCC, op. cit., Vol. XXXI, p. 779.

[228] LDC, op. cit., Vol. 23, p. 602; Charles Thomson to the States, October 16, 1786.

[229] LDC, op. cit., Vol. 23, p. 609; Charles Thomson to the States, October 21, 1786.

[230] LDC, op. cit., Vol. 23, p. 610; Charles Thomson to the States, October 21, 1786. See also: Chapter 3, p. 106.

[231] LDC, op. cit., Vol. 24, p. 27; Charles Thomson to the States, November 11, 1786. See also: JCC, op. cit., Vol. XXXII, p. 1.

[232] JCC, op. cit., Vol. XXXII, p. 11.

[233] JCC, op. cit., Vol. XXXII, p. 74. The Resolution was adopted on February 21, 1787.

[234] LDC, op. cit., Vol. 24, p. 191; Charles Thomson to John Sullivan, March 31, 1787.

[235] LDC, op. cit., Vol. 24, p. 176; Lambert Cadwalader to Charles Stewart, March 27, 1787.

[236] Gaillard Hunt and James Brown Scott, Editors, The Debates in the Federal Convention of 1787 (Prometheus Books, Buffalo, New York, 1987) Vol. 1, pp. 17 & 27.

[237] LDC, op. cit., Vol. 24, p. 276, footnote 1.

[238] JCC, op. cit., Vol. XXXII, pp. 292-297.

[239] LDC, op. cit., Vol. 24, pp. 281; Arthur St. Clair to Charles Thomson, May 18, 1787; and, p. 323, footnote 1. Secretary Thomson was gone from May 6 to June 22, 1787. President St. Clair was gone from May 18 to July 17, 1787.

[240] LDC, op. cit., Vol. 24, pp. 378-379; Charles Thomson to George Morgan, July 28, 1787.

[241] LDC, op. cit., Vol. 24, p. 343; Charles Thomson to William Bingham, June 25, 1787.

[242] JCC, op. cit., Vol. XXXII, p. 297.

[243] LDC, op. cit., Vol. 24, p. 350; Charles Thomson to William Bingham, July 8, 1787.

[244] JCC, op. cit., Vol. XXXII, pp. 334-343.

[245] LDC, op. cit., Vol. 24, p. 379; Charles Thomson to George Morgan, July 28, 1787.

[246] LDC, op. cit., Vol. 24, p. 373, footnote 1.

[247] JCC, op. cit., Vol. XXXIII, p. 392; July 23, 1787.

[248] Hunt, op. cit., Vol. 2, p. 583.

[249] JCC, op. cit., Vol. XXXIII, pp. 487-503.

[250] Chapter 11.

[251] JCC, op. cit., Vol. XXXIII, p. 549. See also: LDC, op. cit., Vol. 24, p. 451; Charles Thomson to the States, September 28, 1787.

[252] JCC, op. cit., Vol. XXXIII, p. 610.

[253] Chapter 13.

[254] LDC, op. cit., Vol. 25, p. 47; Charles Thomson to Arthur St. Clair, April 11, 1788.

[255] JCC, op. cit., Vol. XXXIII, p. 715.

[256] Sol Bloom, Director General, History of the Formation of the Union under the Constitution (Constitution Sesquicentennial Commission, Washington, DC, 1940), p. 60.

[257] Thomson, Hannah, op. cit., p. 38; Hannah Thomson to John Mifflin, March 2, 1788.

[258] JCC, op. cit., Vol. XXXIV, pp. 1 & 9.

[259] Chapter 3.

[260] JCC, op. cit., Vol. XXXIV, pp. 62-65; February 26, 1788.

[261] LDC, op. cit., Vol. 25, p. 63; Charles Thomson to James McHenry, April 19, 1788.

[262] James Grant Wilson and John Fiske, Editors, Appletons' Cyclopaedia of American Biography (D. Appleton and Company, New York, 1887), Vol. 2, p. 326. Ellery had literally stood at Secretary Thomson's side on August 2, 1776, during the signing of the Declaration of Independence: "I was determined to see how they all looked as they signed what might be their death-warrant. I placed myself beside the secretary, Charles Thomson, and eyed each closely as he affixed his name to the document. Undaunted resolution was displayed in every countenance." Like Thomson, Ellery's house was burned by the British during the war.

[263] LDC, op. cit., Vol. 25, p. 114; Charles Thomson to William Ellery, May 26, 1788.

[264] LDC, op. cit., Vol. 25, p. 199; Charles Thomson to John Dickinson, June 30, 1788.

[265] Bloom, op. cit., p. 60.

[266] Bloom, op. cit., p. 60.

[267] LDC, op. cit., Vol. 25, p. 210; Charles Thomson to Samuel McDowell, July 3, 1788.

[268] Thomson, Hannah, op. cit., p. 40; Hannah Thomson to John Mifflin, August 17, 1788.

[269] JCC, op. cit., Vol. XXXIV, p. 523.

[270] LDC, op. cit., Vol. 25, p. 366; Charles Thomson to the States, September 13, 1788.

[271] Bloom, op. cit., p. 224.

[272] JCC, op. cit., Vol. XXXIV, p. 599.

[273] LDC, op. cit., Vol. 25, p. 441; Charles Thomson to the States, October 22, 1788.

[274] JCC, op. cit., Vol. XXXIV, p. 605.

[275] LDC, op. cit., Vol. 25, p. 509; Charles Thomson to Unknown, March 7, 1789.

[276] LDC, op. cit., Vol. 25, pp. 513-514; Charles Thomson to George Read, March 21, 1789. George Read of Delaware had a very mixed record in Revolutionary history. Because he initially opposed Independence when the test vote was taken in the Committee of the Whole on July 1, 1776, Thomas McKean, the other delegate from Delaware had to ask the seriously ill Caesar Rodney to ride through a thunder storm in order to reach Philadelphia the following day to break Delaware's tie in the final vote. (That scene is depicted on the reverse of the Delaware Commerative Quarter.) When the Declaration was finally signed on August 2, 1776, however, Read did add his name. In 1789, even though Read lived closer to New York than many of the newly elected US Senators, he failed to arrive until April 16, after a quorum had finally been established. Like Charles Thomson, Read was also a former student of the Rev. Alison.

[277] Bloom, op. cit., pp. 238-239.

[278] Collections of the New-York Historical Society for the Year 1878, op. cit., p. 249; Charles Thomson to Robert Morris, April 7, 1789.

[279] Collections of the New-York Historical Society for the Year 1878, op. cit., pp. 249-259; Benjamin Franklin to Charles Thomson, December 29, 1788.

[280] Bowling, op. cit., pp. 318-320. Had Senator George Read of Delaware been there on time, as Thomson had pleaded, Thomson would most likely have won the election to be Secretary of the Senate.

[281] LDC, op. cit., Vol. 25, pp. 517-521; Charles Thomson to John Langdon, April 14 & 24, 1789.

[282] Chapter 9. See also: Harley, op. cit, p. 127.

[283] LDC, op. cit., Vol. 25, p. 525, footnote 3. See also: Bowling, op. cit., p. 326-327. Another member of that three person committee, Ralph Izard of South Carolina, also disliked Secretary Thomson.

[284] LDC, op. cit., Vol. 25, p. 523; Charles Thomson's Draft Letter to Congress [never sent], April 30, 1789.

[285] LDC, op. cit., Vol. 25, p. 533; Roger Alden to David Humphreys, May 29, 1789.

[286] As cited in Bowling, op. cit., pp. 327-328.

[287] LDC, op. cit., Vol. 25, pp. 533-534; Charles Thomson to the Board of Treasury, July 17, 1789. The Treasury Board, which challenged any payments to Secretary Thomson after March 31, 1789, included another of the Secretary's enemies, Arthur Lee. The outstanding balance was finally settled by the new Secretary of the Treasury, Alexander Hamilton, on September 29, 1789.

[288] As cited in Bowling, op. cit., pp. 328-330.

[289] LDC, op. cit., Vol. 25, pp. 534-535; Charles Thomson to George Washington, July 23, 1789.

[290] Collections of the New-York Historical Society for the Year 1878, op. cit., p. 250; George Washington to Charles Thomson, July 24, 1789.

[291] John C. Fitzpatrick, The Writings of Washington (Government Printing Office, Washington, DC, 1933), Vol. XXX, p. 505; George Washington to Sir Edward Newenham, January 15, 1790.

[292] Bowling, op. cit., p. 334. See also: Shakespeare's Macbeth, Act III, Scene 4.

[293] As cited in Bowling, op. cit., p. 334; Hannah Thomson to Miss Van Horn, July 1790.

[294] As cited in Harley, op. cit, p. 131; William Maclay's Journal, July 13, 1789. In a slightly similar situation nearly two centuries later, the author of this book asked retired Secretary of State Dean Acheson what his greatest regret was concerning his long and distinguished career. He replied: "Not having the good fortune to die in office." To illustrate his point, Acheson pointed to the State Funeral for his successor, John Foster Dulles, who died of cancer at the end of the Eisenhower Administration.

[295] As cited in Schlenther, op. cit., p. 196; Charles Thomson to Alexander Thomson, July 26, 1792.

[296] Schlenther, op. cit., p. 196.

[297] Collections of the New-York Historical Society for the Year 1878, op. cit., pp. 253-254; George Washington to Charles Thomson, January 31, 1793.

[298] As cited in Hendricks, op. cit., p. 186; Charles Thomson to Alexander Thomson, July 26, 1792.

[299] Albert J. Edmunds, "Charles Thomson's New Testament: A Description of Three MSS. in the Library of the Historical Society of Pennsylvania," The Pennsylvania Magazine of History and Biography, Vol. 15, No. 3 (1891), p. 329.

[300] C. A. Muses, Editor, The Septuagint Bible...in the Translation of Charles Thomson (The Falcon's Wing Press, Indian Hills, Colorado, 1954), pp. ix & xxii. According to Muses, the editions of the Bible associated with St. Jerome, Luther and King James all

drew on a version of the Hebrew Old Testament that was approximately four hundred years newer than the one used to write the Septuagint.

[301] Muses, op. cit., p. xxiii. For example, Muses points out that "the sixth and seventh commandments are reversed in the Septuagint text, and Jesus quoted the same reversed order to the wealthy young man in Luke xviii.20, again showing Jesus' use of the original Semitic text."

[302] After sponsoring vicious newspaper attacks on President John Adams, the two men did not speak for nearly a decade. In private correspondence, Jefferson was also extremely demeaning toward former President Cyrus Griffin even though they had once been good friends.

[303] As cited in Muses, op. cit., p. xi; Charles Thomson to Samuel Miller, January 6, 1801.

[304] As cited in Muses, op. cit., p. xi.

[305] Edmunds, op. cit., p. 331

[306] Muses, op. cit., p. xv.

[307] Muses, op. cit.

[308] Schlenther, op. cit., pp. 211-213.

[309] Schlenther, op. cit., pp. 214-215.

[310] Schlenther, op. cit., p. 215.

[311] As cited in Schlenther, op. cit., p. 216; Charles Thomson to Thomas Jefferson, February 24, 1808.

[312] Schlenther, op. cit., pp. 215-216.

[313] Collections of the New-York Historical Society for the Year 1878, op. cit., pp. 262-263; Thomas Jefferson to Charles Thomson, January 9, 1816; and, pp. 207-208; Thomas Jefferson to Charles Thomson, January 29, 1817.

[314] Collections of the New-York Historical Society for the Year 1878, op. cit., p. 266; Charles Thomson to Thomas Jefferson, (sometime in 1816).

[315] Collections of the New-York Historical Society for the Year 1878, op. cit., pp. 264-265; Charles Thomson to Thomas Jefferson, May 16, 1816.

[316] Hendricks, op. cit., p. 187.

[317] Schlenther, op. cit., pp. 218-222. John Adams and Thomas Jefferson died two years later on July 4, 1826. In 1832, Charles Carroll of Carrollton, a Catholic who was still the richest man in America, was the last Signer of the Declaration of Independence to die. He was one of the founders of the B&O Railroad.

[318] Schlenther, op. cit., pp. 220-223. Even though the graves at Harriton were supposedly

unmarked, John Thomson should have been familiar enough with their arrangement to transport the correct bodies. One of the major business partners in the development of Laurel Hill Cemetery was Nicholas Biddle, the President of the Second Bank of the United States.

319 William Summers and X. Y., "Obituary Notices of Pennsylvania Soldiers of the Revolution," *The Pennsylvania Magazine of History and Biography*, Vol. 38, No. 4 (1914), p. 455. The obituary for Charles Thomson appeared on August 25, 1824. Of the 14 Presidents of the Continental Congress, only his close friend, John Jay, outlived Charles Thomson.

Postscript

THE SECOND
AMERICAN REPUBLIC

1789 - Present

As the Second American Republic began to evolve under the new Constitution, additional States joined the original thirteen in rapid succession. In 1791, Vermont was finally welcomed after its decade-long struggle for recognition. Kentucky was admitted the following year. The proposed State of Franklin, however, was not as successful. Nor, to this day, are the citizens of the District of Columbia. They still struggle under the weight of "Taxation Without Representation" even though they wrote and ratified a constitution for the State of New Columbia in the 1980s, two centuries after the war for Independence had been won.

The Founders would not be shocked that the nation now stretches across the entire continent, though Hawaii would certainly surprise them. Most envisioned a "manifest destiny" long before that phrase was coined. What many of them would find incredulous is the fact that Canada never joined the Union despite congressional invitations and invasions. They would also be amazed that 300,000,000 citizens have been added to the population of the United States since the end of the Revolution.

One recent development that would undoubtedly astonish them would be the current composition of the United States Supreme Court. The Founders, who were overwhelmingly Protestant and profoundly anti-papist, would be flabbergasted that the highest Court now consists of six Catholics, three Jews and not one member of a Protestant denomination.

The Civil War of the 1860s would have come as no surprise to many of the Founders. The regional divisions within the nation were abundantly clear from the opening of the Continental Congress. At one point, Secretary Thomson had even envisioned the outline of regional confederations. Furthermore, as they cobbled together the new Constitution, the Founders also realized that they were leaving the cancer of slavery for future generations to cure, if hey could. But none of the men who struggled to form the new nation could have imagined the extent of the human carnage that terrible war would reap. How many of the Presidents of the Continental Congress would have supported Lincoln's conviction that imposing political union was worth such an unimaginable price in blood? Equally egregious, most would belatedly lament the genocide the new nation carried out against Indian Tribes. Only now, after millions of Native Americans have died or been displaced, are ancient treaties starting to be honored.

The fact that the United States of America would some day take its place as a great and powerful country on the World stage was widely anticipated by many of the Founders. They would be rightfully proud that the concept of representative government which they helped to advance would one day sweep aside most of the monarchies and oligarchies that had repressed individuals for so many millennia. Even they, however, could never have imagined a day when their young fledgling nation would become the sole surviving super power in a nuclear age. To the Founders, who so deeply distrusted standing armies, the concentration of such vast destructive force in the hands of so few would be absolutely abhorrent.

As they wrote and ratified the new Constitution, some feared that the ill-defined presidency under the Second Republic would be inadequate to the great challenges ahead. In sharp contrast, how that office has been used and abused over the past two centuries would likely alarm most of those who were present at its creation. The very lack of specificity in the Constitution has permitted Presidents to do anything they desire unless the Courts, Congress or the People stop them. So many who have held that title have made that point abundantly and alarmingly clear.

Needless to say, none of the Founders ever anticipated a day when an African- American would become President of the United States. The fact that even the city of Charleston, South Carolina voted for Barack Obama would have been far beyond their wildest imagination.

During the Constitutional Convention in 1787, former President Nathaniel Gorham asked: "Can it be supposed that this vast country...will, one hundred and fifty years hence, remain one nation?" Now, nearly two and a half centuries after forty-three delegates elected Peyton Randolph as the first President, the Republic they initiated that early fall morning in 1774 still stands as the United States of America.

ACKNOWLEDGMENT

The two decades of research and writing that I have devoted to this book have truly been a labor of love. It is a humbling experience to finally bring these giants of early American history to life. I have tried my best to tell their remarkable stories. Now, it is for others to fill in the gaps.

Like all students of the American Revolution, I am deeply indebted to the Library of Congress for its 26 volume series: *Letters of Delegates to Congress: 1774-1789*. Not only were the thousands of letters of inestimable value, but the detailed notations added by the Library staff were equally critical in helping to illuminate what I frequently refer to as the black hole of American history.

I am enormously grateful to Judith Chamberlin, my friend and faithful editor, who drew on her years of teaching English to mercilessly underscore my grammatical mistakes. It was a painful but beneficial experience.

My deepest gratitude is also extended to my friend and former student Alex Summer who used his remarkable computer knowledge to frequently save me from my technical illiteracy. In similar fashion, I owe a sincere word of thanks to my very dear friend Deacon Maccubbin for his Macintosh magic. Without them, this book would never have seen the light of day.

I would also like to express my appreciation to Michael Phillips and his staff in the Interlibrary Loan Office at Addlestone Library of the College of Charleston. Their ability to track down even the most obscure document is simply amazing.

My publisher, AuthorHouse, and its professional staff have helped to make this daunting process possible. My friend and Web Master, Randy Bredell, has been tremendously generous with both his time and his talent.

I appreciate the help and guidance that I have received from a wide variety of individuals and institutions. All errors, of course, are exclusively mine.

INDEX

Boston Tea Party xxxiv, xxxv, 12, 27, 83, 105, 106, 124, 163, 190, 280, 307, 361, 363, 435, 587

Boudinot, Elias 179, 184, 218, 298, 312, 319, 320, 322, 334, 337, 347, 349, 350, 351, 352, 353, 354, 355, 356, 357, 359, 367, 375, 382, 450, 502, 522, 523, 570, 598, 616, 628, 634

Boudinot, Elisha 352

Bowdoin, James 83, 458, 476, 479, 481, 485, 488

Bradford, William xvii, 338, 339, 343, 355, 475

Britain xviii, xix, xxi, xxii, xxiii, xxiv, xxv, xxvi, xxvii, xxviii, xxxi, xxxiii, xxxiv, xxxv, xxxviii, xl, xlii, 6, 9, 10, 11, 13, 15, 17, 18, 25, 32, 38, 47, 48, 51, 53, 54, 61, 63, 65, 71, 79, 80, 91, 94, 103, 105, 122, 123, 128, 136, 138, 144, 159, 163, 164, 166, 169, 170, 174, 175, 176, 181, 188, 191, 193, 195, 205, 210, 211, 223, 246, 261, 275, 279, 280, 281, 304, 333, 334, 342, 347, 348, 354, 363, 365, 377, 388, 397, 404, 409, 413, 414, 415, 417, 429, 458, 490, 505, 515, 537, 553, 560, 571, 583, 584, 585, 586, 587, 596, 602, 605

Bruton Parish Church 5, 13, 573

Bull, William, II 47

Burgoyne, John 101, 113

Burke, Edmund 62, 136

Burr, Aaron 81, 183, 320, 324, 349, 555, 573

Bute, Lord xxii, xxiii, xxxix

C

Callender, James 554, 573

Canada xix, xxii, xxxv, 38, 100, 143, 165, 187, 323, 414, 415, 416, 436, 437, 447, 491, 492, 645

Carleton, Guy 297, 299, 304, 334, 455

Carpenters Hall 1, 2, 28, 51

Carroll, Charles 191, 263, 275, 284, 285, 286, 288, 305, 308, 309, 310, 642

Carroll, Daniel 284, 286, 289, 309, 310, 601, 602

Catholic xix, xxxv, 117, 153, 160, 165, 167, 170, 191, 192, 222, 234, 244, 305, 320, 338, 533, 545, 604, 642, 645

Champlain, Samuel de xvii

Chantilly (Virginia) 404, 406, 409, 415, 420, 423, 427

Charles I xviii, 533

Charles II xviii, xix, xxxviii, 64, 402

Charleston xxiv, xxxiv, xl, 12, 40, 42, 43, 44, 45, 47, 48, 49, 50, 51, 52, 53, 54, 55, 56, 57, 58, 59, 65, 66, 67, 68, 69, 92, 100, 112, 115, 117, 118, 119, 120, 121, 122, 123, 124, 125, 126, 128, 129, 134, 138, 139, 146, 149, 151, 152, 153, 170, 187, 214, 221, 222, 261, 264, 284, 308, 332, 473, 499, 537, 563, 566, 596, 597, 598, 637, 646, 647, 661

Chase, Samuel 21, 266, 392, 437, 492, 519, 537, 555, 572

Cherokee Tribe xx, 344, 357

Chisholm v. Georgia 1793 180

Church of England 117, 430, 583

Cincinnati, Ohio 194, 337, 338, 342, 357, 384, 397, 502, 517

City Tavern 1

Clinton, Bill 270, 313

Clinton, George 151, 168, 192, 333, 339, 353, 526, 550, 559, 570, 594, 615, 630

Clinton, Henry 54, 68, 144, 187, 229, 262, 273, 304, 316, 499

College of New Jersey 320, 636

College of William & Mary 34

Common Sense 89, 100, 107, 128, 193, 203, 207

Concord, Massachusetts 19, 26, 84, 85, 125, 165, 205, 245, 323, 448, 490, 585, 590

Connecticut xxi, xxviii, xxxiii, 3, 14, 85, 88, 89, 92, 170, 179, 196, 201, 202, 204, 205, 206, 207, 208, 209, 211, 213, 216, 218, 219, 220, 225, 226, 227, 228, 231, 237, 242, 264, 268, 284, 294, 296, 308, 330, 332, 344, 352, 359, 362, 364, 366, 367, 376, 394, 417, 447, 461, 465, 483, 507, 508, 539, 540, 541, 547, 550, 559, 567, 595, 613, 635

L

Lafayette, Marquis de 23, 97, 116, 130, 150, 187, 294, 311, 334, 353, 430, 443, 497, 521

La Luzerne, Chevalier de 170, 215, 229, 290, 310, 394, 395

Lancaster, Pennsylvania 91, 92, 116, 119, 257, 263, 265, 335, 371, 372, 385, 403, 500, 501, 532, 535, 542, 588, 593

Laurel Hill Cemetery 258, 579, 623, 643

Laurens, Henry 27, 35, 48, 55, 63, 66, 67, 68, 71, 92, 103, 111, 115, 117, 128, 139, 143, 144, 145, 146, 147, 148, 149, 150, 151, 152, 153, 154, 155, 159, 162, 168, 170, 173, 174, 189, 199, 209, 225, 228, 233, 243, 250, 263, 267, 273, 278, 293, 305, 315, 320, 331, 349, 359, 372, 374, 377, 382, 389, 393, 396, 399, 418, 420, 421, 431, 438, 439, 443, 473, 475, 485, 497, 517, 521, 529, 536, 563, 565, 575, 583, 593, 603, 616, 625, 630, 631, 634, 637, 661

Laurens, John 68, 117, 133, 139, 145, 146, 147, 149, 150, 151, 153, 228, 372, 393, 396

Lee, Arthur xxxiii, xxxiv, 106, 113, 132, 143, 168, 331, 408, 418, 419, 422, 432, 434, 438, 439, 442, 535, 536, 594, 598, 607, 641

Lee, Charles 365, 366, 390, 437, 442, 491, 519

Lee-Deane Affair 418, 536, 539, 594, 628, 630

Lee, Francis Lightfoot 21, 34, 117, 417, 419, 425, 436, 438, 439, 441

Lee, Richard Henry xx, xxvi, xl, 2, 8, 12, 14, 21, 25, 27, 30, 33, 34, 51, 64, 100, 108, 132, 133, 138, 165, 166, 168, 177, 190, 194, 207, 230, 246, 283, 289, 349, 367, 391, 401, 403, 405, 408, 413, 414, 415, 416, 417, 421, 422, 423, 425, 426, 427, 429, 431, 432, 433, 434, 435, 436, 437, 438, 439, 440, 441, 442, 443, 450, 451, 462, 473, 479, 506, 508, 520, 536, 539, 542, 543, 544, 565, 594, 606, 612, 613, 616, 618, 631

Lee, Robert E. 23, 233, 403

Lee, Thomas 403, 404, 440, 441, 442

Lee, Thomas Sim 284, 296, 308, 309, 310, 311, 312, 521

Lee, William 418, 427, 433, 434, 435, 436, 438, 441

Leigh, Egerton 122, 148

Lexington, Massachusetts 19, 26, 62, 74, 84, 85, 106, 125, 165, 205, 245, 323, 366, 414, 469, 490, 590

Library of Congress 23, 27, 63, 65, 106, 145, 155, 156, 191, 226, 263, 269, 273, 276, 293, 305, 307, 315, 351, 359, 372, 389, 399, 425, 433, 443, 455, 459, 476, 485, 487, 517, 529, 564, 565, 594, 607, 613, 626, 627, 628, 629, 647

Lincoln, Benjamin 54, 134, 188, 214, 221, 229, 261, 284, 448, 477, 515, 521, 551

Livingston, Robert R. 162, 183, 190, 191, 241, 264, 353, 354, 597, 599, 633

Livingston, William 132, 150, 162, 163, 174, 190, 194, 322, 394, 479, 522

Louis XIV xix, 160, 531, 563

Louis XVI 342, 430, 516, 561, 563

Lovell, James 210, 215, 228, 229, 373, 393, 495, 520

Lynch, Thomas, Sr. 2, 48, 51, 589

M

Madison, James 95, 109, 152, 177, 194, 277, 291, 330, 332, 333, 336, 353, 380, 394, 396, 397, 421, 425, 430, 439, 441, 443, 461, 463, 477, 478, 480, 481, 482, 500, 506, 522, 524, 527, 529, 538, 542, 545, 548, 550, 556, 559, 567, 568, 569, 573, 596, 615, 628, 631, 633

Marshall, John 23, 183, 184, 254, 542, 552, 553, 555, 556, 559, 564, 571, 573

Maryland xxi, xxviii, 18, 116, 217, 230, 252, 267, 268, 273, 275, 276, 277, 278, 279, 280, 281, 282, 283, 284, 285, 286, 287, 288, 289, 290, 292, 296, 298, 299, 300, 305, 306, 307, 308, 309, 310, 313, 319, 330, 332, 333, 336, 355, 361, 371, 376, 378,

O

P

W

Y

THE AUTHOR

Thomas Patrick Chorlton teaches the American Presidency and the Politics of the American Revolution at the College of Charleston, the thirteenth-oldest college in America. It was founded in 1770 by Henry Laurens, the fourth President of the Continental Congress. The college was subsequently incorporated in 1785 by three Signers of the Declaration of Independence and three Signers of the United States Constitution.

The previous decade, Tom taught history and government at the Lake Campus of Columbia College in central Missouri, including courses on the History of the American Revolution as well as Historical Research and Methods.

Tom received his Bachelor's degree in Political Science from St. Louis University in 1968. Following graduation, he served as a Peace Corps teacher in Kenya. Tom completed his Master's degree in Government Administration at Webster University in 1977 while employed as a Local Government Specialist with the St. Louis Area Council of Governments.

During 1975, Tom worked in Washington, DC on the staff of Congressman Melvin Price (D-IL), the Chairman of the House Armed Services Committee. From 1982-87, Tom served as the founding Executive Director of the National Association of Gay & Lesbian Democratic Clubs (the forerunner of today's National Stonewall Democrats). In 1988, Tom ran at-large for the Council of the District of Columbia.

For over 40 years, Tom has traveled extensively across six continents from Khartoum to Katmandu, Easter Island to the Arctic Circle.

As "the World's largest vegetarian," Tom is above all a passionate advocate of Animal Rights. He also delights in live theatre, red wine and, of course, both old and new friends.

Tom and his best friend, Athens, live in Folly Beach, South Carolina, only a short walk from the Atlantic Ocean.

www.firstamericanrepublic.com